Mathematics Applied to Mechanics

Books in this Series

1. Algebra and Number Systems
2. Analytic Geometry and Vectors
3. Statistics and Probability
4. Calculus
5. Numerical Analysis
6. Fortran
7. Mathematics Applied to Mechanics

Mathematics Applied to Mechanics

D. P. Thomas
B.Sc., Ph.D., FR.Met.S.
University of Dundee

Blackie Glasgow and London
Chambers Edinburgh

Blackie & Son Limited Bishopbriggs, Glasgow
450/452 Edgware Road, London W2 1EG

W. & R. Chambers Limited 11 Thistle Street, Edinburgh EH2 1DG

First published 1977

Blackie edition ISBN 0 216 89831 5

Chambers edition ISBN 0 550 75897 6

Printed in Great Britain by Thomson Litho Ltd., East Kilbride, Scotland

Dedicated to
Aldwyth and Elwyn,
Joy,
Jennifer and Siân

Preface

This book provides an introduction to Newtonian Mechanics suitable for students at universities and polytechnics, and also for those specializing in the subject in their final years at school. A primary emphasis has been placed throughout on mathematical models and the equations of motion; a secondary, but important, role being played by the conservation principles. The reader is thereby encouraged to apply to all problems a consistent approach which involves the choice of a frame of reference, the representation of a body's position, velocity and acceleration, the representation of all forces acting on a body, and the application of mathematical techniques to solve the governing equation of motion subject to given initial conditions. It has been assumed that the reader has, or is acquiring, a knowledge of relevant topics in algebra, calculus, geometry and trigonometry. Vectors and differential equations are used throughout the book, and numerical methods are referred to on appropriate occasions.

The reader is urged to have pen and paper at hand. It is good practice to work out on paper the details of any calculation or manipulation. The reading of a mathematical textbook should be different from the reading of a novel.

Graded sets of exercises are provided at the ends of chapters. There is no substitute for the hard work involved in the attempting of exercises. The reader is invited frequently to make a complete analysis of a particular problem rather than to provide information about one aspect, as is usually the case in examination questions. The many worked examples in the text encourage this approach to problems. Examinations do have to be passed, however, so questions set in the appropriate examination held in previous years should be attempted to gain experience.

Three books that may widen horizons and suggest project work are: *Animal Mechanics* by R. McNeill Alexander, Sidgwick and Jackson (1968); *The Physics of Ball Games* by C. B. Daish, The English Universities Press (1972); *Discrete Models* by Donald Greenspan, Addison-Wesley (1973).

Articles that appear in the monthly publication, *The American Journal of Physics*, provide another source of stimulating material.

This book was planned in collaboration with Mr W. T. Blackburn,

Principal Lecturer in Mathematics at Dundee College of Education. His untimely death in 1974 meant that the writing of the book fell to me, but I should like to acknowledge the benefits of his careful analysis of my preliminary ideas.

It gives me much pleasure to express my thanks to Miss R. A. Dudgeon and Mrs A. J. Fraser for preparing the typescript.

D. P. THOMAS

University of Dundee

Contents

Introduction

1

1.1 Mathematical models

When an aeroplane is being designed and developed, many tests and experiments are performed before the prototype takes to the air. Sometimes full-scale or scaled-down models are used in these tests and experiments. For example, tests may be conducted on the strength of parts of the framework subjected to vibrations, or wind-tunnel experiments may be performed to check the effects of the shape of the fuselage at different speeds. The development of a ship, e.g. a supertanker or a lifeboat, includes similar procedures.

Some problems in the physical sciences and engineering cannot be answered by full-scale or scaled-down testing. Weather forecasting, space-flight planning and nuclear-power generation are a few examples. In these cases the development of an abstract model may be useful. Such a model consists of assumptions, axioms, theorems, conclusions and predictions. It is called a "mathematical model". These models are of importance not only in the physical sciences and engineering, but also in business, economics, and the biological and medical sciences.

In geometry, a point, a straight line, and a plane are abstract ideas. They represent a dot on a page, a line drawn on a page with the aid of a ruler, and the page itself. To describe the shape and position of objects in the real world, it is convenient to work with an abstract (euclidean) space that has particular properties. The space consists of a set of elements, called *points*. The distance between two points is defined. Straight lines are collections of points having specified properties. The angle between two intersecting straight lines is defined. The ideas of distance and angle are fundamental. Their development into a mathematical theory is studied under the heading of "Euclidean Geometry" [see J. Hunter, *Analytic Geometry and Vectors*, Blackie/Chambers]. The predictions of the theory may lead to interesting results in the real world, and situations in the real world may suggest the development of theorems. These links between the real world and the abstract mathematical model are important, particularly their two-way nature. A word of warning should be given. Some illustrations may be misleading and confusing in our study of geometry [see E. A. Maxwell, *Fallacies in Mathematics*, p. 22, Cambridge University Press].

Let us consider the extremely complicated problem of describing the motion of the Earth around the Sun. To make any progress we attempt to develop a mathematical model. The model must be sufficiently simple for us to be able to solve the resulting abstract problem (an idealization of the real problem) with the mathematics available to us. This restriction on the model is always present. It depends on the development of mathematical techniques (e.g. algebra, geometry, calculus, numerical analysis) and not only on *our* knowledge of these techniques. Conversely we must not accept an oversimplified mathematical model. Let us examine the constituent parts of a mathematical model in relation to this problem.

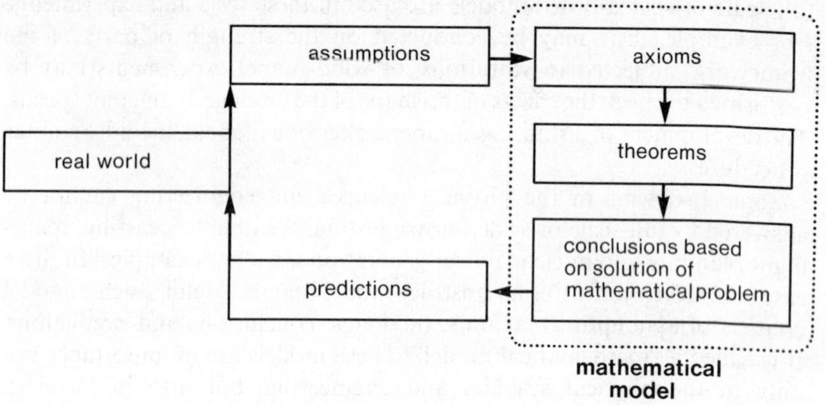

Assumptions	Represent the Earth and the Sun by two points having given properties (mass, initial position, initial velocity). Ignore all other bodies (planets, stars, etc.).
Axioms	Euclidean space Newton's Laws of Motion Newton's Law of Gravitation
Theorems, conclusions	Apply the axioms and solve the resulting mathematical equations (exactly or approximately).
Predictions	Make predictions based on the mathematical model (e.g. the Earth moves round the Sun once a year) and carry out experiments in the real world to test the predictions.

We have assumed that the principal factor in this problem is the gravitational force acting between the Earth and the Sun, and we have ignored all other factors (e.g. the finite dimensions of the Earth and the Sun, the influence of the Moon and the planets). Our model will not predict the spinning of the Earth about its axis, but it will predict that the Earth moves round the Sun once a year.

As a second example let us consider a pendulum made from a ball and a length of string. It is worth while to list some of the possible assumptions. We may suppose that:

(i) The ball is represented by a point having mass (ignoring the shape and dimensions of the ball).
(ii) The string has negligible mass and is of constant length (ignoring the mass of the string and any variations in its length).
(iii) The string is attached to a rigid support situated near the surface of the Earth.
(iv) The only applied force is a constant gravitational force (ignoring the variations of the Earth's gravitational force with height and the presence of other gravitational bodies, e.g. Sun, Moon, planets).
(v) The Earth is at rest (ignoring the effects of the rotation of the Earth).
(vi) The pendulum is in a vacuum (ignoring air resistance).

We shall examine this problem under these six assumptions in chapter 7. Another way to look at the problem is to list the factors that may influence the motion of the pendulum. We may ask ourselves the following questions:

(i) How important are the shape and the size of the ball?
(ii) How is the ball fixed to the string?
(iii) What supports the string? Can the support move?
(iv) Does the string extend?
(v) Does the string have the characteristics of a thread or of a rope? How does the mass of the string compare with that of the ball?
(vi) Is air resistance important?
(vii) What applied forces are acting on the pendulum?

When setting up a mathematical model of a real-world problem, we commonly have to decide which factor is most important and then ignore the other factors. If we were to attempt to incorporate all or most of the factors into our mathematical model, the governing mathematical equations would be so complicated that we would be unable to find even an approximate solution. We expect the predictions based on the mathematical model to be in approximate agreement with the results of experiments in the real world. If the agreement between theory and experiment (carefully executed) is not satisfactory, we must examine our assumptions and our axioms. We may single out another factor as being possibly the most important factor. Alternatively, we may try to incorporate two factors into our mathematical model. Sometimes we may find that the axioms used were inappropriate, e.g. we may have to replace Newton's laws by Einstein's axioms of relativity.

It is our task to discuss in this book

(*a*) the setting up of mathematical models;

(*b*) the statement and application of Newton's laws of motion and Newton's law of gravitation;
(*c*) the derivation of mathematical equations and the development of techniques of solution;
(*d*) the design of experiments to test the conclusions.

We shall devote the main effort to discussions of mathematical models (items *b* and *c*), but we shall attempt to retain an awareness of the connections between the real-world problem and the mathematical model under discussion (items *a* and *d*).

1.2 Coordinate systems and frames of reference

We are interested in the positions and motions of bodies, e.g. an aeroplane or a motor-car. We shall represent a body in an abstract way by means of a collection of points in a three-dimensional euclidean space [see J. Hunter, *Analytic Geometry and Vectors*, Blackie/Chambers]. Each point in a three-dimensional euclidean space is specified by an ordered set of three real numbers, these being the coordinates of the point; and the distance between points obeys Pythagoras's theorem. Each point has a unique set of coordinates relative to a given coordinate system. A coordinate system consists of a chosen point, called the *origin* and represented by $(0, 0, 0)$, and surfaces, called *coordinate surfaces*, on which a given coordinate is held fixed and the other two coordinates are allowed to vary. The simplest example is a cartesian coordinate system. In this case, a general point P has the coordinates (x, y, z), and the coordinate surfaces are planes intersecting at right angles. The coordinate axes are the lines of intersection of the coordinate surfaces corresponding to $x = 0$, $y = 0$, $z = 0$. The coordinate surface corresponding to $x = 0$ is the set of points $\{(0, y, z): -\infty < y < \infty, -\infty < z < \infty\}$. Similarly we define the coordinate surfaces corresponding to $y = 0, z = 0$ respectively. In this way, we see that the x-axis is the set of points $\{(x, 0, 0): -\infty < x < \infty\}$, the y-axis is the set of points $\{(0, y, 0): -\infty < y < \infty\}$ and the z-axis is the set of points $\{(0, 0, z): -\infty < z < \infty\}$. The origin is the point of intersection of the three coordinate axes.

Let the distance between two points A and B be $d(A, B)$. Then

$$d(A, B) = \{(x_A - x_B)^2 + (y_A - y_B)^2 + (z_A - z_B)^2\}^{1/2}$$

where the coordinates of A are (x_A, y_A, z_A) and the coordinates of B are (x_B, y_B, z_B). Sometimes it is convenient to work with part of the three-dimensional space. Particular cases are a plane and a straight line. If a plane is appropriate, we usually use the coordinate surface corresponding to $z = 0$, which contains the x-axis and the y-axis. In this case the distance between two points A, B in the plane is

$$d(A, B) = \{(x_A - x_B)^2 + (y_A - y_B)^2\}^{1/2}$$

and we say that the coordinates of A are (x_A, y_A). The name of the plane is the xy-plane. If a straight line is appropriate, we may take the x-axis (or one of the other axes). The distance between two points A, B on the line is

$$d(A, B) = \{(x_A - x_B)^2\}^{1/2} = |x_A - x_B|$$
$$= \begin{cases} x_A - x_B & \text{if} \quad x_B \leqslant x_A \\ x_B - x_A & \text{if} \quad x_A \leqslant x_B \end{cases}$$

and we say that the coordinate of A is x_A.

In a real-world situation, distances are measured by making comparisons with measuring rods or tape measures. The length of a measuring aid is standardized in terms of a chosen system of units. We shall use SI units (International System of Units) throughout the book. Our unit of length will be the metre (the SI symbol being m). This has been standardized by international agreement in terms of the wavelength of radiation emitted by the krypton-86 atom under specified conditions [see *Quantities, Units and Symbols*, a report by The Symbols Committee of the Royal Society, 1975]. In common terms, the height of a three- to four-year-old child is approximately one metre, and the height of a doorway in a modern house is approximately two metres.

Once we can measure distance, we can specify the coordinates (relative to a chosen cartesian coordinate system) of a point representing the position of a body. Consider a pip of an apple on a table in a room. After measuring, we may say that the pip is (approximately) one metre from the west-facing wall, two metres from the south-facing wall, and three-quarters of a metre from the floor. We are ignoring here the dimensions of the pip itself. (To be more precise we may say that the pip is between 1·000 and 1·003 metres from the west-facing wall, between 1·999 and 2·001 metres from the south-facing wall, and between 0·749 and 0·750 metres from the floor.) If we choose a

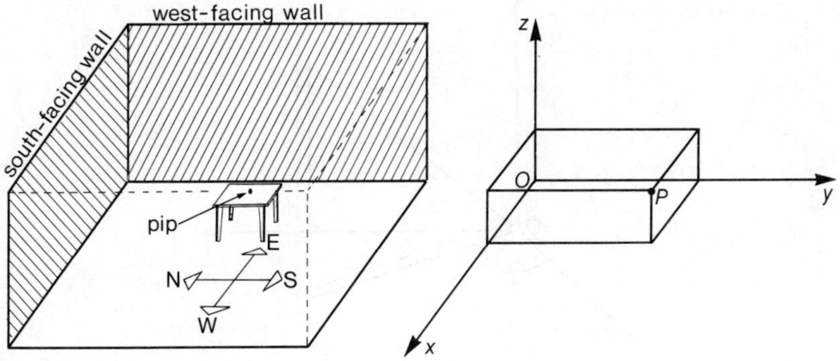

cartesian coordinate system such that the xy-plane represents the floor, the yz-plane represents the west-facing wall and the zx-plane represents the south-facing wall, then we can say that the point with coordinates $(1, 2, \frac{3}{4})$ represents the pip of the apple. We have adopted a scale of measurement in doing this. If we had chosen a different scale, we could have said that the point with coordinates (100, 200, 75) represented the pip of the apple. We see that a cartesian coordinate system is based on the three coordinate axes and a unit of measurement.

Let us consider briefly the measurement of angle. Our measuring instrument is the protractor, and our unit of measurement is the radian (the SI symbol being rad). Consider the acute angle AOB in the figure below. We have an angle of one radian when the length of the circular arc AB equals the radius of the arc. We may note that the degree is an alternative unit of angular measurement, and that 360 degrees are equivalent to 2π radians.

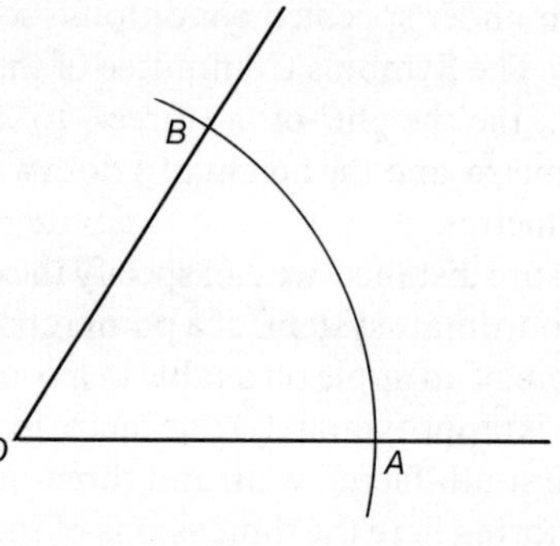

It is convenient in some problems to introduce special systems of coordinates, e.g. cylindrical polar coordinates or spherical polar coor-

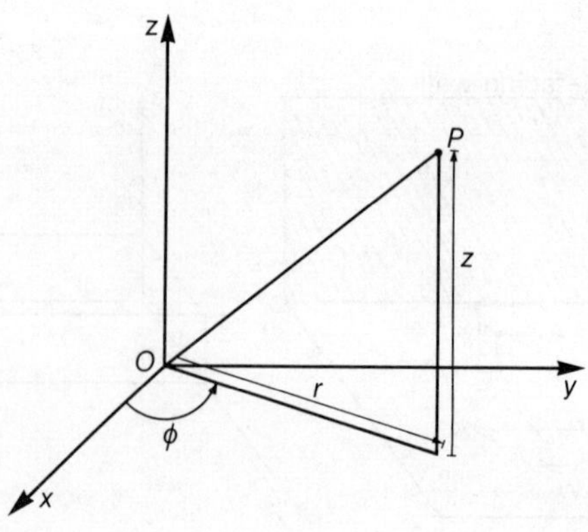

dinates. Cylindrical polar coordinates (r, ϕ, z) are defined in terms of cartesian coordinates (x, y, z) by the equations

$$x = r\cos\phi, \quad y = r\sin\phi, \quad z = z$$

Hence $r^2 = x^2 + y^2$ $(0 \leqslant r < \infty)$ and $\tan\phi = y/x$ $(0 \leqslant \phi < 2\pi)$. The distances are measured in an appropriate unit, and the angle is measured in radians. The coordinate surface corresponding to r equal to a constant is a circular cylinder, and the other two coordinate surfaces are planes.

A special case is the plane polar-coordinate system corresponding to z set equal to zero (or a constant). Then the coordinates are (r, ϕ), where r and ϕ are defined above in terms of the cartesian coordinates x and y. We note that

$$x_A - x_B = r_A\cos\phi_A - r_B\cos\phi_B$$
$$y_A - y_B = r_A\sin\phi_A - r_B\sin\phi_B$$
$$(x_A - x_B)^2 + (y_A - y_B)^2 = r_A^2 + r_B^2 - 2r_A r_B\cos(\phi_A - \phi_B)$$

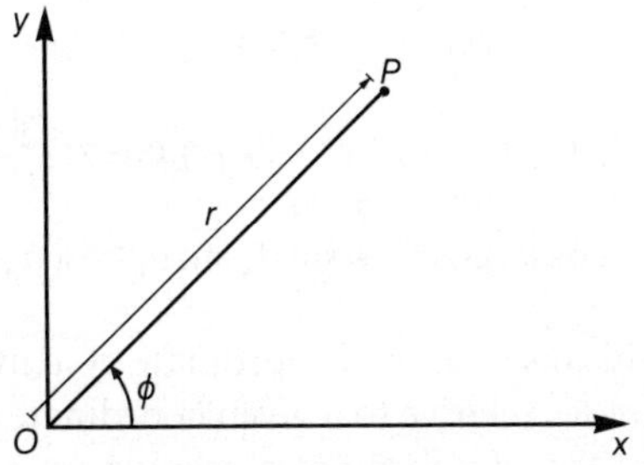

Spherical polar coordinates (r, θ, ϕ) are related to cartesian coordinates (x, y, z) by the equations

$$x = r\sin\theta\cos\phi, \quad y = r\sin\theta\sin\phi, \quad z = r\cos\theta$$

Hence

$$r^2 = x^2 + y^2 + z^2 \quad (0 \leqslant r < \infty)$$
$$\tan\theta = \frac{(x^2+y^2)^{1/2}}{z} \quad (0 \leqslant \theta \leqslant \pi)$$

and

$$\tan\phi = \frac{y}{x} \quad (0 \leqslant \phi < 2\pi)$$

The distances are measured in an appropriate unit, and the angles are measured in radians. The coordinate surface corresponding to r equal to a

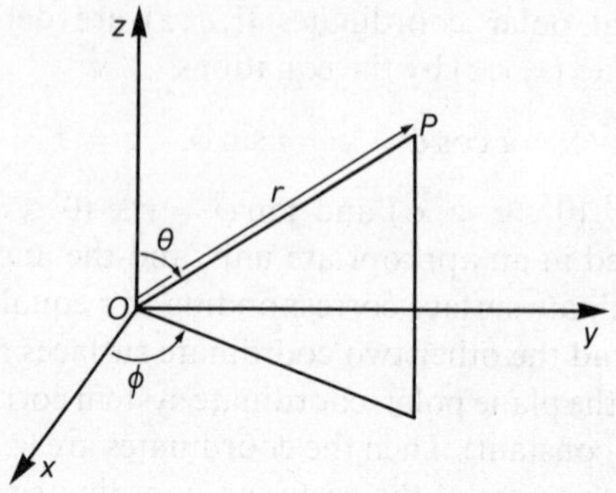

constant is a sphere; the coordinate surface corresponding to θ equal to a constant is a right circular cone, and the coordinate surface corresponding to ϕ equal to a constant is a plane. We note that

$$x_A - x_B = r_A \sin\theta_A \cos\phi_A - r_B \sin\theta_B \cos\phi_B$$
$$y_A - y_B = r_A \sin\theta_A \sin\phi_A - r_B \sin\theta_B \sin\phi_B$$
$$z_A - z_B = r_A \cos\theta_A - r_B \cos\theta_B$$

and

$$d(A, B) = (r_A^2 + r_B^2 - 2r_A r_B \cos\chi)^{1/2}$$

where

$$\cos\chi = \cos\theta_A \cos\theta_B + \sin\theta_A \sin\theta_B \cos(\phi_A - \phi_B)$$

We have seen in this discussion of coordinate systems that a point has a unique set of coordinates relative to a given coordinate system. However, a point has a different set of coordinates relative to a second coordinate system. It is essential to specify a chosen coordinate system at the outset of an investigation. This specified coordinate system is a *frame of reference*.

The idea of a frame of reference is familiar to us in connection with maps. A system of grid lines divides British Ordnance Survey maps into squares. The lines are numbered and provide a single reference system for the whole of Great Britain. A typical reference (correct to a hundred metres) consists of two letters and six digits. The letters refer to a particular square of side a hundred thousand metres, the next three digits give the number of hundred metres east of the western edge of the square, and the last three digits give the number of hundred metres north of the southern edge of the square. This has strong similarities with a two-dimensional system of cartesian coordinates. On a worldwide scale, we use latitudes and longitudes to indicate the position of cities. The frame of reference in this example is based on the equator and a chosen meridian (the one through Greenwich). The position of a city is specified by two angles, the latitude and the longitude.

Latitudes range from 90 degrees south to 90 degrees north, and longitudes range from 180 degrees west to 180 degrees east. A comparison with spherical polar coordinates is obvious.

TYPICAL LATITUDES AND LONGITUDES (MEASURED IN DEGREES AND MINUTES, 60 MINUTES BEING EQUIVALENT TO A DEGREE)

Colombo	Sri Lanka	6 55 N,	79 52 E
Edinburgh	Scotland	55 57 N,	3 12 W
London	England	51 30 N,	0 5 W
Moscow	USSR	55 45 N,	37 42 E
Nairobi	Kenya	1 17 S,	36 50 E
New York	USA	40 40 N,	73 50 W
Rio de Janeiro	Brazil	23 0 S,	43 12 W
San Francisco	USA	37 35 N,	122 30 W
Sydney	Australia	33 53 S,	151 10 E
Tokyo	Japan	35 45 N,	139 45 E

1.3 Time

Our notion of time is based on our experience of such phenomena as the changing of the seasons, the pattern of day and night, and the swinging of a pendulum. These phenomena are periodic, and they afford us means of measuring time in terms of years, days and seconds, for example. The international unit of time is the second (the SI symbol being s). It is defined in terms of the "atomic clock", which involves radiation from a caesium-133 atom. Everyday units of time are the minute (being equivalent to 60 seconds) and the hour (being equivalent to 3600 seconds).

Clocks and watches of various designs are mechanisms that measure time. Their scales of measurement are standardized relative to the second (or units derived from the second, for example, minutes and hours). The accuracy of the mechanisms varies from design to design. Some mechanisms measure to the nearest minute, and others to the nearest hundredth of a second or better.

In Britain, the Greenwich Time Signal and the chimes of Big Ben are broadcast on radio and television each day. A Speaking Clock is available to telephone subscribers. They are aids to good time keeping [see Peter Hood, *How Time is Measured*, second edition, 1969, Oxford University Press].

1.4 Events

An event is a happening (such as a flash of light from a photographer's flash-bulb) that occurs independently of the way in which its positions in space and time are measured. Both its positions are independent of all frames of reference and all clocks.

1.5 Observers

An observer is a person who is equipped to locate the position of an event in space and time, relative to a given frame of reference and a given time scale. He is equipped with measuring rods and a clock, each of which has been standardized relative to units of measurements, for example the metre and the second.

An observer is capable of determining the coordinates of the points of the region of space occupied by the photographer's flash-bulb at any instant of time, and the interval of time during which the bulb emitted light. It is often convenient to idealize and say that the bulb occupied a point in space, and the flash occurred at an instant of time. Adopting this idealization, the observer records the three coordinates and the time of the event.

Would a different observer (with a different frame of reference and a different clock) have made the same recordings? We must analyse the assumptions made about space and time in Newtonian Mechanics before we are able to answer this question. It is important to make this analysis, because the assumptions about space and time in Einstein's Theory of Relativity are different from those in Newtonian Mechanics. Before we examine the assumptions, we can say that both observers would agree that a flash of light had happened.

1.6 Assumptions about space and time

The basic assumptions about space and time in Newtonian Mechanics are

(i) Space is isotropic—there are no preferred directions in space.
(ii) Space and time are homogeneous—there are no special points or regions of space, and there are no special instants of time.
(iii) Time is absolute—the time interval between two events is an absolute invariant, i.e. it is independent of the observer.
(iv) Spatial displacement is absolute—the spatial displacement between two events is the same for all observers.

Returning to our two observers witnessing a flash of light, we see that they would agree about the time at which the event took place, provided their clocks agreed at any other instant, that is the origins of the time scales had been synchronized. Here we are using the absoluteness of time and the fact that the two observers are using the same unit of time. The discussion of their readings of the spatial coordinates is a little more complicated. However, it is sufficient to say now that the observers would agree where the flash occurred in space, provided their frames of reference were properly related. We shall discuss in chapter 2 the relationships between different frames of reference. Our observers, witnessing two flashes of light (that is, two events), would agree about the distance between the two locations. This follows from the absoluteness of spatial displacement.

We note that measurements of time and distance in Newtonian Mechanics are independent. In Relativistic Mechanics, however, there is a dependence between measurement of time and measurement of distance, and the frame of reference associated with an observer consists of a coordinate system *and* a clock.

Kinematics

2

2.1 Velocity and acceleration

In this chapter we shall study the motion of a body. For the time being we shall be interested in how the body moves—the kinematics of the body—and not in the causes of the motion.

At any instant the body can be represented by a set of points in a mathematical model. The elements of the set change when the body moves, and the description of this set will, in general, be complicated. The simplest is that where each element of the set has the same description. This occurs when the motion of the body is translational and when the body does not deform. In this case the motion of the body may be described in terms of the motion of a single representative element. When the motion of the body is more complicated (e.g. the body deforms or the motion has a rotational element), we may no longer concentrate on a single representative element unless we choose to ignore the deformation or rotation.

We shall concentrate on the special case of a set with a single element, from which the general case may be built. We sometimes talk about "a moving point P" rather than "a set P whose single element changes with time" or "a set whose single element P changes with time". To specify the position of the element P of the set at any instant, relative to a chosen frame of reference having a point O as its origin, we use line segments and position vectors [see J. Hunter, *Analytic Geometry and Vectors*, Blackie/Chambers]. The line segment $\overrightarrow{OP}$ is a geometrical representation of the position vector of P relative to O, denoted by $\boldsymbol{r}$.

To emphasize the dependence of the position vector of P on time, we write $\boldsymbol{r}(t)$. At some later time $t+\Delta t$, the position vector $\boldsymbol{r}(t+\Delta t)$ is $\boldsymbol{r}(t)+\Delta \boldsymbol{r}$. The ratio

$$\frac{\boldsymbol{r}(t+\Delta t)-\boldsymbol{r}(t)}{t+\Delta t-t}=\frac{\Delta \boldsymbol{r}}{\Delta t}$$

is called the average velocity of P over the time interval $[t, t+\Delta t]$. We note that the path of P during the time interval is not important. We define the velocity of P at the instant t to be the limit of the average velocity over the time interval $[t, t+\Delta t]$ as Δt tends to zero, i.e. limit of $\{\boldsymbol{r}(t+\Delta t)-\boldsymbol{r}(t)\}/\Delta t$ as Δt tends to zero. Letting $\boldsymbol{u}$ denote the velocity, we write

$$\boldsymbol{u}(t) = \lim_{\Delta t \to 0} \frac{\boldsymbol{r}(t+\Delta t)-\boldsymbol{r}(t)}{\Delta t} = \frac{d\boldsymbol{r}(t)}{dt}$$

The velocity is the time derivative of the position vector. We use a dot to denote a time derivative and write $\boldsymbol{u} = \dot{\boldsymbol{r}}$. We note that average velocity and velocity have the dimensions LT^{-1}, and our unit of measurement is the metre per second, the SI symbol being $\mathrm{m\,s^{-1}}$. The magnitude of the velocity is called the *speed*.

In the same way, we may define an average acceleration over the time interval $[t, t+\Delta t]$,

$$\frac{\boldsymbol{u}(t+\Delta t)-\boldsymbol{u}(t)}{t+\Delta t-t}$$

and the acceleration at the instant t,

$$\lim_{\Delta t \to 0} \frac{\boldsymbol{u}(t+\Delta t)-\boldsymbol{u}(t)}{\Delta t}$$

We shall let $\boldsymbol{a}$ denote the acceleration, i.e.

$$\boldsymbol{a}(t) = \frac{d\boldsymbol{u}(t)}{dt} = \frac{d^2\boldsymbol{r}(t)}{dt^2} \quad \text{or} \quad \boldsymbol{a}(t) = \dot{\boldsymbol{u}}(t) = \ddot{\boldsymbol{r}}(t)$$

Average acceleration and acceleration have the dimensions LT^{-2}, and our unit of measurement is the metre per second per second, the SI symbol $\mathrm{m\,s^{-2}}$.

We shall introduce specific coordinate systems and examine the forms of the velocity and the acceleration of P in terms of the coordinates and the unit vectors perpendicular to the coordinate surfaces.

(i) *Cartesian coordinate system*

$$\boldsymbol{r}(t) = x(t)\boldsymbol{i} + y(t)\boldsymbol{j} + z(t)\boldsymbol{k}$$

where the coordinates depend on time, and $\boldsymbol{i}, \boldsymbol{j}, \boldsymbol{k}$ are unit vectors having constant directions. Then

$$\begin{aligned}
\boldsymbol{u}(t) &= \lim_{\Delta t \to 0} \frac{\boldsymbol{r}(t+\Delta t)-\boldsymbol{r}(t)}{\Delta t} \\
&= \lim_{\Delta t \to 0} \left\{ \frac{x(t+\Delta t)-x(t)}{\Delta t}\boldsymbol{i} + \frac{y(t+\Delta t)-y(t)}{\Delta t}\boldsymbol{j} + \frac{z(t+\Delta t)-z(t)}{\Delta t}\boldsymbol{k} \right\} \\
&= \lim_{\Delta t \to 0} \left\{ \frac{x(t+\Delta t)-x(t)}{\Delta t} \right\}\boldsymbol{i} + \lim_{\Delta t \to 0} \left\{ \frac{y(t+\Delta t)-y(t)}{\Delta t} \right\}\boldsymbol{j} +
\end{aligned}$$

$$+\lim_{\Delta t\to 0}\left\{\frac{z(t+\Delta t)-z(t)}{\Delta t}\right\}\boldsymbol{k}$$

$$=\frac{dx(t)}{dt}\boldsymbol{i}+\frac{dy(t)}{dt}\boldsymbol{j}+\frac{dz(t)}{dt}\boldsymbol{k}=\frac{d\boldsymbol{r}(t)}{dt}$$

$$=\dot{x}(t)\boldsymbol{i}+\dot{y}(t)\boldsymbol{j}+\dot{z}(t)\boldsymbol{k}=\dot{\boldsymbol{r}}(t)$$

Similarly we have

$$\boldsymbol{a}(t)=\frac{d^2x(t)}{dt^2}\boldsymbol{i}+\frac{d^2y(t)}{dt^2}\boldsymbol{j}+\frac{d^2z(t)}{dt^2}\boldsymbol{k}=\frac{d^2\boldsymbol{r}(t)}{dt^2}=\frac{d\boldsymbol{u}(t)}{dt}$$

$$=\ddot{x}(t)\boldsymbol{i}+\ddot{y}(t)\boldsymbol{j}+\ddot{z}(t)\boldsymbol{k}=\ddot{\boldsymbol{r}}(t)=\dot{\boldsymbol{u}}(t)$$

(ii) *Plane polar coordinates*

$$\boldsymbol{r}(t)=r(t)\boldsymbol{e}_r$$

where $\boldsymbol{e}_r=\boldsymbol{i}\cos\phi+\boldsymbol{j}\sin\phi$, and $\boldsymbol{e}_\phi=-\boldsymbol{i}\sin\phi+\boldsymbol{j}\cos\phi$. The unit vectors $\boldsymbol{e}_r$ and $\boldsymbol{e}_\phi$ have constant magnitude and their directions vary with time. Writing

$$\boldsymbol{r}=r\cos\phi\boldsymbol{i}+r\sin\phi\boldsymbol{j}$$

we have

$$\boldsymbol{u}=\dot{\boldsymbol{r}}=(\dot{r}\cos\phi-r\sin\phi\,\dot{\phi})\boldsymbol{i}+(\dot{r}\sin\phi+r\cos\phi\,\dot{\phi})\boldsymbol{j}=\dot{r}\boldsymbol{e}_r+r\dot{\phi}\boldsymbol{e}_\phi$$

and

$$\boldsymbol{a}=\dot{\boldsymbol{u}}=(\ddot{r}\cos\phi-\dot{r}\sin\phi\,\dot{\phi}-\dot{r}\sin\phi\,\dot{\phi}-r\cos\phi\,\dot{\phi}^2-r\sin\phi\,\ddot{\phi})\boldsymbol{i}$$
$$+(\ddot{r}\sin\phi+\dot{r}\cos\phi\,\dot{\phi}+\dot{r}\cos\phi\,\dot{\phi}-r\sin\phi\,\dot{\phi}^2-r\cos\phi\,\ddot{\phi})\boldsymbol{j}$$
$$=(\ddot{r}-r\dot{\phi}^2)\boldsymbol{e}_r+(2\dot{r}\dot{\phi}+r\ddot{\phi})\boldsymbol{e}_\phi$$

The radial components of velocity and acceleration are $\boldsymbol{u}\,.\,\boldsymbol{e}_r$ and $\boldsymbol{a}\,.\,\boldsymbol{e}_r$, and the transverse components are $\boldsymbol{u}\,.\,\boldsymbol{e}_\phi$ and $\boldsymbol{a}\,.\,\boldsymbol{e}_\phi$.

	Radial component	Transverse component
Position vector $\boldsymbol{r}$	r	0
Velocity $\boldsymbol{u}$	$\dot{r}$	$r\dot{\phi}$
Acceleration $\boldsymbol{a}$	$\ddot{r}-r\dot{\phi}^2$	$r\ddot{\phi}+2\dot{r}\dot{\phi}=\frac{1}{r}\frac{d}{dt}(r^2\dot{\phi})$

We note that

$$\dot{\boldsymbol{e}}_r=-\boldsymbol{i}\sin\phi\,\dot{\phi}+\boldsymbol{j}\cos\phi\,\dot{\phi}=\dot{\phi}\boldsymbol{e}_\phi$$

and

$$\dot{\boldsymbol{e}}_\phi=-\boldsymbol{i}\cos\phi\,\dot{\phi}-\boldsymbol{j}\sin\phi\,\dot{\phi}=-\dot{\phi}\boldsymbol{e}_r$$

Hence $\boldsymbol{u} = \dot{r}\boldsymbol{e}_r + r\dot{\boldsymbol{e}}_r$.

Equivalently we have

$$\begin{aligned}\boldsymbol{u}(t) &= \lim_{\Delta t \to 0} \left\{ \frac{r(t+\Delta t)\boldsymbol{e}_r(t+\Delta t) - r(t)\boldsymbol{e}_r(t)}{\Delta t} \right\} \\ &= \lim_{\Delta t \to 0} \left\{ \left(\frac{r(t+\Delta t) - r(t)}{\Delta t} \right) \boldsymbol{e}_r(t+\Delta t) + r(t) \left(\frac{\boldsymbol{e}_r(t+\Delta t) - \boldsymbol{e}_r(t)}{\Delta t} \right) \right\} \\ &= \dot{r}(t)\boldsymbol{e}_r(t) + r(t)\dot{\boldsymbol{e}}_r(t)\end{aligned}$$

Therefore we may write

$$\boldsymbol{r} = r\boldsymbol{e}_r$$

$$\boldsymbol{u} = \dot{\boldsymbol{r}} = \dot{r}\boldsymbol{e}_r + r\dot{\boldsymbol{e}}_r = \dot{r}\boldsymbol{e}_r + r\dot{\phi}\boldsymbol{e}_\phi$$

and

$$\begin{aligned}\boldsymbol{a} = \dot{\boldsymbol{u}} = \ddot{\boldsymbol{r}} &= \ddot{r}\boldsymbol{e}_r + \dot{r}\dot{\boldsymbol{e}}_r + \dot{r}\dot{\phi}\boldsymbol{e}_\phi + r\ddot{\phi}\boldsymbol{e}_\phi + r\dot{\phi}\dot{\boldsymbol{e}}_\phi \\ &= (\ddot{r} - r\dot{\phi}^2)\boldsymbol{e}_r + (2\dot{r}\dot{\phi} + r\ddot{\phi})\boldsymbol{e}_\phi\end{aligned}$$

(iii) *Cylindrical polar coordinates*

The results appropriate to this system of coordinates follow from our previous results.

$$\boldsymbol{r} = r\boldsymbol{e}_r + z\boldsymbol{k}$$

where $\boldsymbol{e}_r = \boldsymbol{i}\cos\phi + \boldsymbol{j}\sin\phi$, and $\boldsymbol{e}_\phi = -\boldsymbol{i}\sin\phi + \boldsymbol{j}\cos\phi$. Hence

$$\boldsymbol{u} = \dot{\boldsymbol{r}} = \dot{r}\boldsymbol{e}_r + r\dot{\phi}\boldsymbol{e}_\phi + \dot{z}\boldsymbol{k}$$

and

$$\boldsymbol{a} = \dot{\boldsymbol{u}} = \ddot{\boldsymbol{r}} = (\ddot{r} - r\dot{\phi}^2)\boldsymbol{e}_r + (2\dot{r}\dot{\phi} + r\ddot{\phi})\boldsymbol{e}_\phi + \ddot{z}\boldsymbol{k}$$

Finally in this section, we comment on the measurement of velocities and accelerations. Provided that we can measure distances (and angles), we are able to determine position vectors; and hence, provided we can also measure time, we are able to determine average velocities. The velocity at an instant is a mathematical idealization based on the idea of limits. It may be approximated by an average value over a short time interval neighbouring the instant. For example, we may say

$$\boldsymbol{u}(t) = \frac{\boldsymbol{r}(t+\Delta t) - \boldsymbol{r}(t-\Delta t)}{2\Delta t} + \text{error term}$$

It follows from Taylor's theorem [see J. Hunter, *Calculus*, Blackie/Chambers] that the error term is proportional to the square of Δt when Δt is small. An easy extension leads to

$$\boldsymbol{a}(t) = \frac{\boldsymbol{u}(t+\Delta t) - \boldsymbol{u}(t-\Delta t)}{2\Delta t} + \text{error term}$$

$$= \frac{r(t+2\Delta t)-2r(t)+r(t-2\Delta t)}{(2\Delta t)^2} + \text{error term}$$

where the final error term is proportional to Δt when Δt is small. Compare this with numerical differentiation of a function [see C. Dixon, *Numerical Analysis*, Blackie/Chambers].

2.2 One-dimensional motion

Let us concentrate on a special case. Consider a set P having a single element, and suppose the set is moving in a straight line. Then at any instant t, the position vector of the point (being the element of the set P) has the form

$$\boldsymbol{r} = g(t)\boldsymbol{e} + \boldsymbol{r}_0$$

where $\boldsymbol{e}$ and $\boldsymbol{r}_0$ are independent of time. We select a coordinate axis that coincides with the path of the set P, determined by the direction of the vector $\boldsymbol{e}$. Let this axis be the x-axis and let the coordinate of the "moving point P" at the instant t be $x(t)$ relative to a specified origin O. Let $\boldsymbol{i}$ be the unit vector in the direction of x increasing. Then

$$\boldsymbol{r} = x(t)\boldsymbol{i}, \quad \boldsymbol{u} = \dot{x}(t)\boldsymbol{i}, \quad \boldsymbol{a} = \ddot{x}(t)\boldsymbol{i}$$

We may omit the vectorial representation in this one-dimensional situation and deal with the components of the vectors. In doing this, we understand that the unit vector $\boldsymbol{i}$ has been omitted and we say that the velocity (or strictly speaking, the velocity component) is $u(t) = \dot{x}(t)$ and the acceleration (or strictly speaking, the acceleration component) is $a(t) = \dot{u}(t) = \ddot{x}(t)$.

Graphical representations are useful aids. If we plot the x-coordinate against time, the slope of the curve, $\dot{x}$, is the velocity. The graph below

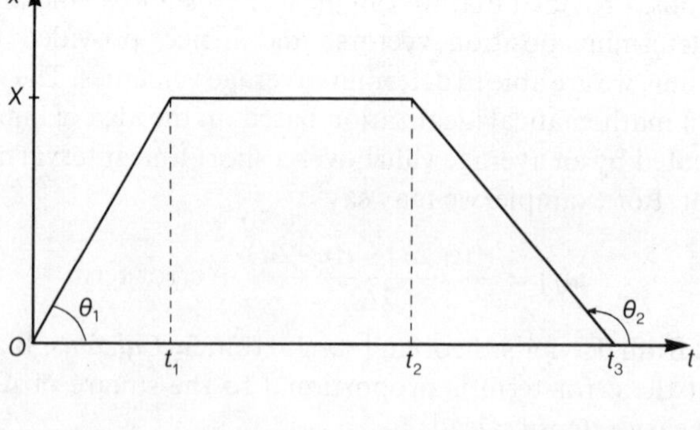

represents the motion of a body (represented by the set P) that starts from the origin O at $t = 0$, moves with constant velocity until $t = t_1$, is stationary between $t = t_1$ and $t = t_2$, and returns to the starting point O with constant velocity. The straight lines making up the graph give rise to discontinuities in slope at $t = t_1$ and $t = t_2$. This indicates discontinuities in the velocity of the body. This is unacceptable because the velocity of a body changes continually. We have ignored the retardation (or deceleration) and the acceleration that take place over very short time intervals surrounding $t = t_1$ and $t = t_2$, respectively. However, the straight-line graph is a useful approximation, provided we recognize our assumptions.

If we plot the velocity u against time, the slope of the curve, $\dot{u}$, is the acceleration, and the area under the curve,

$$\int_{t_B}^{t_E} u(t)dt = \int_{t_B}^{t_E} \dot{x}(t)dt = x(t_E) - x(t_B)$$

gives the change in the x-coordinate during the time interval $[t_B, t_E]$. The second graph is appropriate to the motion described in the previous

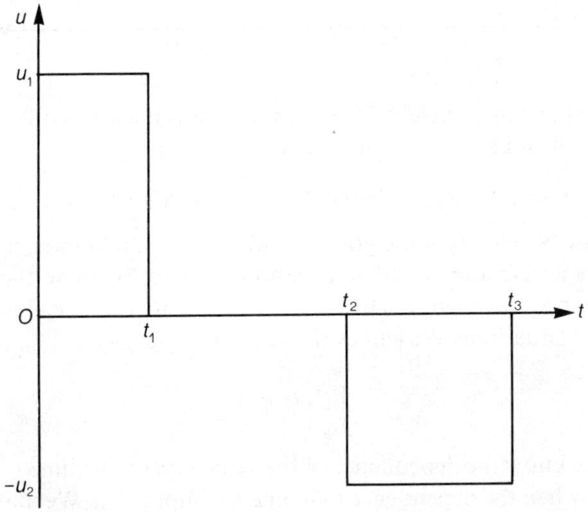

paragraph. It consists of three straight lines parallel to the time axis. The following relations hold between X, t_1, t_2, t_3, θ_1, θ_2, u_1 and u_2, which are introduced in the figures.

$$\tan\theta_1 = \frac{X}{t_1} = u_1 > 0$$

$$\tan\theta_2 = \frac{-X}{t_3 - t_2} = -u_2 < 0$$

and $X = u_1 t_1 = u_2(t_3 - t_2)$. The requirement that the velocity changes continuously suggests that we should smooth away some corners of the rectangles in the second figure (in particular, the corners having coordinates (t_1, u_1), $(t_1, 0)$, $(t_2, 0)$ and $(t_2, -u_2)$).

As another example, consider the graph that describes the motion of a body accelerating with constant acceleration A from rest, moving with maximum velocity U during a time interval, and coming to rest with constant retardation R. We have

$$\tan\theta_1 = A = U/t_1, \quad \tan\theta_2 = -R = -U/(t_3 - t_2)$$

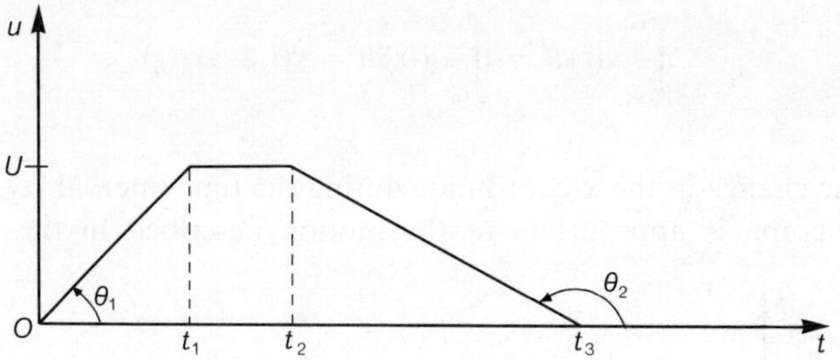

and the total distance travelled from rest to rest is the area under the curve between $t = 0$ and $t = t_3$, which equals

$$\tfrac{1}{2}Ut_1 + U(t_2 - t_1) + \tfrac{1}{2}U(t_3 - t_2) = \tfrac{1}{2}U(t_3 + t_2 - t_1)$$

In the case of velocity–time graphs made up of straight lines, it is easy to read off the accelerations and retardations and to calculate the distance travelled during a journey. However, we have to use calculus in more complicated situations. We can evaluate the integral

$$\int_{t_B}^{t_E} u(t)\,dt$$

provided we know the dependence of the velocity u on the time t. This may not be true when the dependence of u on t is complicated. We may usefully employ an approximate integration method, e.g. the trapezium rule or Simpson's rule [see C. Dixon, *Numerical Analysis*, Blackie/Chambers], when the integrand is complicated or when the velocity is known only at a finite number of instants during the journey.

EXAMPLE

A motor-car accelerates from rest. Times to reach various speeds (measured in kilometres per hour) are measured in seconds. Use the table of results to estimate the distance travelled in the first thirty seconds.

t	0	4·3	7·0	11·2	16·7	23·5	36·9
$u(t)$	0	40	60	80	100	120	140

We assume that the acceleration is constant between each pair of consecutive measurements and use the trapezium rule to evaluate an approximation to the integral

$$\int_0^{30} u(t)dt = \int_0^{23\cdot5} u(t)dt + \int_{23\cdot5}^{30} u(t)dt$$

The approximation (in metres) to

$$\int_0^{23\cdot5} u(t)dt = [\tfrac{1}{2}(4\cdot3)(0+40)+\tfrac{1}{2}(2\cdot7)(40+60)+\tfrac{1}{2}(4\cdot2)(60+80)$$

$$+\tfrac{1}{2}(5\cdot5)(80+100)+\tfrac{1}{2}(6\cdot8)(100+120)]\frac{1000}{3600} = 488\cdot3$$

The average acceleration over the interval $[23\cdot5, 36\cdot9]$ is

$$\frac{(140-120)}{(36\cdot9-23\cdot5)}\cdot\frac{1000}{3600} = 0\cdot4144$$

(the units being m s^{-2}). Hence the approximation (in metres) to

$$\int_{23\cdot5}^{30} u(t)dt = \tfrac{1}{2}(6\cdot5)\left\{120+120+6\cdot5\left(\frac{140-120}{36\cdot9-23\cdot5}\right)\right\}\frac{1000}{3600}$$

$$= \frac{650}{3} + \tfrac{1}{2}(6\cdot5)^2(0\cdot4144) = 225\cdot4$$

Thus the distance travelled in the first thirty seconds is approximately 714 metres.

Sometimes it is useful to consider the velocity to depend on the position, and the position to depend on time. Then the velocity appears as a composition function, i.e.

$$(u \circ x)(t) = u(x(t))$$

Using the chain rule to differentiate this composition function with respect to time, we see that the acceleration a is given by

$$\frac{d}{dt}(u \circ x)(t) = \frac{du(x)}{dx}\frac{dx(t)}{dt} = u(x)\frac{du(x)}{dx}$$

We shall find this alternative expression for the acceleration very useful in later sections.

We note in passing that distance–time graphs are useful in the design of timetables for ’buses, trains and aircraft. We find that a rough sketch is sufficient and we assume that the paths of the vehicles are straight lines. The graphs indicate average velocities between cities and provide no information about instantaneous values of velocity and acceleration. An example is given in which the movements of five trains are illustrated:

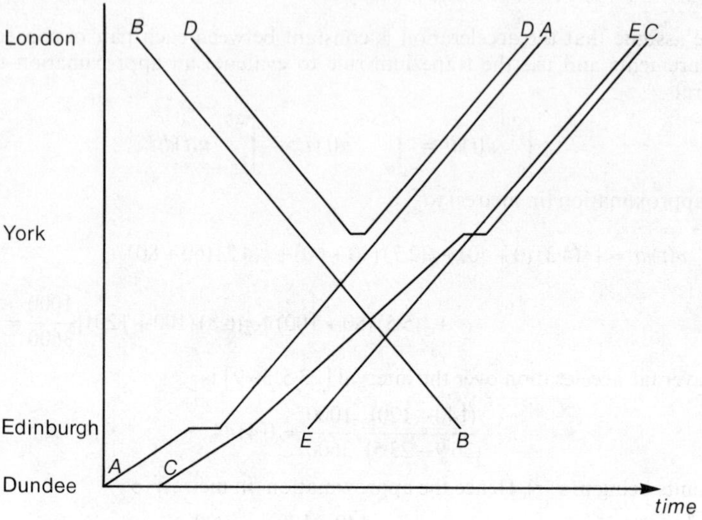

AA Dundee to London, with a stop at Edinburgh;
BB London to Edinburgh, non-stop;
CC Dundee to London, with a stop at York;
DD London to York and return;
EE Edinburgh to London, non-stop (passes *CC* at York, which raises the question of the number of trains that can be handled at York simultaneously).

2.3 Uniformly accelerated motion in a straight line

Suppose that we are given the information that the acceleration of a body, moving in a straight line, is constant during the time interval $[t_0, t_1]$. What can we say about the velocity and the position of the body? We shall see later that this situation arises when bodies fall under the influence of gravity near the surface of the Earth.

First, we assume that we represent the body by the set P, having a single element at any instant, the element being a point of a specified line in euclidean space. Let the x-axis coincide with this specified line. Then the position vector (relative to a chosen origin) $\boldsymbol{r}$ is $x\boldsymbol{i}$, the velocity $\boldsymbol{u}$ is $u\boldsymbol{i}$, where $u = \dot{x}$, and the acceleration $\boldsymbol{a}$ is $a\boldsymbol{i}$, where $a = \dot{u} = \ddot{x}$.

We can write the given information in the form of an equation

$$a(t) = A, \quad t_0 \leqslant t \leqslant t_1$$

where A is a known constant. By setting $a(t) = \dot{u}(t)$, we convert the equation into a differential equation for the unknown velocity component u. Hence

$$\frac{du(t)}{dt} = A, \quad t_0 \leqslant t \leqslant t_1$$

Integration with respect to time leads to

$$\int_{t_0}^{t} \frac{du(t)}{dt}\,dt = \int_{t_0}^{t} A\,dt$$

and

$$u(t) = u(t_0) + A(t-t_0) \quad \text{for} \quad t \in [t_0, t_1]$$

This gives the velocity component at time t in terms of the velocity component at time t_0 and the linear expression. On substituting $u(t) = \dot{x}(t)$, we obtain a differential equation for the x-coordinate, namely

$$\frac{dx(t)}{dt} = u(t_0) + A(t-t_0), \quad t_0 \leqslant t \leqslant t_1$$

Integrating with respect to time again, we find that

$$\int_{t_0}^{t} \frac{dx(t)}{dt}\,dt = \int_{t_0}^{t} \{u(t_0) + A(t-t_0)\}\,dt$$

and

$$x(t) = x(t_0) + u(t_0)(t-t_0) + \tfrac{1}{2}A(t-t_0)^2 \quad \text{for} \quad t \in [t_0, t_1]$$

This is an expression for the x-coordinate at time t in terms of the x-coordinate at time t_0 and the quadratic expression. Hence we can calculate the velocity and the position of the body moving with constant acceleration, provided we know its velocity at an instant and its position at an instant (possibly, a different instant). What we have done is to solve a differential equation ($\ddot{x}(t) = A$) subject to two initial conditions (the values of $x(t)$ and $\dot{x}(t)$ at $t = t_0$).

If we choose the origin of the coordinate axis to be the element of the set P at time t_0, and we measure time from the instant the set P leaves the origin, we may set $t_0 = 0$ and $x(t_0) = 0$. Then our results simplify to

$$u(t) = u_0 + At$$

and

$$x(t) = u_0 t + \tfrac{1}{2}At^2$$

where u_0 is the initial value of the velocity component, namely $u(0)$.

Eliminating the parameter t from the above pair of equations, we obtain an expression between the velocity component u and the coordinate x, namely,

$$x = u_0\left(\frac{u-u_0}{A}\right)+\tfrac{1}{2}A\left(\frac{u-u_0}{A}\right)^2$$

$$\Rightarrow \quad 2Ax = 2u_0(u-u_0)+(u-u_0)^2 = u^2-u_0^2$$

$$\Rightarrow \quad u^2(x) = u_0^2+2Ax$$

This result may be obtained directly from the differential equation

$$a(x) = A, \quad \text{where} \quad a(x) = u(x)\frac{du(x)}{dx}$$

Integration with respect to x gives

$$\int_0^x u(x)\frac{du(x)}{dx}\,dx = \int_0^x A\,dx$$

and $\frac{1}{2}u^2(x)-\frac{1}{2}u_0^2 = Ax$, i.e. $u^2(x) = u_0^2+2Ax$.

2.4 Circular motion

The simplest example of motion along a curved path is a body moving in a circle. Again we represent the body by a set P having a single element at any instant. The appropriate coordinate system is a system of plane polar coordinates having the origin at the centre of the circle.

The element of the set P has the position vector

$$\boldsymbol{r} = r_0\boldsymbol{e}_r, \quad \text{where} \quad \boldsymbol{e}_r = \boldsymbol{i}\cos\phi+\boldsymbol{j}\sin\phi$$

r_0 is the radius of the circle (a constant) and ϕ is an angle varying with time. Either by working from first principles or by applying the results of Section 2.1 to this special case, we find that the velocity and the acceleration are

$$\boldsymbol{u} = \dot{\boldsymbol{r}} = r_0\dot{\phi}\boldsymbol{e}_\phi$$

and

$$\boldsymbol{a} = \dot{\boldsymbol{u}} = \ddot{\boldsymbol{r}} = -r_0\dot{\phi}^2\boldsymbol{e}_r+r_0\ddot{\phi}\boldsymbol{e}_\phi$$

where $\boldsymbol{e}_\phi = -\boldsymbol{i}\sin\phi+\boldsymbol{j}\cos\phi$. We notice that the velocity vector is always perpendicular to the position vector (because the unit vectors $\boldsymbol{e}_r, \boldsymbol{e}_\phi$ are always orthogonal, i.e. $\boldsymbol{e}_r\cdot\boldsymbol{e}_\phi = 0$). Another way of saying this is that the velocity vector has no radial component.

When $\dot{\phi}$ is constant, the magnitude of the velocity vector (the speed) is constant. In this steady motion $\ddot{\phi} = 0$, and the acceleration vector has a radial component and no transverse component. Hence a body moving with constant speed U in a circle of radius r_0 has an acceleration of magnitude U^2/r_0 towards the centre of the circle. Its cartesian coordinates are $x = r_0 \cos\phi$ and $y = r_0 \sin\phi$. Setting the constant value of $\dot{\phi}$ to be ω, we have

$$U = r_0\omega \quad \text{and} \quad \phi = \omega t + \varepsilon$$

where ε is an arbitrary constant of integration. Hence

$$x = r_0 \cos(\omega t + \varepsilon) \quad \text{and} \quad y = r_0 \sin(\omega t + \varepsilon)$$

It is worth noting that

$$\frac{dx}{dt} = -\omega r_0 \sin(\omega t + \varepsilon), \quad \frac{d^2x}{dt^2} = -\omega^2 r_0 \cos(\omega t + \varepsilon) = -\omega^2 x$$

and

$$\frac{dy}{dt} = \omega r_0 \cos(\omega t + \varepsilon), \quad \frac{d^2y}{dt^2} = -\omega^2 r_0 \sin(\omega t + \varepsilon) = -\omega^2 y$$

Therefore $r_0 \cos(\omega t + \varepsilon)$ and $r_0 \sin(\omega t + \varepsilon)$ are both solutions of the differential equation $(d^2x/dt^2) + \omega^2 x = 0$ (i.e. $\ddot{x} + \omega^2 x = 0$). We remember that r_0 and ε are constants. Noting that

$$\cos(\omega t + \varepsilon) = \cos\omega t \cos\varepsilon - \sin\omega t \sin\varepsilon$$

and

$$\sin(\omega t + \varepsilon) = \sin\omega t \cos\varepsilon + \cos\omega t \sin\varepsilon$$

we deduce that $\cos\omega t$ and $\sin\omega t$ are two independent solutions of the differential equation $\ddot{x} + \omega^2 x = 0$. In fact this second-order differential equation has no other independent solution. Its general solution has the form

$$A\cos\omega t + B\sin\omega t$$

where A and B are arbitrary constants. An alternative form is

$$(A^2+B^2)^{1/2}\left\{\frac{A}{(A^2+B^2)^{1/2}}\cos\omega t + \frac{B}{(A^2+B^2)^{1/2}}\sin\omega t\right\}$$

which equals either

$$(A^2+B^2)^{1/2}\sin(\omega t + \delta)$$

with $\sin\delta = A/(A^2+B^2)^{1/2}$ and $\cos\delta = B/(A^2+B^2)^{1/2}$ or

$$(A^2+B^2)^{1/2}\cos(\omega t - \delta)$$

with $\sin\delta = B/(A^2+B^2)^{1/2}$ and $\cos\delta = A/(A^2+B^2)^{1/2}$.

The differential equation $\ddot{x} + \omega^2 x = 0$ has important applications in mechanics: it describes *simple harmonic motion* (SHM). If we plot the coordinate x (or y) against the time t, we obtain a curve that has crests and troughs. The curve lies between the lines $x = -r_0$ and $x = +r_0$ and it repeats itself. r_0 is the amplitude. The time interval between repeated values of x (called the period and denoted by T) is $2\pi/\omega$, because

$$x = r_0 \cos(\omega t + \varepsilon) = r_0 \cos\{\omega(t + 2\pi/\omega) + \varepsilon\}$$
$$= r_0 \cos\{\omega(t + 4\pi/\omega) + \varepsilon\} = \ldots$$

The frequency ν is $1/T$ and the angular frequency ω is $2\pi\nu = 2\pi/T$.

The Earth rotates about the Sun and spins about its axis. The Earth's path around the Sun is almost circular, the radius being $1{\cdot}50 \times 10^{11}$ metres. The time taken by the Earth to move once round the Sun is one year, which equals $3{\cdot}16 \times 10^7$ seconds approximately. Therefore the period, which equals $2\pi/\omega$, is $3{\cdot}16 \times 10^7$ seconds and $\omega = 1{\cdot}99 \times 10^{-7}$ (the unit being rad s^{-1}). Hence the speed U, which equals $r_0\omega$, is $3{\cdot}0 \times 10^4$ m s^{-1} and the acceleration towards the Sun, which equals $r_0\omega^2$ or U^2/r_0, is $0{\cdot}0059$ m s^{-2}. These values are relative to a coordinate system having the Sun at the origin.

We can calculate the velocity and the acceleration of a body fixed on the surface of the Earth relative to a coordinate system about whose z-axis the Earth is rotating daily. We note that it is difficult to find the velocity and acceleration of this body relative to the coordinate system having the Sun at the origin. The Earth rotates about the polar axis approximately once per day. Its period is 86 164 seconds (not 86 400 seconds). Assuming that the Earth is a sphere of radius $6{\cdot}371 \times 10^6$ metres, we can proceed as before. (The equatorial radius is $6{\cdot}378 \times 10^6$ metres and the polar radius is $6{\cdot}357 \times 10^6$ metres.) Therefore $\omega = 7{\cdot}29 \times 10^{-5}$ (the unit being rad s^{-1}). Then for a body at latitude θ, the speed U, which equals $(r_0 \cos\theta)\omega$, is $465 \cos\theta$ m s^{-1} and the acceleration towards the axis, which equals $(r_0 \cos\theta)\omega^2$, is $0{\cdot}0339 \cos\theta$ m s^{-2}.

2.5 Relative motion

In the previous sections of this chapter, the set P (having a single element at any instant) has had assigned a unique position vector relative to the chosen frame of reference. It follows that the velocity of the set P is uniquely specified relative to the chosen frame of reference. However, if we change our frame of reference, we must assign a new position vector and a new velocity to the set P. Consider, for example, a passenger walking along the corridor of an express train rushing through a station. The passenger's velocity relative to the driver seated in the engine-cab is different from the passenger's velocity relative to a porter standing on the station platform. We must be able to relate these velocities.

Suppose we introduce a second frame of reference, and the position vectors of the set P under investigation relative to the two frames are $\boldsymbol{r}$ and

$\boldsymbol{r}'$. If the origin O' of the second frame of reference has the position vector $\boldsymbol{c}$ relative to the first frame of reference, then

$$\overrightarrow{OP} = \overrightarrow{OO'} + \overrightarrow{O'P} \quad \text{and} \quad \boldsymbol{r}(t) = \boldsymbol{c}(t) + \boldsymbol{r}'(t)$$

The relation between the velocities of the set P relative to the two frames clearly follows. It is

$$\frac{d\boldsymbol{r}(t)}{dt} = \frac{d\boldsymbol{c}(t)}{dt} + \frac{d\boldsymbol{r}'(t)}{dt}$$

where the velocity relative to the original frame of reference is $d\boldsymbol{r}(t)/dt$ and the velocity relative to the second frame of reference is $d\boldsymbol{r}'(t)/dt$. Alternatively we may write

$$\boldsymbol{u}(t) = \dot{\boldsymbol{c}}(t) + \boldsymbol{u}'(t)$$

If $\boldsymbol{c}(t)$ is a constant vector (i.e. independent of time), then $\dot{\boldsymbol{c}}(t) = \boldsymbol{0}$ and the two velocities are identical. In all other cases, the two velocities differ, and it is essential to associate the frame of reference with the velocity. The velocity of a body (or of the set P representing the body) has meaning only when it is specified relative to a chosen frame of reference (e.g. $\boldsymbol{u}$ is the velocity relative to the first frame of reference and $\boldsymbol{u}'$ is the velocity relative to the second frame of reference).

We must associate similarly the acceleration of a body with a frame of reference. We see that the accelerations of the set P relative to the two frames of reference are related by the equation

$$\boldsymbol{a}(t) = \ddot{\boldsymbol{c}}(t) + \boldsymbol{a}'(t)$$

where the acceleration relative to the original frame of reference is $\boldsymbol{a}(t)$ and the acceleration relative to the second frame of reference is $\boldsymbol{a}'(t)$. If $\ddot{\boldsymbol{c}}(t) = \boldsymbol{0}$, the two accelerations are identical and

$$\dot{\boldsymbol{c}}(t) = \mathbf{A}, \quad \boldsymbol{c}(t) = \mathbf{A}t + \mathbf{B}$$

where $\mathbf{A}, \mathbf{B}$ are constant vectors. In this case the origin O' is moving in a straight line with constant velocity relative to the original frame of reference.

EXAMPLE

A ship is steaming due north at a constant speed of 20 knots, and a second ship is steaming due east at a constant speed of 10 knots. At noon the second ship is 10 nautical miles north-west of the first ship. Find the shortest subsequent distance between the ships, and the time at which they reach their closest separation.

We select a frame of reference fixed relative to the Earth and discuss the motion of two points, S_1 and S_2, relative to it. Let $\boldsymbol{i}, \boldsymbol{j}$ be unit vectors in the directions due east and due north, respectively, and let the origin O coincide with the position of S_1 at noon. We measure distance in nautical miles, time in hours from noon, and speeds in nautical miles per hour (namely, knots). There are two interpretations of the nautical mile: the United Kingdom version of 1853·18 metres (6080 feet) and the international version of 1852 metres.

Let $\boldsymbol{r}_1, \boldsymbol{r}_2$ be the position vectors of S_1, S_2 relative to O. For all time, we have

$$\dot{\boldsymbol{r}}_1 = 20\boldsymbol{j} \quad \text{and} \quad \dot{\boldsymbol{r}}_2 = 10\boldsymbol{i}$$

Integration of these differential equations leads to

$$\boldsymbol{r}_1 = 20t\boldsymbol{j} + \mathbf{C}_1 \quad \text{and} \quad \boldsymbol{r}_2 = 10t\boldsymbol{i} + \mathbf{C}_2$$

where $\mathbf{C}_1, \mathbf{C}_2$ are constant vectors determined by the positions of S_1, S_2 at noon (i.e. $t = 0$). Therefore

$$\boldsymbol{0} = \mathbf{C}_1 \quad \text{and} \quad 10(-\boldsymbol{i}+\boldsymbol{j})/\sqrt{2} = \mathbf{C}_2$$

Thus

$$\boldsymbol{r}_1 = 20t\boldsymbol{j} \quad \text{and} \quad \boldsymbol{r}_2 = (10t - 5\sqrt{2})\boldsymbol{i} + 5\sqrt{2}\boldsymbol{j}$$

Let D be the distance between S_1 and S_2. Then

$$\begin{aligned} D^2 = |\boldsymbol{r}_1 - \boldsymbol{r}_2|^2 &= (10t - 5\sqrt{2})^2 + (20t - 5\sqrt{2})^2 \\ &= 500t^2 - 300\sqrt{2}t + 100 \\ &= 500\left(t^2 - \frac{3\sqrt{2}}{5}t + \frac{1}{5}\right) \\ &= 500\left\{\left(t - \frac{3\sqrt{2}}{10}\right)^2 + \frac{1}{5} - \frac{9}{50}\right\} \\ &= 500\left(t - \frac{3\sqrt{2}}{10}\right)^2 + 10 \end{aligned}$$

The shortest distance between the two ships is $\sqrt{10}$ nautical miles, and the ships reach their closest separation at $3\sqrt{2}/10$ hours (about 25 minutes 27 seconds) after noon.

An alternative way of finding the minimum of D is to use calculus. Thus

$$\begin{aligned} 2D\frac{dD}{dt} &= 20(10t - 5\sqrt{2}) + 40(20t - 5\sqrt{2}) \\ &= 1000t - 300\sqrt{2} \end{aligned}$$

and either $D = 0$ or $dD/dt = 0$ at $t = 3\sqrt{2}/10$. At $t = 3\sqrt{2}/10$,

$$D^2 = (3\sqrt{2} - 5\sqrt{2})^2 + (6\sqrt{2} - 5\sqrt{2})^2 = 8 + 2 = 10 \quad \text{and} \quad \frac{dD}{dt} = 0$$

Also $2(dD/dt)^2 + 2D(d^2D/dt^2) = 1000$. Therefore D takes a minimum value of $\sqrt{10}$ at $t = 3\sqrt{2}/10$.

Let us look at this example in a more general manner. Suppose that there are two sets P_1 and P_2 (each containing a single element at any instant) and that their position vectors relative to an origin O are $\boldsymbol{r}_1$ and $\boldsymbol{r}_2$. We are given that

$$\dot{\boldsymbol{r}}_1 = \mathbf{U}_1 \quad \text{and} \quad \dot{\boldsymbol{r}}_2 = \mathbf{U}_2 \quad \text{for all time}$$

where $\mathbf{U}_1$ and $\mathbf{U}_2$ are constant vectors, and that $\boldsymbol{r}_1 = \mathbf{C}_1$ and $\boldsymbol{r}_2 = \mathbf{C}_2$ at $t = 0$. Therefore

$$\boldsymbol{r}_1 = \mathbf{U}_1 t + \mathbf{C}_1 \quad \text{and} \quad \boldsymbol{r}_2 = \mathbf{U}_2 t + \mathbf{C}_2 \quad \text{for all time}$$

Let D be the distance between P_1 and P_2 at any time t. Then

$$\begin{aligned} D^2 &= |\boldsymbol{r}_1 - \boldsymbol{r}_2|^2 = |(\mathbf{U}_1 - \mathbf{U}_2)t + (\mathbf{C}_1 - \mathbf{C}_2)|^2 \\ &= |\mathbf{U}_1 - \mathbf{U}_2|^2 t^2 + 2(\mathbf{U}_1 - \mathbf{U}_2).(\mathbf{C}_1 - \mathbf{C}_2)t + |\mathbf{C}_1 - \mathbf{C}_2|^2 \\ &= |\mathbf{U}_1 - \mathbf{U}_2|^2 \left\{ t + \frac{(\mathbf{U}_1 - \mathbf{U}_2).(\mathbf{C}_1 - \mathbf{C}_2)}{|\mathbf{U}_1 - \mathbf{U}_2|^2} \right\}^2 + |\mathbf{C}_1 - \mathbf{C}_2|^2 \\ &\quad - \frac{\{(\mathbf{U}_1 - \mathbf{U}_2).(\mathbf{C}_1 - \mathbf{C}_2)\}^2}{|\mathbf{U}_1 - \mathbf{U}_2|^2} \end{aligned}$$

Hence the shortest distance apart is

$$\left\{ |\mathbf{C}_1 - \mathbf{C}_2|^2 - \frac{\{(\mathbf{U}_1 - \mathbf{U}_2).(\mathbf{C}_1 - \mathbf{C}_2)\}^2}{|\mathbf{U}_1 - \mathbf{U}_2|^2} \right\}^{1/2}$$

and P_1 and P_2 are in this position at

$$t = \frac{-(\mathbf{U}_1 - \mathbf{U}_2).(\mathbf{C}_1 - \mathbf{C}_2)}{|\mathbf{U}_1 - \mathbf{U}_2|^2}$$

We note that $\mathbf{U}_1 - \mathbf{U}_2$ is the velocity of P_1 relative to P_2 and that $\mathbf{C}_1 - \mathbf{C}_2$ is the position vector of P_1 relative to P_2 initially.

2.6 Translation of a frame of reference

We wish to study the motion of one frame of reference relative to another frame of reference. Let the cartesian coordinate system $Oxyz$ be the original frame of reference. As a simple example of a translating frame of reference, consider the cartesian coordinate system $O'x'y'z'$, of which the origin O' travels along the Ox-axis in the direction of x increasing with constant speed u and the axes $O'x', O'y', O'z'$ are parallel to the axes Ox, Oy, Oz, respectively, throughout the motion. Suppose that observers moving with the frames of reference have clocks which they synchronized when the origins, O and O', coincided. Let P be any point, having coordinates (x, y, z) and (x', y', z') relative to the two frames of reference. We seek the relations

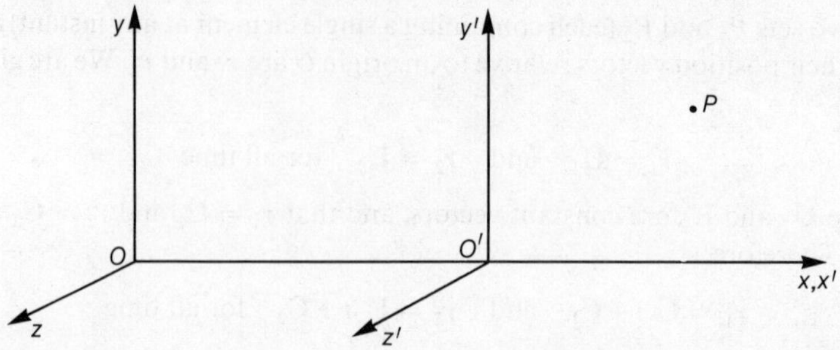

between these coordinates. The coordinates of O' relative to the original frame of reference (based on the coordinate system $Oxyz$) at time t are $(ut, 0, 0)$. By comparing distances and using the absoluteness of displacement, we obtain the relations

$$\begin{aligned} x &= x' + ut & \qquad x' &= x - ut \\ y &= y' & \text{and} \qquad y' &= y \\ z &= z' & z' &= z \end{aligned}$$

The absoluteness of time and the synchronization of the clocks give $t = t'$. Thus we have the Galilean transformation, namely

$$\begin{aligned} x &= x' + ut' & \qquad x' &= x - ut \\ y &= y' & \text{and} \qquad y' &= y \\ z &= z' & z' &= z \\ t &= t' & t' &= t \end{aligned}$$

This becomes $\boldsymbol{r} = \boldsymbol{c} + \boldsymbol{r}'$ in the notation of the previous section, where

$$\begin{aligned} \boldsymbol{r} &= x\boldsymbol{i} + y\boldsymbol{j} + z\boldsymbol{k} \\ \boldsymbol{c} &= ut\boldsymbol{i} \\ \boldsymbol{r}' &= x'\boldsymbol{i}' + y'\boldsymbol{j}' + z'\boldsymbol{k}' \\ \boldsymbol{i} &= \boldsymbol{i}',\ \boldsymbol{j} = \boldsymbol{j}' \text{ and } \boldsymbol{k} = \boldsymbol{k}' \end{aligned}$$

An alternative representation is

$$\boldsymbol{x} = G_u \boldsymbol{x}'$$

where

$$\boldsymbol{x} = \begin{bmatrix} x \\ y \\ z \\ t \end{bmatrix} \qquad G_u = \begin{bmatrix} 1 & 0 & 0 & u \\ 0 & 1 & 0 & 0 \\ 0 & 0 & 1 & 0 \\ 0 & 0 & 0 & 1 \end{bmatrix} \qquad \boldsymbol{x}' = \begin{bmatrix} x' \\ y' \\ z' \\ t' \end{bmatrix}$$

Here $\boldsymbol{x}$ and $\boldsymbol{x}'$ are column vectors, and G_u is a matrix.

In the Special Theory of Relativity, the assumptions about space and time are different from those in Newtonian Mechanics and the corresponding transformation—called the Lorentz transformation—is

$$\begin{aligned} x &= \frac{x'+ut'}{(1-u^2/c^2)^{1/2}} & \qquad & & x' &= \frac{x-ut}{(1-u^2/c^2)^{1/2}} \\ y &= y' & & \text{and} & y' &= y \\ z &= z' & & & z' &= z \\ t &= \frac{t'+ux'/c^2}{(1-u^2/c^2)^{1/2}} & & & t' &= \frac{t-ux/c^2}{(1-u^2/c^2)^{1/2}} \end{aligned}$$

[see W. G. V. Rosser, *An Introduction to the Theory of Relativity*, Butterworth]. An alternative representation is

$$\boldsymbol{x} = L_u \boldsymbol{x}'$$

where

$$L_u = \begin{bmatrix} \gamma(u) & 0 & 0 & u\gamma(u) \\ 0 & 1 & 0 & 0 \\ 0 & 0 & 1 & 0 \\ u\gamma(u)/c^2 & 0 & 0 & \gamma(u) \end{bmatrix}$$

and $\gamma(u) = (1-u^2/c^2)^{-1/2}$. Here c is the speed of light. The speed of light in a vacuum is $2{\cdot}998 \times 10^8$ m s^{-1}. In engineering problems the speeds are very much less than the speed of light, and the Galilean transformation is an excellent approximation to the Lorentz transformation.

Suppose that there is a third frame of reference (based on the cartesian coordinate system $O''x''y''z''$) which is moving relative to the second frame of reference (based on the cartesian coordinate system $O'x'y'z'$) so that the coordinates and times are related by the Galilean transformation

$$\begin{aligned} x' &= x''+vt'' & \qquad & & x'' &= x'-vt' \\ y' &= y'' & & \text{and} & y'' &= y' \\ z' &= z'' & & & z'' &= z' \\ t' &= t'' & & & t'' &= t' \end{aligned}$$

i.e. $x' = G_v x''$. It follows that the transformation between x, y, z, t and x'', y'', z'', t'' is

$$\begin{aligned} x &= x'' + (u+v)t'' \qquad & x'' &= x - (u+v)t \\ y &= y'' \qquad \text{and} & y'' &= y \\ z &= z'' & z'' &= z \\ t &= t'' & t'' &= t \end{aligned}$$

i.e. $x = G_u x' = G_u G_v x'' = G_{u+v} x''$. This is a Galilean transformation with the relative velocity being $u+v$, a simple addition of the two relative velocities.

EXAMPLE

If $x = L_u x'$ and $x' = L_v x''$, show that $x = L_V x''$, where $V = (u+v)/(1+uv/c^2)$.

We have $x = L_u L_v x''$, where

$$L_u L_v = \begin{bmatrix} \gamma(u) & 0 & 0 & u\gamma(u) \\ 0 & 1 & 0 & 0 \\ 0 & 0 & 1 & 0 \\ u\gamma(u)/c^2 & 0 & 0 & \gamma(u) \end{bmatrix} \begin{bmatrix} \gamma(v) & 0 & 0 & v\gamma(v) \\ 0 & 1 & 0 & 0 \\ 0 & 0 & 1 & 0 \\ v\gamma(v)/c^2 & 0 & 0 & \gamma(v) \end{bmatrix}$$

$$= \begin{bmatrix} \gamma(u)\gamma(v)(1+uv/c^2) & 0 & 0 & \gamma(u)\gamma(v)(u+v) \\ 0 & 1 & 0 & 0 \\ 0 & 0 & 1 & 0 \\ \gamma(u)\gamma(v)(u+v)/c^2 & 0 & 0 & \gamma(u)\gamma(v)(1+uv/c^2) \end{bmatrix}$$

The above matrix can be obtained by matrix multiplication or by elimination of the quantities x', y', z', t' in the linear equations. Now

$$\begin{aligned} \gamma(u)\gamma(v) &= (1-u^2/c^2)^{-1/2}(1-v^2/c^2)^{-1/2} \\ &= (1-u^2/c^2-v^2/c^2+u^2v^2/c^4)^{-1/2} \\ &= \{(1+uv/c^2)^2-(u^2+2uv+v^2)/c^2\}^{-1/2} \\ &= (1+uv/c^2)^{-1}\left\{1-\frac{(u+v)^2/c^2}{1+uv/c^2}\right\}^{-1/2} \\ &= (1+uv/c^2)^{-1}\gamma(V) \end{aligned}$$

where $V = (u+v)/(1+uv/c^2)$. Therefore

$$L_u L_v = \begin{bmatrix} \gamma(V) & 0 & 0 & V\gamma(V) \\ 0 & 1 & 0 & 0 \\ 0 & 0 & 1 & 0 \\ V\gamma(V)/c^2 & 0 & 0 & \gamma(V) \end{bmatrix} = L_V$$

The combination of two successive Lorentz transformations in the same direction is a Lorentz transformation with the relative velocity of the origins being $(u+v)/(1+uv/c^2)$.

EXAMPLE

A motor-boat takes time T_1 to travel a distance D up a river flowing with constant speed, and a time T_2 to return to its starting position from the point a distance D upstream. Find the speed (assumed constant) of the motor-boat in still water.

We require two frames of reference, one fixed relative to the banks of the river (assumed straight) and the other moving with the river. Let $Oxyz$ be a coordinate system such that the x-axis represents the river and the origin represents the boat's starting point. Assuming that the river flows with speed u in the x-direction, we introduce the moving frame of reference, based on the coordinate system $O'x'y'z'$ for which

$$x' = x - ut, \quad y' = y, \quad z' = z$$

During its upstream motion, let the motor-boat have the velocity $-U\boldsymbol{i}$ relative to the moving frame of reference. Then the velocity of the motor-boat relative to the fixed frame of reference is $u\boldsymbol{i} + (-U\boldsymbol{i})$, i.e.

$$\dot{\boldsymbol{r}} = -(U-u)\boldsymbol{i} \quad \text{and} \quad \boldsymbol{r} = -(U-u)t\boldsymbol{i}$$

Therefore $\boldsymbol{r} = -D\boldsymbol{i}$ when $(U-u)T_1 = D$. During the downstream motion, the motor-boat has the velocity $U\boldsymbol{i}$ relative to the moving frame of reference. Hence, relative to the fixed frame of reference, we have

$$\dot{\boldsymbol{r}} = u\boldsymbol{i} + U\boldsymbol{i} \quad \text{and} \quad \boldsymbol{r} = (U+u)(t-T_1)\boldsymbol{i} - D\boldsymbol{i}$$

for $t \geqslant T_1$. When $t = T_1 + T_2$, $\boldsymbol{r} = \boldsymbol{0}$; i.e. $(U+u)T_2 = D$.

Solving the governing equations (namely, $U - u = D/T_1$ and $U + u = D/T_2$) for U, we see that

$$U = \frac{D}{2}\left(\frac{1}{T_1} + \frac{1}{T_2}\right)$$

This is the constant speed of the motor-boat in still water. Further, the speed of the river is

$$\frac{D}{2}\left(\frac{1}{T_2} - \frac{1}{T_1}\right)$$

EXAMPLE

A man can swim at a speed of 40 metres per minute in still water. Find how long he will take to swim across a river 150 metres wide and flowing at a speed of 30 metres per minute, if he directs his course so as to reach a point on the opposite bank 15 metres below his starting point.

We choose a fixed frame of reference, $Oxyz$, such that the starting point is the origin O and the finishing point has the position vector $15\boldsymbol{i} + 150\boldsymbol{j}$. Relative to this frame of reference the velocity of the river is $30\boldsymbol{i}$, measured in metres per minutes. We shall take the time to be measured in minutes from the instant the swim begins. The other information given in the question is with respect to a frame of reference moving with the river. Let $O'x'y'z'$, where

$$x' = x - 30t, \quad y' = y, \quad z' = z$$

be the moving coordinate system. The position vector of the swimmer relative to O, $\boldsymbol{r}$, and the position vector of the swimmer relative to O', $\boldsymbol{r}'$, are related by the equation

$$\boldsymbol{r} = \boldsymbol{r}' + 30t\boldsymbol{i}$$

where $\dot{\boldsymbol{r}}' = U(\boldsymbol{i}\cos\theta + \boldsymbol{j}\sin\theta)$, $\boldsymbol{r}' = Ut(\boldsymbol{i}\cos\theta + \boldsymbol{j}\sin\theta)$ and U is the speed of the man swimming in still water ($U = 40$). Therefore $\boldsymbol{r} = (30 + U\cos\theta)t\boldsymbol{i} + (U\sin\theta)t\boldsymbol{j}$.

If $t = T$ is the time for the swimmer to complete his swim, then

$$(30 + U\cos\theta)T\boldsymbol{i} + (U\sin\theta)T\boldsymbol{j} = 15\boldsymbol{i} + 150\boldsymbol{j}, \quad \text{where} \quad U = 40$$

Hence we have to solve the two scalar equations

$$(30 + 40\cos\theta)T = 15, \quad (40\sin\theta)T = 150$$

In particular, $4T\cos\theta = 3(\frac{1}{2} - T)$ and $4T\sin\theta = 15$. Therefore T satisfies the quadratic equations $28T^2 + 36T - 909 = 0$, whose roots are $-6{\cdot}377$ and $5{\cdot}092$. We select the positive root and deduce that the swim lasts approximately 5 minutes 5 seconds.

EXAMPLE

Raindrops are falling vertically downwards with a speed u_R relative to the air. If a west wind blows with a speed u_W, find the direction in which the raindrops appear to fall to a man walking due west at a speed u_M. What is the speed with which the raindrops hit the man's umbrella?

This problem involves three frames of reference: one fixed, one moving with the wind and one moving with the man. The Galilean transformation indicates that the man observes the wind blowing from the west with speed $u_M + u_W$. Also, relative to the man, the vertical component of the raindrops' velocity is u_R. Therefore the required direction is $\tan^{-1}\{(u_M + u_W)/u_R\}$ with the downward vertical and the required speed is $\{(u_M + u_W)^2 + u_R^2\}^{1/2}$.

EXAMPLE

An aeroplane has a speed of 300 kilometres per hour in still air. When the wind blows from the east, the velocity of the aeroplane as observed from the ground is 260 kilometres per hour towards the north-east. Find the speed of the wind.

We introduce two frames of reference, one fixed relative to the ground and the other moving with the wind, that are related by a Galilean transformation. Let $Oxyz$ and $O'x'y'z'$ be the two coordinate systems such that the x and x'-axes point in an easterly direction, the y and y'-axes point in a northerly direction, and the z and z'-axes point vertically upwards. If the coordinate system $Oxyz$ is fixed relative to the ground, we have

$$x' = x + Wt, \quad y' = y, \quad z' = z$$

where W is the speed of the east wind. We are assuming that the corresponding axes coincide at $t = 0$. If $\boldsymbol{r}$ and $\boldsymbol{r}'$ are the position vectors of the aeroplane (to be more precise, the single element set representing the aeroplane) relative to the origins O and O', respectively, we have $\dot{\boldsymbol{r}} = \dot{\boldsymbol{r}}' - W\boldsymbol{i}$. We are told that

$$\dot{\boldsymbol{r}} = 260(\boldsymbol{i} + \boldsymbol{j})/\sqrt{2} \quad \text{and} \quad \dot{\boldsymbol{r}}' = 300(\boldsymbol{i}\cos\theta + \boldsymbol{j}\sin\theta)$$

where the angle θ is unknown. Therefore

$$130\sqrt{2} = 300\cos\theta - W \quad \text{and} \quad 130\sqrt{2} = 300\sin\theta$$

Eliminating θ, we have

$$90\,000 = (130\sqrt{2} + W)^2 + 33\,800 \quad \text{and} \quad W = \pm(56\,200)^{1/2} - 130\sqrt{2}$$

The speed of the east wind is positive (i.e. $W > 0$), so we choose the positive sign and obtain the result that

$$W = 53{\cdot}2$$

The units are kilometres per hour.

EXAMPLE

An aircraft has a maximum speed u in still air. It makes a journey from A due east to a point B, and then back again. If there is a cross wind blowing with constant velocity w from a direction θ south of west, show that the total time taken for the double journey is

$$\frac{2d(u^2 - w^2\sin^2\theta)^{1/2}}{u^2 - w^2}$$

where d is the distance between A and B. Determine the directions in which the aircraft must steer on the outward and return journeys.

We introduce two coordinate systems, $Oxyz$ and $O'x'y'z'$, whose corresponding axes are parallel and which coincide when the aircraft leaves A at $t = 0$. The first frame of reference (based on $Oxyz$) is fixed relative to the ground, and the second is moving with the wind. Let the single-element set representing the aircraft have the position vectors $\boldsymbol{r}$ and $\boldsymbol{r}'$ relative to O and O', respectively. Then

$$\dot{\boldsymbol{r}} = \dot{\boldsymbol{r}}' + w(\boldsymbol{i}\cos\phi + \boldsymbol{j}\sin\phi)$$

where $\boldsymbol{i}$ and $\boldsymbol{j}$ are unit vectors in the directions of east and north, respectively. We are given that

$$\dot{\boldsymbol{r}}' = u(\boldsymbol{i}\cos\theta_1 + \boldsymbol{j}\sin\theta_1)$$

where θ_1 is an angle to be determined.

Assuming that A coincides with O and that B has the position vector $d\boldsymbol{i}$, we have (by integration)

$$\boldsymbol{r} = (u\cos\theta_1 + w\cos\phi)t\boldsymbol{i} + (u\sin\theta_1 + w\sin\phi)t\boldsymbol{j}$$

The aircraft reaches B at $t = t_1$, where

$$d\boldsymbol{i} = (u\cos\theta_1 + w\cos\phi)t_1\boldsymbol{i} + (u\sin\theta_1 + w\sin\phi)t_1\boldsymbol{j}$$

Hence $(u\cos\theta_1 + w\cos\phi)t_1 = d$ and $(u\sin\theta_1 + w\sin\phi)t_1 = 0$.
$t_1 \neq 0$ and $\sin\theta_1 = -(w/u)\sin\phi$. Therefore

$$\cos\theta_1 = \pm\{1 - (w^2/u^2)\sin^2\phi\}^{1/2}$$

and

$$\begin{aligned} u\cos\theta_1 + w\cos\phi &= w\cos\phi \pm (u^2 - w^2\sin^2\phi)^{1/2} \\ &= w\cos\phi \pm (u^2 - w^2 + w^2\cos^2\phi)^{1/2} \end{aligned}$$

With $u > w$ (i.e. the speed of the aircraft in still air greater than the speed of the wind relative to the ground), we must choose the sign so that the easterly component of $\dot{r}$ is positive (i.e. $u\cos\theta + w\cos\phi > 0$). Thus

$$t_1 = \frac{d}{w\cos\phi + (u^2 - w^2\sin^2\phi)^{1/2}}$$

On the return journey, $t > t_1$ and

$$\boldsymbol{r} = (u\cos\theta_2 + w\cos\phi)(t - t_1)\boldsymbol{i} + (u\sin\theta_2 + w\sin\phi)(t - t_1)\boldsymbol{j} + d\boldsymbol{i}$$

The aircraft returns to A (which is coincident with O) at $t = t_1 + t_2$, where

$$\boldsymbol{0} = (u\cos\theta_2 + w\cos\phi)t_2\boldsymbol{i} + (u\sin\theta_2 + w\sin\phi)t_2\boldsymbol{j} + d\boldsymbol{i}$$

Hence $(u\cos\theta_2 + w\cos\phi)t_2 = -d$ and $(u\sin\theta_2 + w\sin\phi)t_2 = 0$. This time we have

$$\sin\theta_2 = -(w/u)\sin\phi$$
$$\cos\theta_2 = \pm\{1 - (w^2/u^2)\sin^2\phi\}^{1/2}$$
$$u\cos\theta_2 + w\cos\phi = w\cos\phi \pm (u^2 - w^2\sin^2\phi)^{1/2}$$

and we choose the negative sign so that $u\cos\theta_2 + w\cos\phi < 0$ (with $u > w$). Thus

$$t_2 = \frac{-d}{w\cos\phi - (u^2 - w^2\sin^2\phi)^{1/2}} \quad \text{and} \quad t_1 + t_2 = \frac{2d(u^2 - w^2\sin^2\phi)^{1/2}}{u^2 - w^2}$$

The angles θ_1 and θ_2 determine the directions in which the aircraft must steer. θ_1 is an angle in the fourth quadrant, and θ_2 is an angle in the third quadrant (this information following from the signs of the sines and cosines). Let

$$0 \leqslant \theta = \tan^{-1}\left\{\frac{w\sin\phi}{(u^2 - w^2\sin^2\phi)^{1/2}}\right\} \leqslant \frac{\pi}{2}$$

On the outward journey the aircraft steers in the direction θ south of east and on the return journey the aircraft steers in the direction θ south of west.

2.7 Rotation of a frame of reference

Consider two cartesian coordinate systems that have a common origin O and a common axis for all time. Suppose further that one coordinate system is rotating about the common axis with respect to the other coordinate system. Let (X, Y, Z) be the coordinates of the system rotating with respect to the system having the coordinates (x, y, z) and let the Oz, OZ axes be

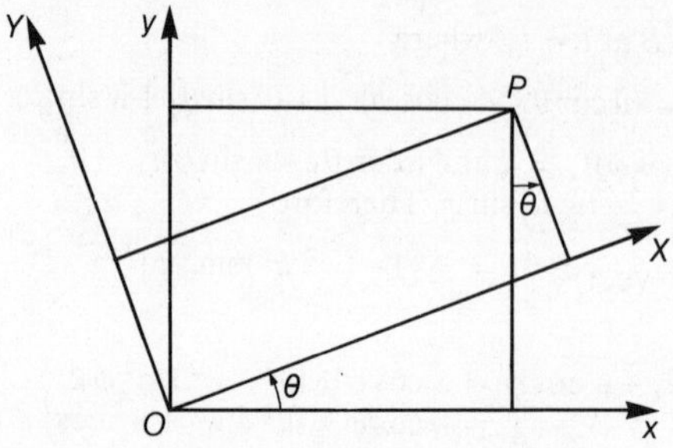

coincident for all time. This means that the plane $z = 0$ coincides with the plane $Z = 0$ for all time. This provides an example of a frame of reference rotating with respect to another frame of reference (which we consider to be fixed).

Consider a set P whose single element at any instant has the coordinates (x, y, z) and (X, Y, Z) with respect to the two systems. The following relations hold:

$$
\begin{aligned}
x &= X\cos\theta - Y\sin\theta \qquad & X &= x\cos\theta + y\sin\theta \\
y &= X\sin\theta + Y\cos\theta \quad \text{and} \quad & Y &= -x\sin\theta + y\cos\theta \\
z &= Z & Z &= z
\end{aligned}
$$

An alternative statement in terms of vectors and a matrix is

$$\boldsymbol{x} = R_\theta \mathbf{X}$$

where

$$\boldsymbol{x} = \begin{bmatrix} x \\ y \\ z \end{bmatrix} \qquad R_\theta = \begin{bmatrix} \cos\theta & -\sin\theta & 0 \\ \sin\theta & \cos\theta & 0 \\ 0 & 0 & 1 \end{bmatrix} \qquad \mathbf{X} = \begin{bmatrix} X \\ Y \\ Z \end{bmatrix}$$

Let $\boldsymbol{i}, \boldsymbol{j}, \boldsymbol{k}$ be unit vectors associated with the directions of the axes of the $Oxyz$ coordinate system, and let $\mathbf{I}, \mathbf{J}, \mathbf{K}$ be unit vectors associated similarly with the $OXYZ$ coordinate system. The position vector of the single element of the set P, relative to the common origin O is

$$
\begin{aligned}
\boldsymbol{r} &= x\boldsymbol{i} + y\boldsymbol{j} + z\boldsymbol{k} \\
&= X\mathbf{I} + Y\mathbf{J} + Z\boldsymbol{k}
\end{aligned}
$$

The relations between the unit vectors are

$$
\begin{aligned}
\boldsymbol{i} &= \mathbf{I}\cos\theta - \mathbf{J}\sin\theta \qquad & \mathbf{I} &= \boldsymbol{i}\cos\theta + \boldsymbol{j}\sin\theta \\
\boldsymbol{j} &= \mathbf{I}\sin\theta + \mathbf{J}\cos\theta \quad \text{and} \quad & \mathbf{J} &= -\boldsymbol{i}\sin\theta + \boldsymbol{j}\cos\theta \\
\boldsymbol{k} &= \mathbf{K} & \mathbf{K} &= \boldsymbol{k}
\end{aligned}
$$

If we assume that the magnitudes and directions of the vectors $\boldsymbol{i}, \boldsymbol{j}, \boldsymbol{k}$ are constant (i.e. the $Oxyz$ coordinate system is the fundamental frame of reference, and the $OXYZ$ coordinate system is rotating about an axis fixed in the fundamental frame of reference, namely the z-axis), then the directions of the unit vectors $\mathbf{I}, \mathbf{J}$ will vary with time. Hence

$$
\begin{aligned}
\dot{\mathbf{I}} &= (-\boldsymbol{i}\sin\theta + \boldsymbol{j}\cos\theta)\dot{\theta} = \dot{\theta}\mathbf{J} \\
\dot{\mathbf{J}} &= (-\boldsymbol{i}\cos\theta - \boldsymbol{j}\sin\theta)\dot{\theta} = -\dot{\theta}\mathbf{I}
\end{aligned}
$$

and

$$\dot{\mathbf{K}} = 0$$

The velocity and the acceleration of P relative to the fundamental frame of reference are

$$\frac{d\boldsymbol{r}}{dt} = \boldsymbol{u} = \dot{x}\boldsymbol{i} + \dot{y}\boldsymbol{j} + \dot{z}\boldsymbol{k}$$

and

$$\frac{d^2\boldsymbol{r}}{dt^2} = \boldsymbol{a} = \ddot{x}\boldsymbol{i} + \ddot{y}\boldsymbol{j} + \ddot{z}\boldsymbol{k}$$

Denoting the velocity and the acceleration of P relative to the rotating frame of reference by $\delta\boldsymbol{r}/\delta t$ and $\delta^2\boldsymbol{r}/\delta t^2$, where

$$\frac{\delta\boldsymbol{r}}{\delta t} = \dot{X}\mathbf{I} + \dot{Y}\mathbf{J} + \dot{Z}\mathbf{K}$$

and

$$\frac{\delta^2\boldsymbol{r}}{\delta t^2} = \ddot{X}\mathbf{I} + \ddot{Y}\mathbf{J} + \ddot{Z}\mathbf{K}$$

we have

$$\begin{aligned}\frac{d\boldsymbol{r}}{dt} &= \{\dot{X}\cos\theta - \dot{Y}\sin\theta - (X\sin\theta + Y\cos\theta)\dot{\theta}\}\boldsymbol{i} \\ &\quad + \{\dot{X}\sin\theta + \dot{Y}\cos\theta + (X\cos\theta - Y\sin\theta)\dot{\theta}\}\boldsymbol{j} + \dot{Z}\boldsymbol{k} \\ &= (\dot{X} - Y\dot{\theta})\mathbf{I} + (\dot{Y} + X\dot{\theta})\mathbf{J} + \dot{Z}\mathbf{K} \\ &= \frac{\delta\boldsymbol{r}}{\delta t} - Y\dot{\theta}\mathbf{I} + X\dot{\theta}\mathbf{J}\end{aligned}$$

or

$$\begin{aligned}\frac{d\boldsymbol{r}}{dt} &= \dot{X}\mathbf{I} + X\dot{\mathbf{I}} + \dot{Y}\mathbf{J} + Y\dot{\mathbf{J}} + \dot{Z}\mathbf{K} + Z\dot{\mathbf{K}} \\ &= \frac{\delta\boldsymbol{r}}{\delta t} - Y\dot{\theta}\mathbf{I} + X\dot{\theta}\mathbf{J}\end{aligned}$$

Similarly we obtain

$$\begin{aligned}\frac{d^2\boldsymbol{r}}{dt^2} &= (\ddot{X} - 2\dot{Y}\dot{\theta} - X\dot{\theta}^2 - Y\ddot{\theta})\mathbf{I} + (\ddot{Y} + 2\dot{X}\dot{\theta} - Y\dot{\theta}^2 + X\ddot{\theta})\mathbf{J} + \ddot{Z}\mathbf{K} \\ &= \frac{\delta^2\boldsymbol{r}}{\delta t^2} - (2\dot{Y}\dot{\theta} + X\dot{\theta}^2 + Y\ddot{\theta})\mathbf{I} + (2\dot{X}\dot{\theta} - Y\dot{\theta}^2 + X\ddot{\theta})\mathbf{J}\end{aligned}$$

We call the vector $\dot{\theta}\boldsymbol{k}$ the angular velocity of the rotating frame of reference and denote it by $\boldsymbol{\omega}$. Then

$$\omega = \dot{\theta}\boldsymbol{k} = \dot{\theta}\mathbf{K}$$

The direction of the angular velocity is obtained by the right-hand corkscrew rule, the index finger giving the appropriate direction along the

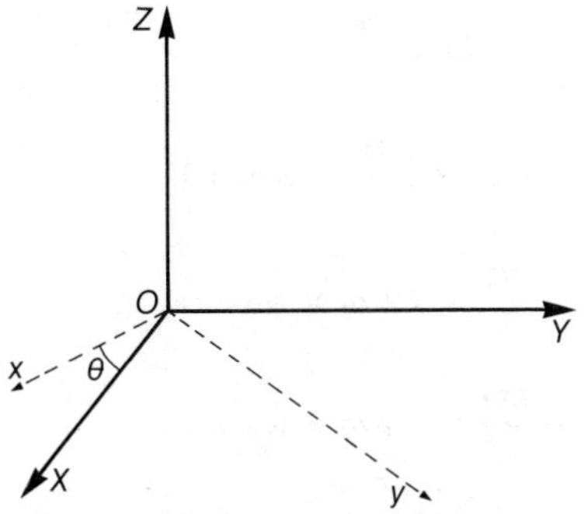

axis of rotation when the right hand is turned in the direction of the rotation (the middle finger and thumb representing the X-axis and Y-axis respectively in this application). Noting that

$$\begin{aligned} -Y\dot{\theta}\mathbf{I}+X\dot{\theta}\mathbf{J} &= -Y\dot{\theta}\mathbf{J}\times\mathbf{K}+X\dot{\theta}\mathbf{K}\times\mathbf{I} \\ &= (\dot{\theta}\mathbf{K})\times(X\mathbf{I}+Y\mathbf{J}) \\ &= (\dot{\theta}\mathbf{K})\times(X\mathbf{I}+Y\mathbf{J}+Z\mathbf{K}) \\ &= \boldsymbol{\omega}\times\boldsymbol{r} \end{aligned}$$

we have

$$\frac{d\boldsymbol{r}}{dt} = \frac{\delta\boldsymbol{r}}{\delta t} + \boldsymbol{\omega}\times\boldsymbol{r}$$

This result is in no way special to the position vector $\boldsymbol{r}$.

It is true that, for any vector $\boldsymbol{v}$,

$$\frac{d\boldsymbol{v}}{dt} = \frac{\delta\boldsymbol{v}}{\delta t} + \boldsymbol{\omega}\times\boldsymbol{v}$$

where

$$\frac{d\boldsymbol{v}}{dt} = \frac{d}{dt}(\boldsymbol{v}\,.\,\boldsymbol{i})\boldsymbol{i} + \frac{d}{dt}(\boldsymbol{v}\,.\,\boldsymbol{j})\boldsymbol{j} + \frac{d}{dt}(\boldsymbol{v}\,.\,\boldsymbol{k})\boldsymbol{k}$$

$$\frac{\delta\boldsymbol{v}}{\delta t} = \frac{d}{dt}(\boldsymbol{v}\,.\,\mathbf{I})\mathbf{I} + \frac{d}{dt}(\boldsymbol{v}\,.\,\mathbf{J})\mathbf{J} + \frac{d}{dt}(\boldsymbol{v}\,.\,\mathbf{K})\mathbf{K}$$

and the vectors $\boldsymbol{i}, \boldsymbol{j}, \boldsymbol{k}, \mathbf{I}, \mathbf{J}, \mathbf{K}, \boldsymbol{\omega}$ have the specifications given earlier in the section. Therefore, in particular,

$$\frac{d\boldsymbol{\omega}}{dt} = \frac{\delta\boldsymbol{\omega}}{\delta t} + \boldsymbol{\omega} \times \boldsymbol{\omega} = \frac{\delta\boldsymbol{\omega}}{\delta t}$$

and

$$\begin{aligned}\frac{d^2\boldsymbol{r}}{dt^2} &= \frac{d}{dt}\left(\frac{d\boldsymbol{r}}{dt}\right) = \frac{\delta}{\delta t}\left(\frac{d\boldsymbol{r}}{dt}\right) + \boldsymbol{\omega} \times \frac{d\boldsymbol{r}}{dt} \\ &= \frac{\delta}{\delta t}\left(\frac{\delta\boldsymbol{r}}{\delta t} + \boldsymbol{\omega} \times \boldsymbol{r}\right) + \boldsymbol{\omega} \times \left(\frac{\delta\boldsymbol{r}}{\delta t} + \boldsymbol{\omega} \times \boldsymbol{r}\right) \\ &= \frac{\delta^2\boldsymbol{r}}{\delta t^2} + 2\boldsymbol{\omega} \times \frac{\delta\boldsymbol{r}}{\delta t} + \frac{\delta\boldsymbol{\omega}}{\delta t} \times \boldsymbol{r} + \boldsymbol{\omega} \times (\boldsymbol{\omega} \times \boldsymbol{r}) \\ &= \frac{\delta^2\boldsymbol{r}}{\delta t^2} + 2\boldsymbol{\omega} \times \frac{\delta\boldsymbol{r}}{\delta t} + \frac{d\boldsymbol{\omega}}{dt} \times \boldsymbol{r} + \boldsymbol{\omega} \times (\boldsymbol{\omega} \times \boldsymbol{r})\end{aligned}$$

If we write the right-hand side of this equation in terms of the unit vectors $\mathbf{I}, \mathbf{J}, \mathbf{K}$, we regain our earlier expression because $\boldsymbol{\omega} \times (\boldsymbol{\omega} \times \boldsymbol{r}) = (\boldsymbol{\omega}.\boldsymbol{r})\boldsymbol{\omega} - (\boldsymbol{\omega}.\boldsymbol{\omega})\boldsymbol{r}$ and

$$\begin{aligned}&2\boldsymbol{\omega} \times \frac{\delta\boldsymbol{r}}{\delta t} + \frac{d\boldsymbol{\omega}}{dt} \times \boldsymbol{r} + \boldsymbol{\omega} \times (\boldsymbol{\omega} \times \boldsymbol{r}) \\ &\quad = 2\dot{\theta}\mathbf{K} \times (\dot{X}\mathbf{I} + \dot{Y}\mathbf{J} + \dot{Z}\mathbf{K}) + \ddot{\theta}\mathbf{K} \times (X\mathbf{I} + Y\mathbf{J} + Z\mathbf{K}) + \dot{\theta}^2 Z\mathbf{K} \\ &\qquad - \dot{\theta}^2(X\mathbf{I} + Y\mathbf{J} + Z\mathbf{K}) \\ &\quad = 2\dot{\theta}\dot{X}\mathbf{J} - 2\dot{\theta}\dot{Y}\mathbf{I} + \ddot{\theta}X\mathbf{J} - \ddot{\theta}Y\mathbf{I} - \dot{\theta}^2(X\mathbf{I} + Y\mathbf{J}) \\ &\quad = -(2\dot{Y}\dot{\theta} + X\dot{\theta}^2 + Y\ddot{\theta})\mathbf{I} + (2\dot{X}\dot{\theta} - Y\dot{\theta}^2 + X\ddot{\theta})\mathbf{J}\end{aligned}$$

EXAMPLE

Space probes are launched from a point on the equator towards (i) the east, (ii) the west, both at an angle of 60 degrees to the surface of the Earth and at a speed of 2·5 km s^{-1} relative to the Earth. Determine in each case the resultant velocity of the probe in magnitude and direction. The radius of the Earth is 6378 km at the equator, and the period of the Earth's rotation about its axis is 23 hours 56 minutes.

This problem fits into the framework of this section if we set the z-axis and Z-axis to coincide with the axis of rotation and we take the origin O to be at the centre of the Earth (i.e. the equatorial plane is given by $z = 0, Z = 0$). We shall assume that at $t = 0$ the x-axis and X-axis coincide, and the position vector associated with the space probe is

$$\boldsymbol{r} = 6{\cdot}378 \times 10^6\boldsymbol{i} = 6{\cdot}378 \times 10^6\mathbf{I}$$

Also at $t = 0$.

$$\frac{\delta \boldsymbol{r}}{\delta t} = 2{\cdot}5 \times 10^3(\mathbf{I}\sin\tfrac{1}{3}\pi + \mathbf{J}\cos\tfrac{1}{3}\pi)$$

for the first probe and

$$\frac{\delta \boldsymbol{r}}{\delta t} = 2{\cdot}5 \times 10^3(\mathbf{I}\sin\tfrac{1}{3}\pi - \mathbf{J}\cos\tfrac{1}{3}\pi)$$

for the second probe. The angular velocity is

$$\boldsymbol{\omega} = \frac{2\pi}{1436 \times 60}\boldsymbol{k} \quad = \frac{2\pi}{1436 \times 60}\mathbf{K}$$

Therefore at $t = 0$

$$\begin{aligned}
\frac{d\boldsymbol{r}}{dt} &= \frac{\delta \boldsymbol{r}}{\delta t} + \boldsymbol{\omega} \times \boldsymbol{r} \\
&= 2{\cdot}5 \times 10^3(\mathbf{I}\sin\tfrac{1}{3}\pi \pm \mathbf{J}\cos\tfrac{1}{3}\pi) + \frac{2\pi}{1436 \times 60}6{\cdot}378 \times 10^6\mathbf{K} \times \mathbf{I} \\
&= 2{\cdot}5 \times 10^3 \times \tfrac{1}{2}(\sqrt{3}\mathbf{I} \pm \mathbf{J}) + 465\mathbf{J} \\
&= 2165\mathbf{I} + (465 \pm 1250)\mathbf{J} \\
&= 2165\boldsymbol{i} + (465 \pm 1250)\boldsymbol{j} \quad \text{because} \quad \mathbf{I} = \boldsymbol{i}, \mathbf{J} = \boldsymbol{j} \quad \text{when} \quad \theta = 0.
\end{aligned}$$

The speed of the first probe is $\{(2165)^2 + (1715)^2\}^{1/2} = 2762$, and the velocity makes an angle with the east of $\tan^{-1}(\frac{2165}{1715}) = 0{\cdot}901$. The speed of the second probe is $\{(2165)^2 + (-785)^2\}^{1/2} = 2303$, and the velocity makes an angle with the west of $\tan^{-1}(\frac{2165}{785}) = 1{\cdot}223$. The speeds are measured in metres per second and the angles are measured in radians.

The essential manipulation can be illustrated in terms of parallelograms which correspond to the addition of two velocities in each part of the problem. A graphical method based on these parallelograms is an alternative approach to this problem.

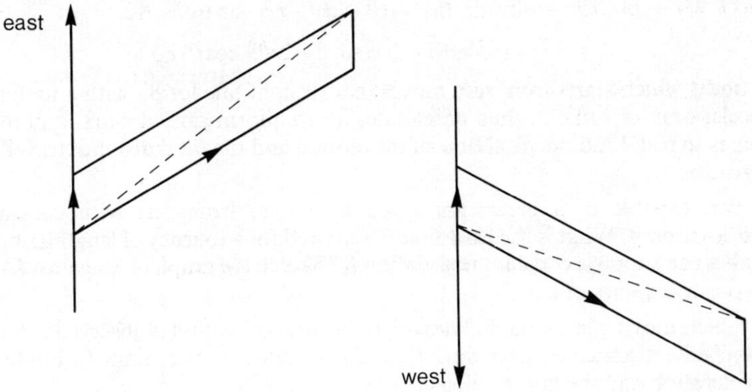

EXERCISES ON CHAPTER 2

1. What distance would a pigeon achieve in one hour, if its average speed were $10\,\text{m}\,\text{s}^{-1}$?

2. A swift flies a distance of 240 km in 4 hours. What is its average speed in (i) kilometres per hour, (ii) metres per second?

3. Show that the equation $\boldsymbol{r} = \boldsymbol{r}_0 + \boldsymbol{h}t$ represents a straight line, where $\boldsymbol{r}$ is the position of a point P, t is the scalar variable, and $\boldsymbol{r}_0$ and $\boldsymbol{h}$ are constant vectors.

4. An aeroplane takes off in an easterly direction and climbs at an angle of 0·2 rad to a height of 2000 m. It then travels north at an air speed of 360 km per hour, climbing at an angle of 0·1 rad, for 3 minutes. Assuming no air currents, find the distance, bearing and elevation of the aeroplane from its point of take-off.

5. A moving point P describes the plane spiral $r = ae^{\phi}$, where a is a positive constant, in such a way that the radial component of its velocity is always inversely proportional to its distance from the origin O. Show that the transverse component of its acceleration is zero and that its radial component is directed towards O and is inversely proportional to the cube of its distance from O.

6. Using spherical polar coordinates, we have

$$\boldsymbol{r} = r\boldsymbol{e}_r$$

where

$$\boldsymbol{e}_r = \boldsymbol{i}\sin\theta\cos\phi + \boldsymbol{j}\sin\theta\sin\phi + \boldsymbol{k}\cos\theta$$

$$\boldsymbol{e}_\theta = \boldsymbol{i}\cos\theta\cos\phi + \boldsymbol{j}\cos\theta\sin\phi - \boldsymbol{k}\sin\theta$$

and

$$\boldsymbol{e}_\phi = -\boldsymbol{i}\sin\phi + \boldsymbol{j}\cos\phi$$

Show that

$$\dot{\boldsymbol{e}}_r = \dot{\theta}\boldsymbol{e}_\theta + \dot{\phi}\boldsymbol{e}_\phi\sin\theta$$

$$\dot{\boldsymbol{e}}_\theta = -\dot{\theta}\boldsymbol{e}_r + \dot{\phi}\,\boldsymbol{e}\;\cos\theta$$

$$\dot{\boldsymbol{e}}_\phi = -\dot{\phi}\boldsymbol{e}_r\sin\theta - \dot{\phi}\,\boldsymbol{e}_\theta\cos\theta$$

$$\boldsymbol{u} = \dot{\boldsymbol{r}} = \dot{r}\boldsymbol{e}_r + r\dot{\theta}\boldsymbol{e}_\theta + r\dot{\phi}\,\boldsymbol{e}_\phi\sin\theta$$

and

$$\boldsymbol{a} = \dot{\boldsymbol{u}} = \ddot{\boldsymbol{r}} = (\ddot{r} - r\dot{\theta}^2 - r\dot{\phi}^2\sin^2\theta)\boldsymbol{e}_r + (r\ddot{\theta} + 2\dot{r}\dot{\theta} - r\dot{\phi}^2\sin\theta\cos\theta)\,\boldsymbol{e}_\theta$$
$$+ (r\ddot{\phi}\sin\theta + 2\dot{r}\dot{\phi}\sin\theta + 2r\dot{\theta}\dot{\phi}\cos\theta)\,\boldsymbol{e}_\phi$$

7. A body, which starts from rest, moves in a straight line for 8 s with a uniform acceleration of $8\,\text{m}\,\text{s}^{-2}$, then decelerates at a uniform rate of $4\,\text{m}\,\text{s}^{-2}$ until it comes to rest. Find the total time of the motion and the total distance travelled by the body.

8. A car, capable of a maximum speed U, moves from rest with constant acceleration A. What is the least time T required for a journey of length L if the brakes can supply a constant retardation R? Sketch the graph of T against L for all positive values of L.

9. A vehicle moving in a straight line with uniform acceleration is observed to have travelled a distance D_1 after time T_1, and a distance D_2 after time T_2. Find the acceleration and the initial velocity.

10. A train has an acceleration of $\frac{1}{2}$ kilometre per hour per second and can decelerate at five times that rate. It is supposed to complete a run of 72 kilometres in 60 minutes by accelerating, then running at a fixed speed and finally slowing down. One day the train started 6 minutes late but arrived on time. By what percentage was the maximum speed increased to achieved this shorter run time?

11. A body moves so that corresponding values of its velocity u (measured in $\mathrm{m\,s^{-1}}$) at time t (measured in s) are those given in the table.

t	0	20	50	70
u	0·0	15·0	12·5	0·0

During the first 20 seconds the acceleration is uniform; during the next 30 seconds the acceleration is variable and $u = at^2 + bt$; during the last 20 seconds the retardation is uniform. Sketch a graph of u against t for the whole motion. Find the numerical values of a and b and determine the time taken to reach the maximum speed. Calculate the total distance travelled from rest to rest.

12. A vehicle starts from rest, attains a maximum speed of $10\,\mathrm{m\,s^{-1}}$ after 30 s and comes to rest again after a further period of 30 s. Calculate the total distance travelled in 60 s when the velocity-time graph is

(i) the arc of a parabolic curve,
(ii) the arc of a sine curve,
(iii) the arc of a circular curve.

Deduce the acceleration-time graph and the initial acceleration in each case.

13. A motor-car accelerates from rest. The times (measured in seconds) to reach various speeds (measured in kilometres per hour) are given in the table. Estimate the distance travelled in the first seven seconds, the average acceleration in the time interval [15·6, 24·0], and the distance travelled in the first twenty seconds.

t	0	1·1	2·5	4·4	7·0	10·7	15·6	24·0
u	0	20	40	60	80	100	120	140

14. A vehicle moving with velocity U comes to rest in two stages. In the first stage, the deceleration is given in terms of the velocity u at any instant by $k(U-u)^{1/2}$, where k is a positive constant; this stage continues until the velocity is reduced to $\frac{8}{9}U$. In the second stage, the deceleration is constant and equal to $\frac{1}{3}kU^{1/2}$. Show that the time taken over the two stages are in the ratio 1:4, and that the distances covered in the two stages are in the ratio 13:24.

15. If $\boldsymbol{r} = \boldsymbol{i}\cos t + \boldsymbol{j}\sin^2 t + \boldsymbol{k}\sin t\cos t$ at time t, show that $|\boldsymbol{r}|$ is constant and that neither $\dot{\boldsymbol{r}}$ nor $\ddot{\boldsymbol{r}}$ is zero for any t.

16. If $\dot{\boldsymbol{r}}$ is always perpendicular to $\boldsymbol{r}$, show that $|\boldsymbol{r}|$ is constant. If $|\boldsymbol{r}|$ is constant for all time, show that

(i) $\boldsymbol{r}$ is perpendicular to $\dot{\boldsymbol{r}}$ whenever $\dot{\boldsymbol{r}} \neq \boldsymbol{0}$,
(ii) $\dot{\boldsymbol{r}} = \boldsymbol{0}$ if and only if either $\ddot{\boldsymbol{r}}$ is perpendicular to $\boldsymbol{r}$, or $\ddot{\boldsymbol{r}} = \boldsymbol{0}$.

17. A set P, having a single element at any instant, moves on a straight line so that its velocity component u is given by $u^2 = \alpha x^2 + \beta x + \gamma$, where x is its coordinate relative to a fixed point on the line and α, β, γ are constants. What are the conditions that the motion is simple harmonic? Find the centre, the amplitude and the angular frequency of the motion.

18. The rise and fall of the tide at a certain harbour may be taken to be simple harmonic, the interval between successive high tides being 12 hours 20 minutes. The harbour entrance has a depth of 10 m at high tide and 4 m at low tide. If low tide occurs at noon, find the earliest time thereafter that a ship drawing 9 m can pass through the entrance.

19. A train, travelling from A to B, a distance of 100 kilometres, reaches its maximum speed, 120 kilometres per hour, by constant acceleration in the first two kilometres, and keeps it up for the rest of the way. A second train, travelling from B to A, reaches the same maximum speed by constant acceleration in the first kilometre, and keeps it up thereafter. If they start from rest at the same instant, find when and where they pass one another. If the start of one train is delayed, and they pass exactly halfway, find which is delayed and by how much.

20. P_1 and P_2 are two sets, each having a single element at any instant and each representing a body in motion. P_1 moves along the x-axis with constant acceleration 3 cm s^{-2}, and P_2 moves along the x-axis with constant velocity 4 cm s^{-1}. When $t = 0$, P_1 and P_2 are at the origin and P_1 has velocity -2 cm s^{-1}. When do P_1 and P_2 next coincide, and what is the greatest distance between them before that?

21. Two ships, S_1 and S_2, are observed at midnight to have the following velocity and position vectors:

Ship S_1: $\boldsymbol{u}_1 = 4\boldsymbol{i}+3\boldsymbol{j}, \quad \boldsymbol{r}_1 = 4\boldsymbol{i}-2\boldsymbol{j}$

Ship S_2: $\boldsymbol{u}_2 = 16\boldsymbol{i}+12\boldsymbol{j}, \quad \boldsymbol{r}_2 = -20\boldsymbol{i}-20\boldsymbol{j}$

where $\boldsymbol{i}, \boldsymbol{j}$ are unit vectors in the directions east and north, respectively, and where the speeds are measured in kilometres per hour and distances in kilometres. Determine the time at which the ships would collide if they both continued on their respective courses (i.e. their velocities remained constant). Where would the collision occur?

22. PO and QO are two straight roads intersecting at right angles at O. Two cyclists, A and B, are riding in the directions of $\overrightarrow{PO}$ and $\overrightarrow{QO}$, respectively, A at 15 kilometres per hour and B at 20 kilometres per hour. When B is at O, A is 5 kilometres from O and is moving towards O. Find the time after B passes O when the cyclists are nearest to each other, and find their least distance apart.

23. From their point of intersection, two straight roads lie due west and 30° west of north respectively. At the same instant that a car travelling at 90 kilometres per hour due west is at the crossing, a second car is 20 kilometres from it and travelling at 60 kilometres per hour towards it from 30° west of north. Find when the cars will be at their shortest distance apart.

24. A ship A is cruising eastwards at 12 knots. At a certain instant another ship B is 4 nautical miles away from A in a direction N 30° E, and 10 minutes later B is again 4 nautical miles away but in a NE direction. Find the magnitude and direction of the velocity of B and find the shortest distance between A and B.

25. A diesel locomotive passes with speed u along a level railway track under a bridge of height H. A car, approaching the bridge with speed v, is at a distance D from the bridge along a level road that is at right angles to the railway track. Calculate the shortest distance between the car and the locomotive.

26. A, B, C are three points whose cartesian coordinates are $(a, 0, 0)$, $(0, a, a)$ and $(0, 0, a)$, respectively. P and Q are two sets, each having a single element at any instant, that represent two moving bodies. P moves from A to C with speed u. At the instant that P leaves A, Q leaves B and moves towards the origin with speed v. Calculate the time elapsing before the closest approach of P and Q. What is the shortest distance between P and Q?

27. An observer A sees an object P at an elevation of 60° and due north-east. From a point B, the object has an elevation of 45° and a direction $\theta°$ west of north. Given that $AP = r$ and $BP = R$, write down expressions for $\overrightarrow{AP}$, $\overrightarrow{BP}$ in terms of their components. If B is 500 m vertically above a point 1·5 km due east of A, find r.

28. A flight controller at an airport is about to talk down an aircraft A_1 whose position vector relative to the control tower is $\mathbf{R}_1$ and whose constant velocity is $\mathbf{U}_1$. At this instant a second aircraft A_2, moving with constant velocity $\mathbf{U}_2$ appears on his radar screen with position vector $\mathbf{R}_2$. When distances are measured in kilometres and speeds in kilometres per hour,

$\mathbf{R}_1 = 20\boldsymbol{i}+10\boldsymbol{j}+6\boldsymbol{k}, \quad \mathbf{U}_1 = -270\boldsymbol{i}-150\boldsymbol{j}$

$\mathbf{R}_2 = -10\boldsymbol{i}-25\boldsymbol{j}+3\boldsymbol{k}, \quad \mathbf{U}_2 = 90\boldsymbol{i}+270\boldsymbol{j}+60\boldsymbol{k}$

Find the position vector of A_1 relative to A_2 at t minutes after A_2 first appears on the radar screen. Hence calculate the shortest distance between the two aircraft.

29. A river flows between parallel banks, 500 metres apart, at a speed of 2 metres per second. An oarsman, who propels his boat at a constant speed of 2 metres per second in still water, wishes to cross from one bank to a point on the opposite bank. If he rows his boat in a fixed direction making a constant angle θ with the bank, obtain θ so that the boat lands 200 metres downstream on the opposite bank. Determine also the time taken to complete the crossing.

30. Raindrops are falling vertically downwards with a speed of 4 metres per second relative to the air. If a north-west wind blows at 32 kilometres per hour, find the direction in which the raindrops appear to fall to a man walking in a north-westerly direction at 4 kilometres per hour. Calculate the speed, in metres per second, with which the raindrops hit the man's umbrella.

31. To a cyclist travelling due north along a straight road at 10 kilometres per hour, the wind appears to blow from the east. If he increases his speed to 18 kilometres per hour, the wind appears to blow from the direction 30° north of east. Find the speed and direction of the wind relative to the ground.

32. A ship travelling east at speed u observes the apparent direction from which the wind blows to be α east of north. When it travels at the same speed due west, the apparent direction of the wind is β east of north. Find the speed and direction of the wind.

33. An aeroplane can complete a course in the form of a square in time $4T$ at a constant speed U when there is no wind. How long will it take to fly over the same course with a wind of speed kU ($k < 1$) blowing (a) parallel to one side, (b) parallel to a diagonal of the square?

34. A helicopter whose speed is U in still air flies horizontally due north from A to B in a wind blowing with speed w from a direction θ east of north. If the distance between A and B is d, show that the time taken is

$$\frac{d}{U^2-w^2}\{(U^2-w^2\sin^2\theta)^{1/2}+w\cos\theta\}$$

If the helicopter completes a horizontal square $ABCD$ and the wind remains unchanged, show that the total time taken is

$$\frac{2d}{U^2-w^2}\{(U^2-w^2\sin^2\theta)^{1/2}+(U^2-w^2\cos^2\theta)^{1/2}\}$$

35. Two single-element sets, S_1 and S_2, represent two ships at sea. S_1 and S_2 start from points A and B, distance D apart, and move with the same constant speed along straight-line courses in a plane containing $\overrightarrow{AB}$, S_2 moving in a straight line perpendicular to $\overrightarrow{AB}$. Show that S_1 can get within a distance d $(< D)$ from S_2 in the shortest time by moving in a direction making an angle $(\frac{1}{2}\pi-\theta)$ with $\overrightarrow{AB}$, where $\tan\frac{1}{2}\theta = d/D$.

36. A rabbit, running with constant speed u along a straight hedge, is chased by a dog running at speed ku $(k > 1)$. The dog starts from a point A distance d from the hedge at the instant when the rabbit is at its nearest point to A. The dog runs so that it is always pointing at the moving rabbit. If r and ϕ are the polar coordinates of the dog with the rabbit as pole ($\phi = 0$ being the direction in which the rabbit is running), show that the differential equation governing the equation of the path of the dog (relative to the rabbit) is

$$\frac{dr}{d\phi} = -r(k\operatorname{cosec}\phi+\cot\phi)$$

Deduce that the equation of the required path is

$$r(\tan\tfrac{1}{2}\phi)^k\sin\phi = d$$

and that the rabbit runs a distance $kd/(k^2-1)$ before it is caught.

Newton's Laws of Motion

3

3.1 Force

Our understanding of force is based on our experience of muscular effort. Our muscles enable us to push and to pull. We exert a force on the ground when we walk or run, and even when we stand still. We are using our muscles to apply forces and our bodies are experiencing forces throughout our lives.

We experience forces applied by natural phenomena. Probably the most important of these is the force due to gravity. It is the gravitational force between the Earth and our bodies that keeps us in our positions relative to the Earth's surface. When we jump up, our muscles exert an extra large force on the Earth's surface for a short time. Our bodies experience an equal and opposite force that causes us to rise. The force due to gravity acts against the upward motion and slows us down. We come to rest momentarily and then we fall back to the Earth's surface by the action of the gravitational force. We hit the Earth's surface and experience a force due to the impact.

The atmosphere in which we live causes us to experience a force. We know the different experiences of walking with the wind and walking against the wind. The difference is certainly apparent when we hold an opened umbrella. If the wind is blowing against us, we have to exert a great effort to move forward. If the wind is blowing with us, we are swept along and we have difficulty in staying on our feet. Even on a still day, we experience this force, called *air resistance*. We have to push the air out of our way when we move, but its effect is very small in still conditions.

The effects of air are very important in aeroplane design. Air passing over the wings provides the *lift*, but the passage of air round the aeroplane also causes *drag*. The lift keeps the aeroplane above the ground, but the drag always tends to slow down the aeroplane. A propeller-driven aeroplane moves forward because the propellers exert a force on the air, and the air exerts an equal and opposite force on the propellers. Jet engines, helicopters and hovercraft all depend on the effects of air. (It is worth mentioning that rocket engines do not.) Parachutes depend on the resistive effects of the atmosphere. They lessen the effects of a fall from a great height by controlling the speed at which a stricken pilot hits the ground. They are in everyday use at airfields where high-speed aeroplanes use them as braking mechanisms when landing on runways.

Examples of the effects of air are common. Car designers attempt to design car bodies to minimize lift and drag, in order to improve road-holding properties and to decrease petrol consumption. The shape of high-speed trains is influenced similarly. The flight of a golf ball depends on the effects of lift and drag. A ball without dimples travels a shorter distance than a ball with dimples. The shape and the distribution of the dimples are important.

We experience another important type of force when we deform the shape of a body, e.g. when we squeeze a rubber ball, or when we stretch or compress a spring. The ball or spring exerts a force on us and tries to regain its original shape. This force, which depends on the internal or molecular properties of the body, is commonly called *elastic*. If the body regains its original shape when the applied force is removed, we say that the body is (perfectly) elastic. If the body takes up its deformed shape when the applied force is removed, we say that the body is (perfectly) plastic. Most materials have properties somewhere between these two extremes.

A rubber band depends for its usefulness on this internal force. It is not important that the rubber band is not perfectly elastic. When a tennis ball bounces, the impact causes a deformation, the ball comes to rest instantaneously, the internal force causes the ball to regain its original (or near original) shape, and the ball imparts a force on the ground; finally, the ball leaves the ground with an upward velocity. The height to which the ball rises depends on the forces acting during the compression, and the restoration of the shape of the ball.

Springs not only have "elastic" properties but also have *damping* properties. Their use in car suspensions is an obvious example. In this application, car designers are interested in minimizing the effects of road vibrations. In contrast, a seismograph is a spring mechanism which is designed to magnify and record the vibrations caused by distant earth-quakes.

Other forces that are important are electric and magnetic forces, and atomic forces. A study of these is outside the scope of this book.

Each of the forces that we have described has a magnitude and a direction. This suggests that it may be possible to use vectors to represent forces in our mathematical models. We shall assume that each force introduced into a mathematical model has

(i) a magnitude
(ii) a direction
(iii) a point of application.

These properties are similar to those possessed by line segments in geometry. Further we shall assume that forces in a mathematical model are represented by vectors. This implies that we have to assign a meaning to

(i) the sum of two vectors (each representing a force)
(ii) the multiplication of a vector (representing a force) by a real number

and we have to adopt the properties of addition of vectors and the properties of scalar multiples [see J. Hunter, *Analytic Geometry and Vectors*, Blackie/Chambers]. Let $\mathbf{F}_1$ and $\mathbf{F}_2$ represent two forces acting at a point. The sum of $\mathbf{F}_1$ and $\mathbf{F}_2$, written $\mathbf{F}_1+\mathbf{F}_2$, is obtained by the parallelogram law of addition (based on the geometrical representations of vectors). There is a zero vector, written $\mathit{0}$, and $-\mathbf{F}_1$ is a vector whose magnitude equals the magnitude of $\mathbf{F}_1$ and whose direction is opposite to the direction of $\mathbf{F}_1$. $p\mathbf{F}_1$ (p a non-zero real number) is a vector whose magnitude is p times the magnitude of $\mathbf{F}_1$ and whose direction is the direction of $\mathbf{F}_1$ if p is positive and the direction of $-\mathbf{F}_1$ if p is negative.

We emphasize the existence of the assumption concerning the vectorial representation of forces in a mathematical model. It is not obvious at this stage that forces in the real world combine in a way that is consistent with the vectorial representation of forces in a mathematical model. The assumption has to be recognized. It may be unacceptable if the predictions of a mathematical model are not consistent with the results of an experiment in the real-world situation; that is, it has the same status as any other assumption.

3.2 Newton's Laws of Motion

Our everyday experiences indicate that forces cause objects to move. We apply a force, by pushing or pulling, to move a piece of furniture from one position to another. Similarly, we might push a broken-down car or motorcycle, and push or pull a trolley round a supermarket. It is important to be able to relate the forces acting on an object with the motion of the object. What is the flight path of a space vehicle? What is the trajectory of a bullet fired from a gun? What is the motion of a clock pendulum? To answer questions of this type, we need to know how a given force influences the motion of an object.

Isaac Newton (1642–1727) postulated his Laws of Motion in the seventeenth century. Newton's Laws have stood the test of time. Predictions based on them have been verified by experiment in very many areas of astronomy, physics and engineering. However, Newton's Laws do not explain all observed phenomena concerning the motion of objects. There are observations concerning the orbit of the planet Mercury that cannot be explained in terms of them. The motion of objects moving with speeds comparable with the speed of light (approximately, $3 \times 10^8\ \mathrm{m\,s^{-1}}$) requires a more sophisticated theory. The behaviour of atoms cannot be explained by the Newtonian Theory. During the twentieth century, the Theory of Relativity and Quantum Theory have been developed to explain phenomena outwith the Newtonian Theory. The Newtonian Theory is a good approximation to Einstein's Theory of Relativity when the speeds are not comparable with the speed of light. It is entirely satisfactory when the dimensions of objects are large compared with the atomic scale and the speeds of objects are much less than the speed of light. In other words, Newton's Laws of Motion apply to our everyday situation.

In our investigation of a particular problem, say the flight path of a space vehicle, we may find that our solution (i.e. the prediction of the mathematical model) is not confirmed by experiment or observation. We may be inclined to think that Newton's Laws are unsatisfactory. This would almost certainly be an incorrect diagnosis. The reason for the discrepancy is much more likely to be our inability to incorporate into our mathematical model a correct description of all the forces acting on the space vehicle. We must be aware of our inability to provide a satisfactory mathematical model of many interesting and important real-world problems. The inadequacy of our mathematical skills soon becomes apparent!

We shall state Newton's Laws of Motion as they apply to a particle. A particle is an idealization introduced into a mathematical model to represent an object of finite dimensions in the real world. It occupies a single point in space at any instant, and possesses one or more properties (e.g. mass). When we model an object (e.g. a motor-car, a tennis ball or a raindrop) by means of a particle, we are ignoring any rotation or deformation that the object may experience in the real-world situation. Our model (based on a particle representation) will predict the translational aspects of the motion of an object of finite dimensions, but will be unable to predict, for example, the spin or the change of shape of a tennis ball during a rally. We recognize that the application of particle dynamics is not confined to the motion of real-world objects of minute size. We shall introduce later another idealized representation of an object of finite dimensions, namely the *rigid body*. A rigid body occupies a finite region of space, and its shape remains unaltered by any applied force. The study of models of deformable bodies, as in the theory of elasticity, is beyond the scope of this book.

Consider a particle P. We associate with P a single-element set, whose kinematics we studied in chapter 2. Relative to a chosen frame of reference, the particle P has a position vector $\boldsymbol{r}$, its velocity is

$$\boldsymbol{u} = \frac{d\boldsymbol{r}}{dt} = \dot{\boldsymbol{r}}$$

and its acceleration is

$$\boldsymbol{a} = \frac{d\boldsymbol{u}}{dt} = \dot{\boldsymbol{u}}$$

Here is a statement of Newton's Laws of Motion.

(1) Every particle remains in a state of rest or remains in motion with constant speed in a straight line unless acted upon by a force.

(2) If a particle is moving with an acceleration $\boldsymbol{a}$ because a force $\mathbf{F}$ is acting on the particle, then

$$m\boldsymbol{a} = \mathbf{F}$$

where m is a time-independent scalar quantity called the *inertial mass* of the particle.

(3) If particle P acts on particle Q with a force $\mathbf{F}$ in a direction along the line joining the particles, while particle Q acts on particle P with a force $\mathbf{G}$, then $\mathbf{F} = -\mathbf{G}$.

An alternative form of the Second Law is

$$\mathbf{F} = m\frac{d\boldsymbol{u}}{dt} = \frac{d\boldsymbol{p}}{dt}$$

where $\boldsymbol{p} = m\boldsymbol{u}$. The vectorial quantity $\boldsymbol{p}$ is called the *linear momentum* of the particle; it equals the inertial mass times the velocity.

In the statements of the Second Law, we have introduced a new quantity, called the *inertial mass of the particle.* Inertial mass is a characteristic of a particle. It reflects the fact that different objects in the real world, moving with the same velocity at a given instant and acted upon by forces of the same magnitudes and directions, behave in different ways. We shall defer a discussion of how we determine the inertial mass of a particle.

We must concern ourselves now with the conditions under which we are permitted to apply Newton's Laws of Motion. Newton's Laws of Motion hold relative to frames of reference that are at rest or are moving with constant velocity. These chosen frames are called *inertial frames of reference.* Can we give an example of an inertial frame of reference? A frame of reference fixed relative to the Earth's surface (a terrestrial frame of reference) is rotating about the Earth's axis which is moving around the Sun. It is clearly not an inertial frame of reference. The astronomical frame of reference, in which the Sun is fixed and which is not rotating relative to the fixed stars, is almost a perfect inertial frame of reference. This seems to imply that we must make all our measurements and observations relative to this frame, even when we are conducting a laboratory experiment. This inconvenience leads us to inquire whether a terrestrial frame of reference may be assumed to be an inertial frame of reference under certain circumstances. In some problems, for example, most engineering problems, the influence of the motion of the Earth around its axis and around the Sun is negligible. Then we may apply Newton's Laws of Motion as if the terrestrial frame were an inertial frame. When we do this we must remember that we are making an approximation, and we are ignoring the motion of the Earth.

The equation of motion relative to one inertial frame of reference is unchanged when the motion is studied relative to a second frame of reference at rest or translating with uniform velocity relative to the inertial frame of reference (cf. the Galilean transformation described in Section 2.6). This second frame is an inertial frame of reference.

Consider an inertial frame of reference (based on the cartesian coordinate system $Oxyz$) and a second frame of reference (based on the cartesian coordinate system $O'x'y'z'$) translating so that corresponding axes are parallel and the origin O' is moving along the Ox-axis with uniform acceleration $A\boldsymbol{i}$ (cf. figure on p. 28). If we take as the zero on the time scale the instant when O and O' coincide, the position vector of O' relative to O, the origin of the inertial frame of reference, is $(\frac{1}{2}At^2+u_0t)\boldsymbol{i}$, where $u_0\boldsymbol{i}$ is the velocity of O' (relative to the inertial frame of reference) at $t=0$. Consider the motion of a particle P, whose position vectors relative to the two frames of reference are $\boldsymbol{r}$ and $\boldsymbol{r}'$. We have

$$\boldsymbol{r} = x\boldsymbol{i}+y\boldsymbol{j}+z\boldsymbol{k}, \quad \boldsymbol{r}' = x'\boldsymbol{i}+y'\boldsymbol{j}+z'\boldsymbol{k}$$

and

$$\boldsymbol{r} = \boldsymbol{r}'+(\tfrac{1}{2}At^2+u_0t)\boldsymbol{i}$$

The equation of motion of the particle P, which must be written relative to the inertial frame of reference, is

$$m\frac{d^2\boldsymbol{r}}{dt^2} = \mathbf{F}$$

We may rewrite this equation in the form

$$m\frac{d^2}{dt^2}\{\boldsymbol{r}'+(\tfrac{1}{2}At^2+u_0t)\boldsymbol{i}\} = \mathbf{F}$$

or

$$m\frac{d^2\boldsymbol{r}'}{dt^2} = \mathbf{F}-mA\boldsymbol{i}$$

When $A=0$, the second frame of reference is an inertial frame of reference and the equation of motion is

$$m\frac{d^2\boldsymbol{r}}{dt^2} = \mathbf{F} \quad \text{or} \quad m\frac{d^2\boldsymbol{r}'}{dt^2} = \mathbf{F}$$

Consider another situation in which there are two frames of reference, an inertial frame of reference (based on the cartesian coordinate system $Oxyz$)

and a frame of reference (based on the cartesian coordinate system $OXYZ$) rotating so that the origins coincide and the axes Oz and OZ coincide for all time (cf. figures on pp. 34 and 37). The position vector of a particle P relative to the two frames is

$$\begin{aligned} \boldsymbol{r} &= x\boldsymbol{i}+y\boldsymbol{j}+z\boldsymbol{k} \\ &= X\mathbf{I}+Y\mathbf{J}+Z\mathbf{K} \end{aligned}$$

where

$$\mathbf{I} = \boldsymbol{i}\cos\theta+\boldsymbol{j}\sin\theta$$

$$\mathbf{J} = -\boldsymbol{i}\sin\theta+\boldsymbol{j}\cos\theta$$

and

$$\mathbf{K} = \boldsymbol{k}$$

If the angular velocity of the rotating frame be $\omega\boldsymbol{k}$, where ω is a constant, and the instant $t = 0$ corresponds to the instant when the corresponding axes coincide, we have $\theta = \omega t$. We know from Section 2.7 that

$$\begin{aligned} \frac{d^2\boldsymbol{r}}{dt^2} &= \ddot{x}\boldsymbol{i}+\ddot{y}\boldsymbol{j}+\ddot{z}\boldsymbol{k} \\ &= (\ddot{X}-2\omega\dot{Y}-\omega^2X)\mathbf{I}+(\ddot{Y}+2\omega\dot{X}-\omega^2Y)\mathbf{J}+\ddot{Z}\mathbf{K} \end{aligned}$$

Therefore the equation of motion of the particle P (having constant inertial mass m),

$$m\frac{d^2\boldsymbol{r}}{dt^2} = \mathbf{F}$$

may be written in the form

$$m(\ddot{x}\boldsymbol{i}+\ddot{y}\boldsymbol{j}+\ddot{z}\boldsymbol{k}) = \mathbf{F}$$

or

$$m(\ddot{X}\mathbf{I}+\ddot{Y}\mathbf{J}+\ddot{Z}\mathbf{K}) = \mathbf{F}+(2\omega\dot{Y}+\omega^2X)\mathbf{I}+(-2\omega\dot{X}+\omega^2Y)\mathbf{J}$$

We have included these two examples concerning an accelerating frame of reference and a rotating frame of reference to illustrate the importance of applying Newton's Laws of Motion relative to inertial frames of reference.

3.3 Newton's Law of Gravitation

Newton postulated that two particles, P and Q, held in isolation from all other particles would each exert a force of attraction on the other particle; the force acting along the line joining the particles, and its magnitude being proportional to the gravitational masses of P and Q, and being inversely proportional to the square of the distance between P and Q.

The force that P exerts on Q is

$$\frac{GMm(\boldsymbol{r}_P - \boldsymbol{r}_Q)}{|\boldsymbol{r}_P - \boldsymbol{r}_Q|^3}$$

and the force that Q exerts on P is

$$\frac{GMm(\boldsymbol{r}_Q - \boldsymbol{r}_P)}{|\boldsymbol{r}_P - \boldsymbol{r}_Q|^3}$$

where G is a universal constant of proportionality, called the *gravitational constant*, $\boldsymbol{r}_P$ and $\boldsymbol{r}_Q$ are the position vectors of P and Q (relative to a common origin) and m and M are the gravitational masses of P and Q. Here we have associated with a particle another characteristic, namely *gravitational mass*, which is a time-independent scalar quantity.

Consider a particle P moving in the gravitational field of a given particle Q fixed relative to an inertial frame of reference. Let the inertial mass of P be m_I and let the gravitational masses of P and Q be m_G and M_G, respectively. Applying Newton's Laws to this situation we have the following equation of motion for the particle P,

$$m_I \ddot{\boldsymbol{r}} = -\frac{GM_G m_G \boldsymbol{r}}{r^3}$$

where $\boldsymbol{r}$ is the position vector of P relative to Q and $r = |\boldsymbol{r}|$. Experiments have shown that inertial mass is proportional to gravitational mass. Therefore a suitable choice of scaling factor allows us to equate inertial mass with gravitational mass. In future, we shall talk about the mass of a particle and drop the subscripts I and G; the equation of motion for the particle P becoming

$$\ddot{\boldsymbol{r}} = -\frac{GM}{r^3}\boldsymbol{r}$$

We have introduced the units of length (the metre, m), time (the second, s) and angle (the radian, rad). It is appropriate to introduce some more units. The unit of mass is the kilogram (the SI symbol being kg); it is the mass of the international prototype of the kilogram. The unit of force is the newton (the SI symbol being N); a particle of mass one kilogram accelerates at the rate of one metre per second per second when acted upon by a force of one newton. This definition follows from the equation of motion for the particle, $m\ddot{\boldsymbol{r}} = \mathbf{F}$. The newton is defined in terms of the base units (metre, kilogram, second), namely one N is equivalent to one $\mathrm{m\,kg\,s^{-2}}$.

The gravitational constant G has the dimensions

$$\frac{(\mathrm{MLT^{-2}})\mathrm{L}^2}{\mathrm{M}^2} = \mathrm{L^3M^{-1}T^{-2}}$$

Its value is found by experiment. We shall use the value

$$6{\cdot}67 \times 10^{-11}\,\mathrm{N\,m^2\,kg^{-2}}.$$

3.4 Uniform gravitational field of force

Consider a body moving near the surface of the Earth. Suppose that we assume that the principal force acting on the body is the force due to the Earth's gravity. We have to choose a model for the Earth and its gravitational field of force. The shape and internal structure of the Earth is very complicated. The shape is rather like a sphere flattened at the north and south poles (cf. an oblate spheroid). The equatorial radius is $6{\cdot}378 \times 10^6$ m and the polar radius is $6{\cdot}357 \times 10^6$ m. We shall assume that the Earth's surface is spherical with radius $6{\cdot}371 \times 10^6$ m. The internal structure may be modelled in various ways, e.g.

(*a*) there are three materials occupying a spherical core of radius $3{\cdot}470 \times 10^6$ m, and two spherical layers of outer radii $6{\cdot}340 \times 10^6$ m and $6{\cdot}371 \times 10^6$ m,
(*b*) there is a single material occupying the sphere,
(*c*) the sphere is hollow and has its total mass concentrated at the centre.

Possibility (*c*) is the simplest representation to adopt, because we can apply Newton's Law of Gravitation directly if we take the moving body to be represented by a particle. The equation of motion for the moving particle in a frame of reference in which the Earth is stationary (assumed to be an inertial frame of reference) is

$$m\ddot{\boldsymbol{r}} = -\frac{GMm}{r^3}\boldsymbol{r}$$

where m is the mass of the particle representing the body, M is the mass of the particle representing the Earth, and $\boldsymbol{r}$ is the position vector of the body relative to the centre of the Earth. This equation is valid for r greater than the radius of the Earth. It can be shown that possibilities (*a*) and (*b*) lead to the same equation of motion [see Section 16.5].

Suppose that we introduce a cartesian coordinate system, whose origin is on the surface of the sphere (representing the Earth) and whose z-axis is along the radial direction out of the sphere. Then the xy-plane is tangential to the sphere at the origin and

$$\boldsymbol{r} = x\boldsymbol{i} + y\boldsymbol{j} + (R+z)\boldsymbol{k}$$

where $\boldsymbol{i}, \boldsymbol{j}, \boldsymbol{k}$ are unit vectors along the coordinate axes and R is the radius of the sphere. Hence the equation of motion (for the particle representing the moving body) becomes

$$\ddot{x}\boldsymbol{i} + \ddot{y}\boldsymbol{j} + \ddot{z}\boldsymbol{k} = \frac{-GM\{x\boldsymbol{i} + y\boldsymbol{j} + (R+z)\boldsymbol{k}\}}{\{x^2 + y^2 + (R+z)^2\}^{3/2}}$$

The three scalar equations are complicated; e.g.

$$\ddot{x} = \frac{-GMx}{\{x^2+y^2+(R+z)^2\}^{3/2}}$$

$\ddot{x}$ depends on x, y and z. $\ddot{y}$ and $\ddot{z}$ have a similar dependence on the coordinates. If the body is moving near the Earth's surface, the coordinates x,y,z are small compared with the radius of the sphere R. Thus we can make some approximations and simplify the equation of motion. We note that the radius in our model of the Earth is $6{\cdot}371 \times 10^6$ m, which is a distance very much greater than the distance encountered in most physical or engineering problems. Using the binomial expansion [see J. Hunter, *Calculus*, Blackie/Chambers], we have

$$\begin{aligned}
\frac{1}{\{x^2+y^2+(R+z)^2\}^{3/2}} &= \frac{1}{\{R^2+2Rz+x^2+y^2+z^2\}^{3/2}} \\
&= \frac{1}{R^3}\left\{1+\left(\frac{2z}{R}+\frac{x^2+y^2+z^2}{R^2}\right)\right\}^{-3/2} \\
&= \frac{1}{R^3}\left[1-\frac{3}{2}\left(\frac{2z}{R}+\frac{x^2+y^2+z^2}{R^2}\right)\right. \\
&\quad +\frac{1}{2!}\left(\frac{-3}{2}\right)\left(\frac{-5}{2}\right)\left(\frac{2z}{R}+\frac{x^2+y^2+z^2}{R^2}\right)^2 \\
&\quad \left. +\text{smaller terms}\right] \\
&= \frac{1}{R^3}\left[1-\frac{3z}{R}-\frac{3}{2R^2}(x^2+y^2-4z^2)\right. \\
&\quad \left. +\text{smaller terms}\right].
\end{aligned}$$

If we ignore terms involving x/R, y/R, z/R, the equation of motion becomes

$$\ddot{x}\boldsymbol{i}+\ddot{y}\boldsymbol{j}+\ddot{z}\boldsymbol{k} = \frac{-GM}{R^2}\boldsymbol{k}$$

Hence $\ddot{x}=0$, $\ddot{y}=0$ and $\ddot{z}=-g$, where

$$g = GM/R^2$$

The symbol g represents the numerical value of the acceleration due to gravity at the surface of the Earth. It is possible to design experiments to find the value of g. We shall adopt the value 9·81 when the units of acceleration are m s^{-2}. We have seen in the chapter on kinematics, Section 2.3, that differential equations of the above form are easy to solve by straightforward integration. The general solutions are

$$x = At + B$$

$$y = Ct + D$$

and

$$z = -\tfrac{1}{2}gt^2 + Et + F$$

where A, B, C, D, E, F are arbitrary constants of integration. At $t = 0$, the position vector is $\boldsymbol{r}_0 = B\boldsymbol{i} + D\boldsymbol{j} + F\boldsymbol{k}$ and the velocity vector is $\boldsymbol{u}_0 = A\boldsymbol{i} + C\boldsymbol{j} + E\boldsymbol{k}$. The vectorial forms of the above results are

$$\ddot{\boldsymbol{r}} = -g\boldsymbol{k}, \quad \dot{\boldsymbol{r}} = -gt\boldsymbol{k} + \boldsymbol{u}_0, \quad \boldsymbol{r} = -\tfrac{1}{2}gt^2\boldsymbol{k} + t\boldsymbol{u}_0 + \boldsymbol{r}_0$$

If we retain terms involving x/R, y/R, z/R, and ignore terms involving $(x/R)^2$, $(y/R)^2$, $(z/R)^2$, the equation of motion becomes

$$\ddot{x}\boldsymbol{i} + \ddot{y}\boldsymbol{j} + \ddot{z}\boldsymbol{k} = -g\left\{\frac{x}{R}\boldsymbol{i} + \frac{y}{R}\boldsymbol{j} + \left(1 - \frac{2z}{R}\right)\right\}\boldsymbol{k}$$

Hence we have to solve

$$\ddot{x} + \Omega^2 x = 0, \quad \ddot{y} + \Omega^2 y = 0 \quad \text{and} \quad \ddot{z} - 2\Omega^2 z = -g$$

where $\Omega^2 = g/R$. We shall quote the general solutions [see J. Hunter, *Calculus*, Blackie/Chambers]

$$x = A'\cos\Omega t + B'\sin\Omega t, \quad y = C'\cos\Omega t + D'\sin\Omega t$$

and

$$z = E'\cosh\sqrt{2}\Omega t + F'\sinh\sqrt{2}\Omega t + \tfrac{1}{2}R$$

where A', B', C', D', E', F' are arbitrary constants of integration. At $t = 0$, the position vector is $A'\boldsymbol{i} + C'\boldsymbol{j} + (E' + \frac{1}{2}R)\boldsymbol{k}$ and the velocity vector is $\Omega(B'\boldsymbol{i} + D'\boldsymbol{j} + \sqrt{2}F'\boldsymbol{k})$. Noting that $\Omega = (g/R)^{1/2} = 0{\cdot}00124$ (the units being s^{-1}), we may usefully expand the general solutions in powers of Ωt when Ωt is small. Hence using the Maclaurin expansions of the cosine, sine, hyperbolic cosine and hyperbolic sine functions [see J. Hunter, *Calculus*, Blackie/Chambers], we have

$$x = A' + B'\Omega t - \tfrac{1}{2}A'(\Omega t)^2 - \ldots$$

$$y = C' + D'\Omega t - \tfrac{1}{2}C'(\Omega t)^2 - \ldots$$

$$z = E' + \tfrac{1}{2}R + \sqrt{2}F'\Omega t + \tfrac{1}{2}2E'(\Omega t)^2 + \tfrac{1}{6}2\sqrt{2}F'(\Omega t)^3 + \ldots$$

We regain our results for the uniform gravitational field of force when we ignore the square of Ωt and smaller terms. Here we note that

$$A = B'\Omega, \quad B = A', \quad C = D'\Omega, \quad D = C', \quad E = \sqrt{2}F'\Omega, \quad F = E' + \tfrac{1}{2}R$$

and, in particular,

$$\tfrac{1}{2}2E'(\Omega t)^2 = (F-\tfrac{1}{2}R)(\Omega t)^2 = -\tfrac{1}{2}gt^2+F(\Omega t)^2$$

If we retain terms involving $(x/R)^2$, $(y/R)^2$, $(z/R)^2$ and ignore terms involving $(x/R)^3$, $(y/R)^3$, $(z/R)^3$, we obtain a set of differential equations that is no easier to solve than the original set of differential equations. A numerical technique, with which to obtain approximate solutions, would be appropriate in this case.

Let us consider a situation in which we can solve the equation of motion in its original form. Suppose that the body is thrown vertically upwards from the origin (on the surface of the Earth) with initial speed u_0. The only force acts vertically. Therefore the body moves along the vertical line for all time (i.e. $\ddot{x} = \dot{x} = x = 0$ and $\ddot{y} = \dot{y} = y = 0$ for all time). The equation of motion for the particle representing the body reduces to

$$\ddot{z} = \frac{-GM}{(z+R)^2}$$

subject to the conditions that $z = 0$, $\dot{z} = u_0$ at $t = 0$. Using the relation $\ddot{z} = \dot{z}(d\dot{z}/dz)$, we can integrate the differential equation directly with respect to z and obtain the result

$$\int_0^z \dot{z}\frac{d\dot{z}}{dz}\,dz = -GM\int_0^z \frac{1}{(z+R)^2}\,dz$$

or

$$\int_{u_0}^{\dot{z}} \dot{z}\,d\dot{z} = GM\left[\frac{1}{z+R}\right]_0^z$$

Hence

$$\dot{z}^2 = u_0^2+2GM\left(\frac{1}{z+R}-\frac{1}{R}\right) = u_0^2-\frac{2GMz}{R(z+R)}$$

$$= u_0^2-\frac{2gRz}{z+R} = u_0^2-\frac{2gz}{1+z/R}$$

where $g = GM/R^2$. Let H be the height to which the body rises above the Earth's surface. Then $z = H$ when $\dot{z} = 0$. Thus

$$u_0^2 = \frac{2gH}{1+H/R} \quad \text{and} \quad H = \frac{u_0^2}{2g-u_0^2/R}$$

If we examine the dependence of H on u_0^2, we find that H increases as u_0^2 increases from zero and H tends to infinity as u_0^2 tends to $2gR$. The initial speed $\sqrt{2gR}$ is called the escape speed (associated with the Earth). Its value is $1{\cdot}12\times10^4$ when the units are $\mathrm{m\,s^{-1}}$. Remember that we have ignored in this model air resistance during the early stages of the motion through the atmosphere, the motion of the Earth, the gravitational fields of force of bodies other than the Earth (e.g. the Moon and the Sun).

It is acceptable in very many situations to take as the set of differential equations governing the motion of a body near the Earth's surface the simplest of those that we deduced from our model of the Earth's gravitational field of force, namely

$$\ddot{x} = 0, \quad \ddot{y} = 0, \quad \ddot{z} = -g$$

In addition, we may ignore the curvature of the Earth's surface and we may take the xy-plane to represent the surface of the Earth. On all future occasions, unless we specify otherwise, we shall assume that the force due to gravity acts vertically downwards and has a magnitude equal to mg, the product of the mass and the acceleration due to gravity. We can apply this model consisting of a uniform gravitational field of force with confidence when the distances involved are much smaller than the radius of the Earth (i.e. when x/R, y/R, z/R are negligible).

EXERCISES ON CHAPTER 3

1. Sketch the curve associated with the function f, where

$$f(z) = \frac{gR^2}{(R+z)^2} \qquad 0 \leqslant z < \infty$$

Calculate the value of $f(z)/f(0)$ when $z/R = 0{\cdot}001, 0{\cdot}01, 0{\cdot}1, 0{\cdot}5, 1$ and relate your results to the variation of the magnitude of the inverse square gravitational force with height above the surface of the Earth.

2. Sketch the curve associated with the function H, where

$$H(x) = \frac{x}{2g - x/R} \qquad 0 \leqslant\ < \infty$$

Explain how the vertical asymptote is associated with the square of the escape speed associated with the Earth.

3. Use the expansion

$$\{2(g+\Delta g)(R+\Delta R)\}^{1/2} = (2gR)^{1/2}\left\{1 + \frac{\Delta g}{g} + \frac{\Delta R}{R} + \frac{\Delta g}{g}\frac{\Delta R}{R}\right\}^{1/2}$$
$$= (2gR)^{1/2}\left\{1 + \frac{\Delta g}{2g} + \frac{\Delta R}{2R} + \ldots\right\}$$

to investigate the influence of inaccuracies in the values of g and R on the calculated value of the escape speed.

4 Projectiles

4.1 Equation of motion

Consider the motion of a body near the surface of the Earth. There are many forces acting on the body. In our first model we shall assume that the only force acting is the uniform gravitational field of force. Further, we shall assume that the terrestrial frame of reference is an inertial frame of reference and we shall represent the body by a particle.

Let the particle have constant mass m and let its position vector be $\boldsymbol{r}$ (relative to a chosen origin O). It is convenient to take the xy-plane to represent the surface of the Earth and to let the direction of z increasing be vertically upwards. Then we represent the force acting on the body by $-mg\boldsymbol{k}$. The equation of motion for the particle is

$$m\frac{d^2\boldsymbol{r}}{dt^2} = -mg\boldsymbol{k} \quad \text{or} \quad m\ddot{\boldsymbol{r}} = -mg\boldsymbol{k}$$

The product mg is called the *weight* of the particle and has the dimensions of force. Integrating the equation of motion with respect to time, we find that

$$\frac{d\boldsymbol{r}}{dt} = \dot{\boldsymbol{r}} = -gt\boldsymbol{k} + \mathbf{A}$$

and

$$\boldsymbol{r} = -\tfrac{1}{2}gt^2\boldsymbol{k} + t\mathbf{A} + \mathbf{B}$$

where $\mathbf{A}, \mathbf{B}$ are constant vectors, being the particle's velocity vector and position vector at $t = 0$.

We notice from the results of integrating the equation of motion that $\dot{\boldsymbol{r}}$ and $\boldsymbol{r} - \mathbf{B}$ are vectors in the vertical plane specified by the pair of vectors, $\boldsymbol{k}$ and $\mathbf{A}$. Therefore the particle moves in this particular vertical plane specified by the vertical to the Earth's surface and the initial velocity of the particle. We shall choose our cartesian coordinate system so that this vertical plane is parallel to the xz-plane. If the initial speed, called the *speed of projection*, is u_0 and the angle of projection is θ, we have

$$\mathbf{A} = u_0(\boldsymbol{i}\cos\theta + \boldsymbol{k}\sin\theta)$$

If the particle is at the origin at $t = 0$, the origin is the point of projection and

$$\mathbf{B} = \mathit{0}$$

Then the particle moves in the xy-plane throughout its motion. Here we have a simple model of a shell being fired from a gun at O such that the barrel of the gun makes an angle θ with the horizontal. Alternatively, we may consider the above to be a simple model of the flight of a ball in tennis or golf (or any other ball game). The solution is

$$\dot{\boldsymbol{r}} = u_0 \cos\theta \boldsymbol{i} + (u_0 \sin\theta - gt)\boldsymbol{k}$$

and

$$\boldsymbol{r} = u_0 t \cos\theta \boldsymbol{i} + (u_0 t \sin\theta - \tfrac{1}{2}gt^2)\boldsymbol{k}$$

An alternative approach to this problem is to write out the equation of motion in terms of its components and to solve the resulting scalar differential equations subject to initial conditions. Adopting this approach, we have

$$m\ddot{x} = 0, \quad m\ddot{y} = 0, \quad m\ddot{z} = -mg$$

subject to

$$x = y = z = 0 \quad \text{at} \quad t = 0$$

and

$$\dot{x} = u_0 \cos\theta, \quad \dot{y} = 0, \quad \dot{z} = u_0 \sin\theta \quad \text{at} \quad t = 0$$

Hence, at time t,

$$\dot{x} = u_0 \cos\theta, \quad \dot{y} = 0, \quad \dot{z} = u_0 \sin\theta - gt$$

and

$$x = u_0 t \cos\theta, \quad y = 0, \quad z = u_0 t \sin\theta - \tfrac{1}{2}gt^2$$

The maximum height corresponding to a given initial velocity is achieved when

$$\frac{dz}{dt} = 0$$

This stationary value, which must be a maximum because

$$\frac{d^2 z}{dt^2} = -g < 0$$

occurs when $t = (u_0/g)\sin\theta$. Hence the maximum height is $\frac{1}{2}(u_0^2/g)\sin^2\theta$. This is less than or equal to $\frac{1}{2}(u_0^2/g)$, the value corresponding to the case $\theta = \frac{1}{2}\pi$.

The particle returns to the surface of the Earth when $z = 0$. This occurs when either $t = 0$ or $t = (2u_0/g)\sin\theta$. The time of flight is $(2u_0/g)\sin\theta$. The range R is the horizontal distance covered by the particle in flight. Hence

$$R = u_0(2u_0/g)\sin\theta\cos\theta = (u_0^2/g)\sin 2\theta$$

The maximum range for a given initial speed u_0 is u_0^2/g and corresponds to an angle of projection of $\frac{1}{4}\pi$. When the range R is less than the maximum range for a given initial speed u_0, there are two possible angles of projection, these being the solutions of $\sin 2\theta = Rg/u_0^2$, namely

$$\tfrac{1}{2}\sin^{-1}(Rg/u_0^2) \quad \text{and} \quad \tfrac{1}{2}\pi - \tfrac{1}{2}\sin^{-1}(Rg/u_0^2)$$

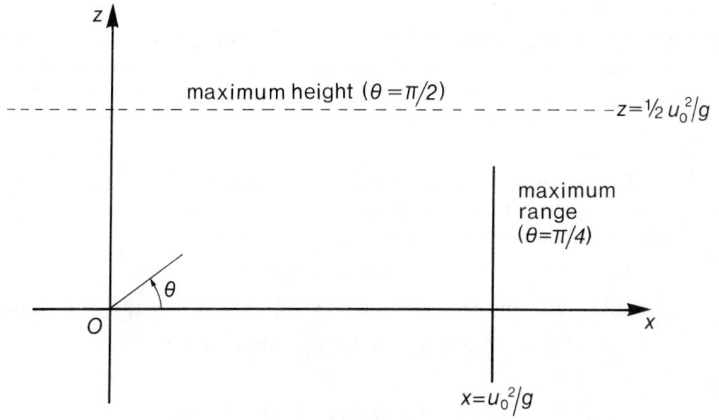

EXAMPLE
A particle is projected vertically upwards at time $t = 0$ and is at a height H at two instants, $t = t_1$ and $t = t_2$. Find the initial speed u_0 and the acceleration due to gravity g.

The upward and downward motions of the particle are governed by

$$m\ddot{\boldsymbol{r}} = -mg\boldsymbol{k}$$

where m is the mass of the particle. The initial conditions are $\dot{\boldsymbol{r}} = u_0\boldsymbol{k}$ and $\boldsymbol{r} = \boldsymbol{0}$ at $t = 0$. Therefore

$$\dot{\boldsymbol{r}} = (u_0 - gt)\boldsymbol{k} \quad \text{and} \quad \boldsymbol{r} = (u_0 t - \tfrac{1}{2}gt^2)\boldsymbol{k}$$

i.e.

$$x = y = 0 \quad \text{and} \quad z = u_0 t - \tfrac{1}{2}gt^2$$

for all time t. We are told that

$$H = u_0 t_1 - \tfrac{1}{2}gt_1^2 \quad \text{and} \quad H = u_0 t_2 - \tfrac{1}{2}gt_2^2$$

i.e. t_1 and t_2 are the roots of $\frac{1}{2}gt^2 - u_0 t + H = 0$. Hence

$$(t - t_1)(t - t_2) = t^2 - (2u_0/g)t + 2H/g$$

and

$$t_1+t_2 = 2u_0/g, \quad t_1t_2 = 2H/g$$

Thus $g = 2H/t_1t_2$ and $u_0 = H(t_1+t_2)/t_1t_2$. Alternatively, we may solve the two simultaneous linear algebraic equations for u_0 and g and obtain the results

$$u_0 = \frac{H(t_1^2-t_2^2)}{t_1^2t_2-t_1t_2^2} = \frac{H(t_1-t_2)(t_1+t_2)}{t_1t_2(t_1-t_2)} = \frac{H(t_1+t_2)}{t_1t_2}$$

and

$$g = \frac{H(t_1-t_2)}{\frac{1}{2}(t_1^2t_2-t_1t_2^2)} = \frac{2H}{t_1t_2}$$

EXAMPLE

A particle is projected, with speed u_0, from a point on a horizontal plane. When the angle of projection is α the particle falls short of a target on the horizontal plane by a distance d_1, and when the angle is β the particle goes beyond the target by a distance d_2. Find the correct angle to hit the target.

We select a system of cartesian coordinates so that the point of projection is at the origin; the target has the position vector $D\boldsymbol{i}$ and the direction vertically upwards corresponds to the direction of increasing z. Then the equation of motion is

$$m\ddot{\boldsymbol{r}} = -mg\boldsymbol{k}$$

and the initial conditions are $\dot{\boldsymbol{r}} = u_0(\boldsymbol{i}\cos\theta+\boldsymbol{k}\sin\theta)$, $\boldsymbol{r} = \boldsymbol{0}$ at $t = 0$. Hence

$$\dot{\boldsymbol{r}} = u_0\cos\theta\boldsymbol{i}+(u_0\sin\theta-gt)\boldsymbol{k}$$

and

$$\boldsymbol{r} = u_0t\cos\theta\boldsymbol{i}+(u_0t\sin\theta-\tfrac{1}{2}gt^2)\boldsymbol{k}$$

Let R be the distance between the point of projection and the point at which the particle strikes the horizontal plane (the range); i.e.

$$R = \boldsymbol{r}.\boldsymbol{i} \quad \text{when} \quad \boldsymbol{r}.\boldsymbol{k} = 0 \quad (t \neq 0)$$

Hence $R = (u_0^2/g)\sin 2\theta$. We are given the information that

$$D-d_1 = (u_0^2/g)\sin 2\alpha \quad \text{and} \quad D+d_2 = (u_0^2/g)\sin 2\beta$$

Hence

$$(u_0^2/g) = \frac{d_1+d_2}{\sin 2\beta-\sin 2\alpha}$$

and

$$D = d_1+\frac{(d_1+d_2)\sin 2\alpha}{\sin 2\beta-\sin 2\alpha} = \frac{d_1\sin 2\beta+d_2\sin 2\alpha}{\sin 2\beta-\sin 2\alpha}$$

The correct angle of projection satisfies

$$D = (u_0^2/g)\sin 2\theta$$

i.e.

$$\sin 2\theta = \frac{d_1\sin 2\beta+d_2\sin 2\alpha}{d_1+d_2}$$

There are two solutions:

$$\tfrac{1}{2}\sin^{-1}\left(\frac{d_1 \sin 2\beta + d_2 \sin 2\alpha}{d_1 + d_2}\right) \quad \text{and} \quad \tfrac{1}{2}\pi - \tfrac{1}{2}\sin^{-1}\left(\frac{d_1 \sin 2\beta + d_2 \sin 2\alpha}{d_1 + d_2}\right)$$

In passing, we note that the speed of projection can be expressed in terms of d_1, d_2, α and β, namely

$$u_0 = \left\{\frac{(d_1 + d_2)g}{\sin 2\beta - \sin 2\alpha}\right\}^{1/2}$$

EXAMPLE

A particle is projected with initial velocity $\boldsymbol{u}_0$ and moves freely under gravity. If it is moving at right angles to its original direction of motion after time t_1 and strikes the horizontal plane through the point of projection after time t_2 (both times being measured from the instant of projection), show that the speed of projection, u_0, is given by

$$u_0^2 = \tfrac{1}{2}g^2 t_1 t_2$$

and the range on the horizontal plane, R, by

$$R = \tfrac{1}{2}g t_2 (2t_1 t_2 - t_2^2)^{1/2}$$

provided $t_1 < t_2 < 2t_1$.

Let $\boldsymbol{r}$ be the position vector of the particle relative to the particle's initial position. The governing equation is

$$\ddot{\boldsymbol{r}} = -g\boldsymbol{k}$$

subject to $\dot{\boldsymbol{r}} = \boldsymbol{u}_0$ and $\boldsymbol{r} = \boldsymbol{0}$ at $t = 0$. Hence

$$\dot{\boldsymbol{r}} = \boldsymbol{u}_0 - gt\boldsymbol{k} \quad \text{and} \quad \boldsymbol{r} = t\boldsymbol{u}_0 - \tfrac{1}{2}gt^2\boldsymbol{k}$$

At $t = t_1$, $\dot{\boldsymbol{r}} \cdot \boldsymbol{u}_0 = 0$ and at $t = t_2$, $\boldsymbol{r} \cdot \boldsymbol{k} = 0$. Hence

$$u_0^2 - gt_1 \boldsymbol{k} \cdot \boldsymbol{u}_0 = 0 \quad \text{and} \quad t_2 \boldsymbol{u}_0 \cdot \boldsymbol{k} - \tfrac{1}{2}gt_2^2 = 0$$

Therefore

$$\boldsymbol{u}_0 \cdot \boldsymbol{k} = \tfrac{1}{2}gt_2 \quad \text{and} \quad u_0^2 = \tfrac{1}{2}g^2 t_1 t_2$$

Next we consider the range R, where

$$R = t_2 \boldsymbol{u}_0 \cdot \boldsymbol{i}$$

with

$$\boldsymbol{u}_0 = (\boldsymbol{u}_0 \cdot \boldsymbol{i})\boldsymbol{i} + (\boldsymbol{u}_0 \cdot \boldsymbol{k})\boldsymbol{k} \quad \text{and} \quad \boldsymbol{i} \cdot \boldsymbol{k} = 0$$

Thus

$$(\boldsymbol{u}_0 \cdot \boldsymbol{i})^2 = u_0^2 - (\boldsymbol{u}_0 \cdot \boldsymbol{k})^2 = \tfrac{1}{2}g^2 t_1 t_2 - (\tfrac{1}{2}gt_2)^2 = \tfrac{1}{4}g^2(2t_1 t_2 - t_2^2)$$

We may take the square root provided $2t_1 > t_2$ and hence

$$R = \tfrac{1}{2}gt_2(2t_1 t_2 - t_2^2)^{1/2}$$

We require the inequality $t_1 < t_2$ so that the particle is moving at right angles to its original direction of motion before it strikes the horizontal plane.

EXAMPLE

A golf ball travels 180 m when struck with a driver with a steel shaft, which produces a club head speed of $43\,\mathrm{m\,s^{-1}}$. It travels 190 m when struck with a driver with a carbon fibre shaft, which produces a club head speed of $46\,\mathrm{m\,s^{-1}}$. Are the predictions of our simple model (in which the effects of air are ignored) consistent with these experimental data?

Let us assume that each driver gives rise to the same angle of projection, α say, and that the club head speed is the speed of projection of the golf ball (to be modelled by a particle).

Let the predicted ranges (the horizontal distances covered to the first bounce) be R_1 and R_2. Then

$$R_1 = \frac{(43)^2}{g}\sin 2\alpha \quad \text{and} \quad R_2 = \frac{(46)^2}{g}\sin 2\alpha$$

Hence

$$\frac{R_2}{R_1} = \frac{(46)^2}{(43)^2} = 1{\cdot}144$$

and $R_2 = 206$ if $R_1 = 180$. (These results remain correct if we assume that the speed of projection is proportional to the club head speed.) Alternatively we may seek the values of R_1 and R_2 that satisfy

$$R_2 = 1{\cdot}144R_1 \quad \text{and} \quad R_2 - R_1 = 10$$

The required values are

$$R_1 = 69{\cdot}2 \quad \text{and} \quad R_2 = 79{\cdot}2$$

The inconsistency between the predictions and the experimental data indicates that our simple model is unacceptable for golf-ball dynamics. In fact, spin and aerodynamical forces play important parts in golf-ball dynamics. [J. M. Davies, "The Aerodynamics of Golf Balls", *Journal of Applied Physics*, **20** (1949) 821–828; D. Williams, "Drag Force on a Golf Ball", *Quarterly Journal of Mechanics and Applied Mathematics*, **12** (1959) 387–392.]

4.2 Geometry of the trajectory

The path of the projectile through space is called the *trajectory*. We have obtained in the previous section a representation of the trajectory in terms of a parameter t, namely time measured from the instant of projection. What geometric properties does the trajectory have? Repeating our earlier results, we have that

$$\boldsymbol{r} = x\boldsymbol{i} + z\boldsymbol{k}$$

where $x = u_0 t\cos\theta$ and $z = u_0 t\sin\theta - \frac{1}{2}gt^2$. Eliminating t, we find that

$$z = x\tan\theta - \frac{g}{2u_0^2}x^2\sec^2\theta$$

Completing the square in x leads to

$$\left(\frac{2u_0^2\cos^2\theta}{g}\right)z = \left(\frac{2u_0^2\sin\theta\cos\theta}{g}\right)x - x^2$$

$$= -\left(x - \frac{u_0^2\sin\theta\cos\theta}{g}\right)^2 + \frac{u_0^4\sin^2\theta\cos^2\theta}{g^2}$$

Hence, we have the equation

$$\left(x - \frac{u_0^2\sin\theta\cos\theta}{g}\right)^2 = \frac{2u_0^2\cos^2\theta}{g}\left(\frac{u_0^2\sin^2\theta}{2g} - z\right)$$

We compare this with the canonical equation of the parabola, namely $Y^2 = 4aX$ [see J. Hunter, *Analytic Geometry and Vectors*, Blackie/Chambers]. Therefore the trajectory is parabolic. Its vertex has the coordinates ($X = Y = 0$)

$$x = \frac{u_0^2}{g}\sin\theta\cos\theta, \quad z = \frac{u_0^2}{2g}\sin^2\theta$$

and corresponds to the point having maximum height above the plane $z = 0$. The coordinates of the focus of the parabola are ($X = a$, $Y = 0$)

$$x = \frac{u_0^2}{g}\sin\theta\cos\theta = \frac{u_0^2}{2g}\sin 2\theta, \quad z = \frac{u_0^2}{2g}(\sin^2\theta - \cos^2\theta) = -\frac{u_0^2}{2g}\cos 2\theta$$

The directrix of the parabola is the line ($X = -a$)

$$\frac{u_0^2}{2g}\sin^2\theta - z = -\frac{u_0^2}{2g}\cos^2\theta$$

i.e.

$$z = \frac{u_0^2}{2g}$$

The position of the directrix is independent of the angle of projection. A particle projected vertically upwards ($\theta = 0$) just reaches the directrix before falling back to the surface of the Earth.

It is useful in some problems to employ the directrix-focus property of the parabolic trajectory, namely, the distance between the particle and the focus equals the perpendicular distance between the particle and the directrix [see J. Hunter, *Analytic Geometry and Vectors*, Blackie/Chambers]. Let us verify this property. The square of the distance between the particle and the focus equals

$$\left\{\frac{u_0^2}{2g}\sin 2\theta - u_0 t\cos\theta\right\}^2 + \left\{-\frac{u_0^2}{2g}\cos 2\theta - u_0 t\sin\theta + \tfrac{1}{2}gt^2\right\}^2$$

$$= \frac{u_0^4}{4g^2}(\sin^2 2\theta + \cos^2 2\theta) - \frac{u_0^3 t}{g}(\sin 2\theta \cos \theta - \cos 2\theta \sin \theta)$$

$$+ u_0^2 t^2(\cos^2 \theta + \sin^2 \theta - \tfrac{1}{2}\cos 2\theta) - u_0 g t^3 \sin \theta + \tfrac{1}{4}g^2 t^4$$

$$= \frac{u_0^4}{4g^2} - \frac{u_0^3 t}{g}\sin \theta + u_0^2 t^2(\tfrac{1}{2} + \sin^2 \theta) - u_0 g t^3 \sin \theta + \tfrac{1}{4}g^2 t^4$$

$$= \left\{\frac{u_0^2}{2g} - u_0 t \sin \theta + \tfrac{1}{2}g t^2\right\}^2$$

which equals the square of the perpendicular distance between the particle and the directrix.

EXAMPLE

Find the minimum speed of projection for a particle to clear a wall of height H when the point of projection is a distance D from the base of the wall and the trajectory is in a plane perpendicular to the wall.

We describe a geometrical approach based on the directrix-focus property of the parabolic trajectory. Let u_0 be the speed of projection. The point of projection and the top of the wall lie on the parabolic trajectory. Consider a circle, centre the point of projection and radius $u_0^2/2g$, and a second circle, centre the top of the wall and radius $u_0^2/2g - H$. Both circles touch the directrix. They may or may not intersect each other. There are three possibilities: the circles intersect at two points, the circles touch at a point, the circles do not intersect. The points of intersection are the foci of the possible parabolic trajectories. There are two possible trajectories if there are two foci; there is one possible trajectory if there is one focus; there are no possible trajectories if there are no foci. These cases correspond to the speed of projection being greater than the minimum value, equal to the minimum value and less than the minimum value. In the limiting case of the minimum speed of projection, the point of projection, the focus and the top of the wall are collinear. By Pythagoras's theorem, we have

$$D^2 + H^2 = \left\{\frac{u_0^2}{2g} + \left(\frac{u_0^2}{2g} - H\right)\right\}^2$$

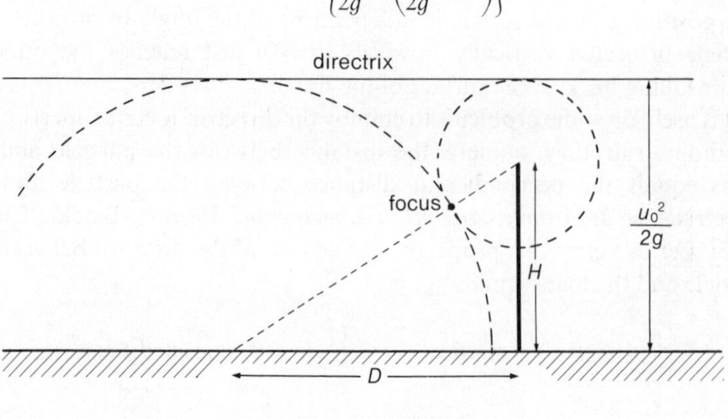

Hence

$$\left(\frac{u_0^2}{g}\right)^2 - 2H\left(\frac{u_0^2}{g}\right) - D^2 = 0 \quad \text{and} \quad \frac{u_0^2}{g} = H \pm (H^2+D^2)^{1/2}$$

We have to select the positive sign to ensure that the right-hand side of the equation is non-negative. Therefore

$$u_0 = [g\{H+(H^2+D^2)^{1/2}\}]^{1/2}$$

This is the minimum speed of projection.

Let us re-examine this problem by the alternative method described in the previous section. When the speed of projection is u_0 and the angle of projection is θ, we know that the coordinates of the general point on the trajectory are

$$x = u_0 t\cos\theta \quad \text{and} \quad z = u_0 t\sin\theta - \tfrac{1}{2}gt^2$$

The trajectory passes through the point having the position vector $D\boldsymbol{i}+H\boldsymbol{k}$, if

$$D = u_0 t\cos\theta \quad \text{and} \quad H = u_0 t\sin\theta - \tfrac{1}{2}gt^2$$

By eliminating t, we have

$$H = D\tan\theta - \tfrac{1}{2}\frac{gD^2}{u_0^2}\sec^2\theta$$

Hence

$$u_0^2 = \frac{gD^2}{2D\sin\theta\cos\theta - 2H\cos^2\theta} = \frac{gD^2}{D\sin 2\theta - H - H\cos 2\theta}$$

and we require $D\sin\theta > H\cos\theta$ so that $u_0^2 > 0$.

Differentiating with respect to θ leads to

$$2u_0\frac{du_0}{d\theta} = \frac{-gD^2(2D\cos 2\theta + 2H\sin 2\theta)}{(D\sin 2\theta - H - H\cos 2\theta)^2}$$

The numerator is zero when

$$D\cos 2\theta + H\sin 2\theta = 0$$

which implies that $\tan 2\theta = -D/H$. Hence 2θ is in the second quadrant (θ is in the first quadrant),

$$\sin 2\theta = D(H^2+D^2)^{-1/2} \quad \text{and} \quad \cos 2\theta = -H(H^2+D^2)^{-1/2}$$

The corresponding value of u_0^2 is

$$\frac{gD^2}{D^2(H^2+D^2)^{-1/2} - H + H^2(H^2+D^2)^{-1/2}} = \frac{gD^2}{(H^2+D^2)^{1/2} - H}$$
$$= g\{(H^2+D^2)^{1/2} + H\}$$

This agrees with our previous result. We note that the second derivative of u_0 with respect to θ takes the positive value

$$\frac{2g^{1/2}D(H^2+D^2)^{1/2}}{\{(H^2+D^2)^{1/2} - H\}^{3/2}}$$

at the stationary point. This confirms that the stationary value of u_0 is a minimum. This approach, based on calculus, gives us information directly about the angle of projection corresponding to the minimum speed of projection. We can obtain the same information from the geometric approach, if we note the position of the focus, in particular the x and z-coordinates of the focus, namely

$$\frac{u_0^2}{2g}\sin 2\theta = \frac{u_0^2}{2g}\cos\alpha \quad \text{and} \quad -\frac{u_0^2}{2g}\cos 2\theta = \frac{u_0^2}{2g}\sin\alpha$$

where $\tan\alpha = H/D$. Thus

$$\tan 2\theta = -\cot\alpha = -D/H$$

4.3 Some additional examples

We shall discuss in this section projectile problems involving vertical cliffs and inclined planes. The governing equation of motion remains the same as that in Section 4.1. Hence we have to solve

$$m\ddot{\boldsymbol{r}} = -mg\boldsymbol{k}$$

subject to given initial conditions. In each problem, it is advisable (but not essential) to choose a convenient system of coordinates, that is, a convenient frame of reference.

EXAMPLE

A gun is mounted on the edge of a vertical cliff, a height H above sea-level. Find the angle of projection to achieve the maximum range out to sea when the speed of projection is u_0.

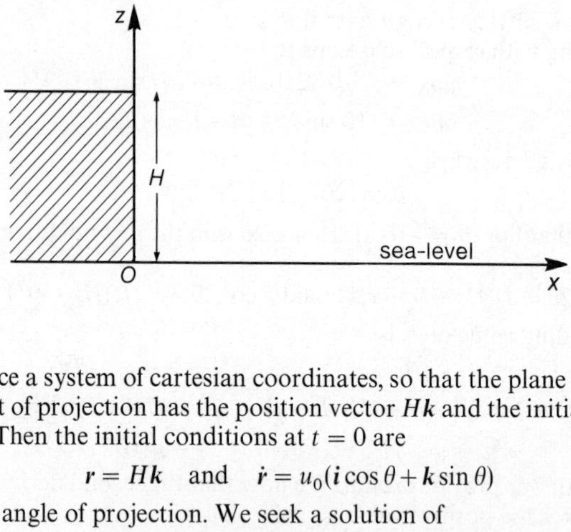

We introduce a system of cartesian coordinates, so that the plane $z = 0$ is at sea-level, the point of projection has the position vector $H\boldsymbol{k}$ and the initial velocity is in the xz-plane. Then the initial conditions at $t = 0$ are

$$\boldsymbol{r} = H\boldsymbol{k} \quad \text{and} \quad \dot{\boldsymbol{r}} = u_0(\boldsymbol{i}\cos\theta + \boldsymbol{k}\sin\theta)$$

where θ is the angle of projection. We seek a solution of

$$\ddot{\boldsymbol{r}} = -g\boldsymbol{k}$$

subject to these initial conditions. Integration with respect to time leads to

$$\dot{\boldsymbol{r}} = u_0\cos\theta\boldsymbol{i} + (u_0\sin\theta - gt)\boldsymbol{k}$$

and

$$\boldsymbol{r} = u_0 t\cos\theta\boldsymbol{i} + (H + u_0 t\sin\theta - \tfrac{1}{2}gt^2)\boldsymbol{k}$$

Alternatively, we may solve the scalar differential equations

$$\ddot{x} = 0 \quad \text{subject to} \quad x = 0,\ \dot{x} = u_0\cos\theta \quad \text{at} \quad t = 0$$

$$\ddot{y} = 0 \quad \text{subject to} \quad y = 0,\ \dot{y} = 0 \quad \text{at} \quad t = 0$$

and

$$\ddot{z} = -g \quad \text{subject to} \quad z = H, \dot{z} = u_0 \sin\theta \quad \text{at} \quad t = 0$$

Hence, at time t,

$$\dot{x} = u_0 \cos\theta, \quad \dot{y} = 0, \quad \dot{z} = u_0 \sin\theta - gt$$

and

$$x = u_0 t \cos\theta, \quad y = 0, \quad z = H + u_0 t \sin\theta - \tfrac{1}{2}gt^2$$

We note that these results are only slightly different from those in Section 4.1, where we used a different frame of reference, and that the trajectory is parabolic.

The particle is at sea-level when $\boldsymbol{r}.\boldsymbol{k} = 0$, i.e. $z = 0$. The range R at sea-level that we are interested in is the value of

$$\boldsymbol{r}.\boldsymbol{i} \quad \text{subject to} \quad \boldsymbol{r}.\boldsymbol{k} = 0$$

$\boldsymbol{r}.\boldsymbol{k} = 0$ leads to

$$\tfrac{1}{2}gt^2 - u_0 t \sin\theta - H = 0$$

which has the roots

$$t = \{u_0 \sin\theta \pm (u_0^2 \sin^2\theta + 2gH)^{1/2}\}/g$$

We must select the positive sign to obtain a positive value for the time taken for the projectile to reach sea-level. Hence the time of flight is

$$\frac{u_0}{g}\left\{\sin\theta + \left(\sin^2\theta + \frac{2gH}{u_0^2}\right)^{1/2}\right\}$$

and the range R (at sea-level) is given by

$$R = \frac{u_0^2}{g}\cos\theta\left\{\sin\theta + \left(\sin^2\theta + \frac{2gH}{u_0^2}\right)^{1/2}\right\}$$

Next we investigate the dependence of R on θ. Differentiating with respect to θ, we find that

$$\frac{dR}{d\theta} = -\frac{u_0^2}{g}\sin\theta\left\{\sin\theta + \left(\sin^2\theta + \frac{2gH}{u_0^2}\right)^{1/2}\right\} + \frac{u_0^2}{g}\cos\theta\left\{\cos\theta + \left(\sin^2\theta + \frac{2gH}{u_0^2}\right)^{-1/2}\sin\theta\cos\theta\right\}$$

Hence $dR/d\theta = 0$ when

$$(1 - 2\sin^2\theta)\left(\sin^2\theta + \frac{2gH}{u_0^2}\right)^{1/2} = \sin\theta\left(\frac{2gH}{u_0^2} - 1 + 2\sin^2\theta\right)$$

Squaring and examining the resulting polynomial in $\sin\theta$, we obtain a second-degree polynomial in $\sin\theta$, namely

$$2\left(1 + \frac{gH}{u_0^2}\right)\sin^2\theta = 1$$

Therefore

$$\sin\theta = \left\{\frac{u_0^2}{2(u_0^2 + gH)}\right\}^{1/2} \qquad \cos\theta = \left\{\frac{u_0^2 + 2gH}{2(u_0^2 + gH)}\right\}^{1/2}$$

and the corresponding stationary value of R is

$$\frac{u_0^2}{g}\left\{\frac{u_0^2+2gH}{2(u_0^2+gH)}\right\}^{1/2}\left[\left\{\frac{u_0^2}{2(u_0^2+gH)}\right\}^{1/2}+\left\{\frac{(u_0^2+2gH)^2}{2u_0^2(u_0^2+gH)}\right\}^{1/2}\right]=\frac{u_0}{g}(u_0^2+2gH)^{1/2}$$

The geometric property of the trajectory indicates that the stationary value is a maximum. (Alternatively, we have to investigate the sign of the second derivative of R at the stationary point.) We note that these results reduce to our earlier results in Section 4.1 when we put $H = 0$. We observe that the maximum range (at sea-level) is achieved for a given speed of projection u_0 when the angle of projection θ equals

$$\tan^{-1}\left\{\left(\frac{u_0^2}{u_0^2+2gH}\right)^{1/2}\right\}$$

which equals $\frac{1}{4}\pi$ when $H = 0$. The range when $\theta = \frac{1}{4}\pi$ equals

$$\frac{u_0}{g}\{\tfrac{1}{2}u_0+(\tfrac{1}{4}u_0^2+gH)^{1/2}\}$$

(and is less than the maximum range $(u_0/g)(u_0^2+2gH)^{1/2}$ provided $0 < (gH)^2$, this condition being obviously true).

EXAMPLE

A gun is mounted on a ship. How far to sea may the ship be so that the gun is able to shell the top of a vertical cliff of height H when the speed of projection is u_0?

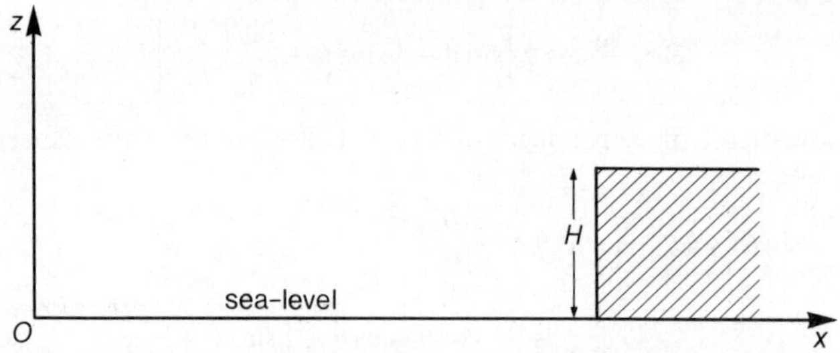

We select a frame of reference, based on a cartesian coordinate system, so that the plane $z = 0$ is at sea-level, the point of projection is at the origin, and the velocity of projection is in the xz-plane. We seek a solution of the differential equation

$$\ddot{\boldsymbol{r}} = -g\boldsymbol{k}$$

subject to the initial conditions at $t = 0$ being

$$\boldsymbol{r} = \boldsymbol{0} \quad \text{and} \quad \dot{\boldsymbol{r}} = u_0(\boldsymbol{i}\cos\theta+\boldsymbol{k}\sin\theta)$$

where θ is the angle of projection. We find by integration that the required solution is

$$\boldsymbol{r} = u_0 t\cos\theta\,\boldsymbol{i}+(u_0 t\sin\theta-\tfrac{1}{2}gt^2)\boldsymbol{k}$$

$\boldsymbol{r}\,.\,\boldsymbol{k} = z = H$ when

$$H-u_0 t\sin\theta+\tfrac{1}{2}gt^2 = 0$$

The two roots of this quadratic equation are

$$t = \{u_0 \sin\theta \pm (u_0^2 \sin^2\theta - 2gH)^{1/2}\}/g$$

Both times are possible, the positive sign corresponding to the larger value of $\boldsymbol{r}.\boldsymbol{i}$ ($= X$ say) for a given angle of projection θ. Hence we are interested in the dependence of X on θ, where

$$X = \frac{u_0^2}{g}\cos\theta\left\{\sin\theta + \left(\sin^2\theta - \frac{2gH}{u_0^2}\right)^{1/2}\right\}$$

and X represents the distance between the base of the vertical cliff and the ship at sea. Making use of the analysis in the previous example (R becomes X if we change the sign of H), we see that the maximum value of X for a given speed of projection u_0 is

$$\frac{u_0}{g}(u_0^2 - 2gH)^{1/2}$$

provided $u_0^2 > 2gH$. This condition requires the speed of projection to be sufficiently large for a height H to be attainable by the projectile. If $u_0^2 = 2gH$, the projectile has to be projected vertically upwards from the base of the vertical cliff (because $\theta = \frac{1}{2}\pi$ and $X = 0$). In geometric terms, the condition $u_0^2 > 2gH$ says that the directrix of the trajectory must be in a horizontal plane above the plane $z = H$.

EXAMPLE

A particle is projected with speed u_0 from a point on an inclined plane. The angle of inclination of the plane to the horizontal is α and the angle of projection is θ with the inclined plane. Find the range up the plane and the time of flight.

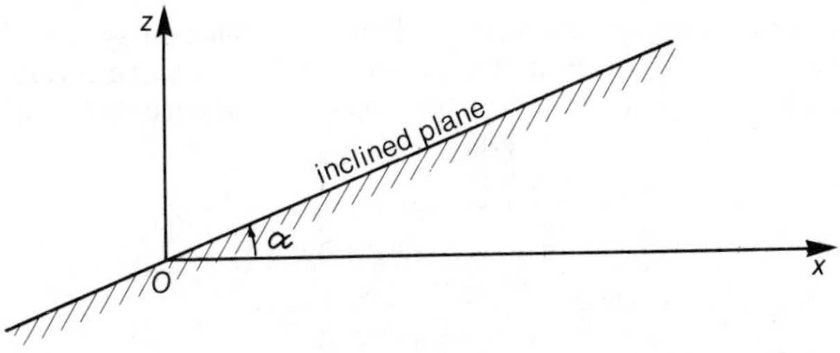

We assume that the motion is in a vertical plane through the line of greatest slope. (This assumption clarifies the definition of the angle α and is not restrictive.) We choose to introduce cartesian coordinate axes so that the origin is at the point of projection, the z-axis is vertical, and the first quadrant of the xz-plane includes the direction of the velocity of projection. The equation of motion is

$$m\ddot{\boldsymbol{r}} = -mg\boldsymbol{k}$$

and the initial conditions at $t = 0$ are

$$\boldsymbol{r} = \boldsymbol{0} \quad \text{and} \quad \dot{\boldsymbol{r}} = u_0\{\boldsymbol{i}\cos(\theta+\alpha) + \boldsymbol{k}\sin(\theta+\alpha)\}$$

Therefore, at time t

$$\dot{\boldsymbol{r}} = u_0\cos(\theta+\alpha)\boldsymbol{i} + \{u_0\sin(\theta+\alpha) - gt\}\boldsymbol{k}$$

and

$$r = u_0 t\cos(\theta+\alpha)\boldsymbol{i} + \{u_0 t\sin(\theta+\alpha) - \tfrac{1}{2}gt^2\}\boldsymbol{k}$$

The particle strikes the inclined plane when

$$r = R\cos\alpha\boldsymbol{i} + R\sin\alpha\boldsymbol{k}$$

where R is the range up the plane. Therefore the time of flight is specified by

$$u_0 t\cos(\theta+\alpha) = R\cos\alpha$$

and

$$u_0 t\sin(\theta+\alpha) - \tfrac{1}{2}gt^2 = R\sin\alpha$$

Eliminating the time of flight between these equations, we have

$$\frac{R\sin(\theta+\alpha)\cos\alpha}{\cos(\theta+\alpha)} - \frac{gR^2\cos^2\alpha}{2u_0^2\cos^2(\theta+\alpha)} = R\sin\alpha$$

This leads to

$$R = 0 \quad \text{or} \quad R = \frac{2u_0^2\sin\theta\cos(\theta+\alpha)}{g\cos^2\alpha}$$

and the corresponding times of flight are zero and $2u_0\sin\theta/g\cos\alpha$. Therefore the required distance up the plane is

$$\frac{2u_0^2\sin\theta\cos(\theta+\alpha)}{g\cos^2\alpha}$$

and the time of flight is

$$\frac{2u_0\sin\theta}{g\cos\alpha}$$

We shall work this problem again and choose a different system of cartesian coordinates. Let the X-axis be up the plane and let the Z-axis be at right angles, so that the origin coincides with the point of projection and the direction of the vector

$$\mathbf{I}\sin\alpha + \mathbf{K}\cos\alpha$$

is vertically upwards. The equation of motion is

$$m\ddot{r} = -mg(\mathbf{I}\sin\alpha + \mathbf{K}\cos\alpha)$$

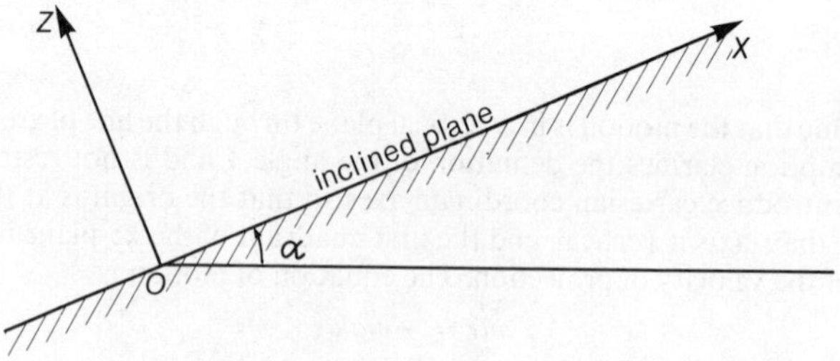

and the initial conditions at $t = 0$ are

$$r = \boldsymbol{0} \quad \text{and} \quad \dot{r} = u_0(\mathbf{I}\cos\theta + \mathbf{K}\sin\theta)$$

Therefore, the required solution satisfying the initial conditions is specified by the pair of equations

$$\dot{\boldsymbol{r}} = (u_0 \cos\theta - gt\sin\alpha)\mathbf{I} + (u_0 \sin\theta - gt\cos\alpha)\mathbf{K}$$

and

$$\boldsymbol{r} = (u_0 t\cos\theta - \tfrac{1}{2}gt^2 \sin\alpha)\mathbf{I} + (u_0 t\sin\theta - \tfrac{1}{2}gt^2\cos\alpha)\mathbf{K}$$

The particle strikes the plane when $\boldsymbol{r} = R\mathbf{I}$, where R is the range up the plane. Thus the appropriate final conditions are

$$R = u_0 t\cos\theta - \tfrac{1}{2}gt^2\sin\alpha$$

and

$$0 = u_0 t\sin\theta - \tfrac{1}{2}gt^2\cos\alpha$$

Ignoring the trivial solution ($t = 0, R = 0$), we see that the time of flight is

$$\frac{2u_0\sin\theta}{g\cos\alpha}$$

and

$$R = \frac{2u_0^2\sin\theta\cos\theta}{g\cos\alpha} - \tfrac{1}{2}g\left(\frac{2u_0\sin\theta}{g\cos\alpha}\right)^2\sin\alpha = \frac{2u_0^2\sin\theta\cos(\theta+\alpha)}{g\cos^2\alpha}$$

We note that the pair of equations governing the range and the time of flight in the second approach is simpler than the pair in the first approach. Our choice of the second frame of reference is responsible for this simplification. It is important to emphasize that the principles and the results are identical in the two approaches.

We may use the above analysis when the particle is projected down the inclined plane, in which case $\theta + \alpha > \tfrac{1}{2}\pi$, $\boldsymbol{r}.\mathbf{I} < 0$ and $R < 0$.

EXERCISES ON CHAPTER 4

1. A particle moving vertically under gravity passes upwards through a point P at $t = t_1$ and downwards through P at $t = t_2$. Where is the particle at $t = 0$ and what is its speed when it passes through P?

2. A ball is dropped (from rest) from the top of a tower. In the last second of its motion it falls a distance $\frac{9}{25}H$, where H is the total height of the tower. Find the total time of fall and evaluate H.

3. A stone is dropped in a well and the impact is heard after time T. Find the depth of the well and show that it is approximately

$$\tfrac{1}{2}gT^2 - \tfrac{1}{2}g^2T^3/U$$

where U is the speed of sound.

Using SI units and the values $T = 1{\cdot}5$ and $U = 332$, find the approximate percentage error in the depth caused by assuming that U is infinite.

4. A load of mass m is raised from rest by a constant vertical force F which acts for a time and then ceases. The load continues to ascend until it comes to rest under the action of gravity after rising a total distance D. Determine the time during which the constant force F acts, and find the maximum speed of the load. Draw a graph of speed against time.

5. A balloon of total mass M has a downward acceleration A_1. How much ballast must be ejected so that the balloon will have an upward acceleration A_2?

6. A balloon rises from rest on the ground with constant acceleration $g/18$. A stone is dropped when the balloon has risen to a height H. Find its maximum height above the ground and the time it takes to reach the ground.

7. A particle is projected upwards with a speed of $50\,\mathrm{m\,s^{-1}}$ at an angle θ to the horizontal, where $\tan\theta = \frac{4}{3}$. Calculate the coordinates of the particle at intervals of one second during the flight. Deduce that

(i) the time of flight is less than 9 seconds,

(ii) the range is greater than 240 metres,

(iii) the maximum height above the ground is greater than $81{\cdot}4$ metres.

8. A shell is fired from a gun with a muzzle speed of $400\,\mathrm{m\,s^{-1}}$. Calculate the maximum range on horizontal ground.

9. A particle is projected at a given angle α from a point on a horizontal plane. If the maximum height attained above the plane is H, find the time interval between the instants when the particle is at a height $H\sin^2\alpha$.

10. A juggler throws up five balls, one after the other, at equal intervals of time T, each ball rising to a height H. The first ball returns to the juggler's hand at time T after the fifth ball was thrown up. Find the height of each ball at the instant when the first ball returns to the juggler's hand.

11. A ball thrown at an angle θ to the horizontal just clears a wall. The horizontal and vertical distances of the top of the wall from the point of projection are X and Z respectively, with $X\tan\theta > Z$. Show that the speed of projection is

$$\frac{X}{\cos\theta}\left\{\frac{g}{2(X\tan\theta - Z)}\right\}^{1/2}$$

and determine the position of the highest point reached.

12. A particle is projected, from a point O on a horizontal plane, with speed u_0 at an angle θ to the horizontal. When it has travelled a horizontal distance $H \cot \alpha$, its height above the plane is H. Show that its distance from O is

$$\frac{2u_0^2 \sin(\theta-\alpha)\cos\theta}{g\cos^2\alpha}$$

Show that, to shell a target on top of a hill of height H above the horizontal plane through the point of projection, the initial speed of the shell must not be less than

$$\{gH(1+\operatorname{cosec}\alpha)\}^{1/2}$$

where α is the angle of elevation of the target from the gun.

13. To convert a try at rugby football, the ball has to be kicked over a bar of height H. Ignoring air resistance, what is the least possible speed of projection, and the corresponding angle of projection, if a try is to be converted from a point at a distance D away from the nearest point directly below the bar? Evaluate the least possible speed of projection for suitable values of H and D.

14. A particle is projected from a point A with speed u_0 at an angle θ to the horizontal. A horizontal belt is moving with speed v from A to B and the particle sticks to the belt if it lands on it but does not affect the motion of the belt. Show that the particle must land on the belt when projected towards B if $u_0^2 < gD$, where D is the distance between A and B.

Investigate the minimum time between A and B in the three cases (i) $v = u_0/35$, (ii) $v = u_0/6$, (iii) $v = u_0$.

15. At a given instant a particle P_1 is dropped from a point A at the top of a vertical cliff, and a particle P_2 is projected from a gun at a point S on a ship at sea. The height of the cliff is H and the distance AS is $(H^2+D^2)^{1/2}$. What are the conditions to be satisfied so that the two particles collide in the air? Deduce that the gunner on the ship must aim at A and that the speed of projection of P_2 must be greater than

$$\{g(H^2+D^2)/2H\}^{1/2}$$

16. A gun which launches a projectile with speed u_0 is situated at a point O on a horizontal plane. A target at a point P on the plane is in such a position that it could be hit by firing at an elevation of $\pi/6$. The target now starts to move along the line OP at a constant speed U and simultaneously the gun fires at an appropriate elevation θ. If the projectile hits the moving target, show that

$$U = u_0(\cos\theta - \tfrac{1}{4}\sqrt{3}\operatorname{cosec}\theta)$$

17. A gunboat is cruising with constant speed U. A gun is mounted at the stern of the vessel so as to point straight backwards and is set at an inclination of θ. If u_0 is the speed of projection of the shell relative to the gun, show that the range with respect to the ship's position when the shell is fired is

$$(u_0/g)(u_0 \sin 2\theta - 2U\sin\theta)$$

Find the angle of elevation for maximum range.

18. A projectile is to be fired from O with speed u at an elevation θ to hit a target A which is in a vertical plane at a distance D from O. Small errors Δu and $\Delta\theta$ are made in the speed and elevation. Calculate approximately at what height the projectile passes over A.

If the target is in the horizontal plane through O, show that the particle will overshoot the target by the approximate distance

$$\frac{2u^2}{g}\left(\frac{\Delta u}{u}\sin 2\theta + \Delta\theta\cos 2\theta\right)$$

19. Two parallel vertical walls have heights H_1 and H_2, and the distance between the tops of the walls is D. A particle is projected from the ground in a plane perpendicular to both walls; the point of projection is not between the walls. Show, by means of the focus-directrix property of the parabolic trajectory, that the particle will clear both walls provided that the speed of projection is greater than

$$\{g(H_1+H_2+D)\}^{1/2}$$

20. A particle is projected, at an angle of elevation θ and with speed $(gH)^{1/2}$, from the top of a hill of height H above a plain. Find the horizontal distance R covered by the particle when it strikes the plain. What is the angle of projection corresponding to the maximum value of R?

21. Two vertical poles AB and CD, the pole CD being 6 metres shorter than the pole AB, stand 8 metres apart with their bases A and C on a horizontal plane. A particle is projected from B (in the vertical plane of the poles) with speed u so that it strikes D. Show that

$$u^2 = \frac{16g(1+\tan^2\theta)}{(3+4\tan\theta)}$$

where θ is the angle of projection. Find the smallest value of u needed to make the particle strike D and the corresponding angle of projection.

22. When a glider is flying at a height of 500 metres above a plain and is rising with a speed of 40 metres per second at an angle of $\pi/6$ radians to the horizontal, a fragment of the fuselage drops off the glider: find (*a*) how long the fragment takes to reach the plain and (*b*) the velocity of the fragment just before impact with the ground.

23. A gun is firing shot, with speed of projection U, from sea-level out to sea. It is then mounted on a cliff of height H and fired at the same inclination α. Find the increase in its range and show that it is approximately $H\cot\alpha$ (provided $U\sin\alpha$ is much greater than $(2gH)^{1/2}$).

24. A ship is cruising in an easterly direction at a speed u. An aircraft, flying horizontally in an easterly direction at a speed U, passes above the ship at a height H. At what distance astern of the ship should a bomb be dropped from the aircraft to hit the ship? What is the position of the aircraft relative to the ship when the bomb strikes the ship?

25. A projectile is discharged, at speed u_0 and elevation 2α to the horizontal, up a plane inclined at α to the horizontal. Show that the time of flight is $2(u_0/g)\tan\alpha$ and that the projectile strikes the plane at an angle ϕ, where

$$\cot\phi = \cot\alpha - 2\tan\alpha$$

26. A particle is projected from a point on a plane which slopes at an angle of $\pi/6$ radians to the horizontal. The particle's initial velocity has magnitude u_0 and its direction is at right angles to the plane. Find where the particle strikes the plane.

27. A particle is projected from a point with speed u_0. It strikes at right angles a plane through the point of projection inclined at an angle α to the horizontal. Find the time of flight. Show that, if the inclined plane had been absent, the particle would have struck the horizontal plane through the point of projection O at a distance

$$\frac{u_0^2 \sin 2\alpha}{g}\left(\frac{1+\sin^2\alpha}{1+3\sin^2\alpha}\right)$$

from O.

28. A particle is projected at an angle θ to the horizontal from the foot of a plane, whose inclination to the horizontal is α ($\theta > \alpha$). Find the value of θ for which the range on the inclined plane is a maximum. Show that this maximum range is

$$\tfrac{1}{2}gT^2$$

where T is the corresponding time of flight.

29. A particle is projected at an angle θ to the horizontal from the top of a plane, whose inclination to the horizontal is α. Find the maximum range down the inclined plane when the speed of projection is u_0. What is the corresponding time of flight? Is the maximum range proportional to the square of the corresponding time of flight?

30. From the rim of a wheel of radius a, which is rotating about a fixed horizontal axis with constant angular speed Ω, particles fly off tangentially with speed $a\Omega$. For a particle flying off at a point where the radius is at an angle θ behind the upward vertical radius, find the greatest height above the centre of the wheel that is attained. Find for what value of θ this height is a maximum. Show that the highest point attained is vertically above the centre of the wheel when θ has this value.

31. Drops of water are thrown tangentially off the rim of a wheel of radius a which is rotating with angular speed Ω in a vertical plane, about its axis which is fixed and horizontal. Show that no drops rise above the level of the highest point of the wheel unless

$$\Omega > (g/a)^{1/2}$$

but that if a horizontal ceiling at height $h > a$ above the axis of the wheel is not to be sprayed with water

$$a\Omega < \{gh + g(h^2 - a^2)^{1/2}\}^{1/2}$$

32. A car is travelling at a constant speed U. Particles of mud are thrown tangentially from points of the back tyres where the tangent makes an angle of Θ or less with the road. The radius of the tyres is a. The lowest point of the windscreen of a following car (also travelling at a constant speed U) is at a height h above the road level. Investigate whether the windscreen is sprayed with mud when it is a distance D behind the rear axle of the leading car. Suggest suitable numerical values for Θ, a and h.

Constant Resistive Forces

5

5.1 Introduction

Let us investigate the influence of some resistive forces. The characteristic property of a resistive force is its opposition to motion. When we walk, the air tends to slow us down. The air resistance is particularly noticeable when we move into a wind. Its magnitude depends on our velocity relative to the air. Similarly, when we push an object across a table top, the object slides (we are ignoring the possibilities of rolling and toppling) and the contact between the two surfaces gives rise to a resistive force—called the *frictional force.* The problem of one surface moving when in contact with another is complex. [See F. Parmer, *American Journal of Physics,* **17** (1949) 181–187, 327–342; and *Encyclopaedic Dictionary of Physics* (ed. J. Thewlis), volume 3, pp. 307–312, Pergamon Press, 1961.] However, our experience helps us to classify surfaces into "smooth" or "rough". We have to exert a greater force to produce sliding when the surfaces are "rough" than when they are "smooth". If the surfaces were (perfectly) smooth, there would be no frictional force to overcome. In many of our models we shall assume that surfaces are (perfectly) smooth and there are no frictional forces. We shall focus our attention in this chapter on constant resistive forces. In chapter 10 we shall examine variable resistive forces.

5.2 Surfaces in contact

Suppose we try to slide a block of wood (or a brick or some other object without the ability to roll) across a table top by applying a force parallel to the table top. When the magnitude of the applied force F_A is not great enough, the block does not move. The forces acting on the block are the applied force, the force due to gravity, and the force due to the contact with the table top (which will be equal and opposite to the force experienced by the table top due to the contact with the block). Let the contact force acting on the block have a normal component N (vertically upwards) and a tangential component F_F. The tangential force, of magnitude F_F, is called the *frictional force.* Its direction is such as to oppose the motion of the block relative to the table top.

We are not considering rolling or toppling, so we may use a particle of mass m to represent the block of wood. We introduce a system of cartesian coordinates so that the table top is in the plane $z = 0$, the constant direction of the applied force is along the positive x-axis, and the region above the table top is the half-space $z > 0$. The equation of motion is

$$m\ddot{\boldsymbol{r}} = (F_A - F_F)\boldsymbol{i} + (N - mg)\boldsymbol{k}$$

when $\boldsymbol{r} = x\boldsymbol{i}$ and the initial conditions at $t = 0$ are $\boldsymbol{r} = \boldsymbol{0}$ and $\boldsymbol{r} = u_0\boldsymbol{i}$. Hence we have

$$m\ddot{x} = F_A - F_F \quad \text{and} \quad N = mg\,.$$

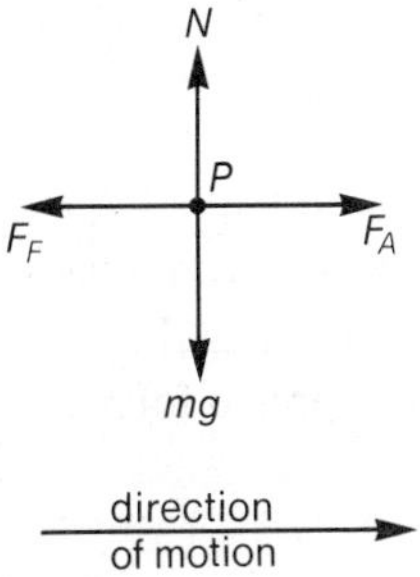

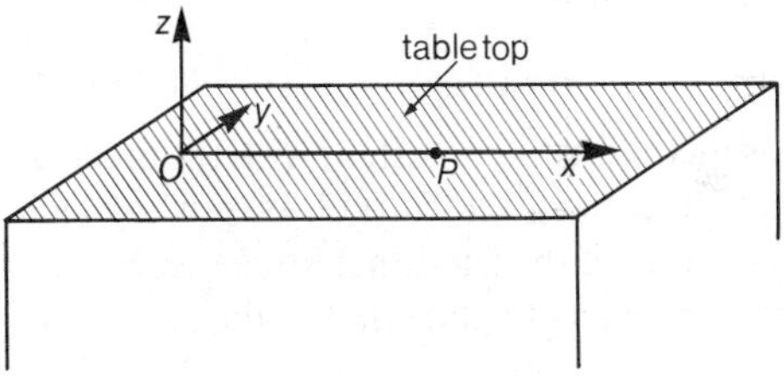

These equations are not sufficient to specify the motion when F_A is given, unless F_F is characterized in an appropriate manner.

Experimental evidence suggests that a reasonable, but oversimplified, characterization of the frictional force is possible when the surfaces are clean and dry (i.e. in particular, are not lubricated). The classical laws of dry friction (or Coulomb friction) are:

(i) The magnitude of the frictional force is proportional to the magnitude of the total force which acts normal to the sliding surface, i.e.

$$F_F = \mu N$$

where μ is the coefficient of kinematic friction.

(ii) The frictional force, for a constant load N, is independent of the area of contact.

(iii) The frictional force is independent of the velocity of sliding.

(iv) The frictional force depends on the nature of the materials in contact.

The coefficient of kinematic friction μ is usually less than one, but it may be greater than one. Tables of μ provide only a guide. A small change in the experimental conditions (e.g. dirt or a drop of oil between two metal surfaces) may alter the value of μ drastically. A μ-value has meaning only in a precise experimental situation. The coefficient of kinematic friction varies with the load. In the problems in this chapter, N and μ will be constant for any pair of surfaces, and so the frictional force will be an example of a constant resistive force.

What can we say about F_F when the block of wood is not moving across the table top? When there is no applied force, there is no frictional force (i.e. $F_F = 0$). As the applied force increases in magnitude, the magnitude of the frictional force increases until a limiting value is reached. We express this by writing

$$F_F \leqslant \mu_s N$$

where μ_s is the coefficient of static friction. For a given load N and a given pair of surfaces,

$$\mu_s > \mu$$

This inequality is consistent with the fact that there is a sudden jerk forward when a piece of furniture is pushed across the floor from rest; the magnitude of the frictional force decreasing slightly as soon as the piece of furniture starts to slide due to the action of a constant applied force.

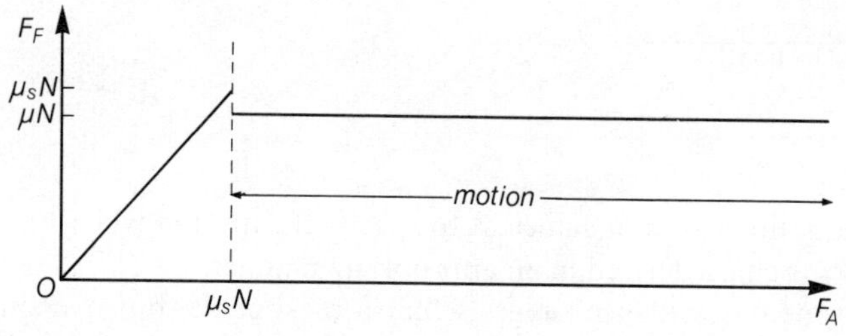

What is the importance of the frictional force between surfaces in contact? Nails, screws, moving belts, brakes (disc and drum varieties) and clutches depend on it. Trains and cars could not start and people could not walk without friction existing. However in some circumstances (especially in machinery) we are interested in the minimization of the effects of friction. Lubricants and bearings are designed for this purpose. The effects of rolling friction are considerably less than the effects of sliding friction. That explains why trains and cars have wheels, and why axles have bearings.

EXAMPLE

A particle P of mass m moves up an inclined plane (along a line of greatest slope) having an inclination α with the horizontal. It starts with a speed u_0 and eventually comes to rest because of the action of a frictional force. Investigate this situation when the coefficient of kinematic friction is μ.

Let us introduce cartesian coordinates so that the particle is at the origin O initially, the particle moves up the plane along the x-axis subsequently and the constant gravitational force is $-mg(\boldsymbol{i}\sin\alpha+\boldsymbol{k}\cos\alpha)$. The contact force acting on P has the form

$$-\mu N\boldsymbol{i}+N\boldsymbol{k}$$

when P is moving up the plane. Hence the equation governing the motion up the plane is

$$m\ddot{\boldsymbol{r}} = -mg(\boldsymbol{i}\sin\alpha+\boldsymbol{k}\cos\alpha)-\mu N\boldsymbol{i}+N\boldsymbol{k}$$

where $\boldsymbol{r} = x\boldsymbol{i}$, and the initial conditions at $t = 0$ are $\boldsymbol{r} = \boldsymbol{0}$ and $\dot{\boldsymbol{r}} = u_0\boldsymbol{i}$. Therefore

$$N = mg\cos\alpha$$

and

$$\ddot{x} = -g(\sin\alpha+\mu\cos\alpha)$$

Integrating with respect to t and using the initial conditions, we obtain

$$\dot{x} = u_0-gt(\sin\alpha+\mu\cos\alpha)$$

and

$$x = u_0t-\tfrac{1}{2}gt^2(\sin\alpha+\mu\cos\alpha)$$

The particle comes to rest when

$$t = \frac{u_0}{g(\sin\alpha+\mu\cos\alpha)} = t_U \text{ (say)}$$

and the distance moved in the time interval $[0, t_U]$ is

$$\frac{u_0^2}{2g(\sin\alpha+\mu\cos\alpha)} = \tfrac{1}{2}u_0t_U = D \text{ (say)}.$$

As soon as the particle comes to rest, the forces acting on the particle change. In particular, the frictional force reverses its direction and opposes the motion of the particle down the inclined plane. The particle will remain at rest if $mg\sin\alpha \leqslant \mu_s N$, where μ_s is the coefficient of static friction and $N = mg\cos\alpha$. Here $\mu_s N$ is the limiting value of the magnitude of the static frictional force. Sometimes it is convenient to set

$$\mu_s = \tan\lambda$$

where λ is the angle of friction. Then the above condition becomes

$$\tan\alpha \leqslant \mu_s = \tan\lambda \quad \text{or} \quad \alpha \leqslant \lambda$$

However, if

$$mg\sin\alpha > \mu_s N = \mu_s mg\cos\alpha$$

(i.e. $\tan\alpha > \mu_s$ or $\alpha > \lambda$) the particle starts to move down the inclined plane and the equation of motion is

$$m\ddot{\boldsymbol{r}} = m\ddot{x}\boldsymbol{i} = -mg(\boldsymbol{i}\sin\alpha+\boldsymbol{k}\cos\alpha)+\mu N\boldsymbol{i}+N\boldsymbol{k}$$

subject to $\boldsymbol{r} = D\boldsymbol{i}$, $\dot{\boldsymbol{r}} = \boldsymbol{0}$ at $t = t_U$. Hence, for $t \geqslant t_U$ we have

$$N = mg\cos\alpha$$

and

$$\ddot{x} = -g(\sin\alpha-\mu\cos\alpha)$$

The required results obtained from this differential equation and the conditions at $t = t_U$ are

$$\dot{x} = -g(t-t_U)(\sin\alpha - \mu\cos\alpha)$$

and

$$x = -\tfrac{1}{2}g(t-t_U)^2(\sin\alpha - \mu\cos\alpha) + D,$$

where $t \geqslant t_U$. The particle returns to the origin O when

$$t - t_U = \left\{\frac{2D}{g(\sin\alpha - \mu\cos\alpha)}\right\}^{1/2} = \frac{u_0}{g(\sin^2\alpha - \mu^2\cos^2\alpha)^{1/2}} = t_D \text{ (say)}$$

and its speed at O is

$$u_0\left\{\frac{\sin\alpha - \mu\cos\alpha}{\sin\alpha + \mu\cos\alpha}\right\}^{1/2}$$

We notice that its initial speed is greater than its return speed.

If the frictional force were absent (i.e. $\mu = 0$), the particle could not remain at rest at the top of the incline, and its return speed would be equal to its initial speed.

Suppose that we are able to measure the value of t_U (the time taken to come to rest) and D (the distance moved up the inclined plane). Can we calculate the values of u_0 and μ in terms of t_U and D? From the relations

$$\frac{u_0}{g(\sin\alpha + \mu\cos\alpha)} = t_U \quad \text{and} \quad \frac{u_0^2}{2g(\sin\alpha + \mu\cos\alpha)} = D$$

we deduce that

$$u_0 = 2D/t_U \quad \text{and} \quad \mu = 2D/(gt_U^2\cos\alpha) - \tan\alpha$$

Suppose that we are able to measure the value of t_U (the time taken to come to rest) and $t_U + t_D$ (the time taken to return to the point of projection). Then the relations

$$\frac{u_0}{g(\sin\alpha + \mu\cos\alpha)} = t_U \quad \text{and} \quad \frac{u_0}{g(\sin^2\alpha - \mu^2\cos^2\alpha)^{1/2}} = t_D$$

lead to

$$\mu = \left(\frac{t_D^2 - t_U^2}{t_D^2 + t_U^2}\right)\tan\alpha \quad \text{and} \quad u_0 = \frac{2gt_U t_D^2 \sin\alpha}{t_D^2 + t_U^2}$$

If measured values of t_U, t_D and D were available, we would be able to test our assumption concerning the form of the frictional force by means of the predicted relation

$$D(t_D^2 + t_U^2) = gt_D^2 t_U^2 \sin\alpha$$

EXAMPLE

A particle of mass m is thrown vertically upwards with initial speed u_0. Investigate its motion under the assumption that air resistance is a resistive force having a constant magnitude F. (In fact, the effects of air on a moving body are complicated and are studied in aerodynamics. In chapter 10 we shall investigate a more realistic model of a projectile being subject to air resistance, when we allow the resistive force to depend on the velocity of the projectile relative to the air.)

Let the z-axis be vertically upwards and let the origin be the point of projection.

For the upward motion, the equation of motion leads to

$$m\ddot{z} = -mg - F$$

subject to $z = 0$, $\dot{z} = u_0$ at $t = 0$. Hence

$$\begin{aligned}\ddot{z} &= -(g+F/m)\\ \dot{z} &= -t(g+F/m)+u_0\\ z &= -\tfrac{1}{2}t^2(g+F/m)+u_0 t\end{aligned}$$

The particle comes to rest when

$$t = \frac{mu_0}{mg+F} = t_U \text{ (say)}$$

and at a height

$$z = \frac{mu_0^2}{2(mg+F)} = \tfrac{1}{2}u_0 t_U = H \text{ (say)}.$$

For the downward motion, the equation of motion reduces to

$$m\ddot{z} = -mg+F$$

subject to $z = H$, $\dot{z} = 0$ at $t = t_U$. Note the change in the direction of the resistive force. Therefore for $t \geqslant t_U$,

$$\begin{aligned}\ddot{z} &= -(g-F/m)\\ \dot{z} &= -t(g-F/m)+t_U(g-F/m) = -(t-t_U)(g-F/m)\\ z &= -\tfrac{1}{2}(t-t_U)^2(g-F/m)+H\end{aligned}$$

The particle returns to the origin, its point of projection, when

$$(t-t_U)^2 = \frac{2H}{g-F/m} = \frac{m^2u_0^2}{(mg)^2-F^2}$$

i.e.

$$\begin{aligned}t &= t_U + \frac{mu_0}{\{(mg)^2-F^2\}^{1/2}} = t_U + t_D\\ &= \frac{mu_0}{mg+F}\left\{1+\left(\frac{mg+F}{mg-F}\right)^{1/2}\right\}\end{aligned}$$

and its return speed is

$$u_0\left(\frac{mg-F}{mg+F}\right)^{1/2}$$

These results indicate that the particle takes a shorter time to go up than to come down, and its return speed is less than its initial speed. (We can obtain them from the results of the previous example by setting $\mu mg\cos\alpha = F$ and $\sin\alpha = 1$.)

EXERCISES ON CHAPTER 5

1. A curling stone of mass m slides on ice. Its initial speed is u_0 and it travels a distance D along a straight path before coming to rest after time T. Assume that a constant resistive force of magnitude F is acting throughout the motion. Show that

$$FT = mu_0$$

Is it true that $FD = \frac{1}{2}mu_0^2$? Derive some relations between D and T.

2. A body, given an initial velocity, slides across a horizontal rough surface. It covers a distance of 36 metres before coming to rest in 7 seconds. Estimate the coefficient of kinematic friction.

3. A block will slide at constant speed down a rough inclined plane of inclination α. What will be its acceleration down a similar inclined plane of inclination β ($\beta > \alpha$) if the frictional resistance is proportional to the normal component of the contact force?

4. A particle of mass m is projected with speed u up a line of greatest slope of a rough plane inclined to the horizontal at an angle α. It returns to the point of projection with speed ku. Show that the distance moved up the plane is

$$\frac{u^2(1+k^2)}{4g \sin \alpha}$$

and find the magnitude of the frictional force (assumed constant).

5. A particle, projected directly down a rough plane inclined at an angle $\tan^{-1}(\frac{5}{12})$ to the horizontal, travels 13 metres before coming to rest. When projected directly up the plane with the same initial speed, it travels 3 metres before coming to rest. Show that the coefficient of friction is $\frac{2}{3}$, and find the speed of projection.

6. ABC is a line of greatest slope down a plane inclined at an angle $\sin^{-1}(\frac{3}{5})$ to the horizontal. Along AB, a distance of 5 metres, the surface is smooth. Along BC the surface of the plane is rough, and the coefficient of kinematic friction between the plane and a block of wood is $\frac{4}{5}$. The block is released from rest at A. Investigate its motion down the inclined plane and draw a graph of its speed against time. What is the total distance travelled?

7. A car (with all wheels locked) skids down a road inclined to the horizontal at an angle of 0·08 radian. It comes to rest along a straight path of length 35 metres. Estimate its initial speed, if a test under similar circumstances results in a police car, initially travelling at 40 kilometres per hour, coming to rest after skidding for a distance of 15 metres. Estimate μ, the coefficient of kinematic friction between the tyres and the road surface. What value of μ would produce a skid distance of 35 metres down the inclined road if the initial speed of the car were 40 kilometres per hour?

8. A particle is projected vertically upwards in a medium whose resistance is constant and equal to k ($k < 1$) times the weight of the particle. Show that the ratio of the times of ascent and descent is

$$\{(1-k)/(1+k)\}^{1/2}$$

9. An object of mass m, after falling from rest during a time interval of length T_1, penetrates a bog and comes to rest at the end of a further time interval of length

T_2. Find the resistance of the bog (assumed constant) and the depth of penetration.

10. A body can just be held without slipping on a fixed inclined plane by an applied force of magnitude F_1 and just dragged up by an applied force of magnitude F_2, where the applied forces act up a line of greatest slope of inclination α to the horizontal. Find the coefficient of static friction.

11. A body of mass M rests on a rough plane of inclination α to the horizontal. A force, whose direction makes an angle $\alpha+\theta$ with the horizontal, is applied to the body. Show that the direction of the force having the least magnitude that will move the body up the plane corresponds to $\theta = \lambda$, where λ is the angle of friction. What is the magnitude of this force? If the direction of the force is kept constant, show that the magnitude of the force may be reduced to $Mg\sin(\alpha-\lambda)\sec 2\lambda$ before the body moves down the plane (provided $\alpha > \lambda$).

12. A block of mass M is placed on a horizontal table, the contact between the block and the table being smooth. A second block of mass m is placed on the first block, the contact between the blocks being rough. A force whose direction is horizontal and whose constant magnitude is F_A is applied to the first block. What is the least value of the coefficient of static friction needed to prevent the second block sliding on the first block?

13. A body lies on a rough horizontal table whose motion is horizontal and simple harmonic of amplitude a and frequency ν. What is the least value of the coefficient of static friction needed to prevent sliding?

14. A block is placed on a horizontal table, the contact between the block and the table being smooth. A second block is placed on the first block, the contact between the blocks being characterized by a coefficient of static friction μ_s. A force is applied to the first block so that the first block moves from rest with constant acceleration A, attains a maximum speed, and comes to rest again with a constant retardation R. Under what conditions on μ_s will the second block be at rest with respect to the first block throughout the described motion?

6 Energy and Work

6.1 Kinetic energy

The kinetic energy of a particle is one half the product of the mass and the square of the speed of the particle. We denote kinetic energy by E_k and we write

$$E_k = \tfrac{1}{2}m\frac{d\boldsymbol{r}}{dt}\cdot\frac{d\boldsymbol{r}}{dt} = \tfrac{1}{2}m\dot{\boldsymbol{r}}\cdot\dot{\boldsymbol{r}} = \tfrac{1}{2}m|\dot{\boldsymbol{r}}|^2$$

This physical quantity depends only on the mass and the kinematics of the particle. Its dimensions are ML^2T^{-2} and the unit of measurement is one newton metre (Nm), which is called one joule (J).

6.2 Work done by a force

Suppose a constant force $\mathbf{F}$ is acting on a particle P which is moving along a straight line in the direction of the unit vector $\boldsymbol{i}$. Let A and B be two points on the path of the particle such that their position vectors are $a\boldsymbol{i}$, $b\boldsymbol{i}$ with $b > a$ (relative to an origin on the straight-line path). The work done by the force $\mathbf{F}$ during the motion of its point of application from A to B is the product of the component of the force in the direction of motion and the distance moved. We use W to denote the work done and we write

$$W = \mathbf{F}\cdot\boldsymbol{i}(b-a) = \mathbf{F}\cdot(b\boldsymbol{i}-a\boldsymbol{i})$$

i.e. the work done by the force is the scalar product of $\mathbf{F}$ and the position vector of B relative to A.

We note that W is zero if $\mathbf{F}$ has no component parallel to the direction of motion of the point of application. For example, there is no work done by the constant gravitational force when a particle moves in a horizontal plane. It is useful to observe that the work done by the force $\mathbf{F}$ during the motion of its point of application from A to a general point on the straight-line path with position vector $x\boldsymbol{i}$ is given by

$$W = \mathbf{F}\cdot(x\boldsymbol{i}-a\boldsymbol{i})$$

Let us generalize our result to the case of a variable force $\mathbf{F}(x)$ acting on a particle P which is moving along a straight line in the direction of the unit vector $\boldsymbol{i}$, i.e. we retain the rectilinear motion of the particle and allow the force to vary. The work done by the force during the motion of its point of application from the general point $x\boldsymbol{i}$ to a neighbouring point $(x+\Delta x)\boldsymbol{i}$ is approximately

$$\mathbf{F}(x).\{(x+\Delta x)\boldsymbol{i}-x\boldsymbol{i}\}$$

Adding these contributions and taking the limit as $||D|| = \max|\Delta x| \to 0$, we find that the work done by the force during the motion of its point of application from A to B is

$$W = \lim_{||D|| \to 0} \sum_{x=a}^{x=b} [\mathbf{F}(x).\{\Delta x\boldsymbol{i}\}] = \int_a^b \mathbf{F}(x).\boldsymbol{i}\,dx$$

which is a Riemann integral [see J. Hunter, *Calculus*, Blackie/Chambers]. Here the integrand is the component of $\mathbf{F}(x)$ in the direction of the unit vector $\boldsymbol{i}$.

Sometimes it is useful to introduce a parameter, such as time. Then, by changing variables, we have

$$W = \int_{t_A}^{t_B} \mathbf{F}(x(t)).\boldsymbol{i}\frac{dx(t)}{dt}\,dt$$

where t_A, t_B are the values of the parameter specified by

$$x(t_A) = a, \quad x(t_B) = b$$

When t denotes time, the integrand is the scalar product of the force and the velocity of the point of application, namely $\mathbf{F}.(\dot{x}\boldsymbol{i})$. Hence the work done by a variable force $\mathbf{F}$ during the motion of its point of application from A to a general point (specified by the position vector $x\boldsymbol{i}$ or the time t at which the point of application is at this point) is

$$\begin{aligned} W &= \int_a^x \mathbf{F}(x).\boldsymbol{i}\,dx \\ &= \int_{t_A}^{t} \mathbf{F}(x(t)).\left(\frac{dx(t)}{dt}\boldsymbol{i}\right)dt \end{aligned}$$

We may generalize our results still further. In particular, suppose a variable force $\mathbf{F}$ is acting on a particle moving along a curve that can be represented in terms of a parameter t, for example time. Let the position vector of the particle at time t be

$$\boldsymbol{r}(t) = x(t)\boldsymbol{i}+y(t)\boldsymbol{j}+z(t)\boldsymbol{k}$$

Our calculation of the work done by the force is based on our taking the limit of the sum of contributions from short straight segments, the union of the segments approximating the curve. This limit is

$$W = \int_{t_A}^{t_B} \mathbf{F}(\boldsymbol{r}(t)).\frac{d\boldsymbol{r}(t)}{dt}\,dt$$

Sometimes we write

$$W = \int_C \mathbf{F}(\boldsymbol{r}).d\boldsymbol{r}$$

where C is the curve from A to B, and we call the integral a *line integral.*

The work done by a force has the dimensions ML^2T^{-2}. The newton metre (Nm) or joule (J) is the unit of measurement.

EXAMPLE

Consider a projectile problem in which the only force acting on the particle of mass m is the constant gravitational force. The equation of motion is

$$m\ddot{\boldsymbol{r}} = \mathbf{F}$$

where $\mathbf{F} = -mg\boldsymbol{k}$.

(i) Suppose that the initial conditions are

$$\boldsymbol{r} = \boldsymbol{0}, \quad \dot{\boldsymbol{r}} = u_0\boldsymbol{k} \quad \text{at} \quad t = 0.$$

Then

$$\dot{\boldsymbol{r}} = (-gt + u_0)\boldsymbol{k}$$
$$\boldsymbol{r} = (-\tfrac{1}{2}gt^2 + u_0 t)\boldsymbol{k}$$

The particle attains its maximum height, $\frac{1}{2}u_0^2/g$, at $t = u_0/g$ and returns to the point of projection at $t = 2u_0/g$. Its motion is confined to the z-axis, and the z-coordinate is specified by

$$z = -\tfrac{1}{2}gt^2 + u_0 t$$

(This is a synopsis of our examination of this problem in Section 4.1.) The kinetic energy of the particle is

$$E_k = \tfrac{1}{2}m\dot{\boldsymbol{r}}.\dot{\boldsymbol{r}} = \tfrac{1}{2}m(u_0 - gt)^2 \quad \text{with} \quad 0 \leqslant t \leqslant 2u_0/g.$$

Noting that

$$-2gz = g^2t^2 - 2gtu_0 = (u_0 - gt)^2 - u_0^2$$

we have the alternative expression

$$E_k = \tfrac{1}{2}mu_0^2 - mgz \quad \text{with} \quad 0 \leqslant z \leqslant \tfrac{1}{2}u_0^2/g.$$

Let W_U, W_D be the work done by the constant gravitational force while the particle is moving upwards and downwards, respectively. Then

$$W_U = \int_0^{u_0/g} \mathbf{F}.\dot{\boldsymbol{r}}\,dt = \int_0^{u_0/g} (-mg)\boldsymbol{k}.\dot{\boldsymbol{r}}\,dt$$

Evaluating the integral, we have

$$\int_0^{u_0/g} \boldsymbol{k}\,.\,\dot{\boldsymbol{r}}\,dt = \int_0^{u_0/g} (-gt+u_0)\,dt = \left[-\tfrac{1}{2}gt^2+u_0 t\right]_0^{u_0/g} = \tfrac{1}{2}u_0^2/g$$

or

$$\int_0^{u_0/g} \boldsymbol{k}\,.\,\dot{\boldsymbol{r}}\,dt = \int_0^{u_0/g} \dot{z}\,dt = \int_0^{u_0^2/2g} dz = \tfrac{1}{2}u_0^2/g$$

Therefore

$$W_U = -\tfrac{1}{2}mu_0^2$$

Similarly, we have

$$\begin{aligned} W_D = \int_{u_0/g}^{2u_0/g} \mathbf{F}\,.\,\dot{\boldsymbol{r}}\,dt &= \int_{u_0/g}^{2u_0/g} (-mg)\boldsymbol{k}\,.\,\dot{\boldsymbol{r}}\,dt \\ &= \int_{u_0^2/2g}^{0} (-mg)\,dz \\ &= \tfrac{1}{2}mu_0^2 \end{aligned}$$

In fact, we could have used our definition in the simplest situation (constant force and straight-line motion), namely "work done" equals "force in the direction of motion" times "distance moved"; that is

$$W_U = (-mg)(\tfrac{1}{2}u_0^2/g) = -\tfrac{1}{2}mu_0^2$$

and

$$W_D = (mg)(\tfrac{1}{2}u_0^2/g) = \tfrac{1}{2}mu_0^2$$

We note that the total work done by the constant gravitational force during the flight of the projectile, W_U+W_D, is zero.

Consider

$$\begin{aligned} W &= \int_0^t \mathbf{F}\,.\,\dot{\boldsymbol{r}}\,dt \\ &= -mg(-\tfrac{1}{2}gt^2+u_0 t) \\ &= \tfrac{1}{2}m(g^2t^2-2gtu_0) \\ &= \tfrac{1}{2}m(u_0-gt)^2-\tfrac{1}{2}mu_0^2 \\ &= -mgz \end{aligned}$$

It follows from our results that

$$E_k - W = \tfrac{1}{2}mu_0^2\,;$$

the right-hand side being the initial kinetic energy of the particle, a constant.

(ii) Suppose the initial conditions are

$$\boldsymbol{r} = \boldsymbol{0}, \quad \dot{\boldsymbol{r}} = u_0(\boldsymbol{i}\cos\theta+\boldsymbol{k}\sin\theta) \quad \text{at} \quad t=0.$$

Summarizing results presented in Sections 4.1 and 4.2, we have

$$\dot{\boldsymbol{r}} = u_0\cos\theta\,\boldsymbol{i}+(u_0\sin\theta-gt)\boldsymbol{k}$$

and

$$\boldsymbol{r} = u_0 t\cos\theta\,\boldsymbol{i}+(u_0 t\sin\theta-\tfrac{1}{2}gt^2)\boldsymbol{k}.$$

The particle reaches its maximum height, $\frac{1}{2}(u_0\sin\theta)^2/g$, at $t=(u_0\sin\theta)/g$ and it returns to the plane $z = 0$ at $t = 2(u_0 \sin\theta)/g$. The motion is in the xz-plane and the trajectory is parabolic. The z-coordinate of the particle is given by

$$z = -\tfrac{1}{2}gt^2 + u_0 t \sin\theta$$

Calculating the quantities E_k, W_U, W_D, W defined in part (i) of this example, we find that

$$E_k = \tfrac{1}{2}m\dot{\boldsymbol{r}}\,.\,\dot{\boldsymbol{r}} = \tfrac{1}{2}m(u_0^2 - 2gtu_0\sin\theta + g^2t^2)$$
$$= \tfrac{1}{2}mu_0^2 - mgz$$

$$W_U = \int_0^{(u_0 \sin\theta)/g} \mathbf{F}\,.\,\dot{\boldsymbol{r}}\,dt = -\tfrac{1}{2}m(u_0\sin\theta)^2$$

$$W_D = \int_{(u_0\sin\theta)/g}^{2(u_0 \sin\theta)/g} \mathbf{F}\,.\,\dot{\boldsymbol{r}}\,dt = \tfrac{1}{2}m(u_0\sin\theta)^2$$

and

$$W = \int_0^t \mathbf{F}\,.\,\dot{\boldsymbol{r}}\,dt = -mg(u_0 t\sin\theta - \tfrac{1}{2}gt^2)$$
$$= -mgz$$

We observe that

$$E_k - W = \tfrac{1}{2}mu_0^2$$

the right-hand side being the kinetic energy at $t = 0$.

It is worth noting that the integrals defining W_U, W_D, W are equivalent to line integrals along curves that are parabolic arcs. The introduction of the parameter t reduces the line integrals to definite integrals, which we can evaluate easily.

EXAMPLE

Consider a particle moving along a rough plane inclined at an angle α to the horizontal. We shall use the coordinate system and notation introduced in our examination of this problem in Section 5.2. When the particle is moving up the plane, the equation of motion is

$$m\ddot{\boldsymbol{r}} = \mathbf{F}$$

where $\boldsymbol{r} = x\boldsymbol{i}$ and $\mathbf{F} = \mathbf{F}_1 + \mathbf{F}_2 + \mathbf{F}_3$ with $\mathbf{F}_1 = -mg(\boldsymbol{i}\sin\alpha + \boldsymbol{k}\cos\alpha)$, $\mathbf{F}_2 = -\mu N\boldsymbol{i}$, $\mathbf{F}_3 = N\boldsymbol{k}$. Using the results of Section 5.2, we find that

$$E_k = \tfrac{1}{2}m\dot{\boldsymbol{r}}\,.\,\dot{\boldsymbol{r}} = \tfrac{1}{2}m\{u_0 - gt(\sin\alpha + \mu\cos\alpha)\}^2$$
$$= \tfrac{1}{2}mu_0^2 - mgx(\sin\alpha + \mu\cos\alpha)$$

$$W_{U_1} = \int_0^{t_U} \mathbf{F}_1\,.\,\dot{\boldsymbol{r}}\,dt = -mg\sin\alpha\int_0^{t_U}\dot{x}\,dt = -mg\sin\alpha\int_0^D dx$$
$$= -mgD\sin\alpha$$

$$W_{U_2} = \int_0^{t_U} \mathbf{F}_2\,.\,\dot{\boldsymbol{r}}\,dt = -\mu mg\cos\alpha\int_0^{t_U}\dot{x}\,dt = -\mu mg\cos\alpha\int_0^D dx$$
$$= -\mu mgD\cos\alpha$$

$$W_{U_3} = \int_0^{t_U} \mathbf{F}_3 \,.\, \dot{\boldsymbol{r}}\, dt = \int_0^{t_U} (mg\boldsymbol{k}\cos\alpha) \,.\, (\dot{x}\boldsymbol{i})\, dt$$
$$= 0$$

$$W_U = \int_0^{t_U} \mathbf{F} \,.\, \dot{\boldsymbol{r}}\, dt = -mg\,D\,(\sin\alpha + \mu\cos\alpha)$$

If $\tan\alpha > \mu_s$, the particle is instantaneously at rest when $t = t_U$ and subsequently moves down the plane. During the downward motion the equation of motion is

$$m\ddot{\boldsymbol{r}} = \mathbf{F}$$

where $\boldsymbol{r} = x\boldsymbol{i}$ and $\mathbf{F} = \mathbf{F}_1 + \mathbf{F}_2 + \mathbf{F}_3$ with $\mathbf{F}_1 = -mg(\boldsymbol{i}\sin\alpha + \boldsymbol{k}\cos\alpha)$, $\mathbf{F}_2 = \mu N\boldsymbol{i}$, $\mathbf{F}_3 = N\boldsymbol{k}$.

Hence for this phase of the motion we have

$$E_k = \tfrac{1}{2}m\dot{\boldsymbol{r}} \,.\, \dot{\boldsymbol{r}} = \tfrac{1}{2}m\{g(\sin\alpha - \mu\cos\alpha)(t - t_U)\}^2$$
$$= mg(\sin\alpha - \mu\cos\alpha)(D - x)$$

$$W_{D_1} = \int_{t_U}^{t_U+t_D} \mathbf{F}_1 \,.\, \dot{\boldsymbol{r}}\, dt = -mg\sin\alpha \int_{t_U}^{t_U+t_D} \dot{x}\, dt = -mg\sin\alpha \int_D^0 dx$$
$$= mg\,D\sin\alpha$$

$$W_{D_2} = \int_{t_U}^{t_U+t_D} \mathbf{F}_2 \,.\, \dot{\boldsymbol{r}}\, dt = \mu mg\cos\alpha \int_{t_U}^{t_U+t_D} \dot{x}\, dt = \mu mg\cos\alpha \int_D^0 dx$$
$$= -\mu mg\,D\cos\alpha$$

$$W_{D_3} = \int_{t_U}^{t_U+t_D} \mathbf{F}_3 \,.\, \dot{\boldsymbol{r}}\, dt = \int_{t_U}^{t_U+t_D} (mg\boldsymbol{k}\cos\alpha) \,.\, (\dot{x}\boldsymbol{i})\, dt$$
$$= 0$$

$$W_D = \int_{t_U}^{t_U+t_D} \mathbf{F} \,.\, \dot{\boldsymbol{r}}\, dt = mg\,D(\sin\alpha - \mu\cos\alpha)$$

In the motion up the plane away from the origin and down the plane back to the origin, the work done by the constant gravitational force $\mathbf{F}_1$ is

$$W_{U_1} + W_{D_1} = 0$$

and the work done by the frictional force $\mathbf{F}_2$ is

$$W_{U_2} + W_{D_2} = -2\mu mg\,D\cos\alpha$$

The normal reaction $\mathbf{F}_3$ does no work during any time interval because its direction is perpendicular to the direction of motion of the point of application.

We note that an alternative approach to the above calculations of work done is that based on the basic definition, "force times distance", because the forces are constant and the point of application moves along a straight line. However note must be taken of the change in the direction of the frictional force $\mathbf{F}_2$.

Consider

$$W = \int_0^t \mathbf{F} \,.\, \dot{\boldsymbol{r}}\, dt.$$

For $0 \leqslant t \leqslant t_U$

$$\mathbf{F}.\dot{\mathbf{r}} = -mg(\sin\alpha + \mu\cos\alpha)\dot{x}$$

and

$$\begin{aligned} W &= -mg(\sin\alpha + \mu\cos\alpha)\int_0^t \dot{x}\,dt \\ &= -mg(\sin\alpha + \mu\cos\alpha)\{u_0 t - \tfrac{1}{2}gt^2(\sin\alpha + \mu\cos\alpha)\} \\ &= -mgx(\sin\alpha + \mu\cos\alpha) \end{aligned}$$

For $t_U \leqslant t \leqslant t_U + t_D$

$$\mathbf{F}.\dot{\mathbf{r}} = -mg(\sin\alpha - \mu\cos\alpha)\dot{x}$$

and

$$\begin{aligned} W &= W_U + \int_{t_U}^t \mathbf{F}.\dot{\mathbf{r}}\,dt \\ &= W_U - mg(\sin\alpha - \mu\cos\alpha)\int_{t_U}^t \dot{x}\,dt \\ &= W_U + \tfrac{1}{2}mg^2(\sin\alpha - \mu\cos\alpha)^2(t - t_U)^2 \\ &= W_U + mg(\sin\alpha - \mu\cos\alpha)(D - x) \end{aligned}$$

We note that the relation

$$E_k - W = \tfrac{1}{2}mu_0^2$$

holds throughout the motion up and down the inclined plane, i.e. when

$$0 \leqslant t \leqslant t_U + t_D.$$

In this example the point of application of the forces starts at the origin of the chosen coordinate system, moves up the plane, comes to rest after travelling a distance D and returns to the origin (provided $\tan\alpha > \mu_s$). During this motion, the total work done by the gravitational force is zero and the total work done by the frictional force equals

$$-2\mu mg\,D\cos\alpha$$

the minus sign appearing because the direction of the frictional force is opposite to the direction of the motion of the point of application. This indicates a fundamental difference between the constant gravitational force and the contact frictional force.

6.3 Conservative forces

In the rough inclined-plane problem discussed in the previous section we have recognized a difference between the constant gravitational force and the contact frictional force. This difference allows us to classify *fields of force*. If the point of application of a force moves round a curve and returns to its starting position, we say that the point has traced out a *closed contour*. A field of force is said to be *conservative* in a region of space if the work done by the force is zero, no matter which closed contour in that region of space the point of application follows. Otherwise a field of force is said to be *non-conservative* or *dissipative*.

We are unable to test every closed contour by carrying out the necessary integration. Fortunately it is possible to decide whether a field of force is conservative or not without evaluating the integrals for every closed contour. This possibility depends on vector analysis and is beyond the scope of this book. Vector analysis allows us to make the classification based on our knowledge of the field of force itself, and not based on the evaluation of an infinite number of line integrals around closed contours.

A force that always opposes the motion of a particle around a closed contour (for example, the contact frictional force in the rough inclined plane problem) is non-conservative. It is an important observation that finding *one* closed contour for which the work done is non-zero is sufficient to show that a field of force is non-conservative.

The constant gravitational field of force is conservative throughout its domain of definition, which is the three-dimensional euclidean space.

6.4 Potential energy

We associate with every conservative field of force **F** a physical quantity called the *potential energy* and denoted by E_p. We define the increase in potential energy during the time interval $[t_1, t_2]$ to be *minus* the work done by the force during $[t_1, t_2]$, i.e.

$$\Bigg| E_p \Bigg|_{t=t_1}^{t=t_2} = -\int_{t_1}^{t_2} \mathbf{F} \cdot \dot{\mathbf{r}}\, dt$$

We are able to define the potential energy at an instant by the indefinite integral

$$E_p = -\int \mathbf{F} \cdot \dot{\mathbf{r}}\, dt$$

This means that the potential energy at an instant is defined up to an additive constant. We are allowed to choose the instant (or the position of the point of application of the force) at which the potential energy is zero. Potential energy has the dimensions ML^2T^{-2} and the unit of measurement is the joule (J).

EXAMPLE

What is the potential energy associated with the constant gravitational field of force?

In this case we may write $\mathbf{F} = -mg\mathbf{k}$. Then

$$E_p = -\int (-mg\mathbf{k}) \cdot \dot{\mathbf{r}}\, dt = mg \int \dot{z}\, dt$$
$$= mgz + A$$

where A is an arbitrary constant.

We may decide that the potential energy is zero when $z = 0$. Then we choose $A = 0$ and we say that the horizontal plane $z = 0$ is the level of zero potential energy associated with the constant gravitational field of force. In general we have $E_p = mg(z-H)$, in which case the horizontal plane $z = H$ is the level of zero potential energy.

6.5 Conservation of energy

Suppose a particle is subjected to a conservative force **F**. The equation of motion is

$$m\ddot{\mathbf{r}} = \mathbf{F}$$

The kinetic energy of the particle is

$$E_k = \tfrac{1}{2}m\dot{\mathbf{r}}\cdot\dot{\mathbf{r}}$$

and the potential energy associated with the conservative force **F** is

$$\begin{aligned} E_p &= -\int \mathbf{F}\cdot\dot{\mathbf{r}}\,dt \\ &= -\int m\ddot{\mathbf{r}}\cdot\dot{\mathbf{r}}\,dt = -\int \tfrac{1}{2}m\frac{d}{dt}(\dot{\mathbf{r}}\cdot\dot{\mathbf{r}})\,dt \\ &= -\tfrac{1}{2}m\dot{\mathbf{r}}\cdot\dot{\mathbf{r}} + A \end{aligned}$$

where A is an arbitrary constant. Hence we have the relation

$$E_k + E_p = A$$

i.e. the sum of the kinetic energy and the potential energy is constant throughout the motion. This is known as the **principle of conservation of (kinetic and potential) energy.** This principle holds only when the force **F** is conservative. It is based on the integration of the equation of motion

$$m\ddot{\mathbf{r}} = \mathbf{F}$$

which implies that

$$m\ddot{\mathbf{r}}\cdot\dot{\mathbf{r}} = \mathbf{F}\cdot\dot{\mathbf{r}}, \quad \int m\ddot{\mathbf{r}}\cdot\dot{\mathbf{r}}\,dt = \int \mathbf{F}\cdot\dot{\mathbf{r}}\,dt + \text{constant}$$

and $E_k + E_p =$ constant.

If the force $\mathbf{F} = \mathbf{F}_1 + \mathbf{F}_2$, where $\mathbf{F}_1$ is conservative and $\mathbf{F}_2$ is non-conservative, we have

$$\int m\ddot{\mathbf{r}}\cdot\dot{\mathbf{r}}\,dt = \int \mathbf{F}_1\cdot\dot{\mathbf{r}}\,dt + \int \mathbf{F}_2\cdot\dot{\mathbf{r}}\,dt + \text{constant}$$

and

$$E_k + E_p = \int \mathbf{F}_2\cdot\dot{\mathbf{r}}\,dt + \text{constant}$$

where E_p is the potential energy associated with the conservative force $\mathbf{F}_1$. The general statement is that **the sum of the kinetic energy of the particle and the potential energy associated with the conservative force equals the sum of a constant and the work done by the non-conservative force acting on the particle.**

EXAMPLE

Consider a projectile in a constant gravitational field of force, in particular the case in which its motion is along a vertical line.

The only force acting on the projectile is conservative. We shall choose the level of zero potential energy to be the plane $z = 0$. Then

$$E_k = \tfrac{1}{2}m\dot{z}^2 \quad \text{and} \quad E_p = mgz\,.$$

The conservation of energy gives

$$\tfrac{1}{2}m\dot{z}^2 + mgz = \text{constant}\,.$$

If $\dot{z} = u_0$ when $z = 0$, the relation governing the motion of the projectile is

$$\tfrac{1}{2}m\dot{z}^2 + mgz = \tfrac{1}{2}mu_0^2$$

i.e.

$$\dot{z}^2 = u_0^2 - 2gz$$

This is obtainable from the equation of motion (discussed in Section 4.1) through the results

$$\dot{z} = u_0 - gt \quad \text{and} \quad z = u_0 t - \tfrac{1}{2}gt^2$$

It is called an *integral of the equation of motion*. Sometimes it is convenient to take the conservation of energy as the governing relation. We should never lose sight of the facts that the fundamental relation is the equation of motion (subject to initial conditions) and that the conservation of energy is a consequence of the equation of motion provided the force is conservative.

EXAMPLE

Let us re-examine the rough inclined-plane problem discussed in Sections 5.2 and 6.2.

Let the level of zero potential energy (associated with the constant gravitational field of force) be the horizontal plane through the point of projection O. Then

$$E_k = \tfrac{1}{2}m\dot{x}^2 \quad \text{and} \quad E_p = mgx\sin\alpha$$

In this example we may not say that the sum, $E_k + E_p$, is constant throughout the motion because a non-conservative force, namely the contact frictional force, is acting on the particle. It follows from the equation of motion (see Section 6.2) that

$$E_k + E_p = \begin{cases} \tfrac{1}{2}mu_0^2 - \mu mgx\cos\alpha & \text{upward motion} \\ \tfrac{1}{2}mu_0^2 - \mu mg(2D - x)\cos\alpha & \text{downward motion} \end{cases}$$

The right-hand side is the sum of the initial kinetic energy ($\tfrac{1}{2}mu_0^2$), the initial potential energy (zero) and the work done by the contact frictional force. When the particle starts from the origin O, the sum of the kinetic and potential energies is $\tfrac{1}{2}mu_0^2$. When the particle returns to O, the sum is

$$\tfrac{1}{2}mu_0^2 - 2\mu mgD\cos\alpha$$

What has happened to the energy $2\mu mgD\cos\alpha$? Heat and noise (principally heat) have been generated during the motion of the particle up and down the rough inclined plane. Some of the initial kinetic energy has been converted into other forms of energy associated with heat and noise, that is, some mechanical energy has been converted into thermal energy and acoustic energy.

The conservation of energy holds and has the form

$$E_k + E_p + (\text{minus work done by the frictional force acting on the particle}) = \tfrac{1}{2}mu_0^2$$

or

$$E_k + E_p + (\text{work done by the frictional force acting on the inclined plane}) = \tfrac{1}{2}mu_0^2$$

or

$$E_k + E_p + (\text{energy associated with heat and noise}) = \tfrac{1}{2}mu_0^2$$

i.e. the sum of the mechanical, thermal and acoustic energies is a constant.

6.6 Power

Suppose a force **F** is causing a particle to move with velocity $\dot{\mathbf{r}}$ relative to an inertial frame of reference, i.e. the point of application of the force has velocity $\dot{\mathbf{r}}$. Then we define the power associated with the force to be the scalar product of the force and the velocity of the point of application. We write

$$P = \mathbf{F} \cdot \dot{\mathbf{r}}$$

We recognize that the power is the time rate of change of the work done by the force. In Section 6.2 we were integrating the power with respect to time to calculate the work done during a given time interval. Power has the dimensions ML^2T^{-3} and the unit of measurement is one joule per second ($J\,s^{-1}$), which is called one watt (W). We note that one horse-power is equivalent to 745·700 watts.

EXAMPLE

A force causes a particle of mass m to move along a straight line. The rate at which work is done by the force is a constant P_0. If the particle starts from rest, what is the velocity of the particle after the particle has moved a distance x?

Suppose the particle is moving along the x-axis and starts from the origin. The equation of motion is

$$m\ddot{x} = F$$

where $F\dot{x} = P_0$. Therefore we have $P_0 = m\dot{x}\ddot{x}$. Setting $\dot{x} = u$ and using $\ddot{x} = u(du/dx)$, we obtain

$$P_0 = mu^2\frac{du}{dx} \quad \text{and} \quad \int_0^x P_0\,dx = \int_0^x mu^2\frac{du}{dx}\,dx = \int_0^u mu^2\,du$$

Hence $P_0 x = \tfrac{1}{3}mu^3$ and $u = (3P_0x/m)^{1/3}$.

Considering our result in the form

$$x^{-1/3}\frac{dx}{dt} = (3P_0/m)^{1/3}$$

and integrating with respect to time, we find that

$$\tfrac{3}{2}x^{2/3} = (3P_0/m)^{1/3}t$$

and

$$x = \frac{2}{3}\left(\frac{2P_0}{m}\right)^{1/2} t^{3/2}.$$

An alternative derivation of this result is based on the integration of

$$P_0 = m\dot{x}\ddot{x} = \tfrac{1}{2}m\frac{d}{dt}(\dot{x}^2)$$

with respect to time. Thus $\frac{1}{2}m\dot{x}^2 = P_0 t$ and $\dot{x} = (2P_0/m)^{1/2}t^{1/2}$. A further integration with respect to time gives

$$x = \frac{2}{3}\left(\frac{2P_0}{m}\right)^{1/2} t^{3/2}$$

In this paragraph we have used the initial conditions

$$x = 0 \quad \text{and} \quad \dot{x} = 0 \quad \text{at} \quad t = 0.$$

EXERCISES ON CHAPTER 6

1. The linear momentum associated with a particle of mass m is $\boldsymbol{p}$ at a given instant. What is the particle's kinetic energy?

2. A force of magnitude 250 newtons moves a body of mass 50 kilograms a distance of 3·6 metres along a straight-line path. Calculate the work done by the force. What is the final speed if the initial speed is zero?

3. A particle moves along straight paths from A to B to C to D in the uniform gravitational field of force specified by $-mg\boldsymbol{k}$. If the position vectors of the points A, B, C and D are

$$\boldsymbol{i}+2\boldsymbol{k},\quad 3\boldsymbol{i}+4\boldsymbol{k},\quad 3\boldsymbol{i}+2\boldsymbol{j}+4\boldsymbol{k}\quad\text{and}\quad 6\boldsymbol{i}+2\boldsymbol{j}+5\boldsymbol{k}$$

respectively, calculate the work done by the gravitational force during the particle's motion from A to D along the given path. Is the work done during the motion from A to D independent of the path taken?

4. A constant force $F_0(\boldsymbol{i}\cos\alpha+\boldsymbol{j}\sin\alpha)$ is applied to a particle during the particle's motion from $-a\boldsymbol{j}$ to $a\boldsymbol{j}$ along the semicircular arc, centre the origin and radius a, passing through $a\boldsymbol{i}$. Write down the integral defining the work done by the force, and hence calculate the work done.

5. A time-varying force $\mathbf{F} = F_0(1+(t/t_0))^{-1/2}\boldsymbol{i}$, where F_0 and t_0 are constants, acts on a particle whose position vector is $\boldsymbol{r} = x_0(1+(t/t_0))^{3/2}\boldsymbol{i}$, where x_0 is constant. Calculate the work done during the time interval $[0, T]$.

6. A force $\mathbf{F} = (F_0+kx)\boldsymbol{i}$, where F_0 and k are constants, acts on a particle whose position vector is $\boldsymbol{r} = x\boldsymbol{i}$. Calculate the work done by the force while the particle moves along the straight-line path from the point having the position vector $x_0\boldsymbol{i}$ to the origin.

7. The resultant force on a train of mass M starting from rest on a straight level track has a constant magnitude F_0 for speeds less than U. For speeds greater than U the power associated with the force has a constant value F_0U. Calculate the time taken to reach a speed $u(>U)$. How far has the train travelled in this time? Express the magnitude of the resultant force acting on the train in terms of the distance moved from the rest position. Use the integral definition to verify that the work done during the second part of the motion is $\frac{1}{2}Mu^2-\frac{1}{2}MU^2$, namely the increase in kinetic energy.

8. A body of mass m moves from rest under the action of a constant horizontal force of magnitude F. At the same instant a second body of the same mass starts from rest under a force which does work at the constant rate P_0. If the bodies have the same speed U after a time T, show that $P_0 = \frac{1}{2}FU$, where $FT = mU$.

Show that the ratio of the speeds of the bodies when they have been moving for a time kT is $k^{1/2}:1$. Find the instant at which the trains have travelled the same distance. Provide for each body sketches of speed against time, and distance against time, for the time interval $[0, 4T]$.

9. A train of mass m moves along a level track. The engine provides a tractive force $\mathbf{F}$ and works at a constant rate P_0. There is a constant resistive force of magnitude R_0 opposing the motion. Show that the equation governing the motion has the form

$$m\dot{x}\ddot{x} = P_0 - R_0\dot{x}\ (\text{provided } \dot{x}\neq 0).$$

The maximum speed occurs when $\dot{x} = 0$ and has the value $P_0/R_0 = U_{max}$. By setting $\dot{x} = u$ and $\ddot{x} = (du/dt)$ and by rewriting the equation in the form

$$\frac{m}{R_0}\left\{\frac{P_0}{P_0 - R_0 u} - 1\right\}\frac{du}{dt} = 1$$

show that the train takes a time interval of length

$$\left\{\ln\left(\frac{1-\alpha}{1-\beta}\right) - (\alpha - \beta)\right\}\frac{mU_{max}}{R_0}$$

to change its speed from αU_{max} to βU_{max}, where $0 < \alpha < \beta < 1$. Similarly, by setting $\ddot{x} = u(du/dx)$ and rewriting the equation in an appropriate way, find the distance moved by the train while increasing its speed from αU_{max} to βU_{max}, where $0 < \alpha < \beta < 1$. Observe that these results are consistent with the fundamental equation

$$[\tfrac{1}{2}m\dot{x}^2] = P_0[t] - R_0[x]$$

i.e. the change in the kinetic energy equals the work done by the tractive force and the resistive force, which we obtain by integrating the governing equation with respect to time.

10. A train of mass 2×10^5 kilograms has a maximum speed of 150 kilometres per hour on the level. If the track resistance is 0·15 newtons per kilogram, find the power of engine. Find the acceleration when the speed is 50 kilometres per hour and the engine is working at its maximum rate.

11. A train travelling with a steady speed u_1 slips a carriage of mass m, and the ultimate steady speed of the train is u_2 with the engine working at the same rate. If the track resistance per unit mass is R, find the mass of the train in its final form. What power is generated by the engine?

12. A car of mass M travels along a level road at a constant speed U before descending a slope inclined to the horizontal at an angle α. The engine of the car works at a constant rate P_0 both on the level and on the slope. Assume that the frictional resistance on the slope equals that on the level, and neglect the air resistance. Hence show that the equation governing the motion of the car down the slope has the form

$$M\ddot{x} = \frac{P_0}{\dot{x}} + Mg\sin\alpha - \frac{P_0}{U}$$

What is the maximum speed attainable in the case when $P_0 > MgU\sin\alpha$?

The Pendulum and Circular Motion

7

7.1 Introduction

The pendulum is a fundamental part of a clock mechanism. Its importance in time keeping is obvious. Another reason for studying the motion of a pendulum is that experiments with pendula afford ways of measuring g, the acceleration due to gravity.

For our purposes, a pendulum consists of a body suspended from a support. The essential feature is that the motion of the body is constrained by the suspension. The designs of pendula are varied and some are complex. Let us consider a pendulum made from a ball and a length of string, which we introduced in Section 1.1 during our discussion of mathematical models. Making the six assumptions listed in Section 1.1, we find that the idealized problem consists of a particle suspended by a light inextensible string from a fixed support in a uniform gravitational field of force. A new feature of this problem is the light inextensible string. What do we mean by the phrase "a light inextensible string"?

Consider a sack of grain suspended by a rope from the ceiling of a mill. When the sack is stationary, the rope is taut and vertical. The rope communicates a force between the ceiling and the sack. The rope appears to be pulling down at the ceiling and pulling up at the sack. The force applied to the ceiling is the sum of the weights of the rope and the sack of grain. The

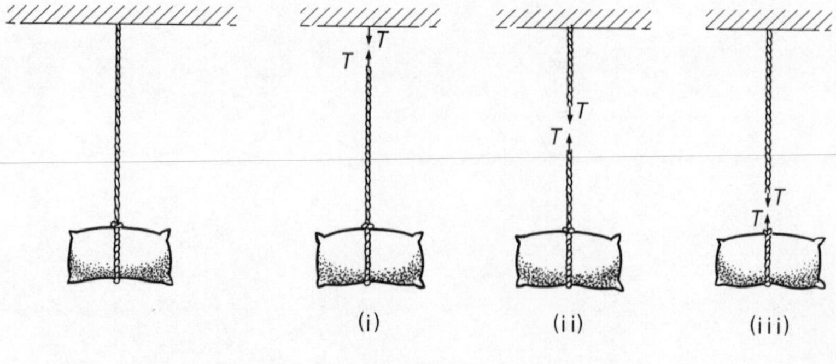

force applied to the sack is equal and opposite to the weight of the sack of grain. We speak of the tension of the rope. The tension, which is a force, varies with position along the length of the rope. To define it we imagine cutting the rope at a given position and applying equal and opposite forces at the cut ends to maintain the cut ends in contact. The force applied to a cut end is called the *tension* in that length of rope at that position. The cuts in the rope (at the top end, at a general position and at the bottom end) have been exaggerated on p. 100 to aid clarity in the illustration of the directions of the tensions (T being positive). If we were to ignore the weight of the rope (on account of it being small compared with the weight of the sack of grain), we see that the tension would be independent of position. In particular, the force applied to the ceiling would be assumed to be the weight of the sack of grain alone. Let us consider two further characteristics of a rope. Firstly, the length of the rope may vary with tension. However, the change in length may be so small that we may choose to ignore it and consider the length to be constant. In that case we speak of an inextensible rope. Secondly a rope may become slack, in which case the tension depends on the mass of the rope. If the rope has negligible mass, we consider the tension to be zero when the rope is slack. We note that the rope suspending the sack of grain is not able to apply either a vertically upward directed force to the ceiling or a vertically downward directed force to the sack of grain. The quantity T introduced in the figure cannot be negative, even when the sack of grain is moving, i.e. a rope cannot support a compression.

We can now collect these properties and give an interpretation of the phrase "a light inextensible string". A string is a suspension which will not support a compression. (In contrast, a rod will withstand forces applied to its end-points that tend either to compress it or extend it.) The qualification that the string is light and inextensible means that we may ignore the mass of the string and any change in length. The lightness of the string implies that the tension does not vary along the length of the string. Hence, the quantity T in the figure would be independent of position along the string and would be greater than or equal to zero. It would, however, depend on time if the sack of grain were moving. A light inextensible string is effectively a geometrical constraint which demands that the distance between the ends of the string is constant when the string is under tension (i.e. when the string is not slack).

Before we analyse our mathematical model of the pendulum we must state what we mean by "a fixed support". A fixed support is a geometrical point fixed relative to the chosen frame of reference. An applied force acts at this point and is equal and opposite to the tension in the string at this point of suspension. The combination of "a fixed support" and "a light inextensible string" implies that the particle lies on a spherical surface, centre the fixed support and radius the length of the string (provided the string is not slack).

7.2 Simple pendulum

Consider the motion of a particle of mass m suspended by a light inextensible string of length l from a given fixed support. We say that we have a simple pendulum when the particle moves on the arc of a circle in a vertical plane through the point of suspension.

The position of the particle is specified by ϕ, the angle the string makes with the downward vertical.

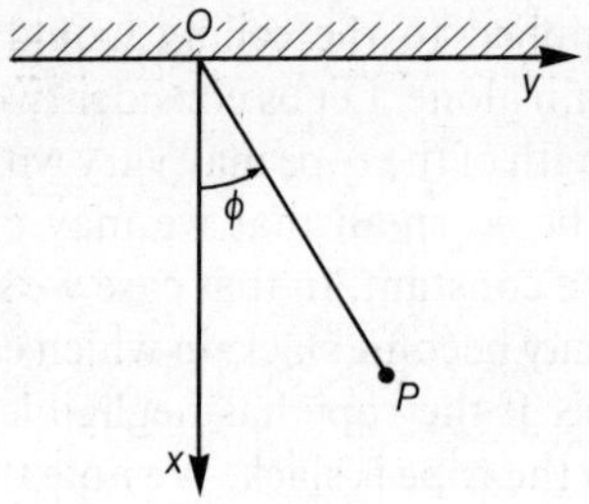

The next task is to introduce a coordinate system. Let us choose cartesian coordinates so that the origin O coincides with the point of suspension, the x-axis is vertically downwards and the y-axis is in the plane of motion. Then the position vector of the particle P relative to the point of suspension O is

$$\boldsymbol{r} = l(\boldsymbol{i}\cos\phi + \boldsymbol{j}\sin\phi)$$

Hence the velocity and the acceleration of the particle are

$$\dot{\boldsymbol{r}} = l(-\boldsymbol{i}\sin\phi\,\dot{\phi} + \boldsymbol{j}\cos\phi\,\dot{\phi})$$

and

$$\ddot{\boldsymbol{r}} = -l(\cos\phi\,\dot{\phi}^2 + \sin\phi\,\ddot{\phi})\boldsymbol{i} + l(-\sin\phi\,\dot{\phi}^2 + \cos\phi\,\ddot{\phi})\boldsymbol{j}$$

The forces acting on the particle are the constant gravitational force and the tension in the string. Let $\mathbf{F}$ denote the total force acting on the particle, where

$$\begin{aligned}\mathbf{F} &= mg\boldsymbol{i} - T(\boldsymbol{i}\cos\phi + \boldsymbol{j}\sin\phi)\\ &= (mg - T\cos\phi)\boldsymbol{i} - T\sin\phi\,\boldsymbol{j}\end{aligned}$$

Here we note the correct signs and the fact that $T \geqslant 0$. The equation of motion $m\ddot{\boldsymbol{r}} = \mathbf{F}$ becomes

$$-ml(\cos\phi\,\dot{\phi}^2 + \sin\phi\,\ddot{\phi})\boldsymbol{i} + ml(-\sin\phi\,\dot{\phi}^2 + \cos\phi\,\ddot{\phi})\boldsymbol{j} = (mg - T\cos\phi)\boldsymbol{i} - T\sin\phi\boldsymbol{j}$$

Examining the components, we have

$$ml\ddot{\phi}\sin\phi + (ml\dot{\phi}^2 - T)\cos\phi + mg = 0$$
$$ml\ddot{\phi}\cos\phi - (ml\dot{\phi}^2 - T)\sin\phi = 0$$

Multiplying the first equation by $\sin\phi$ and the second equation by $\cos\phi$ and adding, leads to

$$ml\ddot{\phi} + mg\sin\phi = 0$$

Similarly we have

$$(ml\dot{\phi}^2 - T) + mg\cos\phi = 0$$

The differential equation governing ϕ is

$$\ddot{\phi} + (g/l)\sin\phi = 0$$

and the equation determining the tension in the string is

$$T = mg\cos\phi + ml\dot{\phi}^2$$

It is worth while to derive this pair of equations by a method based on plane polar coordinates [see Sections 2.1 and 2.4]. The position vector of P relative to O is

$$\boldsymbol{r} = l\boldsymbol{e}_r, \quad \text{where} \quad \boldsymbol{e}_r = \boldsymbol{i}\cos\phi + \boldsymbol{j}\sin\phi$$

The velocity and the acceleration are

$$\dot{\boldsymbol{r}} = l\dot{\phi}\boldsymbol{e}_\phi$$

and

$$\ddot{\boldsymbol{r}} = -l\dot{\phi}^2\boldsymbol{e}_r + l\ddot{\phi}\boldsymbol{e}_\phi$$

where $\boldsymbol{e}_\phi = -\boldsymbol{i}\sin\phi + \boldsymbol{j}\cos\phi$. The force is

$$\mathbf{F} = mg(\boldsymbol{e}_r\cos\phi - \boldsymbol{e}_\phi\sin\phi) - T\boldsymbol{e}_r$$
$$= (mg\cos\phi - T)\boldsymbol{e}_r - mg\sin\phi\boldsymbol{e}_\phi$$

The equation of motion is

$$-ml\dot{\phi}^2\boldsymbol{e}_r + ml\ddot{\phi}\boldsymbol{e}_\phi = (mg\cos\phi - T)\boldsymbol{e}_r - mg\sin\phi\boldsymbol{e}_\phi$$

The radial and transverse components are

$$T = mg\cos\phi + ml\dot{\phi}^2$$

and

$$\ddot{\phi} + (g/l)\sin\phi = 0$$

This derivation is superior to our first derivation. The problem of finding a solution remains.

Suppose that $\phi = \phi_0$ and the pendulum is at rest (i.e. $\dot{\phi} = 0$) at $t = 0$. We seek a solution of the governing differential equation subject to these initial conditions. If ϕ_0 is small, we can make some progress if we assume that ϕ is small for all time, and we replace $\sin\phi$ by ϕ. Then we have to solve

$$\ddot{\phi} + \omega^2\phi = 0, \quad \text{where} \quad \omega^2 = g/l$$

This is the equation governing simple harmonic motion [see Section 2.4]. Its general solution is

$$\phi = A\cos\omega t + B\sin\omega t$$

where the constants A and B are determined by the initial conditions. The equations determining A and B are

$$\phi_0 = A \quad \text{and} \quad 0 = \omega B$$

Thus we find that the required solution, satisfying the differential equation and the given initial conditions, is

$$\phi = \phi_0\cos\omega t$$

The variation of ϕ with time is simple harmonic. The tension in the string is

$$T = mg\cos(\phi_0\cos\omega t) + ml(-\omega\phi_0\sin\omega t)^2$$

Remembering that ϕ_0 is small and using the Maclaurin expansion of the cosine function [see J. Hunter, *Calculus*, Blackie/Chambers], we have

$$\begin{aligned} T &= mg\{1 - \tfrac{1}{2}\phi_0^2\cos^2\omega t + \text{smaller terms}\} + ml\omega^2\phi_0^2\sin^2\omega t \\ &= mg + mg\phi_0^2(\sin^2\omega t - \tfrac{1}{2}\cos^2\omega t) + \text{smaller terms} \end{aligned}$$

We see that the tension is approximately constant and equal to the weight of the particle, namely mg. Our approximate solution is

$$\phi = \phi_0\cos\{(g/l)^{1/2}t\} \quad \text{and} \quad T = mg$$

It is acceptable provided the initial angular displacement is small, less than a tenth of a radian, say. The simple pendulum oscillates about the position $\phi = 0$, the amplitude of the oscillations is ϕ_0, which is constant, and the period of the oscillations is $2\pi/\omega$, which equals $2\pi(l/g)^{1/2}$. We observe that the period is independent of the mass of the particle, and that the period depends on the length of the string and the acceleration due to gravity. If we perform a simple pendulum experiment and take careful measurements of the period and of the length of the string, then we may obtain a value for g, the acceleration due to gravity. Our mathematical model predicts that the amplitude of the oscillations is constant. This is inconsistent with our observation of a laboratory situation, in which the amplitude of the oscillations decreases as time increases. This inconsistency can be explained by the fact that we have not incorporated the effects of the air surrounding the pendulum into the mathematical model.

7.3 Large-amplitude oscillations

Let us investigate the possibility of avoiding the introduction of the assumption concerning the smallness of the amplitude of the oscillations of the simple pendulum. The crucial step is the observation that

$$\ddot{\phi} = \frac{d^2\phi}{dt^2} = \frac{d\dot{\phi}}{d\phi}\frac{d\phi}{dt} = \dot{\phi}\frac{d\dot{\phi}}{d\phi} = \frac{d}{d\phi}(\tfrac{1}{2}\dot{\phi}^2)$$

We have encountered a similar result in Sections 2.2 and 2.3. Hence using this result we find that the differential equation

$$\ddot{\phi} + (g/l)\sin\phi = 0$$

becomes

$$\frac{d}{d\phi}(\tfrac{1}{2}\dot{\phi}^2) + \omega^2 \sin\phi = 0$$

where $\omega^2 = g/l$. An integration with respect to ϕ gives

$$\tfrac{1}{2}\dot{\phi}^2 - \omega^2\cos\phi = \text{constant}$$

When the initial conditions are $\phi = \phi_0$ and $\dot{\phi} = 0$ at $t = 0$, we have

$$\tfrac{1}{2}\dot{\phi}^2 = \omega^2(\cos\phi - \cos\phi_0)$$

and the tension in the string is

$$\begin{aligned} T &= mg\cos\phi + 2ml\omega^2(\cos\phi - \cos\phi_0) \\ &= mg(3\cos\phi - 2\cos\phi_0) \end{aligned}$$

We still have to find the manner in which the angle ϕ varies with the time t. We deduce from the equation

$$\dot{\phi}^2 = 2\omega^2(\cos\phi - \cos\phi_0)$$

that

$$\dot{\phi} = \pm\omega(2\cos\phi - 2\cos\phi_0)^{1/2}$$

While ϕ decreases from its initial value ϕ_0 to zero, $\dot{\phi}$ is negative and the negative sign is appropriate. Hence

$$\frac{1}{(2\cos\phi - 2\cos\phi_0)^{1/2}}\frac{d\phi}{dt} = -\omega$$

Integrating with respect to t leads to

$$\int_0^t \frac{1}{(2\cos\phi - 2\cos\phi_0)^{1/2}}\frac{d\phi}{dt}\,dt = -\omega\int_0^t dt$$

Thus

$$\int_{\phi_0}^{\phi}\frac{1}{(2\cos\phi - 2\cos\phi_0)^{1/2}}\,d\phi = -\omega t$$

In particular the time taken by the pendulum to swing from $\phi = \phi_0$ to $\phi = 0$ is

$$\frac{1}{\omega}\int_0^{\phi_0}\frac{1}{(2\cos\phi - 2\cos\phi_0)^{1/2}}\,d\phi = \frac{1}{2}\left(\frac{l}{g}\right)^{1/2}\int_0^{\phi_0}\frac{1}{(\sin^2\frac{1}{2}\phi_0 - \sin^2\frac{1}{2}\phi)^{1/2}}\,d\phi$$

This integral cannot be evaluated by analytical means because the integrand does not have an anti-derivative expressible in terms of elementary functions. It is an elliptic integral, numerical values of which are available in published tables or are obtainable at computer centres by means of a library procedure or subroutine. Let us obtain an approximation when ϕ_0 is small. Using a change of variable ($\sin\frac{1}{2}\phi = \sin\frac{1}{2}\phi_0 \sin u$), the binomial expansion and the Maclaurin expansion [see J. Hunter, *Calculus*, Blackie/Chambers], we have

$$\begin{aligned}
&\frac{1}{2}\left(\frac{l}{g}\right)^{1/2}\int_0^{\phi_0}\frac{1}{(\sin^2\frac{1}{2}\phi_0 - \sin^2\frac{1}{2}\phi)^{1/2}}\,d\phi \\
&\quad= \left(\frac{l}{g}\right)^{1/2}\int_0^{\pi/2}\frac{1}{(1-\sin^2\frac{1}{2}\phi_0\sin^2 u)^{1/2}}\,du \\
&\quad= \left(\frac{l}{g}\right)^{1/2}\int_0^{\pi/2}\{1+\tfrac{1}{2}\sin^2\tfrac{1}{2}\phi_0\sin^2 u + \tfrac{3}{8}\sin^4\tfrac{1}{2}\phi_0\sin^4 u + \ldots\}\,du \\
&\quad= \left(\frac{l}{g}\right)^{1/2}\{\tfrac{1}{2}\pi + \tfrac{1}{8}\pi\sin^2\tfrac{1}{2}\phi_0 + \text{smaller terms}\} \\
&\quad= \frac{\pi}{2}\left(\frac{l}{g}\right)^{1/2}\{1+\tfrac{1}{16}\phi_0^2 + \text{smaller terms}\}
\end{aligned}$$

This result suggests that the period of a simple pendulum, namely

$$2\left(\frac{l}{g}\right)^{1/2}\int_0^{\phi_0}\frac{1}{(\sin^2\frac{1}{2}\phi_0 - \sin^2\frac{1}{2}\phi)^{1/2}}\,d\phi$$

is greater than the approximate value $2\pi(l/g)^{1/2}$, which we calculated in the previous section (on the basis of the assumption that the motion is simple harmonic). The percentage increase is approximately $\frac{1}{16}$ per cent when the amplitude of the oscillations is 0·1 radian and $\frac{25}{16}$ per cent when the amplitude of the oscillations is 0·5 radian. A better estimate of the percentage increase in the second case is

$$100\{\tfrac{1}{4}\sin^2(0{\cdot}25)+\tfrac{9}{64}\sin^4(0{\cdot}25)\} \text{ percent}$$

i.e. 1·58 per cent.

To summarize this section, we have found an expression for $\dot{\phi}$ in terms of ϕ, but we have failed to represent ϕ explicitly in terms of t. However, the result involving the elliptic integral gives t explicitly in terms of ϕ. The motion of the simple pendulum is oscillatory but is not simple harmonic.

7.4 Conservation of energy

The forces acting on the particle in the simple pendulum problem are the constant gravitational force and the tension in the string. The equation of motion is

$$-ml\dot{\phi}^2\boldsymbol{e}_r+ml\ddot{\phi}\boldsymbol{e}_\phi = (mg\cos\phi - T)\boldsymbol{e}_r - mg\sin\phi\boldsymbol{e}_\phi$$

and the velocity of the particle is $\dot{\boldsymbol{r}} = l\dot{\phi}\boldsymbol{e}_\phi$. Forming the scalar product of both sides of the equation of motion with the velocity vector and integrating with respect to time, we obtain the result

$$\int ml^2\dot{\phi}\,\ddot{\phi}\,dt = -\int mgl\sin\phi\,\dot{\phi}\,dt + \text{constant}$$

i.e. $\frac{1}{2}ml^2\dot{\phi}^2 - mgl\cos\phi = \text{constant}$. The first term is the kinetic energy of the particle

$$E_k = \tfrac{1}{2}m\dot{\boldsymbol{r}}\,.\,\dot{\boldsymbol{r}} = \tfrac{1}{2}ml^2\dot{\phi}^2$$

and the second term is the potential energy of the particle situated in the constant gravitational field of force,

$$E_p = -mgl\cos\phi = -mgx$$

where $x = l\cos\phi$ [see figure on p. 102]. Here we have chosen the level of zero potential energy to be the horizontal plane through the point of suspension.

Therefore we have the principle of conservation of (kinetic and potential) energy, namely

$$E_k + E_p = \text{constant}$$

We note that the tension does no work because its direction is perpendicular to the direction of motion of the point of application for all time. If the initial conditions are $\phi = \phi_0$ and $\dot{\phi} = 0$, the constant energy is

$$-mgl\cos\phi_0$$

and the conservation of energy gives

$$\tfrac{1}{2}ml^2\dot{\phi}^2 = mgl(\cos\phi - \cos\phi_0)$$

i.e. $\dot{\phi}^2 = 2\omega^2(\cos\phi - \cos\phi_0)$, where $\omega^2 = g/l$. We recognize that we encountered this result in the previous section when we obtained an integral of the differential equation

$$\ddot{\phi} + \omega^2 \sin\phi = 0$$

This is not surprising because the principal of conservation of (kinetic and potential) energy is an integral of the equation of motion when the forces acting on the particle are conservative [see Section 6.4].

The relation based on the conservation of energy applies to the motion of a particle in a circle in a vertical plane, because we have not assumed in this section that the oscillations of the pendulum have a small amplitude.

EXAMPLE

A piece of metal of mass m hangs in equilibrium at one end of an inextensible string of length l while the other end of the string is fixed. Given that the piece of metal is projected horizontally with speed u_0, determine an expression for the tension. What is the minimum value of u_0 for the piece of metal to make complete revolutions?

Referring to the coordinate system in the figure on p. 102, we see that the equation of motion for the particle (representing the piece of metal) is

$$m(-l\dot{\phi}^2\mathbf{e}_r + l\ddot{\phi}\mathbf{e}_\phi) = mg(\mathbf{e}_r\cos\phi - \mathbf{e}_\phi\sin\phi) - T\mathbf{e}_r$$

and the initial conditions are $\phi = 0$, $l\dot{\phi} = u_0$ at $t = 0$. Hence $T = mg\cos\phi + ml\dot{\phi}^2$. We can express $\dot{\phi}^2$ in terms of ϕ by obtaining an integral of the governing differential equation

$$l\ddot{\phi} + g\sin\phi = 0$$

or, equivalently, by using the conservation of energy. Thus we find that

$$\tfrac{1}{2}(l\dot{\phi})^2 - gl\cos\phi = \text{constant}$$

and that the constant equals $\tfrac{1}{2}u_0^2 - gl$ in view of the given initial conditions. Therefore

$$(l\dot{\phi})^2 = u_0^2 - 2gl(1-\cos\phi)$$

and

$$T = \frac{mu_0^2}{l} + mg(3\cos\phi - 2)$$

The particle will make complete revolutions provided the speed is non-zero for all angles ϕ, and the tension is positive for all angles ϕ. Therefore we require

$$(l\dot{\phi})^2 > 0 \quad \text{and} \quad T > 0 \quad \text{for all angles } \phi$$

The first condition is satisfied when $u_0^2 > 4gl$, and the second condition is satisfied when $u_0^2 > 5gl$. Hence the particle makes complete revolutions when $u_0^2 \geqslant 5gl$; we may include the case $u_0^2 = 5gl$, for which the tension is zero instantaneously at $\phi = \pi$, the highest point of the circle.

What happens when $u_0^2 < 5gl$? Either the speed becomes zero or the tension becomes zero for a value of ϕ less than π. For $u_0^2 \leqslant 2gl$, the speed is zero at $\phi = \phi_S$, where

$$\cos\phi_S = \frac{2gl-u_0^2}{2gl} \geqslant 0 \quad \text{and} \quad 0 < \phi_S \leqslant \tfrac{1}{2}\pi$$

and the tension is zero at $\phi = \phi_T$, where

$$\cos\phi_T = \frac{2gl-u_0^2}{3gl} \geqslant 0 \quad \text{and} \quad 0 < \phi_T \leqslant \tfrac{1}{2}\pi$$

Further $\phi_S < \phi_T$ for $u_0^2 < 2gl$ and $\phi_S = \phi_T = \frac{1}{2}\pi$ for $u_0^2 = 2gl$. Therefore the tension is positive throughout the motion of the particle when $u_0^2 < 2gl$; in this case

$$|\phi| \leqslant \phi_S = \cos^{-1}\left(\frac{2gl-u_0^2}{2gl}\right) < \tfrac{1}{2}\pi$$

In the limiting case of $u_0^2 = 2gl$, the tension is positive throughout the motion of the particle, except when the speed and the tension are both zero instantaneously at $\phi = \frac{1}{2}\pi$; in this case

$$|\phi| \leqslant \phi_S = \phi_T = \tfrac{1}{2}\pi$$

For $2gl < u_0^2 < 5gl$,

$$\cos\phi_T = -\frac{u_0^2-2gl}{3gl} < 0 \quad \text{and} \quad \tfrac{1}{2}\pi < \phi_T < \pi$$

If $2gl < u_0^2 \leqslant 4gl$, ϕ_S satisfies

$$\cos\phi_S = -\frac{u_0^2-2gl}{2gl} < 0 \quad \text{and} \quad \tfrac{1}{2}\pi < \phi_T < \phi_S < \pi$$

and if $4gl < u_0^2$, ϕ_S is undefined because $\cos\phi_S < -1$ and the speed is never zero. Therefore the string becomes slack before the speed decreases to zero when $2gl < u_0^2 < 5gl$; in this case

$$0 \leqslant \phi \leqslant \phi_T \quad \text{with} \quad \tfrac{1}{2}\pi < \phi_T = \cos^{-1}\left(\frac{2gl-u_0^2}{3gl}\right) < \pi$$

Hence the particle behaves like the bob of a pendulum during the first part of its motion and then as a projectile moving under the action of uniform gravity. Its path is the union of the arc of a circle and the arc of a parabola. The initial conditions for the projectile motion are

$$\boldsymbol{r} = l(\boldsymbol{i}\cos\phi_T + \boldsymbol{j}\sin\phi_T)$$

and

$$\dot{\boldsymbol{r}} = \left(\frac{u_0^2-2gl}{3}\right)^{1/2}(-\boldsymbol{i}\sin\phi_T + \boldsymbol{j}\cos\phi_T)$$

We may solve the equation of motion

$$m(\ddot{x}\boldsymbol{i} + \ddot{y}\boldsymbol{j}) = mg\boldsymbol{i}$$

subject to these initial conditions at $t = t_0$ (say). The principle of conservation of energy appropriate to this projectile motion is

$$\tfrac{1}{2}m(\dot{x}^2+\dot{y}^2) - mgx = \tfrac{1}{2}m\frac{(u_0^2-2gl)}{3} - mgl\cos\phi_T = \tfrac{1}{2}mu_0^2 - mgl$$

subject to the condition that

$$\dot{y} = \left(\frac{u_0^2 - 2gl}{3}\right)^{1/2} \cos \phi_T$$

its initial value at $t = t_0$; $\dot{y}$ is constant because $\ddot{y} = 0$. We deduce, in particular, that $\dot{x} = 0$ when

$$\tfrac{1}{2}m\left(\frac{u_0^2 - 2gl}{3}\right)\cos^2 \phi_T - mgx = \tfrac{1}{2}mu_0^2 - mgl$$

i.e.

$$x = l - \tfrac{1}{2}\frac{u_0^2}{g} + \tfrac{1}{6}\left(\frac{u_0^2}{g} - 2l\right)\left(\frac{u_0^2 - 2gl}{3gl}\right)^2$$

Thus the stationary value of x is

$$l - \tfrac{3}{2}l + \tfrac{1}{6}l(\tfrac{1}{3})^2 = -\tfrac{13}{27}l \quad \text{when} \quad u_0^2 = 3gl$$

and

$$l - 2l + \tfrac{1}{3}l(\tfrac{2}{3})^2 = -\tfrac{23}{27}l \quad \text{when} \quad u_0^2 = 4gl$$

Therefore the maximum height above the level of projection is

$$\tfrac{40}{27}l \quad \text{when} \quad u_0^2 = 3gl$$

and

$$\tfrac{50}{27}l \quad \text{when} \quad u_0^2 = 4gl$$

EXAMPLE

A smooth hoop, in the shape of a circle of radius l is fixed in a vertical plane. A bead of mass m is threaded on the hoop and is projected horizontally with speed u_0 from the lowest point on the hoop. Find an expression for the force exerted by the hoop on the bead. What is the minimum value of u_0 for the bead to make complete revolutions?

The forces acting on the particle (representing the bead) are the uniform gravitational force and the contact force, which is normal to the hoop because the hoop is smooth. Using the coordinate system in the figure on p. 102, we write down the equation of motion

$$m(-l\dot{\phi}^2\boldsymbol{e}_r + l\ddot{\phi}\boldsymbol{e}_\phi) = mg(\boldsymbol{e}_r \cos \phi - \boldsymbol{e}_\phi \sin \phi) - N\boldsymbol{e}_r$$

and the initial conditions, which are $\phi = 0$, $l\dot{\phi} = u_0$ at $t = 0$. The contact force exerted by the hoop on the bead is represented by $-N\boldsymbol{e}_r$. This problem is exactly the same as the previous example except that N may take any value (cf. the condition on T). Proceeding as in the previous example, we find that

$$(l\dot{\phi})^2 = u_0^2 - 2gl(1 - \cos \phi)$$

$$N = \frac{mu_0^2}{l} + mg(3 \cos \phi - 2)$$

and the condition for complete revolutions is $u_0^2 > 4gl$.

To illustrate the differences between these similar examples, we shall examine the present example in the special case when $u_0^2 = 3gl$. We have

$$(l\dot{\phi})^2 = gl(1 + 2\cos \phi)$$

and

$$N = mg(1+3\cos\phi)$$

The speed becomes zero when $\phi = \pm\cos^{-1}(-\frac{1}{2}) = \pm\frac{2}{3}\pi$ and the motion of the bead is confined to the arc of the hoop specified by $-\frac{2}{3}\pi \leqslant \phi \leqslant \frac{2}{3}\pi$. During this motion the value of N changes from $4mg$ at $\phi = 0$ (the lowest point of the hoop) to $-\frac{1}{2}mg$ at $\phi = \pm\frac{2}{3}\pi$ (the highest points attained by the bead).

7.5 Simple pendulum with a moving support

Suppose the point of suspension of a simple pendulum moves in a prescribed manner in the vertical plane of the pendulum. We are interested in the effect the motion of the support has on the motion of the pendulum bob. This is a complicated topic, so we shall develop the preliminary stages of an investigation. We shall be concerned primarily with the derivation of the differential equations governing the problem, and with the validity of the application of the principle of conservation of energy.

We choose an inertial frame of reference based on a system of cartesian coordinates with origin O. The vertical plane in which the motion takes place will be the xy-plane. Let the point of suspension Q have the position vector $\mathbf{R}$ relative to O. Then the position vector of the particle P, representing the bob of the pendulum, relative to O is

$$\boldsymbol{r} = \mathbf{R}+l(\boldsymbol{i}\cos\phi+\boldsymbol{j}\sin\phi)$$

where $\mathbf{R} = X\boldsymbol{i}+Y\boldsymbol{j}$ and l is the length of the string. We are assuming that the string never becomes slack.

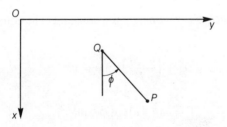

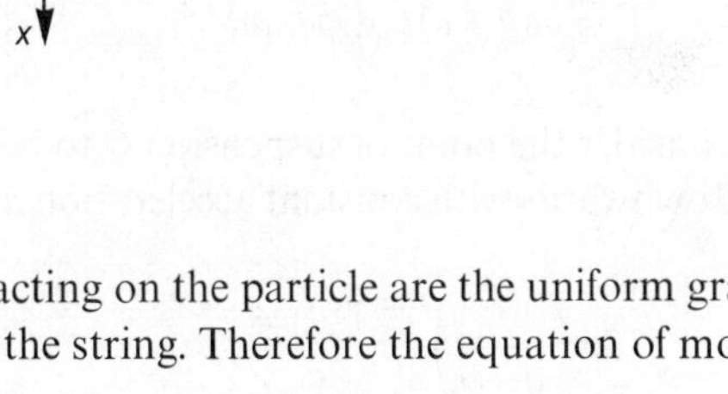

The forces acting on the particle are the uniform gravitational force and the tension in the string. Therefore the equation of motion is

$$m\ddot{\boldsymbol{r}} = mg\boldsymbol{i}-T(\boldsymbol{i}\cos\phi+\boldsymbol{j}\sin\phi)$$

where

$$\ddot{\boldsymbol{r}} = \{\ddot{X}-l(\cos\phi\,\dot{\phi}^2+\sin\phi\,\ddot{\phi})\}\boldsymbol{i}+\{\ddot{Y}+l(-\sin\phi\,\dot{\phi}^2+\cos\phi\,\ddot{\phi}\}\boldsymbol{j}$$

Using the unit vectors $\boldsymbol{e}_r$ and $\boldsymbol{e}_\phi$, where

$$\boldsymbol{i} = \boldsymbol{e}_r \cos\phi - \boldsymbol{e}_\phi \sin\phi, \quad \boldsymbol{j} = \boldsymbol{e}_r \sin\phi + \boldsymbol{e}_\phi \cos\phi$$

we see that

$$\ddot{\phi} + (\omega^2 - \ddot{X}/l)\sin\phi + (\ddot{Y}/l)\cos\phi = 0$$

and

$$T = mg\cos\phi + ml\dot{\phi}^2 - m(\ddot{X}\cos\phi + \ddot{Y}\sin\phi)$$

where $\omega^2 = g/l$. We are assuming that we have knowledge of the forms of $\ddot{X}$ and $\ddot{Y}$ (in terms of time, say) based on the prescribed manner in which the support Q is moving in the given vertical plane. The form of the differential equation governing ϕ is complicated in general. Let us examine some special cases.

Case (i) $X = u_0 t$, $Y = v_0 t$, where u_0, v_0 are constants. The equations reduce to

$$\ddot{\phi} + \omega^2 \sin\phi = 0$$

and

$$T = mg\cos\phi + ml\dot{\phi}^2$$

which we have studied in previous sections of this chapter. This is an illustration of the fact that Newton's Laws of Motion are invariant under a Galilean transformation.

Case (ii) $X = \frac{1}{2}at^2$, $Y = 0$, where a is a constant. The equations reduce to

$$\ddot{\phi} + \left(\frac{g-a}{l}\right)\sin\phi = 0$$

and

$$T = m(g-a)\cos\phi + ml\dot{\phi}^2$$

In this case we may consider the point of suspension Q to be a hook on the roof of a lift moving downwards with constant acceleration $a\boldsymbol{i}$. The period is

$$2\pi\left(\frac{l}{g-a}\right)^{1/2} \quad (a < g)$$

when the amplitude of the oscillations is small. This is greater than $2\pi(l/g)^{1/2}$ if $0 < a < g$ and less than $2\pi(l/g)^{1/2}$ if $a < 0$. We note that the character of the differential equation changes if $g \leqslant a$.

Case (iii) $X = 0$, $Y = \frac{1}{2}at^2$, where a is a constant. The equations reduce to

$$\ddot{\phi} + \omega^2 \sin\phi + (a/l)\cos\phi = 0$$

and

$$T = mg\cos\phi + ml\dot{\phi}^2 - ma\sin\phi$$

We can simplify the differential equation by noting that

$$\begin{aligned}\omega^2 \sin\phi + \frac{a}{l}\cos\phi &= \frac{(g^2+a^2)^{1/2}}{l}\left\{\frac{g}{(g^2+a^2)^{1/2}}\sin\phi + \frac{a}{(g^2+a^2)^{1/2}}\cos\phi\right\}\\ &= \frac{(g^2+a^2)^{1/2}}{l}\sin(\phi+\delta)\end{aligned}$$

where $\cos\delta = g/(g^2+a^2)^{1/2}$, $\sin\delta = a/(g^2+a^2)^{1/2}$, and by letting $\Phi = \phi+\delta$. Thus

$$\ddot{\Phi} + \{(g^2+a^2)^{1/2}/l\}\sin\Phi = 0$$

and

$$T = m(g^2+a^2)^{1/2}\cos\Phi + ml\dot{\Phi}^2.$$

These equations arise when we make a study of a gantry crane. The particle P represents the load, and the moving point of suspension Q represents the crab moving along the horizontal rails. The constant a relates to a constant horizontal force applied to the crab, and l represents the constant distance the load is away from the crab. In general, the horizontal force applied to the crab and the length of the wire rope suspending the load from the crab are variables which enable the crane driver to control the movement of the load. The mathematical study of this control problem is outside the scope of this book.

Case (iv) $X = \varepsilon l \sin\Omega t$, $Y = 0$, where ε, Ω are constants. The equations reduce to

$$\ddot{\phi} + (\omega^2 + \varepsilon\Omega^2 \sin\Omega t)\sin\phi = 0$$

and

$$T = m(g + \varepsilon l\Omega^2 \sin\Omega t)\cos\phi + ml\dot{\phi}^2$$

The differential equation is complicated even if we assume that the ϕ is small. It has a periodic coefficient.

Case (v) $X = 0$, $Y = \varepsilon l \sin\Omega t$, where ε, Ω are constants. The equations reduce to

$$\ddot{\phi} + \omega^2 \sin\phi - \varepsilon\Omega^2 \sin\Omega t\cos\phi = 0$$

and

$$T = mg\cos\phi + ml\dot{\phi}^2 + m\varepsilon l\Omega^2 \sin\Omega t \sin\phi$$

When we assume that ϕ is small, the differential equation becomes a linear differential equation of second order with constant coefficients, namely

$$\ddot{\phi} + \omega^2\phi = \varepsilon\Omega^2 \sin\Omega t$$

whose general solution is the sum of the complementary function and a particular integral [see J. Hunter, *Calculus*, Blackie/Chambers]. In fact, the general solution is

$$\phi = \begin{cases} A\cos\omega t + B\sin\omega t + \dfrac{\varepsilon\Omega^2}{\omega^2 - \Omega^2}\sin\Omega t, & \omega \neq \Omega \\ A\cos\omega t + B\sin\omega t - \frac{1}{2}\varepsilon\omega t\cos\omega t, & \omega = \Omega \end{cases}$$

where A and B are parameters to be determined by the initial conditions. When $\omega = \Omega$, the amplitude of the oscillations increases linearly with time, and our assumption about the smallness of ϕ does not remain valid for all time. This is an example of a resonance phenomenon.

Let us examine the validity of the principle of conservation of mechanical energy when the point of suspension of a simple pendulum is moving in a prescribed manner. Writing the equation of motion of the particle P in the form

$$m\ddot{\mathbf{r}} = \mathbf{F}_1 + \mathbf{F}_2$$

where $\mathbf{F}_1 = mg\mathbf{i}$ and $\mathbf{F}_2 = -T(\mathbf{i}\cos\phi + \mathbf{j}\sin\phi)$, we have

$$\int m\dot{\mathbf{r}}\,.\,\ddot{\mathbf{r}}\,dt = \int \mathbf{F}_1\,.\,\dot{\mathbf{r}}\,dt + \int \mathbf{F}_2\,.\,\dot{\mathbf{r}}\,dt + \text{constant}$$

Next we proceed as in Section 7.4 and examine each of these integrals.

$$\int m\mathbf{r}\,.\,\ddot{\mathbf{r}}\,dt = \int m\frac{d}{dt}(\tfrac{1}{2}\dot{\mathbf{r}}\,.\,\dot{\mathbf{r}})\,dt = \tfrac{1}{2}m\dot{\mathbf{r}}\,.\,\dot{\mathbf{r}} + \text{constant}$$
$$= E_k + \text{constant}$$

where $E_k = \frac{1}{2}m\dot{\mathbf{r}}\,.\,\dot{\mathbf{r}} = \frac{1}{2}m(\dot{X}^2 + \dot{Y}^2 - 2l\dot{X}\dot{\phi}\sin\phi + 2l\dot{Y}\dot{\phi}\cos\phi + l^2\dot{\phi}^2)$.

$$\int \mathbf{F}_1\,.\,\dot{\mathbf{r}}\,dt = \int mg\dot{x}\,dt = mgx + \text{constant}$$
$$= -E_p + \text{constant}$$

where $E_p = -mg(X + l\cos\phi)$. We have chosen the level of zero potential energy associated with the uniform gravitational field of force to be the fixed horizontal plane through the origin O, namely the plane $x = 0$. The third integral is

$$\int \mathbf{F}_2 \cdot \dot{\mathbf{r}}\, dt = -\int T(\dot{x}\cos\phi + \dot{y}\sin\phi)\, dt$$

$$= -\int T(\dot{X}\cos\phi + \dot{Y}\sin\phi)\, dt$$

$$= -\int T(\boldsymbol{i}\cos\phi + \boldsymbol{j}\sin\phi) \cdot \dot{\mathbf{R}}\, dt$$

The last expression looks like the work done by a force

$$-T(\boldsymbol{i}\cos\phi + \boldsymbol{j}\sin\phi) = -T\boldsymbol{e}_r$$

acting at the point Q. In fact the point Q is moved by an applied force that is equal in magnitude and opposite in direction to the tension of the string acting at Q. Hence the applied force acting at Q equals the tension of the string acting at P, namely $-T\boldsymbol{e}_r$. Therefore the third integral is the work done by the applied force acting at Q and causing the point of suspension Q to move in the prescribed manner. Collecting these integrals together, we have

$$E_k + E_p = \text{work done by applied force acting at } Q + \text{constant}$$

It is instructive to determine the explicit form of this relation in our special case (i), in which the point of suspension Q is moving with a constant velocity.

$$E_k = \tfrac{1}{2}m\{u_0^2 + v_0^2 - 2u_0 l\dot{\phi}\sin\phi + 2v_0 l\dot{\phi}\cos\phi + l^2\dot{\phi}^2\}$$

$$E_p = -mg(u_0 t + l\cos\phi)$$

and

$$\int \mathbf{F}_2 \cdot \dot{\mathbf{r}}\, dt = -\int T(u_0\cos\phi + v_0\sin\phi)\, dt$$

$$= -u_0\int (mg\cos^2\phi + ml\dot{\phi}^2\cos\phi)\, dt$$

$$-v_0\int (mg\cos\phi\sin\phi + ml\dot{\phi}^2\sin\phi)\, dt$$

$$= -u_0\int\left\{mg + m\frac{d}{dt}(l\dot{\phi}\sin\phi) - m(g\sin\phi + l\ddot{\phi})\sin\phi\right\} dt$$

$$-v_0\int\left\{m\frac{d}{dt}(-l\dot{\phi}\cos\phi) + m(g\sin\phi + l\ddot{\phi})\cos\phi\right\} dt$$

$$= -u_0\int\left\{mg + m\frac{d}{dt}(l\dot{\phi}\sin\phi)\right\} dt$$

$$-v_0\int m\frac{d}{dt}(-l\dot{\phi}\cos\phi)\, dt$$

$$= -mgu_0 t - mu_0 l\dot{\phi}\sin\phi + mv_0 l\dot{\phi}\cos\phi + \text{constant}$$

Terms cancel out and the relation reduces to

$$\tfrac{1}{2}ml^2\dot{\phi}^2 - mgl\cos\phi = \text{constant}$$

This we recognize to be the principle of conservation of mechanical energy relative to a frame of reference moving with Q, the horizontal plane through Q being the level of zero potential energy [see Section 7.4]. This moving frame is inertial because u_0 and v_0 are constant. This example illustrates the fact that the choice of an appropriate inertial frame of reference is important in order to simplify the mathematical analysis, but the choice does not influence the motion of the particle P. In a given problem, we select an inertial frame of reference and choose a level of zero potential energy (associated with the uniform gravitational field of force) that is fixed relative to the selected inertial frame of reference.

We conclude this section by examining a second illustrative example, namely case (ii) in which the point of suspension is moving along a vertical line with constant acceleration.

$$E_k = \tfrac{1}{2}m(a^2t^2 - 2atl\dot{\phi}\sin\phi + l^2\dot{\phi}^2)$$

$$E_p = -mg(\tfrac{1}{2}at^2 + l\cos\phi)$$

and

$$\begin{aligned}\int \mathbf{F}_2 \cdot \dot{r}\, dt &= -\int T\, at\cos\phi\, dt \\ &= -a\int \{m(g-a)\cos\phi + ml\dot{\phi}^2\} t\cos\phi\, dt \\ &= -a\int \left\{ m(g-a) + m\frac{d}{dt}(l\dot{\phi}\sin\phi)\right\} t\, dt \\ &= -m(g-a)\tfrac{1}{2}at^2 - ma\int t\frac{d}{dt}(l\dot{\phi}\sin\phi)\, dt \\ &= -m(g-a)\tfrac{1}{2}at^2 - matl\dot{\phi}\sin\phi - mal\cos\phi + \text{constant}\end{aligned}$$

We have integrated the last integral by parts [see J. Hunter, *Calculus*, Blackie/Chambers]. Collecting the terms together, we see that the relation simplifies to

$$\tfrac{1}{2}ml^2\dot{\phi}^2 - m(g-a)l\cos\phi = \text{constant}$$

We observe that we could obtain this result more simply by multiplying the differential equation

$$l\ddot{\phi} + (g-a)\sin\phi = 0$$

by $\dot{\phi}$ and integrating with respect to time.

The examples in chapter 6 concerning a resistive force, and the examples in this section concerning an externally applied force with a moving point of application, give a warning regarding the indiscriminate use of the principle of conservation of mechanical energy. We may use the equation of motion relative to an inertial frame of reference on all occasions. We are permitted to use the relation

$$E_k + E_p = \text{constant}$$

in a certain class of problems, i.e. when the forces are conservative—there must be no dissipative force that drains mechanical energy, and there must be no applied force that supplies mechanical energy.

7.6 Spherical pendulum

Let us investigate the possibility of generalizing our results for the simple pendulum and of allowing the bob of mass m to move freely at the end of the inextensible string of length l, i.e. we are lifting our restriction that the bob must move in a given vertical plane through the point of suspension. We shall assume that the point of suspension is fixed relative to an inertial frame of reference. We choose a system of cartesian coordinates whose origin O is at the point of suspension and whose z-axis is vertical and is directed downwards.

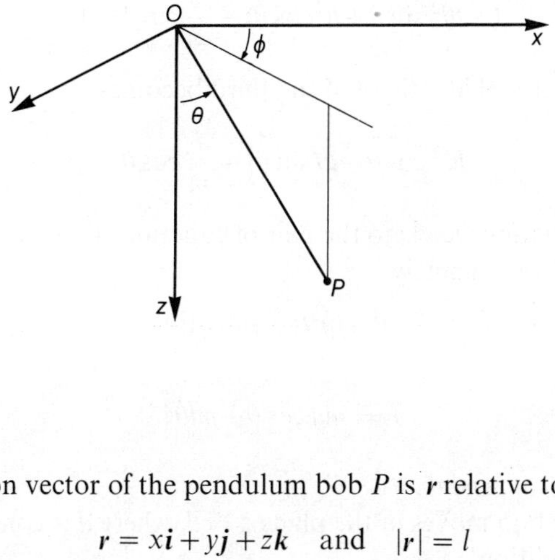

The position vector of the pendulum bob P is $\boldsymbol{r}$ relative to O, where

$$\boldsymbol{r} = x\boldsymbol{i} + y\boldsymbol{j} + z\boldsymbol{k} \quad \text{and} \quad |\boldsymbol{r}| = l$$

The equation of motion for the particle P, of mass m (which represents the pendulum bob), is

$$m\ddot{\boldsymbol{r}} = mg\boldsymbol{k} - \frac{T\boldsymbol{r}}{|\boldsymbol{r}|} \quad \text{with} \quad |\boldsymbol{r}| = l$$

Considering the cartesian component, we have

$$\ddot{x} = -\frac{Tx}{ml}$$

$$\ddot{y} = -\frac{Ty}{ml}$$

$$\ddot{z} = g - \frac{Tz}{ml}$$

subject to the condition that $(x^2+y^2+z^2)^{1/2} = l$. This system of ordinary differential equations is complicated by the constraint that the particle lies on the surface of a sphere, centre the origin O and radius l. We shall examine some special cases.

Case (a) Simple pendulum in the xz-plane
We introduce the polar angle θ, such that

$$x = l\sin\theta, \quad y = 0 \quad \text{and} \quad z = l\cos\theta$$

The position of the simple pendulum in the xz-plane is specified uniquely by the angle θ. The first differential equation becomes

$$(-l\dot{\theta}^2\sin\theta + l\ddot{\theta}\cos\theta) + \frac{T}{m}\sin\theta = 0$$

the second is a trivial identity and the third becomes

$$(-l\dot{\theta}^2\cos\theta - l\ddot{\theta}\sin\theta) + \frac{T}{m}\cos\theta = g$$

This pair of equations leads to the pair of equations that we derived in our earlier investigation, namely

$$\ddot{\theta} + (g/l)\sin\theta = 0$$

and

$$T = mg\cos\theta + ml\dot{\theta}^2$$

Case (b) Conical pendulum
In this case the bob moves in the plane $z = d$, where d is constant and less than l. The condition

$$x^2+y^2+z^2 = l^2$$

reduces to

$$x^2+y^2 = l^2-d^2 > 0$$

The bob describes a circular path of radius $(l^2-d^2)^{1/2}$ in the plane $z = d$. Hence we may set

$$x = (l^2-d^2)^{1/2}\cos\phi, \quad y = (l^2-d^2)^{1/2}\sin\phi, \quad z = d$$

The governing differential equations are

$$(-\dot{\phi}^2 \cos\phi - \ddot{\phi}\sin\phi) + \frac{T}{ml}\cos\phi = 0$$

$$(-\dot{\phi}^2 \sin\phi + \ddot{\phi}\cos\phi) + \frac{T}{ml}\sin\phi = 0$$

$$0 = g - \frac{Td}{ml}$$

Solving for $\dot{\phi}^2$ and $\ddot{\phi}$, we find that

$$\dot{\phi}^2 = \frac{T}{ml} = \frac{g}{d}, \quad \ddot{\phi} = 0$$

We deduce that the period of a conical pendulum is

$$2\pi(d/g)^{1/2}$$

where d is the distance between the point of suspension and the horizontal plane in which the bob moves. We note that the tension is constant. These results for the conical pendulum are exact; we have introduced no approximation in their derivation.

Case (*c*) *Spherical pendulum*

The governing differential equations are difficult to solve exactly. We shall obtain an approximate solution valid when the bob is slightly disturbed from the point having the position vector $l\mathbf{k}$. In passing, we note that the bob may be at rest at this point for all time because

$$\dot{x} = x = \dot{y} = y = \dot{z} = 0, \quad z = l, \quad T = mg$$

are particular solutions of the governing equations. This position is a position of equilibrium.

We shall assume that x and y are small compared to l. The z-coordinate satisfies the quadratic equation

$$z^2 = (l^2 - x^2 - y^2)$$

the two solutions being $\pm(l^2 - x^2 - y^2)^{1/2}$. The positive sign corresponds to the equilibrium position being discussed. (The negative sign corresponds to a position of equilibrium, whose position vector is $-l\mathbf{k}$, in the case of a particle sliding on the smooth exterior surface of a sphere, centre the origin and radius l.) Hence we have

$$\begin{aligned} z &= l\{1 - (x^2 + y^2)/l^2\}^{1/2} \\ &= l - (x^2 + y^2)/2l + \text{smaller terms} \end{aligned}$$

We see that $(z-l)/l$ is comparable with the square of the small quantities x/l, y/l. If we take x/l, y/l to be first-order terms, then $(z-l)/l$ is a second-order term. We note that

$$\dot{z}/l = -(x\dot{x}+y\dot{y})/l^2 + \text{smaller terms}$$

and

$$\ddot{z}/l = -(x\ddot{x}+\dot{x}^2+y\ddot{y}+\dot{y}^2)/l^2 + \text{smaller terms}$$

We assume that the velocity of the bob is small, i.e. that $\dot{x}/l$ and $\dot{y}/l$ are first-order terms and that $\dot{z}/l$ is a second-order term. Further we assume that $\ddot{x}/l$ and $\ddot{y}/l$ are first-order terms and that $\ddot{z}/l$ is a second-order term. To obtain an approximate solution, we shall ignore second-order terms. Thus the governing equations reduce to

$$\ddot{x}+(T/ml)x = 0$$

$$\ddot{y}+(T/ml)y = 0$$

$$T = mg \quad \text{and} \quad z = l$$

Substituting for T and setting $\omega^2 = g/l$, we have

$$\ddot{x}+\omega^2 x = 0 \quad \text{and} \quad \ddot{y}+\omega^2 y = 0$$

If the bob starts from a point whose x- and y-coordinates are x_0 and y_0 and if the initial velocity of the bob is

$$u_0\boldsymbol{i}+v_0\boldsymbol{j}$$

then the required solutions of the differential equations, i.e. the solutions satisfying the differential equations (governing simple harmonic motion) and the initial conditions, are

$$x = x_0\cos\omega t+(u_0/\omega)\sin\omega t$$

and

$$y = y_0\cos\omega t+(v_0/\omega)\sin\omega t$$

To find the equation of the curve traced out in the xy-plane we eliminate the parameter t by noting that

$$\sin\omega t = \frac{\omega(xy_0-yx_0)}{(u_0y_0-v_0x_0)} \quad \text{and} \quad \cos\omega t = \frac{(u_0y-v_0x)}{(u_0y_0-v_0x_0)}$$

Thus we find that

$$\omega^2(xy_0-yx_0)^2+(u_0y-v_0x)^2 = (u_0y_0-v_0x_0)^2$$

which reduces to

$$x^2(\omega^2y_0^2+v_0^2)-2xy(x_0y_0\omega^2+u_0v_0)+y^2(\omega^2x_0^2+u_0^2) = (u_0y_0-v_0x_0)^2$$

It is possible to demonstrate that this equation represents an ellipse. To achieve this we introduce the transformation of coordinates

$$x = X\cos\theta - Y\sin\theta$$
$$y = X\sin\theta + Y\cos\theta$$

We choose θ so that the coefficient of the XY-term is zero, and we verify that the resulting equation has the form

$$\frac{X^2}{a^2} + \frac{Y^2}{b^2} = 1$$

[see J. Hunter, *Analytic Geometry and Vectors*, Blackie/Chambers].

Let us examine the consequence of some special choices of the initial conditions:

(i) $y_0 = 0$, $u_0 = 0$.

$$x = x_0 \cos\omega t, \quad y = (v_0/\omega)\sin\omega t \quad \text{and} \quad \frac{x^2}{x_0^2} + \frac{y^2}{(v_0/\omega)^2} = 1$$

which is the equation of an ellipse. If $v_0 = x_0\omega$, the ellipse reduces to a circle and the spherical pendulum becomes a conical pendulum.

(ii) $u_0 = 0$, $v_0 = 0$.

$$x = x_0 \cos\omega t, \quad y = y_0 \cos\omega t \quad \text{and} \quad y = (y_0/x_0)x$$

which is the equation of a straight line. The spherical pendulum is behaving as a simple pendulum.

Throughout this discussion of the approximate solution of the spherical-pendulum problem we have assumed that the oscillations have small amplitudes.

EXAMPLE

A particle moves on the smooth interior surface of a hemispherical bowl. Write down the equation of motion in terms of two angular coordinates.

We introduce spherical polar coordinates (r, θ, ϕ) such that the origin O is at the centre of the spherical surface, part of which represents the interior surface of the bowl, and the polar axis is vertically downwards. Then the surface of the bowl is

$$\{\{(r,\theta,\phi): r = a, \quad 0 \leqslant \theta \leqslant \tfrac{1}{2}\pi, \quad 0 \leqslant \phi < 2\pi\}$$

The position vector of the particle P relative to O is

$$\boldsymbol{r} = a\boldsymbol{e}_r$$

where $e_r = \boldsymbol{i}\sin\theta\cos\phi + \boldsymbol{j}\sin\theta\sin\phi + \boldsymbol{k}\cos\theta$ and $\boldsymbol{i}, \boldsymbol{j}, \boldsymbol{k}$ are the unit vectors associated with the axes of the cartesian coordinate system illustrated on p. 117. The equation of motion of the particle P (of mass m) is

$$m\ddot{\boldsymbol{r}} = mg\boldsymbol{k} - N\boldsymbol{e}_r$$
$$= mg(\boldsymbol{e}_r \cos\theta - \boldsymbol{e}_\theta \sin\theta) - N\boldsymbol{e}_r$$

where $-N\boldsymbol{e}_r$ represents the contact force exerted by the smooth surface on the particle and

$$\ddot{\boldsymbol{r}} = -a(\dot{\theta}^2 + \dot{\phi}^2 \sin^2\theta)\boldsymbol{e}_r + a(\ddot{\theta} - \dot{\phi}^2 \sin\theta\cos\theta)\boldsymbol{e}_\theta + a(\ddot{\phi}\sin\theta + 2\dot{\theta}\dot{\phi}\cos\theta)\boldsymbol{e}_\phi$$

[see exercise 6 at the end of chapter 2]. Hence the differential equations governing the motion are

$$\ddot{\theta} - \dot{\phi}^2 \sin\theta\cos\theta + \omega^2 \sin\theta = 0$$
$$\ddot{\phi}\sin\theta + 2\dot{\theta}\dot{\phi}\cos\theta = 0$$

and

$$N = mg\cos\theta + ma(\dot{\theta}^2 + \dot{\phi}^2 \sin^2\theta)$$

where $\omega^2 = g/a$. We note that integration of the second equation with respect to time leads to

$$\dot{\phi}\sin^2\theta = \text{constant} = C_1 \text{ (say)}$$

provided $\theta \neq 0$. Therefore we have

$$\ddot{\theta} - \frac{C_1^2 \cos\theta}{\sin^3\theta} + \omega^2 \sin\theta = 0$$

and

$$N = mg\cos\theta + ma\left(\dot{\theta}^2 + \frac{C_1^2}{\sin^2\theta}\right)$$

provided $\theta \neq 0$. Further integration with respect to time gives

$$\tfrac{1}{2}\dot{\theta}^2 - \frac{C_1^2}{2\sin^2\theta} - \omega^2\cos\theta = \text{constant} = C_2 \text{ (say)}$$

provided $\dot{\theta} \neq 0$. Thus

$$N = \begin{cases} 3mga\cos\theta + 2ma(C_2 + C_1^2/\sin^2\theta) & \dot{\theta} \neq 0 \\ mg/\cos\theta & \dot{\theta} = 0 \end{cases}$$

We recognize in the above analysis the special results for the simple pendulum ($\dot{\phi} = 0$) and the conical pendulum ($\dot{\theta} = 0$).

Finally we apply the principle of the conservation of energy, which is applicable to this problem because the surface of the bowl is smooth. Noting that the velocity of the particle is

$$\dot{\boldsymbol{r}} = a(\dot{\theta}\boldsymbol{e}_\theta + \dot{\phi}\boldsymbol{e}_\phi \sin\theta)$$

we have

$$E_k = \tfrac{1}{2}ma^2(\dot{\theta}^2 + \dot{\phi}^2 \sin^2\theta)$$

and

$$E_p = -mga\cos\theta + mga$$

when we choose the level of zero potential energy to be the horizontal plane through the lowest point of the hemispherical surface. Thus

$$\tfrac{1}{2}ma^2(\dot{\theta}^2 + \dot{\phi}^2 \sin^2\theta) - mga\cos\theta = \text{constant}$$

We need to use the equation of motion to make any further progress. The time derivative of the above result is

$$\dot{\theta}(\ddot{\theta}+\dot{\phi}^2 \sin\theta\cos\theta+\omega^2\sin\theta)+\dot{\phi}\ddot{\phi}\sin^2\theta = 0$$

i.e.

$$\dot{\theta}(\ddot{\theta}-\dot{\phi}^2 \sin\theta\cos\theta+\omega^2\sin\theta)+\dot{\phi}(\ddot{\phi}+2\dot{\theta}\dot{\phi}\cos\theta)\sin\theta = 0$$

which we recognize to be a combination of the differential equations obtained earlier from the equation of motion. This is an expected result because the principle of the conservation of energy is derived from the equation of motion by the process of integration (in fact, the integration with respect to time of the scalar product of the velocity vector with the equation of motion).

EXERCISES ON CHAPTER 7

1. A simple pendulum is performing small-amplitude oscillations with a period of two seconds. What is its length?

2. Calculate the period of a simple pendulum, of length two metres, performing small-amplitude oscillations near the surface of the Moon. What is the length of the simple pendulum whose period is two seconds in a lunar experiment. (Take the acceleration due to gravity near the surface of the Moon to be $1{\cdot}62\,\mathrm{m\,s^{-2}}$.)

3. Assume that the period of a simple pendulum is proportional to the product

$$m^{\alpha} l^{\beta} g^{\gamma}$$

where m is the mass of the bob, l is the length of the pendulum and g is the acceleration due to gravity. Use an argument based on dimensions to show that

$$\alpha = 0, \quad \beta = \tfrac{1}{2}, \quad \gamma = -\tfrac{1}{2}$$

4. Let ϕ_1 and ϕ_2 be two solutions of the differential equation

$$\ddot{\phi} + \omega^2 \phi = 0$$

i.e.

$$\ddot{\phi}_1 + \omega^2 \phi_1 = 0 \quad \text{and} \quad \ddot{\phi}_2 + \omega^2 \phi_2 = 0$$

Is $\phi = a\phi_1 + b\phi_2$, where a and b are any real numbers, a solution of the differential equation?

5. Suppose that ϕ_1 and ϕ_2 are two solutions of the differential equation

$$\ddot{\phi} + \omega^2 \sin \phi = 0$$

Is $\phi = \phi_1 + \phi_2$ a solution of the differential equation in general?

6. A small piece of metal of mass $0{\cdot}25$ kg hangs in equilibrium at one end of an inextensible string of length 1 m while the other end of the vertical string is fixed. Given that the piece of metal is projected horizontally with speed $8\,\mathrm{m\,s^{-1}}$, determine the minimum and maximum values of the tension. How large can the speed of projection be if the string breaks when the tension exceeds 50 N?

7. A particle of mass m is attached to one end B of a light inextensible string of length l, the other end of which is tied to a fixed point A. When the string is taut and horizontal, the particle is projected vertically downwards with speed u. When the string becomes vertical, it wraps itself round a small smooth peg C at a depth a ($<l$) below A. Show that the tension in the string, when $\angle ABC = \pi - \phi$, is

$$3mg\cos\phi + (mu^2 + 2mga)/(l-a)$$

Find the least value of u if the lower portion of the string is to reach the upward vertical. Verify that this minimum value is zero when $a = \tfrac{3}{4}l$ and is $(\tfrac{1}{2}gl)^{1/2}$ when $a = \tfrac{1}{2}l$.

8. A smooth hoop, in the shape of a circle of radius a, is fixed in a vertical plane. A bead, which is threaded on the hoop, passes the highest point of the hoop with a speed of $(3ga)^{1/2}$. Find its speed when it passes the lowest point. Show that the force exerted by the hoop on the bead when the bead is at its lowest point is four times the force exerted by the hoop when the bead is at its highest point.

9. A bead sliding on a fixed smooth vertical circular wire is making complete revolutions. If the ratio of the greatest to the least speed is n:1 ($n < \sqrt{5}$), find the ratio of the greatest to the least force exerted by the wire on the bead. What is the significance of the condition $n < \sqrt{5}$?

10. A particle is projected with speed u_0 from the lowest point of a fixed hollow sphere of radius a so that it slides on the smooth inner surface. Show that the particle leaves the spherical surface if

$$-1 < \cos\phi_T = (2mga - mu_0^2)/3mga < 0$$

i.e. if $2ga < u_0^2 < 5ga$.

Find the height above the starting point at which the particle leaves the spherical surface when $u_0 = (\frac{7}{2}ga)^{1/2}$. In this special case investigate the projectile motion and show that the particle strikes the spherical surface again at the starting point.

11. A particle P is projected horizontally with speed $u_0 < (ga)^{1/2}$ from the top of a smooth fixed sphere of centre O and radius a. Find the angle between $\overrightarrow{OP}$ and the upward vertical at the instant when the particle leaves the sphere. Describe the motion of the particle if $u_0 \geqslant (ga)^{1/2}$.

12. A body of mass m describes a circle, on a smooth horizontal table, at the end of a light inextensible cord of length l. If the maximum tension that the cord can sustain is T_M, calculate the maximum number of revolutions per second that the body can make. What is the magnitude of the contact force between the body and the table?

13. A piece of metal of mass m is attached by a light inextensible string of length l to a fixed support. It is set in steady motion such that its path is a horizontal circle and the string makes an angle of $\frac{1}{3}\pi$ with the downward vertical. Calculate the period of this conical pendulum. What is the magnitude of the tension in the string?

14. The string of a conical pendulum can support n times the weight of the bob, without breaking. Show that the least possible value of the period of the conical pendulum is $2\pi(l/ng)^{1/2}$, where l is the length of the string.

15. A particle P, attached by a light inextensible string to a fixed point A, is describing uniformly a horizontal circle whose centre O is vertically below A and distance d from A. Prove that the angular speed of P about O is $(g/d)^{1/2}$.

In a second experiment P is joined by a second light inextensible string, of the same length as the first string, to a fixed point B vertically below A and O and distance $2d$ below A. The angular speed of P about O is now made equal to $2(g/d)^{1/2}$ and is kept steady at this new value. Find the ratio of the tensions in the two strings, AO and OB, in the new motion.

16. On a horizontal curve of radius a, a railway track is banked so that there is no lateral force on the rails when the speed of the train is u_0. (i) Show that the angle of the banking α satisfies

$$\tan\alpha = u_0^2/ga$$

Complete the following table of α, measured in radians, for various values of u_0 and a, measured in $\mathrm{m\,s^{-1}}$ and m respectively.

u_0 \ a	400	800	2000	4000
10	0·025			
30		0·114		
50			0·127	

(ii) Find the magnitude of the lateral force exerted by carriage of mass m travelling round the curve at speed U.

17. A bead of mass m slides on a rough vertical circular wire of radius a. The coefficient of kinematic friction between the bead and the wire is μ. The bead is projected with speed $a\omega$ from the lowest point of the wire. Deduce from the equation of motion for a particle representing the bead that the governing differential equation has the form

$$\frac{d\dot{\phi}^2}{d\phi} + 2\mu\dot{\phi}^2 = -\frac{2g}{a}(\sin\phi + \mu\cos\phi)$$

provided $0 < \dot{\phi}$ and $0 < a\dot{\phi}^2 + g\cos\phi$. Show that the solution of this linear first-order differential equation (see J. Hunter, *Calculus*, Blackie/Chambers) that satisfies the initial condition $\dot{\phi}^2 = \omega^2$ at $\phi = 0$ is

$$\dot{\phi}^2 = -\frac{2g}{a}\left\{\frac{(2\mu^2-1)\cos\phi + 3\mu\sin\phi}{1+4\mu^2}\right\} + \left\{\omega^2 + \frac{2g}{a}\left(\frac{2\mu^2-1}{1+4\mu^2}\right)\right\}e^{-2\mu\phi}$$

This first phase of the motion ends when ϕ satisfies the equation

$$0 = a\dot{\phi}^2 + g\cos\phi = 3g\left\{\frac{\cos\phi - 2\mu\sin\phi}{1+4\mu^2}\right\} + \left\{a\omega^2 + 2g\left(\frac{2\mu^2-1}{1+4\mu^2}\right)\right\}e^{-2\mu\phi}$$

We would have to solve this equation by iteration [see C. Dixon, *Numerical Analysis*, Blackie/Chambers] to find the appropriate value of ϕ. What is the differential equation that governs the second phase of the motion (when $a\dot{\phi}^2 + g\cos\phi < 0$)?

18. A bead slides on a fixed rough horizontal circular wire of radius a, the coefficient of kinematic friction being μ. It is projected with speed $a\omega$ from a point of the wire. Show that, if the effects of gravity are ignored, the governing differential equation, which is first order and separable, is

$$\frac{d\phi}{dt} = \omega e^{-\mu\phi}$$

where ϕ is the angle turned through by the position vector of the particle (representing the bead) relative to the centre of the circle (representing the wire). Deduce that the bead returns to the point of projection after a time

$$(e^{2\mu\pi} - 1)/\mu\omega$$

Does this model, in which the effects of gravity are ignored, predict that the bead comes to rest? Incorporate a uniform gravitational field of force into a revised model and show that

$$\left(\frac{d\phi}{dt}\right)^2 = \omega^2 \cosh 2\mu\phi - (\omega^4 + g^2/a^2)^{1/2} \sinh 2\mu\phi$$

19. The position of a particle, which slides on a rough circular wire, is given by the polar coordinates (a, ϕ), the centre of the circle being the origin. The particle of mass m is pulled by a constant tangential force of magnitude F_0. Consider its motion under the assumption that gravity may be neglected.

If the particle has speed $(2aF_0/\mu m)^{1/2}$ when $\phi = 0$, show that its subsequent speed is

$$(aF_0/\mu m)^{1/2}(1 + e^{-2\mu\phi})^{1/2}$$

Find the subsequent speed of the particle in the case when the initial speed is zero at $\phi = 0$.

20. A rope is wrapped round a rough post of circular cross-section. Consider a small element of the rope when the rope is about to slip and the effects of gravity are neglected. Show that the tension T and the polar angle ϕ satisfy

$$(T + \Delta T)\cos \Delta\phi = T + \mu_s(T + \Delta T)\sin \Delta\phi + \text{smaller terms}$$

where μ_s is the limiting value of the coefficient of static friction. Deduce that

$$\frac{dT}{d\phi} = \lim_{\Delta\phi \to 0} \frac{\Delta T}{\Delta\phi} = \mu_s T$$

and

$$T(\phi) = T(0)e^{\mu_s \phi}$$

We notice that the tension is independent of the angle if the contact between the rope and the post is smooth.

A typical value for μ_s for a hemp rope around a metal post is 0·3. Evaluate

$$T(2\pi)/T(0), \quad T(4\pi)/T(0), \quad T(6\pi)/T(0)$$

in this case. A force of 10,000 N is applied at one end of this rope. What is the minimum number of complete turns that should be on the post, if the maximum force available at the other end is 50 N and no slipping is to occur?

Elastic Forces

8

8.1 Introduction

Let us consider springs and strings whose lengths change when forces are applied to their ends. We shall suppose that a spring is a helix of wire, and a string is a strand of rubber. A spring can be extended or compressed. A string can be extended but cannot be compressed. Such strings are known as *extensible strings.* When applied forces cause the length of a spring (or string) to change, there are forces acting within the spring (or string) material that tend to restore the spring (or string) to its original length. We seek a mathematical description of the restoring force.

8.2 Springs

Firstly we shall consider springs. Suppose one end of a spring is attached to a fixed support so that the spring hangs freely. A body of mass m is attached to the free end of the spring. The spring becomes extended because the gravitational field of force acts on the body. If a body of mass M ($M > m$) replaces the first body, the spring will have an increased extension. The spring is characterized by the way in which its length is related to the applied forces, namely the reaction at the fixed support and the weight of the attached body. If we ignore the mass of the spring, then the magnitude of the reaction at the fixed support equals the weight of the attached body. Many springs have a relation between length and applied force that is approximately linear, provided the applied force is not excessive. If the applied force is excessively large, the spring will become permanently extended and will not regain its original length when the applied force ceases to act. An applied force of a sufficiently large magnitude will cause the spring material to fracture.

In adopting a model of a spring we shall make some assumptions:

(i) The length of a spring placed on a smooth horizontal table equals its length when suspended by one end from a fixed support. This length is called the natural length of the spring and is denoted by l. This assumption amounts to ignoring the mass of the spring. All the springs in our mathematical model will be light, i.e. of negligible mass.

(ii) The relation between applied force and length is Hooke's Law, which states that **the applied force is proportional to the extension**, where the extension equals the actual length minus the natural length. When the spring is compressed, its actual length is less than its natural length, and the extension is negative. Suppose that one end of the spring is fixed at a point O, the origin of a system of cartesian coordinates, and the other end of the spring is at P, a point on the x-axis having the position vector $x\boldsymbol{i}$ relative to the origin O. An applied force $F_A\boldsymbol{i}$ acts at P (and the consequent reaction of the fixed support on the end of the spring at O is $-F_A\boldsymbol{i}$). Hooke's Law gives

$$F_A\boldsymbol{i} = k(x-l)\boldsymbol{i}$$

i.e.

$$F_A = k(x-l)$$

where k is the stiffness of the spring. The dimensions of stiffness are MT^{-2} and the unit of measurement is $\mathrm{N\,m}^{-1}$. This statement of Hooke's Law applies in a static situation only. When the length of the spring varies with time, we have to adopt a variation of the above statement of Hooke's Law. This alternative statement, which is valid in static and dynamic situations, relates the extension and the elastic restoring force, which is the internal force tending to restore the length of the spring to its natural length. Denoting the elastic restoring force acting at P by $F_R\boldsymbol{i}$, we have

$$F_R\boldsymbol{i} = -k(x-l)\boldsymbol{i}$$

i.e.

$$F_R = -k(x-l)$$

The elastic restoring force acting at P is equal and opposite to the tension in the spring at the end P, denoted by $T\boldsymbol{i}$. Therefore we have

$$T = k(x-l)$$

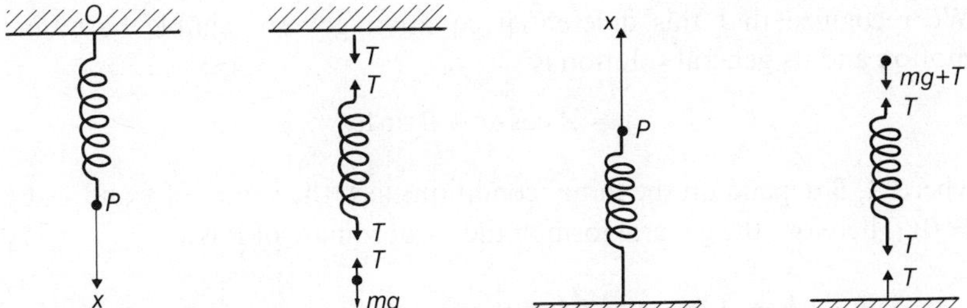

(i) (ii) (iii) (iv)

We note that T is positive when the spring is extended, and is negative when the spring is compressed.

Consider two simple situations, one in which a body is suspended from a fixed support by a spring, and the other in which a body is supported by a spring above a fixed horizontal floor. We shall use a particle of mass m to denote the body. In the first instance we shall assume that the system is in equilibrium, i.e. the particle is at rest for all time. In the first case, illustrated in figure (i), the equation of motion reduces to

$$\boldsymbol{0} = mg\boldsymbol{i} - T\boldsymbol{i}$$

where $T = k(x-l) > 0$. Hence $x = l + mg/k$ gives the equilibrium position. In the second case, illustrated in figure (iii), the equation of motion reduces to

$$\boldsymbol{0} = -mg\boldsymbol{i} - T\boldsymbol{i}$$

where $T = k(x-l) < 0$. Hence $x = l - mg/k$ gives the equilibrium position. Now assume that the particle P moves along the vertical axis through O. The equation of motion for the particle is

$$m\ddot{x} = mg - T = mg - k(x-l) \quad \text{in the first case}$$

and

$$m\ddot{x} = -mg - T = -mg - k(x-l) \quad \text{in the second case.}$$

These reduce respectively to

$$m\ddot{x} + kx = kl + mg$$

and

$$m\ddot{x} + kx = kl - mg$$

Setting $b = l + mg/k$, $x = y + b$ and $\omega^2 = k/m$, we rewrite the first of these differential equations in the form

$$\ddot{y} + \omega^2 y = 0$$

We recognize that this differential equation governs simple harmonic motion and its general solution is

$$y = A\cos\omega t + B\sin\omega t$$

where A, B depend on the initial conditions (e.g. the values of y and $\dot{y}$ at $t = 0$). Therefore the general form of the x-coordinate of P is

$$\begin{aligned} x = y + b &= A\cos\omega t + B\sin\omega t + b \\ &= A\cos\{(k/m)^{1/2}t\} + B\sin\{(k/m)^{1/2}t\} + l + mg/k \end{aligned}$$

The particle P oscillates about its equilibrium position, the period of the oscillations being $2\pi/\omega$, which equals

$$2\pi(m/k)^{1/2}$$

We note that

$$T = k(x-l) = mg + Ak\cos\{(k/m)^{1/2}t\} + Bk\{\sin(k/m)^{1/2}t\}$$

We can treat the second differential equation, namely

$$m\ddot{x} + kx = kl - mg$$

in the same way. The general results are

$$x = A\cos\{(k/m)^{1/2}t\} + B\{\sin(k/m)^{1/2}t\} + l - mg/k$$

and

$$T = -mg + Ak\cos\{(k/m)^{1/2}t\} + Bk\sin\{(k/m)^{1/2}t\}$$

where A, B are specified in terms of the values of x and $\dot{x}$ at $t = 0$ (say).

EXAMPLE

A particle of mass m is suspended from a fixed support by a spring of natural length l and stiffness k. It moves along a vertical line through the point of suspension such that its speed is u_0 when it passes in a downward direction through the equilibrium position. Obtain a description of the motion and determine the tension in the spring.

Using the coordinate system illustrated in figure (i), we see that the equation of motion of the particle leads to

$$m\ddot{x} = mg - T$$

where $T = k(x-l)$. This is the appropriate differential equation because there are two forces acting on the particle, namely the uniform gravitational force $mg\boldsymbol{i}$ and the elastic restoring force $-T\boldsymbol{i}$, where $T\boldsymbol{i}$ represents the tension in the spring at the end attached to the particle. The equilibrium position (determined by the solution of the differential equation that is consistent with the conditions $\ddot{x} = \dot{x} = 0$ for all time) is

$$x = l + mg/k$$

Hence the given initial conditions are

$$x = l + mg/k \quad \text{and} \quad \dot{x} = u_0 > 0 \quad \text{at} \quad t = 0.$$

The general solution of the differential equation

$$\ddot{x} + \omega^2 x = g + l\omega^2, \quad \text{where} \quad \omega^2 = k/m$$

is

$$x = l + g/\omega^2 + A\cos\omega t + B\sin\omega t.$$

A particular integral is $l + g/\omega^2$ and the complementary function is $A\cos\omega t + B\sin\omega t$. Imposing the initial conditions, we find that A and B satisfy

$$l + g/\omega^2 = l + g/\omega^2 + A$$

and

$$u_0 = B\omega$$

Thus $A = 0$, $B = u_0/\omega$ and the required solution is

$$x = l+g/\omega^2+(u_0/\omega)\sin\omega t$$

We deduce that

$$T = k\{g/\omega^2+(u_0/\omega)\sin\omega t\}$$

The maximum and minimum values of x are

$$l+g/\omega^2+u_0/\omega \quad \text{and} \quad l+g/\omega^2-u_0/\omega$$

which equal $l+mg/k+u_0(m/k)^{1/2}$ and $l+mg/k-u_0(m/k)^{1/2}$. We note that the spring is extended throughout the motion provided $mg/k > u_0/(m/k)^{1/2}$, i.e. $0 < u_0 < g(m/k)^{1/2}$. If we allow u_0 to increase beyond $g(m/k)^{1/2}$, the spring is extended sometimes and is compressed at other times. The maximum permitted value of u_0 is

$$l\omega+g/\omega = l(k/m)^{1/2}+g(m/k)^{1/2} = (mg+kl)/(mk)^{1/2}$$

which coincides with the x-coordinate taking values between zero and $2(l+mg/k)$. For this value of u_0 the minimum length of the spring is zero (which is impossible to achieve in an experiment).

The maximum and minimum values of T are

$$k(g/\omega^2+u_0/\omega) \quad \text{and} \quad k(g/\omega^2-u_0/\omega)$$

which equal $mg+u_0(mk)^{1/2}$ and $mg-u_0(mk)^{1/2}$. A further constraint on u_0 arises if Hooke's Law does not apply for all values of T within these limits. For example, the tension at which the spring breaks may be attained.

8.3 Extensible strings

Let us now investigate similar problems in which the spring is replaced by an extensible string. The essential feature that we must note is that a string cannot withstand a compression. We shall study strings of negligible mass to which Hooke's Law is applicable. Referring to the coordinate system illustrated in figure (i), we represent the tension in the string at P by $T\mathbf{i}$, where

$$T = \frac{\lambda}{l}(x-l)$$

l is the natural length of the string and λ is the modulus of elasticity. The modulus of elasticity has the dimensions of force, MLT^{-2}, and its unit of measurement is the newton. This definition of T is valid for $x \geqslant l$. If $0 < x < l$, the string is slack and we set T equal to zero (because we are ignoring the mass of the string).

EXAMPLE

A particle of mass m is suspended from a fixed support by an extensible string of natural length l and modulus of elasticity λ. It is pulled down a distance d below its equilibrium position and is released with zero velocity. Does the string become slack at any time?

We choose to use the coordinate system illustrated in figure (i). Then the governing differential equation is

$$m\ddot{x} = mg - \frac{\lambda}{l}(x-l)$$

Rewriting this equation, we have

$$\ddot{x} + \omega^2 x = g + \omega^2 l$$

where $\omega^2 = \lambda/ml$. The equilibrium position is specified by

$$x = l + g/\omega^2 = l + mgl/\lambda$$

Therefore the initial conditions are

$$x = l + g/\omega^2 + d \quad \text{and} \quad \dot{x} = 0 \quad \text{at} \quad t = 0.$$

The general solution of the differential equation is

$$x = l + g/\omega^2 + A\cos\omega t + B\sin\omega t$$

and A, B satisfy the equations

$$l + g/\omega^2 + d = l + g/\omega^2 + A \quad \text{and} \quad 0 = \omega B$$

Hence $A = d$, $B = 0$ and the required solution is

$$x = l + g/\omega^2 + d\cos\omega t = l + mgl/\lambda + d\cos\{(\lambda/ml)^{1/2}t\}.$$

The tension in the string is given by

$$T = \frac{\lambda}{l}(x-l) = mg + \lambda(d/l)\cos\{(\lambda/ml)^{1/2}t\}$$

$T = 0$ if there exists a value of t such that

$$\cos\{(\lambda/ml)^{1/2}t\} = -\frac{mgl}{\lambda d}$$

This equation has real solutions provided $mgl < \lambda d$. Therefore the string will become slack if $d > mgl/\lambda$. We note that mgl/λ is the equilibrium extension.

Let us examine the particular case in which $\lambda = 4mg$ and $d = \frac{1}{2}l$. Substituting these values in our previously found solutions, we find that

$$x = l[\tfrac{5}{4} + \tfrac{1}{2}\cos\{2(g/l)^{1/2}t\}]$$

and

$$T = mg[1 + 2\cos\{2(g/l)^{1/2}t\}]$$

Initially $x = \frac{7}{4}l$ and $T = 3mg$. The string becomes slack when $T = 0$. To determine the time at which $T = 0$ we have to solve the equation

$$\cos\{2(g/l)^{1/2}t\} = -\tfrac{1}{2}$$

The smallest positive solution is $2(g/l)^{1/2}t = \frac{2}{3}\pi$, i.e. $t = \frac{1}{3}\pi(l/g)^{1/2}$. At this time, $t = t_0$ (say),

$$x = l \quad \text{and} \quad \dot{x} = -(gl)^{1/2}\sin(\tfrac{2}{3}\pi) = -\tfrac{1}{2}(3gl)^{1/2}.$$

For $t > t_0$, the string is slack and the particle is moving upwards subject to a single force, the uniform gravitational force. Hence the governing differential equation for the projectile motion is

$$\ddot{x} = g$$

and the initial conditions are

$$x = l \quad \text{and} \quad \dot{x} = -\tfrac{1}{2}(3gl)^{1/2} \quad \text{at} \quad t = t_0 = \tfrac{1}{3}\pi(l/g)^{1/2}.$$

We deduce that the required solution is

$$\dot{x} = g(t-t_0) - \tfrac{1}{2}(3gl)^{1/2}$$

and

$$x = \tfrac{1}{2}g(t-t_0)^2 - \tfrac{1}{2}(3gl)^{1/2}(t-t_0) + l$$

This is valid provided $x < l$. We see that

$$\dot{x} = 0 \quad \text{when} \quad t = t_0 + \tfrac{1}{2}(3l/g)^{1/2} = (\tfrac{1}{3}\pi + \tfrac{1}{2}\sqrt{3})(l/g)^{1/2}$$

and the corresponding value of x is

$$\tfrac{1}{2}g(\tfrac{3}{4}l/g) - \tfrac{1}{2}(\tfrac{3}{2}l) + l = \tfrac{5}{8}l$$

Therefore the particle rises to a point $\frac{5}{8}l$ below the fixed support. The particle then falls under gravity for $\frac{5}{8}l \leqslant x \leqslant l$ and continues to fall under gravity and the elastic restoring force for $l \leqslant x \leqslant \frac{7}{4}l$. The motion is confined to the interval

$$\tfrac{5}{8}l \leqslant x \leqslant \tfrac{7}{4}l$$

and the period of the oscillations is

$$(\tfrac{2}{3}\pi + \sqrt{3})(l/g)^{1/2}$$

Finally we note the corresponding results for an equivalent spring, whose natural length is l and whose stiffness is $4mg/l$. The motion of the particle is confined to the interval

$$\tfrac{3}{4}l \leqslant x \leqslant \tfrac{7}{4}l$$

and the period of the oscillations is $\pi(l/g)^{1/2}$. This example illustrates the essential difference between a spring and an extensible string.

8.4 An energy equation

Let us re-examine the spring problem discussed in Section 8.2 and illustrated by figure (i). The governing differential equation is

$$m\ddot{x} = mg - k(x-l)$$

Multiplying by $\dot{x}$ and integrating with respect to t (or, equivalently, noting that $\ddot{x} = d(\frac{1}{2}\dot{x}^2)/dx$ and integrating with respect to x), we have

$$\tfrac{1}{2}m\dot{x}^2 = mgx - \tfrac{1}{2}k(x-l)^2 + \text{constant}$$

Hence

$$\tfrac{1}{2}m\dot{x}^2 - mgx + \tfrac{1}{2}k(x-l)^2 = \text{constant}$$

The first term is the kinetic energy of the particle, and the second term is the potential energy of the particle associated with the uniform gravitational field of force. The third term is called the *potential energy of the spring*. We have adjusted the constant so that the potential energy of the spring is zero when $x = l$ (the natural length of the spring). The potential energy of the spring equals

$$\int_l^x k(x-l)\,dx = \int_l^x T\,dx = -\int_l^x F_R\,dx$$

which is minus the work done by the elastic restoring force $F_R\,\boldsymbol{i}$, as the point of application P moves from $l\boldsymbol{i}$ to $x\boldsymbol{i}$. We are assuming that the elastic restoring force is a conservative force. Let us justify this assumption. Suppose that a spring OP, of natural length l and stiffness k, has its end O

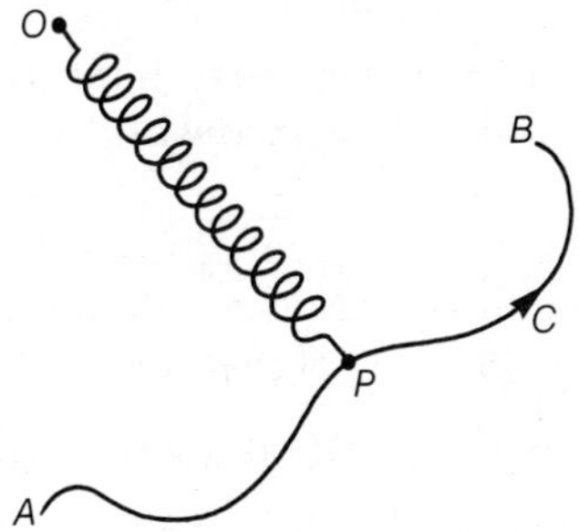

fixed and its end P variable. Let $\boldsymbol{r}$ be the position vector of the point P relative to O. The spring lies along the straight line between O and P. Then the elastic restoring force acting at P equals

$$k(|\boldsymbol{r}|-l)\,(-\boldsymbol{r}/|\boldsymbol{r}|) = -k(r-l)\boldsymbol{r}/r$$

where $|\boldsymbol{r}| = r$. Suppose P moves along a curve C from A to B. The work done by the elastic restoring force $\mathbf{F}_R$ is

$$\int_C \mathbf{F}_R \cdot d\boldsymbol{r} = \int_{t_A}^{t_B} \mathbf{F}_R \cdot \dot{\boldsymbol{r}}\,dt$$

$$= \int_{t_A}^{t_B} \left\{-k(r-l)\frac{\boldsymbol{r}\cdot\dot{\boldsymbol{r}}}{r}\right\} dt$$

Using the fact that $\boldsymbol{r}\cdot\dot{\boldsymbol{r}} = r\dot{r}$ (because $\boldsymbol{r}\cdot\boldsymbol{r} = r^2$), we have

$$\int_C \mathbf{F}_R \cdot d\boldsymbol{r} = \int_{t_A}^{t_B} \left\{-k(r-l)\frac{dr}{dt}\right\} dt$$

$$= \int_{r_A}^{r_B} \{-k(r-l)\}\,dr$$

$$= \tfrac{1}{2}k(r_A-l)^2 - \tfrac{1}{2}k(r_B-l)^2$$

This result is independent of the path C between A and B, and is zero for any closed curve. Therefore we may say that the elastic restoring force is a conservative force, and we may define the potential energy associated with this conservative force to be one half of the product of the stiffness and the square of the extension of the spring.

Letting E_k be the kinetic energy and E_p be the potential energy (associated with the uniform gravitational force and the elastic restoring force), we have a convenient statement of the conservation of energy

$$E_k + E_p = \text{constant}$$

where $E_k = \frac{1}{2}m\dot{x}^2$ and $E_p = -mg(x-l)+\frac{1}{2}k(x-l)^2$. Note that we have adjusted the constant so that E_p is zero when the spring is at its natural length.

When we are studying the equivalent problem for an extensible string of natural length l and modulus of elasticity λ, the above analysis carries over. The statement of the conservation of energy is

$$\tfrac{1}{2}m\dot{x}^2 - mg(x-l)+\tfrac{1}{2}(\lambda/l)(x-l)^2 = \text{constant}$$

which is valid provided the string is stretched, i.e. when $x > l$.

EXAMPLE

A particle of mass m is suspended from a fixed support by a spring of natural length l and stiffness k. It moves along a vertical line through the point of suspension. At a given instant the length of the spring is L and the speed of the particle is u_0. Write down the energy equation and consider any possible deductions.

Using the coordinate system illustrated in figure (i), we are able to write

$$E_k = \tfrac{1}{2}m\dot{x}^2$$

and

$$E_p = -mg(x-l)+\tfrac{1}{2}k(x-l)^2.$$

We note that the first term in the expression for the potential energy is positive when $x < l$, i.e. when the particle is above the level of zero potential energy. Hence the conservation of energy gives

$$E_k + E_p = \tfrac{1}{2}m\dot{x}^2 - mg(x-l)+\tfrac{1}{2}k(x-l)^2 = \text{constant}$$

We use the initial conditions, namely $x = L$ and $\dot{x} = u_0$, to evaluate the constant, which equals

$$\tfrac{1}{2}mu_0^2 - mg(L-l)+\tfrac{1}{2}k(L-l)^2$$

Therefore

$$\begin{aligned}\tfrac{1}{2}m\dot{x}^2 &= mg(x-l)-\tfrac{1}{2}k(x-l)^2+\tfrac{1}{2}mu_0^2-mg(L-l)+\tfrac{1}{2}k(L-l)^2\\ &= \tfrac{1}{2}mu_0^2+mg(x-L)-\tfrac{1}{2}k(x^2-2xl-L^2+2Ll)\\ &= -\tfrac{1}{2}kx^2+x(mg+kl)+\tfrac{1}{2}kL^2-L(mg+kl)+\tfrac{1}{2}mu_0^2\end{aligned}$$

Introducing the equilibrium length b, which equals $l+mg/k$, we have

$$\begin{aligned}\tfrac{1}{2}m\dot{x}^2 &= -\tfrac{1}{2}kx^2+bkx+\tfrac{1}{2}kL^2-bkL+\tfrac{1}{2}mu_0^2\\ &= -\tfrac{1}{2}k(x-b)^2+\tfrac{1}{2}kL^2-bkL+\tfrac{1}{2}kb^2+\tfrac{1}{2}mu_0^2\\ &= -\tfrac{1}{2}k(x-b)^2+\tfrac{1}{2}k(L-b)^2+\tfrac{1}{2}mu_0^2\end{aligned}$$

The right-hand side of this equation is a polynomial in x of degree two (and is a difference of squares). The allowable values of x are those for which the right-hand side is positive. They are between the two zeros of the quadratic equation

$$-\tfrac{1}{2}k(x-b)^2+\tfrac{1}{2}k(L-b)^2+\tfrac{1}{2}mu_0^2 = 0$$

which are

$$b-\{(L-b)^2+mu_0^2/k\}^{1/2} \quad \text{and} \quad b+\{(L-b)^2+mu_0^2/k\}^{1/2}$$

We deduce that the particle will oscillate about its equilibrium position, namely $x = b$, and that the amplitude of the oscillations is

$$\{(L-b)^2+mu_0^2/k\}^{1/2} = A_0 \text{ (say)}.$$

We obtained a special case of this result with $L = b$ in the example in Section 8.2.

Hence we may write

$$\dot{x}^2 = \frac{k}{m}\{A_0^2-(x-b)^2\}$$

Thus

$$\dot{x} = \pm\left[\frac{k}{m}\{A_0^2-(x-b)^2\}\right]^{1/2}$$

or

$$\frac{1}{\{A_0^2-(x-b)^2\}^{1/2}}\frac{dx}{dt} = \pm\left(\frac{k}{m}\right)^{1/2}.$$

We must choose the correct sign for the appropriate stage of the motion (either x is increasing or x is decreasing). Then we can integrate the equation with respect to t and obtain a relation between x and t. If we choose the positive sign, we find that

$$\int\frac{1}{\{A_0^2-(x-b)^2\}^{1/2}}\frac{dx}{dt}\,dt = \left(\frac{k}{m}\right)^{1/2} t+\text{constant}$$

Using the substitution

$$x-b = A_0\sin v, \quad 0 \leqslant v \leqslant \tfrac{1}{2}\pi$$

we convert the integral into

$$\int\frac{1}{A_0\cos v}A_0\cos v\frac{dv}{dx}\frac{dx}{dt}\,dt = v = \sin^{-1}\left(\frac{x-b}{A_0}\right)$$

Thus

$$x-b = A_0\sin\{(k/m)^{1/2}t+\text{constant}\}$$

where the constant is specified by the initial conditions. If $x = L$ and $\dot{x} = u_0$ at $t = 0$,

$$L-b = A_0\sin\{\text{constant}\} \quad \text{and} \quad u_0 = A_0(k/m)^{1/2}\cos\{\text{constant}\}.$$

Therefore

$$\begin{aligned}x-b &= A_0[\sin\{(k/m)^{1/2}t\}\cos\{\text{constant}\}+\cos\{(k/m)^{1/2}t\}\sin\{\text{constant}\}]\\ &= u_0(m/k)^{1/2}\sin\{(k/m)^{1/2}t\}+(L-b)\cos\{(k/m)^{1/2}t\}\end{aligned}$$

where $b = l+mg/k$, is an explicit expression for x in terms of t.

In the last paragraph we have been successful in solving the first-order differential equation in which $\dot{x}$ is given in terms of x and so obtaining an explicit expression for x in terms of t. The more usual way to derive this explicit expression for x in terms of t is to solve the second-order differential equation obtained from the equation of motion (cf. Section 8.2). The energy equation is a particularly convenient starting point when we require information about speeds and distances, and we do not require the length of time intervals (e.g. the period of oscillations) or the form of forces (e.g. the tension in a spring or string).

EXAMPLE

A particle of mass m is suspended from a fixed support by an extensible string of natural length l and modulus of elasticity $4mg$. It is pulled down a distance $\frac{7}{4}l$ below the fixed support and is released with zero velocity. What distance does the particle move before it is instantaneously at rest again?

We have answered this question in the example in Section 8.3. There we took the equation of motion as the starting point and found an explicit expression for the coordinate of the particle in terms of time. Let us re-examine the problem and use the conservation of energy. We must remember that the problem involves a string, which may become slack.

The energy equation (specified in terms of the x-coordinate illustrated in figure (i)) is

$$\begin{aligned}\tfrac{1}{2}m\dot{x}^2 - mg(x-l) + \tfrac{1}{2}(4mg/l)(x-l)^2 \\ = \text{constant} = 0 - \tfrac{3}{4}mgl + \tfrac{9}{8}mgl = \tfrac{3}{8}mgl\end{aligned}$$

This is valid provided $x \geqslant l$. We make the important observation that

$$\tfrac{1}{2}m\dot{x}^2 = \tfrac{3}{8}mgl \quad \text{when} \quad x = l$$

i.e. the particle has the speed $\frac{1}{2}(3gl)^{1/2}$ when the string becomes slack. Hence this form of the energy equation is valid for $l \leqslant x \leqslant \frac{7}{4}l$. When $x \leqslant l$ the valid form of the energy equation is

$$\tfrac{1}{2}m\dot{x}^2 - mg(x-l) = \text{constant} = \tfrac{3}{8}mgl + 0 = \tfrac{3}{8}mgl$$

We deduce from this equation that $\dot{x} = 0$ when

$$x = l - \tfrac{3}{8}l = \tfrac{5}{8}l$$

and that x must not be less than $\frac{5}{8}l$. Therefore we conclude that the motion of the particle is confined between $x = \frac{5}{8}l$ and $x = \frac{7}{4}l$, and that the distance between two consecutive positions of instantaneous rest is $\frac{9}{8}l$.

8.5 Some alternatives to Hooke's Law

Let us examine some alternatives to Hooke's Law (the linear relation between extension and the elastic restoring force). We shall retain the elastic condition but shall allow the relation between the extension and the restoring force (or tension) to be non-linear. In particular, consider the vertical motion of a particle suspended from a fixed support by a spring. Using the coordinate system illustrated in figure (i), we see that the equation of motion of the particle reduces to

$$m\ddot{x} = mg - T$$

Suppose that

$$T = k(x-l) + \alpha(x-l)^2$$

where k is the stiffness, l is the natural length and α is the parameter associated with the non-linear term. Here k is positive, but α may be positive or negative. The dimensions of α are $\mathrm{ML^{-1}T^{-2}}$ and the unit of measurement is $\mathrm{N\,m^{-2}}$. Therefore the governing differential equation is

$$m\ddot{x} + k(x-l) + \alpha(x-l)^2 = mg$$

If x_1 and x_2 are two independent solutions, $x_1 + x_2$ is not a solution (unless $\alpha = 0$). We say that the differential equation is non-linear. What information can we derive from this non-linear differential equation?

Firstly we shall examine the possible existence of one or more equilibrium positions. Let $x = x_0$ represent an equilibrium position, i.e. $x = x_0$, $\dot{x} = \ddot{x} = 0$ is a solution of the differential equation. Hence

$$k(x_0 - l) + \alpha(x_0 - l)^2 = mg$$

The solutions of this quadratic equation are

$$x_0 = l + \left\{\frac{(k^2 + 4mg\alpha)^{1/2} - k}{2\alpha}\right\}$$

and

$$x_0 = l - \left\{\frac{(k^2 + 4mg\alpha)^{1/2} + k}{2\alpha}\right\}$$

Hence there are two equilibrium positions (in general) but no equilibrium position exists if $\alpha < 0$ and $k^2 < -4mg\alpha$. However, if the non-linear parameter is small in magnitude ($k^2 \gg 4mg|\alpha|$), there is one acceptable equilibrium position corresponding to

$$x_0 = l + \frac{mg}{k} - \frac{m^2g^2\alpha}{k^3} + \dots$$

which is a small distance away from the equilibrium position in the linear case ($\alpha = 0$).

Secondly we shall derive an energy equation. We may not be able to obtain directly an explicit relation between x and t from the non-linear differential equation

$$m\ddot{x} + k(x-l) + \alpha(x-l)^2 = mg$$

but we are able to find an expression for $\dot{x}$ in terms of x. Proceeding as in Section 8.4, we obtain the result

$$\tfrac{1}{2}m\dot{x}^2 - mg(x-l) + \tfrac{1}{2}k(x-l)^2 + \tfrac{1}{3}\alpha(x-l)^3 = \text{constant}$$

The first term is the kinetic energy of the particle, and the second term is the potential energy associated with the uniform gravitational field of force. The elastic restoring force, which we may represent in general by

$$-\{k(r-l) + \alpha(r-l)^2\}\mathbf{r}/r$$

is conservative and the potential energy associated with this conservative force is

$$\tfrac{1}{2}k(r-l)^2 + \tfrac{1}{3}\alpha(r-l)^3$$

Therefore we have the statement of the conservation of energy for this particular problem, namely

$$E_k + E_p = \text{constant}$$

where $E_k = \frac{1}{2}m\dot{x}^2$ and $E_p = -mg(x-l) + \frac{1}{2}k(x-l)^2 + \frac{1}{3}\alpha(x-l)^3$. We may deduce that

$$\tfrac{1}{2}m\dot{x}^2 = \text{constant} + mg(x-l) - \tfrac{1}{2}k(x-l)^2 - \tfrac{1}{3}\alpha(x-l)^3$$

and that allowable values of x satisfy

$$0 \leqslant \text{constant} + mg(x-l) - \tfrac{1}{2}k(x-l)^2 - \tfrac{1}{3}\alpha(x-l)^3$$

where the constant depends on the initial conditions. Suppose that the initial conditions are $x = l$, $\dot{x} = u_0$ at $t = 0$. Then we seek solutions of the cubic equation

$$\tfrac{1}{2}mu_0^2 + mg(x-l) - \tfrac{1}{2}k(x-l)^2 - \tfrac{1}{3}\alpha(x-l)^3 = 0$$

to determine the ranges of the allowable values of x. If this equation has three real roots, it is possible for the particle to perform oscillations of finite amplitude. However, if there is only a single real root, no oscillations of finite amplitude are possible.

We shall examine in detail a modification of a linear spring problem reported in Section 8.3. The initial conditions are

$$x = \tfrac{7}{4}l, \quad \dot{x} = 0 \quad \text{at} \quad t = 0$$

and the stiffness of the spring is $4mg/l$. We shall select various values for α and seek the possibility of the particle performing finite-amplitude oscillations. We know that when $\alpha = 0$, the centre of the oscillations is the equilibrium position $x = \frac{5}{4}l$ and the amplitude of the oscillations is $\frac{1}{2}l$, i.e. the allowable values of x are in the interval $[\frac{3}{4}l, \frac{7}{4}l]$.

For a given value of α, the constant equals

$$\tfrac{9}{64}\alpha l^3 + \tfrac{9}{8}mgl - \tfrac{3}{4}mgl = \tfrac{9}{64}\alpha l^3 + \tfrac{3}{8}mgl$$

and we have

$$\tfrac{1}{2}m\dot{x}^2 = \tfrac{1}{64}(9\alpha l^3 + 24mgl) + mg(x-l) - 2mg(x-l)^2/l - \tfrac{1}{3}\alpha(x-l)^3$$

Setting $X = (x-l)/l$ and rearranging, we obtain

$$\dot{x}^2 = gl\left\{\tfrac{3}{4} + 2X - 4X^2 + \frac{\alpha l^2}{mg}(\tfrac{9}{32} - \tfrac{2}{3}X^3)\right\}$$

The next step is to find values of X for which the right-hand side is positive. We remember that $\dot{x}^2 \geqslant 0$ for $X \in [-\frac{1}{4}, \frac{3}{4}]$ when $\alpha = 0$. When α is nonzero, it is necessary to find the roots of the cubic equation

$$\tfrac{3}{4} + 2X - 4X^2 + \gamma(\tfrac{9}{32} - \tfrac{2}{3}X^3) = 0$$

where $\alpha = \gamma mg/l^2$. We may use a numerical technique, e.g. a simple search for sign changes followed by the process of iteration [see C. Dixon, *Numerical Analysis*, Blackie/Chambers]. However, it is convenient to note that the initial conditions in this example indicate that $X = \frac{3}{4}$ is a root of the cubic equation. Therefore, we write the cubic equation in the form

$$(X - \tfrac{3}{4})\{\tfrac{2}{3}\gamma X^2 + (\tfrac{1}{2}\gamma + 4)X + (\tfrac{3}{8}\gamma + 1)\} = 0$$

and determine the second and third roots. Also we examine

$$\ddot{x} = g - 4g(x-l)/l - \alpha(x-l)^2/m$$

$$= g\left(1 - 4X - \frac{\alpha l^2}{mg}X^2\right) = g(1 - 4X - \gamma X^2)$$

to find the positions of equilibrium, which are given by the roots of

$$\gamma X^2 + 4X - 1 = 0$$

The zeros of $\dot{x}$ and the zero of $\ddot{x}$ for various values of $\gamma = \alpha l^2/mg$ are presented in the table. If we use the information to help us to plot graphs of

$\gamma = \alpha l^2/mg$	Values of X for which $\dot{x}^2 = 0$			Values of X for which $\ddot{x} = 0$	
−5·0			0·750		
−4·0			0·750	0·500	0·500
−3·6	0·205	0·712	0·750	0·380	0·731
−3·55555556	0·1875	0·750	0·750	0·375	0·750
−3·5	0·168	0·750	0·796	0·369	0·773
−1·0	−0·173	0·750	5·42	0·268	3·73
−0·1	−0·243	0·750	59·5	0·252	39·7
0	−0·250	0·750		0·250	
0·1	−60·5	−0·257	0·750	−40·2	0·248
1·0	−6·43	−0·321	0·750	−4·24	0·236
5·5	−1·03	−0·811	0·750	−0·924	0·197
5·59244677	−0·911	−0·911	0·750	−0·911	0·196
5·6			0·750	−0·910	0·196
6·0			0·750	−0·860	0·194

$\dot{x}^2/gl$ against $X = (x-l)/l$ for various values of $\gamma = \alpha l^2/mg$, we are able to make the following deductions:

(i) when $\gamma < -\frac{32}{9}$, the particle falls for all time,

(ii) when $\gamma = -\frac{32}{9}$, the particle remains at its initial position, which is an equilibrium position, for all time,

(iii) when $-\frac{32}{9} < \gamma < (8+16\sqrt{7})/9$, the particle performs finite amplitude oscillations,

(iv) when $\gamma = (8+16\sqrt{7})/9$, the particle moves upwards and comes to rest at an equilibrium position, where it remains for all time,

(v) when $(8+16\sqrt{7})/9 < \gamma$, the particle moves upwards for all time.

We have encountered in this analysis situations that are different from the situations that arise when the spring obeys Hooke's Law. These new situations exist because the governing differential equation is non-linear.

A second possible replacement of Hooke's Law is

$$T = k(x-l)+\beta(x-l)^3$$

where k is the stiffness, l is the natural length and β is the parameter associated with the non-linear term. In this case the differential equation governing our illustrative problem is

$$m\ddot{x}+k(x-l)+\beta(x-l)^3 = mg$$

which is non-linear. We can obtain an energy equation, and we can search for equilibrium positions and the possibility of finite-amplitude oscillations. This work involves finding the zeros of polynomial equations of degrees three and four.

In this section we have obtained some qualitative information about the motion of a particle suspended from a fixed support by an elastic spring that obeys a non-linear generalization of Hooke's Law, e.g. the motion is, or is not, oscillatory. This has been possible, even though we have not had available any quantitative information, e.g. the explicit form of x in terms of t. We have employed some elementary ideas of phase plane analysis, the aim of which is the construction and the interpretation of graphs representing the relation between $\dot{x}$ and x for a variety of initial conditions [see W. E. Boyce, R. C. DiPrima, *Elementary Differential Equations and Boundary Value Problems*, 2nd ed., chapter 9, Wiley].

EXERCISES ON CHAPTER 8

1. A body is suspended from a fixed support by a light spring and is set in vertical motion. Show that the period of oscillation is

$$2\pi(e/g)^{1/2}$$

where e is the equilibrium extension produced by the weight of the attached body.

2. A light spiral spring has unstretched length l. One end of the spring is attached to a fixed support at O, while a body of mass m is attached to the other end of the spring so that the spring is vertical and extends a distance $\frac{1}{9}l$ when the body has been placed in the equilibrium position A. Calculate the stiffness of the spring. If the body is displaced a small distance d from A in the direction $\overrightarrow{OA}$ and released from rest, find the period of the subsequent motion and the speed of the body as it passes through the equilibrium position A.

3. The motion of a particle is governed by the differential equation

$$\ddot{x} = -4x$$

The conditions at $t = 0$ are $x = 2$ and $\dot{x} = 4$. Find the period and the amplitude of the oscillations. What is the first positive value of t for which $x = 0$?

4. A spring of natural length l would suffer extensions e_1 and e_2 respectively when supporting each of two particles P_1 and P_2 in equilibrium. If both particles are hanging in equilibrium and P_2 falls off, show that after time t the depth of P_1 below the upper end of the spring is

$$l+e_1+e_2\cos\{(g/e_1)^{1/2}t\}$$

provided $l+e_1 > e_2$.

5. A light string is carrying a particle P of mass M. When an extra particle Q of mass m $(M > m)$ is attached, the new equilibrium position is a distance d below the previous equilibrium position. If the particle Q is suddenly taken off, find an expression for the period of oscillations of the particle P. What is the tension in the string when the particle P is a distance D $(D < 2d)$ above the lowest point? Show that the speed of the particle P in that position is

$$\{(2d-D)Dmg/dM\}^{1/2}$$

6. To measure the modulus of elasticity λ of a light string of natural length l, an experimenter suspends from it a body of mass m and observes the frequency ν of oscillations about the position of equilibrium. Express λ in terms of l, m and ν.

If l and m may each be in error by one percent, and ν may be in error by two percent, what is the maximum possible percentage error in λ?

7. An elastic string AB of natural length l is fixed at A and is of length $2l$ if it carries a particle of mass M at rest at B. What is the string's modulus of elasticity?

A single particle of mass m is attached to B and is dropped from A. Show that the period of the subsequent motion is

$$2\left[\left(\frac{2l}{g}\right)^{1/2}+\left(\frac{ml}{Mg}\right)^{1/2}\left\{\pi-\cos^{-1}\left(\frac{m}{m+2M}\right)^{1/2}\right\}\right]$$

Find the distance between A and the lowest point reached by the particle. Confirm your answer by recalculating the distance by means of the energy equation.

8. A particle of mass m is attached to one end of an elastic string of unstretched length l and modulus of elasticity $2mg$. It hangs in equilibrium under gravity and the elastic restoring force of the string. Determine the particle's position of equilibrium relative to the fixed support.

The particle is set in motion from its equilibrium position so that it is moving towards the fixed support, and its initial speed is $(\frac{3}{2}gl)^{1/2}$. Prove that the string will become slack after a time $(l/2g)^{1/2} \sin^{-1}(3^{-1/2})$ and that the particle will rise for a further time $(l/g)^{1/2}$. What is the position of the particle at the end of this time?

3. A nylon climbing rope of length 35 metres is stretched in a laboratory experiment by a known applied force. The relation between the applied force F_A (measured in newtons) and the corresponding extension e (measured in metres) is given in the following table:

e	0	1	2	3	4	5	6	7	8	9	10
$F_A(e)$	0	1600	2400	3000	3600	4100	4600	5200	5700	6400	8000

Express the energy stored in the rope when it is extended by 10 metres as a definite integral and then use Simpson's rule to obtain an estimate of the value.

A climber of mass 64 kilograms is climbing on a vertical rock-face above the point to which he is securely attached by the rope of length 35 metres, whose characteristics are described above. The climber slips and falls freely. He is brought to rest for the first time by the action of his climbing rope (which does not break) when the rope has been extended by 10 metres. When the climber slipped, how high was he above the point on the rock-face to which his rope is attached?

Calculate the speed of the climber at the instant when the rope became taut, and estimate the average deceleration of the climber from that instant until he came to rest instantaneously.

10. Two light springs, each of natural length l, are joined by a small link of mass m. The whole system is stretched between two fixed points A and B, where A is at a distance $2l+h$ vertically above B. The upper spring has stiffness k_1 and the lower spring has stiffness k_2. Show that the link's equilibrium position is at a distance

$$\frac{mg+k_1 l+k_2(l+h)}{k_1+k_2}$$

below A. Verify that both springs are extended if $mg < k_1 h$. Determine the condition that guarantees that the link's equilibrium position is above B.

If the link is slightly displaced towards A and is released from rest, show that the subsequent motion is simple harmonic and find the period of the oscillations.

11. A particle of mass m moves along a straight line through a fixed point O under the action of a single force, which is directed towards O and is of magnitude $m\omega^2|\overrightarrow{OP}|$, where ω is a constant. It starts from rest at A, where $|\overrightarrow{OA}| = d$. Show that the particle has speed u when its displacement from O is x such that

$$u^2 = \omega^2(d^2 - x^2)$$

What is the particle's maximum distance from A?

12. A particle of mass m is attached to one end of a spring of natural length l and stiffness k, the other end of the spring being fixed to a point O on a smooth horizontal table. The particle is held on the table at a distance $\frac{3}{2}l$ from O and is then released. What is the shortest distance between the particle and the fixed point O? Show that the particle again passes through its starting point after time $2\pi(m/k)^{1/2}$.

13. A particle of mass m is attached to one end of an elastic string of natural length l and modulus of elasticity λ, the other end of the string being fixed at a point O on a smooth horizontal table. The particle is held on the table at a distance $\frac{3}{2}l$ from O and is then released. How far does the particle travel before it is again at rest? Show that the particle returns to its starting point after time $(2\pi+8)(ml/\lambda)^{1/2}$.

14. A particle P of mass m is attached by two elastic strings to two fixed points A and B on a smooth horizontal table where $|\overrightarrow{AB}| = 4l$. The string AP has natural length l and modulus λ_1, and the string PB has natural length $2l$ and modulus λ_2. Find the equilibrium position of the particle, and prove that the period of oscillation along the line AB is

$$2\pi\left(\frac{2ml}{2\lambda_1+\lambda_2}\right)^{1/2}$$

Does the string AP become slack if the particle is released from rest at the mid-point of AB?

15. An elastic string of natural length l and modulus of elasticity λ is stretched, and its ends are attached to two fixed points on a smooth horizontal table. A particle of mass m is tied to a point dividing the string in the ratio $n:1$. Find the period of oscillation in the line of the string when both parts of the string are extended throughout the motion. What value of n gives the maximum period?

16. In an experiment to test car seat belts, a seat with a belted dummy is at rest until it is suddenly moved backwards with a horizontal acceleration $100\,\text{m s}^{-2}$. The belt breaks if the tension in it reaches 9000 N. Consider a mathematical model in which we ignore gravity and regard the belted dummy as a particle of mass 60 kg attached to a movable point (representing the seat) by a spring of natural length 0·5 m and stiffness $400\,\text{N m}^{-1}$. Show that the belt must break if the initial length of the spring is its natural length. For what length of time is the dummy attached to the seat, and what is the speed of the dummy when the belt breaks?

17. An elastic string of natural length $2l$ and modulus of elasticity λ is stretched between two fixed points A and B on a smooth horizontal table, the distance between A and B being $4l$. A particle of mass m is attached to the mid-point of the string. Find the period of small oscillations if the particle is moved along the table a small distance away from its equilibrium position in a direction perpendicular to the direction $\overrightarrow{AB}$ and is released from rest. What is the significance of the assumption regarding the amplitude of the oscillations?

18. A particle of mass m is suspended from a fixed support by an extensible string of natural length l and modulus of elasticity λ. The particle moves in a horizontal circle with angular speed ω, maintaining a constant distance L from the point of suspension. If θ is the angle that the string makes with the downward vertical, show that

$$\lambda(L-l)\cos\theta = mgl \quad \text{and} \quad L\cos\theta = g/\omega^2$$

The extensible string breaks if the tension reaches $6mg$. Find the value of λ if the string breaks when $\omega^2 = 4g/l$.

19. A body of mass m is placed on a rough horizontal table, the coefficient of kinematic friction being μ. It is attached by a spring of natural length l and stiffness k to a fixed point O on the table. Initially the body is released from rest at a point whose distance from O is $2l$. Assume that the body starts to move towards O and show that the equation of motion has the form

$$m\ddot{x}+kx = \begin{cases} kl+\mu mg & \dot{x}<0 \\ kl-\mu mg & \dot{x}>0 \end{cases}$$

Hence deduce that the body next comes to rest at a point whose distance from O is $2\mu mg/k$.

What is the condition that guarantees that the body moves from its initial position?

20. A and B are two points on the same horizontal level. Two light identical elastic strings, each of natural length l, have one end attached to A and B respectively and the other ends to a small link of mass m. The strings support the link in equilibrium at C, where the distance between C and the line AB is l and the extension of each string is l. What is the modulus of elasticity?

The link is given a small vertical displacement away from its equilibrium position C and released. Show that the period of small-amplitude oscillations is $4\pi(l/5g)^{1/2}$.

If the link is released from rest a small distance d below C, what is its speed when it passes through C?

21. A small bead of mass m can slide on a smooth circular hoop of radius R. The hoop is fixed in a vertical plane and the bead is attached to the lowest point of the hoop by an extensible string of natural length R and modulus of elasticity mg. The bead is projected from the highest point of the hoop with speed $(\frac{1}{2}gR)^{1/2}$.

Find the speed of the bead when the string becomes slack. Show that bead passes through the lowest point of the hoop with speed $(\frac{11}{2}gR)^{1/2}$.

22. The motion of a particle is governed by the differential equation

$$\ddot{x}+7x+6x^2 = 0$$

Where are the equilibrium positions? If the initial conditions are

$$\dot{x} = \tfrac{3}{2}, \quad x = 0 \quad \text{at} \quad t = 0$$

show that the particle performs finite-amplitude oscillations such that $-\frac{3}{4} \leqslant x \leqslant \frac{1}{2}$.

Orbits 9

9.1 Introduction

Astronomy has interested man for centuries. The planets (Mercury, Venus, Earth, Mars, Jupiter, Saturn, Uranus, Neptune and Pluto) have been studied extensively. About eighty years prior to Newton's statements of the laws of motion and the law of gravity, Johannes Kepler (1571–1630) formulated his laws of planetary motion. Kepler's laws are empirical. Here is a convenient statement of them.

(i) Every planet moves in an orbit which is an ellipse with the Sun at one focus.
(ii) The radius vector drawn from the Sun to any planet sweeps out equal areas in equal times.
(iii) The squares of the periods of revolution of the planets are proportional to the cubes of the semi-major axes of their orbits.

Spaceflight is a subject of current interest. Satellites orbiting around the Earth allow television signals to be transmitted between ground stations that are thousands of kilometres apart. Astronauts have landed on the Moon. Man is able to carry out experiments in a space-laboratory orbiting around the Earth. Unmanned spacecraft have been sent from Earth to neighbouring planets. Interplanetary flight by man will be achieved in the foreseeable future.

In this chapter we shall introduce and examine a simple model of a planet moving relative to the Sun, or a satellite moving relative to a planet. We shall use two particles, one of which is fixed relative to an inertial frame of reference, and we shall adopt Newton's law of gravitation (introduced in Section 3.3). The particle moving relative to the inertial frame of reference experiences a single force, namely the gravitational force of attraction between the two particles. When we are using this model to examine the motion of a planet (e.g. Mercury) around the Sun, we are ignoring the other planets and satellites. We can apply this model to the problem of a man-made satellite orbiting around the Earth, provided we note that we are ignoring the Sun, the other planets and their satellites, the Moon, the oblateness of the Earth and the resistive effects of the Earth's atmosphere. In addition, there are the assumptions that one body (e.g. the Sun or the Earth) is fixed relative to an inertial frame of reference and that both bodies are representable by particles.

9.2 Equation of motion

A particle S of mass M is fixed at the origin of an inertial frame of reference. A particle P of mass m is free to move under the gravitational force of attraction. Let $\boldsymbol{r}$ denote the position vector of P relative to S. The equation of motion for the particle P is

$$m\ddot{\boldsymbol{r}} = -\frac{GMm\boldsymbol{r}}{r^3}$$

We encountered this equation in chapter 3, where we obtained a solution in a special case (straight-line motion of P away from S). Let us now examine all possible solutions.

We note that

$$\boldsymbol{r}\times(m\ddot{\boldsymbol{r}}) = -\frac{GMm}{r^3}\boldsymbol{r}\times\boldsymbol{r} = \boldsymbol{0}$$

Introducing $\mathbf{L}$ to denote the angular momentum of the particle P about the origin of the inertial frame of reference, we define

$$\mathbf{L} = \boldsymbol{r}\times(m\dot{\boldsymbol{r}}) = m(\boldsymbol{r}\times\dot{\boldsymbol{r}})$$

and we deduce that

$$\dot{\mathbf{L}} = \dot{\boldsymbol{r}}\times(m\dot{\boldsymbol{r}})+\boldsymbol{r}\times(m\ddot{\boldsymbol{r}}) = \boldsymbol{r}\times(m\ddot{\boldsymbol{r}}) = \boldsymbol{0}$$

Hence $\mathbf{L}$ is constant, its constant value being determined by initial conditions at $t = 0$, say. Further,

$$\boldsymbol{r}.\mathbf{L} = m\boldsymbol{r}.(\boldsymbol{r}\times\dot{\boldsymbol{r}}) = m\dot{\boldsymbol{r}}.(\boldsymbol{r}\times\boldsymbol{r}) = 0$$

Therefore the motion of P is confined to a plane, the normal to the plane having the direction of the constant angular-momentum vector. We introduce plane-polar coordinates (r, ϕ) to describe the motion of the particle P relative to S, which is at the origin of the coordinate system. Thus we have

$$\boldsymbol{r} = r\boldsymbol{e}_r$$

$$\dot{\boldsymbol{r}} = \dot{r}\boldsymbol{e}_r + r\dot{\phi}\boldsymbol{e}_\phi$$

$$\ddot{\boldsymbol{r}} = (\ddot{r}-r\dot{\phi}^2)\boldsymbol{e}_r + (r\ddot{\phi}+2\dot{r}\dot{\phi})\boldsymbol{e}_\phi$$

The equation of motion reduces to the pair of governing differential equations, namely

$$m(\ddot{r} - r\dot{\phi}^2) = -\frac{GMm}{r^2}$$

and

$$m(r\ddot{\phi} + 2\dot{r}\dot{\phi}) = 0$$

In terms of this representation of $\boldsymbol{r}$, we see that

$$\mathbf{L} = mr^2\dot{\phi}\boldsymbol{e}_r \times \boldsymbol{e}_\phi = mr^2\dot{\phi}\boldsymbol{k}$$

where $\boldsymbol{k} = \boldsymbol{e}_r \times \boldsymbol{e}_\phi$ and that

$$\dot{\mathbf{L}} = (2mr\dot{r}\dot{\phi} + mr^2\ddot{\phi})\boldsymbol{k} = mr(r\ddot{\phi} + 2\dot{r}\dot{\phi})\boldsymbol{k}$$

The second of the governing differential equations shows that

$$\dot{\mathbf{L}} = \boldsymbol{0}$$

which is a statement of the conservation of angular momentum about the origin of the inertial frame of reference. Hence we may write

$$r^2\dot{\phi} = \mathbf{L}.\boldsymbol{k}/m = L_0 \text{ (say)}$$

where L_0 is a constant determined by the initial conditions. L_0 is the (initial) value of the component of the angular-momentum vector per unit mass. Using the result

$$r\dot{\phi}^2 = L_0^2/r^3$$

we may rewrite the first of the governing differential equations in the form

$$\ddot{r} - \frac{L_0^2}{r^3} = -\frac{GM}{r^2}$$

This equation and the initial conditions determine r in terms of t. Then the equation

$$\dot{\phi} = L_0/r^2$$

and the initial conditions determine ϕ in terms of t. In general, it is a difficult task to determine explicit relations for r and ϕ in terms of t.

9.3 Energy equation

Noting that $\ddot{r} = d(\frac{1}{2}\dot{r}^2)/dr$ and integrating the equation

$$\ddot{r} - \frac{L_0}{r^3} = -\frac{GM}{r^2}$$

with respect to r, we find that

$$\tfrac{1}{2}\dot{r}^2 + \tfrac{1}{2}\frac{L_0^2}{r^2} = \frac{GM}{r} + \text{constant}$$

where the constant is determined by the initial conditions. An equivalent way of obtaining this result is to integrate

$$\left(\ddot{r} - \frac{L_0}{r^3}\right)\dot{r} = -\frac{GM}{r^2}\dot{r}$$

with respect to time. This is essentially the same as the following approach.

If we form the scalar product of the equation of motion with the velocity vector, we obtain

$$m\ddot{\mathbf{r}}\,.\,\dot{\mathbf{r}} = -\frac{GMm}{r^3}\,\mathbf{r}\,.\,\dot{\mathbf{r}}$$

An integration with respect to time gives

$$\int \frac{d}{dt}\left\{\tfrac{1}{2}m\dot{\mathbf{r}}\,.\,\dot{\mathbf{r}} - \frac{GMm}{r}\right\}dt = \text{constant}$$

i.e. $\tfrac{1}{2}m\dot{\mathbf{r}}\,.\,\dot{\mathbf{r}} - (GMm/r) = \text{constant}.$

The first term of this equation is the kinetic energy of the particle, and the second term is the particle's potential energy associated with the gravitational force of attraction. The inverse-square gravitational field of force

$$\mathbf{F} = -\frac{GMm}{r^3}\,\mathbf{r}$$

is conservative, cf. the vector form of Hooke's law in Section 8.4. Hence we write

$$E_k = \tfrac{1}{2}m\dot{\mathbf{r}}\,.\,\dot{\mathbf{r}} = \tfrac{1}{2}m(\dot{r}^2 + r^2\dot{\phi}^2) = \tfrac{1}{2}m(\dot{r}^2 + L_0^2/r^2)$$

and

$$E_p = -GMm/r$$

The conservation of energy,

$$E_k + E_p = \text{constant}$$

applies to our present study. This gives us a relation for $\dot{r}$ in terms of r, which we may attempt to solve to obtain an explicit relation for r in terms of t.

9.4 Linear motion and circular orbits

Let us investigate whether it is possible for the particle P to travel along a straight line or around a circular path. We know from our earlier investigations in Section 3.4 that linear motion is possible.

Suppose that $\phi = \phi_0$ for all time, then the governing differential equations reduce to

$$\ddot{r} = -\frac{GM}{r^2}$$

and a trivial identity. The energy equation becomes

$$\tfrac{1}{2}\dot{r}^2 - \frac{GM}{r} = \text{constant}$$

Initial conditions that lead to this special case of linear motion are

$$\mathbf{r} = R\mathbf{e}_r \quad \text{and} \quad \dot{\mathbf{r}} = u_0\,\mathbf{e}_r \quad \text{at} \quad t = 0$$

i.e.

$$r = R, \quad \phi = \phi_0, \quad \dot{r} = u_0, \quad \dot{\phi} = 0 \quad \text{at} \quad t = 0.$$

Then $L_0 = 0$ and

$$\dot{r}^2 = u_0^2 + 2GM\left(\frac{1}{r} - \frac{1}{R}\right)$$

As $r \to \infty$, $\dot{r}^2 \to u_0^2 - 2GM/R$ provided $u_0^2 \geqslant 2GM/R$. If the particle S is representing a spherical planet of mass M and radius R, we say that $(2GM/R)^{1/2}$ is the escape speed. It is the minimum initial speed necessary for the body represented by the particle P to possess in order to leave the surface of the planet and never to return. It is convenient to note that

$$GM/R^2 = g$$

where g is the acceleration due to gravity at the surface of the planet. Hence, in particular,

$$\dot{r}^2 = u_0^2 + 2gR\left(\frac{R}{r} - 1\right)$$

and the escape speed equals $(2gR)^{1/2}$.

EXAMPLE

A body is projected vertically upwards with speed $(gR)^{1/2}$ from the surface of the Earth, where g is the acceleration due to gravity at the Earth's surface and R is the radius of the Earth. Verify that the body achieves a height R above the Earth and calculate the time taken to reach this height.

It follows from the conservation of energy that

$$\dot{r}^2 = gR\left(\frac{2R}{r} - 1\right)$$

Hence $\dot{r} = 0$ when $r = 2R$. During the upward motion from $r = R$ to $r = 2R$,

$$\dot{r} = \{gR(2R - r)/r\}^{1/2}$$

Therefore

$$\left(\frac{r}{2R - r}\right)^{1/2} \dot{r} = (gR)^{1/2}$$

Suppose $r = R$, $\dot{r} = (gR)^{1/2}$ at $t = 0$ and $r = 2R$, $\dot{r} = 0$ at $t = T$. Integration of the differential equation with respect to time leads to

$$\int_0^T \left(\frac{r}{2R-r}\right)^{1/2} \dot{r}\,dt = \int_R^{2R} \left(\frac{r}{2R-r}\right)^{1/2} dr = (gR)^{1/2} \int_0^T dt = (gR)^{1/2} T$$

Substituting $r = 2R\sin^2\theta$ with $\theta \in [\frac{1}{4}\pi, \frac{1}{2}\pi]$, we find that

$$T = \frac{1}{(gR)^{1/2}} \int_{\pi/4}^{\pi/2} \left(\frac{2R\sin^2\theta}{2R\cos^2\theta}\right)^{1/2} 4R\sin\theta\cos\theta\,d\theta$$

$$= 2\left(\frac{R}{g}\right)^{1/2} \int_{\pi/4}^{\pi/2} (1-\cos 2\theta)\,d\theta = \left(\frac{R}{g}\right)^{1/2} (\tfrac{1}{2}\pi + 1)$$

The body takes about 34·5 minutes to reach its maximum height ($r = 2R$) above the surface of the Earth. It takes the same time to return to Earth.

Let us re-examine this example when the initial speed equals $(2gR)^{1/2}$. In this case the energy equation becomes

$$\dot{r}^2 = 2gR^2/r$$

and during the upward motion

$$r^{1/2}\dot{r} = (2gR^2)^{1/2}$$

Suppose that $r = R$ at $t = 0$ and $r = R + H$ at $t = T$. Then we see that

$$\int_0^T r^{1/2}\dot{r}\,dt = \int_R^{R+H} r^{1/2}\,dr = (2gR^2)^{1/2} T$$

and

$$T = \frac{1}{(2gR^2)^{1/2}} \tfrac{2}{3}\{(R+H)^{3/2} - R^{3/2}\}$$

In particular, when $H = R$

$$T = \left(\frac{R}{g}\right)^{1/2} \left(\frac{4 - 2^{1/2}}{3}\right)$$

Hence the time taken to travel from $r = R$ to $r = 2R$ is about 11·6 minutes. It is important to note that $T \to \infty$ as $H \to \infty$.

What is the time taken to travel from $r = R$ to $r = 2R$ when the initial speed is greater than $(2gR)^{1/2}$? Suppose that the initial speed equals $(\frac{5}{2}gR)^{1/2}$, for example. The energy equation leads to

$$\dot{r}^2 = gR\left(\frac{2R}{r} + \tfrac{1}{2}\right)$$

and during the upward motion

$$\left(\frac{2r}{4R+r}\right)^{1/2} \dot{r} = (gR)^{1/2}$$

Suppose that $r = R$ at $t = 0$ and $r = 2R$ at $t = T$. Then we have

$$\int_0^T \left(\frac{2r}{4R+r}\right)^{1/2} \dot{r}\,dt = \int_R^{2R} \left(\frac{2r}{4R+r}\right)^{1/2} dr = (gR)^{1/2} T$$

Substituting $r = 4R\sinh^2 u$, where $u \in [u_1, u_2]$ with $u_1 = \sinh^{-1}(1/2)$ and $u_2 = \sinh^{-1}(1/2^{1/2})$, we find that

$$T = \frac{1}{(gR)^{1/2}} \int_{u_1}^{u_2} \left(\frac{8R\sinh^2 u}{4R\cosh^2 u}\right)^{1/2} 8R\sinh u\cosh u\,du$$

$$= 4\left(\frac{2R}{g}\right)^{1/2} \int_{u_1}^{u_2} (\cosh 2u - 1)\,du$$

$$= 4\left(\frac{2R}{g}\right)^{1/2} \left\{\frac{3^{1/2}}{2} - \frac{5^{1/2}}{4} - u_2 + u_1\right\}$$

$$= 4\left(\frac{2R}{g}\right)^{1/2} \left\{\frac{3^{1/2}}{2} - \frac{5^{1/2}}{4} - \ln\left(\frac{1+3^{1/2}}{2^{1/2}}\right) + \ln\left(\frac{1+5^{1/2}}{2}\right)\right\}$$

Hence the time taken to travel from $r = R$ to $r = 2R$ is about 9·9 minutes.

Suppose that $r = r_0$ for all time. In this special case of circular motion the governing differential equations are

$$r_0\dot{\phi}^2 = \frac{GM}{r_0^2} \quad \text{and} \quad r_0\ddot{\phi} = 0$$

Therefore $\dot{\phi}$ has the constant value $\pm(GM/r_0^3)^{1/2}$. We shall assume that ϕ is increasing with time and we shall select the positive sign. In this case $L_0 = (GMr_0)^{1/2}$. The appropriate form of the energy equation is

$$\tfrac{1}{2}mr_0^2\dot{\phi}^2 - \frac{GMm}{r_0} = \text{constant}$$

which confirms that $\dot{\phi}$ is constant. Suitable initial conditions that produce this special case of circular motion are

$$\mathbf{r} = r_0\mathbf{e}_r \quad \text{and} \quad \dot{\mathbf{r}} = u_0\mathbf{e} \quad \text{at} \quad t = 0$$

i.e. $r = r_0, \phi = 0, \dot{r} = 0, \dot{\phi} = u_0/r_0$ at $t = 0$. Here we must have $r_0^3\dot{\phi}^2 = GM$, i.e. $r_0u_0^2 = GM$. If we use $GM = gR^2$ and set $r_0 = R+H$, we have

$$u_0^2 = \frac{gR^2}{R+H}$$

and

$$\dot{\phi} = \left\{\frac{gR^2}{(R+H)^3}\right\}^{1/2} = \frac{R}{R+H}\left(\frac{g}{R+H}\right)^{1/2} = \frac{u_0}{R+H}$$

The period of revolution T is $2\pi/\dot{\phi}$, i.e.

$$T = \frac{2\pi(R+H)}{R}\left(\frac{R+H}{g}\right)^{1/2}.$$

In this special case we are able to write down the explicit relations for r and ϕ in terms of t, namely

$$r = R+H \quad \text{and} \quad \phi = \left\{\frac{gR^2}{(R+H)^3}\right\}^{1/2} t$$

EXAMPLE

A communications satellite is to be stationed over the equator of the Earth so that it will appear (to an observer at the equator) to be stationary in the sky. Estimate the height of the satellite.

The isosynchronous satellite has the same angular speed as the Earth has about its axis, i.e. its period of revolution is one day or, more precisely, 86 164 seconds. Therefore we have to solve

$$\frac{2\pi}{(gR^2)^{1/2}}(R+H)^{3/2} = 86\,164$$

for H. If we use the equatorial radius and the equatorial value of the acceleration due to gravity, namely 6378 kilometres and 9·78 metres per second per second, we find that the estimated height above the surface of the Earth is 35 800 kilometres. If we take the period of revolution to be 86 400 seconds, the radius of the Earth to be 6371 kilometres and the acceleration due to gravity to be 9·81 metres per second per second, the calculated value of the height is 35 900 kilometres. The tabulated value of the height of the isosynchronous satellite above the Earth is 35 770 kilometres.

We can estimate the minimum number of isosynchronous satellites that have to be positioned so that every location on the equator is in the view of at least one satellite. Consider the arc of the equator that is in the view of a given isosynchronous satellite. This arc subtends an angle Φ at the centre of the Earth, where

$$\cos\left(\tfrac{1}{2}\Phi\right) = \frac{R}{R+H} = 0{\cdot}1516$$

i.e. Φ equals 2·84 radians. Noting that

$$2\Phi < 2\pi < 3\Phi$$

we deduce that three isosynchronous satellites are required. These three satellites would permit communications between most locations situated between latitude 81° north and latitude 81° south; these are overestimates because we have not allowed for the oblateness of the Earth and for the shape of the surface area in direct view of each satellite (cf. the intersection of a cone and a sphere).

9.5 General orbits

We seek a general solution of the differential equations

$$\ddot{r} - \frac{L_0^2}{r^3} = -\frac{GM}{r^2} \quad \text{and} \quad \dot{\phi} = \frac{L_0}{r^2}$$

where L_0 is a constant determined by the initial conditions. We shall explore the possibility of expressing r in terms of ϕ.

Using

$$\dot{r} = \frac{dr}{d\phi}\dot{\phi} = \frac{L_0}{r^2}\frac{dr}{d\phi}$$

and

$$\ddot{r} = \left\{\frac{L_0}{r^2}\frac{d^2r}{d\phi^2} - \frac{2L_0}{r^3}\left(\frac{dr}{d\phi}\right)^2\right\}\dot{\phi} = \frac{L_0^2}{r^4}\frac{d^2r}{d\phi^2} - \frac{2L_0^2}{r^5}\left(\frac{dr}{d\phi}\right)^2$$

we find that the first of the differential equations becomes

$$\frac{d^2r}{d\phi^2} - \frac{2}{r}\left(\frac{dr}{d\phi}\right)^2 = -\frac{GMr^2}{L_0^2}$$

which has no attractive features. However, we are able to make some progress by considering $1/r$ rather than r. It is customary to set $u = (1/r)$. (In this Section u represents the reciprocal of r and is not a speed or a velocity component.) Then

$$\dot{r} = -\frac{1}{u^2}\frac{du}{d\phi}\dot{\phi} = -L_0\frac{du}{d\phi}$$

and

$$\ddot{r} = -L_0\frac{d^2u}{d\phi^2}\dot{\phi} = -L_0^2u^2\frac{d^2u}{d\phi^2}$$

The first differential equation transforms into

$$\frac{d^2u}{d\phi^2} + u = \frac{GM}{L_0^2}$$

which is a second-order linear differential equation with a constant inhomogeneous term. Therefore the general solution, which is the sum of the complementary function and a particular integral, is

$$u = A\cos\phi + B\sin\phi + \frac{GM}{L_0^2}$$

where A and B are determined by the initial conditions. In this way we obtain an explicit expression for r in terms of ϕ.

We can write the energy equation, derived in Section 9.3, in the form

$$\frac{1}{2}\left(\dot{r}^2 + \frac{L_0^2}{r^2}\right) - \frac{GM}{r} = E_0$$

where E_0 is a constant that equals the initial value of the total energy per unit mass. Using

$$\dot{r} = \frac{L_0}{r^2}\frac{dr}{d\phi}$$

we see that the energy equation gives

$$\left\{\frac{L_0^2}{r^2(2E_0r^2 + 2GMr - L_0^2)}\right\}^{1/2}\frac{dr}{d\phi} = \pm 1$$

An integration with respect to ϕ leads to an integral with respect to r that is manageable provided we set $r = 1/u$. We achieve the same result by substituting

$$r = \frac{1}{u} \quad \text{and} \quad \dot{r} = -L_0 \frac{du}{d\phi}$$

in the energy equation and integrating with respect to ϕ. Thus

$$\left\{ \frac{L_0^2}{2E_0 + 2GMu - L_0^2 u^2} \right\}^{1/2} \frac{du}{d\phi} = \pm 1$$

and

$$u = \pm \left\{ \left(\frac{GM}{L_0^2} \right)^2 + \frac{2E_0}{L_0^2} \right\}^{1/2} \sin(\phi + C) + \frac{GM}{L_0^2}$$

where C is determined by the initial conditions. This manipulation involves an inverse sine integral [see J. Hunter, *Calculus*, Blackie/Chambers]. We recognize that this result agrees with the general solution of the differential equation

$$\frac{d^2u}{d\phi^2} + u = \frac{GM}{L_0^2}$$

It is much easier to solve this differential equation than to manipulate the energy equation.

Suppose that the initial conditions are

$$r = r_0, \quad \dot{r} = 0, \quad \phi = 0, \quad \dot{\phi} = L_0/r_0^2 \quad \text{at} \quad t = 0.$$

It follows that

$$u = \frac{1}{r_0}, \quad \frac{du}{d\phi} = 0, \quad \phi = 0, \quad \dot{\phi} = L_0/r_0^2 \quad \text{at} \quad t = 0.$$

The required solution of

$$\frac{d^2u}{d\phi^2} + u = \frac{GM}{L_0^2}$$

is

$$u = A\cos\phi + B\sin\phi + \frac{GM}{L_0^2}$$

where

$$\frac{1}{r_0} = A + \frac{GM}{L_0^2} \quad \text{and} \quad 0 = B, \quad \text{i.e.}$$

$$u = \left(\frac{1}{r_0} - \frac{GM}{L_0^2} \right) \cos\phi + \frac{GM}{L_0^2}$$

or

$$r = \frac{L_0^2/GM}{1 + (L_0^2/GMr_0 - 1)\cos\phi}$$

In this case, we see that the energy equation and the initial conditions lead to

$$\frac{1}{2}\frac{L_0^2}{r_0^2} - \frac{GM}{r_0} = E_0$$

and that

$$\left(\frac{GM}{L_0^2}\right)^2 + \frac{2E_0}{L_0^2} = \left(\frac{GM}{L_0^2} - \frac{1}{r_0}\right)^2$$

i.e.

$$E_0 = \frac{1}{2}\left(\frac{GM}{L_0}\right)^2 \{(L_0^2/GMr_0 - 1)^2 - 1\}$$

It is convenient to introduce some notation. We shall set in this case

$$|L_0^2/GMr_0 - 1| = e \quad \text{and} \quad L_0^2/GM = l.$$

Then we have

$$r = \frac{l}{1 \pm e\cos\phi} \quad \text{and} \quad E_0 = \frac{GM}{2l}(e^2 - 1)$$

the first equation being the equation of the orbit of particle P relative to the fixed particle S. The equation of the orbit is expressed in polar coordinates, r and ϕ, the origin of the coordinate system being at S. The positive sign is appropriate if $L_0^2 > GMr_0$, and the negative sign is appropriate if $L_0^2 < GMr_0$. The second equation expresses E_0, the constant total energy per unit mass, in terms of the two new parameters, e and l. We note that L_0, the constant angular momentum per unit mass, equals $(GMl)^{1/2}$.

A major topic is the description of the geometrical properties of the orbit of the particle P about the fixed particle S. The equation

$$r = \frac{l}{1 + e\cos\phi}$$

is the polar equation of a conic (e.g. an ellipse, a parabola, a hyperbola) [see J. Hunter, *Analytic Geometry and Vectors*, Blackie/Chambers]. We shall discuss the polar equation of a conic in the next section and examine elliptic, parabolic and hyperbolic orbits in subsequent sections.

9.6 Polar equation of a conic

A conic (or conic section) is a plane curve characterized by the focus-directrix property. The focus is a fixed point, S (say), and the directrix is a given straight line which does not pass through S. Let P be a point of the plane determined by the focus and the directrix, and let M be the projection of P on the directrix. A set of points

$$\{P : |\overrightarrow{PS}| = e|\overrightarrow{PM}|, e > 0\}$$

is called a conic. The positive real number e is called the eccentricity of the conic. The conic is an ellipse if $e < 1$, a parabola if $e = 1$ and a hyperbola if $e > 1$ [see J. Hunter, *Analytic Geometry and Vectors*, Blackie/Chambers].

It is usual to introduce cartesian coordinates and obtain the canonical equations, namely

$$\frac{x^2}{a^2} + \frac{y^2}{b^2} = 1, \quad y^2 = 4ax, \quad \frac{x^2}{a^2} - \frac{y^2}{b^2} = 1.$$

Let us summarize the results.

(i) *Ellipse* $e < 1$
The focus has the cartesian coordinates $(ae, 0)$ and the directrix is the line $x = a/e$. (The ellipse has a second focus $(-ae, 0)$ and a corresponding directrix $x = -a/e$.) The canonical equation is

$$\frac{x^2}{a^2} + \frac{y^2}{b^2} = 1$$

where $b = a(1-e^2)^{1/2}$, the definition of b following from the focus-directrix property. The ellipse is a closed curve.

(ii) *Parabola* $e = 1$
The focus has the cartesian coordinates $(a, 0)$ and the directrix is the line $x = -a$. The canonical equation is $y^2 = 4ax$.

(iii) *Hyperbola* $e > 1$
The focus has the cartesian coordinates $(ae, 0)$ and the directrix is the line $x = a/e$. (The hyperbola has a second focus $(-ae, 0)$ and a corresponding directrix $x = -a/e$.) The canonical equation is

$$\frac{x^2}{a^2} - \frac{y^2}{b^2} = 1$$

where $b = a(e^2-1)^{1/2}$, the definition of b following from the focus-directrix property. The hyperbola has two branches.

To obtain the polar equation of a conic, we introduce plane-polar coordinates (r, ϕ) whose origin is the focus S. We set

$$x = ae + r\cos\phi \quad \text{and} \quad y = r\sin\phi.$$

(i) *Ellipse* $e < 1$

$$|\overrightarrow{PS}| = r \quad \text{and} \quad e|\overrightarrow{PM}| = e(a/e - x) = a - ex.$$

Thus the polar equation is

$$r = \frac{a(1-e^2)}{1+e\cos\phi}$$

(ii) *Parabola* $e = 1$

$$|\vec{PS}| = r \quad \text{and} \quad e|\vec{PM}| = a+x.$$

Thus the polar equation is

$$r = \frac{2a}{1-\cos\phi}$$

(iii) *Hyperbola* $e > 0$

For the branch nearer the focus S

$$|\vec{PS}| = r, \quad e|\vec{PM}| = e(x-a/e) = ex-a$$

and the polar equation is

$$r = \frac{a(e^2-1)}{1-e\cos\phi}$$

For the second branch,

$$|\vec{PS}| = r, \quad e|\vec{PM}| = e(a/e-x) = a-ex$$

and the polar equation is

$$r = -\frac{a(e^2-1)}{1+e\cos\phi}$$

A latus rectum is the chord through a focus that is parallel to the directrix. We denote its length by $2l$, i.e. l is the length of a semi-latus rectum. We see from the polar equations (or from the canonical equations) that

$$l = \begin{cases} a(1-e^2) = b^2/a & \text{ellipse} \\ 2a & \text{parabola} \\ a(e^2-1) = b^2/a & \text{hyperbola} \end{cases}$$

Thus we may write the canonical equations in the forms

Ellipse $e < 1$ $\qquad r = \dfrac{l}{1+e\cos\phi}$

Parabola $e = 1$ $\qquad r = \dfrac{l}{1-\cos\phi}$

Hyperbola $e > 1$ $\qquad r = \dfrac{l}{1-e\cos\phi}$ and $r = \dfrac{-l}{1+e\cos\phi}$

In some applications it is convenient to introduce polar coordinates (r, ϕ) defined by

$$x = ae - r\cos\phi \quad \text{and} \quad y = r\sin\phi .$$

The polar equations appropriate to this definition are

Ellipse $e < 1$ $\qquad r = \dfrac{l}{1 - e\cos\phi}$

Parabola $e = 1$ $\qquad r = \dfrac{l}{1 + \cos\phi}$

Hyperbola $e > 1$ $\qquad r = \dfrac{l}{1 + e\cos\phi}$ and $r = \dfrac{-l}{1 - e\cos\phi}$

9.7 Elliptic orbits

We are in a position to recognize that the orbit appropriate to the initial conditions specified in Section 9.5 is elliptic if

$$|L_0^2/GMr_0 - 1| = e < 1$$

This condition gives

$$0 < L_0^2 < 2GMr_0$$

This is equivalent to saying that $E_0 < 0$. In Section 9.4 we have considered the special case in which $L_0^2 = GMr_0$ and $e = 0$, i.e. the orbit is circular. Elliptic orbits are the only closed orbits to be associated with the inverse-square law of attraction. They are particularly important in connection with studies of the solar system. If a body were moving on a parabolic or hyperbolic path, it would eventually become outside the influence of the Sun. Our model predicts that all the planets have elliptic orbits with the Sun situated at a focus (cf. Kepler's first law).

Let us work out details when $L_0^2 = \frac{1}{2}GMr_0$. In this case $E_0 = -\frac{3}{4}GM/r_0$, $e = \frac{1}{2}$ and $l = \frac{1}{2}r_0$. The polar equation of the ellipse is

$$r = \frac{\frac{1}{2}r_0}{1 - \frac{1}{2}\cos\phi} = \frac{r_0}{2 - \cos\phi}$$

We deduce that

$$\dot{r} = \frac{-r_0\sin\phi}{(2 - \cos\phi)^2}\,\dot{\phi} = -\left(\frac{GM}{2r_0}\right)^{1/2}\sin\phi$$

and that $\dot{r} = 0$ when $\sin\phi = 0$. When $\phi = 0$, $r = r_0$ and $\dot{r} = 0$. When $\phi = \pi$, $r = \frac{1}{3}r_0$ and $\dot{r} = 0$. It follows that $a = \frac{1}{2}(r_0 + \frac{1}{3}r_0) = \frac{2}{3}r_0$ and $b = \frac{2}{3}r_0(1 - \frac{1}{4})^{1/2}$ $= r_0/3^{1/2}$.

A point of an orbit at which $\dot{r} = 0$ is called an *apse*. The velocity vector is perpendicular to the position vector at an apse (because $\dot{\boldsymbol{r}}.\boldsymbol{r} = \dot{r}r = 0$ at an apse). In the case of a planet moving round the Sun, the point of the planet's orbit closest to the Sun is called the *perihelion* and the point of the orbit farthest from the Sun is called the *aphelion*. In the case of a satellite (e.g. the Moon or a space laboratory) moving round the Earth, the point of the satellite's orbit closest to the Earth is called the *perigee* and the point of the orbit farthest from the Earth is called the *apogee*.

We may deduce from the energy equation that the speed of the particle has a stationary valve at an apse. Hence the conservation of angular momentum indicates that the speed takes its maximum value at the point of closest approach (the perihelion or the perigee) and takes its minimum value at the other apse (the aphelion or the apogee). In the particular elliptic orbit being studied, the maximum speed is $3(GM/2r_0)^{1/2}$ at $(\frac{1}{3}r_0, \pi)$ and the minimum speed is $(GM/2r_0)^{1/2}$, the initial speed, at $(r_0, 0)$.

Let T denote the period of rotation, i.e. the time taken by the particle to move once around the elliptic orbit. Using

$$r^2\dot{\phi} = L_0 = (GMl)^{1/2} \quad \text{and} \quad r = \frac{l}{1+e\cos\phi}$$

we have

$$\int_0^T \frac{1}{(1+e\cos\phi)^2}\dot{\phi}\,dt = \left(\frac{GM}{l^3}\right)^{1/2}\int_0^T dt$$

Therefore

$$\begin{aligned} T &= \left(\frac{l^3}{GM}\right)^{1/2}\int_0^{2\pi}\frac{1}{(1+e\cos\phi)^2}\,d\phi \\ &= \left(\frac{l^3}{GM}\right)^{1/2}\left\{\int_0^{\pi}\frac{1}{(1+e\cos\phi)^2}\,d\phi + \int_{\pi}^{2\pi}\frac{1}{(1+e\cos\phi)^2}\,d\phi\right\} \\ &= 2\left(\frac{l^3}{GM}\right)^{1/2}\int_0^{\pi}\frac{1}{(1+e\cos\phi)^2}\,d\phi \end{aligned}$$

Changing into half-angles and setting $t = \tan(\frac{1}{2}\phi)$, we find that

$$\begin{aligned} T &= 4\left(\frac{l^3}{GM}\right)^{1/2}\int_0^{\infty}\frac{1+t^2}{\{1+e+(1-e)t^2\}^2}\,dt \\ &= 4\left(\frac{l^3}{GM}\right)^{1/2}\int_0^{\infty}\frac{d}{dt}\left[\frac{1}{(1-e^2)^{3/2}}\tan^{-1}\left\{\left(\frac{1-e}{1+e}\right)^{1/2}t\right\}\right. \\ &\qquad \left. - \frac{et}{(1-e^2)\{(1+e)+(1-e)t^2\}}\right]dt \end{aligned}$$

$$= 4\left(\frac{l^3}{GM}\right)^{1/2}\frac{\pi}{2}\frac{1}{(1-e^2)^{3/2}}$$

$$= 2\pi\left(\frac{a^3}{GM}\right)^{1/2} = \frac{2\pi ab}{L_0}$$

This result agrees with Kepler's third law.

Suppose the polar coordinates of the particle P change from (r, ϕ) to $(r+\Delta r, \phi+\Delta\phi)$ in time Δt. Let ΔA be the area swept out by $\overrightarrow{SP}$ during this change of position. ΔA is approximately equal to the area of a triangle. Therefore

$$\Delta A = \tfrac{1}{2}(r+\Delta r)r\Delta\phi + \text{smaller terms}$$

and

$$\frac{\Delta A}{\Delta t} = \tfrac{1}{2}r^2\frac{\Delta\phi}{\Delta t} + \text{smaller terms}.$$

Thus

$$\frac{dA}{dt} = \lim_{\Delta t\to 0}\frac{\Delta A}{\Delta t} = \tfrac{1}{2}r^2\dot{\phi} = \tfrac{1}{2}L_0$$

and

$$A = \tfrac{1}{2}L_0 t + \text{constant}$$

We see that equal areas are swept out in equal time intervals (cf. Kepler's second law). Hence we may deduce that the period of revolution T for a particle in an elliptic orbit is twice the area of the ellipse divided by L_0. The area of the ellipse equals

$$\int_0^T \tfrac{1}{2}r^2\dot{\phi}\,dt = \int_0^{2\pi}\tfrac{1}{2}r^2\,d\phi = \tfrac{1}{2}l^2\int_0^{2\pi}\frac{1}{(1+e\cos\phi)^2}\,d\phi$$

We encountered this integral in the previous paragraph. We are able to calculate the area of the ellipse more easily by using the cartesian coordinates associated with the canonical equation for the ellipse. Thus the area of the ellipse equals

$$\int_{-a}^{a} 2b(1-x^2/a^2)^{1/2}\,dx = ab\int_{-\pi/2}^{\pi/2} 2\cos^2\theta\,d\theta$$

$$= ab\int_{-\pi/2}^{\pi/2}(1+\cos 2\theta)\,d\theta = \pi ab$$

Hence $T = 2\pi ab/L_0$. This confirms the equivalent calculation in the previous paragraph.

EXAMPLE

A particle P is moving relative to a fixed particle S and is experiencing an inverse-square gravitational force. Initially $|\overrightarrow{PS}| = r_0$ and the velocity of P relative to S is perpendicular to PS and has magnitude $(3GM/2r_0)^{1/2}$, where M is the mass of the particle S. Use the conservation of energy to show that $r_0 \leqslant |\overrightarrow{PS}| \leqslant 3r_0$.

What instantaneous change in speed is necessary (i) at the apse $|\overrightarrow{PS}| = 3r_0$ to put the particle P in a circular orbit of radius $3r_0$, (ii) at the apse $|\overrightarrow{PS}| = r_0$ to put the particle P in a circular orbit of radius r_0?

Introducing plane-polar coordinates relative to the fixed point S, we find that the equation of motion of the particle P is

$$m(\ddot{r} - r\dot{\phi}^2)\mathbf{e}_r + m(r\ddot{\phi} + 2\dot{r}\dot{\phi})\mathbf{e}_\phi = -\frac{GMm}{r^2}\mathbf{e}_r$$

Hence the statements of conservation of angular momentum and conservation of energy are

$$r^2\dot{\phi} = L_0 \quad \text{and} \quad \tfrac{1}{2}(\dot{r}^2 + r^2\dot{\phi}^2) - \frac{GM}{r} = E_0$$

The initial conditions give

$$L_0 = (3GMr_0/2)^{1/2} \quad \text{and} \quad E_0 = -GM/4r_0$$

Therefore

$$\dot{r}^2 = -\frac{GM}{2r_0} + \frac{2GM}{r} - \frac{3GMr_0}{2r^2}$$

$$= \frac{GM}{2r_0r^2}(-r^2 + 4rr_0 - 3r_0^2) = \frac{GM}{2r_0r^2}(r - r_0)(3r_0 - r)$$

We see that $\dot{r}^2 \geqslant 0$ provided $r_0 \leqslant r \leqslant 3r_0$ and that the orbit of P has an apse at $r = r_0$ (the initial position) and at $r = 3r_0$.

At $r = 3r_0$, $\dot{r} = 0$ and $r\dot{\phi} = (GM/6r_0)^{1/2}$. The orbital speed corresponding to a circular orbit of radius $3r_0$ is $(GM/3r_0)^{1/2}$. The required instantaneous increase in speed at the apse to achieve the transfer to the circular orbit is

$$\tfrac{1}{3}(2^{1/2} - 1)(3GM/2r_0)^{1/2}.$$

At $r = r_0$, $\dot{r} = 0$ and $r\dot{\phi} = (3GM/2r_0)^{1/2}$. The orbital speed corresponding to a circular orbit of radius r_0 is $(GM/r_0)^{1/2}$. Therefore we require an instantaneous decrease in speed at the apse $r = r_0$ to transfer the particle P to a circular orbit of radius r_0.

This example illustrates the transfer of a spacecraft (represented by the particle P) between a circular orbit of radius r_0 and a circular orbit of radius $3r_0$. Suppose two planets are moving around the Sun in circular orbits. We can apply the ideas of this example to calculate the elliptic orbit of a spacecraft to be transferred from one planet to another (provided we let the particle S represent the Sun and ignore the gravitational forces associated with the planets).

EXAMPLE

Consider the problem of putting a satellite into a circular orbit around the Earth.

Suppose that the satellite is projected from the surface of the Earth with speed U and that the direction of projection makes an angle α with the upward vertical. (This is a simplification of the first stage of the motion during which the satellite is part of a rocket-propelled launch vehicle.) Derive a condition for the orbit to be elliptical and find the positions of the apses. What instantaneous change in speed is appropriate at the apogee to put the satellite into a circular orbit? What is the radius of this circular orbit?

We introduce plane-polar coordinates (r, ϕ) relative to the centre of the Earth so that the initial position has the coordinates $(R, 0)$, where R is the radius of the Earth. We find the equation of the orbit by setting $r = 1/u$ and solving

$$\frac{d^2u}{d\phi^2} + u = \frac{GM}{L_0^2}$$

subject to the (initial) conditions at $\phi = 0$, namely

$$u = \frac{1}{R}, \quad L_0 = RU \sin\alpha \quad \text{and} \quad \frac{du}{d\phi} = \frac{-\cos\alpha}{R\sin\alpha}$$

Hence

$$u = A\cos\phi + B\sin\phi + \frac{GM}{(RU\sin\alpha)^2}$$

where

$$\frac{1}{R} = A + \frac{GM}{(RU\sin\alpha)^2} \quad \text{and} \quad \frac{-\cos\alpha}{R\sin\alpha} = B$$

i.e.

$$\begin{aligned} u &= \left\{\frac{1}{R} - \frac{GM}{(RU\sin\alpha)^2}\right\}\cos\phi - \frac{\cos\alpha}{R\sin\alpha}\sin\phi + \frac{GM}{(RU\sin\alpha)^2} \\ &= \left\{\frac{1}{R} - \frac{g}{U^2\sin^2\alpha}\right\}\cos\phi - \frac{\cos\alpha}{R\sin\alpha}\sin\phi + \frac{g}{U^2\sin^2\alpha} \end{aligned}$$

because $GM = gR^2$. Thus

$$r = \frac{l}{1 - e\cos(\phi - \phi_0)}$$

where

$$\begin{aligned} l &= (U^2/g)\sin^2\alpha \\ e &= \left\{1 - \frac{U\sin\alpha^2}{gR}(2gR - U^2)\right\}^{1/2} \\ e\cos\phi_0 &= 1 - (U^2/gR)\sin^2\alpha \end{aligned}$$

and

$$e\sin\phi_0 = (U^2/gR)\sin\alpha\cos\alpha$$

The orbit is elliptical (i.e. $e < 1$) provided $U^2 < 2gR$. We deduce from the relation

$$\dot{r} = -\frac{eL_0}{l}\sin(\phi - \phi_0)$$

that there are apses when $\phi = \phi_0$ and $\phi = \phi_0 + \pi$. At $\phi = \phi_0$, $r = l/(1-e)$, $\dot{r} = 0$ and $r\dot{\phi} = L_0/r = (1-e)L_0/l$; and at $\phi = \phi_0 + \pi$, $r = l/(1+e)$, $\dot{r} = 0$ and $r\dot{\phi} = (1+e)L_0/l$. Remembering that $e > 0$, we see that the coordinates of the apogee are $(l/(1-e), \phi_0)$.

The satellite may be transferred to a circular orbit of radius $l/(1-e)$ by means of an instantaneous increase of speed at the apogee, the final speed being $\{(1-e)gR^2/l\}^{1/2}$.

We note that the radius of the circular orbit is

$$\frac{l}{1-e} = \frac{R}{\left(\dfrac{gR}{U^2 \sin^2 \alpha}\right) - \left\{\left(\dfrac{gR}{U^2 \sin^2 \alpha} - 1\right)^2 + \dfrac{U^2 \cos^2 \alpha}{U^2 \sin^2 \alpha}\right\}^{1/2}}$$

where $U \sin \alpha$ is the horizontal component of the initial velocity and $U \cos \alpha$ is the vertical component of the initial velocity. We may interpret $U \sin \alpha$ to be the Earth's rotational speed at the launch-site and $U \cos \alpha$ to be the speed provided by the rocket-propelled launch vehicle. In this case, once the launch-site has been selected, the altitude of the satellite depends on only the speed provided by the launch vehicle, namely $U \cos \alpha$.

9.8 Parabolic and hyperbolic orbits

We shall complete our discussion of the possible orbits associated with an inverse-square force of attraction by considering some illustrative examples.

EXAMPLE

A particle P is moving relative to a fixed point S. A particle of mass M is stationed at S. The only force acting on P is an inverse-square gravitational force associated with the two particles. The speed of the particle P is $(2GM/r_0)^{1/2}$ when $|\overrightarrow{SP}| = r_0$. Investigate the orbit of P.

We introduce plane-polar coordinates so that the origin is situated at S and the coordinates of P are (r, ϕ). The initial conditions may be written in the form

$$r = r_0, \quad \phi = 0, \quad \dot{r} = (2GM/r_0)^{1/2} \cos \alpha, \quad r\dot{\phi} = (2GM/r_0)^{1/2} \sin \alpha.$$

Hence $L_0 = r^2\dot{\phi} = (2GMr_0)^{1/2} \sin \alpha$ and the differential equation governing the orbit is

$$\frac{d^2u}{d\phi^2} + u = \frac{GM}{L_0^2} = \frac{1}{2r_0 \sin^2 \alpha}$$

where $u = 1/r$. We seek a solution that satisfies

$$u = \frac{1}{r_0} \quad \text{and} \quad \frac{du}{d\phi} = -\frac{\dot{r}}{L_0} = -\frac{\cos \alpha}{r_0 \sin \alpha} \quad \text{at} \quad \phi = 0$$

The required solution is

$$u = A \cos \phi + B \sin \phi + \frac{1}{2r_0 \sin^2 \alpha}$$

where

$$\frac{1}{r_0} = A + \frac{1}{2r_0 \sin^2 \alpha} \quad \text{and} \quad -\frac{\cos \alpha}{r_0 \sin \alpha} = B$$

Thus we find that

$$r = \frac{2r_0 \sin^2 \alpha}{1 - \cos(\phi - 2\alpha)}$$

Therefore

$$\dot{r} = -\frac{2r_0 \sin^2 \alpha \sin(\phi - 2\alpha)}{\{1-\cos(\phi-2\alpha)\}^2}\,\dot{\phi} = -\left(\frac{GM}{2r_0 \sin^2 \alpha}\right)^{1/2} \sin(\phi - 2\alpha)$$

and $\dot{r} = 0$ when $\sin(\phi - 2\alpha) = 0$. There is only one apse, which has the coordinates $(r_0 \sin^2 \alpha, \pi + 2\alpha)$. The orbit of the particle P is parabolic, and the shortest distance between P and S is $r_0 \sin^2 \alpha$. We note that as $\phi \to 2\alpha$, $r \to \infty$, $\dot{r} \to 0$ and $r\dot{\phi} \to 0$.

Let us examine the energy equation, namely

$$\tfrac{1}{2}(\dot{r}^2 + r^2\dot{\phi}^2) - \frac{GM}{r} = E_0$$

The initial conditions indicate that

$$E_0 = \frac{1}{2}\left(\frac{2GM}{r_0}\cos^2 \alpha + \frac{2GM}{r_0}\sin^2 \alpha\right) - \frac{GM}{r_0} = 0$$

The zero value of E_0 is a characteristic property of the parabolic orbit.

EXAMPLE

A particle P is moving in a gravitational field of force associated with a fixed particle S of mass M. Initially $|\overrightarrow{SP}| = r_0$, the initial speed of P is $2(GM/r_0)^{1/2}$ and the direction of the initial velocity is perpendicular to $\overrightarrow{SP}$. Find the equation of the subsequent orbit.

We introduce plane-polar coordinates whose origin coincides with the position of the particle S. The equation of motion of the particle P leads to the relations

$$\ddot{r} - r\dot{\phi}^2 = -\frac{GM}{r^2} \quad \text{and} \quad r^2\dot{\phi} = L_0$$

Using the initial conditions we find that $L_0 = 2(GMr_0)^{1/2}$. Introducing

$$r = \frac{1}{u}, \quad \dot{r} = -L_0\frac{du}{d\phi} \quad \text{and} \quad \ddot{r} = -u^2L_0^2\frac{d^2u}{d\phi^2}$$

we obtain the differential equation

$$\frac{d^2u}{d\phi^2} + u = \frac{GM}{L_0^2} = \frac{1}{4r_0}$$

Solving this differential equation and imposing the initial conditions, namely

$$u = \frac{1}{r_0} \quad \text{and} \quad \frac{du}{d\phi} = 0 \quad \text{at} \quad \phi = 0$$

lead to

$$u = \frac{1}{4r_0}(3\cos\phi + 1)$$

Therefore the polar equation of the orbit of P is

$$r = \frac{4r_0}{1 + 3\cos\phi}$$

This is the equation of a hyperbola, the eccentricity being 3 and the length of the semi-latus rectum being $4r_0$.

The energy equation takes the form

$$\tfrac{1}{2}(\dot{r}+r^2\dot{\phi}^2)-\frac{GM}{r}=\frac{1}{2}\left(\dot{r}^2+\frac{L_0}{r^2}\right)-\frac{GM}{r}=E_0$$

where $E_0 = GM/r_0$. We may deduce from this that

$$\dot{r}^2=\frac{2GM}{r^2 r_0}(r-r_0)(r+2r_0)$$

Hence there is one apse, this being at $r = r_0$, and $r \geqslant r_0$ for all time. An alternative expression for $\dot{r}$ is

$$\dot{r}=\frac{4r_0}{(1+3\cos\phi)^2}(3\sin\phi)\dot{\phi}=\frac{3}{2}\left(\frac{GM}{r_0}\right)^{1/2}\sin\phi$$

The coordinates of the apse are $(r_0, 0)$.

The hyperbola has asymptotes. We note that

$$r\to\infty \quad \text{as} \quad \phi\to\pi-\cos^{-1}\tfrac{1}{3}$$

As $\phi\to\pi-\cos^{-1}\frac{1}{3}$

$$r\dot{\phi}=\frac{L_0}{r}\to 0 \quad \text{and} \quad \dot{r}\to\left(\frac{2GM}{r_0}\right)^{1/2}$$

The second asymptote corresponds to $\phi = -\pi+\cos^{-1}\frac{1}{3}$, i.e. the branch of the hyperbola along which the particle P is moving is confined to the sector

$$-\pi+\cos^{-1}\tfrac{1}{3}<\phi<\pi-\cos^{-1}\tfrac{1}{3}$$

When P is a long way from S, it appears to be moving with speed $(2GM/r_0)^{1/2}$ along an asymptote. Letting d denote the perpendicular distance from S to an asymptote, we may write

$$L_0=(2GM/r_0)^{1/2}d$$

and deduce that $d = 2^{1/2}r_0$.

We may use the relation $r^2\dot{\phi} = L_0$ together with the polar equation of the orbit to calculate the time taken by the particle P to move along various parts of its orbit. For instance, the length of the time interval during which P is between the apse and the end of the latus rectum ($r_0 \leqslant |\overrightarrow{SP}| \leqslant 4r_0$) equals

$$\frac{1}{L_0}\int_0^{\pi/2} r^2\,d\phi=\frac{16r_0^2}{L_0}\int_0^{\pi/2}\frac{1}{(1+3\cos\phi)^2}\,d\phi$$

$$=\left(\frac{r_0^3}{GM}\right)^{1/2}\left(3+\frac{1}{2^{1/2}}\ln(2^{1/2}-1)\right)$$

We may confirm this answer by noting that the area swept out by the radius vector is

$$\tfrac{1}{2}\int_0^{\pi/2} r^2\,d\phi=\int_{r_0/2}^{3r_0/2} y\,dx$$

where $y = 2^{1/2}(4x^2-r_0^2)^{1/2}$, and evaluating the integral with the aid of the substitution $2x = r_0\cosh v$.

EXERCISES ON CHAPTER 9

1. An object is projected vertically from the surface of the Earth so that it just reaches a height above the Earth's surface equal to three times the radius of the Earth. Calculate the speed of projection. How long is the time interval during which the object is above the Earth?

2. A projectile is given a velocity vertically upwards from the surface of the Moon. Find the least value of the speed of projection such that the projectile never returns to the Moon. Assume that the acceleration due to gravity at the surface of the Moon is $1{\cdot}62\,\mathrm{m\,s^{-2}}$ and that the radius of the Moon is 1738 km.

3. Calculate the escape speed associated with the planet Jupiter. Assume that the acceleration due to gravity at the surface of Jupiter is $26\,\mathrm{m\,s^{-2}}$ and that the radius of Jupiter is 70 000 km.

4. A satellite is travelling in a circular orbit at an altitude of 1600 kilometres above the surface of the Earth. What is its period of revolution?

5. A spacecraft is travelling in a circular orbit at an altitude of 225 kilometres above the surface of the Earth. What is its speed? Show that it travels once round the Earth every 89 minutes.

6. A lunar module is moving in a circular orbit about the Moon at a height of 16 kilometres above the lunar surface. Show that the speed of the module is approximately 6000 kilometres per hour. Estimate the time it takes the module to complete an orbit.

7. An artificial satellite is in a circular orbit at a height H above the surface of the Earth. Let u_1 and u_2 be the calculated values of the speed of the satellite when it is assumed that gravitational field of force (i) is uniform and (ii) obeys an inverse-square law. Show that $u_1 > u_2$ and calculate $(u_1 - u_2)/u_2$.

8. Assuming that the planets move in circular orbits under an inverse-square attraction to a fixed Sun, show that the squares of their periods of revolution are proportional to the cubes of the orbital radii.

9. A space platform is to be placed in a circular orbit round the equator of Venus. How far from the surface of the planet must the platform be placed if it is to appear stationary to an observer fixed at the equator? You may use the following approximate values:

Venus's period of revolution about its axis is $2{\cdot}1 \times 10^7$ seconds, the equatorial radius of Venus is 6000 kilometres, the acceleration due to gravity at a point on the equator of Venus is 8·9 metres per second per second.

10. What is the altitude of an isosynchronous satellite associated with the planet Jupiter? Use the data given in question 3 and the fact that Jupiter's period of revolution about its axis is $3{\cdot}5 \times 10^4$ seconds.

11. Two satellites are moving in circular orbits around a planet. Their altitudes and their periods of revolution are H_1, H_2, and T_1, T_2, respectively. Find an expression for the radius of the planet and show that the acceleration due to gravity at the surface of the planet is

$$\frac{4\pi^2(H_2-H_1)^3}{(T_2^{2/3}-T_1^{2/3})(H_2T_1^{2/3}-H_1T_2^{2/3})^2}$$

(Ignore the gravitational force that one satellite exerts on the other satellite.)

Suppose that the planet is Earth and that the altitudes are 515 km, 1450 km and the periods are 95 minutes, 115 minutes. Estimate the radius of the Earth and the value of g.

12. A particle is attracted to a fixed point S by a force of magnitude μ/r^2 per unit mass, μ being a positive constant and r being the distance from S. It is projected from a point A, where $|\overrightarrow{AS}| = d$. The initial velocity has magnitude $(\mu/d)^{1/2}$ and its direction makes an angle $(\frac{1}{2}\pi - \alpha)$ with $\overrightarrow{AS}$ where $0 \leqslant \alpha < \frac{1}{2}\pi$. If $\alpha = 0$, show that the particle moves in a circular orbit about S. If $\alpha \neq 0$, find the maximum value and the minimum value of the distance between S and the particle in the subsequent motion.

13. A particle is moving in a plane under an attraction to a fixed point S of magnitude μ/r^2 per unit mass, where μ is a positive constant and r is the distance from S. Initially the particle is projected from Q with speed U, the direction of the initial velocity being perpendicular to $\overrightarrow{SQ}$ and $|\overrightarrow{SQ}|$ equalling D. If $U^2 < 2\mu/D$, show that the orbit meets the directed line passing through S and having the direction of $\overrightarrow{QS}$ at R where

$$|\overrightarrow{SR}| = \frac{U^2D^2}{2\mu - U^2D}$$

14. A satellite is moving in an elliptic orbit around the Earth, whose average radius is 6371 km. The altitude of its perigee is 251 km and the altitude of its apogee is 995 km. Calculate the length of the semi-major axis, and hence estimate the satellite's period of revolution. What is the value of the eccentricity of the orbit?

15. A satellite is moving in an elliptic orbit around the Earth. The distance of its perigee from the centre of the Earth is 6622 km and the distance of its apogee from the centre of the Earth is 48 200 km. Use this information to estimate the orbital parameters a, e, $l = a(1-e^2)$. Calculate the speed of the satellite at the perigee and at the apogee (from the relation $L_0^2 = gR^2l$). Show that the period of revolution in the elliptic orbit is about 12 hours 33 minutes.

16. The period of revolution of a satellite around its parent body in an elliptic orbit depends upon the length of the semi-major axis of the ellipse a, the gravitational constant G, and the mass of the parent body M. Use dimensional analysis to determine the form of Kepler's third law, which relates these quantities.

17. The perigee and the apogee of a satellite are at altitudes 213 km and 359 km respectively, and the satellite's period of revolution is 90·1 minutes. The perigee and the apogee of a second satellite are at altitudes 206 km and 294 km respectively. Use Kepler's third law to estimate the second satellite's period of revolution.

18. A satellite is moving in a circular orbit at a height H above the Earth's surface. Find an expression for its orbital speed U.

The firing of retro-rockets reduces the satellite's speed to kU $(0 < k < 1)$ and puts the satellite into an elliptic orbit. Show that the satellite will collide with the Earth if

$$k^2 \leqslant 2R/(2R+H)$$

where R is the radius of the Earth.

19. Assume that the Earth's orbit around the Sun is circular. The radius of the orbit is $1{\cdot}495 \times 10^{11}$ m, and the value of the product of the gravitational constant G

and the mass of the Sun is $1{\cdot}326 \times 10^{20}\,\mathrm{m^3\,s^{-2}}$. Calculate the Earth's orbital speed.

Assume that the orbit of Mars around the Sun is circular and in the same plane as the Earth's orbit. The radius of the orbit of Mars is 1·523 times the radius of the Earth's orbit. A satellite is to be transferred from an orbit around the Earth to an orbit around Mars. Calculate the eccentricity of the elliptical transfer-orbit that is tangential to the orbits of the Earth and Mars. Show that the satellite's flight time is $2{\cdot}235 \times 10^7$ s (about 259 days) and that the satellite's orbital speed at the perihelion is $32{\cdot}7\,\mathrm{km\,s^{-1}}$. Deduce that the satellite has to be given an instantaneous increase in speed of $2{\cdot}9\,\mathrm{km\,s^{-1}}$ to transfer it from its orbit around the Earth to its elliptic transfer-orbit. What is the satellite's orbital speed at the aphelion?

20. Show that for an ellipse the distance from a focus to a point at the end of the minor axis is equal to one half the length of the major axis.

The eccentricity of the Earth's orbit round the Sun is 0·0167. Consider areas swept out by the radius vector from the Sun to the Earth, and hence deduce that the Earth's distance from the Sun exceeds the length of the semi-major axis of the orbit during 0·505 316 years (nearly two days more than half a year).

21. A particle P describes a parabolic orbit about a fixed particle S of mass M. The minimum distance between P and S is a. Show that L_0 equals $(2GMa)^{1/2}$, where L_0 is the magnitude of the angular momentum per unit mass about the centre of attraction S possessed by the particle P. Find the length of the time interval during which $|\overrightarrow{SP}| \leqslant 2a$.

22. A spacecraft has an elliptic orbit around the Earth. The eccentricity of the ellipse is e and the length of the semi-major axis is a. Write down the positions of the apses in terms of polar coordinates. Hence determine E_0 and L_0, where

$$\frac{1}{2}\left(\dot{r}^2 + \frac{L_0^2}{r^2}\right) - \frac{GM}{r} = E_0$$

It is decided to double the speed at the end of the minor axis at which the spacecraft is heading towards the Earth. Show that the energy equation associated with the new orbit is

$$\tfrac{1}{2}\dot{r}^2 + \frac{2GMa(1-e^2)}{r^2} - \frac{GM}{r} = \frac{GM}{a}$$

What is the new minimum distance between the spacecraft and the centre of the Earth? Is the new orbit elliptic?

23. A particle P of unit mass is attracted by a force of magnitude μ/r^2 towards the origin O, where μ is a positive constant and $r = |\overrightarrow{OP}|$. It is approaching with speed $(\mu/d)^{1/2}$ from a great distance and is travelling so as to pass O at a perpendicular distance d in the absence of the attractive force. Show that the minimum value of $|\overrightarrow{OP}|$ is $(2^{1/2}-1)\,d$. Find the speed of the particle at the apse.

24. A particle is moving under the influence of an inverse-square law of repulsion, its equation of motion being

$$(\ddot{r} - r\dot{\phi}^2)\mathbf{e}_r + (r\ddot{\phi} + 2\dot{r}\dot{\phi})\mathbf{e}_\phi = (\mu/r^2)\mathbf{e}_r$$

where μ is a positive constant. Deduce that $r^2\dot{\phi} = L_0$, where L_0 is a constant, and that

$$\frac{d^2u}{d\phi^2} + u = -\frac{\mu}{L_0^2}$$

where $u = 1/r$.

Describe the motion of the particle when the initial conditions are

$$r = r_0, \quad \phi = 0, \quad \dot{r} = 0 \quad \text{and} \quad \dot{\phi} = u_0/r_0$$

25. A particle is moving in the Oxy plane under the influence of an attraction towards O of magnitude μ/r^3 per unit mass, r being its distance from O and μ being a positive constant. Write down the equation of motion in terms of polar coordinates (r, ϕ) and derive the differential equation that gives u $(= 1/r)$ in terms of ϕ.

Consider the general solution of this differential equation and determine the condition under which the particle's orbit can be circular.

26. A particle is attracted to the point S by a force of magnitude μ/r^4 per unit mass, where μ is a positive constant and r is the distance of the particle from S. The particle is projected from $r = r_0$ with a velocity whose magnitude is $(7\mu/9r_0^3)^{1/2}$ and whose direction is perpendicular to the radius vector. Show that the initial value of $\ddot{r}$ is negative, and deduce that $\dot{r}$ is negative for all subsequent time.

Find the value of r, other than $r = r_0$, that corresponds to an apse, and deduce that the particle does not reach this position.

27. A particle of mass m rests on a smooth horizontal table and is attached to a fixed point on the table by a light elastic string of modulus mg and natural length r_0. Initially the string is just taut and the particle is projected along the table in a direction perpendicular to the line of the string with speed $2(\frac{1}{3}gr_0)^{1/2}$. Show that, if r is the length of the string at time t,

$$\ddot{r} = \frac{4gr_0^3}{3r^3} - \frac{g(r-r_0)}{r_0}$$

Prove that the string will extend until its length is $2r_0$ and that the speed of the particle is then half its initial speed.

28. An elastic string has one end fastened to a smooth horizontal table at O and the other end attached to a particle P of mass m. The natural length of the string is r_0 and the modulus of elasticity is λ. When $|\overrightarrow{OP}| = 2r_0$ the particle is projected along the table at right angles to the string. Prove that the string will never attain its natural length in the subsequent motion if the initial speed is greater than $(\lambda r_0/3m)^{1/2}$.

29. A particle P of mass m is attracted by a force of magnitude $m\mu r$ to a fixed point O, where μ is a positive constant and $r = |\overrightarrow{OP}|$. Derive the differential equation

$$\frac{d^2u}{d\phi^2} + u = \frac{\mu}{L_0^2 u^3}$$

where $u = 1/r$, r and ϕ are polar coordinates and L_0 is a constant.

The particle is describing a circle, centre at O and radius r_0. Determine the value of L_0. The particle is slightly disturbed without altering L_0. Show that $u = 1/r_0 + x$, where

$$\frac{d^2x}{d\phi^2} + 4x = 0 \quad \text{provided} \quad xr_0 \ll 1.$$

30. A particle of unit mass moves steadily around a circular orbit of radius r_0 under the influence of an attraction of magnitude $g(r)/r^3$ towards the centre of the circle, where $g'(r_0) > 0$. Derive the equation that governs small oscillations about the steady motion, and show that the period of these oscillations is approximately equal to $2\pi\{r_0^3/g'(r_0)\}^{1/2}$.

Suppose $g(r) = \mu/r$, where μ is a positive constant. Show that a circular orbit is possible. What happens if the particle is slightly disturbed from its circular orbit without any alteration to the angular momentum?

10 Variable Resistive Forces

10.1 Introduction

When an object moves through a liquid or a gas it experiences a resistive force—called the *drag*. Some examples are an aeroplane flying through the air, a ship cruising across the ocean, and a submarine patrolling under the surface of the sea. The motion of an object through a fluid (a liquid or a gas) is complex; it comes under the subject heading of "Fluid Dynamics".

There is experimental evidence that the drag depends on the speed of the object relative to the fluid, and acts against the motion of the object through the fluid. The dependence of the drag upon the relative speed is complicated. We shall consider some approximate relations between the drag and the relative speed. The principal relations are

(i) the drag is proportional to the relative speed and
(ii) the drag is proportional to the square of the relative speed.

The first relation is a reasonable approximation for low relative speeds, and the second is appropriate for high relative speeds. It is important to use the relative speed, i.e. the speed of the object relative to the fluid. The fluid may be moving relative to our frame of reference. We appreciate this when we select a golf club to play a shot with the wind, in still conditions or against the wind.

10.2 Horizontal motion

Suppose that we wish to investigate the effect of drag on the motion of a motor-car along a horizontal straight road. We introduce a particle of mass m to represent the motor-car and the x-axis to represent the road. There will be a normal reaction between the car and the road equal to the weight of the car. The equation governing the horizontal motion is

$$m\ddot{x} = F(\dot{x})$$

where the horizontal component of the force F depends on the velocity component $\dot{x}$. Setting $u = \dot{x}$ and noting that

$$\ddot{x} = \frac{du}{dt} \quad \text{and} \quad \ddot{x} = u\frac{du}{dx}$$

we may write the governing equation in the forms

$$m\frac{du}{dt} = F(u) \quad \text{and} \quad mu\frac{du}{dx} = F(u)$$

We solve the differential equation in its first form when we seek information about the velocity u in terms of the time t. Thus

$$\int_{t_1}^{t_2} \frac{m}{F(u)}\frac{du}{dt}\,dt = \int_{t_1}^{t_2} dt$$

i.e.

$$t_2 - t_1 = m\int_{u_1}^{u_2} \frac{1}{F(u)}\,du$$

where $u_1 = u(t_1)$ and $u_2 = u(t_2)$. The derivation of an implicit relation between velocity and time is complete when we have evaluated the integral with respect to u.

Manipulating the second form in a similar manner, we obtain

$$\int_{x_1}^{x_2} \frac{mu}{F(u)}\frac{du}{dx}\,dx = \int_{x_1}^{x_2} dx$$

i.e.

$$x_2 - x_1 = m\int_{u_1}^{u_2} \frac{u}{F(u)}\,du$$

where $u_1 = u(x_1)$ and $u_2 = u(x_2)$. This provides an implicit relation between velocity and position, if we are able to evaluate the integral with respect to u. The success of this approach rests on our ability to evaluate certain integrals.

Let us examine some special cases when the only horizontal force acting on the motor-car is the drag. Suppose that there is no wind and the drag is proportional to the speed of the motor-car. We write

$$F(\dot{x}) = \begin{cases} -k_1\dot{x} & \dot{x} > 0 \\ +k_1(-\dot{x}) & \dot{x} < 0 \end{cases} \quad (k_1 > 0)$$
$$= -k_1\dot{x}$$

When there is no wind and the drag is proportional to the square of the speed of the motor-car, we have

$$F(\dot{x}) = \begin{cases} -k_2\dot{x}^2 & \dot{x} > 0 \\ +k_2(-\dot{x})^2 & \dot{x} < 0 \end{cases} \quad (k_2 > 0)$$
$$= -k_2\dot{x}|\dot{x}|$$

It is essential to choose the sign appropriate to the representation of a resistive force (the direction of the drag is opposite to the direction of the velocity of the object relative to the fluid). The dimensions of the proportionality parameter k_1 are $MLT^{-2}(LT^{-1})^{-1} = MT^{-1}$ and those of k_2 are $MLT^{-2}(LT^{-1})^{-2} = ML^{-1}$.

EXAMPLE

A motor-car of mass m is travelling at speed u_0 along a horizontal straight road when the clutch is disengaged. Investigate the subsequent motion of the car if the only horizontal force acting on the car is the aerodynamic drag. Suppose that (i) the drag is proportional to the speed and (ii) the drag is proportional to the square of the speed.

We introduce the x-axis so that the initial conditions are $x = 0$ and $\dot{x} = u_0$ at $t = 0$.

(i) the governing differential equation is

$$m\ddot{x} = -k_1\dot{x}$$

Using $\dot{x} = u$ and $\ddot{x} = du/dt$, we have

$$\frac{1}{u}\frac{du}{dt} = -\frac{k_1}{m} \quad \text{and} \quad \ln u = -\frac{k_1}{m}t + C$$

where $\ln u_0 = C$. Therefore

$$\ln(u/u_0) = -\frac{k_1}{m}t \quad \text{and} \quad u = u_0\, e^{-k_1 t/m}$$

Substituting $\ddot{x} = u(du/dx)$, we obtain

$$\frac{du}{dx} = -\frac{k_1}{m} \quad \text{and} \quad u = -\frac{k_1 x}{m} + C$$

where $u_0 = C$. Hence $u = u_0 - k_1 x/m$. We note that this model predicts that

$$u \to 0 \quad \text{as} \quad t \to \infty \quad \text{and} \quad x \to mu_0/k_1$$

(ii) The governing differential equation is

$$m\ddot{x} = -k_2\dot{x}^2$$

because $\dot{x} > 0$. Proceeding as in part (i) we find that

$$\frac{1}{u^2}\frac{du}{dt} = -\frac{k_2}{m}, \quad \frac{1}{u} = \frac{k_2}{m}t + \frac{1}{u_0}$$

and

$$\frac{1}{u}\frac{du}{dx} = -\frac{k_2}{m}, \quad \ln u = -\frac{k_2}{m}x + \ln u_0$$

Therefore the required relations are

$$u = \frac{u_0}{1 + (k_2 u_0/m)t} \quad \text{and} \quad u = u_0\, e^{-k_2 x/m}$$

In this case the prediction is that

$$u \to 0 \quad \text{as} \quad t \to \infty \quad \text{and} \quad x \to \infty$$

To complete this investigation we shall seek the relation between x and t.

(i) Integrating

$$\dot{x} = u_0 e^{-k_1 t/m}$$

with respect to t and imposing the initial conditions we obtain

$$x = \frac{mu_0}{k_1}(1 - e^{-k_1 t/m})$$

This is consistent with our previous results

$$u = \begin{cases} u_0 e^{-k_1 t/m} \\ u_0 - k_1 x/m \end{cases}$$

(ii) Similarly, we deduce from

$$\dot{x} = \frac{u_0}{1 + (k_2 u_0/m)t}$$

and the initial conditions that

$$x = \frac{m}{k_2} \ln\left(1 + \frac{k_2 u_0}{m} t\right)$$

We note that we had shown previously that

$$u = \begin{cases} \dfrac{u_0}{1 + (k_2 u_0/m)t} \\ u_0 e^{-k_2 x/m} \end{cases}$$

EXAMPLE

A train of mass m moves along a horizontal straight track against a resistance whose magnitude is ku when the train's speed is u. It starts from rest. The engine can either (i) exert a constant tractive force F or (ii) work at a constant rate P. Investigate the motion in each case.

We represent the train by a particle of mass m and we introduce the x-axis to represent the track. The initial conditions are

$$x = 0 \quad \text{and} \quad \dot{x} = 0 \quad \text{at} \quad t = 0$$

We assume that the direction of the tractive force coincides with the direction of x increasing.

(i) The governing differential equation is

$$m\ddot{x} = F - k\dot{x}$$

Introducing $\dot{x} = u$ and $\ddot{x} = du/dt$, we have

$$m\frac{du}{dt} = F - ku$$

We may rewrite this first-order differential equation as either

$$m\frac{du}{dt} + ku = F \quad \text{(linear)}$$

or

$$\frac{m}{F - ku}\frac{du}{dt} = 1 \quad \text{(separable)}$$

The general solution is

$$u = \frac{F}{k} + Ce^{-kt/m}$$

[see J. Hunter, *Calculus*, Blackie/Chambers]. The solution satisfying the initial conditions is

$$u = \frac{F}{k}(1 - e^{-kt/m})$$

This indicates that $u \to F/k$ as $t \to \infty$. We shall let U denote F/k, which is called the *terminal speed*. The train never attains the terminal speed. We note that the value of the terminal speed may be obtained by setting $\ddot{x} = 0$ in the governing differential equation.

Integrating

$$\dot{x} = U(1 - e^{-kt/m})$$

with respect to t we obtain

$$x = Ut + \frac{mU}{k}e^{-kt/m} + C$$

where $0 = mU/k + C$ (the initial conditions determining the value of C). Hence

$$x = Ut - \frac{mU}{k}(1 - e^{-kt/m})$$

To find a relation between u and x, we examine

$$mu\frac{du}{dx} = F - ku$$

This is a first-order differential equation that is separable. Integrating the separated form of the equation

$$\frac{m}{k}\left\{\frac{F}{F-ku} - 1\right\}\frac{du}{dx} = 1$$

with respect to x leads to

$$\frac{m}{k}\left\{-\frac{F}{k}\ln(F-ku) - u\right\} = x + C$$

The value of C appropriate to the initial conditions is $-(mF/k^2)\ln F$. Therefore the solution satisfying the initial conditions is

$$\frac{m}{k}\left\{U\ln\left(\frac{U}{U-u}\right) - u\right\} = x$$

This is an explicit relation for x in terms of u (or an implicit relation for u in terms of x).

For example, we may deduce from these results the values of x and t corresponding to $\dot{x} = \frac{1}{2}U$. The train travels a distance

$$\frac{mF}{k^2}(\ln 2 - \tfrac{1}{2})$$

in time

$$\frac{m}{k}\ln 2$$

to attain half its terminal speed, the terminal speed being F/k. Similarly it is easy to evaluate the values of x and $\dot{x}$ corresponding to a given value of t. The evaluation of t and $\dot{x}$ corresponding to a given value of x involves us in the numerical solution of non-linear equations [see C. Dixon, *Numerical Analysis*, Blackie/Chambers].

(ii) The differential equation governing the motion is

$$m\ddot{x} = \frac{P}{\dot{x}} - k\dot{x}$$

Setting $\dot{x} = u$ and $\ddot{x} = du/dt$, we obtain

$$\frac{mu}{P-ku^2}\frac{du}{dt} = 1$$

This is a first-order differential equation that is separable. Integrating with respect to t, we find that

$$-\frac{1}{2}\frac{m}{k}\ln(P-ku^2) = t+C$$

The imposition of the initial conditions leads to

$$-\frac{1}{2}\frac{m}{k}\ln P = C$$

Therefore

$$\frac{1}{2}\frac{m}{k}\ln\left(\frac{P}{P-ku^2}\right) = t \quad \text{and} \quad u^2 = \frac{P}{k}(1-e^{-2kt/m})$$

We see that the terminal speed U equals $(P/k)^{1/2}$.

To solve

$$\dot{x} = U(1-e^{-2kt/m})^{1/2}$$

we integrate the equation with respect to t and obtain

$$x = U\int (1-e^{-2kt/m})^{1/2}\,dt + C$$

$$= \frac{mU}{k}\left|\ \tfrac{1}{2}\ln\left\{\frac{1+(1-e^{-2kt/m})^{1/2}}{1-(1-e^{-2kt/m})^{1/2}}\right\} - (1-e^{-2kt/m})^{1/2}\ \right| + C$$

We have used the substitution $(1-e^{-2kt/m})^{1/2} = s$ to evaluate the integral. The initial conditions require that $C = 0$. This gives us an explicit expression for x in terms of t.

To obtain a relation between u and x, we return to the governing differential equation and use $\ddot{x} = u(du/dx)$. Thus we have

$$\frac{m}{k}\frac{u^2}{U^2-u^2}\frac{du}{dx} = 1$$

An integration with respect to x leads to

$$\frac{m}{k}\left\{\tfrac{1}{2}U\ln\left(\frac{U+u}{U-u}\right) - u\right\} = x+C$$

The initial conditions indicate that $C = 0$.

We note that the relations that we have derived are consistent, and we deduce that the train travels a distance

$$\frac{m}{k}\left(\frac{P}{k}\right)^{1/2}(\tfrac{1}{2}\ln 3-\tfrac{1}{2})$$

in time

$$\frac{1}{2}\frac{m}{k}\ln(\tfrac{4}{3})=\frac{m}{k}(\ln 2-\tfrac{1}{2}\ln 3)$$

to attain half its terminal speed, the terminal speed being $(P/k)^{1/2}$.

We shall terminate this investigation by calculating the work done by each of the tractive forces. In part (i) the work done by the tractive force equals

$$Fx=\int_0^t F\dot{x}\,dt=\int_0^t (m\ddot{x}+k\dot{x})\dot{x}\,dt$$

$$=E_k+k\int_0^t \dot{x}^2\,dt$$

where E_k is the kinetic energy of the particle, namely $\frac{1}{2}m\dot{x}^2$. In part (ii) the work done by the tractive force equals

$$Pt=\int_0^t \frac{P}{\dot{x}}\dot{x}\,dt=\int_0^t (m\ddot{x}+k\dot{x})\dot{x}\,dt$$

$$=E_k+k\int_0^t \dot{x}^2\,dt$$

Suppose the two forces produce the same terminal speed U, i.e. $F = kU$ and $P = kU^2$. The values of the work done by the first and second tractive forces to attain half the terminal speed are

$$mU^2(\ln 2-\tfrac{1}{2})\quad\text{and}\quad mU^2(\ln 2-\tfrac{1}{2}\ln 3)$$

respectively (approximately, $0{\cdot}193\,mU^2$ and $0{\cdot}144\,mU^2$).

10.3 Aerodynamic drag proportional to speed

We studied in chapter 4 the motion of projectiles subject to the uniform gravitational field of force. What influence does aerodynamic drag have on the motion of a projectile? We shall attempt to answer this question in this section and the next section. First we shall assume that the aerodynamic drag is proportional to the speed of the projectile relative to the air, which may be moving relative to the chosen inertial frame of reference.

Suppose that a particle P of mass m is projected from O, the origin of a system of cartesian coordinates, and assume that the particle's initial velocity is in the xz-plane. The x-axis is horizontal and the direction of z increasing is vertically upwards. The particle's position vector relative to O is $\boldsymbol{r}$. The projectile experiences two forces, the gravitational force represented by $-mg\boldsymbol{k}$ and the aerodynamic drag of a stationary atmosphere represented by $-k_1\dot{\boldsymbol{r}}$. The positive parameter k_1 has the dimensions MT^{-1}.

The equation of motion is

$$m\ddot{\boldsymbol{r}} = -mg\boldsymbol{k} - k_1\dot{\boldsymbol{r}}$$

and the initial conditions at $t = 0$ are

$$\boldsymbol{r} = \boldsymbol{0} \quad \text{and} \quad \dot{\boldsymbol{r}} = u_0(\boldsymbol{i}\cos\theta + \boldsymbol{k}\sin\theta)$$

where u_0 is the speed of projection and θ is the angle of projection.

We may rewrite the equation of motion in terms of three scalar differential equations, namely

$$m\ddot{x} + k_1\dot{x} = 0$$

$$m\ddot{y} + k_1\dot{y} = 0$$

$$m\ddot{z} + k_1\dot{z} = -mg$$

Each of these equations is a linear first-order differential equation for a velocity component in terms of time. We may apply the integrating-factor method to each differential equation to obtain its general solution, the integrating factor being $e^{k_1 t/m}$ [see J. Hunter, *Calculus*, Blackie/Chambers]. Equivalently we may treat the equation of motion in a similar manner. We rearrange the equation of motion and multiply by the integrating factor $e^{k_1 t/m}$. Thus we have

$$(m\ddot{\boldsymbol{r}} + k_1\dot{\boldsymbol{r}})e^{k_1 t/m} = -mg\boldsymbol{k}\, e^{k_1 t/m}$$

i.e.

$$\frac{d}{dt}\{\dot{\boldsymbol{r}}\, e^{k_1 t/m}\} = -g\boldsymbol{k}\, e^{k_1 t/m}$$

Integration with respect to t leads to

$$\dot{\boldsymbol{r}}\, e^{k_1 t/m} = -\frac{mg}{k_1}\boldsymbol{k}\, e^{k_1 t/m} + \mathbf{A}$$

where $\mathbf{A}$ is a vector of integration, determined by the initial conditions. We find that

$$u_0(\boldsymbol{i}\cos\theta + \boldsymbol{k}\sin\theta) = -\frac{mg}{k_1}\boldsymbol{k} + \mathbf{A}$$

and

$$\dot{\boldsymbol{r}} = -\frac{mg}{k_1}\boldsymbol{k}(1 - e^{-k_1 t/m}) + u_0(\boldsymbol{i}\cos\theta + \boldsymbol{k}\sin\theta)\, e^{-k_1 t/m}$$

We note that $\dot{\boldsymbol{r}} \to -(mg/k_1)\boldsymbol{k}$ as $t \to \infty$. We denote the terminal speed (mg/k_1) by U. The terminal velocity $-U\boldsymbol{k}$ is independent of the velocity of projection.

We integrate with respect to t the above expression for $\dot{\boldsymbol{r}}$ in terms of t. Hence we have

$$\boldsymbol{r} = -\frac{mg}{k_1}\boldsymbol{k}\left(t+\frac{m}{k_1}e^{-k_1t/m}\right)-\frac{mu_0}{k_1}(\boldsymbol{i}\cos\theta+\boldsymbol{k}\sin\theta)\,e^{-k_1t/m}+\mathbf{B}$$

where

$$\boldsymbol{0} = -\frac{m^2g}{k_1^2}\boldsymbol{k}-\frac{mu_0}{k_1}(\boldsymbol{i}\cos\theta+\boldsymbol{k}\sin\theta)+\mathbf{B}$$

The required expression for the position vector in terms of time is

$$\boldsymbol{r} = -\frac{mgt}{k_1}\boldsymbol{k}+\left\{\frac{mu_0\cos\theta}{k_1}\boldsymbol{i}+\left(\frac{m^2g}{k_1^2}+\frac{mu_0\sin\theta}{k_1}\right)\boldsymbol{k}\right\}(1-e^{-k_1t/m})$$

We note that the components of these results are

$$\dot{\boldsymbol{r}}\,.\,\boldsymbol{i} = \dot{x} = u_0\cos\theta\,e^{-k_1t/m}$$

$$\boldsymbol{r}\,.\,\boldsymbol{i} = x = \frac{mu_0\cos\theta}{k_1}(1-e^{-k_1t/m})$$

$$\dot{\boldsymbol{r}}\,.\,\boldsymbol{j} = \dot{y} = 0$$

$$\boldsymbol{r}\,.\,\boldsymbol{j} = y = 0$$

$$\dot{\boldsymbol{r}}\,.\,\boldsymbol{k} = \dot{z} = u_0\sin\theta\,e^{-k_1t/m}-\frac{mg}{k_1}(1-e^{-k_1t/m})$$

$$\boldsymbol{r}\,.\,\boldsymbol{k} = z = \left(\frac{mu_0\sin\theta}{k_1}+\frac{m^2g}{k_1^2}\right)(1-e^{-k_1t/m})-\frac{mg}{k_1}t$$

The problem of determining $\dot{x}$ and x is separate from the problem of determining $\dot{z}$ and z. We see this by writing out a full description of each problem, namely

to solve $m\ddot{x}+k_1\dot{x} = 0$

subject to $x = 0$ and $\dot{x} = u_0\cos\theta$ at $t = 0$ and

to solve $m\ddot{z}+k_1\dot{z} = -mg$

subject to $z = 0$ and $\dot{z} = u_0\sin\theta$ at $t = 0$

Let us examine our solution. As $t\to\infty$

$$x\to\frac{mu_0\cos\theta}{k_1} \qquad z\to-\infty$$

$$\dot{x}\to 0 \qquad \dot{z}\to-\frac{mg}{k_1} = -U$$

The new fact that emerges here is that the x-coordinate has a finite upper bound. (The comparable results for the parabolic trajectory corresponding to $k_1 = 0$ are

$$x \to \infty, \quad z \to -\infty, \quad \dot{x} = u_0 \cos\theta, \quad \dot{z} \to -\infty \quad \text{as} \quad t \to \infty.)$$

We have noted already the phenomenon of the terminal velocity $-U\mathbf{k}$ that exists when we incorporate air resistance into the mathematical model.

The maximum height occurs when $\dot{z} = 0$. Solving the equation $\dot{z} = 0$, we have

$$e^{-k_1 t/m} = \frac{mg/k_1}{u_0 \sin\theta + mg/k_1} = \frac{U}{u_0 \sin\theta + U}$$

and

$$t = \frac{m}{k_1} \ln\{1 + (u_0/U)\sin\theta\}$$

Hence the x and z-coordinates of the highest point of the trajectory are

$$\frac{mu_0^2 \sin\theta\cos\theta}{k_1(u_0\sin\theta + U)} = \frac{u_0^2 \sin\theta\cos\theta}{g\{1 + (u_0/U)\sin\theta\}}$$

and

$$\frac{m}{k_1}\left(u_0\sin\theta + \frac{mg}{k_1}\right)\left(\frac{u_0\sin\theta}{u_0\sin\theta + U}\right) - \frac{m^2 g}{k_1^2}\ln\{1 + (u_0/U)\sin\theta\}$$

$$= \frac{Uu_0\sin\theta}{g} - \frac{U^2}{g}\ln\{1 + (u_0/U)\sin\theta\}$$

respectively.

To determine the range of the projectile we have to find the value of x when $z = 0$. The equation $z = 0$ becomes

$$\{1 + (u_0/U)\sin\theta\}(1 - e^{-k_1 t/m}) = k_1 t/m$$

One solution of this equation is $t = 0$. There is a second solution, corresponding to the time of flight, $t = T$ say. We have to solve the transcendental equation

$$1 - \frac{\tau}{1 + (u_0/U)\sin\theta} = e^{-\tau}$$

where $\tau = k_1 T/m = gT/U$. An iteration method is a suitable technique to (improve a first approximation and) obtain a satisfactory approximation to the time of flight [see C. Dixon, *Numerical Analysis*, Blackie/Chambers]. We note that the range equals

$$\frac{u_0 T \cos\theta}{1+(u_0/U)\sin\theta}$$

When τ is large, i.e. $gT \gg U$, we may ignore the exponential term $e^{-\tau}$ and obtain a good approximation to the time of flight from the equation

$$1 - \frac{\tau}{1+(u_0/U)\sin\theta} = 0$$

Thus we find that T is approximately equal to $(U + u_0 \sin\theta)/g$ and that the range is approximately equal to $(Uu_0/g)\cos\theta$. Our approximation to the velocity at $t = T$ is the terminal velocity $-U\mathbf{k}$.

Suppose $k_1 t/m \ll 1$ (and $t > 0$), i.e. $gt \ll U$. This condition applies when the aerodynamic drag has little effect. Using the expansion

$$e^{-k_1 t/m} = 1 - \frac{k_1 t}{m} + \frac{1}{2}\left(\frac{k_1 t}{m}\right)^2 - \frac{1}{6}\left(\frac{k_1 t}{m}\right)^3 + \ldots$$

we find that

$$\dot{x} = u_0 \cos\theta\left\{1 - \frac{k_1 t}{m} + \ldots\right\}$$

$$x = u_0 t \cos\theta\left\{1 - \frac{k_1 t}{2m} + \ldots\right\}$$

$$\dot{z} = u_0 \sin\theta\left\{1 - \frac{k_1 t}{m} + \ldots\right\} - gt\left\{1 - \frac{k_1 t}{2m} + \ldots\right\}$$

$$z = u_0 t \sin\theta\left\{1 - \frac{k_1 t}{2m} + \ldots\right\} - \tfrac{1}{2}gt^2\left\{1 - \frac{k_1 t}{3m} + \ldots\right\}$$

The terms independent of k_1 arose in chapter 4 in our study of the projectile's trajectory in the special case of no aerodynamic drag. The highest point of the trajectory has the coordinates

$$x = \frac{u_0^2}{g}\sin\theta\cos\theta\left\{1 - \frac{k_1 u_0}{mg}\sin\theta + \ldots\right\}$$

and

$$z = \frac{1}{2}\frac{u_0^2}{g}\sin^2\theta\left\{1 - \frac{2}{3}\frac{k_1 u_0}{mg}\sin\theta + \ldots\right\}$$

and the projectile is at its maximum height when

$$t = \frac{u_0}{g}\sin\theta\left\{1 - \frac{1}{2}\frac{k_1 u_0}{mg}\sin\theta + \ldots\right\}.$$

Here we have used the expansions

$$\{1+(u_0/U)\sin\theta\}^{-1} = 1 - \frac{k_1 u_0}{mg}\sin\theta + \ldots$$

and

$$\ln\{1+(u_0/U)\sin\theta\} = \frac{k_1 u_0}{mg}\sin\theta \times \left\{1 - \frac{1}{2}\frac{k_1 u_0}{mg}\sin\theta + \frac{1}{3}\left(\frac{k_1 u_0 \sin\theta}{mg}\right)^2 - \ldots\right\}$$

[see J. Hunter, *Calculus*, Blackie/Chambers]. Solving the equation $z = 0$, we find that the time of flight equals

$$\frac{2u_0}{g}\sin\theta\left\{1 - \frac{1}{3}\frac{k_1 u_0}{mg}\sin\theta + \ldots\right\}$$

Our approximation to the range is

$$2\frac{u_0^2}{g}\sin\theta\cos\theta\left\{1 - \frac{4}{3}\frac{k_1 u_0}{mg}\sin\theta + \ldots\right\}$$

and our approximation to the final velocity is

$$u_0\cos\theta\left\{1 - 2\frac{k_1 u_0}{mg}\sin\theta + \ldots\right\}\boldsymbol{i} - u_0\sin\theta\left\{1 - \frac{2}{3}\frac{k_1 u_0}{mg}\sin\theta + \ldots\right\}\boldsymbol{k}$$

We note that $k_1 u_0/mg = u_0/U$ and we have assumed that $u_0/U \ll 1$ in the derivation of the above approximations.

EXAMPLE

A particle is thrown vertically upwards with speed u_0 in a medium for which the resistance is proportional to the particle's speed. The particle's terminal speed is U. Find a relation between the particle's speed and its height above the point of projection.

We introduce the z-axis with the direction of $\boldsymbol{k}$ vertically upwards and the origin coinciding with the point of projection. The equation governing the particle's motion is

$$m\ddot{z} = -mg - k_1\dot{z}$$

where m is the mass of the particle and $mg/k_1 = U$. Setting $\dot{z} = u$ and using $\ddot{z} = \dot{z}(d\dot{z}/dz) = u(du/dz)$, we have

$$\frac{mu}{mg + k_1 u}\frac{du}{dz} = -1$$

This is a first-order differential equation (determining u in terms of z) that is separable. An integration with respect to z leads to

$$\frac{U}{g}\{u-U\ln(U+u)\} = -z+A$$

The imposition of the initial condition, namely $u = u_0$ at $z = 0$, gives

$$\frac{U}{g}\{u_0-U\ln(U+u_0)\} = A$$

The required relation is

$$z = \frac{U}{g}\left\{(u_0-u)-U\ln\left(\frac{U+u_0}{U+u}\right)\right\}$$

where $u = \dot{z}$. The maximum height, which corresponds to $u = 0$, is

$$\frac{U}{g}\{u_0-U\ln(1+u_0/U)\} = H \text{ (say)}$$

Multiplying the governing differential equation by $\dot{z}$ and integrating with respect to t, we find that

$$\tfrac{1}{2}m\dot{z}^2+mgz = \tfrac{1}{2}mu_0^2 - \int_0^t k_1\dot{z}^2\,dt$$

We may deduce that the energy dissipated during the upward motion equals

$$\tfrac{1}{2}mu_0^2-mgH$$

Noting that

$$\int_0^t k_1\dot{z}^2\,dt = \int_0^t k_1\dot{z}\frac{dz}{dt}\,dt = \int_0^z k_1\dot{z}\,dz$$

we see that the energy loss equals

$$\int_0^H k_1 u\,dz$$

We do not have an explicit expression for u in terms of z, so we are unable to evaluate the integral directly. However, a direct evaluation of

$$\int_0^t k_1\dot{z}^2\,dt$$

is possible when we use the relation for $\dot{z}$ in terms of t.

Finally we try to calculate the speed that the particle has on its return to the point of projection. The final speed is a solution of $z = 0$. One solution of the equation

$$\left\{(u_0-u)-U\ln\left(\frac{U+u_0}{U+u}\right)\right\} = 0$$

is $u = u_0$. The final speed is the second solution of this transcendental equation, which we may rewrite in the form

$$e^{-\sigma} = 1-\frac{\sigma}{1+u_0/U}$$

where $\sigma = (u_0-u)/U$. We have to use a numerical method to find an approximation to the final speed.

EXAMPLE

A parachutist leaves an aircraft flying horizontally with speed 300 kilometres per hour. His terminal speed is $5\,\mathrm{m\,s^{-1}}$. Describe the motion of the parachutist. Assume that there is no wind and that the parachute opens immediately the parachutist leaves the aircraft.

We introduce cartesian coordinates and suppose that the aircraft is flying along the x-axis in the direction of x increasing and that the parachutist leaves the aircraft at the origin O at $t = 0$. The initial velocity of the parachutist is the velocity of the aircraft. Assuming that the aerodynamic drag is proportional to speed, we obtain the equation of motion (for a particle representing the parachutist)

$$m\ddot{\boldsymbol{r}} = -mg\boldsymbol{k} - k_1\dot{\boldsymbol{r}}$$

The initial conditions are $\boldsymbol{r} = \boldsymbol{0}$ and $\dot{\boldsymbol{r}} = u_0\boldsymbol{i}$ at $t = 0$. Therefore the required solution is

$$\boldsymbol{r} = \frac{mu_0}{k_1}(1 - e^{-k_1 t/m})\boldsymbol{i} - \left\{\frac{mgt}{k_1} - \frac{m^2 g}{k_1^2}(1 - e^{-k_1 t/m})\right\}\boldsymbol{k}$$

We note that the terminal velocity is $-(mg/k_1)\boldsymbol{k}$. Therefore k_1/m equals $\frac{1}{5}g$. Substituting for the particular values of u_0 and k_1/m, we find that

$$\boldsymbol{r} = \frac{1250}{3g}(1 - e^{-gt/5})\boldsymbol{i} - \left\{5t - \frac{25}{g}(1 - e^{-gt/5})\right\}\boldsymbol{k}$$

and

$$\dot{\boldsymbol{r}} = \frac{250}{3}e^{-gt/5}\boldsymbol{i} - 5(1 - e^{-gt/5})\boldsymbol{k}$$

t (s)	x (m)	$\dot{x}$ ($\mathrm{m\,s^{-1}}$)	z (m)	$\dot{z}$ ($\mathrm{m\,s^{-1}}$)
0·0	0·00	83·333	0·00	0·000
1·0	36·50	11·715	−2·81	−4·297
2·0	41·63	1·647	−7·52	−4·901
3·0	42·36	0·232	−12·46	−4·986
4·0	42·46	0·033	−17·45	−4·998
5·0	42·47	0·005	−22·45	−5·000
10·0	42·47	0·000	−47·45	−5·000

The tabulated results show that after five seconds the parachutist is moving vertically downwards with his terminal speed and that the parachutist drops 1000 metres in 200·5 seconds.

We have ignored the phase of the motion before the parachute opens. Assume that the parachutist falls for $t \in [0, t_0]$ in a random posture, the associated terminal speed being $54\,\mathrm{m\,s^{-1}}$, and that the parachute opens instantaneously at $t = t_0$. The results corresponding to delay times of 5 seconds and 10 seconds are given in the tables. We see that the parachutist is moving with his terminal speed about five seconds after the parachute opens (because $e^{-g} < e^{-9 \cdot 8} = 0{\cdot}000\,0555$).

t (s)	x (m)	$\dot{x}$ (m s^{-1})	z (m)	$\dot{z}$ (m s^{-1})
		$t_0 = 5$		
0·0	0·00	83·333	0·00	0·000
1·0	76·20	69·490	−4·62	−8·971
2·0	139·75	57·946	−17·44	−16·451
3·0	192·73	48·320	−37·11	−22·688
4·0	236·92	40·293	−62·48	−27·890
5·0	273·76	33·600	−92·60	−32·227
6·0	288·48	4·723	−109·53	−8·828
7·0	290·55	0·664	−116·20	−5·538
8·0	290·84	0·093	−121·44	−5·076
9·0	290·88	0·013	−126·47	−5·011
10·0	290·89	0·002	−131·48	−5·001
20·0	290·89	0·000	−181·48	−5·000

		$t_0 = 10$		
0·0	0·00	83·333	0·00	0·000
5·0	273·76	33·600	−92·60	−32·227
6·0	304·49	28·018	−126·69	−35·844
7·0	330·11	22·364	−164·09	−38·860
8·0	351·47	19·482	−204·25	−41·375
9·0	369·29	16·246	−246·70	−43·473
10·0	384·14	13·547	−291·07	−45·221
11·0	390·08	1·904	−313·69	−10·654
12·0	390·91	0·268	−321·17	−5·795
13·0	391·03	0·038	−326·52	−5·112
14·0	391·05	0·005	−331·57	−5·016
15·0	391·05	0·001	−336·57	−5·002
20·0	391·05	0·000	−361·58	−5·000

10.4 Aerodynamic drag proportional to the square of speed

We continue to examine the motion of a projectile through a stationary atmosphere. In this section we shall assume that the aerodynamic drag is proportional to the square of the projectile's speed relative to the air. There is experimental evidence to suggest that this relation is generally applicable and that the linear relation considered in Section 10.3 is applicable to small projectiles whose speeds are less than 24 m s^{-1} or greater than 330 m s^{-1} (the speed of sound).

Consider a particle of mass m moving in a vertical plane (the xz-plane, say). Let $\boldsymbol{r}$ be its position vector relative to the origin of the coordinate system. The initial conditions at $t = 0$ are

$$\boldsymbol{r} = \boldsymbol{0} \quad \text{and} \quad \dot{\boldsymbol{r}} = u_0(\boldsymbol{i}\cos\theta + \boldsymbol{k}\sin\theta)$$

The projectile experiences two forces, the gravitational force represented by $-mg\mathbf{k}$ and the aerodynamic drag represented by $-k_2|\dot{\mathbf{r}}|\dot{\mathbf{r}}$. The positive parameter k_2 has the dimensions ML^{-1}. We note that the representation of the drag is correct; its magnitude is proportional to the square of the speed and its direction is opposite to the direction of motion. The equation of motion is

$$m\ddot{\mathbf{r}} = -mg\mathbf{k} - k_2|\dot{\mathbf{r}}|\dot{\mathbf{r}}$$

In practice the value of k_2 varies with the speed of the projectile. We shall assume that k_2 takes a constant value throughout the motion.

The motion of the particle is confined to the xz-plane (because the initial position and the initial velocity are in the xz-plane and there is no force perpendicular to the xz-plane). The governing differential equations are

$$m\ddot{x} + k_2(\dot{x}^2 + \dot{z}^2)^{1/2}\dot{x} = 0$$

and

$$m\ddot{z} + k_2(\dot{x}^2 + \dot{z}^2)^{1/2}\dot{z} = -mg$$

They form a pair of simultaneous first-order non-linear differential equations (relating $\dot{x}$ and $\dot{z}$ to t). We have no analytical methods of solution available. We could consider the possibility of using a numerical method to obtain an approximate solution. The differential equations indicate the existence of a terminal velocity $-(mg/k_2)^{1/2}\mathbf{k}$.

We are able to apply an analytical method of solution when the motion is confined to a vertical line. In this special case

$$\theta = \tfrac{1}{2}\pi, \quad x = \dot{x} = 0, \quad (\dot{x}^2 + \dot{z}^2)^{1/2} = |\dot{z}|$$

and z satisfies

$$m\ddot{z} + k_2|\dot{z}|\dot{z} = -mg$$

subject to $z = 0$ and $\dot{z} = u_0$ at $t = 0$. In the upward motion, $\dot{z} > 0$ and the differential equation becomes

$$m\ddot{z} + k_2\dot{z}^2 = -mg$$

In the downward motion, $\dot{z} < 0$ and the governing equation is

$$m\ddot{z} - k_2\dot{z}^2 = -mg$$

The sign of the term representing the drag is very important. The second differential equation leads us to expect a terminal speed U equalling $(mg/k_2)^{1/2}$.

First we shall examine the upward motion. Setting $\dot{z} = u$ and using $\ddot{z} = du/dt$, we change the governing differential equation into

$$\frac{m}{k_2}\left(\frac{1}{u^2+mg/k_2}\right)\frac{du}{dt}=-1; \quad \text{i.e.} \quad \frac{1}{u^2+U^2}\frac{du}{dt}=-\frac{g}{U^2}$$

Integration with respect to t gives

$$\frac{1}{U}\tan^{-1}\left(\frac{u}{U}\right)=-\frac{gt}{U^2}+A$$

Imposing the initial condition, namely $u = u_0$ at $t = 0$, we have

$$\frac{1}{U}\tan^{-1}\left(\frac{u_0}{U}\right)=A$$

Therefore

$$\tan^{-1}\left(\frac{u}{U}\right)=-\frac{gt}{U}+\tan^{-1}\left(\frac{u_0}{U}\right)$$

and

$$u=U\tan\left\{\tan^{-1}\left(\frac{u_0}{U}\right)-\frac{gt}{U}\right\}$$

Letting T_U denote the time to attain the maximum height, we have

$$T_U=\frac{U}{g}\tan^{-1}\left(\frac{u_0}{U}\right) \quad \text{and} \quad u=U\tan\left\{\frac{g}{U}(T_U-t)\right\}$$

Hence

$$\frac{dz}{dt}=U\tan\left\{\frac{g}{U}(T_U-t)\right\}$$

Integrating with respect to t, we obtain

$$z=\frac{U^2}{g}\ln\left|\cos\left\{\frac{g}{U}(T_U-t)\right\}\right|+B$$

The condition that $z = 0$ at $t = 0$ shows that

$$0=\frac{U^2}{g}\ln\left[\cos\left\{\frac{gT_U}{U}\right\}\right]+B$$

Thus, we have

$$z=\frac{U^2}{g}\ln\left|\frac{\cos\{g(T_U-t)/U\}}{\cos\{gT_U/U\}}\right|$$

When $t = T_U$, $z = H$, where H denotes the maximum height. Therefore

$$H=\frac{U^2}{g}\ln\left[\frac{1}{\cos\{gT_U/U\}}\right]$$

where $\tan\{gT_U/U\} = u_0/U$, i.e.

$$H = \frac{U^2}{2g}\ln(1+u_0^2/U^2)$$

During the downward motion, the governing equation is

$$m\ddot{z} - k_2\dot{z}^2 = -mg$$

subject to $z = H$ and $\dot{z} = 0$ at $t = T_U$. The drag is acting vertically upwards when the particle is falling and the signs are correct in the differential equation. Setting $\dot{z} = u$ and treating the differential equation as a first-order equation of separable type, we have

$$\frac{m}{k_2}\left(\frac{1}{mg/k_2 - u^2}\right)\frac{du}{dt} = -1; \quad \text{i.e.} \quad \frac{1}{U^2-u^2}\frac{du}{dt} = -\frac{g}{U^2}$$

Using partial fractions and integrating with respect to t, we find that

$$\frac{1}{2U}\ln\left(\frac{U+u}{U-u}\right) = -\frac{gt}{U^2} + A$$

The value of A is given by $0 = -gT_U/U^2 + A$. Thus we have

$$\ln\left(\frac{U+u}{U-u}\right) = -\frac{2g}{U}(t-T_U)$$

and

$$u = -U\left\{\frac{1-e^{-2g(t-T_U)/U}}{1+e^{-2g(t-T_U)/U}}\right\} = -U\tanh\{g(t-T_U)/U\}$$

This confirms our expectation that $\dot{z} \to -U$ as $t \to \infty$. The next step (to determine z in terms of t) requires us to integrate

$$\begin{aligned}\frac{dz}{dt} &= -U\tanh\{g(t-T_U)/U\}\\ &= -\frac{U^2}{g}\frac{d}{dt}\ln[\cosh\{g(t-T_U)/U\}]\end{aligned}$$

with respect to t. The required result is

$$z = -\frac{U^2}{g}\ln[\cosh\{g(t-T_U)/U\}] + B$$

where $H = B$. Hence we have

$$z = \frac{U^2}{g}\{\tfrac{1}{2}\ln(1+u_0^2/U^2) - \ln[\cosh\{g(t-T_U)/U\}]\}$$

Suppose that the particle returns to its point of projection when $t = T_U + T_D$. Then

$$\cosh\{gT_D/U\} = (1+u_0^2/U^2)^{1/2}$$

i.e.

$$T_D = \frac{U}{g}\cosh^{-1}\{(1+u_0^2/U^2)^{1/2}\}$$

$$= \frac{U}{g}\ln\{(1+u_0^2/U^2)^{1/2}+u_0/U\}$$

We note that at $t = T_U + T_D$

$$\dot{z} = -U\tanh\{gT_D/U\} = \frac{-U\{(1+u_0^2/U^2)-1\}^{1/2}}{(1+u_0^2/U^2)^{1/2}} = \frac{-u_0}{(1+u_0^2/U^2)^{1/2}}$$

When the drag is proportional to the square of speed, we experience no difficulty in obtaining the time of flight and the speed with which the particle returns to the point of projection; cf. the transcendental equations in Section 10.3.

EXAMPLE

A particle is thrown vertically upwards with speed u_0 in a medium for which the resistance is proportional to the square of the particle's speed. The particle's terminal speed is U. What is the relation between the particle's speed and its height above the point of projection?

We introduce the z-axis with the direction of $\boldsymbol{k}$ vertically upwards and the origin coinciding with the point of projection. We have to solve

$$m\ddot{z} = -mg - k_2\dot{z}^2 \quad \text{when} \quad \dot{z} > 0$$

and

$$m\ddot{z} = -mg + k_2\dot{z}^2 \quad \text{when} \quad \dot{z} < 0$$

It is convenient to set $\dot{z} = u$ and to use $\ddot{z} = u(du/dz)$. First we shall consider the upward motion, which is subject to the initial condition $u = u_0$ at $z = 0$. The differential equation becomes

$$\left(\frac{2u}{U^2+u^2}\right)\frac{du}{dz} = -\frac{2g}{U^2}$$

where $U^2 = mg/k_2$. This leads to

$$\ln(U^2+u^2) = -\frac{2gz}{U^2} + A$$

where $\ln(U^2+u_0^2) = A$. Thus we have

$$\ln\left(\frac{U^2+u^2}{U^2+u_0^2}\right) = -\frac{2gz}{U^2}$$

and

$$u^2 = u_0^2 e^{-2gz/U^2} - U^2(1-e^{-2gz/U^2})$$

At the end of the upward motion, we find that

$$\dot{z} = 0 \quad \text{and} \quad z = H = \frac{U^2}{2g}\ln(1+u_0^2/U^2)$$

These are the initial conditions for the downward motion, which is governed by the differential equation

$$\left(\frac{2u}{U^2-u^2}\right)\frac{du}{dz} = -\frac{2g}{U^2}$$

Integrating with respect to z, we find that

$$-\ln(U^2-u^2) = -\frac{2gz}{U^2} + B$$

where

$$-\ln U^2 = -\frac{2gH}{U^2} + B$$

Substituting for B and H leads to

$$\ln\left(\frac{U^2}{U^2-u^2}\right) - \ln(1+u_0^2/U^2) = -\frac{2gz}{U^2}$$

Hence we obtain

$$\ln\left(\frac{U^4}{(U^2-u^2)(U^2+u_0^2)}\right) = -\frac{2gz}{U^2}$$

and

$$u^2 = U^2\left\{1 - \frac{e^{2gz/U^2}}{(1+u_0^2/U^2)}\right\}$$

When the particle returns to the point of projection

$$u = -\frac{u_0}{(1+u_0^2/U^2)^{1/2}}$$

We may deduce that the energy dissipated during the upward motion is

$$\tfrac{1}{2}mu_0^2 - mgH = \tfrac{1}{2}mu_0^2 - \tfrac{1}{2}mU^2\ln(1+u_0^2/U^2)$$

and the energy dissipated during the downward motion is

$$mgH - \frac{\tfrac{1}{2}mu_0^2}{(1+u_0^2/U^2)} = \tfrac{1}{2}mU^2\ln(1+u_0^2/U^2) - \frac{\tfrac{1}{2}mu_0^2}{(1+u_0^2/U^2)}$$

The total loss of energy during the complete journey is

$$\tfrac{1}{2}mu_0^2/(1+U^2/u_0^2)$$

EXAMPLE

A parachutist drops from a balloon moored at an altitude of 500 m. He falls in a spread-eagle position for $t \in [0, t_0]$, the associated terminal speed being 54 m s^{-1}. He opens his parachute to brake his fall and to achieve a terminal speed of 5 m s^{-1}. Assume that the aerodynamic drag is proportional to the square of speed. Investigate the parachutist's descent when the delay time t_0 is zero, 5 s and 10 s.

We introduce the z-axis so that the balloon is represented by the origin and the ground is represented by the plane $z = -H$. The equation governing the motion (of a particle of mass m representing the parachutist) has the form

$$m\ddot{z} = -mg + k_2\dot{z}^2$$

For $t \in [0, t_0]$ and the associated terminal speed U_1, we find that

$$\dot{z} = -U_1 \tanh(gt/U_1)$$

and

$$z = -\frac{U_1^2}{g} \ln\{\cosh(gt/U_1)\}$$

At $t = t_0$

$$\dot{z} = -U_1 \tanh(gt_0/U_1) = u_0 \text{ (say)}$$

and

$$z = -\frac{U_1^2}{g} \ln\{\cosh(gt/U_1)\} = z_0 \text{ (say)}$$

For $t > t_0$ and the associated terminal speed U_2, we find that

$$\dot{z} = -U_2\left[\frac{U_2 \sinh\{g(t-t_0)/U_2\} - u_0 \cosh\{g(t-t_0)/U_2\}}{U_2 \cosh\{g(t-t_0)/U_2\} - u_0 \sinh\{g(t-t_0)/U_2\}}\right]$$

and

$$z = z_0 - \frac{U_2^2}{g} \ln[\cosh\{g(t-t_0)/U_2\} - (u_0/U_2)\sinh\{g(t-t_0)/U_2\}]$$

Suppose that $z = -H$ when $t = T$. Then we have that

$$\cosh\{g(t-t_0)/U_2\} - (u_0/U_2)\sinh\{g(T-t_0)/U_2\} = e^{g(H+z_0)/U_2^2}$$

It follows that

$$T = t_0 + \frac{U_2}{g} \ln\left[\frac{e^{g(H+z_0)/U_2^2} + \{e^{2g(H+z_0)/U_2^2} + (u_0/U_2)^2 - 1\}^{1/2}}{1 - u_0/U_2}\right]$$

$$= t_0 + \frac{(H+z_0)}{U_2} + \frac{U_2}{g} \ln\left[\frac{1 + [1 + \{(u_0/U_2)^2 - 1\}\, e^{-2g(H+z_0)/U_2^2}]^{1/2}}{1 - u_0/U_2}\right]$$

	$t_0 = 0$		$t_0 = 5$		$t_0 = 10$	
t (s)	z (m)	$\dot{z}$ (m s^{-1})	z (m)	$\dot{z}$ (m s^{-1})	z (m)	$\dot{z}$ (m s^{-1})
0·0	0·00	0·000	0·00	0·000	0·00	0·000
1·0	−3·28	−4·806	−4·88	−9·703		
2·0	−8·23	−4·996	−19·20	−18·800		
3·0	−13·23	−5·000	−42·12	−26·825		
4·0	−18·23	−5·000	−72·41	−33·535		
5·0	−23·23	−5·000	−108·74	−38·898	−108·74	−38·898
6·0			−117·47	−5·155	−149·80	−43·031
7·0			−122·51	−5·003	−194·46	−46·129
8·0			−127·51	−5·000	−241·78	−48·403
9·0			−132·51	−5·000	−291·05	−50·046
10·0	−48·23	−5·000	−137·51	−5·000	−341·72	−51·219
11·0					−351·08	−5·165
12·0					−356·12	−5·003
13·0					−361·12	−5·000
14·0					−366·12	−5·000
15·0					−371·12	−5·000
20·0	−98·23	−5·000	−187·51	−5·000	−396·12	−5·000

The tabulated results correspond to the delay time being zero, 5 s and 10 s. The values of the time of descent are 100·4 s, 82·5 s and 40·8 s, respectively. The corresponding times to descend 500 m, based on a linear law for the aerodynamic drag, can be deduced from the tables in Section 10.3. They are 100·5 s, 83·7 s and 47·7 s, respectively. We note the similarity when the delay time is either zero or 5 s and we note the difference when the delay time is 10 s. The difference suggests a dangerous experiment to test the mathematical model! Finally, we recognize that we have assumed that the parachute opens instantaneously. This assumption leads to an overestimate of the descent times.

10.5 Numerical methods

We noted in Section 10.4 the non-availability of analytical methods to solve the two-dimensional problem of a projectile subjected to aerodynamic drag proportional to the square of the speed of the projectile. Let us explore the possibility of obtaining approximate results by means of numerical methods. To make the development of the numerical methods as simple as possible we shall consider in the first instance the one-dimensional problem of an object dropped from a height H above the ground.

We introduce the z-axis so that the plane $z = 0$ represents the ground and the initial conditions at $t = 0$ are $z = H$ (>0) and $\dot{z} = 0$. The differential equation governing the motion of a particle representing the object of mass m is

$$w(t_n) = w_n + \text{error term}$$

$$m\ddot{z} = -mg + R$$

where R represents aerodynamic drag (i.e. $R > 0$). We shall be interested in the three cases

$$\text{(i) } R = 0, \quad \text{(ii) } R = k_1|\dot{z}|, \quad \text{(iii) } R = k_2\dot{z}^2$$

Setting $\dot{z} = w$, we have to solve

$$m\frac{dw}{dt} = -mg + R(w)$$

and

$$\frac{dz}{dt} = w$$

where

$$R(w) = \begin{cases} 0 & \text{case (i)} \\ -k_1 w & \text{case (ii)} \\ k_2 w^2 & \text{case (iii)} \end{cases}$$

These are two first-order differential equations for w and z in terms of t. First we solve for w and then we solve for z.

Consider

$$\frac{dw}{dt} = f(w) = F(t)$$

where $F(t) = f(w(t)) = (f \circ w)(t)$. Integrating with respect to t from $t = T_1$ to $t = T_2$, we obtain

$$w(T_2) - w(T_1) = \int_{T_1}^{T_2} \frac{dw}{dt}\, dt = \int_{T_1}^{T_2} F(t)\, dt$$

The next step is to use an approximation to the integral, which is usually based on a polynomial approximation to the integrand [see C. Dixon, *Numerical Analysis*, Blackie/Chambers]. It is convenient for us to use

$$\int_{T_1}^{T_2} F(t)\, dt = (T_2 - T_1)F(T_1) + \text{truncation error}$$

Thus we obtain

$$w(T_2) = w(T_1) + (T_2 - T_1)F(T_1) + \text{truncation error}$$

This gives us information about w at $t = T_2$ in terms of information at $t = T_1$ and the truncation error.

We introduce the sequence

$$t_0, t_1, t_2, \ldots, t_n, t_{n+1}, \ldots$$

where $t_n = n\Delta t$ and Δt is the length of a given time interval. Then we set

$$w(t_n) = w_n + \text{error term}$$

where $w(t_n)$ is the exact value of w at $t = t_n$ and w_n is an approximation to w at $t = t_n$. The approximation technique described in the previous paragraph is applied to the interval $[t_n, t_{n+1}]$. Thus we define the elements of the sequence

$$w_0, w_1, w_2, \ldots, w_n, w_{n+1}, \ldots$$

by the recurrence relation

$$w_{n+1} = w_n + \Delta t\, f(w_n) \quad (n = 0, 1, 2, \ldots)$$

subject to the initial condition $w_0 = w(0) = 0$. This is Euler's method. The forms of the recurrence relation corresponding to the three cases are

(i) $f(w) = -g$

$$w_{n+1} = w_n - g\Delta t \quad \text{with} \quad w_0 = 0$$

(ii) $f(w) = -g - k_1 w/m = -g(1+w/U)$, where $U = mg/k_1$

$$w_{n+1} = w_n - g\Delta t(1+w_n/U)$$
$$= (1-g\Delta t/U)w_n - g\Delta t \quad \text{with} \quad w_0 = 0$$

(iii) $f(w) = -g + k_2 w^2/m = -g(1-w^2/U^2)$, where $U^2 = mg/k_2$

$$w_{n+1} = w_n - g\Delta t(1-w_n^2/U^2)$$
$$= (g\Delta t/U^2)w_n^2 + w_n - g\Delta t \quad \text{with} \quad w_0 = 0$$

In this way we are able to obtain a sequence of approximations to w (corresponding to the times $t = t_0, t_1, t_2, \ldots, t_n, t_{n+1}, \ldots$) by a step-by-step process.

Setting z_n to denote an approximation to z at $t = t_n$, we have

$$z(t_n) = z_n + \text{error term}$$

and

$$z(t_{n+1}) - z(t_n) = \int_{t_n}^{t_{n+1}} \frac{dz}{dt}\,dt = \int_{t_n}^{t_{n+1}} w(t)\,dt$$

We use the trapezium approximation to the integral and define the elements of the sequence

$$z_0, z_1, z_2, \ldots, z_n, z_{n+1}, \ldots$$

by the recurrence relation

$$z_{n+1} = z_n + \tfrac{1}{2}\Delta t\{w(t_n) + w(t_{n+1})\} \quad (n = 0, 1, 2, \ldots)$$

subject to the initial condition $z_0 = z(0) = H$. The exact values of w are not available so we adopt the modified recurrence relation

$$z_{n+1} = z_n + \tfrac{1}{2}\Delta t(w_n + w_{n+1}) \quad (n = 0, 1, 2, \ldots)$$

with $z_0 = H$.

We calculate the approximations in the order

$$w_1, z_1, w_2, z_2, \ldots, w_n, z_n, w_{n+1}, z_{n+1}, \ldots$$

It is a straightforward matter to write an appropriate computer program.

In case (i) we find that

$$w_1 = 0 - g\Delta t = -g\Delta t$$
$$w_2 = -g\Delta t - g\Delta t = -2g\Delta t$$
$$w_3 = -2g\Delta t - g\Delta t = -3g\Delta t, \text{ etc.}$$

We may prove, by induction, that $w_n = -ng\Delta t = -gt_n$. Therefore

$$z_1 = H + \tfrac{1}{2}\Delta t\{0 + (-g\Delta t)\} = H - \tfrac{1}{2}g(\Delta t)^2$$

$$z_2 = H - \tfrac{1}{2}g(\Delta t)^2 + \tfrac{1}{2}\Delta t\{(-g\Delta t)+(-2g\Delta t)\} = H - \tfrac{1}{2}g(2\Delta t)^2$$
$$z_3 = H - \tfrac{1}{2}g(2\Delta t)^2 + \tfrac{1}{2}\Delta t\{(-2g\Delta t)+(-3g\Delta t)\} = H - \tfrac{1}{2}g(3\Delta t)^2, \text{ etc.}$$

A proof by induction shows that $z_n = H - \frac{1}{2}gt_n^2$. We deduce that in this special case the numerical method that we have described leads to the exact values of w and z; i.e. $w_n = w(t_n) = \dot{z}(t_n)$ and $z_n = z(t_n)$. The analysis of the errors, $w(t_n) - w_n$ and $z(t_n) - z_n$, in the general case is beyond the scope of this book [see J. D. Lambert, *Computational Methods in Ordinary Differential Equations*, Wiley].

A verbal description of the recurrence relation based on Euler's method is that average acceleration over the time interval $[t_n, t_{n+1}]$, namely $(w_{n+1} - w_n)/\Delta t$, equals the force per unit mass at $t = t_n$. We may interpret this as a discrete analogue of Newton's second law of motion. Our second recurrence relation states that the average velocity over the time interval $[t_n, t_{n+1}]$, namely $(z_{n+1} - z_n)/\Delta t$, equals the mean of the values of the velocity at $t = t_n$ and $t = t_{n+1}$. The development of discrete models and numerical methods is an interesting topic [see D. Greenspan, *Discrete Models*, Addison-Wesley].

Finally we apply this simple numerical method to the two-dimensional projectile problem formulated in Section 10.4. Let

$$\boldsymbol{r} = x\boldsymbol{i} + z\boldsymbol{k}, \quad \dot{\boldsymbol{r}} = u\boldsymbol{i} + w\boldsymbol{k}$$

and let x_n, z_n, u_n, w_n denote approximations to the exact values $x(t_n), z(t_n), u(t_n), w(t_n)$. The recurrence relations are

$$\begin{aligned} u_{n+1} &= u_n - g\Delta t(u_n^2 + w_n^2)^{1/2} u_n/U^2 \\ w_{n+1} &= w_n - g\Delta t\{1 + (u_n^2 + w_n^2)^{1/2} w_n/U^2\} \\ x_{n+1} &= x_n + \tfrac{1}{2}\Delta t(u_n + u_{n+1}) \\ z_{n+1} &= z_n + \tfrac{1}{2}\Delta t(w_n + w_{n+1}) \end{aligned}$$

where

$$u_0 = u(0) = u_0 \cos\theta \qquad w_0 = w(0) = u_0 \sin\theta$$
$$x_0 = x(0) = 0 \qquad z_0 = z(0) = 0$$

and $U^2 = mg/k_2$. In particular, we reconsider the example in Section 10.3, in which a parachutist drops from an aircraft flying horizontally. The table gives details about the first ten seconds of the motion. We present three sets of results corresponding to $\Delta t = 0{\cdot}01$, $0{\cdot}001$ and $0{\cdot}0001$. We have to choose small values of Δt so that, in particular, the recurrence relation defining u_{n+1} is a satisfactory replacement of the differential equation

$$\frac{du}{dt} = -g(u^2 + w^2)^{1/2} u/U^2$$

The horizontal motion in the first second is very sensitive to the size of Δt. We have used a computer to provide the results for $t \leqslant 5$. We deduce from the table that the horizontal range is about 10 m and the time it takes the parachutist to descend 100 m is 201 s. When the drag is proportional to the speed the corresponding results are 42 m and 201 s.

	t (s)	x_n (m)	u_n (m s^{-1})	z_n (m)	w_n (m s^{-1})
$\Delta t = 0{\cdot}01$	0·0	0·00	83·333	0·00	0·000
	1·0	7·97	1·744	−2·49	−4·299
	2·0	8·75	0·254	−7·28	−4·973
	3·0	8·86	0·035	−12·27	−4·999
	4·0	8·88	0·005	−17·27	−5·000
	5·0	8·88	0·001	−22·27	−5·000
	10·0	8·88	0·000	−47·27	−5·000
$\Delta t = 0{\cdot}001$	0·0	0·00	83·333	0·00	0·000
	1·0	8·69	1·844	−2·43	−4·244
	2·0	9·52	0·274	−7·19	−4·969
	3·0	9·64	0·038	−12·18	−4·999
	4·0	9·66	0·005	−17·18	−5·000
	5·0	9·66	0·001	−22·18	−5·000
	10·0	9·66	0·000	−47·18	−5·000
$\Delta t = 0{\cdot}0001$	0·0	0·00	83·333	0·00	0·000
	1·0	8·76	1·853	−2·42	−4·239
	2·0	9·59	0·276	−7·18	−4·969
	3·0	9·72	0·039	−12·17	−4·999
	4·0	9·73	0·005	−17·17	−5·000
	5·0	9·73	0·001	−22·17	−5·000
	10·0	9·73	0·000	−47·17	−5·000

EXERCISES ON CHAPTER 10

1. A particle of mass m is moving in a straight line subject to a resistive force whose magnitude equals $R+ku$ when the particle's speed is u, where R and k are given positive parameters. The particle is set moving with speed u_0. It travels a distance X before coming to rest in a time T. Show that

$$T = \frac{m}{k}\ln\left(1+\frac{ku_0}{R}\right) \quad \text{and} \quad X = \frac{1}{k}(mu_0 - RT)$$

2. A car of mass m starts from rest and moves in a straight line under a constant propelling force F and against a resistive force mku, where k is a positive constant and u is the speed at time t. Determine the value of the car's terminal speed U.

Show that the car attains a third of the terminal speed after travelling a distance

$$\frac{U}{k}(\ln \tfrac{3}{2} - \tfrac{1}{3})$$

and attains two-thirds of the terminal speed after travelling an additional distance

$$\frac{U}{k}(\ln 2 - \tfrac{1}{3})$$

Determine the lengths of the time intervals corresponding to these distances.

3. A motor-car, initially at rest, moves along a straight road. It is propelled by a force that is proportional to the time t and is retarded by a force that is proportional to the speed. Show that the motion of the car is governed by the differential equation

$$\frac{du}{dt} + ku = \alpha t$$

where α and k are positive constants and u is the car's velocity at time t.

Find the solution of this differential equation that satisfies the initial condition and deduce that

$$u = \tfrac{1}{2}\alpha t^2(1 - \tfrac{1}{3}kt + \ldots)$$

when $kt \ll 1$.

4. A particle of mass m moves along the x-axis under the action of a resistive force $mk\dot{x}^2$, where k is a given positive parameter. It is projected from the origin with speed u_0 at $t = 0$. Show that half the initial kinetic energy of the particle will be dissipated when $t = (2^{1/2} - 1)/ku_0$. How far will the particle have moved in this time?

5. A ship of mass M is driven by a propeller that exerts a constant thrust F. If the resistance to motion is ku^2 at speed u, where k is a positive constant, find the starting acceleration and the terminal speed. Show that the power is less than $(F^3/k)^{1/2}$.

Evaluate M, F and k in the case when the starting acceleration is $0{\cdot}1\ \text{m s}^{-2}$, the terminal speed is 30 kilometres per hour and the maximum power is 2×10^7 W.

6. A train of mass m moves along a horizontal straight track against a resistive force that is ku^2 when the train's speed is u. The engine works at a constant rate P. Show that the equation of motion leads to the differential equations

$$\frac{mu^2}{P-ku^3}\frac{du}{dx} = 1 \quad \text{and} \quad \frac{mu}{P-ku^3}\frac{du}{dt} = 1$$

Find a solution of the first differential equation that satisfies the condition $u = 0$ at $x = 0$. Deduce that the terminal speed U is $(P/k)^{1/3}$.

Verify that the solution of the second differential equation that satisfies the condition $u = 0$ at $t = 0$ is given by the implicit relation

$$\frac{m}{3kU}\left[\tfrac{1}{2}\ln\left(\frac{u^2+uU+U^2}{u^2-2uU+U^2}\right) + 3^{1/2}\left\{\frac{\pi}{6} - \tan^{-1}\left(\frac{2u+U}{3^{1/2}U}\right)\right\}\right] = t$$

Show that the work done by the tractive force while the train accelerates from rest to half the terminal speed is

$$m(P/k)^{2/3}\left[\tfrac{1}{6}\ln 7 + \frac{1}{3^{1/2}}\left\{\frac{\pi}{6} - \tan^{-1}\left(\frac{2}{3^{1/2}}\right)\right\}\right]$$

i.e. approximately $0{\cdot}132\,mU^2$.

7. A motor-car of mass 840 kg has a maximum speed on the level of 150 kilometres per hour when the engine is working at its maximum rate of 45 000 W. The aerodynamic drag is proportional to the square of the car's speed. Find the inclination to the horizontal of the steepest hill that the car can ascend at a steady speed of 50 kilometres per hour.

8. A particle of unit mass moves along the x-axis under a force of magnitude $\mu|x|$ attracting it to the origin O and a resistive force of magnitude $k\dot{x}^2$. The particle starts from rest at a distance d from the origin O. Show that the governing differential equation has the form

$$\frac{du^2}{dx} - 2ku^2 = -2\mu x$$

where $u = \dot{x} < 0$. Deduce that the square of the speed of the particle when the particle first reaches O is

$$2\mu\int_0^d xe^{-2kx}\,dx = \frac{\mu}{2k^2}\{1-(1+2kd)e^{-2kd}\}$$

Derive the identity

$$\tfrac{1}{2}u^2 = \int_0^t ku^3\,dt + \tfrac{1}{2}\mu(d^2-x^2)$$

where $u = \dot{x} < 0$ and $x \geqslant 0$, and show that the work done against the resistive force (i.e. the energy dissipated) during the motion from the initial position to the origin O is approximately $\tfrac{2}{3}\mu kd^2(1-\tfrac{3}{4}kd+\ldots)$ when $kd \ll 1$.

9. Assume that the motion of a ship is opposed by a drag that is proportional to the cube of the ship's speed through the water. It is found that, when the engines of a ship of mass M travelling at a steady speed U are stopped, the ship's speed is reduced to $\tfrac{1}{4}U$ in a distance d. Determine the power of the engines.

What is the corresponding value of the power when we assume that the drag is proportional to the square of the ship's speed?

10. To test the resistance to motion, an object is projected along a straight path on a horizontal surface and the time t taken to travel a distance x from a fixed point O on the path is measured for different values of x.

It is found that the experimental results lie on a curve whose equation is

$$t = a_1 x + a_2 x^2$$

where a_1 and a_2 are positive parameters. Determine the initial speed and show that there is a resistive force proportional to the cube of the speed.

11. A particle moves along a horizontal straight line against a resistive force that is proportional to the nth power of the speed. What is the condition on the value of n that the particle moves only a finite distance?

12. A particle of mass m moves through a medium which offers resistance $k_1 u + k_3 u^3$, where u is the particle's speed and k_1 and k_3 are positive parameters. The particle is projected with speed u_0. The resistance is the only force acting. Show that the total distance travelled before the particle comes to rest is

$$\frac{m}{(k_1 k_3)^{1/2}} \tan^{-1}\left\{\left(\frac{k_3}{k_1}\right)^{1/2} u_0\right\}$$

What is the length of the time interval during which the particle's speed reduces from u_0 to $\frac{1}{2}u_0$?

13. A ship with engines stopped is gliding to rest. It experiences a resistive force proportional to the square of its speed for speeds above 0·5 m s^{-1} and a resistive force proportional to its speed for speeds less than 0·5 m s^{-1}. Initially the ship's speed is 3 m s^{-1} and it is 2 m s^{-1} after 60 s. Show that the distance travelled before the ship comes to rest is 1005 m.

What is the ship's speed and how far has the ship travelled after 46 minutes?

14. A particle is projected vertically upwards in a medium whose resistance is proportional to the particle's speed. If the speed of projection is the same as the terminal speed U, show that the time T taken to attain the greatest height H is $(U/g)\ln 2$ and that

$$gH = U^2 - UgT$$

15. A particle is thrown vertically upwards with speed u_0 in a medium for which the resistance is proportional to the particle's speed. The particle's terminal speed is U. Find the length of the time interval during which the particle is moving upwards, and show that the height that the particle attains is

$$\frac{Uu_0}{g} - \frac{U^2}{g}\ln(1 + u_0/U)$$

Hence calculate the amount of energy dissipated during the upward motion.

If the particle returns to the point of projection with speed u after a time T from the instant of projection, show that

$$gT = u_0 + u$$

16. A sky-diver is falling in a head-down position, his speed being 80 m s^{-1}. At an altitude of 670 m, he opens his parachute to achieve a terminal speed of 5 m s^{-1}. Assume that the aerodynamic drag is proportional to speed. Calculate his altitude and his speed five seconds after the opening of the parachute (assumed to be an instantaneous operation) and estimate the total time of descent.

17. An experimenter drops from a helium balloon at a high altitude and attains a speed of 274 m s^{-1} at an altitude of 5330 m. His parachute opens automatically at this altitude and his decent by parachute to the Earth's surface lasts 547 s. Estimate his terminal speed, based on the assumption that the aerodynamic drag is proportional to speed.

18. A parachutist-in-training drops from a balloon moored at an altitude of 300 m. He falls in a spread-eagle position for the first three seconds, the associated terminal speed being 54 m s^{-1}. He opens his parachute to brake his fall and to achieve a terminal speed of 5 m s^{-1}. Assume that the aerodynamic drag is proportional to speed (in both phases of the motion). Calculate the parachutist's speed and altitude at the end of his free fall.

What are his speed and altitude eight seconds after leaving the balloon? Estimate his total descent time.

19. An aeroplane flying horizontally with speed u_0 releases a canister of mass m at an altitude H. Assume that the air resistance is ku when the canister's speed is u. Show that the horizontal and vertical distances travelled by the canister in time t are

$$\frac{mu_0}{k}(1-e^{-kt/m}) \quad \text{and} \quad \frac{m^2 g}{k^2}(e^{-kt/m}-1+kt/m)$$

respectively.

If the square and higher powers of kt/m are negligible, show that the canister reaches the ground when t approximately equals $a+bk$, where

$$a = (2H/g)^{1/2} \quad \text{and} \quad b = H/(3mg)$$

after having covered a horizontal distance approximately equal to $u_0(a-2bk)$.

20. Two particles P_1 and P_2, each of mass m, move in a vertical plane, their position vectors with respect to an origin being respectively $\boldsymbol{r}_1$ and $\boldsymbol{r}_2$ at time t. During the motion each particle is subjected to the uniform gravitational field of force and a resistive force whose magnitude is ku when the particle's speed is u. At $t = 0$

$$\boldsymbol{r}_1 = \boldsymbol{r}_0, \quad \dot{\boldsymbol{r}}_1 = \boldsymbol{u}_0 \quad \text{and} \quad \boldsymbol{r}_2 = \mathbf{R}_0, \quad \dot{\boldsymbol{r}}_2 = \mathbf{U}_0$$

Show that a necessary condition for P_1 and P_2 to collide is that $\boldsymbol{u}_0 - \mathbf{U}_0$ and $\boldsymbol{r}_0 - \mathbf{R}_0$ are parallel.

If $\boldsymbol{r}_0 - \mathbf{R}_0 = \alpha(\mathbf{U}_0 - \boldsymbol{u}_0)$, where $0 < \alpha k < m$, and the vertical component of $\boldsymbol{u}_0$ is u_v in the upward direction, show that the collision occurs when t equals

$$\frac{m}{k}\ln\left(\frac{m}{m-\alpha k}\right)$$

and that P_2 hits P_1 while P_1 is rising if

$$u_v > \frac{\alpha mg}{m-\alpha k}$$

21. A particle of mass m is projected vertically upwards in a medium for which the resistance at speed u is $mg(u/u_0)^2$, where u_0 is a constant. If the initial speed is u_0, show that the maximum height is $(u_0^2/2g)\ln 2$ and that the particle returns to the point of projection with speed $2^{-1/2}u_0$.

What is the length of the time interval during which the particle is above the point of projection?

22. A stone of mass m is thrown upwards with speed u_0. Show that, if the air resistance is proportional to the square of the speed and is equal to the weight of the stone at speed U, the stone's maximum height is $(U^2/2g)\ln(1+u_0^2/U^2)$. Calculate the work done against the resistive force during the upward motion.

23. A particle is projected along a smooth horizontal straight wire with speed u_0 away from a point O on the wire. It is subject to a constant force a per unit mass towards O and to a variable resistance bu^2 per unit mass, where b is a positive parameter and u is the particle's speed in the subsequent motion. Show that it comes instantaneously to rest after a time

$$\left(\frac{1}{ab}\right)^{1/2} \tan^{-1}\left\{\left(\frac{b}{a}\right)^{1/2} u_0\right\}$$

What is the particle's speed when the particle first returns to O?

24. An object of mass m is projected vertically upwards from the Earth's surface. On its upward journey its speed u is related to its altitude x by the formula

$$u = (be^{-2gx/a} - a)^{1/2}$$

where a and b are given positive parameters ($a < b$). Find the maximum height attained by the object. Show that the aerodynamic drag is represented by $-mgu^2/a$. Express a and b in terms of the initial speed u_0 and the terminal speed U.

25. A sky-diver is falling in a spread-eagle position, his speed being $54\,\mathrm{m\,s^{-1}}$. He opens his parachute at an altitude of 670 m, the terminal speed associated with the subsequent motion being $5\,\mathrm{m\,s^{-1}}$. Assume that the aerodynamic drag is proportional to the square of the sky-diver's speed and that the parachute opens instantaneously. Show that the sky-diver's altitude and speed three seconds after the opening of the parachute are

$$670 - \left[15 + \frac{25}{g}\{\ln(5{\cdot}9) + \ln(1 - \tfrac{49}{59}e^{-6g/5})\}\right] = 650{\cdot}5$$

and

$$5\{1 + (49/59)e^{-6g/5}\}/\{1 - (49/59)e^{-6g/5}\} = 5{\cdot}000$$

the units being m and $\mathrm{m\,s^{-1}}$, respectively. Estimate the time of the descent by parachute.

What would the descent time be if the sky-diver's speed were $80\,\mathrm{m\,s^{-1}}$ at the instant the parachute opens at an altitude of 670 m?

26. A parachutist leaves a balloon moored at an altitude of 300 m and falls freely in a spread-eagle position for the first three seconds, the associated terminal speed being $54\,\mathrm{m\,s^{-1}}$. Then the parachute opens instantaneously to achieve a terminal speed of $5\,\mathrm{m\,s^{-1}}$. Assume that the air resistance is proportional to the square of the parachutist's speed in both phases of the descent. What is the total time of descent, and what are the values of the parachutist's speed and altitude at the end of the free-fall phase?

27. In a delayed-drop experiment, the experimenter is descending with speed $274\,\mathrm{m\,s^{-1}}$ at an altitude of 5330 m. His parachute opens automatically at this altitude and his descent by parachute to the Earth's surface lasts 547 s. Assume that the aerodynamic drag is proportional to the square of the experimenter's speed. Show that the terminal speed U satisfies

$$\cosh(547g/U) + (274/U)\sinh(547g/U) = e^{5330g/U^2}$$

Derive from this the approximate relation

$$f(U) = \ln(\tfrac{1}{2}+137/U) - g(5330-547U)/U^2 = 0$$

Evaluate $f(9{\cdot}6), f(9{\cdot}7), f(9{\cdot}8)$ and obtain an estimate of U.

28. The results of an experiment suggest that the resistive force experienced by an object moving with speed u relative to a fluid is proportional to the product

$$\rho^{\alpha} u^{\beta} S^{\gamma}$$

where ρ is the mass of the fluid per unit volume and S is the projected area of the object perpendicular to the direction of motion. Use an argument based on dimensional analysis to determine the values of the indices α, β and γ.

29. A metal sphere of radius R is falling with a terminal speed U in a fluid.

(i) What is the terminal speed of each of N identical spheres made from a volume $\tfrac{4}{3}\pi R^3$ of the metal?

(ii) What is the terminal speed of a sphere of radius R/M made from the metal?

(Assume that the expression for the drag given in the previous question applies.)

30. An aeroplane is travelling horizontally with speed u_0. A canister with an attached parachute is released from the aeroplane. On account of the parachute, the motion of the canister is opposed by a force equal to the canister's weight. Show that the governing differential equations may be written in the form

$$\ddot{x} = -\frac{g\dot{x}}{(\dot{x}^2+\dot{z}^2)^{1/2}} \quad \text{and} \quad \ddot{z} = -g - \frac{g\dot{z}}{(\dot{x}^2+\dot{z}^2)^{1/2}}$$

Substitute $\dot{x} = u\cos\psi$ and $\dot{z} = -u\sin\psi$, where $0 \leqslant u$ and $0 \leqslant \psi \leqslant \tfrac{1}{2}\pi$, and deduce that

$$u = \frac{u_0}{1+\sin\psi}$$

What is the maximum value of $|\dot{z}|$?

31. Show that the solution of the recurrence relation

$$w_{n+1} = \alpha w_n + \beta \quad \text{with} \quad w_0 = 0$$

where α and β are given constants, is

$$w_n = \begin{cases} \beta(1-\alpha^n)/(1-\alpha) & \alpha \neq 1 \\ n\beta & \alpha = 1 \end{cases}$$

Hence solve

$$w_{n+1} = (1-g\Delta t/U)w_n - g\Delta t \quad \text{with} \quad w_0 = 0$$

Thus show that the recurrence relation

$$z_{n+1} = z_n + \tfrac{1}{2}\Delta t(w_n + w_{n+1}) \quad \text{with} \quad z_0 = 0$$

reduces to

$$z_{n+1} = z_n - U\Delta t\{1-(1-g\Delta t/2U)(1-g\Delta t/U)^n\}$$

with $z_0 = 0$ and hence find an expression for z_n.

Given that

$$w(t) = -U(1-e^{-gt/U})$$

and

$$z(t) = -Ut + (U^2/g)(1 - e^{-gt/U})$$

show that the global truncation errors $w(n\Delta t) - w_n$ and $z(n\Delta t) - z_n$ are proportional to Δt for any fixed value of n, n being a positive integer.

32. A balloon is moored at an altitude of 2100 m. A sky-diver drops from the balloon in a spread-eagle position, the associated terminal speed being $54\,\mathrm{m\,s^{-1}}$. He opens his parachute at an altitude of 700 m. Use a numerical method to estimate his speed when the parachute opens, and the length of the time interval during which he is free-falling. Assume that the aerodynamic drag is proportional to (i) the sky-diver's speed, and (ii) the square of the sky-diver's speed.

Forced Damped Oscillations

11

11.1 Introduction

In chapter 8 we discussed the vertical motion of a body suspended from a fixed support by a spring. We assumed that the spring was elastic and obeyed Hooke's Law. The main conclusion was that the body performed simple harmonic motion, the amplitude of the oscillations being constant for all time. We know from our experience of the physical situation that the oscillations have a decaying amplitude, and the vertical motion eventually ceases to exist. Let us construct a revised model that will predict the decaying amplitude of the oscillations.

There are two main causes of the decaying amplitude. Firstly there is the effect of the air. This is a variable resistive force, which we introduced in the previous chapter and which depends on the speed of body relative to the air. Secondly the spring will not be ideal, i.e. it will not be a perfectly elastic spring satisfying Hooke's Law. We shall represent a (real) spring by a combination of an "ideal" spring and a dashpot in parallel. A *dashpot*, sometimes called a *fluid damper*, is a container of viscous fluid, e.g. an oil or glycerine, through which a piston moves. The motion of the piston through the viscous fluid is impeded by a resistive force that depends on the velocity of the piston relative to the container. We assume that the mass of the dashpot (i.e. the container, the fluid and the piston) is negligible, and we continue to assume that the mass of the "ideal" spring is negligible. These assumptions are acceptable provided the mass of the body is much greater than the mass of the suspending spring. Mechanisms to close doors and to prevent slamming consist of a spring and a fluid damper.

We assume that the resistive force is proportional to velocity (i.e. the aerodynamic drag is proportional to the velocity of the body through the air, and the viscous drag is proportional to the velocity of the piston relative to the container). This linear relation is valid provided the speed is small. Its incorporation into the revised mathematical model leads to predictions of oscillations having decaying amplitudes.

11.2 Damped oscillations

Consider the vertical motion of a body suspended from a fixed support by a spring. We shall examine a mathematical model in which a particle is suspended from a fixed support by a combination of a spring and a dashpot in parallel. We assume that the line AB in the figure is horizontal throughout the motion. We introduce a z-axis so that its origin is at the level of the fixed support and the direction of z increasing is vertically downwards.

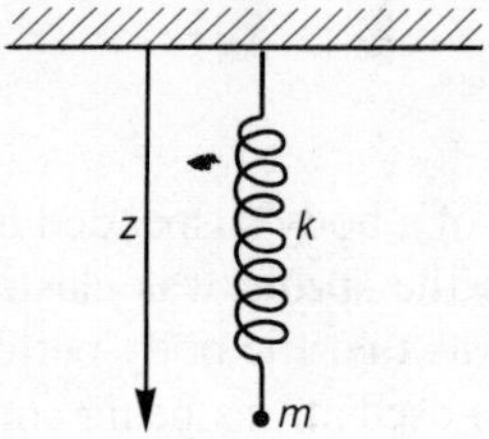

THE ORIGINAL MODEL

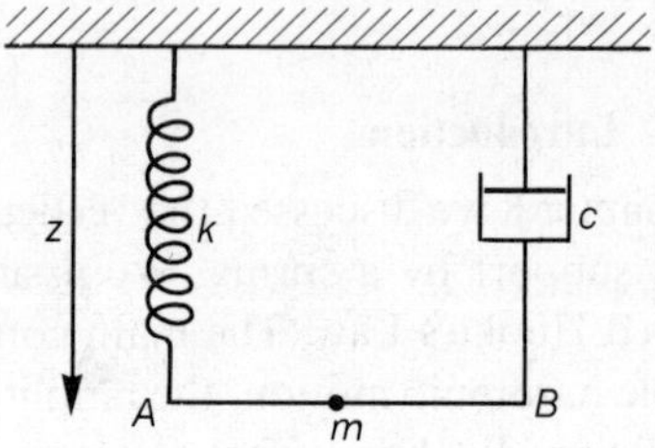

THE REVISED MODEL

There are three forces acting on the particle, namely the uniform gravitational force, the elastic restoring force and the viscous drag. Assuming that the motion of the particle is constrained to lie along the z-axis (or a line parallel to the z-axis), we represent the uniform gravitational force by $mg\boldsymbol{k}$ and the elastic restoring force by $-k(z-l)\boldsymbol{k}$, where k is the stiffness of the spring and l is the natural length of the spring. We represent the viscous drag by $-c\dot{z}\boldsymbol{k}$, where c is the (viscous) damping coefficient, which is a positive parameter having the dimensions MT^{-1}. This representation of the viscous drag is correct because the viscous drag is proportional to $|\dot{z}|$ (the speed of the piston relative to the container) and opposes the motion of the particle. The differential equation governing the motion of the particle of mass m is

$$m\ddot{z} = mg - k(z-l) - c\dot{z}$$

Therefore we seek solutions of

$$m\ddot{z} + c\dot{z} + kz = mg + kl$$

which is a second-order linear differential equation with constant coefficients [see J. Hunter, *Calculus*, Blackie/Chambers]. The general solution consists of a particular integral and the complementary function. The inhomogeneous term, $mg+kl$, is constant so we see that

$$z = (mg+kl)/k = l + mg/k$$

is a particular integral. This solution happens to define the equilibrium position of the particle. To find the complementary function we set $z = Ae^{\alpha t}$

in the homogeneous equation

$$m\ddot{z}+c\dot{z}+kz=0$$

and we obtain the auxiliary equation

$$m\alpha^2+c\alpha+k=0$$

The roots of the auxiliary equation are

$$\frac{-c\pm(c^2-4mk)^{1/2}}{2m}$$

There are three cases to consider, namely $c<2(mk)^{1/2}$, $c=2(mk)^{1/2}$ and $2(mk)^{1/2}<c$.

Case (i). Weakly damped (or underdamped) $(0\leqslant c<2(mk)^{1/2})$
The roots of the auxiliary equation are complex conjugates and the complementary function is

$$[A\cos\{(4mk-c^2)^{1/2}t/2m\}+B\sin\{(4mk-c^2)^{1/2}t/2m\}]\exp(-ct/2m)$$

Case (ii). Critically damped $(c=2(mk)^{1/2})$
The roots are real and equal and the complementary function is

$$(A+Bt)\exp(-ct/2m)$$

Case (iii). Strongly damped (or overdamped) $(2(mk)^{1/2}<c)$
The roots are real and distinct and the complementary function is

$$A\exp[-\{c-(c^2-4mk)^{1/2}\}t/2m]+B\exp[-\{c+(c^2-4mk)^{1/2}\}t/2m]$$

Let us now find the solution in each of the three cases that satisfies the initial conditions

$$z=l+mg/k+d \quad\text{and}\quad \dot{z}=0 \quad\text{at}\quad t=0\ (d>0).$$

Case (i). Weakly damped $(0\leqslant c<2(mk)^{1/2})$
It is convenient to reintroduce $\omega=(k/m)^{1/2}$ and to set

$$\delta=c/2m \quad\text{and}\quad \bar{\omega}=(4mk-c^2)^{1/2}/2m=(1-c^2/4mk)^{1/2}\omega$$

The required solution is

$$z=l+mg/k+(A\cos\bar{\omega}t+B\sin\bar{\omega}t)e^{-\delta t}$$

where

$$l+mg/k+d=l+mg/k+A$$

and

$$0=-\delta A+\bar{\omega}B$$

i.e. $A=d$ and $B=\delta d/\bar{\omega}$. Thus we obtain

$$z=l+g/\omega^2+d(\cos\bar{\omega}t+(\delta/\bar{\omega})\sin\bar{\omega}t)e^{-\delta t}$$

We write

$$\cos\bar{\omega}t+(\delta/\bar{\omega})\sin\bar{\omega}t=\frac{(\delta^2+\bar{\omega}^2)^{1/2}}{\bar{\omega}}\left\{\frac{\bar{\omega}\cos\bar{\omega}t+\delta\sin\bar{\omega}t}{(\delta^2+\bar{\omega}^2)^{1/2}}\right\}$$
$$=(1+\delta^2/\bar{\omega}^2)^{1/2}\sin(\bar{\omega}t+\varepsilon)$$

where $\cos\varepsilon=\delta/(\delta^2+\bar{\omega}^2)^{1/2}$ and $\sin\varepsilon=\bar{\omega}/(\delta^2+\bar{\omega}^2)^{1/2}$. Noting that $\delta^2+\bar{\omega}^2=\omega^2$, we find that the required solution is

$$z=l+g/\omega^2+(\omega d/\bar{\omega})\sin(\bar{\omega}t+\varepsilon)\,e^{-\delta t}$$

This solution represents periodic motion whose amplitude decays with increasing time. The period is

$$\frac{2\pi}{\bar{\omega}}=\frac{2}{\omega}(1-c^2/4mk)^{-1/2}=2\pi\left(\frac{m}{k}\right)^{1/2}(1-c^2/4mk)^{-1/2}$$

and the amplitude of the oscillatory term

$$(\omega d/\bar{\omega})\,e^{-\delta t}=d(1-c^2/4mk)^{-1/2}\,e^{-ct/2m}$$

As $t\to\infty$, $z\to l+mg/k$, the equilibrium value. Further $z=l+mg/k$ when $\sin(\bar{\omega}t+\varepsilon)=0$, i.e. $t=(N\pi-\varepsilon)/\bar{\omega}$ $(N=1,2,3,\dots)$, and $\dot{z}=0$ when $\tan(\bar{\omega}t+\varepsilon)=\bar{\omega}/\delta=\tan\varepsilon$, i.e. $t=N\pi/\bar{\omega}$ $(N=0,1,2,\dots)$. Let $z=z_N$ when $t=N\pi/\bar{\omega}$. Then

$$z_N=l+g/\omega^2+(\omega d/\bar{\omega})(-1)^N(\sin\varepsilon)\,e^{-\delta N\pi/\bar{\omega}}$$
$$=l+g/\omega^2+(-1)^N d\,e^{-\delta N\pi/\bar{\omega}}$$

The local maxima are z_{2M} $(M=0,1,2,\dots)$ and the local minima are z_{2M+1} $(M=0,1,2,\dots)$. We note that

$$\frac{z_{2M}-l-g/\omega^2}{z_{2M+2}-l-g/\omega^2}=\frac{z_{2M+1}-l-g/\omega^2}{z_{2M+3}-l-g/\omega^2}=e^{2\pi\delta/\bar{\omega}}$$

The argument of the exponential function is called the *logarithmic decrement* and is denoted by Λ, i.e.

$$z_N=l+g/\omega^2+(-1)^N d\,e^{-N\Lambda/2}$$

The particle comes to rest after travelling a distance

$$d+(de^{-\Lambda/2}+de^{-\Lambda/2})+(de^{-2\Lambda/2}+de^{-2\Lambda/2})+(de^{-3\Lambda/2}+de^{-3\Lambda/2})+\dots$$
$$=d+2d(e^{-\Lambda/2}+e^{-\Lambda}+e^{-3\Lambda/2}+\dots)$$
$$=d+2de^{-\Lambda/2}/(1-e^{-\Lambda/2})=d(1+e^{-\Lambda/2})/(1-e^{-\Lambda/2})$$
$$=d\coth(\Lambda/4)=d\coth\{\tfrac{1}{2}\pi(4mk/c^2-1)^{1/2}\}$$

It takes an infinite time to travel this finite distance. Suppose that the period T is measured and the logarithmic decrement Λ is estimated from experimental data. Then we find that

$$c = 2m\delta = 2m\Lambda/T$$

and

$$k = m\bar{\omega}^2 + c^2/4m = m(4\pi^2 + \Lambda^2)/T^2$$

where m is the mass of the body (represented by the particle). This is a feasible way of calculating the characteristics of the suspension.

Case (ii). Critically damped ($c = 2(mk)^{1/2}$)
The solution satisfying the given initial conditions is

$$z = l + mg/k + (A + Bt)\,e^{-\delta t}$$

where

$$l + mg/k + d = l + mg/k + A$$

and

$$0 = -\delta A + B$$

i.e. $A = d$ and $B = \delta d$. Hence we have

$$z = l + g/\omega^2 + d(1 + \delta t)\,e^{-\delta t}$$

and

$$\dot{z} = -d\,\delta^2 t\,e^{-\delta t}$$

There are no oscillations. At $t \to \infty$, $z \to l + g/\omega^2 = l + mg/k$ and $\dot{z} \to 0$. For all $t > 0$, $z > l + mg/k$, the equilibrium value. Therefore the particle travels a distance d in an infinite time before coming to rest.

Case (iii). Strongly damped ($2(mk)^{1/2} < c$)
We set $\alpha_1 = \{c - (c^2 - 4mk)^{1/2}\}/2m$ and $\alpha_2 = \{c + (c^2 - 4mk)^{1/2}\}/2m$. The required solution is

$$z = l + mg/k + A\,e^{-\alpha_1 t} + B\,e^{-\alpha_2 t}$$

where

$$l + mg/k + d = l + mg/k + A + B$$

and

$$0 = -\alpha_1 A - \alpha_2 B$$

i.e.

$$A = \alpha_2 d/(\alpha_2 - \alpha_1) \quad \text{and} \quad B = -\alpha_1 d/(\alpha_2 - \alpha_1)$$

This leads to

$$z = l + g/\omega^2 + d(\alpha_2\,e^{-\alpha_1 t} - \alpha_1\,e^{-\alpha_2 t})/(\alpha_2 - \alpha_1)$$

and

$$\dot{z} = -\alpha_1\alpha_2\,d(e^{-\alpha_1 t} - e^{-\alpha_2 t})/(\alpha_2 - \alpha_1).$$

There are no oscillations. As $t \to \infty$, $z \to l + mg/k$ and $\dot{z} \to 0$. There are no solutions of

$$\alpha_2 e^{-\alpha_1 t} - \alpha_1 e^{-\alpha_2 t} = 0$$

and we note that $\alpha_2 > \alpha_1$. Therefore $z > l + mg/k$ for all $t \geqslant 0$ and the particle travels a distance d in an infinite time before coming to rest.

Let us return to the differential equation governing the motion of the particle, namely

$$m\ddot{z} + c\dot{z} + k(z - l) = mg$$

and let us derive an expression for the sum of the kinetic energy and the potential energy. Multiplying the differential equation by $\dot{z}$ and integrating with respect to time, we find that

$$E_k + E_p + \int_0^t c\dot{z}^2 \, dt = \text{constant}$$

where $E_k = \frac{1}{2}m\dot{z}^2$ and $E_p = -mgz + \frac{1}{2}k(z-l)^2$.

We deduce that the sum of the kinetic energy and the potential energy, $E_k + E_p$, decreases with time. In fact

$$\frac{d}{dt}(E_k + E_p) = -c\dot{z}^2 .$$

The resistive force causes some of the mechanical energy to be converted into thermal energy (and acoustic energy).

11.3 Forced oscillations

In many situations a force is applied to an oscillating system. The applied force influences the motion of the system. The form of the applied force is known, and a description of the motion is required. Sometimes the inverse problem is posed, in which the nature of the motion is known and a description of the applied force is required.

We begin by assuming that there is no damping. Consider a particle suspended from a fixed support by a spring and subjected to a known applied force. Referring to the figure on page 208, "the original model", we introduce the z-axis with its origin at the level of the fixed support and the direction of z increasing vertically downwards. We assume that the applied force experienced by the particle is $F(t)\boldsymbol{k}$, where F is a known function. The differential equation governing the vertical motion of the particle is

$$m\ddot{z} = mg - k(z - l) + F(t)$$

where m denotes the mass of the particle, k the stiffness of the spring and l the natural length of the spring. Thus we have to solve

$$m\ddot{z}+kz = mg+kl+F(t)$$

which is an inhomogeneous second-order linear differential equation with constant coefficients. The general solution is the sum of the complementary function

$$A\cos\omega t+B\sin\omega t$$

where A, B are arbitrary constants and $\omega = (k/m)^{1/2}$, and a particular integral. To enable us to complete the solution, we assume that the applied force has a harmonic time-dependence, i.e.

$$F(t) = F_0\cos\Omega t$$

where F_0 and Ω are known parameters with constant values. This is an important special case. Assuming that a particular integral is a linear combination of $\cos\Omega t$, $\sin\Omega t$ and a constant, we employ the method of undetermined coefficients [see J. Hunter, *Calculus*, Blackie/Chambers] and find that

$$l+g/\omega^2+\{F_0/m(\omega^2-\Omega^2)\}\cos\Omega t$$

is a particular integral. Thus the general solution is

$$z = A\cos\omega t+B\sin\omega t+l+\frac{g}{\omega^2}+\frac{F_0}{m(\omega^2-\Omega^2)}\cos\Omega t$$

Suppose the initial conditions at $t = 0$ are $z = l+g/\omega^2+d$ and $\dot{z} = u_0$. Then A and B satisfy

$$d = A+F_0/m(\omega^2-\Omega^2) \quad\text{and}\quad u_0 = \omega B$$

The required solution is

$$z = l+\frac{g}{\omega^2}+\left\{d-\frac{F_0}{m(\omega^2-\Omega^2)}\right\}\cos\omega t+\frac{u_0}{\omega}\sin\omega t+\frac{F_0}{m(\omega^2-\Omega^2)}\cos\Omega t$$

This representation shows that the resultant motion about the equilibrium position ($z = l+g/\omega^2$) is the sum of two oscillatory motions having different angular frequencies and different amplitudes. When Ω, the angular frequency of the applied force, equals ω, the natural angular frequency, the above solution is not valid (without some modification). It is appropriate to seek a particular integral that is a linear combination of $t\cos\omega t$, $t\sin\omega t$ and a constant. We find that the required solution is

$$z = A\cos\omega t+B\sin\omega t+l+\frac{g}{\omega^2}+\frac{F_0}{2m\omega}t\sin\omega t$$

where $d = A$ and $u_0 = \omega B$, i.e.

$$z = l + \frac{g}{\omega^2} + d\cos\omega t + \frac{u_0}{\omega}\sin\omega t + \frac{F_0}{2m\omega}t\sin\omega t$$

This is obtainable from the previous case by a limiting process because

$$\frac{\cos\Omega t - \cos\omega t}{\omega^2 - \Omega^2} = \left\{\frac{2\sin\frac{1}{2}(\omega-\Omega)t}{(\omega-\Omega)t}\right\}\frac{t\sin\frac{1}{2}(\omega+\Omega)t}{\omega+\Omega} \rightarrow \frac{t\sin\omega t}{2\omega}$$

as $\Omega \rightarrow \omega$ [see J. Hunter, *Calculus*, Blackie/Chambers]. We note that the term $(F_0/2m\omega)t\sin\omega t$ has an amplitude that increases linearly with time. The oscillations of the particle become more and more violent as time increases, until the spring yields. This is a resonance phenomenon.

We shall examine some special cases.

(i) $\Omega \neq \omega$, $d = 0$, $u_0 = 0$

The solution is

$$z = l + \frac{g}{\omega^2} + \frac{F_0}{m(\omega^2 - \Omega^2)}(\cos\Omega t - \cos\omega t)$$

$$= l + \frac{g}{\omega^2} + \frac{2F_0}{m(\omega^2 - \Omega^2)}\sin\tfrac{1}{2}(\omega-\Omega)t\sin\tfrac{1}{2}(\omega+\Omega)t\,.$$

When Ω is approximately equal to ω, we write $\Omega = \omega(1-h)$, where $|h| \ll 1$, and the solution becomes

$$z = l + g/\omega^2 + K(t)\sin(1 - \tfrac{1}{2}h)\omega t$$

where

$$K(t) = \frac{2F_0}{m\omega^2(2h - h^2)}\sin\tfrac{1}{2}h\omega t$$

The amplitude of the oscillatory term is K and is slowly varying, the associated period being $4\pi/|h|\omega$. Here we have the combination of two oscillations whose amplitudes are equal and whose angular frequencies are nearly equal. This type of oscillatory motion (possessing an amplitude having a harmonic time-dependence) exhibits what is called a *beat*. The phenomenon of beats occurs in acoustics when two tuning forks of nearly equal frequency are sounded simultaneously. Any variation of the amplitude with time is called *amplitude modulation* (cf. A.M. radio transmission).

$$z = l + \frac{g}{\omega^2} + \left\{d - \frac{F_0}{m(\omega^2 - \Omega^2)}\right\}\cos\omega t + \frac{F_0}{m(\omega^2 - \Omega^2)}\cos\Omega t$$

$$= l + \frac{g}{\omega^2} + \left\{d - \frac{F_0}{m(\omega^2 - \Omega^2)}\right\}\{\cos\tfrac{1}{2}(\omega+\Omega)t\cos\tfrac{1}{2}(\omega-\Omega)t$$
$$- \sin\tfrac{1}{2}(\omega+\Omega)t\sin\tfrac{1}{2}(\omega-\Omega)t\}$$

$$+ \frac{F_0}{m(\omega^2 - \Omega^2)}\{\cos\tfrac{1}{2}(\omega+\Omega)t\cos\tfrac{1}{2}(\omega-\Omega)t + \sin\tfrac{1}{2}(\omega+\Omega)t\sin\tfrac{1}{2}(\omega-\Omega)t\}\,.$$

$$= l+\frac{g}{\omega^2}+d\cos\tfrac{1}{2}(\omega-\Omega)t\cos\tfrac{1}{2}(\omega+\Omega)t$$
$$+\left\{\frac{2F_0}{m(\omega^2-\Omega^2)}-d\right\}\sin\tfrac{1}{2}(\omega-\Omega)t\sin\tfrac{1}{2}(\omega+\Omega)t$$
$$= l+g/\omega^2+K(t)\cos\{\tfrac{1}{2}(\omega+\Omega)t-\varepsilon(t)\}$$

where

$$K(t)\cos\varepsilon(t) = d\cos\tfrac{1}{2}(\omega-\Omega)t$$

and

$$K(t)\sin\varepsilon(t) = \left\{\frac{2F_0}{m(\omega^2-\Omega^2)}-d\right\}\sin\tfrac{1}{2}(\omega-\Omega)t\,.$$

This is a generalization of the phenomenon of beats. The amplitude K and the phase angle ε vary with time. The variation of the phase angle with time is called *phase modulation.* The third type of modulation, namely *frequency modulation* (cf. F.M. radio transmission), occurs when the frequency (or angular frequency) depends on time.

11.4 Forced damped oscillations

We wish to incorporate into a model the resistive force introduced in Section 11.2 and the applied force introduced in Section 11.3. Consider a particle suspended from a fixed support by a mechanism (consisting of a spring and a dashpot in parallel) and subjected to a known applied force. Referring to the illustration of "the revised model" on page 208, we introduce the z-axis with its origin at the level of the fixed support and the direction of z increasing vertically downwards. The differential equation governing the vertical motion of the particle is

$$m\ddot{z} = mg-k(z-l)-c\dot{z}+F(t)$$

This may be rewritten in the form

$$m\ddot{z}+c\dot{z}+kz = mg+kl+F(t)$$

Its general solution is the sum of the complementary function, which we have discussed in Section 11.2, and a particular integral. We shall assume that the applied force has a harmonic time-dependence and write $F(t) = F_0\cos\Omega t$. A particular integral, in this special case, will be

$$l+mg/k+P\cos\Omega t+Q\sin\Omega t$$

where

$$m(-P\Omega^2\cos\Omega t-Q\Omega^2\sin\Omega t)+c(-P\Omega\sin\Omega t+Q\Omega\cos\Omega t)$$
$$+k(l+mg/k+P\cos\Omega t+Q\sin\Omega t) = mg+kl+F_0\cos\Omega t$$

It follows that P and Q satisfy the simultaneous linear equations

$$P(-m\Omega^2+k)+Qc\Omega = F_0$$
$$-Pc\Omega+Q(-m\Omega^2+k) = 0$$

Therefore

$$P = \frac{F_0(k-m\Omega^2)}{(k-m\Omega^2)^2+c^2\Omega^2} \quad \text{and} \quad Q = \frac{F_0 c\Omega}{(k-m\Omega^2)^2+c^2\Omega^2}$$

It is convenient to write

$$\begin{aligned} P\cos\Omega t + Q\sin\Omega t &= K\cos(\Omega t - \varepsilon) \\ &= K(\cos\Omega t\cos\varepsilon + \sin\Omega t\sin\varepsilon) \end{aligned}$$

where $P = K\cos\varepsilon$ and $Q = K\sin\varepsilon$. Thus

$$K = \frac{F_0}{\{(k-m\Omega^2)^2+c^2\Omega^2\}^{1/2}}$$

$$\cos\varepsilon = (k-m\Omega^2)K/F_0 \quad \text{and} \quad \sin\varepsilon = c\Omega K/F_0$$

Hence a particular integral is

$$l + mg/k + K\cos(\Omega t - \varepsilon)$$

where the amplitude K and the phase angle ε are defined above. This part of the solution persists for all time, in contrast to the complementary function, which decays exponentially as time increases. Therefore, whatever the initial conditions (that determine the complementary function), the motion of the particle is eventually described by the particular integral. The forced oscillations (the undamped oscillations depending on the applied force $F_0\cos\Omega t$) dominate the motion of the particle about the equilibrium position $z = l + mg/k$ and exist for all time. They are independent of the initial conditions.

Let us consider how K, the amplitude of the forced oscillations, depends on Ω, the angular frequency of the applied force. We note that

$$\begin{aligned} (k-m\Omega^2)^2+c^2\Omega^2 &= m^2\Omega^4 + (c^2-2mk)\Omega^2 + k^2 \\ &= m^2\left\{\Omega^2 + \frac{c^2}{2m^2} - \frac{k}{m}\right\}^2 + k^2\left\{1 - \left(1 - \frac{c^2}{2mk}\right)^2\right\} \end{aligned}$$

Hence we deduce that K has a maximum when

$$\Omega^2 = \frac{k}{m} - \frac{c^2}{2m^2} = \left(1 - \frac{c^2}{2mk}\right)\frac{k}{m} = \left(1 - \frac{c^2}{2mk}\right)\omega^2$$

provided $c < (2mk)^{1/2}$; the maximum value being

$$\frac{F_0/k}{\left\{1 - \left(1 - \frac{c^2}{2mk}\right)^2\right\}^{1/2}}$$

This is a resonance effect. It occurs when the damping is weak (because c

$< (2mk)^{1/2} < 2(mk)^{1/2}$). When $(2mk)^{1/2} < c$ (the damping may be weak, critical or strong), K has a maximum when $\Omega = 0$, the maximum value being F_0/k.

When a system is performing forced damped oscillations there are three important angular frequencies, namely

(i) $\omega = (k/m)^{1/2}$, the undamped natural angular frequency,

(ii) $\bar{\omega} = (1-(c^2/4mk))^{1/2}\omega$, the angular frequency of the damped oscillations,

(iii) $(1-(c^2/2mk))^{1/2}\omega$, the angular frequency of the applied force associated with maximum-amplitude forced oscillations.

EXAMPLE

A particle of mass m is suspended from a fixed support by a mechanism consisting of a spring and a dashpot in parallel. The spring has stiffness $m\omega^2$ and natural length l, and the dashpot's damping coefficient is $m\omega$. At $t = 0$ the particle is at rest in its equilibrium position, and the application of a vertical force $F_0 \sin \Omega t$ to the particle commences. Investigate the subsequent motion of the particle.

The motion of the particle will be along a vertical line through the equilibrium position. We introduce a z-axis (cf. diagram on page 208) with respect to which the differential equation governing the particle's motion is

$$m\ddot{z} = mg - m\omega^2(z-l) - m\omega\dot{z} + F_0 \sin \Omega t$$

The initial conditions at $t = 0$ are $z = l + g/\omega^2$ and $\dot{z} = 0$. The complementary function is

$$\{A \cos(3^{1/2}\,\omega t/2) + B \sin(3^{1/2}\,\omega t/2)\}\, e^{-\omega t/2}$$

and a particular integral is

$$l + g/\omega^2 - \frac{F_0\{\omega\Omega \cos \Omega t - (\omega^2 - \Omega^2) \sin \Omega t\}}{m(\omega^4 - \omega^2\Omega^2 + \Omega^4)}$$

The imposition of the initial conditions leads to the required solution

$$z = l + g/\omega^2 - \frac{F_0\{\omega\Omega \cos \Omega t - (\omega^2 - \Omega^2) \sin \Omega t\}}{m(\omega^4 - \omega^2\Omega^2 + \Omega^4)}$$
$$+ \frac{F_0\Omega\{3^{1/2}\omega^2 \cos(3^{1/2}\,\omega t/2) - (\omega^2 - 2\Omega^2) \sin(3^{1/2}\,\omega t/2)\}\, e^{-\omega t/2}}{3^{1/2} m\omega(\omega^4 - \omega^2\Omega^2 + \Omega^4)}$$

The amplitude of the forced oscillations is

$$\frac{F_0/m}{(\omega^4 - \omega^2\Omega^2 + \Omega^4)^{1/2}} = \frac{F_0/m}{\{(\Omega^2 - \frac{1}{2}\omega^2)^2 + \frac{3}{4}\omega^4\}^{1/2}}$$

which takes its maximum value, $2F_0/3^{1/2}m\omega^2$, when $\Omega = \omega/2^{1/2}$. As $t \to \infty$, ωt increases and the damped oscillations decay exponentially. The forced oscillations dominate eventually and the damped oscillations become negligible.

The force exerted by the system on the fixed support is $\{m\omega^2(z-l) + m\omega\dot{z}\}\mathbf{k}$. When the damped oscillations have decayed, we find that

$$m\omega^2(z-l) + m\omega\dot{z} = mg + \frac{F_0(\omega^4 \sin \Omega t - \omega\Omega^3 \cos \Omega t)}{(\omega^4 - \omega^2\Omega^2 + \Omega^4)}$$

The amplitude of the oscillating force is

$$\frac{F_0(\omega^8+\omega^2\Omega^6)^{1/2}}{\omega^4-\omega^2\Omega^2+\Omega^4} = F_0\left(\frac{\omega^4+\omega^2\Omega^2}{\omega^4-\omega^2\Omega^2+\Omega^4}\right)^{1/2}$$

We can show by differentiation with respect to Ω that this amplitude has a maximum when $\Omega = (3^{1/2}-1)^{1/2}\omega$, the maximum value being $F_0(1+2/3^{1/2})^{1/2}$ which is approximately $1{\cdot}47\,F_0$. Therefore the fixed support has to withstand an oscillating force of maximum magnitude $mg+1{\cdot}47\,F_0$ when $\Omega = 0{\cdot}86\,\omega$. We note that the amplitude is less than F_0 when $2^{1/2}\omega < \Omega$.

This example is related to the problem of determining the effect that the running of a machine has on the machine's foundation. The only change to the above analysis that is necessary is the reversal of the sign of g. Then the fixed support represents the machine's foundation, the combination of spring and dashpot represents the machine's mounting, and the applied force represents the force exerted by the machine on the mounting. The important design problem is to choose the characteristics of the mounting (the stiffness of the spring and the dashpot's damping coefficient) so that the effects of the applied force transmitted to the foundation by the mounting are minimized. In general, we have to solve

$$m\ddot{z}+c\dot{z}+kz = -mg+kl+F_0\sin(\Omega t+\varepsilon)$$

and consider the magnitude of $k(z-l)+c\dot{z}$, particularly the contribution from the forced oscillations. It is clearly undesirable to have the vibrations of an automobile's engine transmitted to the chassis and the passengers. The rubber engine mountings are designed to isolate the engine's vibrations.

11.5 Moving support

Suppose a body is supported above a horizontal platform by a spring or a spring-dashpot combination, and the platform is made to move vertically in a prescribed manner relative to an inertial frame of reference. We seek a

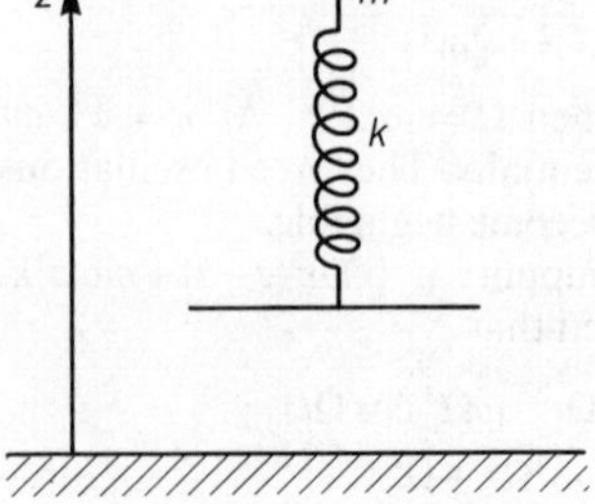

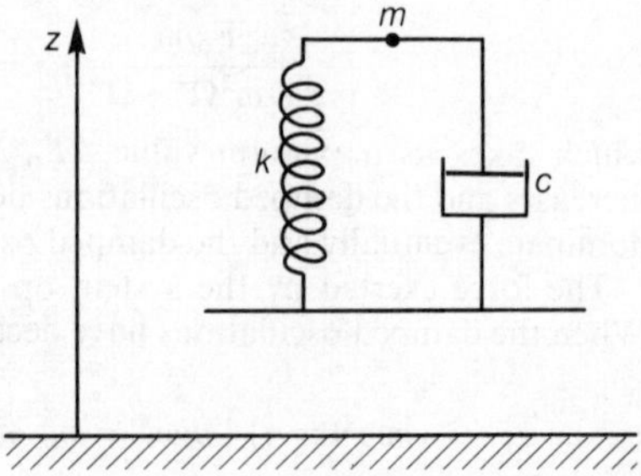

description of the body's motion relative to the moving platform (or relative to the inertial frame of reference). Let the z-axis be a vertical axis whose origin is fixed relative to the inertial frame of reference and let the direction of the associated unit vector $\boldsymbol{k}$ be vertically upwards. At time t the height of the platform above the plane $z = 0$ is $Z(t)$, where Z is a known function. If the z-coordinate of the particle representing the body is z, then the length of the spring is $z - Z$. The dashpot's piston has the velocity $\dot{z}\boldsymbol{k}$ relative to the inertial frame of reference, and the dashpot's fluid container has the velocity $\dot{Z}\boldsymbol{k}$ relative to the inertial frame of reference, i.e. the velocity of the piston relative to the container is $(\dot{z} - \dot{Z})\boldsymbol{k}$.

The differential equation governing the vertical motion of the particle relative to the inertial frame of reference is

$$m\ddot{z} = -mg - k(z - Z - l) - c(\dot{z} - \dot{Z})$$

where m is the particle's mass, k and l are the spring's stiffness and natural length, and c is the dashpot's damping coefficient. Hence we have to solve

$$m\ddot{z} + c\dot{z} + kz = -mg + k(Z + l) + c\dot{Z}$$

or

$$m(\ddot{z} - \ddot{Z}) + c(\dot{z} - \dot{Z}) + k(z - Z) = -mg + kl - m\ddot{Z}$$

namely a second-order linear differential equation with constant coefficients whose inhomogeneous term is a prescribed function of time. Suppose $Z = Z_0 + d\cos\Omega t$, where Z_0, d and Ω are known parameters. The general solution will consist of damped oscillations (the complementary function) and forced oscillations (the particular integral). When the damped oscillations have decayed away, we have

$$\begin{aligned} z - Z &= l - mg/k + \frac{md\Omega^2\{(k - m\Omega^2)\cos\Omega t + c\Omega\sin\Omega t\}}{(k - m\Omega^2)^2 + c^2\Omega^2} \\ &= l - mg/k + K\cos(\Omega t - \varepsilon) \end{aligned}$$

where

$$K = \frac{md\Omega^2}{\{(k - m\Omega^2)^2 + c^2\Omega^2\}^{1/2}}$$

$$\cos\varepsilon = (k - m\Omega^2)K/md\Omega^2 \quad \text{and} \quad \sin\varepsilon = c\Omega K/md\Omega^2$$

(cf. Section 11.4).

Let us examine how K, the amplitude of the forced oscillations, depends on Ω, the angular frequency associated with the movement of the platform. We note that $K = 0$ when $\Omega = 0$ and $K \to d$ as $\Omega \to \infty$. We have to resort to calculus to obtain knowledge about any stationary value. Therefore we obtain

$$\frac{dK}{d\Omega} = \frac{md\Omega[2\{(k-m\Omega^2)^2+c^2\Omega^2\}-\{-2m\Omega^2(k-m\Omega^2)+c^2\Omega^2\}]}{\{(k-m\Omega^2)^2+c^2\Omega^2\}^{3/2}}$$

and find that $(dK/d\Omega) = 0$ when $md\Omega[2k^2+(c^2-2mk)\Omega^2] = 0$. $\Omega = 0$ gives the minimum value, $K = 0$. When $c^2 < 2mk$ a second stationary value exists, this being a maximum,

$$K = \frac{2mkd}{c(4mk-c^2)^{1/2}}$$

at $\Omega = \{2k^2/(2mk-c^2)\}^{1/2} = \omega(1-c^2/2mk)^{-1/2}$, where $\omega = (k/m)^{1/2}$.

When we consider a body suspended by a spring-dashpot combination from a movable horizontal platform, we have a simple model of a seismograph. The earlier analysis of this section is easily adapted. However,

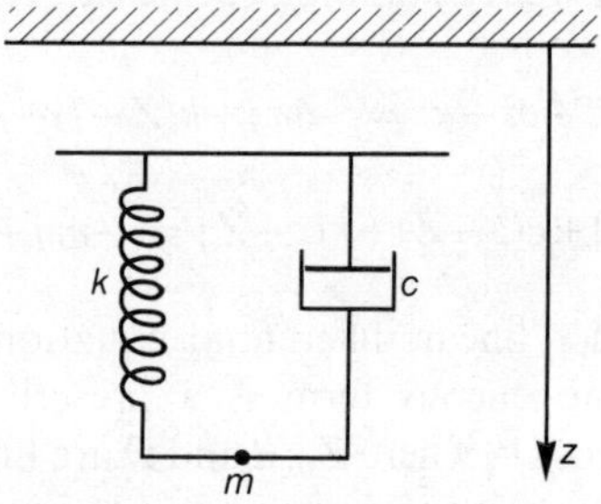

we have an inverse problem in the sense that we seek information about the earthquake (i.e. d and Ω) in terms of the parameters m, k and c and the measured quantities K and ε. Note that the measurements are made relative to the moving platform. It is convenient to write $\Omega = \omega/h_M$, where

$$h_M = (1-c^2/2mk)^{1/2} \quad \text{or} \quad c^2 = 2mk(1-h_M^2)$$

Suppose that we are able to measure K_M, the maximum value of the amplitude of the forced oscillations relative to the platform which occurs when $\Omega = \omega/h_M$; i.e.

$$K_M = \frac{d}{(1-h_M^4)^{1/2}}$$

K_M is a good approximation to d when h_M is small. To make use of this fact we choose ω to be small so that $h_M = \omega/\Omega \ll 1$ and we choose c to be just less than $(2mk)^{1/2} = 2^{1/2}m\omega$. Thus we have

$$d = K_M(1 - \tfrac{1}{2}h_M^4 + \ldots) \quad \text{and} \quad \Omega = \omega/h_M$$

where $h_M = (1 - c^2/2mk)^{1/2}$ and $\omega = (k/m)^{1/2}$. Suppose that we are unable to measure K_M but that we are able to measure K, which equals

$$\frac{md\Omega^2}{\{(k - m\Omega^2)^2 + c^2\Omega^2\}^{1/2}}$$

If we choose c to be equal or nearly equal to $(2mk)^{1/2}$, we may set

$$c^2 = 2mk(1+h) \quad \text{with} \quad 0 \leqslant |h| \ll 1$$

and we find that

$$K = \frac{md\Omega^2}{(k^2 + 2mkh\Omega^2 + m^2\Omega^4)^{1/2}} = \frac{d}{(1 + 2h\omega^2/\Omega^2 + \omega^4/\Omega^4)^{1/2}}$$

Therefore provided we choose m and k so that $\omega^2 \ll \Omega^2$, we see that K is a good approximation to d. This is the principal result concerning a seismograph. In practice the specification of Z is much more complicated than $Z(t) = Z_0 + d\cos\Omega t$. Several time harmonic terms will be necessary to represent the platform's movement caused by an earthquake. Our analysis is adequate provided we may ignore all but the dominant term.

11.6 Related topics

We have been examining in this chapter mechanical systems whose motion is governed by a differential equation of the form

$$m\ddot{z} + c\dot{z} + kz = F(t)$$

This differential equation arises in studies of electrical circuits. Consider a circuit in which a resistor (of resistance R), a capacitor (of capacitance C), an inductor (of inductance L) and a generator (providing a time-varying electromotive force E) are connected in series. Kirchhoff's Laws apply to this problem and govern the charge Q on the capacitor and the flow of current I, where $I = (dQ/dt)$. Thus we obtain the relation

$$L\frac{dI}{dt} + RI + \frac{1}{C}Q = E(t)$$

and the second-order linear differential equation

$$L\ddot{Q} + R\dot{Q} + \frac{1}{C}Q = E(t)$$

The mathematical analysis that we have applied to solve oscillatory problems in mechanics is applicable to electrical circuit problems [see D. S. Jones, *Electrical and Mechanical Oscillations*, Routledge and Kegan Paul].

Here we have an example of two physical problems having an identical mathematical formulation. This mathematical equivalence between the mechanical problem and the electrical problem is the basis of the analogue computer. By designing appropriate circuits, and monitoring the continuously varying electrical quantities, we are able to simulate the motion of an equivalent mechanical system [see G. M. Phillips and P. J. Taylor, *Computers*, Methuen].

EXERCISES ON CHAPTER 11

1. Use the transformation $z = X\exp(-ct/2m)$ to convert the differential equation

$$m\ddot{z}+c\dot{z}+kz = 0$$

into the differential equation

$$\ddot{X}-KX = 0$$

Express K in terms of m, c and k.

2. Solve the differential equations

(i) $\ddot{z}+2\dot{z}+17z = 0$
(ii) $\ddot{z}+2\dot{z}+z = 0$
(iii) $\ddot{z}+5\dot{z}+4z = 0$

subject to the initial conditions at $t = 0$, $z = z_0$ and $\dot{z} = u_0$.

3. Solve the differential equations

(i) $m\ddot{z}+kz = 0$
(ii) $m\ddot{z}+c\dot{z} = 0$
(iii) $m\ddot{z}+c\dot{z}+kz = 0$

subject to the initial conditions at $t = 0$, $z = 0$ and $\dot{z} = u_0$, where m, k, c are positive parameters and $c < 2(mk)^{1/2}$.

4. A particle executes damped oscillations in a straight line under a restoring force proportional to the distance of the particle from a fixed point O on the line and a resistive force proportional to the speed of the particle. Write down the differential equation governing its motion. The motion commences at $t = 0$ with the particle being projected from O with speed u_0. The particle travels a distance d before coming to rest (instantaneously) for the first time at $t = t_1$. Find expressions for d and t_1.

5. The damped oscillations of a body are described by the solution of the differential equation

$$\ddot{x}+2a\omega\dot{x}+\omega^2 x = 0 \quad (a\in(0,1), 0<\omega)$$

subject to $x = d$ and $\dot{x} = 0$ at $t = 0$. Show that

$$x = \frac{d}{(1-a^2)^{1/2}}[(1-a^2)^{1/2}\cos\{\omega(1-a^2)^{1/2}t\}+a\sin\{\omega(1-a^2)^{1/2}t\}]\,e^{-a\omega t}$$

and

$$\dot{x} = -\frac{\omega d}{(1-a^2)^{1/2}}\sin\{\omega(1-a)^{1/2}t\}\,e^{-a\omega t}$$

How far has the body travelled when it passes through the equilibrium position for the Nth time? Denote this distance by D_N and calculate the ratio $(D_\infty - D_5)/D_\infty$ when (i) $a = 0{\cdot}01$, (ii) $a = 0{\cdot}5$.

6. A body of mass m is suspended from a fixed support by a light spring which hangs vertically. The spring has unstretched length l and stiffness $m\delta^2$. Determine the equilibrium position. When the body is moving with speed u along a vertical line, the motion is resisted by a damping force of magnitude $2m\delta u$.

(i) The body is projected downwards with speed u_0 from a position that is a distance d below the equilibrium position. What is the maximum length of the spring?

(ii) The body is projected upwards with speed u_0 from a position that is a distance d below the equilibrium position. What is the minimum length of the spring?

7. A body of mass m is on a rough horizontal belt that moves with constant speed U. The body is connected by a horizontal spring of stiffness $m\omega^2$ to a fixed support. The frictional resistance between the body and the belt is $\frac{10}{3}m\omega$ times the difference in velocity between the body and the belt. Write down the equation of motion and determine the equilibrium position.

If the body is projected from its position of equilibrium with speed u_0 in the direction of the motion of the belt, show that the body's subsequent displacement is

$$\frac{3u_0}{8\omega}(e^{-\omega t/3} - e^{-3\omega t})$$

8. A body of mass m is suspended from a fixed support by a spring of natural length l_1 and stiffness k_1. It is attached to a fixed point B vertically below A, the point of suspension, by a spring (of natural length l_2 and stiffness k_2) and a fluid damper (whose damping coefficient is c) in parallel. The distance between A and B is d. What is the distance between A and the position of equilibrium?

The body is set in motion along the vertical line through the equilibrium position. Under what condition will it perform damped oscillations?

9. An object of mass m is attached by two identical suspension mechanisms to two fixed points, A and B. A and B are on the same horizontal level and the distance between A and B is $6d$. Consider each suspension mechanism to be a spring of natural length l and stiffness k in parallel with a dashpot whose damping coefficient is c. The equilibrium position is a distance $4d$ below the horizontal line through A and B. Show that

$$k = \tfrac{1}{8}mg/(d - \tfrac{1}{5}l)$$

The differential equation governing the motion of the subject along a vertical line through the equilibrium position is

$$m\ddot{z} = mg - 2kz\{1 - l/(9d^2 + z^2)^{1/2}\} - 2c\dot{z}\, z^2/(9d^2 + z^2)$$

Suppose that the object is pulled down a small distance below the equilibrium position and released from rest. Set $z = 4d + x$ and derive the approximate relation

$$m\ddot{x} + \tfrac{32}{25}c\dot{x} + \frac{mg}{100d}\left(\frac{125d - 9l}{5d - l}\right)x = 0$$

Under what condition will there be no oscillations?

10. The bob of a simple pendulum of length l is of mass m and is subject to aerodynamic drag of magnitude $k_1 \times$(speed) in small deviations from the vertical. The bob is given a small horizontal velocity u_0 when it is vertically below the point of suspension. Find the speed with which the bob returns to its initial position after a complete cycle if $k_1 < 2m(g/l)^{1/2}$.

11. Solve the differential equations

(i) $m\ddot{z} + kz = F_0 \sin \Omega t, \quad \Omega \neq (k/m)^{1/2}$

(ii) $m\ddot{z}+kz = F_0 \sin \omega t, \quad \omega = (k/m)^{1/2}$
subject to the initial conditions at $t = 0$, $z = 0$ and $\dot{z} = 0$.

12. Solve the differential equation

$$\ddot{z}+\omega^2 z = (F_0/m)(1+\Omega t)$$

subject to the initial conditions at $t = 0$, $z = z_0$ and $\dot{z} = u_0$.
Show that, when $\omega t \ll 1$ and $\Omega t \ll 1$,

$$z = z_0(1-\tfrac{1}{2}\omega^2 t^2+\ldots)+u_0 t(1-\tfrac{1}{6}\omega^2 t^2+\ldots)+\tfrac{1}{2}(F_0/m)t^2(1+\tfrac{1}{3}\Omega t-\tfrac{1}{12}\omega^2 t^2+\ldots)$$

13. A particle of mass m is suspended from a fixed support by a spring of stiffness k and natural length l. At $t = 0$ the particle is at rest in its equilibrium position. A constant force of magnitude F_0 is applied to the particle in the downward direction during the time interval $[0, t_0]$. Show that at $t = t_0$, the extension of the spring is

$$g/\omega^2+(F_0/m\omega^2)(1-\cos \omega t_0) \quad \text{where} \quad \omega^2 = k/m.$$

What is the speed of the particle at $t = t_0$? Hence show that when $t_0 \leqslant t$ the extension of the spring is

$$(g/\omega^2)\cos \omega(t-t_0)+(2F_0/m\omega^2)\sin \tfrac{1}{2}\omega t_0 \sin \omega(t-\tfrac{1}{2}t_0)-l\{1-\cos \omega(t-t_0)\}$$

14. A particle of mass m is attached to one end of a spring that supports it above a fixed horizontal table. The spring's stiffness is k and its natural length is l. What is the length of the spring when the particle is in equilibrium? The application of a vertical force $F_0 \sin \Omega t$ to the particle commences at $t = 0$; F_0 and Ω are parameters with known positive values. Determine the length of the spring during the subsequent motion for the case $\Omega \neq (k/m)^{1/2}$.
Show that the particle remains above the table when $\Omega = 2(k/m)^{1/2}$ provided

$$F_0 \cos \tfrac{1}{6}\pi < (kl-mg)$$

15. A spring of stiffness k and natural length l is in a vertical position with its lower end fixed to a horizontal table. A particle of mass m is placed (not fixed) on the upper end of the spring. A force $F_0 \sin 2\omega t$, where $\omega^2 = k/l$, is applied in a vertical direction to the upper end of the spring. At $t = 0$ the particle is at rest and the length of the spring is $l-mg/k$. Investigate the subsequent motion. In particular, show that the particle remains in contact with the upper end of the spring provided

$$F_0(\sin \omega t-2\sin 2\omega t) < \tfrac{3}{2}mg$$

for all $t \geqslant 0$. This condition is certainly satisfied provided $F_0 < \tfrac{1}{2}mg$. Are larger values of F_0 permissible?

16. Solve the differential equation

$$m\ddot{z}+c\dot{z} = F_0 \sin \Omega t$$

subject to the initial conditions at $t = 0$, $z = z_0$ and $\dot{z} = 0$. What is the amplitude of the forced oscillations?

17. Solve the differential equation

$$\ddot{z}+5\dot{z}+4z = 150\cos 3t$$

subject to the initial conditions at $t = 0$, $z = z_0$ and $\dot{z} = u_0$.

18. A particle of mass m is suspended from a fixed platform by a mechanism consisting of a spring of stiffness $27m\tilde{\omega}^2$ and a dashpot whose damping coefficient is $6m\tilde{\omega}$. A vertical force $F_0 \cos \Omega t$ is applied to the particle. Show that the amplitude of the forced oscillations of the particle is a maximum when $\Omega = 3\tilde{\omega}$.

What is the maximum value of the forced oscillations' amplitude?

19. A particle of mass m moves along the x-axis. Its motion is governed by the differential equation

$$m\ddot{x} = -18m\tilde{\omega}^2(x-l) - 2m\tilde{\omega}\dot{x} + F_0 \sin \Omega t$$

Show that the greatest amplitude of the forced oscillations occurs when $\Omega = 4\tilde{\omega}$ and determine its magnitude.

20. A particle of mass m moves along the z-axis. The differential equation governing its motion is

$$m\ddot{z} = mg - m\tilde{\omega}^2(z-l) - 4m\tilde{\omega}\dot{z} + F_0 \sin(\Omega t + \varepsilon)$$

Determine the maximum value of the amplitude of the particle's forced oscillations as Ω increases from zero.

21. The mounting of a body of mass m can be regarded as equivalent to a spring of stiffness k connected between the body and the floor, and a dashpot with damping coefficient c also connected between the body and the floor. A vertical force $F_0 \sin \Omega t$ is applied to the body. For what range of Ω will the amplitude of the force transmitted to the floor by the forced oscillations be greater than F_0?

22. Solve the differential equation

$$\ddot{z} = -g - \omega^2(z - Z - l)$$

subject to the initial conditions at $t = 0$, $z = Z_0 + d + l - g/\omega^2$ and $\dot{z} = 0$, in the two cases

(i) $Z = Z_0 + d \cos \Omega t \quad (\Omega \neq \omega)$ (ii) $Z = Z_0 + d \cos \omega t$

23. A particle of mass m is fixed to the upper end of a vertical spring, whose stiffness is $m\omega^2$ and natural length is l. The lower end of the spring is fixed to a horizontal platform. The platform is made to move vertically so that the platform's displacement is $d \sin 2\omega t$ (relative to an inertial frame of reference). At $t = 0$ the length of the spring is $l - g/\omega^2$ and the particle is at rest relative to the platform. Show that in the subsequent motion the length of the spring is not less than $l - g/\omega^2 - 2d3^{1/2}$ and not greater than $l - g/\omega^2 + 2d3^{1/2}$.

24. Solve the differential equation

$$\ddot{z} + \omega^2 z = \omega^2 d \sin 3\omega t$$

subject to the initial conditions at $t = 0$, $z = \dot{z} = 0$.

25. A particle of mass m is suspended from a platform by a spring of stiffness $24m\tilde{\omega}^2$. A dashpot whose damping coefficient is $4m\tilde{\omega}$, is also connected between the particle and the platform. The platform is made to oscillate vertically, its displacement at time t being $d \sin \Omega t$. Show that the amplitude of the forced oscillations of the particle relative to the platform is a maximum when $\Omega = 6\tilde{\omega}$.

What is the maximum value of the amplitude?

26. A particle of mass m is suspended by a spring of stiffness $m\omega^2$ and natural length l from a moving horizontal platform. The platform moves vertically upwards with constant speed u_0. The particle experiences aerodynamic drag of magnitude $m\omega$ times its speed (relative to the stationary medium). At $t = 0$, the length of the spring is $l+g/\omega^2$ and the particle is at rest relative to the platform. Find the terminal speed of the particle and show that the maximum extension of the spring is

$$\frac{g}{\omega^2}+\frac{u_0}{\omega}\{1+e^{-3^{1/2}\pi/6}\}$$

27. In a simple model of a seismograph, a body is suspended from a movable platform by a spring and dashpot combination. The mass of the body is m, the stiffness of the spring is $m\omega^2$ and the damping coefficient associated with the dashpot is $1{\cdot}4\,m\omega$. Show that K, the amplitude of the forced oscillations of the body relative to the oscillating platform, is

$$\frac{d}{(1-0{\cdot}04\,\omega^2/\Omega^2+\omega^4/\Omega^4)^{1/2}}$$

when the displacement of the platform is $d\cos\Omega t$.

Evaluate $(d-K)/d$ when (i) $\Omega = \omega$, (ii) $\Omega = 2\omega$, (iii) $\Omega = 4\omega$.

28. A particle of mass m, moving in a horizontal plane, is attracted to a fixed point O of the plane by a force of magnitude $m\omega^2 r$, where $r = |\boldsymbol{r}|$ and $\boldsymbol{r}$ is the position vector of the particle relative to O. It experiences a resistive force of magnitude $k_1|\dot{\boldsymbol{r}}|$. Show that the equation of motion is

$$m\ddot{\boldsymbol{r}} = -m\omega^2\boldsymbol{r}-k_1\dot{\boldsymbol{r}}+(N-mg)\boldsymbol{k}$$

where $\boldsymbol{r} = x\boldsymbol{i}+y\boldsymbol{j}$ and $N\boldsymbol{k}$ is the normal reaction exerted by the plane on the particle. Deduce that N equals the weight of the particle throughout the motion.

The initial conditions at $t = 0$ are $\boldsymbol{r} = x_0\boldsymbol{i}$ and $\dot{\boldsymbol{r}} = u_0\boldsymbol{j}$. Find $\boldsymbol{r}$ in each of the three cases

(i) $k_1 = m\omega$, (ii) $k_1 = 2m\omega$, (iii) $k_1 = 4m\omega$.

29. A particle is moving on a horizontal table. The differential equation governing its motion is

$$\ddot{\boldsymbol{r}}+3\dot{\boldsymbol{r}}+2\boldsymbol{r} = \boldsymbol{0}$$

where $\boldsymbol{r}$ is the position vector of the particle relative to a fixed point on the table. At $t = 0$, $\boldsymbol{r} = x_0\boldsymbol{i}$ and $\dot{\boldsymbol{r}} = u_0\boldsymbol{j}$. Show that

$$\boldsymbol{r} = (2x_0\boldsymbol{i}+u_0\boldsymbol{j})e^{-t}-(x_0\boldsymbol{i}+u_0\boldsymbol{j})e^{-2t}$$

Introduce plane polar coordinates and establish the results

$$r^2\dot{\phi} = x_0 u_0 e^{-3t}$$

and

$$\ddot{r}+3\dot{r}+2r = \frac{x_0^2 u_0^2}{r^3}e^{-6t}$$

30. A satellite of mass m moves round the Earth of mass M and experiences atmospheric drag. Consider a model in which the equation of motion is

$$m\ddot{\boldsymbol{r}} = -\frac{GMm\boldsymbol{r}}{r^3}-\frac{k_1\dot{\boldsymbol{r}}}{r^2}$$

where k_1, the parameter associated with the resistive force, is small. At $t = 0$, the initial conditions are $r = r_0$, $\phi = 0$, $\dot{r} = 0$, $\dot{\phi} = L_0/r_0^2$. Show that

$$r^2\dot{\phi} = L_0-\frac{k_1}{m}\phi$$

and

$$\frac{d^2u}{d\phi^2}+u=\frac{GM}{(L_0-k_1\phi/m)^2}=\frac{GM}{L_0^2}\left(1+\frac{2k_1\phi}{mL_0}+\dots\right)$$

where $r = 1/u$. Ignore second and higher powers of $k_1\phi/mL_0$ and obtain the solution

$$u=\frac{1}{r_0}\cos\phi+\frac{GM}{L_0^2}(1-\cos\phi)+\frac{2k_1GM}{mL_0^3}(\phi-\sin\phi)$$

[For alternative models incorporating atmospheric drag, see D. King-Hele, *Theory of Satellite Orbits in an Atmosphere*, Butterworth.]

12 Lifts and Turntables

12.1 Lifts

Consider a lift in motion relative to an inertial frame of reference. The lift starts from rest and rises with a constant acceleration a during the time interval $[0, t_1]$. It then rises with constant speed during the time interval (t_1, t_1+t_2), before being uniformly retarded and coming to rest after rising a total height H in a journey time of $t_1+t_2+t_3$.

It is convenient to introduce a vertical axis, say the z-axis with z increasing in an upwards direction. Suppose that the floor of the lift is in the plane $z=0$ at $t=0$ and is in the plane $z=Z(t)$ at $t\in[0, t_1+t_2+t_3]$. We consider the three stages of the motion in turn:

(i) $t\in[0, t_1]$

$$\ddot{Z}(t)=a,\quad \dot{Z}(t)=at,\quad Z(t)=\tfrac{1}{2}at^2$$

(ii) $t\in(t_1, t_1+t_2)$

$$\ddot{Z}(t)=0,\quad \dot{Z}(t)=at_1,\quad Z(t)=at_1(t-t_1)+\tfrac{1}{2}at_1^2$$

(iii) $t\in[t_1+t_2, t_1+t_2+t_3]$

$$\ddot{Z}(t)=-\frac{at_1}{t_3},\quad \dot{Z}(t)=-\frac{at_1}{t_3}(t-t_1-t_2)+at_1$$

$$Z(t)=-\tfrac{1}{2}\frac{at_1}{t_3}(t-t_1-t_2)^2+at_1(t-t_1-t_2)+at_1t_2+\tfrac{1}{2}at_1^2$$

Thus we have

$$Z(t)=\begin{cases}\tfrac{1}{2}at^2 & 0\leqslant t\leqslant t_1\\ at_1(t-\tfrac{1}{2}t_1) & t_1\leqslant t\leqslant t_1+t_2\\ -\tfrac{1}{2}\dfrac{at_1}{t_3}(t-t_1-t_2)^2+at_1(t-\tfrac{1}{2}t_1) & t_1+t_2\leqslant t\leqslant t_1+t_2+t_3\end{cases}$$

We note that the constant speed during the second stage of the motion is at_1

and that the uniform retardation during the third stage is at_1/t_3. The total height H equals $\frac{1}{2}at_1(t_1+2t_2+t_3)$.

Suppose a passenger of mass m is standing in the lift. We introduce a particle to represent the passenger. Let the z-coordinate of the particle be z. Provided the passenger is standing still, we may set $z = Z+d$, where d is a constant. The equation of motion for the particle is

$$m\ddot{z}\mathbf{k} = (-mg+N)\mathbf{k}$$

where $N\mathbf{k}$ represents the reaction of the floor on the passenger. Thus

$$N = mg+m\ddot{z} = mg+m\ddot{Z}$$

i.e.

$$N = \begin{cases} m(g+a) & 0 \leqslant t \leqslant t_1 \\ mg & t_1 < t < t_1+t_2 \\ m(g-at_1/t_3) & t_1+t_2 \leqslant t \leqslant t_1+t_2+t_3 \end{cases}$$

If the mass of the lift cage is M and the tension in the suspending cable at the end attached to the cage is T, then the equation governing the motion of the lift cage is

$$M\ddot{Z} = T-Mg-N$$

Hence

$$T = Mg+M\ddot{Z}+N$$

i.e.

$$T = \begin{cases} (M+m)(g+a) & 0 \leqslant t \leqslant t_1 \\ (M+m)g & t_1 < t < t_1+t_2 \\ (M+m)(g-at_1/t_3) & t_1+t_2 \leqslant t \leqslant t_1+t_2+t_3 \end{cases}$$

Our model is an oversimplification because the discontinuities in the tension of the cable are unacceptable. In practice the tension varies continuously, but rapidly in the neighbourhoods of $t = t_1$ and $t = t_1+t_2$. There is a consequent change in the form of $\ddot{Z}$. A more realistic problem is to solve

$$m\ddot{Z} = -mg+N$$

and

$$M\ddot{Z} = -Mg-N+T$$

where T is a control variable governed by the characteristics of the winding machine. It follows that

$$(m+M)\ddot{Z} = -(m+M)g+T$$

and

$$N = mT/(m+M).$$

The results in the previous paragraph do accord reasonably with our experience of standing in a rising lift.

Let us examine another lift problem, in which the motion of the lift is prescribed by the previously defined function Z. A particle of mass m is supported above the floor of the lift by a spring of stiffness $m\omega^2$ and natural length l. The spring is vertical, with its lower end attached to the floor and the particle attached to its upper end. The differential equation governing the vertical motion of the particle (relative to the inertial frame of reference based on the z-axis) is

$$m\ddot{z} = -mg-m\omega^2(z-Z-l)$$

i.e.

$$\ddot{z}+\omega^2 z = -g+l\omega^2+Z\omega^2$$

or

$$(\ddot{z}-\ddot{Z})+\omega^2(z-Z) = -g+l\omega^2-\ddot{Z}$$

We have to analyse each of the three stages in turn and ensure that z and $\dot{z}$ are continuous at $t = t_1$ and at $t = t_1+t_2$, the instants at which $\ddot{Z}$ is discontinuous (and Z and $\dot{Z}$ are continuous). Suppose that the initial conditions at $t = 0$ are $z = l-g/\omega^2$, $\dot{z} = 0$.

(i) $t \in [0, t_1]$

The differential equation is

$$\ddot{z}+\omega^2 z = -g+l\omega^2+\tfrac{1}{2}a\omega^2 t^2$$

Its complementary function is $A\cos\omega t+B\sin\omega t$. We use the method of undetermined coefficients to find a particular integral. Setting

$$z = C_0+C_1 t+C_2 t^2$$

and substituting into the differential equation, we obtain

$$2C_2+\omega^2(C_0+C_1 t+C_2 t^2) = -g+l\omega^2+\tfrac{1}{2}a\omega^2 t^2$$

i.e.

$$C_2 = \tfrac{1}{2}a, \quad C_1 = 0 \quad \text{and} \quad C_0 = l-g/\omega^2-a/\omega^2.$$

Thus the general solution is

$$A\cos\omega t+B\sin\omega t+l-g/\omega^2-a/\omega^2+\tfrac{1}{2}at^2$$

Imposing the initial conditions at $t = 0$ leads to

$$l-g/\omega^2 = A+l-g/\omega^2-a/\omega^2$$

and

$$0 = B\omega.$$

Therefore the required solution is

$$z = l-(g+a)/\omega^2+(a/\omega^2)\cos\omega t+\tfrac{1}{2}at^2$$

and the length of the spring, $z-Z$, equals

$$l-(g+a)/\omega^2+(a/\omega^2)\cos\omega t$$

At $t = t_1$

$$z = l-(g+a)/\omega^2+(a/\omega^2)\cos\omega t_1+\tfrac{1}{2}at_1^2$$

and

$$\dot{z} = -(a/\omega)\sin\omega t_1+at_1.$$

(ii) $t\in(t_1, t_1+t_2)$

The differential equation is

$$\ddot{z}+\omega^2 z = -g+l\omega^2+a\omega^2 t_1(t-\tfrac{1}{2}t_1)$$

It is convenient to write the complementary function in the form $A\cos\omega(t-t_1)+B\sin\omega(t-t_1)$. A particular integral is

$$l-g/\omega^2+at_1(t-\tfrac{1}{2}t_1)$$

We are able to satisfy the condition that z and $\dot{z}$ are continuous at $t = t_1$ provided we choose A and B such that

$$l-(g+a)/\omega^2+(a/\omega^2)\cos\omega t_1+\tfrac{1}{2}at_1^2 = A+l-g/\omega^2+\tfrac{1}{2}at_1^2$$

and

$$-(a/\omega)\sin\omega t_1+at_1 = B\omega+at_1.$$

Therefore the required solution is

$$z = -(a/\omega^2)\{(1-\cos\omega t_1)\cos\omega(t-t_1)+\sin\omega t_1\sin\omega(t-t_1)\}$$
$$+l-g/\omega^2+at_1(t-\tfrac{1}{2}t_1).$$

This simplifies to

$$z = l-g/\omega^2-(2a/\omega^2)\sin\tfrac{1}{2}\omega t_1\sin\omega(t-\tfrac{1}{2}t_1)+at_1(t-\tfrac{1}{2}t_1)$$

and the length of the spring is

$$l-g/\omega^2-(2a/\omega^2)\sin\tfrac{1}{2}\omega t_1\sin\omega(t-\tfrac{1}{2}t_1)$$

At $t = t_1+t_2$

$$z = l-g/\omega^2-(2a/\omega^2)\sin\tfrac{1}{2}\omega t_1\sin\omega(\tfrac{1}{2}t_1+t_2)+at_1(\tfrac{1}{2}t_1+t_2)$$

and

$$\dot{z} = -(2a/\omega)\sin\tfrac{1}{2}\omega t_1\cos\omega(\tfrac{1}{2}t_1+t_2)+at_1.$$

(iii) $t \in [t_1+t_2, t_1+t_2+t_3]$
The differential equation is

$$\ddot{z}+\omega^2 z = -g+l\omega^2+a\omega^2 t_1\{-\tfrac{1}{2}(t-t_1-t_2)^2/t_3+t-\tfrac{1}{2}t_1\}$$

Writing the complementary function in the form

$$A\cos\omega(t-t_1-t_2)+B\sin\omega(t-t_1-t_2)$$

and using the particular integral

$$l-g/\omega^2+at_1\{-\tfrac{1}{2}(t-t_1-t_2)^2/t_3+t-\tfrac{1}{2}t_1\}+at_1/\omega^2 t_3$$

we obtain two equations for A and B when we impose the continuity conditions at $t = t_1+t_2$. Thus we have

$$-(2a/\omega^2)\sin\tfrac{1}{2}\omega t_1 \sin\omega(\tfrac{1}{2}t_1+t_2) = A+at_1/\omega^2 t_3$$

and

$$-(2a/\omega)\sin\tfrac{1}{2}\omega t_1 \cos\omega(\tfrac{1}{2}t_1+t_2) = B\omega\,.$$

We find that the required solution is

$$z = l-(g-at_1/t_3)/\omega^2-(2a/\omega^2)\sin\tfrac{1}{2}\omega t_1 \sin\omega(t-\tfrac{1}{2}t_1)$$
$$-(at_1/\omega^2 t_3)\cos\omega(t-t_1-t_2)+at_1\{-\tfrac{1}{2}(t-t_1-t_2)^2/t_3+t-\tfrac{1}{2}t_1\}$$

and the length of the spring is

$$l-(g-at_1/t_3)/\omega^2-(2a/\omega^2)\sin\tfrac{1}{2}\omega t_1 \sin\omega(t-\tfrac{1}{2}t_1)$$
$$-(at_1/\omega^2 t_3)\cos\omega(t-t_1-t_2)$$

We summarize the results by noting that the length of spring varies within the following limits

(i) $t \in [0, t_1]$

$$l-(g+a)/\omega^2 \pm a/\omega^2$$

(ii) $t \in [t_1, t_1+t_2]$

$$l-g/\omega^2 \pm (2a/\omega^2)\sin\tfrac{1}{2}\omega t_1$$

(iii) $t \,\varepsilon\, [t_1+t_2, t_1+t_2+t_3]$

$$l-(g-at_1/t_3)/\omega^2$$
$$\pm(a/\omega^2)[4\sin\tfrac{1}{2}\omega t_1\{\sin\tfrac{1}{2}\omega t_1+(t_1/t_3)\sin\omega(\tfrac{1}{2}t_1+t_2)\}+(t_1/t_3)^2]^{1/2}.$$

We notice the three equilibrium lengths corresponding to the three stages of the motion, namely

$$l-(g+a)/\omega^2, \quad l-g/\omega^2, \quad l-(g-at_1/t_3)/\omega^2$$

The conversion of these lengths into forces by means of Hooke's law is the basis of the bathroom scales (or similar measuring instruments) which measures force, namely weight, but whose calibration indicates the measurement of mass. In such instruments there is a damping mechanism which causes the indicator to come to rest quite quickly to facilitate a reading. Our model predicts oscillations about the equilibrium position persisting for ever. We shall revise our model by introducing a dash-pot, whose damping coefficient is c, in parallel with the vertical spring. The appropriate differential equation is

$$m\ddot{z} = -mg - m\omega^2(z-Z-l) - c(\dot{z}-\dot{Z})$$

i.e.

$$m\ddot{z} + c\dot{z} + m\omega^2 z = -m(g-l\omega^2) + c\dot{Z} + m\omega^2 Z$$

or

$$m(\ddot{z}-\ddot{Z}) + c(\dot{z}-\dot{Z}) + m\omega^2(z-Z) = -m(g-l\omega^2+\ddot{Z})$$

This governs the vertical motion of the particle mounted above the floor of the lift cabin by means of the spring/dash-pot combination. It is similar to differential equations that we studied in chapter 11. Its complementary function represents damped oscillations, and a particular integral indicates the equilibrium position and represents any forced oscillations. In the case of the three-stage motion, particular integrals associated with the second alternative form of the differential equation are

$$l-(g+a)/\omega^2, \quad l-g/\omega^2, \quad l-(g-at_1/t_3)/\omega^2$$

these being the equilibrium values of the distance of the particle above the floor. They agree with our results obtained earlier. We note that there are no forced oscillations when $\ddot{Z}$ is constant (or piecewise constant).

12.2 Turntables

A frame of reference rotating with respect to an inertial frame of reference is not an inertial frame of reference. Consequently we are not permitted to apply Newton's Laws of Motion to relate an acceleration measured relative to a rotating frame with an applied force. It is essential to use an acceleration measured relative to an inertial frame when we apply Newton's Laws. Up to now we have ignored the effects of the rotations of the Earth about its axis and about the Sun. Let us consider some problems in which a frame of reference is rotating with respect to an inertial frame of reference. We shall investigate some turntable problems (e.g. associated with a record player, a spin dryer or a fairground roundabout) before examining the effects of the Earth's daily rotation about the polar axis.

Consider two cartesian coordinate systems that have a common origin O

and a common axis for all time. Let (X, Y, Z) be the coordinates of the system that is rotating with respect to an inertial frame of reference having the coordinates (x, y, z) so that the Oz and OZ-axes are coincident for all

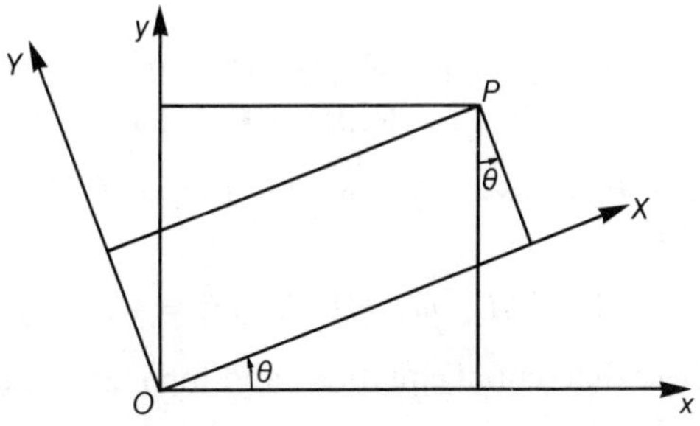

time. We have investigated the kinematic relations between these frames of reference in Section 2.7. Let $\boldsymbol{r}$ be the position vector (relative to the origin O) of a particle P. Then

$$\begin{aligned}\boldsymbol{r} &= x\boldsymbol{i}+y\boldsymbol{j}+z\boldsymbol{k}\\ &= X\mathbf{I}+Y\mathbf{J}+Z\mathbf{K}\end{aligned}$$

where $\mathbf{I} = \boldsymbol{i}\cos\theta+\boldsymbol{j}\sin\theta$, $\mathbf{J} = -\boldsymbol{i}\sin\theta+\boldsymbol{j}\cos\theta$, $\mathbf{K} = \boldsymbol{k}$. It follows that

$$\begin{aligned}\dot{\boldsymbol{r}} &= \dot{x}\boldsymbol{i}+\dot{y}\boldsymbol{j}+\dot{z}\boldsymbol{k}\\ &= (\dot{X}-Y\dot{\theta})\mathbf{I}+(\dot{Y}+X\dot{\theta})\mathbf{J}+\dot{Z}\mathbf{K}\\ &= \frac{\delta\boldsymbol{r}}{\delta t}+\boldsymbol{\omega}\times\boldsymbol{r}\end{aligned}$$

and

$$\begin{aligned}\ddot{\boldsymbol{r}} &= \ddot{x}\boldsymbol{i}+\ddot{y}\boldsymbol{j}+\ddot{z}\boldsymbol{k}\\ &= (\ddot{X}-2\dot{Y}\dot{\theta}-Y\ddot{\theta}-X\dot{\theta}^2)\mathbf{I}+(\ddot{Y}+2\dot{X}\dot{\theta}+X\ddot{\theta}-Y\dot{\theta}^2)\mathbf{J}+\ddot{Z}\mathbf{K}\\ &= \frac{\delta^2\boldsymbol{r}}{\delta t^2}+2\boldsymbol{\omega}\times\frac{\delta\boldsymbol{r}}{\delta t}+\dot{\boldsymbol{\omega}}\times\boldsymbol{r}+\boldsymbol{\omega}\times(\boldsymbol{\omega}\times\boldsymbol{r})\end{aligned}$$

where

$$\boldsymbol{\omega} = \dot{\theta}\boldsymbol{k} = \dot{\theta}\mathbf{K},\ (\delta\boldsymbol{r}/\delta t) = \dot{X}\mathbf{I}+\dot{Y}\mathbf{J}+\dot{Z}\mathbf{K} \text{ and } (\delta^2\boldsymbol{r}/\delta t^2) = \ddot{X}\mathbf{I}+\ddot{Y}\mathbf{J}+\ddot{Z}\mathbf{K}.$$

We assume that we know how θ varies with time. In many applications $\dot{\theta}$ has a constant value, ω say.

If the particle P of mass m is moving relative to the inertial frame of reference (based on the coordinate system $Oxyz$) and $\mathbf{F}$ represents the applied force acting on the particle, then the equation of motion is

$$m\ddot{\boldsymbol{r}} = \mathbf{F}$$

where

$$\begin{aligned} F &= (\mathbf{F}\,.\,\boldsymbol{i})\boldsymbol{i}+(\mathbf{F}\,.\,\boldsymbol{j})\boldsymbol{j}+(\mathbf{F}\,.\,\boldsymbol{k})\boldsymbol{k} \\ &= (\mathbf{F}\,.\,\mathbf{I})\mathbf{I}+(\mathbf{F}\,.\,\mathbf{J})\mathbf{J}+(\mathbf{F}\,.\,\mathbf{K})\mathbf{K} \end{aligned}$$

The coordinates of P relative to the inertial frame of reference satisfy the differential equations

$$m\ddot{x} = \mathbf{F}\,.\,\boldsymbol{i}, \quad m\ddot{y} = \mathbf{F}\,.\,\boldsymbol{j}, \quad m\ddot{z} = \mathbf{F}\,.\,\boldsymbol{k}$$

We may solve these differential equations and then use the relations

$$X = x\cos\theta + y\sin\theta, \quad Y = -x\sin\theta + y\cos\theta, \quad Z = z$$

to find X, Y, Z (the coordinates of P relative to the rotating frame of reference). However, it is usually preferable to analyse directly the differential equations governing X, Y, Z, namely

$$m(\ddot{X} - X\dot{\theta}^2 - 2\dot{Y}\dot{\theta} - Y\ddot{\theta}) = \mathbf{F}\,.\,\mathbf{I}$$

$$m(\ddot{Y} - Y\dot{\theta}^2 + 2\dot{X}\dot{\theta} + X\ddot{\theta}) = \mathbf{F}\,.\,\mathbf{J}, \quad m\ddot{Z} = \mathbf{F}\,.\,\mathbf{K}$$

We note that the equation of motion $m\ddot{\boldsymbol{r}} = \mathbf{F}$ may be written in the form

$$m\frac{\delta^2\boldsymbol{r}}{\delta t^2} = \mathbf{F} - 2m\omega \times \frac{\delta\boldsymbol{r}}{\delta t} - m\dot{\omega} \times \boldsymbol{r} - m\omega \times (\omega \times \boldsymbol{r})$$

The left-hand side is the product of the particle's mass and the particle's acceleration relative to the rotating frame of reference. The right-hand side has the appearance of a force. We emphasize that **F** represents the total force acting on the particle and the other three terms are "apparent forces". The second term,

$$-2m\omega \times \frac{\delta\boldsymbol{r}}{\delta t}$$

is called the *Coriolis force* and the last term,

$$-m\omega \times (\omega \times r) = -m(\omega\,.\,r)\omega + m(\omega\,.\,\omega)\boldsymbol{r}$$

is called the *centrigugal force* (an apparent force directed away from the axis of rotation).

EXAMPLE

A ring can slide on a spoke of a wheel that revolves in a horizontal plane about a vertical axis through its centre with constant angular speed ω. The ring starts from rest relative to the wheel at a distance d from the centre and the contact between the ring and the spoke is smooth. Investigate the ring's motion relative to the spoke.

We let the origin O coincide with the centre of the wheel and let the OX-axis represent the spoke on which the ring slides. Let $\boldsymbol{r}$ be the position vector relative to O of a particle P (of mass m) representing the ring. Then

$$\boldsymbol{r} = X\mathbf{I}$$

We introduce an inertial frame of reference based on the cartesian coordinate system $Oxyz$ so that

$$\mathbf{I} = \boldsymbol{i}\cos\theta + \boldsymbol{j}\sin\theta, \quad \mathbf{J} = -\boldsymbol{i}\sin\theta + \boldsymbol{j}\cos\theta, \quad \mathbf{K} = \boldsymbol{k},$$

where $\dot{\theta} = \omega$ and $\theta = \omega t$. Hence

$$\dot{\boldsymbol{r}} = \dot{X}\mathbf{I} + \omega X\mathbf{J} \quad \text{and} \quad \ddot{\boldsymbol{r}} = (\ddot{X} - \omega^2 X)\mathbf{I} + 2\omega\dot{X}\mathbf{J}$$

Alternative expressions are

$$\boldsymbol{r} = x\boldsymbol{i} + y\boldsymbol{j}, \quad \dot{\boldsymbol{r}} = \dot{x}\boldsymbol{i} + \dot{y}\boldsymbol{j}, \quad \ddot{\boldsymbol{r}} = \ddot{x}\boldsymbol{i} + \ddot{y}\boldsymbol{j}$$

subject to the constraints $x = X\cos\omega t$, $y = X\sin\omega t$.

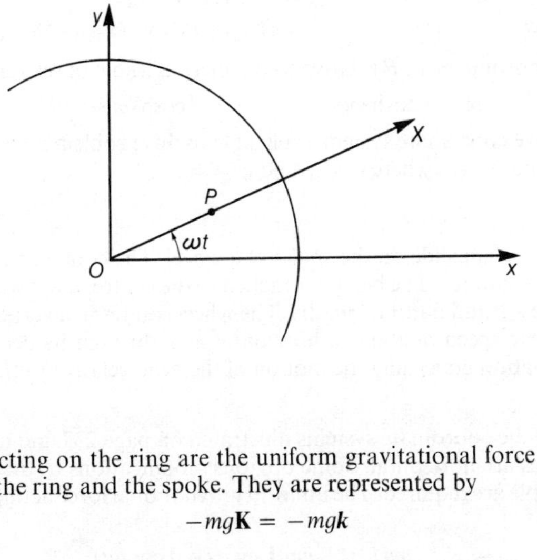

The forces acting on the ring are the uniform gravitational force and a contact force between the ring and the spoke. They are represented by

$$-mg\mathbf{K} = -mg\boldsymbol{k}$$

and

$$N_2\mathbf{J} + N_3\mathbf{K} = N_2(-\boldsymbol{i}\sin\omega t + \boldsymbol{j}\cos\omega t) + N_3\boldsymbol{k}$$

respectively. The contact between the ring and the spoke is smooth, therefore the contact force has no component along the spoke (in the direction of **I**). Thus the total force acting on the particle P is represented by

$$\begin{aligned}\mathbf{F} &= N_2\mathbf{J} + (N_3 - mg)\mathbf{K} \\ &= -(N_2\sin\omega t)\boldsymbol{i} + (N_2\cos\omega t)\boldsymbol{j} + (N_3 - mg)\boldsymbol{k}\end{aligned}$$

The equation of motion, $m\ddot{\boldsymbol{r}} = \mathbf{F}$, is

$$m\ddot{x}\boldsymbol{i} \quad m\ddot{y}\boldsymbol{j} = -(N_2\sin\omega t)\boldsymbol{i} + (N_2\cos\omega t)\boldsymbol{j} + (N_3 - mg)\boldsymbol{k}$$

subject to the constraints $x = X\cos\omega t$, $y = X\sin\omega t$. An equivalent form is

$$m(\ddot{X} - \omega^2 X)\mathbf{I} + 2m\omega\dot{X}\mathbf{J} = N_2\mathbf{J} + (N_3 - mg)\mathbf{K}$$

which is preferable because it leads easily to the three scalar equations

$$\ddot{X} - \omega^2 X = 0, \quad N_2 = 2m\omega\dot{X}, \quad N_3 = mg$$

The X-coordinate is governed by the second-order linear differential equation with constant coefficients, $\ddot{X} - \omega^2 X = 0$, whose general solution is a linear combination of $e^{\omega t}$ and $e^{-\omega t}$ (or $\cosh \omega t$ and $\sinh \omega t$).

Suppose that the ring starts from rest relative to the spoke at a distance d from the centre of the wheel. In this case the initial conditions at $t = 0$ are $X = d$ and $\dot{X} = 0$. Thus the required solution is

$$X = A\,e^{\omega t} + B\,e^{-\omega t}$$

where $d = A + B$ and $0 = \omega A - \omega B$; i.e. $A = B = \frac{1}{2}d$ and $X = d\cosh \omega t$. It follows that $N_2 = 2m\omega^2 d \sinh \omega t$. We note that X and N_2 increase as t increases. We expect the ring to move along the spoke away from the axis of rotation. For example,

$$\begin{aligned} X = 2d \quad \text{when} \quad t = T_2 &= (1/\omega)\cosh^{-1}(2) \\ &= (1/\omega)\ln(2 + 3^{1/2}) = (1{\cdot}317)/\omega \end{aligned}$$

and

$$\begin{aligned} X = 3d \quad \text{when} \quad t = T_3 &= (1/\omega)\cosh^{-1}(3) \\ &= (1/\omega)\ln(3 + 8^{1/2}) = (1{\cdot}764)/\omega \end{aligned}$$

We note the coordinates of P relative to the inertial frame of reference, namely

$$x = d\cosh \omega t \cos \omega t, \quad y = d\cosh \omega t \sin \omega t$$

An alternative coordinate system applicable to this problem is a system of plane-polar coordinates (r, ϕ), where $r = X$ and $\phi = \omega t$.

EXAMPLE

A bead of mass m can slide on the spoke of a wheel. The contact between the bead and the spoke is smooth. The bead is attached to the centre of the wheel by a helical spring of stiffness k and natural length l. The wheel rotates in a vertical plane with a constant angular speed ω about a horizontal axis through its centre. Derive the differential equation governing the motion of the bead relative to the spoke.

We shall use the coordinate systems illustrated on page 237 and understand that the Oz, OZ-axes are horizontal. Some obvious modifications to the analysis of the previous example are required. The uniform gravitational force acting on the bead is represented by

$$-mg\boldsymbol{j} = -mg(\mathbf{I}\sin \omega t + \mathbf{J}\cos \omega t)$$

the contact force by

$$N_2(-\boldsymbol{i}\sin \omega t + \boldsymbol{j}\cos \omega t) = N_2\mathbf{J}$$

and the elastic force by

$$-k(|\boldsymbol{r}| - l)(\boldsymbol{i}\cos \omega t + \boldsymbol{j}\sin \omega t) = -k(X - l)\mathbf{I}$$

Therefore the total force acting on the particle P (representing the bead) is given by

$$\begin{aligned} \mathbf{F} &= -\{N_2 \sin \omega t + k(|\boldsymbol{r}| - l)\cos \omega t\}\boldsymbol{i} - \{mg - N_2\cos \omega t + k(|\boldsymbol{r}| - l)\sin \omega t\}\boldsymbol{j} \\ &= -\{mg\sin \omega t + k(X - l)\}\mathbf{I} - \{mg\cos \omega t - N_2\}\mathbf{J} \end{aligned}$$

Using the result

$$\ddot{\boldsymbol{r}} = (\ddot{X} - \omega^2 X)\mathbf{I} + 2\omega\dot{X}\mathbf{J}$$

we see that the equation of motion, $m\ddot{r} = F$, leads to the scalar equations

$$m\ddot{X} + (k - m\omega^2)X = kl - mg \sin \omega t$$

and

$$N_2 = mg \cos \omega t + 2m\omega\dot{X}$$

Here we have a second-order linear differential equation with constant coefficients. We note the time-harmonic forcing term on the right-hand side of the differential equation. This derivation is based on the assumption that the bead is never in contact with the rim of the wheel.

EXAMPLE

A block of wood is placed on a rough horizontal plate that is rotating about a vertical axis. The contact force between the block and the plate is characterized by the coefficient of static friction μ_s and the coefficient of kinematic friction μ. Estimate the greatest steady angular speed ω that the plate can have without the block slipping, and derive the equation of motion when the block is moving relative to the plate.

We introduce a particle of mass m to represent the block of wood and use the coordinate systems $Oxyz$, $OXYZ$ illustrated on page 237. The appropriate equation of motion is $m\ddot{r} = \mathbf{F}$, where

$$\ddot{r} = (\ddot{X} - 2\dot{Y}\dot{\theta} - Y\ddot{\theta} - X\dot{\theta}^2)\mathbf{I} + (\ddot{Y} + 2\dot{X}\dot{\theta} + X\ddot{\theta} - Y\dot{\theta}^2)\mathbf{J}$$

and $\mathbf{F} = \mathbf{F}_F + (N - mg)\mathbf{K}$. The vector $\mathbf{F}_F$ represents the frictional force acting on the block of wood. In the first part of the problem we are concerned with the case of uniform angular speed and no slipping, that is

$$\ddot{\theta} = 0, \quad \dot{\theta} = \omega, \quad \ddot{X} = \dot{X} = 0, \quad \ddot{Y} = \dot{Y} = 0 \quad \text{and} \quad |\mathbf{F}_F| < \mu_s N.$$

Thus we have

$$-mX\omega^2\mathbf{I} - mY\omega^2\mathbf{J} = \mathbf{F}_F \quad \text{and} \quad |\mathbf{F}_F| < \mu_s mg$$

We deduce that $\omega < (\mu_s mg/d)^{1/2}$, where $d = (X^2 + Y^2)^{1/2}$ which is the distance between the particle and the axis of rotation.

When the block is moving relative to the plate, $|\mathbf{F}_F| = \mu N$, $\mathbf{F}_F = -\mu N(\dot{X}\mathbf{I} + \dot{Y}\mathbf{J})/(\dot{X}^2 + \dot{Y}^2)^{1/2}$ and $N = mg$. Hence the equation of motion gives rise to a pair of simultaneous second-order non-linear differential equations, namely

$$\left(\ddot{X} + \frac{\mu g\dot{X}}{(\dot{X}^2 + \dot{Y}^2)^{1/2}} - \dot{\theta}^2 X\right) - (2\dot{\theta}\dot{Y} + \ddot{\theta}Y) = 0$$

$$(2\dot{\theta}\dot{X} + \ddot{\theta}X) + \left(\ddot{Y} + \frac{\mu g\dot{Y}}{(\dot{X}^2 + \dot{Y}^2)^{1/2}} - \dot{\theta}^2 Y\right) = 0$$

No analytical method of solution is available even when $\dot{\theta} = \omega$ and $\ddot{\theta} = 0$. When the resistive force is a drag proportional to the speed of the particle relative to the plate,

$$\mathbf{F} = -k_1(\dot{X}\mathbf{I} + \dot{Y}\mathbf{J}) + (N - mg)\mathbf{K}$$

and the governing differential equations are

$$(m\ddot{X} + k_1\dot{X} - m\dot{\theta}^2 X) - m(2\dot{\theta}\dot{Y} + \ddot{\theta}Y) = 0$$
$$m(2\dot{\theta}\dot{X} + \ddot{\theta}X) + (m\ddot{Y} + k_1\dot{Y} - m\dot{\theta}^2 Y) = 0$$

When $\dot{\theta}$ and k_1 are constant, these equations are simultaneous second-order linear differential equations with constant coefficients, for which an analytical method of solution is available.

Let us investigate a special case in which the contact between the block of wood and the rotating plate is smooth. In this case $\mathbf{F} = (N - mg)\mathbf{K}$. If we use $\boldsymbol{r} = X\mathbf{I} + Y\mathbf{J}$, we obtain

$$(\ddot{X} - \dot{\theta}^2 X) - (2\dot{\theta}\dot{Y} + \ddot{\theta}Y) = 0$$
$$(2\dot{\theta}\dot{X} + \ddot{\theta}X) + (\ddot{Y} - \dot{\theta}^2 Y) = 0$$

and if we use $\boldsymbol{r} = x\boldsymbol{i} + y\boldsymbol{j}$, we obtain $\ddot{x} = 0$, $\ddot{y} = 0$. The second alternative is preferable in this case. Suppose that at $t = 0$

$$\boldsymbol{r} = d\boldsymbol{i} \quad \text{and} \quad \dot{\boldsymbol{r}} = u_0\boldsymbol{j}$$

Therefore $\dot{\boldsymbol{r}} = u_0\boldsymbol{j}$ and $\boldsymbol{r} = d\boldsymbol{i} + u_0 t\boldsymbol{j}$ for all time. We can find the expressions for X and Y by means of

$$X = x\cos\theta + y\sin\theta = d\cos\theta + u_0 t\sin\theta$$

and

$$Y = -x\sin\theta + y\cos\theta = -d\sin\theta + u_0 t\cos\theta$$

i.e.

$$\boldsymbol{r} = (d\cos\theta + u_0 t\sin\theta)\mathbf{I} + (-d\sin\theta + u_0 t\cos\theta)\mathbf{J}$$

where θ is a specified function of the time t. A less-attractive way to obtain this result is to solve the simultaneous differential equations

$$(\ddot{X} - \dot{\theta}^2 X) - (2\dot{\theta}\dot{Y} + \ddot{\theta}Y) = 0, \quad (2\dot{\theta}\dot{X} + \ddot{\theta}X) + (\ddot{Y} - \dot{\theta}^2 Y) = 0$$

subject to the initial conditions at $t = 0$

$$X = d, \quad \dot{X} = 0, \quad Y = 0, \quad \dot{Y} = u_0 - d(\dot{\theta})_{t=0}, \quad \theta = 0.$$

Let us assume for the purpose of illustration that the answer is unknown to us and that the angular speed is constant (say, $\dot{\theta} = \omega$). Then we have to solve

$$\ddot{X} - \omega^2 X - 2\omega\dot{Y} = 0, \quad 2\omega\dot{X} + \ddot{Y} - \omega^2 Y = 0$$

subject to $X = d$, $\dot{X} = 0$, $Y = 0$, $\dot{Y} = u_0 - \omega d$ at $t = 0$. The elimination of X leads to

$$
\begin{aligned}
0 &= 2\omega\frac{d}{dt}(\ddot{X} - \omega^2 X - 2\omega\dot{Y}) \\
&= \left(\frac{d^2}{dt^2} - \omega^2\right)(2\omega\dot{X}) - 4\omega^2\frac{d^2Y}{dt^2} \\
&= \left(\frac{d^2}{dt^2} - \omega^2\right)(-\ddot{Y} + \omega^2 Y) - 4\omega^2\frac{d^2Y}{dt^2} \\
&= -\frac{d^4Y}{dt^4} + 2\omega^2\frac{d^2Y}{dt^2} - \omega^4 Y - 4\omega^2\frac{d^2Y}{dt^2} \\
&= -\left(\frac{d^4Y}{dt^4} + 2\omega^2\frac{d^2Y}{dt^2} + \omega^4 Y\right) = -\left(\frac{d^2}{dt^2} + \omega^2\right)\left(\frac{d^2Y}{dt^2} + \omega^2 Y\right).
\end{aligned}
$$

Hence

$$\frac{d^2Y}{dt^2} + \omega^2 Y = A_1\cos\omega t + B_1\sin\omega t$$

and

$$Y = (A_2 - B_1 t/2\omega)\cos\omega t + (B_2 + A_1 t/2\omega)\sin\omega t$$

In a similar manner we find that

$$\frac{d^2X}{dt^2} + \omega^2 X = \bar{A}_1 \cos\omega t + \bar{B}_1 \sin\omega t$$

and

$$X = (\bar{A}_2 - \bar{B}_1 t/2\omega)\cos\omega t + (\bar{B}_2 + \bar{A}_1 t/2\omega)\sin\omega t$$

We have introduced eight constants, which we may determine by means of the two simultaneous differential equations and the four initial conditions. The differential equations become

$$\begin{aligned}&-2\omega^2\{(\bar{A}_2 - \bar{B}_1 t/2\omega)\cos\omega t + (\bar{B}_2 + \bar{A}_1 t/2\omega)\sin\omega t\}\\ &+\{\bar{A}_1 \cos\omega t + \bar{B}_1 \sin\omega t\}\\ &-2\omega\{(-\omega A_2 + B_1 t/2 + A_1/2\omega)\sin\omega t + (\omega B_2 + A_1 t/2 - B_1/2\omega)\cos\omega t\} = 0\end{aligned}$$

and

$$\begin{aligned}&2\omega\{(-\omega\bar{A}_2 + \bar{B}_1 t/2 + \bar{A}_1/2\omega)\sin\omega t + (\omega\bar{B}_2 + \bar{A}_1 t/2 - \bar{B}_1/2\omega)\cos\omega t\}\\ &-2\omega^2\{(A_2 - B_1 t/2\omega)\cos\omega t + (B_2 + A_1 t/2\omega)\sin\omega t\}\\ &+\{A_1 \cos\omega t + B_1 \sin\omega t\} = 0\end{aligned}$$

Each of these equations holds for all time provided

$$-2\omega^2\bar{A}_2 + \bar{A}_1 - 2\omega^2 B_2 + B_1 = 0, \quad \omega\bar{B}_1 - \omega A_1 = 0$$
$$-2\omega^2\bar{B}_2 + \bar{B}_1 + 2\omega^2 A_2 - A_1 = 0, \quad -\omega\bar{A}_1 - \omega B_1 = 0$$

i.e.

$$\bar{A}_1 = -B_1, \quad \bar{B}_1 = A_1, \quad \bar{A}_2 = -B_2, \quad \bar{B}_2 = A_2$$

Then the initial conditions lead to the equations

$$d = \bar{A}_2, \quad 0 = -\bar{B}_1/2\omega, \quad 0 = A_2, \quad u_0 - \omega d = -B_1/2\omega + \omega B_2$$

i.e.

$$A_1 = \bar{B}_1 = 0, \quad B_1 = -\bar{A}_1 = -2\omega u_0$$
$$A_2 = \bar{B}_2 = 0, \quad B_2 = -\bar{A}_2 = -d$$

Thus we obtain the results

$$X = d\cos\omega t + u_0 t \sin\omega t$$
$$Y = u_0 t\cos\omega t - d\sin\omega t$$

which agree with our earlier results when $\dot{\theta} = \omega$ and $\theta = \omega t$. We emphasize that the particle is moving with constant speed along a straight line relative to the fixed coordinate system $Oxyz$ (the inertial frame of reference) because it is experiencing a zero total force.

EXAMPLE

An object is dropped from a height H above a point on the Earth's surface whose latitude is $\frac{1}{2}\pi - \theta$. Investigate its motion based on the assumption that the Earth is a sphere rotating with constant angular speed ω about an axis fixed in an inertial frame of reference.

We introduce a cartesian coordinate system $Oxyz$ such that the origin O is at the centre of the Earth and the Oz-axis is the fixed axis of rotation. We are ignoring the Earth's motion around the Sun. Let Q be a point on the surface at latitude $\frac{1}{2}\pi - \theta$. We take the position vector of Q relative to O to be

$$\boldsymbol{r}_Q = R(\boldsymbol{i}\sin\theta\cos\omega t + \boldsymbol{j}\sin\theta\sin\omega t + \boldsymbol{k}\cos\theta)$$

where R is the radius of the sphere representing the Earth. Next we introduce a moving cartesian coordinate system $QXYZ$, such that the QX-axis points in the southerly direction, the QY-axis in the easterly direction, and the QZ-axis is vertically upwards (relative to the observer at Q in the northern hemisphere);

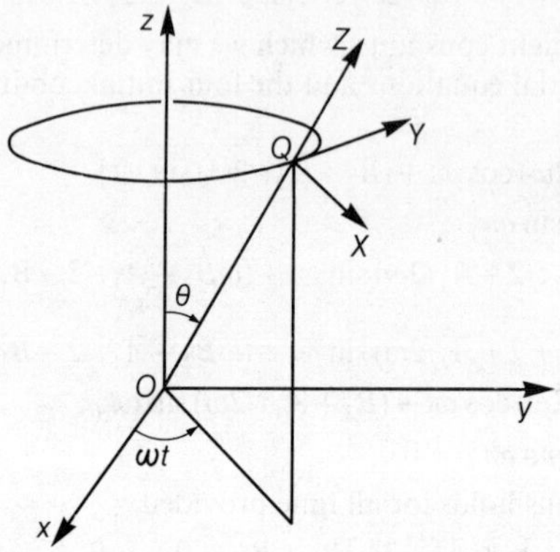

i.e.

$$x = \{X\cos\theta + (R+Z)\sin\theta\}\cos\omega t - Y\sin\omega t$$
$$y = \{X\cos\theta + (R+Z)\sin\theta\}\sin\omega t + Y\cos\omega t$$
$$z = -X\sin\theta + (R+Z)\cos\theta$$

where θ and ω are constants. Hence we obtain expressions for the position vector of a particle P relative to O, namely

$$\begin{aligned}\boldsymbol{r} &= x\boldsymbol{i} + y\boldsymbol{j} + z\boldsymbol{k}\\ &= \boldsymbol{r}_Q + X\mathbf{I} + Y\mathbf{J} + Z\mathbf{K} = X\mathbf{I} + Y\mathbf{J} + (R+Z)\mathbf{K}\end{aligned}$$

where

$$\mathbf{I} = \boldsymbol{i}\cos\theta\cos\omega t + \boldsymbol{j}\cos\theta\sin\omega t - \boldsymbol{k}\sin\theta$$
$$\mathbf{J} = -\boldsymbol{i}\sin\omega t + \boldsymbol{j}\cos\omega t$$
$$\mathbf{K} = \boldsymbol{i}\sin\theta\cos\omega t + \boldsymbol{j}\sin\theta\sin\omega t + \boldsymbol{k}\cos\theta$$

It follows that the velocity vector and acceleration vector of P relative to O are

$$\begin{aligned}\dot{\boldsymbol{r}} &= \dot{x}\boldsymbol{i} + \dot{y}\boldsymbol{j} + \dot{z}\boldsymbol{k}\\ &= (\dot{X} - \omega Y\cos\theta)\mathbf{I} + (\dot{Y} + \omega X\cos\theta + \omega(R+Z)\sin\theta)\mathbf{J} + (\dot{Z} - \omega Y\sin\theta)\mathbf{K}\end{aligned}$$

and

$$\begin{aligned}\ddot{\boldsymbol{r}} &= \ddot{x}\boldsymbol{i} + \ddot{y}\boldsymbol{j} + \ddot{z}\boldsymbol{k}\\ &= (\ddot{X} - 2\omega\dot{Y}\cos\theta - \omega^2 X\cos^2\theta - \omega^2(R+Z)\sin\theta\cos\theta)\mathbf{I}\\ &\quad + (\ddot{Y} + 2\omega\dot{X}\cos\theta + 2\omega\dot{Z}\sin\theta - \omega^2 Y)\mathbf{J}\\ &\quad + (\ddot{Z} - 2\omega\dot{Y}\sin\theta - \omega^2 X\sin\theta\cos\theta - \omega^2(R+Z)\sin^2\theta)\mathbf{K}\end{aligned}$$

We shall assume that the force $\mathbf{F}$ acting on the particle P of mass m (representing the falling object) is the Earth's gravity (and no other force). Therefore

$$\mathbf{F} = -\frac{GMm}{r^3}\mathbf{r} = -GMm\frac{X\mathbf{I}+Y\mathbf{J}+(R+Z)\mathbf{K}}{\{X^2+Y^2+(R+Z)^2\}^{3/2}}$$

$$= -\frac{GMm}{R^3}\{X\mathbf{I}+Y\mathbf{J}+(R+Z)\mathbf{K}\}\left\{1+\frac{2Z}{R}+\frac{X^2+Y^2+Z^2}{R^2}\right\}^{-3/2}$$

$$= -mg\left\{\frac{X}{R}\mathbf{I}+\frac{Y}{R}\mathbf{J}+\left(1-\frac{2Z}{R}\right)\mathbf{K}\right\}+\text{smaller terms}$$

where $GM/R^2 = g$ and X, Y, Z are small compared with R. The governing differential equations obtained from the equation of motion, $m\ddot{\mathbf{r}} = \mathbf{F}$, are

$$\ddot{X}+\left(\frac{g}{R}-\omega^2\cos^2\theta\right)X-2\omega\dot{Y}\cos\theta-\omega^2Z\sin\theta\cos\theta = \omega^2R\sin\theta\cos\theta$$

$$\ddot{Y}+\left(\frac{g}{R}-\omega^2\right)Y+2\omega\dot{X}\cos\theta+2\omega\dot{Z}\sin\theta = 0$$

$$\ddot{Z}-\left(\frac{2g}{R}+\omega^2\sin^2\theta\right)Z-2\omega\dot{Y}\sin\theta-\omega^2X\sin\theta\cos\theta = -g+\omega^2R\sin^2\theta$$

The initial conditions at $t = 0$ are $X = \dot{X} = 0$, $Y = \dot{Y} = 0$, $Z = H$, $\dot{Z} = 0$. This is a complicated system of linear differential equations to solve. We note that $\omega = 7{\cdot}29 \times 10^{-5}$ (the units being rad s^{-1}), $\omega^2 = 5{\cdot}31\times10^{-9}$ (rad^2 s^{-2}), $g/R = 1{\cdot}54\times10^{-6}$ (s^{-2}), $\omega^2R = 3{\cdot}39\times10^{-2}$ (m s^{-2}). In this way we choose to ignore some of the terms and we expect the dominant rotational effects to be governed by the simplified system

$$\ddot{X}-2\omega\dot{Y}\cos\theta = \omega^2R\sin\theta\cos\theta$$

$$\ddot{Y}+2\omega\dot{X}\cos\theta+2\omega\dot{Z}\sin\theta = 0$$

$$\ddot{Z}-2\omega\dot{Y}\sin\theta = -g+\omega^2R\sin^2\theta$$

Integrating the first of these equations with respect to t and using the initial conditions, we find that

$$\dot{X}-2\omega Y\cos\theta = \omega^2Rt\sin\theta\cos\theta$$

The second equation becomes

$$\ddot{Y}+2\omega(2\omega Y\cos\theta+\omega^2Rt\sin\theta\cos\theta)\cos\theta+2\omega\dot{Z}\sin\theta = 0$$

which we reduce to

$$\ddot{Y}+2\omega\dot{Z}\sin\theta = 0$$

Hence

$$\dot{Y}+2\omega Z\sin\theta = 2\omega H\sin\theta$$

and the third differential equation becomes

$$\ddot{Z}-2\omega(-2\omega Z\sin\theta+2\omega H\sin\theta)\sin\theta = -g+\omega^2R\sin^2\theta$$

which we reduce to

$$\ddot{Z} = -g+\omega^2R\sin^2\theta$$

Therefore

$$\dot{Z} = -(g-\omega^2R\sin^2\theta)t$$

and

$$Z = -\tfrac{1}{2}(g-\omega^2R\sin^2\theta)t^2+H$$

It follows that

$$\dot{Y} = \omega(g - \omega^2 R \sin^2\theta)t^2 \sin\theta, \quad Y = \tfrac{1}{3}\omega(g - \omega^2 R \sin^2\theta)t^3 \sin\theta$$

and

$$\dot{X} = \tfrac{2}{3}\omega^2(g - \omega^2 R \sin^2\theta)t^3 \sin\theta\cos\theta + \omega^2 Rt \sin\theta\cos\theta$$
$$X = \tfrac{1}{6}\omega^2(g - \omega^2 R \sin^2\theta)t^4 \sin\theta\cos\theta + \tfrac{1}{2}\omega^2 Rt^2 \sin\theta\cos\theta$$

The particle reaches the plane $Z = 0$ (representing the surface of the Earth) when

$$t = \{2H/(g - \omega^2 R \sin^2\theta)\}^{1/2}$$

The other coordinates at this instant are

$$\begin{aligned} X &= \omega^2(\tfrac{2}{3}H^2 + HR)\sin\theta\cos\theta/(g - \omega^2 R\sin^2\theta) \\ &= \omega^2(HR/g)\sin\theta\cos\theta + \text{smaller terms} \end{aligned}$$

and

$$\begin{aligned} Y &= \tfrac{2}{3}\omega\{2H^3/(g - \omega^2 R\sin^2\theta)\}^{1/2}\sin\theta \\ &= \tfrac{2}{3}\omega(2H^3/g)^{1/2}\sin\theta + \text{smaller terms} \end{aligned}$$

Our analysis predicts that the object will land at a point to the south and east of the point vertically below the initial position. For example, if the initial height is 10 metres

$$\omega^2 HR/g = 3{\cdot}5 \times 10^{-2} \quad \text{and} \quad \tfrac{2}{3}\omega(2H^3/g)^{1/2} = 6{\cdot}9 \times 10^{-4}$$

(the units being metres) and if the initial height is 1000 metres

$$\omega^2 HR/g = 3{\cdot}5 \quad \text{and} \quad \tfrac{2}{3}\omega(2H^3/g)^{1/2} = 6{\cdot}9 \times 10^{-1}$$

(the units being metres). In this example the deflection to the east is caused by the *Coriolis force* and the deflection to the south is caused by the *centrifugal force*. In the southern hemisphere ($\tfrac{1}{2}\pi < \theta < \pi$), the deflection caused by the "centrifugal force" is to the north.

EXERCISES ON CHAPTER 12

1. A passenger of mass m stands in a lift. Find the reaction of the floor on the passenger when the lift is moving upwards with an acceleration a.

2. A lift starts from rest and moves upwards with a constant acceleration $2\,\mathrm{m\,s^{-2}}$ for two seconds. Then it decelerates uniformly for four seconds before coming to rest. Through what distance has the lift moved during its journey lasting six seconds?

Determine the reaction of the floor on a passenger of mass 56 kg during the journey.

3. An object of mass m is suspended from the ceiling of a lift cabin by a spring of stiffness k and natural length l. It hangs in equilibrium. The lift starts from rest and descends with an acceleration a. Calculate the length of the spring during the lift's descent.

4. An object of mass m is mounted above the floor of a lift cabin by a vertical spring of stiffness k and natural length l. It is at rest and the length of the spring is l when the lift starts to move from rest. The lift ascends with constant acceleration a. Determine the extension of the spring during the lift's ascent.

5. A lift starts from rest and moves upwards with constant acceleration to achieve a maximum speed U in time T. It decelerates uniformly and comes to rest after a further time T. Show that the lift has risen a distance UT.

An object of mass m is suspended from the ceiling of the lift cabin by a spring of stiffness k and natural length l. It was hanging in equilibrium when the lift began to move. Investigate the length of the spring during the lift's journey from rest to rest.

6. Simplify the differential equation

$$m\ddot{z} = -mg - k(z - Z - l) - c(\dot{z} - \dot{Z})$$

where $Z = u_0 t + \frac{1}{2}at^2$, and hence obtain a particular integral of the form $A_0 + A_1 t + A_2 t^2$. Check your answer by noting that $y = z - Z$ satisfies

$$m\ddot{y} + c\dot{y} + ky = kl - m(g + a)$$

7. A spring balance, situated in a lift possessing an upward acceleration a, gives a reading M for the mass of an object. What is the true mass of the object?

8. A parcel of mass 10 kg is placed on a spring balance situated on the floor of a lift. What is the mass indicated by the balance when the lift is ascending

(a) with acceleration $1\,\mathrm{m\,s^{-2}}$, (b) with retardation $1\,\mathrm{m\,s^{-2}}$?

9. A crate of mass m is suspended from the roof of a lift cabin by means of a spring balance. When the lift rises from the bottom of a vertical shaft, the reading on the balance indicates a mass m_1 for a time t_1 and a mass m_2 for a further time t_2. While the lift slows down to rest during a time interval of length t_3, the reading on the balance indicates a mass m_3. Show that

$$m = (m_1 t_1 + m_2 t_2 + m_3 t_3)/(t_1 + t_2 + t_3)$$

[Assume that the acceleration is constant in each of the three time intervals and that the changes in the reading of the balance occur instantaneously.]

Take the readings of the balance to be 88 kg, 80 kg and 72 kg and the lengths of the corresponding time intervals to be 4 s, 16 s, and 4 s. What is the mass of the crate and how far has the lift ascended?

10. If $x = R_\theta \mathbf{X}$, where

$$x = \begin{bmatrix} x \\ y \\ z \end{bmatrix}, \quad R_\theta = \begin{bmatrix} \cos\theta & -\sin\theta & 0 \\ \sin\theta & \cos\theta & 0 \\ 0 & 0 & 1 \end{bmatrix}, \quad \mathbf{X} = \begin{bmatrix} X \\ Y \\ Z \end{bmatrix}$$

show that $\dot{x} = R_\theta \dot{\mathbf{X}} + \dot{R}_\theta \mathbf{X}$, where

$$\dot{x} = \begin{bmatrix} \dot{x} \\ \dot{y} \\ \dot{z} \end{bmatrix}, \quad \dot{R}_\theta = \dot{\theta} \begin{bmatrix} -\sin\theta & -\cos\theta & 0 \\ \cos\theta & -\sin\theta & 0 \\ 0 & 0 & 0 \end{bmatrix}, \quad \dot{\mathbf{X}} = \begin{bmatrix} \dot{X} \\ \dot{Y} \\ \dot{Z} \end{bmatrix}$$

Deduce that $\mathbf{X} = R_\theta^{-1} x$ and $\dot{\mathbf{X}} = R_\theta^{-1}\dot{x} - R_\theta^{-1}\dot{R}_\theta R_\theta^{-1} x$ and determine the form of R_θ^{-1} and $R_\theta^{-1}\dot{R}_\theta R_\theta^{-1}$.

11. A bead can slide on a straight wire of length $2d$. The wire rotates in a horizontal plane with constant angular speed ω about a vertical axis through one of its ends, and the contact between the bead and the wire is smooth. The bead is projected from the midpoint of the wire towards the axis of rotation with an initial speed $\frac{1}{2}\omega d$ relative to the wire. Find the shortest distance between the bead and the axis of rotation. How long does the bead remain on the wire?

12. A bead can slide in a straight narrow tube. The tube rotates in a horizontal plane with angular speed $\omega_0(1+\alpha t)$ about a vertical axis through one of its ends, where t represents the time and ω_0, α are parameters independent of time. The contact between the bead and the tube is smooth. Show that the differential equation governing the bead's motion relative to the tube is

$$\frac{d^2X}{dt^2} - \omega_0^2(1+\alpha t)^2 X = 0$$

13. A bead can slide in a straight narrow tube. The tube rotates in a horizontal plane with constant angular speed ω about a vertical axis through one of its ends. There is a frictional force between the bead and the tube characterized by the coefficient of friction μ. Determine the differential equation governing the motion of the bead along the tube.

The bead is projected from the axis of rotation with a speed u_0 relative to the tube. Show that its motion along the tube is described approximately by the differential equation

$$\ddot{X} + 2\mu\omega\dot{X} - \omega^2 X = 0 \quad \text{when} \quad \omega u_0 \gg g$$

Find the required solution. Obtain a differential equation that describes approximately the bead's motion along the tube when $\omega u_0 \ll g$.

14. A ball-bearing can move through a viscous fluid contained in a straight narrow tube. The tube rotates in a horizontal plane with constant angular speed ω about a vertical axis through one of its ends. The ball-bearing's motion through the fluid is impeded by a resistive force proportional to the speed of the ball-bearing relative to the fluid. Show that the differential equation governing the ball-bearing's motion along the tube is

$$m\ddot{X} + k_1\dot{X} - m\omega^2 X = 0$$

where m is the mass of the ball-bearing and k_1 is a positive parameter.

15. A bead of mass m can slide on the spoke of a wheel of radius R_0. The contact between the bead and the spoke is smooth. The bead is attached to the centre of the wheel by a helical spring of stiffness k and natural length l. The wheel rotates in a horizontal plane with a constant angular speed ω about a vertical axis through its centre. Does the bead have an equilibrium position relative to the rotating wheel?

16. A straight wire AB of length $3l$ rotates in a horizontal plane with constant angular speed ω about a vertical axis through A. A bead of mass m is threaded on the wire and is attached to B by a helical spring of natural length l and stiffness $17m\omega^2$. It is held at the midpoint of the wire and is released from rest relative to the wire. Determine the period and amplitude of its oscillatory motion relative to the wire. [Assume that any frictional force is negligible.]

17. A straight wire AB of length $2l$ rotates in a horizontal plane with constant angular speed ω about a vertical axis through A. A bead of mass m is threaded on the wire and is attached to A by a helical spring of natural length l and stiffness $m\omega^2$. It is projected from the midpoint of AB towards A with speed $l\omega$ relative to the wire. Assume that there are no frictional forces and determine the duration for which the bead remains on the wire. What is the maximum magnitude of the contact force between the wire and the bead?

18. A bead can slide on a straight wire of length l. The wire rotates in a vertical plane with constant angular speed ω about a horizontal axis through one of its ends, and the contact between the bead and the wire is smooth. The bead is at a distance $d(<l)$ from the axis of rotation and at rest relative to the wire when the wire is vertically above the axis of rotation. Show that the bead leaves the wire after time T, where

$$(2\omega^2 d - g)\cosh \omega T + g \cos \omega T = 2\omega^2 l$$

provided the bead has not been in contact with the axis of rotation. (A sufficient condition for the bead not to have been in contact with the axis of rotation is $\omega^2 d > g$.)

19. A block of mass m can move along a straight narrow groove cut in a horizontal table, which rotates with constant angular speed ω about a vertical axis. The distance between the groove and the point on the table through which the axis passes is d. The contact between the block and the groove is smooth. Initially the block is a distance d from the axis and is moving with speed u_0 along the groove in the same sense as that of the rotation of the table. Show that the magnitude of the horizontal component of the contact force between the block and the groove is

$$m\omega^2 d + 2m\omega u_0 \cosh \omega t$$

20. A ball-bearing of mass m can move in a circular groove cut in a horizontal table, which rotates with constant angular speed ω about a vertical axis. Assume that a circle of radius R represents the groove, and that the distance between the centre of the circle and the axis of rotation is d. If the contact between the ball-bearing and the groove is smooth, show that the horizontal component of the contact force between the ball-bearing and the groove is

$$m\{(\omega + \dot{\phi})^2 R + \omega^2 d \cos \phi\}$$

where $R\ddot{\phi} + \omega^2 d \sin \phi = 0$ and $\phi = 0, \pi$ correspond to positions of equilibrium. Deduce that the period of small oscillations about the position on the groove at the greatest distance from the axis of rotation is

$$\frac{2\pi}{\omega}\left(\frac{R}{d}\right)^{1/2}$$

21. A smooth horizontal table is rotating with constant angular speed ω about a vertical axis through a point O of it. A particle of mass m is attracted to a point A of the table by a force of magnitude k times the particle's distance from A. Show that its motion relative to the table is governed by the simultaneous differential equations

$$m\ddot{X}+(k-m\omega^2)X-2m\omega\,\dot{Y}=kd$$
$$2m\omega\dot{X}+m\,\ddot{Y}+(k-m\omega^2)Y=0$$

where the OX, OY-axes are fixed relative to the table, A is on the OX-axis and $|\overrightarrow{OA}|=d$.

22. Verify that

$$X=\tfrac{4}{3}d(1-\cos^3\omega t),\quad Y=-\tfrac{4}{3}d\sin^3\omega t$$

satisfy the simultaneous differential equations

$$\ddot{X}+3\omega^2X-2\omega\,\dot{Y}=4\omega^2d,\qquad \ddot{Y}+3\omega^2Y+2\omega\dot{X}=0$$

What are the values of X, $\dot{X}$, Y, $\dot{Y}$ at $t=0$?

23. A particle of mass m moves on a smooth horizontal table which is fixed relative to an inertial frame of reference based on the cartesian coordinate system $Oxyz$. It is attracted to a point A by a force of magnitude $4m\omega^2$ times its distance from A, where ω is a constant. The point A moves in the plane of the table so that its coordinates relatives to the axes Ox, Oy fixed in the plane of the table are

$$x=d\cos\omega t,\quad y=d\sin\omega t$$

where d is a constant. Show that the motion of the particle is governed by

$$\ddot{x}+4\omega^2x=4\omega^2d\cos\omega t,\quad \ddot{y}+4\omega^2y=4\omega^2d\sin\omega t$$

Find the solutions that satisfy the condition that the particle is at rest at the origin O at $t=0$ and evaluate

$$X=x\cos\omega t+y\sin\omega t,\quad Y=-x\sin\omega t+y\cos\omega t$$

24. A particle of mass m moves on a smooth horizontal table, which is fixed relative to an inertial frame of reference based on the cartesian coordinate system $Oxyz$. It is attached to a point A by means of a spring of stiffness k and natural length l. The point A moves in the plane of the table so that its coordinates relative to the axes Ox, Oy fixed in the plane of the table are

$$x=d\cos\omega t,\quad y=d\sin\omega t$$

where d is a constant. Show that the motion of the particle is governed by

$$m\ddot{x}+kx=kd\cos\omega t+\frac{kl(x-d\cos\omega t)}{\{(x-d\cos\omega t)^2+(y-d\sin\omega t)^2\}^{1/2}}$$
$$m\ddot{y}+ky=kd\sin\omega t+\frac{kl(y-d\sin\omega t)}{\{(x-d\cos\omega t)^2+(y-d\sin\omega t)^2\}^{1/2}}$$

What are the corresponding differential equations associated with the coordinates X, Y, where $X=x\cos\omega t+y\sin\omega t$, $Y=-x\sin\omega t+y\cos\omega t$?

25. The point of suspension of a simple pendulum of length l is moving in a horizontal circle of radius R with constant angular speed ω. Show that when the bob is at rest relative to the point of suspension, the tension T in the suspension and the angle ϕ that the suspension makes with the downward vertical satisfy

$$T\cos\phi = mg \quad \text{and} \quad (T - m\omega^2 l)\sin\phi = m\omega^2 R$$

where m is the mass of the bob. Estimate the value of T when $l \ll R$.

26. Find the time derivatives of **I**, **J**, **K**, where

$$\mathbf{I} = \boldsymbol{i}\cos\theta\cos\omega t + \boldsymbol{j}\cos\theta\sin\omega t - \boldsymbol{k}\sin\theta$$
$$\mathbf{J} = -\boldsymbol{i}\sin\omega t + \boldsymbol{j}\cos\omega t$$
$$\mathbf{K} = \boldsymbol{i}\sin\theta\cos\omega t + \boldsymbol{j}\sin\theta\sin\omega t + \boldsymbol{k}\cos\theta$$

$\boldsymbol{i}, \boldsymbol{j}, \boldsymbol{k}$ are constant unit vectors and θ, ω are constants.

27. Convert the differential-equation problem

$$\ddot{X}(t) = 2\omega\dot{Y}(t)\cos\theta$$
$$\ddot{Y}(t) = -2\omega\dot{X}(t)\cos\theta - 2\omega\dot{Z}(t)\sin\theta$$
$$\ddot{Z}(t) = -g + 2\omega\dot{Y}(t)\sin\theta$$

and $X(0) = Y(0) = 0$, $Z(0) = H$, $\dot{X}(0) = \dot{Y}(0) = \dot{Z}(0) = 0$ into the integral-equation problem

$$X(t) = 2\omega\int_0^t Y(x)\,dx\cos\theta$$

$$Y(t) = 2\omega H\sin\theta - 2\omega\int_0^t X(x)dx\cos\theta - 2\omega\int_0^t Z(x)dx\sin\theta$$

$$Z(t) = H - \tfrac{1}{2}gt^2 + 2\omega\int_0^t Y(x)dx\sin\theta$$

28. Calculate $Z_1(t)$, $Y_1(t)$, $X_1(t)$, $Z_2(t)$, $Y_2(t)$, $X_2(t)$, $Z_3(t)$, $Y_3(t)$, $X_3(t)$, where

$$Z_{n+1}(t) = H - \tfrac{1}{2}gt^2 + 2\omega\int_0^t Y_n(x)dx\sin\theta$$

$$Y_{n+1}(t) = 2\omega H\sin\theta - 2\omega\int_0^t X_n(x)dx\cos\theta - 2\omega\int_0^t Z_n(x)dx\sin\theta$$

$$X_{n+1}(t) = 2\omega\int_0^t Y_n(x)\,dx\cos\theta$$

and $Z_0(t) = 0$, $Y_0(t) = 0$, $X_0(t) = 0$. (Neglect terms involving ω^2.)

29. Find an approximate solution to the differential-equation problem (arising from a projectile problem on a rotating Earth)

$$\ddot{X}(t) = 2\omega\dot{Y}(t)\cos\theta$$
$$\ddot{Y}(t) = -2\omega\dot{X}(t)\cos\theta - 2\omega\dot{Z}(t)\sin\theta$$
$$\ddot{Z}(t) = -g + 2\omega\dot{Y}(t)\sin\theta$$

and $X(0) = Y(0) = Z(0) = 0$, $\dot{X}(0) = u_1$, $\dot{Y}(0) = u_2$, $\dot{Z}(0) = u_3$ based on the assumption that terms involving ω^2 are negligible.

30. A projectile is fixed towards the east and at an angle α to the horizontal. The speed of projection relative to the Earth is u_0 and the point of projection is in the northern hemisphere at latitude θ. Find the maximum height and the range of the projectile when terms involving the square of the Earth's angular speed about the polar axis are negligible.

Systems of Particles

13

13.1 Introduction

In earlier chapters we have been concerned primarily with the motion of a single body represented by a particle. On occasions we have encountered problems involving two bodies, one of which has been fixed and stationary relative to an inertial frame of reference (cf. the model in chapter 9 that predicts the orbit of a planet relative to the Sun). This section is concerned with a study of the motion of a system of two particles in a general setting. This forms the basis of a study of the motion of a system of many particles, which in turn leads to a study of the motion of a particular class of bodies having finite dimensions, namely the class of rigid bodies.

P_1 and P_2 are two particles having masses m_1 and m_2 and position vectors $\boldsymbol{r}_1$ and $\boldsymbol{r}_2$ (relative to the origin O of an inertial frame of reference). Their equations of motion are

$$m_1\ddot{\boldsymbol{r}}_1 = \mathbf{F}_1 \quad \text{and} \quad m_2\ddot{\boldsymbol{r}}_2 = \mathbf{F}_2$$

where $\mathbf{F}_1$ represents the total force acting on P_1 and $\mathbf{F}_2$ represents the total force acting on P_2. We may write

$$\mathbf{F}_1 = \mathbf{F}_1^E + \mathbf{F}_1^I \quad \text{and} \quad \mathbf{F}_2 = \mathbf{F}_2^E + \mathbf{F}_2^I$$

where $\mathbf{F}_1^E$, $\mathbf{F}_2^E$ represent external forces (e.g. a gravitational force due to a third body at rest in the inertial frame of reference) and $\mathbf{F}_1^I$, $\mathbf{F}_2^I$ represent internal forces (e.g. their mutual gravitational forces or elastic forces if the particles are connected by a spring). Newton's third law of motion gives

$$\mathbf{F}_1^I = -\mathbf{F}_2^I$$

Further we assume that the internal forces are directed along the line joining the particles, i.e.

$$\mathbf{F}_1^I = F_1^I(\boldsymbol{r}_2 - \boldsymbol{r}_1)/|\boldsymbol{r}_2 - \boldsymbol{r}_1|, \quad \mathbf{F}_1^I \times (\boldsymbol{r}_2 - \boldsymbol{r}_1) = \boldsymbol{0}$$

Adding the two equations of motion, we have

$$m_1\ddot{\boldsymbol{r}}_1 + m_2\ddot{\boldsymbol{r}}_2 = \mathbf{F}_1 + \mathbf{F}_2 = \mathbf{F}_1^E + \mathbf{F}_1^I + \mathbf{F}_2^E + \mathbf{F}_2^I = \mathbf{F}_1^E + \mathbf{F}_2^E$$

because $\mathbf{F}_1^I + \mathbf{F}_2^I = \boldsymbol{0}$. We define the vector $\boldsymbol{r}_c$, called the position vector of the centre of mass C of the system of two particles, by the relation

$$(m_1 + m_2)\boldsymbol{r}_c = m_1 \boldsymbol{r}_1 + m_2 \boldsymbol{r}_2$$

Then we have

$$(m_1 + m_2)\ddot{\boldsymbol{r}}_c = m_1 \ddot{\boldsymbol{r}}_1 + m_2 \ddot{\boldsymbol{r}}_2 = \mathbf{F}_1^E + \mathbf{F}_2^E$$

or

$$m\ddot{\boldsymbol{r}}_c = \mathbf{F}^E$$

where $m = m_1 + m_2$ and $\mathbf{F}^E = \mathbf{F}_1^E + \mathbf{F}_2^E$.

We deduce that the centre of mass moves as if a particle of mass m were located at C and were acted upon by the force $\mathbf{F}^E$, where m is the total mass of the system and $\mathbf{F}^E$ is the sum of the external forces acting on the system. The centre of mass is on the straight line between P_1 and P_2 because

$$\boldsymbol{r}_c = \boldsymbol{r}_1 + \frac{m_2}{m_1 + m_2}(\boldsymbol{r}_2 - \boldsymbol{r}_1) = \boldsymbol{r}_2 + \frac{m_1}{m_1 + m_2}(\boldsymbol{r}_1 - \boldsymbol{r}_2)$$

The linear momentum of the system of two particles is the sum of the linear momenta of the two particles, i.e.

$$\boldsymbol{p} = m_1 \dot{\boldsymbol{r}}_1 + m_2 \dot{\boldsymbol{r}}_2 = (m_1 + m_2)\dot{\boldsymbol{r}}_c = m\dot{\boldsymbol{r}}_c$$

It follows that $\dot{\boldsymbol{p}} = m_1 \ddot{\boldsymbol{r}}_1 + m_2 \ddot{\boldsymbol{r}}_2 = m\ddot{\boldsymbol{r}}_c = \mathbf{F}^E$. The rate of change of linear momentum of the system equals the sum of the external forces acting on the system.

The kinetic energy of the system of two particles is the sum of the kinetic energies of the two particles, i.e.

$$\begin{aligned}
E_k &= \tfrac{1}{2}m_1 \dot{\boldsymbol{r}}_1 \cdot \dot{\boldsymbol{r}}_1 + \tfrac{1}{2}m_2 \dot{\boldsymbol{r}}_2 \cdot \dot{\boldsymbol{r}}_2 \\
&= \tfrac{1}{2}m_1 \left\{ \dot{\boldsymbol{r}}_c - \frac{m_2}{m_1 + m_2}(\dot{\boldsymbol{r}}_2 - \dot{\boldsymbol{r}}_1) \right\} \cdot \left\{ \dot{\boldsymbol{r}}_c - \frac{m_2}{m_1 + m_2}(\dot{\boldsymbol{r}}_2 - \dot{\boldsymbol{r}}_1) \right\} \\
&\quad + \tfrac{1}{2}m_2 \left\{ \dot{\boldsymbol{r}}_c + \frac{m_1}{m_1 + m_2}(\dot{\boldsymbol{r}}_2 - \dot{\boldsymbol{r}}_1) \right\} \cdot \left\{ \dot{\boldsymbol{r}}_c + \frac{m_1}{m_1 + m_2}(\dot{\boldsymbol{r}}_2 - \dot{\boldsymbol{r}}_1) \right\} \\
&= \tfrac{1}{2}(m_1 + m_2)\dot{\boldsymbol{r}}_c \cdot \dot{\boldsymbol{r}}_c + \frac{m_1 m_2^2 + m_2 m_1^2}{2(m_1 + m_2)^2}(\dot{\boldsymbol{r}}_2 - \dot{\boldsymbol{r}}_1) \cdot (\dot{\boldsymbol{r}}_2 - \dot{\boldsymbol{r}}_1) \\
&= \tfrac{1}{2}m\dot{\boldsymbol{r}}_c \cdot \dot{\boldsymbol{r}}_c + \{\tfrac{1}{2}m_1(\dot{\boldsymbol{r}}_1 - \dot{\boldsymbol{r}}_c) \cdot (\dot{\boldsymbol{r}}_1 - \dot{\boldsymbol{r}}_c) + \tfrac{1}{2}m_2(\dot{\boldsymbol{r}}_2 - \dot{\boldsymbol{r}}_c) \cdot (\dot{\boldsymbol{r}}_2 - \dot{\boldsymbol{r}}_c)\}
\end{aligned}$$

The first term is called the *kinetic energy of the centre of mass* (the total mass assumed to be located at the centre of mass) and the second term is called the *kinetic energy associated with the particles' motion relative to the centre of mass*. We obtain (from the equations of motion) the relation

$$m_1\dot{\boldsymbol{r}}_1\cdot\ddot{\boldsymbol{r}}_1+m_2\dot{\boldsymbol{r}}_2\cdot\ddot{\boldsymbol{r}}_2=\dot{\boldsymbol{r}}_1\cdot\mathbf{F}_1+\dot{\boldsymbol{r}}_2\cdot\mathbf{F}_2$$

i.e.

$$\frac{d}{dt}(\tfrac{1}{2}m_1\dot{\boldsymbol{r}}_1\cdot\dot{\boldsymbol{r}}_1+\tfrac{1}{2}m_2\dot{\boldsymbol{r}}_2\cdot\dot{\boldsymbol{r}}_2)=\frac{dE_k}{dt}=\dot{\boldsymbol{r}}_1\cdot\mathbf{F}_1+\dot{\boldsymbol{r}}_2\cdot\mathbf{F}_2$$

Therefore

$$\Big[E_k\Big]_{t=t_1}^{t=t_2}=\int_{t_1}^{t_2}(\mathbf{F}_1\cdot\dot{\boldsymbol{r}}_1+\mathbf{F}_2\cdot\dot{\boldsymbol{r}}_2)\,dt$$

The increase in the kinetic energy of the system equals the work done by all the external and internal forces acting on the system.

The angular momentum (or the moment of linear momentum) of the system of two particles about a point A, having position vector $\boldsymbol{r}_A$ relative to the origin O of the inertial frame of reference, is the sum of the particles' angular momenta about A, i.e.

$$\begin{aligned}\mathbf{L}&=(\boldsymbol{r}_1-\boldsymbol{r}_A)\times m_1\dot{\boldsymbol{r}}_1+(\boldsymbol{r}_2-\boldsymbol{r}_A)\times m_2\dot{\boldsymbol{r}}_2\\&=\left\{\boldsymbol{r}_c-\boldsymbol{r}_A-\frac{m_2}{m_1+m_2}(\boldsymbol{r}_2-\boldsymbol{r}_1)\right\}\times m_1\left\{\dot{\boldsymbol{r}}_c-\frac{m_2}{m_1+m_2}(\dot{\boldsymbol{r}}_2-\dot{\boldsymbol{r}}_1)\right\}\\&=\left\{\boldsymbol{r}_c-\boldsymbol{r}_A+\frac{m_1}{m_1+m_2}(\boldsymbol{r}_2-\boldsymbol{r}_1)\right\}\times m_2\left\{\dot{\boldsymbol{r}}_c+\frac{m_1}{m_1+m_2}(\dot{\boldsymbol{r}}_2-\dot{\boldsymbol{r}}_1)\right\}\\&=(\boldsymbol{r}_c-\boldsymbol{r}_A)\times(m_1+m_2)\dot{\boldsymbol{r}}_c+\frac{m_1m_2^2+m_2m_1^2}{(m_1+m_2)^2}(\boldsymbol{r}_2-\boldsymbol{r}_1)\times(\dot{\boldsymbol{r}}_2-\dot{\boldsymbol{r}}_1)\\&=(\boldsymbol{r}_c-\boldsymbol{r}_A)\times m\dot{\boldsymbol{r}}_c+\{(\boldsymbol{r}_1-\boldsymbol{r}_c)\times m_1(\dot{\boldsymbol{r}}_1-\dot{\boldsymbol{r}}_c)+(\boldsymbol{r}_2-\boldsymbol{r}_c)\times m_2(\dot{\boldsymbol{r}}_2-\dot{\boldsymbol{r}}_c)\}\end{aligned}$$

The first term, $(\boldsymbol{r}_c-\boldsymbol{r}_A)\times\boldsymbol{p}$, is the *angular momentum* (or the moment of linear momentum) *of the centre of mass C* (the total mass assumed to be concentrated at the centre of mass) *about A*, and the second term is the *angular momentum relative to C* (i.e. the moment about C of the linear momenta associated with the particles' motion relative to C). Differentiating with respect to time and using the equations of motion, we find that

$$\begin{aligned}\dot{\mathbf{L}}&=\{(\dot{\boldsymbol{r}}_1-\dot{\boldsymbol{r}}_A)\times m_1\dot{\boldsymbol{r}}_1+(\boldsymbol{r}_1-\boldsymbol{r}_A)\times m_1\ddot{\boldsymbol{r}}_1\}\\&\quad+\{(\dot{\boldsymbol{r}}_2-\dot{\boldsymbol{r}}_A)\times m_2\dot{\boldsymbol{r}}_2+(\boldsymbol{r}_2-\boldsymbol{r}_A)\times m_2\ddot{\boldsymbol{r}}_2\}\\&=-\dot{\boldsymbol{r}}_A\times(m_1\dot{\boldsymbol{r}}_1+m_2\dot{\boldsymbol{r}}_2)+(\boldsymbol{r}_1-\boldsymbol{r}_A)\times m_1\ddot{\boldsymbol{r}}_1+(\boldsymbol{r}_2-\boldsymbol{r}_A)\times m_2\ddot{\boldsymbol{r}}_2\\&=-\dot{\boldsymbol{r}}_A\times m\dot{\boldsymbol{r}}_c+(\boldsymbol{r}_1-\boldsymbol{r}_A)\times(\mathbf{F}_1^E+\mathbf{F}_1^I)+(\boldsymbol{r}_2-\boldsymbol{r}_A)\times(\mathbf{F}_2^E+\mathbf{F}_2^I)\\&=-\dot{\boldsymbol{r}}_A\times\boldsymbol{p}+(\boldsymbol{r}_1-\boldsymbol{r}_A)\times\mathbf{F}_1^E+(\boldsymbol{r}_2-\boldsymbol{r}_A)\times\mathbf{F}_2^E\end{aligned}$$

because

$$(\boldsymbol{r}_1-\boldsymbol{r}_A)\times\mathbf{F}_1^I+(\boldsymbol{r}_2-\boldsymbol{r}_A)\times\mathbf{F}_2^I=(\boldsymbol{r}_1-\boldsymbol{r}_A)\times\mathbf{F}_1^I+(\boldsymbol{r}_2-\boldsymbol{r}_A)\times(-\mathbf{F}_1^I)$$
$$=-(\boldsymbol{r}_2-\boldsymbol{r}_1)\times\mathbf{F}_1^I-\boldsymbol{r}_A\times(\mathbf{F}_1^I-\mathbf{F}_1^I)=\boldsymbol{0}$$

on account of the assumed properties of the internal forces.

The first term in the expression for the rate of change of angular momentum vanishes when $\dot{\boldsymbol{r}}_A\times\dot{\boldsymbol{r}}_c=\boldsymbol{0}$; e.g. when the point A is at rest (i.e. $\dot{\boldsymbol{r}}_A=\boldsymbol{0}$) or when the point A is the centre of mass C (i.e. $\boldsymbol{r}_A=\boldsymbol{r}_c$). Then we have

$$\dot{\mathbf{L}}=\mathbf{M}^E$$

where $\mathbf{M}^E=(\boldsymbol{r}_1-\boldsymbol{r}_A)\times\mathbf{F}_1^E+(\boldsymbol{r}_2-\boldsymbol{r}_A)\times\mathbf{F}_2^E$, namely the sum of the moments about A of the external forces acting on the particles, provided $\dot{\boldsymbol{r}}_A\times\dot{\boldsymbol{r}}_c=\boldsymbol{0}$. It is common practice in applications to choose A to be either O (the origin of the inertial frame of reference) or C (the centre of mass of the system of particles).

There are six coordinates determining the positions of the two particles. The problem is governed by the two equations of motion

$$m_1\ddot{\boldsymbol{r}}_1=\mathbf{F}_1 \quad\text{and}\quad m_2\ddot{\boldsymbol{r}}_2=\mathbf{F}_2$$

from which we have derived the important results

$$\dot{\boldsymbol{p}}=\mathbf{F}^E \quad\text{and}\quad \dot{\mathbf{L}}=\mathbf{M}^E$$

the latter result being valid provided $\dot{\boldsymbol{r}}_A\times\dot{\boldsymbol{r}}_c=\boldsymbol{0}$.

EXAMPLE

A particle S of mass M and a particle P of mass m move under the influence of their mutual gravitational field of force. Their positions and velocities are known at a given instant. Investigate their subsequent motion.

We introduce an inertial frame of reference whose origin O coincides with the position of S at $t=0$. Let $\boldsymbol{r}_s$, $\boldsymbol{r}_p$ be the position vectors of S and P relative to O. The equation of motion of S is

$$M\ddot{\boldsymbol{r}}_s=+\frac{GMm(\boldsymbol{r}_p-\boldsymbol{r}_s)}{|\boldsymbol{r}_p-\boldsymbol{r}_s|^3}$$

and the equation of motion of P is

$$m\ddot{\boldsymbol{r}}_p=-\frac{GMm(\boldsymbol{r}_p-\boldsymbol{r}_s)}{|\boldsymbol{r}_p-\boldsymbol{r}_s|^3}$$

The forces are internal forces. Introducing the centre of mass of the system, whose position vector $\boldsymbol{r}_c$ is given by

$$(m+M)\boldsymbol{r}_c=m\boldsymbol{r}_p+M\boldsymbol{r}_s$$

and adding the equations of motion, we find that

$$(m+M)\ddot{\boldsymbol{r}}_c=\boldsymbol{0} \quad\text{and}\quad \boldsymbol{r}_c=\mathbf{A}t+\mathbf{B}$$

where **A**, **B** are vectors determined by the initial conditions. If $\boldsymbol{r}_p = \boldsymbol{r}_0$, $\dot{\boldsymbol{r}}_p = \boldsymbol{u}_0$, $\boldsymbol{r}_s = \boldsymbol{0}$, $\dot{\boldsymbol{r}}_s = \mathbf{U}_0$ at $t = 0$,

$$\mathbf{A} = (m\boldsymbol{u}_0 + M\mathbf{U}_0)/(m+M) \quad \text{and} \quad \mathbf{B} = m\boldsymbol{r}_0/(m+M)$$

We see that the centre of mass is moving with constant speed in a straight line relative to our chosen inertial frame of reference. It is convenient in this problem to set

$$\boldsymbol{r}_s = \boldsymbol{r}_c + (\boldsymbol{r}_s - \boldsymbol{r}_c) = \boldsymbol{r}_c - m\boldsymbol{r}/(m+M)$$

and

$$\boldsymbol{r}_p = \boldsymbol{r}_c + (\boldsymbol{r}_p - \boldsymbol{r}_c) = \boldsymbol{r}_c + M\boldsymbol{r}/(m+M)$$

where $\boldsymbol{r} = \boldsymbol{r}_p - \boldsymbol{r}_s$. We have an expression for $\boldsymbol{r}_c$ and we need to solve for $\boldsymbol{r}$ in order to determine $\boldsymbol{r}_s$ and $\boldsymbol{r}_p$.

Using the equations of motion, we obtain the equation

$$\ddot{\boldsymbol{r}} = \ddot{\boldsymbol{r}}_p - \ddot{\boldsymbol{r}}_s = -\frac{G(M+m)(\boldsymbol{r}_p - \boldsymbol{r}_s)}{|\boldsymbol{r}_p - \boldsymbol{r}_s|^3}$$

i.e.

$$\ddot{\boldsymbol{r}} = -\frac{G(M+m)\boldsymbol{r}}{r^3}$$

where $r = |\boldsymbol{r}| = |\boldsymbol{r}_p - \boldsymbol{r}_s|$. This is similar to the equation of motion we obtained in Section 9.2 when we assumed that the particle S was fixed at the origin O of the inertial frame of reference. Following the argument presented in Section 9.2, we note that the time derivative of $\boldsymbol{r} \times \dot{\boldsymbol{r}}$ is zero and that $\boldsymbol{r} \cdot (\boldsymbol{r} \times \dot{\boldsymbol{r}}) = \boldsymbol{0}$. Thus $\boldsymbol{r}$ is always perpendicular to the initial value of $\boldsymbol{r} \times \dot{\boldsymbol{r}}$, namely $\boldsymbol{r}_0 \times (\boldsymbol{u}_0 - \mathbf{U}_0)$; and at $t = 0$, $\boldsymbol{r} = \boldsymbol{r}_0$ and $\dot{\boldsymbol{r}} = \boldsymbol{u}_0 - \mathbf{U}_0$. The analysis of chapter 9 is available to us during our determination of $\boldsymbol{r}$.

This investigation simplifies to the investigation commenced in Section 9.2, when we assume that $\mathbf{U}_0 = \boldsymbol{0}$ and $m \ll M$.

13.2 A system of many particles

Consider N particles $P_1, P_2, \ldots, P_i, \ldots, P_N$, where particle P_i has mass m_i and position vector $\boldsymbol{r}_i$ relative to the origin O of an inertial frame of reference. The equations of motion are

$$m_1 \ddot{\boldsymbol{r}}_1 = \mathbf{F}_1^E + \mathbf{F}_1^I, \quad m_2 \ddot{\boldsymbol{r}}_2 = \mathbf{F}_2^E + \mathbf{F}_2^I, \ldots,$$
$$m_i \ddot{\boldsymbol{r}}_i = \mathbf{F}_i^E + \mathbf{F}_i^I, \ldots, \quad m_N \ddot{\boldsymbol{r}}_N = \mathbf{F}_N^E + \mathbf{F}_N^I$$

where $\mathbf{F}_1^E, \mathbf{F}_2^E, \ldots, \mathbf{F}_i^E, \ldots, \mathbf{F}_N^E$ represent the external forces acting on the individual particles and $\mathbf{F}_1^I, \mathbf{F}_2^I, \ldots, \mathbf{F}_i^I, \ldots, \mathbf{F}_N^I$ represent the internal forces (e.g. mutual gravitational forces or elastic forces due to spring connectors) acting on the individual particles. Adding these equations leads to

$$\sum_{i=1}^{N} m_i \ddot{\boldsymbol{r}}_i = \sum_{i=1}^{N} (\mathbf{F}_i^E + \mathbf{F}_i^I) = \sum_{i=1}^{N} \mathbf{F}_i^E + \sum_{i=1}^{N} \mathbf{F}_i^I$$

The sum of the internal forces must be zero by Newton's third law. We introduce the centre of mass C having the position vector $\boldsymbol{r}_c$ relative to O given by

$$m\boldsymbol{r}_c = \sum_{i=1}^{N} m_i \boldsymbol{r}_i$$

where

$$m = \sum_{i=1}^{N} m_i$$

Thus we obtain

$$m\ddot{\boldsymbol{r}}_c = \mathbf{F}^E$$

where

$$\mathbf{F}^E = \sum_{i=1}^{N} \mathbf{F}_i^E$$

and we deduce that the centre of mass moves as if a particle of mass m were situated at the centre of mass and were subjected to an applied force $\mathbf{F}^E$.

The linear momentum of the system of N particles is

$$\boldsymbol{p} = \sum_{i=1}^{N} m_i \dot{\boldsymbol{r}}_i = m\dot{\boldsymbol{r}}_c$$

We note that

$$\dot{\boldsymbol{p}} = \sum_{i=1}^{N} m_i \ddot{\boldsymbol{r}}_i = m\ddot{\boldsymbol{r}}_c = \mathbf{F}^E$$

The kinetic energy of the system is

$$E_k = \tfrac{1}{2} \sum_{i=1}^{N} m_i \dot{\boldsymbol{r}}_i \cdot \dot{\boldsymbol{r}}_i$$

Writing $\boldsymbol{r}_i = \boldsymbol{r}_c + (\boldsymbol{r}_i - \boldsymbol{r}_c)$, we have that

$$\begin{aligned} E_k &= \tfrac{1}{2} \sum_{i=1}^{N} m_i \{\dot{\boldsymbol{r}}_c + (\dot{\boldsymbol{r}}_i - \dot{\boldsymbol{r}}_c)\} \cdot \{\dot{\boldsymbol{r}}_c + (\dot{\boldsymbol{r}}_i - \dot{\boldsymbol{r}}_c)\} \\ &= \tfrac{1}{2} \sum_{i=1}^{N} m_i \dot{\boldsymbol{r}}_c \cdot \dot{\boldsymbol{r}}_c + \sum_{i=1}^{N} m_i \dot{\boldsymbol{r}}_c \cdot (\dot{\boldsymbol{r}}_i - \dot{\boldsymbol{r}}_c) + \tfrac{1}{2} \sum_{i=1}^{N} m_i (\dot{\boldsymbol{r}}_i - \dot{\boldsymbol{r}}_c) \cdot (\dot{\boldsymbol{r}}_i - \dot{\boldsymbol{r}}_c) \\ &= \tfrac{1}{2} m \dot{\boldsymbol{r}}_c \cdot \dot{\boldsymbol{r}}_c + \tfrac{1}{2} \sum_{i=1}^{N} m_i (\dot{\boldsymbol{r}}_i - \dot{\boldsymbol{r}}_c) \cdot (\dot{\boldsymbol{r}}_i - \dot{\boldsymbol{r}}_c) \end{aligned}$$

because

$$\sum_{i=1}^{N} m_i \dot{\boldsymbol{r}}_c \cdot (\dot{\boldsymbol{r}}_i - \dot{\boldsymbol{r}}_c) = \dot{\boldsymbol{r}}_c \cdot \boldsymbol{p} - m\dot{\boldsymbol{r}}_c \cdot \dot{\boldsymbol{r}}_c = \dot{\boldsymbol{r}}_c \cdot (\boldsymbol{p} - m\dot{\boldsymbol{r}}_c) = \boldsymbol{0}$$

The two parts of the expression for the kinetic energy of the system correspond to the motion of the centre of mass and the motion of the system of particles relative to the centre of mass. We observe that

$$\dot{E}_k = \sum_{i=1}^{N} (m_i \ddot{\boldsymbol{r}}_i) \cdot \dot{\boldsymbol{r}}_i = \sum_{i=1}^{N} (\mathbf{F}_i^E + \mathbf{F}_i^I) \cdot \dot{\boldsymbol{r}}_i$$

and

$$\Big[E_k \Big]_{t=t_1}^{t=t_2} = \sum_{i=1}^{N} \int_{t_1}^{t_2} (\mathbf{F}_i^E + \mathbf{F}_i^I) \cdot \dot{\boldsymbol{r}}_i \, dt$$

The increase in the kinetic energy of the system equals the total work done by all the external and internal forces acting on the system.

The angular momentum of the system about the point A (having the position vector $\boldsymbol{r}_A$ relative to O) is

$$\begin{aligned}
\mathbf{L} &= \sum_{i=1}^{N} (\boldsymbol{r}_i - \boldsymbol{r}_A) \times m_i \dot{\boldsymbol{r}}_i \\
&= \sum_{i=1}^{N} \{\boldsymbol{r}_c - \boldsymbol{r}_A + (\boldsymbol{r}_i - \boldsymbol{r}_c)\} \times m_i \{\dot{\boldsymbol{r}}_c + (\dot{\boldsymbol{r}}_i - \dot{\boldsymbol{r}}_c)\} \\
&= (\boldsymbol{r}_c - \boldsymbol{r}_A) \times m \dot{\boldsymbol{r}}_c + (\boldsymbol{r}_c - \boldsymbol{r}_A) \times \sum_{i=1}^{N} m_i (\dot{\boldsymbol{r}}_i - \dot{\boldsymbol{r}}_c) \\
&\quad + \left\{ \sum_{i=1}^{N} m_i (\boldsymbol{r}_i - \boldsymbol{r}_c) \right\} \times \dot{\boldsymbol{r}}_c + \sum_{i=1}^{N} (\boldsymbol{r}_i - \boldsymbol{r}_c) \times m_i (\dot{\boldsymbol{r}}_i - \dot{\boldsymbol{r}}_c) \\
&= (\boldsymbol{r}_c - \boldsymbol{r}_A) \times \boldsymbol{p} + \sum_{i=1}^{N} (\boldsymbol{r}_i - \boldsymbol{r}_c) \times m_i (\dot{\boldsymbol{r}}_i - \dot{\boldsymbol{r}}_c)
\end{aligned}$$

because

$$\sum_{i=1}^{N} m_i (\dot{\boldsymbol{r}}_i - \dot{\boldsymbol{r}}_c) = \boldsymbol{p} - m \dot{\boldsymbol{r}}_c = \boldsymbol{0}$$

and

$$\sum_{i=1}^{N} m_i (\boldsymbol{r}_i - \boldsymbol{r}_c) = m \boldsymbol{r}_c - m \boldsymbol{r}_c = \boldsymbol{0}$$

The final form of the expression for $\mathbf{L}$ shows the contributions of the motion of the centre of mass and the motion of the system relative to the centre of mass. The rate of change of angular momentum is

$$\begin{aligned}
\dot{\mathbf{L}} &= \sum_{i=1}^{N} \{(\dot{\boldsymbol{r}}_i - \dot{\boldsymbol{r}}_A) \times m_i \dot{\boldsymbol{r}}_i + (\boldsymbol{r}_i - \boldsymbol{r}_A) \times m_i \ddot{\boldsymbol{r}}_i\} \\
&= -\dot{\boldsymbol{r}}_A \times \sum_{i=1}^{N} m_i \dot{\boldsymbol{r}}_i + \sum_{i=1}^{N} (\boldsymbol{r}_i - \boldsymbol{r}_A) \times (\mathbf{F}_i^E + \mathbf{F}_i^I)
\end{aligned}$$

$$= -\dot{\boldsymbol{r}}_A \times \boldsymbol{p} + \sum_{i=1}^{N} (\boldsymbol{r}_i - \boldsymbol{r}_A) \times \mathbf{F}_i^E$$

because

$$\sum_{i=1}^{N} (\boldsymbol{r}_i - \boldsymbol{r}_A) \times \mathbf{F}_i^I = \boldsymbol{0}$$

We note that the argument applied in the case of two particles in Section 13.1 applies to any pair of the N particles and that the internal forces are such that

$$\mathbf{F}_i^I = \sum_{\substack{j=1 \\ j \neq i}}^{N} \mathbf{F}_{ij}^I$$

with $\mathbf{F}_{ij}^I = -\mathbf{F}_{ji}^I$ and $(\boldsymbol{r}_j - \boldsymbol{r}_i) \times \mathbf{F}_{ij}^I = \boldsymbol{0}$.

The expression for $\dot{\mathbf{L}}$ simplifies when $\dot{\boldsymbol{r}}_A \times \boldsymbol{p} = \boldsymbol{0}$; i.e. when $\dot{\boldsymbol{r}}_A \times \dot{\boldsymbol{r}}_c = \boldsymbol{0}$, the rate of change of angular momentum about A is equal to the sum of the moments about A of the external forces acting on the particles.

In the case of a system of N particles, there are N vector equations of motion determining the $3N$ scalar coordinates that specify the positions of the particles relative to the inertial frame of reference. Two important results derived from the equations of motion are

$$\dot{\boldsymbol{p}} = \mathbf{F}^E \quad \text{and} \quad \dot{\mathbf{L}} = \mathbf{M}^E$$

(the latter result being valid provided $\dot{\boldsymbol{r}}_A \times \dot{\boldsymbol{r}}_c = \boldsymbol{0}$), where

$$\mathbf{F}^E = \sum_{i=1}^{N} \mathbf{F}_1^E \quad \text{and} \quad \mathbf{M}^E = \sum_{i=1}^{N} (\boldsymbol{r}_i - \boldsymbol{r}_A) \times \mathbf{F}_i^E$$

When the total force is zero, $\dot{\boldsymbol{p}} = \boldsymbol{0}$ and the linear momentum of the system is conserved. When the sum of the moments of the external forces (about a fixed point or about the centre of mass) is zero, $\dot{\mathbf{L}} = \boldsymbol{0}$ and the angular momentum of the system about the chosen point is conserved.

EXAMPLE

Consider the motion of three particles subject to their mutual gravitational fields of force.

This is one of the classic problems in dynamics. It is clearly associated with a model to predict the motion of the Sun, the Earth and the Moon, or to predict the interactions between planets. The general problem has defied attempts by eminent scientists to find an exact solution. Approximate solutions exist, and exact solutions of restricted versions (i.e. particles in particular configurations) are available.

Let the particles have masses m_1, m_2, m_3 and position vectors $\boldsymbol{r}_1$, $\boldsymbol{r}_2$, $\boldsymbol{r}_3$ relative to an inertial frame of reference. The equations of motion are

$$m_1\ddot{\boldsymbol{r}}_1 = -\frac{Gm_1m_2(\boldsymbol{r}_1-\boldsymbol{r}_2)}{|\boldsymbol{r}_1-\boldsymbol{r}_2|^3}-\frac{Gm_1m_3(\boldsymbol{r}_1-\boldsymbol{r}_3)}{|\boldsymbol{r}_1-\boldsymbol{r}_3|^3}$$

$$m_2\ddot{\boldsymbol{r}}_2 = -\frac{Gm_2m_3(\boldsymbol{r}_2-\boldsymbol{r}_3)}{|\boldsymbol{r}_2-\boldsymbol{r}_3|^3}-\frac{Gm_2m_1(\boldsymbol{r}_2-\boldsymbol{r}_1)}{|\boldsymbol{r}_2-\boldsymbol{r}_1|^3}$$

$$m_3\ddot{\boldsymbol{r}}_3 = -\frac{Gm_3m_1(\boldsymbol{r}_3-\boldsymbol{r}_1)}{|\boldsymbol{r}_3-\boldsymbol{r}_1|^3}-\frac{Gm_3m_2(\boldsymbol{r}_3-\boldsymbol{r}_2)}{|\boldsymbol{r}_3-\boldsymbol{r}_2|^3}$$

They and the initial conditions govern the nine coordinates defining the positions of the particles.

One fact that is easily deducible is that the centre of mass of the system of three particles moves with constant speed along a straight line. If $\boldsymbol{r}_c$ is the position vector of the centre of mass,

$$(m_1+m_2+m_3)\boldsymbol{r}_c = m_1\boldsymbol{r}_1+m_2\boldsymbol{r}_2+m_3\boldsymbol{r}_3$$

$$(m_1+m_2+m_3)\ddot{\boldsymbol{r}}_c = m_1\ddot{\boldsymbol{r}}_1+m_2\ddot{\boldsymbol{r}}_2+m_3\ddot{\boldsymbol{r}}_3 = \boldsymbol{0}$$

and $\boldsymbol{r}_c = \mathbf{A}t+\mathbf{B}$, where $\mathbf{A}$ and $\mathbf{B}$ are vectors determined by the initial conditions.

13.3 Systems of connected particles

Let us turn our attention to some problems in which two or more bodies are connected by strings or springs. We shall discuss models in which the bodies are represented by particles, and we shall assume that the connectors are of negligible mass and are either inextensible or perfectly elastic.

Suppose two objects are attached to the ends of a piece of string which passes over a fixed horizontal peg. Let us investigate the motion when the string is taut and the system is released from rest. We recognize that the system may not move when released, because the objects have equal masses or there is a sufficiently large frictional force caused by the contact between the string and the peg. We shall assume that the string has negligible mass, its length is constant, and the peg has a circular cross-section.

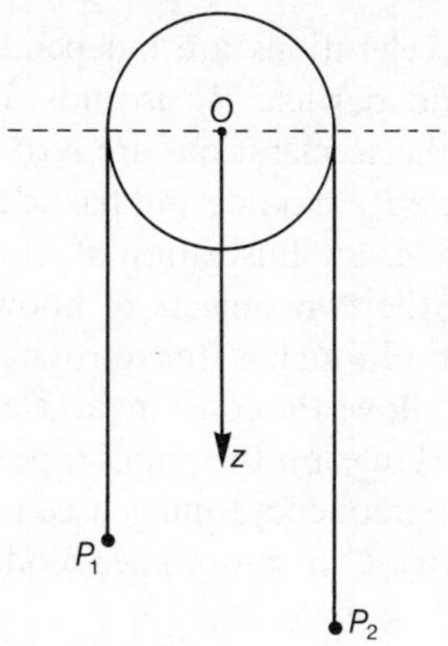

Let the particles P_1 and P_2 represent the objects attached to the string. We introduce a z-coordinate whose origin is at the centre of the peg and which increases in the vertically downward direction. Let z_1 and z_2 be the z-coordinates of the particles P_1 and P_2. We note that each particle will move along a vertical line through its initial position of rest. Further z_1+z_2 is a constant because the string has a constant length. Therefore only one coordinate is necessary to determine the position of the system of particles.

Each particle experiences two forces, namely the uniform gravitational force and the tension in the string. Let P_1 have mass m_1 and let P_2 have mass m_2. The equations of motion are

$$m_1\ddot{z}_1\boldsymbol{k} = (m_1g-T_1)\boldsymbol{k}, \quad m_2\ddot{z}_2\boldsymbol{k} = (m_2g-T_2)\boldsymbol{k},$$

where T_1 is the tension in the string at the end attached to P_1, and T_2 is the tension in the string at the end attached to P_2. We have introduced four unknowns, namely z_1, z_2, T_1 and T_2, and we have three relations, namely the condition that the string is inextensible and the two equations of motion. The fourth relation is determined by the contact between the string and the peg. We shall assume that the peg is smooth, in which case $T_1 = T_2$ (cf. question 20, chapter 7) and the tension is uniform throughout the length of the string. Setting $T_1 = T_2 = T$, we have to solve

$$m_1\ddot{z}_1 = m_1g-T, \quad m_2\ddot{z}_2 = m_2g-T$$

subject to the constraint that z_1+z_2 equals a constant. It follows that $\ddot{z}_1 + \ddot{z}_2 = 0$ and that

$$\left(g-\frac{T}{m_1}\right)+\left(g-\frac{T}{m_2}\right) = 0$$

i.e. $T = 2m_1m_2g/(m_1+m_2)$. Therefore

$$\ddot{z}_1 = -\ddot{z}_2 = (m_1-m_2)g/(m_1+m_2)$$

The tension and the accelerations are independent of time. If $m_1 > m_2$, particle P_1 descends and particle P_2 ascends. If $m_1 = m_2$, the particles remain at rest (because the accelerations are zero and the initial speeds are zero). If $m_1 < m_2$, particle P_1 ascends and particle P_2 descends.

The diagram on p. 259 is an illustration of Atwood's machine, in which the connector between the two objects of known mass is a paper tape passing over a pulley wheel which is free to rotate about a fixed horizontal axis. Atwood's machine allows the constant acceleration of the objects to be measured (from the markings on the paper tape made by a pen vibrating horizontally with known frequency) and is used to provide a value of g, the acceleration due to gravity. Our smooth peg model ignores the effect of the motion of the pulley.

Let us re-examine the problem when the peg is rough and the contact force between the string and the peg is characterized by the coefficient of static friction μ_s and the coefficient of kinetic friction $\mu(\leqslant \mu_s)$. Suppose that there is no motion when the system is released at rest. Then $T_1 = m_1 g$ and $T_2 = m_2 g$. If $m_1 > m_2$, $T_1 = T_2 + F_F$, where F_F is a frictional force derived from the contact between the string and the rough peg. The string is not slipping on the rough peg, therefore $T_1 < T_2\, e^{\pi\mu_s}$ (cf. question 20, chapter 7), $m_1 < m_2\, e^{\pi\mu_s}$ and $F_F < T_2(e^{\pi\mu_s} - 1)$. If the string is slipping and the particles are moving, $T_1 = T_2\, e^{\pi\mu}$. In this case we have to solve

$$m_1 \ddot{z}_1 = m_1 g - T_1, \quad m_2 \ddot{z}_2 = m_2 g - T_2$$

subject to $\ddot{z}_1 + \ddot{z}_2 = 0$ and $T_1 = T_2\, e^{\pi\mu}$. We find that

$$T_1 = T_2\, e^{\pi\mu} = 2m_1 m_2 g/(m\, e^{-\pi\mu} + m_2)$$

and

$$\ddot{z}_1 = -\ddot{z}_2 = (m_1\, e^{-\pi\mu} - m_2)g/(m_1\, e^{-\pi\mu} + m_2)$$

provided $m_1 > m_2\, e^{\pi\mu_s}$. The tensions and accelerations are independent of time.

EXAMPLE

Two particles P_1 and P_2, whose masses are m_1 and m_2, are connected by a light inextensible string of length $2l$. The string passes through a small hole O in a smooth horizontal table; P_1 slides on the table and P_2 moves along a vertical line through O. At a given instant, P is moving in a direction perpendicular to $\overrightarrow{OP}$, with speed u_0 and P_2 is at rest at a distance $d(< 2l)$ below O, the string being taut. Investigate the motion of the system.

We introduce plane-polar coordinates, r and ϕ, to define the position of P_1 on the table relative to O and a coordinate z to define the position P_2 below O. The string's inextensibility implies that $r + z = 2l$.

The equations of motion are

$$m_1\{(\ddot{r} - r\dot{\phi}^2)\boldsymbol{e}_r + (r\ddot{\phi} + 2\dot{r}\dot{\phi})\boldsymbol{e}_\phi\} = -T_1 \boldsymbol{e}_r + (m_1 g - N)\boldsymbol{k}$$

and

$$m_2 \ddot{z}\boldsymbol{k} = (m_2 g - T_2)\boldsymbol{k}$$

where T_1 and T_2 are the tensions at the ends of the string and N is the normal reaction of the table upon the particle P_1. We assume that there is no frictional force at the hole, so that $T_1 = T_2 = T$ (say). Thus we have to solve

$$m_1(\ddot{r} - r\dot{\phi}^2) = -T$$

$$m_1(r\ddot{\phi} + 2\dot{r}\dot{\phi}) = \frac{m_1}{r}\frac{d}{dt}(r^2\dot{\phi}) = 0$$

$$0 = m_1 g - N$$

$$m_2 \ddot{z} = m_2 g - T$$

subject to the constraint $r+z = 2l$ and the initial conditions at $t = 0$

$$z = d, \quad \dot{z} = 0, \quad r = 2l-d, \quad \dot{r} = 0, \quad (2l-d)\dot{\phi} = u_0$$

It follows that $N = m_1 g$ and

$$0 = \ddot{r}+\ddot{z} = \left(r\dot{\phi}^2 - \frac{T}{m_1}\right)+\left(g - \frac{T}{m_2}\right)$$

i.e.

$$T = m_1 m_2(g+r\dot{\phi}^2)/(m_1+m_2)$$

Using this expression for T and the fact that $r^2\dot{\phi}$ has a constant value, namely $(2l-d)u_0$, we find that

$$\ddot{r} = (m_1 r\dot{\phi}^2 - m_2 g)/(m_1+m_2)$$

$$= \left(\frac{m_1(2l-d)^2 u_0^2}{r^3} - m_2 g\right)\Big/ (m_1+m_2)$$

The direction of the initial acceleration of P_2 is upwards provided $u_0^2 > (m_2/m_1)g(2l-d)$. Integrating with respect to r leads to

$$\tfrac{1}{2}\dot{r}^2 = \left(-\frac{m_1(2l-d)^2 u_0^2}{2r^2} - m_2 g r\right)\Big/ (m_1+m_2)+C$$

where the constant C equals $(\frac{1}{2}m_1 u_0^2+m_2 g(2l-d))/(m_1+m_2)$. Thus

$$\tfrac{1}{2}(m_1+m_2)\dot{r}^2 = \tfrac{1}{2}m_1 u_0^2\left\{1 - \frac{(2l-d)^2}{r^2}\right\} + m_2 g\{(2l-d)-r\}$$

$$= \frac{(r-2l+d)}{r^2}\{\tfrac{1}{2}m_1 u_0^2(r+2l-d)-m_2 g r^2\}$$

This is equivalent to the statement of the conservation of energy

$$\tfrac{1}{2}m_1(\dot{r}^2+r^2\dot{\phi}^2)+\tfrac{1}{2}m_2\dot{z}^2-m_2 g z = \text{constant} = \tfrac{1}{2}m_1 u_0^2 - m_2 g d$$

with $r^2\dot{\phi} = (2l-d)u_0$. We note that P_2 just reaches the hole O (i.e. $\dot{r} = 0$ at $r = 2l$) if $u_0^2 = 8(m_2/m_1)gl^2/(4l-d)$ which is greater than $(m_2/m_1)g(2l-d)$. If $u_0^2 = (m_2/m_1)g(2l-d)$, we find that

$$\ddot{r} = \frac{m_2 g}{(m_1+m_2)}\left(\frac{(2l-d)^3}{r^3} - 1\right)$$

and

$$\dot{r}^2 = -\frac{m_2 g}{(m_1+m_2)}(r-2l+d)^2(2r+2l-d)$$

In this case $\ddot{r} = \dot{r} = 0$ and $r = 2l-d$; i.e. the particle P_2 remains stationary and the particle P_1 moves in a circular orbit. If $u_0^2 < (m_2/m_1)g(2l-d)$, the direction of the initial acceleration of P_2 is downwards.

Finally we note that

$$\dot{r}^2 = \frac{2m_2 g}{(m_1+m_2)}\frac{(r-2l+d)}{r^2}(\alpha - r)(r+\beta)$$

and that $\dot{r}^2 \geqslant 0$ for values of r between α and $2l-d$, where α is the unique positive root of the quadratic equation

$$m_2 g r^2 - \tfrac{1}{2}m_1 u_0^2 r - \tfrac{1}{2}m_1 u_0^2(2l-d) = 0$$

EXAMPLE

A particle P_1 of mass m_1 is suspended from a fixed support by means of a spring of natural length l_1 and stiffness k_1. A particle P_2 of mass m_2 is joined to P_1 by means of a spring of natural length l_2 and stiffness k_2. Consider the motion of the system when the particles and the springs are on a vertical line through the point of suspension.

We need two coordinates to describe the position of the system of particles. We introduce a z-axis such that its origin O is at the level of the fixed support, and the direction of z increasing is downwards. Then the position vectors of P_1 and P_2 relative to O are $\boldsymbol{r}_1 = z_1\boldsymbol{k}$ and $\boldsymbol{r}_2 = z_2\boldsymbol{k}$. Let T_1 be the tension in the upper spring and let T_2 be the tension in the lower spring. It follows from Hooke's law that

$$T_1 = k_1(z_1 - l_1) \quad \text{and} \quad T_2 = k_2(z_2 - z_1 - l_2)$$

The equations of motion (along a vertical line through the point of suspension) are

$$m_1\ddot{\boldsymbol{r}}_1 = (m_1 g - T_1 + T_2)\boldsymbol{k}$$

and

$$m_2\ddot{\boldsymbol{r}}_2 = (m_2 g - T_2)\boldsymbol{k}$$

Thus we have to solve the system of differential equations

$$m_1\ddot{z}_1 + (k_1 + k_2)z_1 - k_2 z_2 = m_1 g + k_1 l_1 - k_2 l_2$$
$$m_2\ddot{z}_2 + k_2 z_2 - k_2 z_1 = m_2 g + k_2 l_2$$

To find the position of equilibrium of the system ($\dot{z}_1 = \ddot{z}_1 = \dot{z}_2 = \ddot{z}_2 = 0$) we solve a pair of simultaneous algebraic equations (namely, the differential equations with $\ddot{z}_1$ and $\ddot{z}_2$ set equal to zero) and find that

$$z_1 = l_1 + (m_1 + m_2)g/k_1$$

and

$$z_2 = l_1 + l_2 + (m_1 + m_2)g/k_1 + m_2 g/k_2$$

The upper spring has an extension $(m_1 + m_2)g/k_1$ and the lower spring has an extension $m_2 g/k_2$.

Let us examine the differential equations in the special case when $m_1 = 0$ (when the particle P_2 is suspended by two springs in series). The first differential equation becomes the condition that the tension is continuous, i.e. $T_1 = T_2$. Therefore the governing differential equation is

$$m_2\ddot{z}_2 + k_2 z_2 - k_2 z_1 = m_2 g + k_2 l_2$$

where $(k_1 + k_2)z_1 = k_1 l_1 - k_2 l_2 + k_2 z_2$. This reduces to

$$m_2\ddot{z}_2 + \frac{k_1 k_2}{k_1 + k_2} z_2 = m_2 g + \frac{k_1 k_2}{k_1 + k_2}(l_1 + l_2)$$

Setting $\Omega^2 = k_1 k_2/(k_1 + k_2)m_2$, we have

$$\ddot{z}_2 + \Omega^2 z_2 = g + \Omega^2(l_1 + l_2)$$

the general solution of which is

$$z_2 = A\cos\Omega t + B\sin\Omega t + l_1 + l_2 + g/\Omega^2$$

with the constants A and B depending on the initial conditions. The suspension of the particle P_2, namely a pair of springs in series, is equivalent to a single spring of natural length l and stiffness k, where

$$l = l_1 + l_2 \quad \text{and} \quad \frac{1}{k} = \frac{1}{k_1} + \frac{1}{k_2}$$

The equilibrium values of z_1 and z_2 provide us with particular integrals of the simultaneous differential equations. We expect the complementary functions to represent oscillations and to have the forms

$$A_1 \cos \omega t + B_1 \sin \omega t \quad \text{and} \quad A_2 \cos \omega t + B_2 \sin \omega t$$

where A_1, A_2, B_1 and B_2 depend on the initial conditions and the angular frequency ω is to be determined. Substituting these forms into the homogeneous simultaneous differential equations, we find that

$$\begin{bmatrix} k_1 + k_2 - m_1\omega^2 & -k_2 \\ -k_2 & k_2 - m_2\omega^2 \end{bmatrix} \begin{bmatrix} A_1 \\ A_2 \end{bmatrix} = \begin{bmatrix} 0 \\ 0 \end{bmatrix}$$

and

$$\begin{bmatrix} k_1 + k_2 - m_1\omega^2 & -k_2 \\ -k_2 & k_2 - m_2\omega^2 \end{bmatrix} \begin{bmatrix} B_1 \\ B_2 \end{bmatrix} = \begin{bmatrix} 0 \\ 0 \end{bmatrix}$$

These systems of algebraic equations have non-trivial solutions provided

$$(k_1 + k_2 - m_1\omega^2)(k_2 - m_2\omega^2) - (-k_2)^2 = 0$$

This condition is a quadratic polynomial equation for ω^2. Therefore there are two possible angular frequencies, say Ω_1 and Ω_2, and each complementary function (one corresponding to z_1 and one corresponding to z_2) is the sum of two terms, one representing an oscillation with angular frequency Ω_1 and the other representing an oscillation with angular frequency Ω_2. The frequencies $\Omega_1/2\pi$ and $\Omega_2/2\pi$ are called the *normal frequencies*.

Consider the special case

$$m_1 = m_2 = m \quad \text{and} \quad k_1 = k_2 = k$$

for the purposes of illustration. The quadratic polynomial equation for ω^2,

$$(2k - m\omega^2)(k - m\omega^2) - k^2 = 0$$

has the roots

$$\omega^2 = \Omega_1^2 = \tfrac{1}{2}(3 - 5^{1/2})k/m \quad \text{and} \quad \omega^2 = \Omega_2^2 = \tfrac{1}{2}(3 + 5^{1/2})k/m$$

i.e.

$$\Omega_1 = \tfrac{1}{2}(5^{1/2} - 1)(k/m)^{1/2} \quad \text{and} \quad \Omega_2 = \tfrac{1}{2}(5^{1/2} + 1)(k/m)^{1/2}$$

Therefore we have

$$z_1 = l_1 + 2mg/k + (A_1 \cos \Omega_1 t + B_1 \sin \Omega_1 t) + (C_1 \cos \Omega_2 t + D_1 \sin \Omega_2 t)$$

and

$$z_2 = l_1 + l_2 + 3mg/k + (A_2 \cos \Omega_1 t + B_2 \sin \Omega_1 t) + (C_2 \cos \Omega_2 t + D_2 \sin \Omega_2 t)$$

which are solutions of the simultaneous differential equations provided

$$(2k - m\Omega_1^2)A_1 = kA_2, \quad (2k - m\Omega_1^2)B_1 = kB_2$$
$$(2k - m\Omega_2^2)C_1 = kC_2, \quad (2k - m\Omega_2^2)D_1 = kD_2$$

i.e.

$$A_2 = \tfrac{1}{2}(1 + 5^{1/2})A_1, \quad B_2 = \tfrac{1}{2}(1 + 5^{1/2})B_1$$
$$C_2 = \tfrac{1}{2}(1 - 5^{1/2})C_1, \quad D_2 = \tfrac{1}{2}(1 - 5^{1/2})D_1$$

The initial conditions determine the four constants A_1, B_1, C_1 and D_1. If $C_1 = D_1 = 0$, z_1 and z_2 depend on the normal frequency $\Omega_1/2\pi$ and if $A_1 = B_1 = 0$, z_1 and z_2 depend on the normal frequency $\Omega_2/2\pi$. These special cases are called the *normal modes of vibration.* In general z_1 and z_2 depend on both normal frequencies.

EXERCISES ON CHAPTER 13

1. A particle of mass M is moving with a uniform speed $10\,\mathrm{m\,s^{-1}}$ in an easterly direction and a particle of mass $3M$ is moving with a uniform speed $10\,\mathrm{m\,s^{-1}}$ in a northerly direction. Calculate the magnitude and direction of the velocity of the centre of mass of the system.

2. A particle of mass m is moving with constant speed u around a circular orbit of radius R. A particle of mass M is stationary at the centre of the orbit. Describe the motion of the centre of mass of the system.

3. Particles P_1 and P_2 have masses m and $2m$ and position vectors $\boldsymbol{r}_1$ and $\boldsymbol{r}_2$, where

$$\boldsymbol{r}_1 = R(\boldsymbol{i}\cos\omega_1 t+\boldsymbol{j}\sin\omega_1 t)$$
$$\boldsymbol{r}_2 = \tfrac{1}{2}R(\boldsymbol{i}\cos\omega_2 t+\boldsymbol{j}\sin\omega_2 t)$$

and R, ω_1 and ω_2 are constants. What time elapses before the centre of mass coincides with the origin on the first occasion? Determine the position vector of P_1 at that instant, in the case when $\omega_2 = 3\omega_1$.

4. Three identical particles are situated at the vertices of a triangle. Show that the centre of mass is situated at the point of intersection of the medians of the triangle.

5. Two particles, whose masses are m_1 and m_2, exert on each other equal gravitational attractive forces of magnitude Gm_1m_2/r^2 when they are separated by a distance r. Initially they are at rest and at a distance r_0 apart. If there are no other forces acting on the system, show that the centre of mass is fixed. Determine the speed of one particle relative to the other when the particles are separated by a distance r.

6. Two particles, whose masses are m_1 and m_2, exert on each other equal repulsive forces of magnitude $\mu m_1m_2/r^2$, where μ is a constant and r is the distance between the particles. They experience no other forces. Initially they are at rest and at a distance r_0 apart. Is the centre of mass stationary? Show that, when the particles are separated by a distance r, the speed of one particle relative to the other is

$$\left\{2\mu(m_1+m_2)\left(\frac{1}{r_0}-\frac{1}{r}\right)\right\}^{1/2}$$

7. Two particles of masses m_1 and m_2 are moving in a uniform gravitational field and are experiencing their mutual gravitational force of attraction. Show that the centre of mass behaves like a projectile in the uniform gravitational field. Obtain a differential equation satisfied by $\boldsymbol{r}$, the position vector of one particle relative to the other particle.

Show that the vertical motion and the horizontal motion are independent of each other in the case when the particles are dropped from two points at a given height above the Earth's surface.

8. A particle of mass M is fixed at the origin O of an inertial frame of reference. Two particles having masses m_1 and m_2 are in motion subject to their mutual gravitational field and the gravitational field associated with the fixed particle. Their position vectors relative to O are $\boldsymbol{r}_1$ and $\boldsymbol{r}_2$. Show that

$$\ddot{\boldsymbol{r}}_1 = -\frac{GM\boldsymbol{r}_1}{r_1^3}+\frac{Gm_2\boldsymbol{r}}{r^3}$$

and

$$\ddot{r} = -G\left\{\frac{m_1+m_2}{r^3}+\frac{M}{|r+r_1|^3}\right\}r+GM\left\{\frac{1}{r_1^3}-\frac{1}{|r+r_1|^3}\right\}r_1$$

where $r = r_2 - r_1, r_1 = |r_1|, r = |r|$.

9. Two satellites P and Q each of mass m are describing uniformly a circular orbit of radius R about a fixed body S of mass M such that S is always at the midpoint of the line joining P and Q. Show that their period of revolution is

$$2\pi\{R^3/G(M+\tfrac{1}{4}m)\}^{1/2}$$

Is it necessary to apply a force to S to maintain its stationary position?

10. Three satellites each of mass m are describing uniformly a circular orbit of radius R about a fixed body S of mass M. They are always at the vertices of an equilateral triangle and S is in the plane of the orbit. Determine the speed at which the satellites move.

What is the corresponding result when there are four identical satellites at the corners of a square, each satellite describing uniformly a circular orbit of radius R about a fixed body?

11. An inextensible string AB of negligible mass passes over a fixed smooth peg. A body of mass 4 kg is attached to the end A and a body of mass 5 kg is attached to the end B. Initially the string is taut and the system is at rest with end A at a distance 2 m below the peg. Show that the tension in the string is 43·6 N. Determine the time taken for the end A to reach the peg.

12. Bodies P_1 and P_2, of masses M and $M+m$, are attached to the ends of a light inextensible string which passes over a fixed smooth peg. A rider of mass $2m$ carried by P_1 can be removed by a ring through which P_1 passes freely. The system is released from rest when P_1 is at a point A above the ring. It comes to rest instantaneously when P_1 is at a point B below the ring. Show that

$$g = 8(1+M/m)d/t^2$$

where d is the distance between A and B and t is the time taken by P_1 to move from A to B.

13. A light inextensible string AB passes over a fixed smooth peg. A body of mass M is attached to the end A and a light pulley is attached to the end B. Over the pulley passes a light inextensible string to whose ends are attached bodies of masses m_1 and m_2. Show that the acceleration of the body of mass M will be zero if $M = 4m_1 m_2/(m_1+m_2)$.

14. Two smooth inclined planes meet at a horizontal ridge along which is fixed a smooth peg. A body B_1 of mass M is connected by a light inextensible string to a body B_2 of mass m. B_1 lies on the plane inclined at an angle α to the horizontal and B_2 lies on the plane inclined at an angle β to the horizontal. The string passes from B_1 to B_2 along the lines of greatest slope, and over the smooth peg at the ridge. Calculate the tension in the string and deduce that the accelerations of B_1 and B_2 down the slopes are

$$g(M\sin\alpha - m\sin\beta)/(M+m), \quad g(m\sin\beta - M\sin\alpha)/(M+m)$$

15. A body B_1 of mass m_1 is connected by a light inextensible string to a body B_2 of mass m_2. B_1 lies on a rough plane inclined at an angle α to the horizontal. The string passes from B_1 along the line of greatest slope and over a smooth peg fixed along the horizontal top edge of the plane, and B_2 hangs vertically. The contact between the body B_1 and the rough plane is characterized by the coefficient of kinematic friction μ. Initially the string is taut and the bodies are at rest. Show that the tension in the string is

$$m_1 m_2 g(1+\sin\alpha+\mu\cos\alpha)/(m_1+m_2)$$

when B_1 is moving up the plane. What is the tension when B_1 is moving down the plane?

16. A body of mass m rests on a rough horizontal table, the coefficients of static and kinematic friction being μ_s and μ. It is connected by a light inextensible string to a body of mass M which hangs over the edge of the table. There is a smooth peg fixed along the edge which is perpendicular to the plane of the string. The system is initially at rest with the body of mass m a distance d from the edge of the table. Show that there is no motion provided $M \leqslant m\mu_s$. If $M > m\mu_s$, determine the time at which the body falls from the table.

17. Two beads of masses m and $2m$ are connected by a string of constant length πR and are placed in a vertical circular tube of radius R. The contact between the beads and the tube is smooth. The string lies in the upper half of the tube when the beads are released from rest. Show that when the radius to the lighter bead makes an angle ϕ with the horizontal, the tension in the string is $\frac{4}{3}mg\cos\phi$, the reaction of the tube on the lighter bead is $\frac{1}{3}mg\sin\phi$ and the reaction of the tube on the heavier bead is $\frac{10}{3}mg\sin\phi$.

18. Two beads of masses m and $2m$ are connected by a string of constant length $\frac{1}{3}\pi R$ and are placed on a fixed circular cylinder whose radius is R and whose axis is horizontal. The contact between the beads and the cylinder is smooth, and the string is in a plane perpendicular to the cylinder's axis. The string is taut and the beads are symmetrically placed on the surface of the cylinder when the system is released from rest. Show that the heavier bead leaves the surface when it has travelled a distance $0{\cdot}573R$ over the surface (when the system has turned through an angle of $32{\cdot}8°$).

19. Two beads of masses M, m slide on a smooth circular hoop of radius R which is fixed in a vertical plane. They are connected by a straight wire of length $2R\sin\alpha$ and of negligible mass. Initially the wire is horizontal and at rest. Find the tension in the wire when the wire has turned through an angle ϕ and show that

$$R\dot{\phi}^2 = 2g[(1-\cos\phi)\cos\alpha+\{(M-m)/(M+m)\}\sin\phi\sin\alpha]$$

20. Two bodies of masses m_1 and m_2 are attached to a rope which hangs over a fixed rough peg whose axis is horizontal and whose cross-section is circular. The rope is in a plane perpendicular to the axis of the peg. The contact between the rope, which has negligible mass, and the peg is characterized by the coefficient of static friction μ_s. The system is released with the bodies hanging at rest. Show that the system remains at rest provided

$$e^{-\pi\mu_s} \leqslant m_1/m_2 \leqslant e^{\pi\mu_s}$$

21. Two particles, each of mass m, are connected by a light inextensible string of length $2l$ which passes through a small hole O in a smooth horizontal table. Particle P_1 can slide on the table while particle P_2 hangs freely (moving along a vertical line through O). Initially P_2 is at rest at a distance l below O and P_1 is moving with speed u_0 in a direction perpendicular to $\overrightarrow{OP_1}$. Find the tension in the string and show that

$$\ddot{r} = \tfrac{1}{2}\left(\frac{u_0^2 l^2}{r^3} - g\right)$$

and

$$\dot{r}^2 = \frac{r-l}{r^2}\{\tfrac{1}{2}u_0^2(r+l) - gr^2\}$$

where $r = |\overrightarrow{OP}_1|$. Deduce that $\frac{1}{3}l \leqslant r \leqslant l$ when $u_0^2 = \frac{1}{6}gl$.

22. Two bodies of masses m_1 and m_2 can slide along a smooth horizontal straight track. They are connected by a spring of stiffness k and natural length l. Initially the length of the spring is $\frac{1}{2}l$ and the bodies are projected with speeds u_1 and u_2 in the same direction along the track. Determine the constant speed with which the centre of mass of the system moves, and show that the length of the spring is

$$l(1 - \tfrac{1}{2}\cos\Omega t) + \frac{u_2 - u_1}{\Omega}\sin\Omega t$$

where

$$\Omega^2 = k\left(\frac{1}{m_1} + \frac{1}{m_2}\right)$$

23. Two particles P_1 and P_2 of masses m_1 and m_2 are connected by a spring of stiffness k and natural length l. Initially the system is released from rest with P_1 vertically above P_2 and the spring compressed to a length $\alpha l (0 < \alpha < 1)$. Show that in time t particle P_1 has moved a distance

$$\tfrac{1}{2}gt^2 - \frac{m_2}{m_1 + m_2}(1-\alpha)l(1 - \cos\Omega t)$$

and P_2 has moved a distance

$$\tfrac{1}{2}gt^2 + \frac{m_1}{m_1 + m_2}(1-\alpha)l(1 - \cos\Omega t)$$

where

$$\Omega^2 = k\left(\frac{1}{m_1} + \frac{1}{m_2}\right)$$

What is the length of the spring in the special case when $\alpha = 1$?

24. Two particles P_1 and P_2, each of mass m, are connected by a spring of stiffness k and natural length l. A and B are two fixed points on a smooth horizontal table, the distance between A and B being $3l$. The particles can slide on the table with P_1 connected to A and P_2 connected to B, each connector being a spring of stiffness k and natural length l. Determine the normal frequencies associated with the motion of the particles along the line joining A and B.

At a given instant P_1 is released from rest at a distance $\frac{3}{4}l$ from A and P_2 is released from rest at a distance $\frac{3}{4}l$ from B. Find the length of the middle spring in the subsequent motion.

25. A particle P_1 of mass m_1 is suspended by a light inextensible string of length l_1 from a fixed support. A second particle P_2 of mass m_2 is suspended from P_1 by a light inextensible string of length l_2. Show that small-amplitude oscillations of the system about the equilibrium position in a vertical plane through the point of suspension are governed by

$$m_1 l_1 \ddot{\phi}_1 = -(m_1+m_2)g\phi_1 + m_2 g\phi_2$$

and

$$m_2(l_1\ddot{\phi}_1 + l_2\ddot{\phi}_2) = -m_2 g\phi_2$$

where ϕ_1 and ϕ_2 are the angles that the upper and lower strings make with the downward vertical.

Show that the normal frequencies associated with the double pendulum for which $m_1 = m_2 = m$ and $l_1 = l_2 = l$ are

$$\frac{1}{2\pi}((2-2^{1/2})g/l)^{1/2} \quad \text{and} \quad \frac{1}{2\pi}((2+2^{1/2})g/l)^{1/2}$$

Impulses

14

14.1 Introduction

This chapter is devoted to problems in which two bodies (e.g. billiard balls, curling stones, motor vehicles) collide with each other. In particular, we shall investigate the effects of the collision on the motions of the bodies, and we shall suggest suitable ways of describing the effects of the changes in the shapes of the bodies during the complicated collision process.

Suppose that we consider the problem of two billiard balls (or two curling stones) moving towards each other. The balls collide and their motions are changed. When the balls come into contact, each ball experiences a contact force (in addition to any other applied forces such as the gravitational force and the reaction of the table). The contact force that one ball experiences will be equal and opposite to the contact force experienced by the other ball. The time interval during which the balls are in contact is very small (unless the balls adhere to each other). During this very small time interval the motions of the balls are very complicated. The shapes change during the time interval, the final shapes being in general different from the initial shapes. We wish to suggest a model that will predict the motions of the balls after the collision (given the description of the motions before the collision), but we will not attempt to predict the complicated changes in shape during the collision.

We shall make the assumptions that the balls are not spinning and that the surfaces of the balls are smooth. (These assumptions over-simplify the physical situation, because many shots in billiards and snooker depend on spin and transfer of spin by frictional forces to produce their magical effects.) Thus we may use particles to represent the balls and the fact that the contact forces acting during the collision period act along the line joining the centres of the balls. The collision may be *head-on*, in which case the directions of the velocities of the balls before the collision are parallel to the direction of the line joining the centres of the balls. We refer to any other collision as an *oblique collision.* We shall begin our discussion of collisions by considering a "head-on" collision in which one ball is at rest before the collision.

Let us assume that the particles are moving in a horizontal plane (representing the billiard table), one particle P_1 of mass m_1 moving with uniform velocity before the collision, and the other particle P_2 of mass m_2 being at rest before the "head-on" collision. We choose cartesian coordinates so that the z-axis is vertically upwards, P_1 is moving along the x-axis and P_2 is at the origin O before the collision. Let $\boldsymbol{r}_1$ and $\boldsymbol{r}_2$ be the position vectors of P_1 and P_2 relative to O. Before the collision, which starts to occur at $t = 0$,

$$\boldsymbol{r}_1 = u_0 t\boldsymbol{i} \quad \text{and} \quad \boldsymbol{r}_2 = \boldsymbol{0}$$

The equations of motion are

$$m_1 \ddot{\boldsymbol{r}}_1 = -F_c(t)\boldsymbol{i} + (N_1 - m_1 g)\boldsymbol{k}$$

and

$$m_2 \ddot{\boldsymbol{r}}_2 = F_c(t)\boldsymbol{i} + (N_2 - m_2 g)\boldsymbol{k}$$

where $\boldsymbol{r}_1 = x_1 \boldsymbol{i} + y_1 \boldsymbol{j}$, $\boldsymbol{r}_2 = x_2 \boldsymbol{i} + y_2 \boldsymbol{j}$ and $F_c(t)$ is zero except for a short time interval $[0, \tau]$ during which the particles are in contact. We note that $N_1 = m_1 g$ and $N_2 = m_2 g$. Therefore we have to solve

$$m_1(\ddot{x}_1 \boldsymbol{i} + \ddot{y}_1 \boldsymbol{j}) = -F_c(t)\boldsymbol{i}$$

and

$$m_2(\ddot{x}_2 \boldsymbol{i} + \ddot{y}_2 \boldsymbol{j}) = F_c(t)\boldsymbol{i}$$

subject to the initial conditions at $t = 0$

$$x_1 = x_2 = y_1 = y_2 = 0, \quad \dot{x}_1 = u_0, \quad \dot{x}_2 = \dot{y}_1 = \dot{y}_2 = 0.$$

We remind ourselves that we have no knowledge of the explicit form of the function F_c. We may deduce easily that $y_1 = y_2 = 0$ for all time; i.e. the motions of P_1 and P_2 are confined to the x-axis and are governed by

$$m_1 \ddot{x}_1 = -F_c(t) \quad \text{and} \quad m_2 \ddot{x}_2 = F_c(t)$$

subject to $x_1 = 0$, $\dot{x}_1 = u_0$ and $x_2 = \dot{x}_2 = 0$ at $t = 0$. Adding the differential equations and integrating with respect to t, we find that

$$m_1 \dot{x}_1 + m_2 \dot{x}_2 = m_1 u_0 \quad \text{and} \quad m_1 x_1 + m_2 x_2 = m_1 u_0 t$$

i.e.

$$(m_1 + m_2)\dot{x}_c = m_1 u_0 \quad \text{and} \quad (m_1 + m_2)x_c = m_1 u_0 t$$

where $x_c = (m_1 x_1 + m_2 x_2)/(m_1 + m_2)$, the x-coordinate of the centre of mass of the system of two particles P_1 and P_2. A summary of these results is

$$m_1(\dot{x}_1 \boldsymbol{i} + \dot{y}_1 \boldsymbol{j}) + m_2(\dot{x}_2 \boldsymbol{i} + \dot{y}_2 \boldsymbol{j}) = m_1 u_0 \boldsymbol{i}$$

which is a statement that the *total linear momentum after the collision equals the total linear momentum before the collision.* The conservation of linear momentum for the system of particles has an important role in our present investigation.

Let us now try to determine the velocities of the particles after the collision. Integrating

$$m_1 \ddot{\boldsymbol{r}}_1 = -F_c(t)\boldsymbol{i} \quad \text{and} \quad m_2 \ddot{\boldsymbol{r}}_2 = F_c(t)\boldsymbol{i}$$

with respect to t from just before $t = 0$ to any time after $t = \tau$, we find that

$$m_1(\dot{x}_1 \boldsymbol{i} + \dot{y}_1 \boldsymbol{j}) - m_1 u_0 \boldsymbol{i} = -\int_0^\tau F_c(t)dt\boldsymbol{i}$$

and

$$m_2(\dot{x}_2 \boldsymbol{i} + \dot{y}_2 \boldsymbol{j}) - \boldsymbol{0} = \int_0^\tau F_c(t)dt\boldsymbol{i}$$

from which we deduce that $\dot{y}_1 = \dot{y}_2 = 0$ for all time $t > \tau$. The integral of the contact force with respect to time is called an *impulse*. Any force which acts for a short time is called an *impulsive force*. Impulses are vector valued quantities and are measured in units of the newton second (N s or kg m s^{-1}). The impulse experienced by each particle equals the change in the particle's linear momentum; i.e.

$$\mathbf{J}_1 = -\int_0^\tau F_c(t)dt\boldsymbol{i} = [m_1 \dot{\boldsymbol{r}}_1]$$

and

$$\mathbf{J}_2 = \int_0^\tau F_c(t)dt\boldsymbol{i} = [m_2 \dot{\boldsymbol{r}}_2]$$

We regain the conservation of linear momentum for the system of particles when we note that $\mathbf{J}_1 = -\mathbf{J}_2$. Somehow we have to overcome the unavailability of any further information about $\mathbf{J}_1$ and $\mathbf{J}_2$. We achieve this by introducing an empirical law (attributed to Newton) which attempts to take account of the ways the colliding bodies deform during the time of the collision. We introduce the coefficient of restitution e (which is a positive dimensionless parameter) by the definition

$$-e = \frac{\text{The component of the relative velocity after the collision in the direction of the impulse}}{\text{The component of the relative velocity before the collision in the direction of the impulse}}$$

In our particular problem this becomes

$$-e = \frac{(\dot{\boldsymbol{r}}_1 - \dot{\boldsymbol{r}}_2)\cdot\boldsymbol{i}}{u_0 - 0} = \frac{\dot{x}_1 - \dot{x}_2}{u_0 - 0}; \quad \text{i.e.} \quad \dot{x}_1 - \dot{x}_2 = -e(u_0 - 0)$$

Now we have two linear equations determining $\dot{x}_1$ and $\dot{x}_2$, namely

$$m_1\dot{x}_1 + m_2\dot{x}_2 = m_1 u_0$$
$$\dot{x}_1 - \dot{x}_2 = -eu_0$$

Thus

$$\dot{x}_1 = (m_1 - em_2)u_0/(m_1+m_2) \quad \text{and} \quad \dot{x}_2 = (1+e)m_1 u_0/(m_1+m_2)$$

The velocity component $\dot{x}_2$ is always positive, and the velocity component $\dot{x}_1$ is positive provided $m_1 > em_2$. If $m_1 = m_2$ and $e = 1$, we have a special case in which

$$\dot{x}_1 = 0 \quad \text{and} \quad \dot{x}_2 = u_0$$

Experiments show that e is never as large as unity. The coefficient of restitution depends on the two bodies, the relative velocity before the collision and the temperature of the bodies. All squash players know of the necessity of the "warm-up", but golfers may not know that the coefficient of restitution decreases as the club-head speed increases. The following table gives some typical values of the coefficient of restitution.

"cool" squash ball and racquet	0·25
"warm" squash ball and racquet	0·32
two wooden balls	0·50
two steel balls	0·55
golf ball and club (professional golfer)	0·74
golf ball and club (handicap golfer)	0·79
two ivory balls	0·89
two synthetic rubber balls	0·92

It is convenient to consider on some occasions the extreme values of e:

(i) $e = 0$ in which case the bodies adhere and move off with the same velocity after the collision.
(ii) $e = 1$ in which case we say that the bodies are perfectly elastic (a mathematical idealization).

Our knowledge of the velocities before and after the collision enables us to determine the impulses. We find that

$$\mathbf{J}_1 = m_1(\dot{x}_1 - u_0)\boldsymbol{i} = -\{(1+e)m_1 m_2 u_0/(m_1+m_2)\}\boldsymbol{i}$$

and

$$\mathbf{J}_2 = m_2(\dot{x}_2 - 0)\boldsymbol{i} = \{(1+e)m_1 m_2 u_0/(m_1+m_2)\}\boldsymbol{i} = -\mathbf{J}_1$$

Let us consider the energy of the system of particles before and after the collision. The particles are moving in a horizontal plane, and the potential energy has a constant value. The kinetic energy of the system before the collision is $\frac{1}{2}m_1 u_0^2$ and the kinetic energy of the system after the collision is $\frac{1}{2}m_1 \dot{x}_1^2 + \frac{1}{2}m_2 \dot{x}_2^2$, which equals

$$\frac{m_1(m_1 - em_2)^2 u_0^2}{2(m_1+m_2)^2} + \frac{m_2(1+e)^2 m_1^2 u_0^2}{2(m_1+m_2)^2} = \tfrac{1}{2}m_1 u_0^2 \left\{\frac{(m_1 - em_2)^2 + (1+e)^2 m_1 m_2}{(m_1+m_2)^2}\right\}$$

$$= \tfrac{1}{2}m_1 u_0^2 \left\{\frac{m_1 + e^2 m_2}{m_1+m_2}\right\}$$

The increase in the kinetic energy of the system equals

$$-\tfrac{1}{2}m_1 u_0^2 \left\{\frac{(1-e^2)m_2}{m_1+m_2}\right\}$$

Heat and sound are generated during the collision, so there must be a loss in the mechanical energy (the sum of the kinetic energy and the potential energy). The increase in the kinetic energy is negative provided $e^2 < 1$. This is consistent with our earlier remark that the coefficient of restitution is never as large as unity in an experimental situation. We see from an integration of the individual equations of motion that the increase in the kinetic energy of the system equals

$$-\int_0^\tau F_c(t)\boldsymbol{i}\,.\,\dot{\boldsymbol{r}}_1\,dt + \int_0^\tau F_c(t)\boldsymbol{i}\,.\,\dot{\boldsymbol{r}}_2\,dt = -\int_0^\tau F_c(t)(\dot{x}_1 - \dot{x}_2)dt$$

namely the work done by the contact forces during the collision. The magnitude of the work done by the contact forces during the compression (or deformation) stage of the collision is greater than the magnitude of the work done by the contact forces during the expansion (or restitution) stage of the collision; the sign of the work done is negative during the former stage and is positive during the latter stage. Therefore the total work done is negative, and there is a loss in the kinetic energy of the system.

We emphasize that *the linear momentum of the system is conserved*, but the *energy of the system is not conserved* in this collision problem.

Before we move to another example it is worth while to look again at the coefficient of restitution. Suppose the deformation takes place during the time interval $[0, \tau_1)$ and the restitution takes place during the time interval $(\tau_1, \tau]$. We shall define the coefficient of restitution to be

$$e = \frac{\displaystyle\int_{\tau_1}^{\tau} F_c(t)dt}{\displaystyle\int_0^{\tau_1} F_c(t)dt} = \frac{\text{impulse during restitution}}{\text{impulse during deformation}}$$

and show that this definition is consistent with our earlier definition of e. It follows from the individual equations of motion that

$$e = \frac{-\int_{\tau_1}^{\tau} m_1 \ddot{\boldsymbol{r}}_1 \cdot \boldsymbol{i}\, dt}{-\int_{0}^{\tau_1} m_1 \ddot{\boldsymbol{r}}_1 \cdot \boldsymbol{i}\, dt} = \frac{\dot{x}_1 - \dot{x}_1(\tau_1)}{\dot{x}_1(\tau_1) - u_0}$$

and

$$e = \frac{\int_{\tau_1}^{\tau} m_2 \ddot{\boldsymbol{r}}_2 \cdot \boldsymbol{i}\, dt}{\int_{0}^{\tau_1} m_2 \ddot{\boldsymbol{r}}_2 \cdot dt} = \frac{\dot{x}_2 - \dot{x}_2(\tau_1)}{\dot{x}_2(\tau_1) - 0}$$

The bodies are moving with the same velocity at $t = \tau_1$; i.e. $\dot{x}_1(\tau_1) = \dot{x}_2(\tau_1)$. Solving these equations we find that

$$\dot{x}_1 - \dot{x}_2 = -eu_0$$

and

$$\dot{x}_1(\tau_1) = \dot{x}_2(\tau_1) = \dot{x}_2 u_0/(u_0 - \dot{x}_1 + \dot{x}_2).$$

The former result agrees with our earlier definition of the coefficient of restitution.

EXAMPLE

Two particles of masses m_1 and m_2 are moving along the x-axis with uniform velocities $u_1\boldsymbol{i}$ and $u_2\boldsymbol{i}$. They collide "head-on", the coefficient of restitution associated with the collision being e. Determine the velocities of the particles after the collision and calculate the loss in the kinetic energy of the system of two particles.

The equations of motion are

$$m_1 \ddot{\boldsymbol{r}}_1 = -F_c(t)\boldsymbol{i} \quad \text{and} \quad m_2 \ddot{\boldsymbol{r}}_2 = F_c(t)\boldsymbol{i}$$

during the collision and are

$$m_1 \ddot{\boldsymbol{r}}_1 = \boldsymbol{0} \quad \text{and} \quad m_2 \ddot{\boldsymbol{r}}_2 = \boldsymbol{0}$$

before and after the collision. At any time it is true that

$$m_1 \ddot{\boldsymbol{r}}_1 + m_2 \ddot{\boldsymbol{r}}_2 = \boldsymbol{0}$$

The conservation of linear momentum for the system follows from this statement, namely

$$m_1 \dot{\boldsymbol{r}}_1 + m_2 \dot{\boldsymbol{r}}_2 = (m_1 u_1 + m_2 u_2)\boldsymbol{i}$$

where $\dot{\boldsymbol{r}}_1$ and $\dot{\boldsymbol{r}}_2$ are the velocities of the particles. We deduce that the velocities of the particles after the collision are $\dot{x}_1\boldsymbol{i}$ and $\dot{x}_2\boldsymbol{i}$, where

$$m_1 \dot{x}_1 + m_2 \dot{x}_2 = m_1 u_1 + m_2 u_2$$

Introducing the coefficient of restitution we have

$$\dot{x}_1 - \dot{x}_2 = -e(u_1 - u_2)$$

which is the second equation that we require to be able to determine $\dot{x}_1$ and $\dot{x}_2$. Hence

$$(m_1 + m_2)\dot{x}_1 = (m_1 - em_2)u_1 + (1+e)m_2 u_2$$

and

$$(m_1 + m_2)\dot{x}_2 = (1+e)m_1 u_1 + (m_2 - em_1)u_2$$

The kinetic energy of the system of particles before the collision is

$$\tfrac{1}{2}m_1 u_1^2 + \tfrac{1}{2}m_2 u_2^2$$

and the kinetic energy of the system after the collision is

$$\tfrac{1}{2}m_1 \left\{\frac{(m_1 - em_2)u_1 + (1+e)m_2 u_2}{m_1 + m_2}\right\}^2 + \tfrac{1}{2}m_2 \left\{\frac{(1+e)m_1 u_1 + (m_2 - em_1)u_2}{m_1 + m_2}\right\}^2$$

$$= \tfrac{1}{2}m_1 u_1^2 \left\{\frac{m_1 + e^2 m_2}{m_1 + m_2}\right\} + \frac{(1-e^2)m_1 m_2 u_1 u_2}{m_1 + m_2} + \tfrac{1}{2}m_2 u_2^2 \left\{\frac{e^2 m_1 + m_2}{m_1 + m_2}\right\}$$

Therefore the loss in the kinetic energy of the system is

$$\tfrac{1}{2}m_1 u_1^2 \left\{\frac{(1-e^2)m_2}{m_1 + m_2}\right\} - \frac{(1-e^2)m_1 m_2 u_1 u_2}{m_1 + m_2} + \tfrac{1}{2}m_2 u_2^2 \left\{\frac{(1-e^2)m_1}{m_1 + m_2}\right\}$$

$$= \frac{(1-e^2)m_1 m_2 (u_1 - u_2)^2}{2(m_1 + m_2)}$$

Let us consider the motion of the centre of mass of the system of two particles before and after the collision. The centre of mass has the position vector $\boldsymbol{r}_c$, where

$$(m_1 + m_2)\boldsymbol{r}_c = m_1 \boldsymbol{r}_1 + m_2 \boldsymbol{r}_2$$

Its velocity before the collision is

$$\left(\frac{m_1 u_1 + m_2 u_2}{m_1 + m_2}\right)\boldsymbol{i}$$

and its velocity after the collision is

$$\left(\frac{m_1 \dot{x}_1 + m_2 \dot{x}_2}{m_1 + m_2}\right)\boldsymbol{i}$$

Using the conservation of linear momentum for the system, we deduce that these two velocities are identical and that the motion of the centre of mass is not altered by the collision. This allows us the possibility of using a frame of reference in which the centre of mass is at rest, this frame being an inertial frame of reference.

EXAMPLE

Investigate the oblique collision of two billiard balls.

We assume that the balls are smooth and that the billiard table is horizontal and represented by the xy-plane. The impulsive forces will be normal to each spherical surface at the point of contact; i.e. the impulses are directed along the line of centres, which we shall represent by the x-axis (say). We introduce two particles, whose masses are m_1 and m_2, to represent the balls. Suppose the velocities of the particles before the collision are

$$u_1\mathbf{i}+v_1\mathbf{j} \quad\text{and}\quad u_2\mathbf{i}+v_2\mathbf{j}$$

Let the particles' velocities after the collision be

$$\dot{x}_1\mathbf{i}+\dot{y}_1\mathbf{j} \quad\text{and}\quad \dot{x}_2\mathbf{i}+\dot{y}_2\mathbf{j}$$

The equations of motion are

$$m_1(\ddot{x}_1\mathbf{i}+\ddot{y}_1\mathbf{j}) = -F_c(t)\mathbf{i}$$

and

$$m_2(\ddot{x}_2\mathbf{i}+\ddot{y}_2\mathbf{j}) = F_c(t)\mathbf{i}$$

during the collision period and are

$$m_1(\ddot{x}_1\mathbf{i}+\ddot{y}_1\mathbf{j}) = \mathbf{0} \quad\text{and}\quad m_2(\ddot{x}_2\mathbf{i}+\ddot{y}_2\mathbf{j}) = \mathbf{0}$$

before and after the collision. We deduce from the individual equations of motion that the linear momentum of each particle in a direction perpendicular to the direction of the impulse is unaltered by the collision; i.e.

$$m_1 v_1 = m_1\dot{y}_1 \quad\text{and}\quad m_2 v_2 = m_2\dot{y}_2$$

Therefore $\dot{y}_1 = v_1$ and $\dot{y}_2 = v_2$. Using the conservation of linear momentum for the system of particles, we find that

$$m_1\dot{x}_1+m_2\dot{x}_2 = m_1u_1+m_2u_2$$

Finally the empirical law (which applies to motion in the direction of the impulse) gives

$$\dot{x}_1-\dot{x}_2 = -e(u_1-u_2)$$

These two linear equations determining $\dot{x}_1$ and $\dot{x}_2$ arose in our previous example (which was concerned with a "head-on" collision). Their solutions are

$$\dot{x}_1 = \{(m_1-em_2)u_1+(1+e)m_2u_2\}/(m_1+m_2)$$

and

$$\dot{x}_2 = \{(1+e)m_1u_1+(m_2-em_1)u_2\}/(m_1+m_2)$$

The loss in kinetic energy of the system equals

$$\{\tfrac{1}{2}m_1(u_1^2+v_1^2)+\tfrac{1}{2}m_2(u_2^2+v_2^2)\}-\{\tfrac{1}{2}m_1(\dot{x}_1^2+\dot{y}_1^2)+\tfrac{1}{2}m_2(\dot{x}_2^2+\dot{y}_2^2)\}$$
$$= \tfrac{1}{2}m_1(u_1^2-\dot{x}_1^2)+\tfrac{1}{2}m_2(u_2^2-\dot{x}_2^2)$$
$$= \frac{(1-e^2)m_1m_2(u_1-u_2)^2}{2(m_1+m_2)}$$

the result following from the calculation in the previous example.

In a usual situation in billiards, the balls have identical masses and one ball is at rest before the collision; i.e. $m_1 = m_2$ and $u_2 = v_2 = 0$. The velocities before the collision are

$$u_1\mathbf{i}+v_1\mathbf{j} \quad\text{and}\quad \mathbf{0}$$

and the velocities after the collision are

$$\tfrac{1}{2}(1-e)u_1\mathbf{i}+v_1\mathbf{j} \quad\text{and}\quad \tfrac{1}{2}(1+e)u_1\mathbf{i}$$

The stationary particle acquires a velocity in the direction of the impulse, and the moving particle experiences a change in direction, its directions before and after the collision being at angles α and β to the x-axis, respectively, where $\tan\alpha = v_1/u_1$ and $\tan\beta = 2v_1/(1-e)u_1$. Thus

$$\tan(\beta-\alpha) = \frac{\tan\beta - \tan\alpha}{1+\tan\beta\tan\alpha} = \frac{(1+e)\tan\alpha}{1-e+2\tan^2\alpha}$$

To find out how $(\beta-\alpha)$ varies with α (e fixed), we differentiate and obtain

$$\sec^2(\beta-\alpha)\frac{d(\beta-\alpha)}{d\alpha} = \left\{\frac{(1-e^2)-2(1+e)\tan^2\alpha}{(1-e+2\tan^2\alpha)^2}\right\}\sec^2\alpha$$

Hence $\beta-\alpha$ has a stationary value, which occurs when

$$\tan^2\alpha = \tfrac{1}{2}(1-e)$$

With $\alpha\in[0,\frac{1}{2}\pi]$, $\beta-\alpha$ has a maximum value $\tan^{-1}\{(1+e)/(8-8e)^{1/2}\}$ occurring at $\alpha = \tan^{-1}[\{(1-e)/2\}^{1/2}]$. For example, when $e = 0{\cdot}89$, the maximum angle through which the moving ball can be deflected is 1·11 radians (63·6°), the corresponding value of α being 0·23 radian ($v_1 = 0{\cdot}2345u_1$) and the corresponding value of β being 1·34 radians ($\dot{x}_1 = 0{\cdot}055u_1$, $\dot{y} = 0{\cdot}2345u_1$).

EXAMPLE

Discuss the collision between a puck and the boundary fence of the ice rink (or a ball and the cushion of a billiard table).

We shall assume that the contact between the puck and the fence is smooth, and that the fence is immovable. Let the horizontal surface of ice be represented by the xy-plane, the x-axis representing the boundary fence and the y-axis being directed into the ice rink. We represent the puck with a particle of mass m. Suppose that the particle's speed is $u_0\boldsymbol{i} - v_0\boldsymbol{j}$ before the collision, and let the particle's speed after the collision be $\dot{x}\boldsymbol{i}+\dot{y}\boldsymbol{j}$. The equation of motion of the particle is

$$m(\ddot{x}\boldsymbol{i}+\ddot{y}\boldsymbol{j}) = F_c(t)\boldsymbol{j}$$

where $F_c(t)$ is zero except during the time interval $[0,\tau]$ when the puck is in contact with the boundary fence. Integrating with respect to time, we find that

$$\mathbf{J} = \int_0^\tau F_c(t)dt\boldsymbol{j} = m(\dot{x}-u_0)\boldsymbol{i} + m(\dot{y}+v_0)\boldsymbol{j}$$

from which we deduce that

$$\dot{x} = u_0 \quad \text{and} \quad \mathbf{J} = m(\dot{y}+v_0)\boldsymbol{j}$$

To determine $\dot{y}$ we introduce the empirical law that $\dot{y} = -e(-v_0)$, where e is the coefficient of restitution. This law is based on the assumption that the fence is immovable. It is consistent with the limit of the results in the two-ball "head-on" collision problem as the ratio of the masses of the balls increases, the heavier ball having been stationary before the collision. Thus we find that the particle's velocity after the collision is $u_0\boldsymbol{i}+ev_0\boldsymbol{j}$; the impulse experienced by the particle is $mv_0(1+e)\boldsymbol{j}$; and the loss in the particle's kinetic energy is $\frac{1}{2}mv_0^2(1-e^2)$.

14.2 A bouncing ball

A ball is released at a given height above a floor. It falls, strikes the floor and bounces up. How high does the ball bounce? We shall base our attempt to answer this question on the assumption that the ball and the floor have smooth surfaces. Let a particle of mass m represent the ball which is initially at a height H above the floor. We choose the direction of a z-axis to be vertically upwards and the plane $z = 0$ to represent the floor. The particle's equation of motion before the collision is

$$m\ddot{z}\mathbf{k} = -mg\mathbf{k}$$

and the initial conditions are $z = H$ and $\dot{z} = 0$ at $t = 0$. It follows that when $z = 0, t = (2H/g)^{1/2} = t_0$ (say) and $\dot{z} = -(2gH)^{1/2}$. The equation of motion during the collision which takes place during the time interval $[t_0, t_0+\tau]$ is

$$m\ddot{z}\mathbf{k} = -mg\mathbf{k}+F_c(t)\mathbf{k}$$

where $F_c(t)\mathbf{k}$ represents the contact force experienced by the ball. Hence

$$\begin{aligned}\mathbf{J} &= \int_{t_0}^{t_0+\tau} F_c(t)dt\mathbf{k} = m\int_{t_0}^{t_0+\tau} \{\ddot{z}+g\}dt\mathbf{k} \\ &= \{m\dot{z}+m(2gH)^{1/2}+mg\tau\}\mathbf{k}\end{aligned}$$

By introducing the coefficient of restitution e, where

$$-e = \dot{z}/(-(2gH)^{1/2})$$

we have $\dot{z} = e(2gH)^{1/2}$ and the impulse $\mathbf{J}$ equals

$$\{(1+e)m(2gH)^{1/2}+mg\tau\}\mathbf{k} = mg\{(1+e)t_0+\tau\}\mathbf{k}$$

which approximately equals $mg(1+e)t_0\mathbf{k}$ because $\tau \ll t_0$. Therefore the particle has an upward velocity of magnitude $e(2gH)^{1/2}$ after the collision. If we assume that the particle is at $z = 0$ after the collision (this being equivalent to ignoring the deformed shape of the ball in the physical problem), we can calculate the height to which the particle rises. The governing equation of motion is $m\ddot{z}\mathbf{k} = -mg\mathbf{k}$ and the energy equation is

$$\tfrac{1}{2}m\dot{z}^2+mgz = \tfrac{1}{2}m(e^2 2gH) = e^2 mgH$$

Hence $\dot{z} = 0$ at $z = e^2H = h$ (say). This gives

$$h = e^2H \quad \text{or} \quad e = (h/H)^{1/2}$$

It is possible to design an experiment to test whether the coefficient of restitution is independent of the impact velocity (which depends on the height H). It is found that the coefficient of restitution depends on the impact velocity. Accurate estimates of the velocity before and after the collision can be obtained by photo-electric devices triggering timing mechanisms.

Let us examine the alternative definition of the coefficient of restitution given in the previous section, namely

$$e = \frac{\int_{t_0+\tau_1}^{t_0+\tau} F_c(t)dt}{\int_{t_0}^{t_0+\tau_1} F_c(t)dt} = \frac{\dot{z} - \dot{z}(t_0+\tau_1) + g(\tau-\tau_1)}{\dot{z}(t_0+\tau_1) - (-(2gH)^{1/2}) + g\tau_1} = \frac{\dot{z} + g(\tau-\tau_1)}{(2gH)^{1/2} + g\tau_1}$$

because $\dot{z}(t_0+\tau_1) = 0$ (the floor being immovable and the particle's speed at the end of the deformation stage being zero). We regain the empirical law used in this section if we ignore the terms $g(\tau-\tau_1)$ and $g\tau_1$, which are very small compared with $(2gH)^{1/2}$ and $\dot{z}$, the speeds before and after the collision. A preferable interpretation of the alternative definition is

$$e = \frac{\int_{t_0+\tau_1}^{t_0+\tau} (F_c(t) - mg)dt}{\int_{t_0}^{t_0+\tau_1} (F_c(t) - mg)dt} = \frac{\dot{z} - \dot{z}(t_0+\tau_1)}{\dot{z}(t_0+\tau_1) - (-(2gH)^{1/2})} = \frac{\dot{z}}{(2gH)^{1/2}}$$

EXAMPLE

A projectile is projected from a point on a smooth floor. It strikes the floor and bounces, the coefficient of restitution being e. Investigate the motion.

We introduce cartesian coordinate axes Ox and Oz so that the point of projection is at the origin O and the initial velocity is $u_0(\boldsymbol{i}\cos\theta + \boldsymbol{k}\sin\theta)$. The equation of motion of the particle of mass m representing the projectile is $m\ddot{\boldsymbol{r}} = -mg\boldsymbol{k}$ and the initial conditions are

$$\boldsymbol{r} = \boldsymbol{0} \quad \text{and} \quad \dot{\boldsymbol{r}} = u_0(\boldsymbol{i}\cos\theta + \boldsymbol{k}\sin\theta) \quad \text{at} \quad t = 0$$

Integrating with respect to time and using the initial conditions, we find that

$$\dot{\boldsymbol{r}} = u_0\cos\theta\boldsymbol{i} + (u_0\sin\theta - gt)\boldsymbol{k}$$

and

$$\boldsymbol{r} = u_0 t\cos\theta\boldsymbol{i} + (u_0 t\sin\theta - \tfrac{1}{2}gt^2)\boldsymbol{k}$$

these results being valid before the first bounce. The maximum height reached before the first bounce is $\frac{1}{2}(u_0^2/g)\sin^2\theta$ and the first bounce occurs when $t = 2(u_0/g)\sin\theta$. The site of the first bounce has position vector

$$\boldsymbol{r} = (u_0^2/g)\sin 2\theta\boldsymbol{i}$$

and the velocity just before the projectile strikes the ground is

$$u_0(\boldsymbol{i}\cos\theta - \boldsymbol{k}\sin\theta)$$

The velocity just after the projectile strikes the ground is

$$u_0(\boldsymbol{i}\cos\theta + \boldsymbol{k}e\sin\theta)$$

We can reanalyse the motion of the particle as a projectile between the first and second bounces. The maximum height reached between the first and second bounces is $\frac{1}{2}(e^2u_0^2/g)\sin^2\theta$ and the second bounce occurs at a time $2(eu_0/g)\sin\theta$ after the first bounce, at $t = (1+e)2(u_0/g)\sin\theta$. The site of the second bounce has the position vector

$$(1+e)(u_0^2/g)\sin 2\theta\boldsymbol{i}$$

and the velocities just before and just after the second bounce are

$$u_0(\boldsymbol{i}\cos\theta - \boldsymbol{k}e\sin\theta) \quad \text{and} \quad u_0(\boldsymbol{i}\cos\theta + \boldsymbol{k}e^2\sin\theta)$$

Let H_n be the maximum height reached between the $(n-1)$th and nth bounce and let R_n be the range achieved at the nth bounce. We find that

$$H_n = \tfrac{1}{2}e^{2(n-1)}(u_0^2/g)\sin^2\theta = e^{2(n-1)}H_1$$

and that

$$\begin{aligned} R_n &= (1+e+e^2+\ldots+e^{n-1})(u_0^2/g)\sin 2\theta \\ &= \{(1-e^n)/(1-e)\}(u_0^2/g)\sin 2\theta \\ &< \{1/(1-e)\}(u_0^2/g)\sin 2\theta = R_1/(1-e). \end{aligned}$$

	n	1	2	3	4	5	10
$e = 0{\cdot}3$	H_n/H_1	1·00	0·090	0·008	0·000	0·000	0·000
	R_n/R_1	1·00	1·30	1·39	1·42	1·43	1·43
$e = 0{\cdot}5$	H_n/H_1	1·00	0·250	0·063	0·016	0·004	0·000
	R_n/R_1	1·00	1·50	1·75	1·88	1·94	2·00
$e = 0{\cdot}9$	H_n/H_1	1·00	0·810	0·656	0·531	0·430	0·150
	R_n/R_1	1·00	1·90	2·71	3·44	4·10	6·52

This investigation ignores the dimensions of the projectile (e.g. a ball) and remains valid until the projectile ceases to bounce (and starts to slide on the smooth floor with speed $u_0\cos\theta$). It predicts that the projectile begins to slide at $t = \{1/(1-e)\}2(u_0/g)\sin\theta$, the projectile's distance from the point of projection being $\{1/(1-e)\}(u_0^2/g)\sin 2\theta$.

14.3 Recoil of a gun

Consider what happens when a gun is fired. There is a chemical reaction or an explosion, in which energy is released. Gases expand and give rise to a force that propels the bullet out of the barrel of the gun. The gun experiences a force equal and opposite to the force propelling the bullet. It is this force that causes the gun to recoil. Anyone firing a rifle at a shooting range will have experienced on the shoulder a fierce reaction that lasts a short time.

We shall attempt to model this situation by introducing two particles, one of mass M representing the gun, and one of mass m representing the bullet. The particles experience equal and opposite impulsive forces, the description of which is complicated. We shall not provide any information about the bullet's motion in the barrel, which depends on a precise description of the propelling force caused by the expanding gases (and on the rifling of the barrel). Suppose that the gun and the bullet are at rest initially and that the propelling force experienced by the bullet is represented by $F_c(t)\boldsymbol{i}$, where $\boldsymbol{i}$ is the unit vector associated with the x-axis. The equations of motion for the particles are

$$m\ddot{\boldsymbol{r}}_B = F_c(t)\boldsymbol{i} \quad \text{and} \quad M\ddot{\boldsymbol{r}}_G = -F_c(t)\boldsymbol{i}$$

where $\boldsymbol{r}_B = x_B\boldsymbol{i}$ and $\boldsymbol{r}_G = x_G\boldsymbol{i}$. Adding these equations and integrating with respect to time, we obtain the statement of the conservation of linear momentum of the system of two particles, namely

$$m\dot{\boldsymbol{r}}_B + M\dot{\boldsymbol{r}}_G = (m\dot{x}_B + M\dot{x}_G)\boldsymbol{i} = \boldsymbol{0}$$

It is convenient to set $\dot{x}_B = u$ and $\dot{x}_G = -U$, then

$$mu = MU$$

where u, U are the speeds when the bullet leaves the barrel at $t = \tau$. The mass of the gun is much greater than the mass of the bullet, therefore the speed of the bullet is much greater than the speed of the gun. The bullet moves in one direction and the gun moves in the opposite direction.

The impulse experienced by the bullet is

$$\mathbf{J} = \int_0^\tau F_c(t)dt\boldsymbol{i} = \int_0^\tau m\ddot{x}_B dt\boldsymbol{i} = mu\boldsymbol{i}$$

and the impulse experienced by the gun is

$$-\int_0^\tau F_c(t)dt\boldsymbol{i} = \int_0^\tau M\ddot{x}_G dt\boldsymbol{i} = -MU\boldsymbol{i} = -\mathbf{J}$$

The bullet acquires the kinetic energy $\frac{1}{2}mu^2$ and the gun acquires the kinetic energy $\frac{1}{2}MU^2$. The kinetic energy of the system, $\frac{1}{2}mu^2 + \frac{1}{2}MU^2$, represents only part of the energy released by the chemical reaction. Considerable noise and heat are generated when a gun is fired.

In this simple model we have ignored gravity and any recoil mechanism designed to dissipate the kinetic energy acquired by the gun. This section shows an application of the conservation of linear momentum of a system of particles and introduces the fundamental concept of rocket motion, which we discuss in the next chapter.

EXERCISES ON CHAPTER 14

1. Calculate the impulse $\mathbf{J} = \int_0^\tau F(t)dt$ in the three cases

(i) $\mathbf{F}(t) = F_0 \boldsymbol{i}$ $\quad t \in [0, \tau]$

(ii) $\mathbf{F}(t) = \begin{cases} \{F_0 t/\tau_0\}\boldsymbol{i} & t \in [0, \tau_0] \\ \{F_0(\tau - t)/(\tau - \tau_0)\}\boldsymbol{i} & t \in [\tau_0, \tau] \end{cases}$

(iii) $\mathbf{F}(t) = F_0\{1 - (2t/\tau - 1)^2\}\boldsymbol{i}$ $\quad t \in [0, \tau]$

where F_0 and τ_0 are constants.

2. A body of mass 3 kg acquires a speed of 0·5 m s^{-1} by means of a hammer striking it. Assuming that the duration of the impact is 0·001 s and that the magnitude of the contact force increases at a constant rate from zero to a maximum F_M and then decreases at a constant rate to zero, determine F_M.

3. Two smooth spheres S_1, S_2, having the same size and the same mass, are at rest on a horizontal table. S_1 is projected with speed u_0 along the table to have a "head-on" collision with S_2. What are their speeds after the collision if the coefficient of restitution is $\frac{1}{2}$?

4. Three smooth spheres S_1, S_2, S_3 have the same size and their masses are M, M, m. They are at rest on a horizontal table and their centres are collinear (S_2 being between S_1 and S_3). If S_1 is projected along the table to have a "head-on" collision with S_2, show that there will be two and only two collisions provided

$$m < 2eM/(1+e^2)$$

where e is the coefficient of restitution for both collisions.

5. Three perfectly elastic spheres S_1, S_2, S_3 have masses $4m$, m, $4m$ respectively. They are at rest on a horizontal table, their centres being collinear. S_2 is between S_1 and S_3. S_2 is projected with speed u_0 to have a "head-on" collision with S_3. How many collisions occur and what are the spheres' final speeds?

6. Two perfectly elastic beads slide on a fixed smooth horizontal circular hoop. Their masses are $2m$ and m. The beads are projected with speeds u_0 and $5u_0$ in opposite directions round the hoop, and the first collision takes place at A. Where does the next collision take place? Does the twenty-fifth collision take place at A?

7. Two beads B_1, B_2, having masses m and $2m$, slide on a smooth horizontal circular wire, of radius R. At a given instant B_1 is projected from a point A on the wire with speed u_0 in the anticlockwise direction, and B_2 is projected from a point diametrically opposite to A with speed $2u_0$ in the clockwise direction. How far does B_1 travel before the first collision? If the coefficient of restitution is $\frac{1}{2}$, show that B_1 travels a distance $8\pi R/3$ and B_2 travels a distance $\frac{2}{3}\pi R$ during the time interval between the first and second collisions. What are the velocities of the beads just after the second collision?

8. Two identical smooth spheres are moving on a horizontal table with uniform velocities $u_0(\boldsymbol{i}+2\boldsymbol{j})$ and $u_0(-2\boldsymbol{i}+3\boldsymbol{j})$. They collide when the line joining their centres is parallel to the direction of the vector $\boldsymbol{i}$. If the coefficient of restitution between the spheres is $\frac{1}{3}$, find the velocities of the spheres after the collision.

Show that the loss in kinetic energy is $2mu_0^2$, where m is the mass of each sphere.

9. Two perfectly elastic smooth spheres of equal mass are on a horizontal table. One is at rest before being struck obliquely by the other. Show that the directions of motion after the collision are orthogonal.

10. A body of mass m moving with velocity $u_0(2\boldsymbol{i}-\boldsymbol{j})$ collides with a second body of mass $2m$ moving with velocity $u_0(-4\boldsymbol{i}+2\boldsymbol{j})$. The two bodies adhere and move on together. Use the conservation of linear momentum for the system to determine the common velocity after the collision.

11. A motor-car of mass m was travelling north at a speed u_0. At a crossroads it was involved in an accident with a delivery van of mass $4m$, which had been travelling east. The collision caused the vehicles to lock together and skid off the road in a north-easterly direction. Estimate the speed of the delivery van before the accident.

12. A ball B strikes an identical ball which is stationary. If the coefficient of restitution between the balls is $\frac{1}{2}$, determine the maximum angle through which the path of B can be deflected.

13. A smooth ball moves at speed u_0 on a horizontal table and strikes an identical ball which is stationary on the table at a distance from a vertical cushion, the impulse on each ball being along the line of centres and perpendicular to the cushion. The coefficient of restitution for all collisions is $\frac{3}{4}$. Find the velocities of each ball after they have collided with each other on two occasions.

14. Two smooth spheres S_1 and S_2 of equal radii and of masses m, M lie on a floor between two parallel walls, the line of centres being perpendicular to the walls. S_1 is projected with speed u_0 so as to have a "head-on" collision with S_2. Show that each sphere moves off to strike its adjacent wall before a second collision between the spheres takes place provided $e > m/M$, where e is the coefficient of restitution for all collisions. Calculate the speeds of S_1 and S_2 after they have collided with each other on the second occasion, and show that they are moving in the same direction.

15. A billiard ball has an oblique collision with a cushion and moves on to collide obliquely with a cushion that is perpendicular to the first cushion. Show that the direction of the motion after the collision with the second cushion is parallel to the original direction of motion. (Ignore any frictional forces.)

16. A ball is projected downwards with speed u_0 from a height H above a floor. Show that the height of its first bounce is

$$e^2(H+u_0^2/2g)$$

where e is the coefficient of restitution associated with the ball's collision with the floor.

17. A small ball is dropped from a height H above a table. Show that it will continue to bounce for a time

$$\left(\frac{1+e}{1-e}\right)\left(\frac{2H}{g}\right)^{1/2}$$

where e is the coefficient of restitution associated with every collision. What distance is covered in that time?

18. A ball of mass m strikes a smooth floor. The velocity of the ball just before the collision has magnitude u_0 and its direction makes an angle θ with the horizontal. The coefficient of restitution associated with the ball's collision with the floor is e. Find the loss in the kinetic enrgy due to the collision.

19. A ball starts from rest and slides a distance d down a smooth plane inclined at an angle α to the horizontal before striking a smooth horizontal plane at the foot of the inclined plane. The coefficient of restitution between the ball and the horizontal plane is e. Show that the range of the ball's first bounce on the horizontal plane is $4ed \sin^2 \alpha \cos \alpha$.

20. The ceiling of a room is at a height H above the floor. A ball is projected, from a point on the floor, with speed $4(gH)^{1/2}$ at an inclination $\frac{1}{6}\pi$ with the horizontal. It hits the ceiling and the range of its first bounce on the floor is R. Assume that the contact between the ball and the ceiling is smooth and that the coefficient of restitution between the ball and the ceiling is $\frac{1}{2}$. Show that $R > 5H$.

21. A ball is projected, from a point on the floor, with speed $2(gd)^{1/2}$ at an inclination $\frac{1}{4}\pi$ to the horizontal. It strikes a fixed vertical wall, whose plane is perpendicular to the plane of motion and is a distance d from the point of projection. Assume that the contact between the ball and the wall is smooth. Show that the ball strikes the floor between the wall and the point of projection if the coefficient of restitution between the ball and the wall is less than $\frac{1}{3}$.

22. A and B are fixed points in a horizontal plane and are separated by a distance $2R$. Initially two spherical balls, S_1 and S_2, each of mass m and of radius R, hang vertically from A and B by means of identical light inextensible strings AC and BD. The ball S_1 is then raised so that the string AC is taut and is turned through an angle $\frac{1}{2}\pi$ radians in the vertical plane through A and B. It is released from rest. The ball S_2 rises after the collision until the string BD has turned through an angle α. Show that the coefficient of restitution between the balls is

$$2(1-\cos \alpha)^{1/2}-1$$

Evaluate the coefficient when α has the value (i) 1·0 radian, (ii) 1·2 radians, (iii) 1·4 radians.

23. A bead of mass $2m$ rests at the highest point of a smooth vertical circular wire of radius R and a bead of mass m is at the lowest point. The upper bead is slightly disturbed and slides down the wire to collide with the lower bead. The coefficient of restitution between the beads is $\frac{1}{4}$. Show that the bead of mass m and the bead of mass $2m$ rise to heights $\frac{25}{18}R$ and $\frac{49}{72}R$ above the lowest point of the wire before coming to rest. What is the loss in energy at this first collision?

24. A bullet is fired horizontally into the bob of a simple pendulum of length one metre. It becomes embedded in the bob and a maximum deflection of $\frac{1}{3}\pi$ radians results. The mass of the bullet is 0·013 kg and the mass of the bob is 0·75 kg. Calculate the initial speed of the bullet. (Assume that the bullet comes to rest in the bob before the bob and the bullet have swung through an appreciable angle away from the vertical.)

25. A particle of mass m is at rest on a smooth table and is attached to a fixed point O of the table by means of a spring of natural length l and stiffness k. At $t = 0$ the spring is stretched to a length $l+d < 2l$ and the particle is released from rest. At $t = t_0$ the particle is moving away from O and its distance from O is $l+d_0$. Find the particle's speed at $t = t_0$.

During the time interval $[t_0, t_0+\tau]$ a constant force, whose magnitude is F and whose direction is away from O along the line of spring, is applied to the particle. Find the amplitude of the simple harmonic motion when $t_0+\tau < t$. Show that when $F \to \infty$ and $\tau \to 0$ so that $F\tau$ has a finite value J, this amplitude tends to

$$\left[d_0^2+\left\{\frac{J}{(mk)^{1/2}}+(d^2-d_0^2)^{1/2}\right\}^2\right]^{1/2}$$

Show that the limiting value of the amplitude is consistent with the amplitude obtained when an instantaneous impulse is applied at $t = t_0$, the magnitude of the impulse being J and the direction being away from O along the line of the spring. (An instantaneous impulse provides a change in velocity without a change in position.)

26. Two particles of masses M and m are connected by an elastic string of natural length l and modulus λ. They are at rest on a smooth table and the distance between them is l. The particle of mass M receives an instantaneous impulse of magnitude J in a direction away from the other particle. Show that the greatest extension of the string in the subsequent motion is

$$J\{ml/\lambda M(M+m)\}^{1/2}$$

27. Two particles each of mass m are connected by an elastic string of natural length l and modulus λ. They are placed on a smooth table and the string is just taut. Equal and opposite instantaneous impulses of magnitude J are simultaneously applied to the particles along the line of the string so as to extend the string. Find the greatest extension of the string and the time taken to attain it.

28. A body of mass $4m$ is moving on a smooth table with uniform velocity, the magnitude of which is u_0. Without the action of any external force, an internal explosion breaks the body into two fragments, and a fragment of mass $3m$ continues to move in the original direction but with a speed $2u_0$. Find the velocity of the fragment of mass m and calculate the kinetic energy generated by the explosion.

Verify that at any time after the explosion the centre of mass of the two fragments is in the position that the original body would have reached had there not been an explosion.

29. A gun of mass M discharges a shell of mass m in a horizontal direction. The kinetic energy generated by the explosion is such as would be sufficient to project the shell vertically to a height H. Show that the speed with which the gun begins to recoil is $\{2m^2gH/M(M+m)\}^{1/2}$.

30. A projectile of mass $5m$ is projected from a point O and moves under the action of the uniform gravitational force. During its motion the projectile is split by an internal explosion into two fragments of masses m and $4m$. Immediately after the explosion the direction of the velocity of the fragment of mass $4m$ is unaltered, and the magnitude is increased. If E is the kinetic energy generated by the explosion and u_0 is the speed of the projectile immediately before the explosion, find the speed of each fragment immediately after the explosion. Is it possible for the fragment of mass m to return to O in the case when the projectile's trajectory before the explosion is not vertical?

Rocket Motion

15

15.1 Introduction

Rockets are used in many different areas, for example firework displays, signalling, carrying a line to a ship in distress, warfare and space exploration. We wish to discuss their motion. The new feature introduced in this chapter is a time-varying mass. The fundamental characteristic of a rocket engine is that a rocket engine requires no atmosphere (cf. a propeller engine or a jet engine). A chemical reaction converts a liquid or solid fuel into a gas which is emitted at a very high velocity. The gas emitted from the engine moves in one direction, and the engine and the attached craft move in the opposite direction, this phenomenon being similar to that which we encountered in the gun-bullet problem in the previous chapter. At any instant the mass of the rocket consists of the mass of the payload (e.g. the communications satellite to be put into orbit), the mass of the structure, and the mass of the unused fuel. The fuel is being used up during a burn, and the mass of the rocket is being diminished. We have to take account of the time-varying mass, because the mass of the fuel may be nine-tenths of the mass of the rocket at the start of the ignition process. We note that the mass of the system, that is the rocket and the emitted gas, is constant.

Our statement of Newton's Laws of Motion in chapter 3 apply to particles whose masses are independent of time. We have discussed many applications in the subsequent chapters. Our present task is new. It is to derive an equation governing the motion of a body that has a mass dependent on time. More precisely we have to investigate the motion of a body whose mass is varying continuously with time. As a prelude we shall consider some problems in which the mass of a body varies discontinuously with time. Then by examining our results and using a limiting process, we shall derive the equation governing the motion of a rocket.

15.2 Discontinuous increase of mass

We shall commence by considering the motion of a body that experiences a number of collisions, in each of which a once stationary body adheres to the moving body. Suppose a body of mass M is gliding along a smooth horizontal track with speed U and there are a number of bodies situated at rest on the track in front of the moving body. Let the x-axis represent the track, and let the motion be in the direction of x increasing. Suppose that there are n stationary particles having masses, $m_1, m_2, m_3, \ldots, m_n$ and having x-coordinates $x_1, x_2, x_3, \ldots, x_n$. Let X be the x-coordinate of the particle representing the moving body.

Before the first collision

$$M\ddot{X}(t) = 0, \quad \dot{X}(t) = U \quad \text{and} \quad X(t) = Ut$$

During the first collision, we have the equations governing the motion of the two particles involved in the collision, namely

$$M\ddot{X}(t) = -F_c(t) \quad \text{and} \quad m_1\ddot{x}_1(t) = F_c(t)$$

where F_c represents the contact force associated with the collision. Adding these equations and integrating with respect to time, we obtain the statement of the conservation of linear momentum of the system, namely

$$(M+m_1)\dot{X}_1 = MU$$

Here we have used the fact that the bodies adhere, and we have let $\dot{X}$ denote the velocity of the composite body after the first collision.

Applying these arguments to each collision in turn, we see that the velocity of the composite body after each collision is obtainable from the conservation of linear momentum. Thus we have

$$\begin{aligned}
(M+m_1+m_2)\dot{X}_2 &= (M+m_1)\dot{X}_1 \\
(M+m_1+m_2+m_3)\dot{X}_3 &= (M+m_1+m_2)\dot{X}_2 \\
&\vdots \\
(M+m_1+m_2+\ldots+m_n)\dot{X}_n &= (M+m_1+m_2+\ldots+m_{n-1})\dot{X}_{n-1}
\end{aligned}$$

The linear momentum of the composite body at any instant equals MU, the initial linear momentum.

It is convenient to think of the first collision being during the interval (t_0, t_1), the second collision during $(t_1, t_2), \ldots$ and the nth collision during (t_{n-1}, t_n). If we assume that the collisions are instantaneous and occur when $t = t_{c1}, t_{c2}, t_{c3}, \ldots, t_{cn}$, we can determine X, the coordinate associated with the composite body whose mass is increasing discontinuously at each collision. We find that

$$X(t) = \begin{cases} Ut & t \in [0, t_{c1}) \\ Ut_{c1} = x_1 & t = t_{c1} \\ x_1 + \dot{X}_1(t - t_{c1}) & t \in (t_{c1}, t_{c2}) \\ x_1 + \dot{X}_1(t_{c2} - t_{c1}) = x_2 & t = t_{c2} \\ x_2 + \dot{X}_2(t - t_{c2}) & t \in (t_{c2}, t_{c3}) \\ x_2 + \dot{X}_2(t_{c3} - t_{c2}) = x_3 & t = t_{c3} \end{cases}$$

and so on. The graph of X against t is a piecewise continuous straight line, the slope decreasing discontinuously at $t = t_{c1}, t_{c2}, t_{c3}, \ldots, t_{cn}$.

Let us re-examine this problem when a force of constant magnitude F per unit mass is applied to the moving body. We shall assume that the collisions occur instantaneously. Before the first collision

$$M\ddot{X}(t) = MF, \quad \dot{X}(t) = U + Ft \quad \text{and} \quad X(t) = Ut + \tfrac{1}{2}Ft^2$$

The first collision occurs when $t = t_{c1}$ and $X(t_{c1}) = Ut_{c1} + \frac{1}{2}Ft_{c1}^2 = x_1$. The conservation of linear momentum is applicable to the instantaneous collision process. Thus we find that

$$(M + m_1)\dot{X}_1 = M(U + Ft_{c1})$$

where $\dot{X}_1$ is the velocity of the composite body just after the first collision, and $U + Ft_{c1}$ is the velocity just before the first collision. The equation governing the motion of the composite body between the first and second collisions is

$$(M + m_1)\ddot{X}(t) = (M + m_1)F \quad t \in (t_{c1}, t_{c2})$$

Hence for $t \in (t_{c1}, t_{c2})$

$$\dot{X}(t) = \dot{X}_1 + F(t - t_{c1}) \quad \text{and} \quad X(t) = x_1 + \dot{X}_1(t - t_{c1}) + \tfrac{1}{2}F(t - t_{c1})^2$$

The second collision occurs when $t = t_{c2}$ and

$$X(t_{c2}) = x_1 + \dot{X}_1(t_{c2} - t_{c1}) + \tfrac{1}{2}F(t_{c2} - t_{c1})^2 = x_2$$

It follows that

$$\begin{aligned} (M + m_1 + m_2)\dot{X}_2 &= (M + m_1)\{\dot{X}_1 + F(t_{c2} - t_{c1})\} \\ &= M(U + Ft_{c1}) + (M + m_1)F(t_{c2} - t_{c1}) \\ &= M(U + Ft_{c2}) + m_1 F(t_{c2} - t_{c1}) \end{aligned}$$

and that for $t \in (t_{c2}, t_{c3})$

$$\begin{aligned} (M + m_1 + m_2)\ddot{X}(t) &= (M + m_1 + m_2)F \\ \dot{X}(t) &= \dot{X}_2 + F(t - t_{c2}) \end{aligned}$$

and

$$X(t) = x_2 + \dot{X}_2(t - t_{c2}) + \tfrac{1}{2}F(t - t_{c2})^2$$

The third collision occurs when $t = t_{c3}$ and

$$X(t_{c3}) = x_2 + \dot{X}_2(t_{c3} - t_{c2}) + \tfrac{1}{2}F(t_{c3} - t_{c2})^2 = x_3$$

A further application of the conservation of linear momentum leads to

$$\begin{aligned}(M + m_1 + m_2 + m_3)\dot{X}_3 &= (M + m_1 + m_2)\{\dot{X}_2 + F(t_{c3} - t_{c2})\} \\ &= M(U + Ft_{c2}) + m_1 F(t_{c2} - t_{c1}) \\ &\quad + (M + m_1 + m_2)F(t_{c3} - t_{c2}) \\ &= M(U + Ft_{c3}) + m_1 F(t_{c3} - t_{c1}) + m_2 F(t_{c3} - t_{c2})\end{aligned}$$

The pattern is clear. The graph of X against t consists of continuous parabolic arcs, the slope being discontinuous at $t = t_{c1}, t_{c2}, t_{c3}, \ldots, t_{cn}$.

15.3 Discontinuous decrease of mass

Suppose a composite body moves and experiences a number of internal explosions, the effect of each explosion being the ejection of a fragment with a given velocity relative to the composite body. Initially the composite body of mass M is moving along a smooth horizontal track with speed U. Let the x-axis represent the track, and let the x-coordinate of the particle representing the composite body be X.

Before the first explosion

$$M\ddot{X}(t) = 0, \quad \dot{X}(t) = U \quad \text{and} \quad X(t) = Ut$$

During the first explosion, the equations governing the motion of the two particles resulting after the explosion are

$$(M - m_1)\ddot{X}(t) = F_c(t) \quad \text{and} \quad m_1\ddot{x}(t) = -F_c(t)$$

where F_c represents the contact force associated with the explosion. Hence the appropriate statement of the conservation of linear momentum of the system of two particles (representing the composite body and the first fragment) is

$$(M - m_1)\dot{X}_1 + m_1(\dot{X}_1 - c) = (M - m_1)U + m_1 U$$

i.e.

$$M\dot{X}_1 = MU + m_1 c$$

where $\dot{X}_1$ is the velocity of the composite body after the first fragment of mass m_1 has been ejected with velocity $-c$ relative to the composite body.

Repeating this argument for each ejection we find that

$$
\begin{aligned}
(M-m_1)\dot{X}_2 &= (M-m_1)\dot{X}_1+m_2c \\
&= MU+m_1(c-\dot{X}_1)+m_2c \\
(M-m_1-m_2)\dot{X}_3 &= (M-m_1-m_2)\dot{X}_2+m_3c \\
&= MU+m_1(c-\dot{X}_1)+m_2(c-\dot{X}_2)+m_3c \\
&\ \ \vdots \\
(M-m_1-m_2-\ldots-m_{n-1})\dot{X}_n &= (M-m_1-m_2-\ldots-m_{n-1})\dot{X}_{n-1}+m_n c \\
&= MU+m_1(c-\dot{X}_1)+\ldots \\
&\quad +m_{n-1}(c-\dot{X}_{n-1})+m_n c
\end{aligned}
$$

The velocity of the composite body increases discontinuously provided $c > 0$ and the graph of X against t is a piecewise continuous straight line.

We shall follow the presentation in the previous section and re-examine the problem when a force of constant magnitude F per unit mass is applied to the composite body. We shall assume that the explosions occur instantaneously when $t = t_{e1}, t_{e2}, \ldots, t_{en}$ and $X = X_1, X_2, \ldots, X_n$. Before the first explosion

$$M\ddot{X}(t) = MF, \quad \dot{X}(t) = U+Ft \quad \text{and} \quad X(t) = Ut+\tfrac{1}{2}Ft^2$$

The first explosion occurs when $t = t_{e1}$ and $X(t_{e1}) = Ut_{e1}+\frac{1}{2}Ft_{e1} = X_1$. The conservation of linear momentum is applicable to the instantaneous explosion process. This leads to

$$M\dot{X}_1 = M(U+Ft_{e1})+m_1c$$

where $\dot{X}_1$ is the velocity of the composite body just after the first explosion, and $U+Ft_{e1}$ is the velocity just before the first explosion. The equation governing the motion of the composite body between the first and second explosion is

$$(M-m_1)\ddot{X}(t) = (M-m_1)F \quad t \in (t_{e1}, t_{e2})$$

Therefore for $t \in (t_{e1}, t_{e2})$

$$\dot{X}(t) = \dot{X}_1+F(t-t_{e1})$$

and

$$X(t) = X_1+\dot{X}_1(t-t_{e1})+\tfrac{1}{2}F(t-t_{e1})^2$$

The second explosion occurs when $t = t_{e2}$ and

$$X(t_{e2}) = X_1+\dot{X}_1(t_{e2}-t_{e1})+\tfrac{1}{2}F(t_{e2}-t_{e1})^2 = X_2$$

An application of the conservation of linear momentum gives

$$(M-m_1)\dot{X}_2 = (M-m)\{\dot{X}_1+F(t_{e2}-t_{e1})\}+m_2c$$
$$= M(U+Ft_{e2})+m_1\{c-\dot{X}_1-F(t_{e2}-t_{e1})\}+m_2c$$

Hence for $t \in (t_{e2}, t_{e3})$

$$(M-m_1-m_2)\ddot{X}(t) = (M-m_1-m_2)F$$
$$\dot{X}_1(t) = \dot{X}_2+F(t-t_{e2})$$

and

$$X(t) = X_2+\dot{X}_2(t-t_{e2})+\tfrac{1}{2}F(t-t_{e2})^2$$

The third explosion occurs when $t = t_{e3}$ and

$$X(t_{e3}) = X_2+\dot{X}_2(t_{e3}-t_{e2})+\tfrac{1}{2}F(t_{e3}-t_{e2})^2 = X_3$$

A further application of the conservation of linear momentum leads to

$$(M-m_1-m_2)\dot{X}_3 = (M-m_1-m_2)\{\dot{X}_2+F(t_{e3}-t_{e2})\}+m_3c$$
$$= M(U+Ft_{e3})+m_1\{c-\dot{X}_1-F(t_{e3}-t_{e1})\}$$
$$+m_2\{c-\dot{X}_2-F(t_{e3}-t_{e2})\}+m_3c$$

Without proceeding any further we recognize that the graph of X against t consists of continuous parabolic arcs, the slope being discontinuous at $t = t_{e1}, t_{e2}, t_{e3}, \ldots, t_{en}$.

15.4 Continuous variation of mass

In the days of steam, locomotives pulling express trains used to pick up water from a trough situated between the rails. The locomotive was in motion, its mass was increasing continuously during the replenishing process, and the water was at rest in the trough. This is a continuous analogue of the problems we discussed in Section 15.2.

At time t the mass of the composite body is $M(t)$ and the velocity of the composite body is $U(t)$. In our problems in Section 15.2 n collisions took place in the time interval $[t_0, t_n]$. We shall set $t_n = t_0+\Delta t$.

When there is no external force, we have

$$M(t_0) = M \qquad U(t_0) = U$$
$$M(t_n) = M+m_1+m_2+\ldots+m_n \qquad U(t_n) = \dot{X}_n$$

and

$$M(t_0+\Delta t)U(t_0+\Delta t) = M(t_n)U(t_n)$$
$$= M(t_0)U(t_0)$$

i.e.

$$M(t_0)\{U(t_0+\Delta t)-U(t_0)\}+\{M(t_0+\Delta t)-M(t_0)\}U(t_0+\Delta t) = 0$$

Dividing by Δt and taking the limit as Δt tends to zero, we obtain the result

$$M(t_0)\frac{dU(t)}{dt}\bigg|_{t=t_0} + \frac{dM(t)}{dt}\bigg|_{t=t_0} U(t_0) = 0$$

This is true for any instant t_0. Therefore the differential equation governing the motion is

$$M(t)\frac{dU(t)}{dt} + \frac{dM(t)}{dt}U(t) = \frac{d}{dt}\{M(t)U(t)\} = 0$$

This is appropriate when the material to be picked up by the moving body is stationary and there is no external force in the direction of motion.

When a force of constant magnitude F per unit mass is applied in the direction of motion, we have to modify the above analysis. We note that

$$M(t_0) = M \qquad U(t_0) = U + Ft_0$$

and

$$M(t_n) = M + m_1 + m_2 + \ldots + m_n \quad U(t_n) = \dot{X}_n + F(t_n - t_{cn})$$

It follows from Section 15.2 that

$$\begin{aligned} M(t_0+\Delta t)U(t_0+\Delta t) &= M(t_n)U(t_n) \\ &= M(t_n)\dot{X}_n + M(t_n)F(t_n - t_{cn}) \\ &= M(t_0)(U+Ft_{cn}) + m_1F(t_{cn}-t_{c1}) + m_2F(t_{cn}-t_{c2}) \\ &\quad + \ldots + m_{n-1}F(t_{cn}-t_{c(n-1)}) + M(t_n)F(t_n-t_{cn}) \\ &= M(t_0)\{U(t_0)+F\Delta t\} + m_1F(t_0+\Delta t - t_{c1}) \\ &\quad + m_2F(t_0+\Delta t-t_{c2}) + \ldots + m_nF(t_0+\Delta t - t_{cn}) \end{aligned}$$

i.e.

$$\begin{aligned} M(t_0)\{U(t_0+\Delta t) - U(t_0)\} + \{M(t_0+\Delta t) - M(t_0)\}U(t_0+\Delta t) - M(t_0)F\Delta t \\ = m_1F(t_0+\Delta t-t_{c1}) + m_2F(t_0+\Delta t - t_{c2}) + \ldots + m_nF(t_0+\Delta t-t_{cn}) \end{aligned}$$

The terms on the right-hand side play no part in the limiting process. We can show that this is plausible by considering the special case in which

$$t_{ci} = t_0 + \frac{i\Delta t}{n} - \frac{\Delta t}{2n} \quad \text{and} \quad m_i = \frac{M(t_0+\Delta t) - M(t_0)}{n} \quad (i = 1, 2, \ldots, n)$$

In this special case the right-hand side equals

$$\left\{\frac{M(t_0+\Delta t)-M(t_0)}{n}\right\}F\left\{\left(1-\frac{1}{n}+\frac{1}{2n}\right)+\left(1-\frac{2}{n}+\frac{1}{2n}\right)+\ldots + \left(1-\frac{n}{n}+\frac{1}{2n}\right)\right\}\Delta t$$

$$= \Delta t\{M(t_0+\Delta t)-M(t_0)\}\, F\frac{1}{n}\left\{\frac{n}{2}\left(1-\frac{1}{n}\right)+\frac{1}{2}\right\}$$

$$= \tfrac{1}{2}\Delta t\{M(t_0+\Delta t)-M(t_0)\}F$$

Thus we find that the differential equation governing the motion is

$$M(t)\frac{dU(t)}{dt}+\frac{dM(t)}{dt}U(t)-M(t)F=0$$

i.e.

$$\frac{d}{dt}\{M(t)U(t)\}=M(t)F$$

EXAMPLE

A spherical raindrop falls under the influence of gravity through a stationary cloud. The increase in its volume per unit time is equal to α times its surface area. If at $t = 0$ the raindrop is at rest and has radius r_0, find the velocity acquired and the distance fallen in time t.

We introduce a z-axis so that the plane $z = 0$ represents the surface of the Earth and the direction of z increasing is vertically upwards. At $t = 0$ the z-coordinate of the centre of the raindrop is H.

At time t, the raindrop has radius $r(t)$, surface area $S(t)$, volume $V(t)$ and mass $M(t)$, where

$$S(t)=4\pi r^2(t),\quad V(t)=\tfrac{4}{3}\pi r^3(t),\quad M(t)=\rho_0 V(t)$$

and ρ_0 is the constant mass per unit volume (N.B. ρ_0 is called the *density* of the raindrop). Using the information that

$$\frac{dV(t)}{dt}=\alpha S(t)$$

we see that $dr(t)/dt = \alpha$. Hence $r(t) = r_0+\alpha t$ and

$$M(t)=\tfrac{4}{3}\pi\rho_0(r_0+\alpha t)^3$$

The equation governing the raindrop's motion through the stationary cloud is

$$\frac{d}{dt}\left\{M(t)\frac{dz(t)}{dt}\right\}=-M(t)g$$

Substituting for $M(t)$ and integrating with respect to time, we find that

$$M(t)\frac{dz(t)}{dt}=-\frac{g}{4\alpha}M(t)\,(r_0+\alpha t)+A$$

where

$$0=-gM(0)r_0/4\alpha+A$$

Thus

$$\frac{dz(t)}{dt}=-\frac{g}{4\alpha}\left\{(r_0+\alpha t)-\frac{r_0^4}{(r_0+\alpha t)^3}\right\}$$

It follows that

$$z(t) = H - \frac{g}{4\alpha^2}\left\{\tfrac{1}{2}(r_0+\alpha t)^2 + \tfrac{1}{2}\frac{r_0^4}{(r_0+\alpha t)^2}\right\} + \frac{g r_0^2}{4\alpha^2}$$

and the distance fallen in time t is

$$H - z(t) = \frac{g}{8\alpha^2}\left\{(r_0+\alpha t) - \frac{r_0^2}{(r_0+\alpha t)}\right\}^2$$

Let us derive the equation governing the motion of a rocket subject to (i) no external force and (ii) a force of constant magnitude per unit mass applied in the direction of motion. In the previous section we discussed the discontinuous analogues in which n ejections of fragments took place in the time interval $[t_0, t_n]$.

When there is no external force, we have

$$M(t_0) = M \qquad U(t_0) = U$$
$$M(t_n) = M - m_1 - m_2 - \ldots - m_n \qquad U(t_n) = \dot{X}_n$$

and

$$\begin{aligned} M(t_0+\Delta t)U(t_0+\Delta t) &= M(t_n)U(t_n) \\ &= M(t_0)U(t_0) + m_1(c-\dot{X}_1) + m_2(c-\dot{X}_2) + \ldots \\ &\quad + m_n(c-\dot{X}_n) \end{aligned}$$

i.e.

$$\begin{aligned} M(t_0)\{U(t_0+\Delta t) - U(t_0)\} & \\ + \{M(t_0+\Delta t) - M(t_0)\}&\{U(t_0+\Delta t) + c - U(t_0+\Delta t)\} \\ = m_1(\dot{X}_n - \dot{X}_1) &+ m_2(\dot{X}_n - \dot{X}_2) + \ldots + m_{n-1}(\dot{X}_n - \dot{X}_{n-1}) \end{aligned}$$

The terms on the right-hand side have the same order as

$$\{M(t_0+\Delta t) - M(t_0)\}\{U(t_0+\Delta t) - U(t_0)\}$$

and play no part in the limiting process. Thus we obtain the equation governing the motion of a rocket subject to no external force

$$M(t)\frac{dU(t)}{dt} + c\frac{dM(t)}{dt} = 0$$

i.e.

$$\frac{d}{dt}\{M(t)U(t)\} = \frac{dM(t)}{dt}\{U(t) - c\}$$

We note that $U(t) - c$ is the velocity of the ejected gas at time t relative to the inertial frame of reference, and that $U(t)$ and c are both positive (or both negative).

When there is a constant force of magnitude F per unit mass applied in the direction of motion, we note that

$$M(t_0) = M \qquad U(t_0) = U + Ft_0$$
$$M(t_n) = M - m_1 - m_2 - \ldots - m_n \quad U(t_n) = \dot{X}_n + F(t_n - t_{en})$$

and

$$M(t_0 + \Delta t)U(t_0 + \Delta t) = M(t_n)U(t_n)$$
$$= M(t_n)\dot{X}_n + M(t_n)F(t_n - t_{en})$$
$$= M(t_0)(U + Ft_{en}) + m_1\{c - \dot{X}_1 - F(t_{en} - t_{e1})\}$$
$$+ m_2\{c - \dot{X}_2 - F(t_{en} - t_{e2})\} + \ldots + m_n\{c - \dot{X}_n\}$$
$$+ M(t_n)F(t_n - t_{en})$$
$$= M(t_0)\{U(t_0) + F\Delta t\} + m_1\{c - \dot{X}_1 - F(t_0 + \Delta t - t_{e1})\}$$
$$+ m_2\{c - \dot{X}_2 - F(t_0 + \Delta t - t_{e2})\} + \ldots + m_n\{c - \dot{X}_n - F(t_0 + \Delta t - t_{en})\}$$

i.e.

$$M(t_0)\{U(t_0 + \Delta t) - U(t_0)\} + \{M(t_0 + \Delta t) - M(t_0)\}$$
$$\times \{U(t_0 + \Delta t) + c - U(t_0 + \Delta t)\} - M(t_0)F\Delta t$$
$$= m_1\{\dot{X}_n - \dot{X}_1 - F(t_{en} - t_{e1})\} + m_2\{\dot{X}_n - \dot{X}_2 - F(t_{en} - t_{e2})\}$$
$$+ \ldots + m_{n-1}\{\dot{X}_n - \dot{X}_{n-1} - F(t_{en} - t_{e(n-1)})\}$$

Applying the limiting process, we find that the terms on the right-hand side make no contribution (cf. our comments about previous right-hand sides) and that the required equation is

$$M(t)\frac{dU(t)}{dt} + c\frac{dM(t)}{dt} - M(t)F = 0$$

i.e.

$$\frac{d}{dt}\{M(t)U(t)\} = \frac{dM(t)}{dt}\{U(t) - c\} + M(t)F$$

We shall be able to use this differential equation to analyse the motion of a rocket in a uniform gravitational field.

We wish to present a simplified derivation of the equation governing the motion of a rocket experiencing a force of constant magnitude F per unit mass. What follows is our previous derivation with n set equal to one.

We consider a single instantaneous ejection at $t = t_{e1}$, where $t_0 < t_{e1}$

$< t_0+\Delta t$. Before the ejection, the body of mass $M(t_0)$ has the equation of motion

$$M(t_0)\ddot{X}(t) = M(t_0)F$$

and its velocity is $\dot{X}(t) = U(t_0)+F(t-t_0)$.

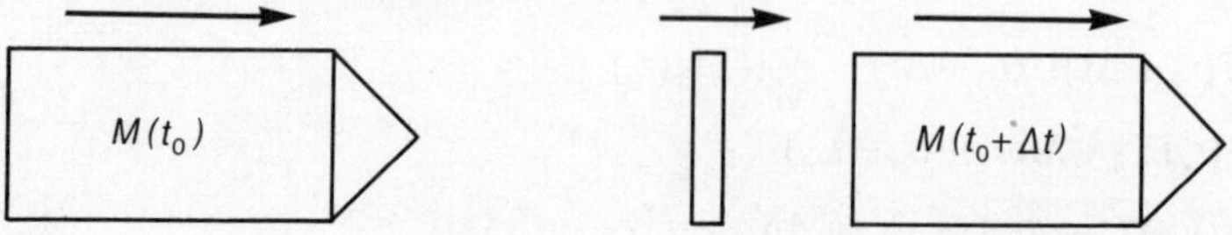

The conservation of linear momentum applies to the instantaneous ejection of a fragment of mass $M(t_0)-M(t_0+\Delta t)$ with velocity $-c$ relative to the body. Thus we have

$$M(t_0+\Delta t)\dot{X}_1+\{M(t_0)-M(t_0+\Delta t)\}(\dot{X}_1-c) = M(t_0)\{U(t_0)+F(t_{e1}-t_0)\}$$

i.e.

$$M(t_0)\dot{X}_1 = M(t_0)\{U(t_0)+F(t_{e1}-t_0)\}+\{M(t_0)-M(t_0+\Delta t)\}c$$

After the ejection, the body of mass $M(t_0+\Delta t)$ has the equation of motion

$$M(t_0+\Delta t)\ddot{X}(t) = M(t_0+\Delta t)F$$

and its velocity is $\dot{X}(t) = \dot{X}_1+F(t-t_{e1})$. The change in linear momentum during the time interval $[t_0, t_0+\Delta t]$ is

$$\begin{aligned} &M(t_0+\Delta t)U(t_0+\Delta t)-M(t_0)U(t_0)\\ &\quad = M(t_0+\Delta t)\{\dot{X}_1+F(t_0+\Delta t-t_{e1})\}-M(t_0)U(t_0)\\ &\quad = M(t_0+\Delta t)\left\{U(t_0)+F(t_{e1}-t_0)+c-\frac{M(t_0+\Delta t)}{M(t_0)}c+F(t_0+\Delta t-t_{e1})\right\}\\ &\qquad - M(t_0)U(t_0)\\ &\quad = \{M(t_0+\Delta t)-M(t_0)\}\left\{U(t_0)-\frac{M(t_0+\Delta t)}{M(t_0)}c\right\}+M(t_0+\Delta t)F\Delta t \end{aligned}$$

Rearranging this relation we find that

$$\begin{aligned} &M(t_0)\{U(t_0+\Delta t)-U(t_0)\}+\{M(t_0+\Delta t)-M(t_0)\}\\ &\qquad\times\left\{U(t_0+\Delta t)-U(t_0)+\frac{M(t_0+\Delta t)}{M(t_0)}c\right\} = M(t_0+\Delta t)F\Delta t \end{aligned}$$

Dividing by Δt and letting Δt tend to zero, we obtain the differential equation

$$M(t)\frac{dU(t)}{dt}+c\frac{dM(t)}{dt}=M(t)F$$

at $t=t_0$. We shall attempt to solve this equation in the next section.

Before leaving this section let us comment on the statement that a fragment is ejected instantaneously with velocity $-c$ relative to the body. We have interpreted this to mean that the velocity of the fragment immediately after the injection is $\dot{X}_1-c$, where $\dot{X}_1$ is the velocity of the body immediately after the ejection (see figure). There is some ambiguity in the statement of the fragment's velocity. One might interpret the statement to mean that the velocity of the fragment immediately after the ejection is $U(t_0)+F(t_{e1}-t_0)-c$, where $U(t_0)+F(t_{e1}-t_0)$ is the velocity of the body (and the fragment) immediately before the ejection. Then the conservation of linear momentum applied to the instantaneous ejection gives

$$\begin{aligned}M(t_0+\Delta t)\dot{X}_1+\{M(t_0)-M(t_0+\Delta t)\}\,\{U(t_0)+F(t_{e1}-t_0)-c\}\\ =M(t_0)\{U(t_0)+F(t_{e1}-t_0)\}\end{aligned}$$

i.e.

$$M(t_0+\Delta t)\dot{X}_1=M(t_0+\Delta t)\{U(t_0)+F(t_{e1}-t_0)\}+\{M(t_0)-M(t_0+\Delta t)\}c$$

and the change in linear momentum during the time interval $[t_0,t_0+\Delta t]$ is

$$\begin{aligned}&M(t_0+\Delta t)U(t_0+\Delta t)-M(t_0)U(t_0)\\ &\quad=M(t_0+\Delta t)\{\dot{X}_1+F(t_0+\Delta t-t_{e1})\}-M(t_0)U(t_0)\\ &\quad=M(t_0+\Delta t)\,\{U(t_0)+F\Delta t\}+\{M(t_0)-M(t_0+\Delta t)\}c-M(t_0)U(t_0)\end{aligned}$$

A suitable rearrangement is

$$\begin{aligned}M(t_0)\,\{U(t_0+\Delta t)-U(t_0)\}+\{M(t_0+\Delta t)-M(t_0)\}\\ \times\{U(t_0+\Delta t)-U(t_0)+c\}=M(t_0+\Delta t)F\Delta t\end{aligned}$$

and the differential equation resulting from the limiting process is

$$M(t)\frac{dU(t)}{dt}+c\frac{dM(t)}{dt}=M(t)F$$

which we obtained earlier.

EXAMPLE

A spaceship S of mass M is moving with velocity **U** under the action of no external forces. In order to alter the direction of motion, an instantaneous rocket burn takes place, during which gas of mass m is ejected with velocity $\mathbf{U}+\boldsymbol{u}$, the direction of $\boldsymbol{u}$ being inclined at an angle α to the direction of $\mathbf{U}$. Through what angle is the direction of the spaceship deviated?

Suppose that the mass of the spaceship is $M-m$ and the velocity of the spaceship is $\mathbf{V}$ after the ejection. The conservation of linear momentum gives

$$(M-m)\mathbf{V}+m(\mathbf{U}+\boldsymbol{u}) = M\mathbf{U}$$

i.e.

$$(M-m)\mathbf{V} = (M-m)\mathbf{U}-m\boldsymbol{u}$$

Introducing cartesian coordinate axes, relative to which the velocities are

$$\mathbf{U} = U\boldsymbol{i}, \quad \boldsymbol{u} = u(\boldsymbol{i}\cos\alpha+\boldsymbol{j}\sin\alpha), \quad \mathbf{V} = V_1\boldsymbol{i}+V_2\boldsymbol{j}$$

we obtain the two scalar equations

$$(M-m)V_1 = (M-m)U-mu\cos\alpha \quad \text{and} \quad (M-m)V_2 = -mu\sin\alpha$$

The direction of the spaceship has been turned through an angle ϕ, where

$$\tan\phi = \frac{V_2}{V_1} = \frac{-mu\sin\alpha}{(M-m)U-mu\cos\alpha}$$

The new speed of the spaceship is $(V_1^2+V_2^2)^{1/2}$, which equals

$$\left\{U^2-\frac{2m}{M-m}Uu\cos\alpha+\frac{m^2}{(M-m)^2}u^2\right\}^{1/2}$$

i.e.

$$|\mathbf{V}| = \left\{\left(\mathbf{U}-\frac{m}{M-m}\boldsymbol{u}\right).\left(\mathbf{U}-\frac{m}{M-m}\boldsymbol{u}\right)\right\}^{1/2}$$

15.5 Rocket motion

We are in a position to consider some simple problems involving the motion of a rocket. We shall suppose that the rocket is moving upwards along a vertical line in a uniform gravitational field of force. We shall ignore the motion of the Earth, the variation of the gravitational force with height above the Earth's surface, and the resistive effects of the atmosphere.

We introduce a z-axis so that the plane $z = 0$ represents the surface of the Earth, and the direction of z increasing is vertically upwards. The position vector of the particle representing the rocket (relative to the origin O) is $\boldsymbol{r} = z\boldsymbol{k}$. At $t = 0$ the ignition process begins and $\boldsymbol{r} = \dot{\boldsymbol{r}} = \boldsymbol{0}$.

Let the mass of the payload be M_P, the mass of the rocket structure be M_S, the rocket's total mass be M_0 at $t = 0$, and the rocket's total mass at burnout (say at $t = t_B$) be M_B. At time t the rocket's total mass is $M(t)$, and the mass of the unused fuel is $M_F(t)$. It follows that

$$M_0 = M_P+M_S+M_F(0)$$

$$M(t) = M_P+M_S+M_F(t)$$

and

$$M_B = M_P + M_S$$

i.e.

$$M_F(0) = M_0 - M_B \quad \text{and} \quad M_F(t_B) = 0$$

We note that the time derivative of M equals the time derivative of M_F and is negative.

The differential equation governing the motion of the particle representing the rocket (the payload, the structure and the fuel) is

$$M(t)\frac{du(t)}{dt} = -c\frac{dM(t)}{dt} - M(t)g$$

where $u(t) = \dot{z}(t)$. The speed of the ejected gas relative to the rocket is c, which we assume to be a known constant. The term $-c\,dM(t)/dt$, which is positive, is called the *thrust* of the rocket engine. The differential equation is valid as soon as lift-off occurs. Lift-off occurs immediately the ignition process begins at $t = 0$ provided

$$-c\frac{dM(t)}{dt}\bigg|_{t=0} > M_0 g$$

i.e. provided the initial thrust is greater than the initial weight. This condition may not be satisfied, in which case the rocket remains supported by the launching gantry until lift-off. Lift-off occurs before the rocket burns out at $t = t_B$ provided

$$-c\frac{dM(t)}{dt} > M(t)g$$

for some $t \in [0, t_B)$.

Assuming that lift-off occurs at $t = 0$, we have

$$\int_0^t \frac{du(t)}{dt}dt = -\int_0^t \left\{\frac{c}{M(t)}\frac{dM(t)}{dt} + g\right\}dt, \quad 0 \leqslant t \leqslant t_B$$

and

$$u(t) = c\ln\{M_0/M(t)\} - gt, \quad 0 \leqslant t \leqslant t_B$$

At $t = t_B$, no fuel remains and the velocity at burnout is

$$u_B = c\ln(M_0/M_B) - gt_B$$

To find $z(t)$ from the differential equation

$$\frac{dz(t)}{dt} = c\ln\{M_0/M(t)\} - gt, \quad 0 \leqslant t \leqslant t_B$$

and the initial condition $z(0) = 0$, we have to know the explicit form of $M(t)$. A possible form is

$$M(t) = M_0 - \beta t$$

where β is independent of time,

$$\frac{dM(t)}{dt} = -\beta \quad \text{and} \quad \beta t_B = M_0 - M_B = M_F(0)$$

In this case the thrust of the rocket engine has the constant value $c\beta$. Substituting for $M(t)$ and integrating by parts we find that

$$\begin{aligned} z(t) &= \int_0^t [c \ln \{M_0/(M_0 - \beta t)\} - gt]\,dt \\ &= \left| ct \ln \{M_0/(M_0 - \beta t)\} \right|_0^t - c\int_0^t \frac{\beta t}{M_0 - \beta t}\,dt - \left| \tfrac{1}{2}gt^2 \right|_0^t \\ &= ct \ln \{M_0/(M_0 - \beta t)\} + c\left| t + \frac{M_0}{\beta} \ln (M_0 - \beta t) \right|_0^t - \tfrac{1}{2}gt^2 \\ &= ct - \frac{c}{\beta}(M_0 - \beta t) \ln \{M_0/(M_0 - \beta t)\} - \tfrac{1}{2}gt^2 \end{aligned}$$

where $0 \leqslant t \leqslant t_B$. In particular, at $t = t_B$,

$$\begin{aligned} u_B &= c \ln \{M_0/(M_0 - \beta t_B)\} - gt_B \\ &= c \ln (M_0/M_B) - g(M_0 - M_B)/\beta \end{aligned}$$

and

$$\begin{aligned} z_B &= ct_B - \frac{c}{\beta}(M_0 - \beta t_B) \ln \{M_0/(M_0 - \beta t_B)\} - \tfrac{1}{2}gt_B^2 \\ &= \frac{c(M_0 - M_B)}{\beta} - \frac{cM_B}{\beta} \ln (M_0/M_B) - \tfrac{1}{2}\frac{g(M_0 - M_B)^2}{\beta^2} \end{aligned}$$

Let us evaluate these expressions for typical values of c, M_0/M_B, t_B, e.g. $2800\,\mathrm{m\,s^{-1}}$, 4, 150 s respectively. Then

$$M_B = \tfrac{1}{4}M_0 \quad \text{and} \quad M_0/\beta = 200\,\mathrm{s}$$

Thus we find that

$$u_B = 2800 \ln 4 - 150g = 3882 - 1472 = 2410$$

and

$$\begin{aligned} z_B &= 2800(150 - 50 \ln 4) - \tfrac{1}{2}\,22500g \\ &= 225\,900 - 110\,400 = 115\,500 \end{aligned}$$

the units being m s^{-1} and m, respectively. The predicted altitude at burnout is 115·5 kilometres and the predicted velocity at burnout is 2·41 kilometres per second. We note the restrictive effect of gravity, and we expect the predictions to be overestimates because we have ignored the atmospheric drag.

The rocket continues to rise after burnout, and the differential equation governing its motion is

$$M_B \frac{d^2 z}{dt^2} = -\frac{M_B g R^2}{(R+z)^2}$$

where R is the radius of the Earth. We have chosen to incorporate the inverse-square law of gravity into this phase of the rocket's motion. The appropriate form of the energy equation is

$$\tfrac{1}{2} M_B u^2 - \frac{M_B g R^2}{R+z} = \tfrac{1}{2} M_B u_B^2 - \frac{M_B g R^2}{R+z_B}$$

At the rocket's highest altitude, $u = 0$ and $z = z_{\max}$, where

$$\frac{R}{R+z_{\max}} = \frac{R}{R+z_B} - \frac{u_B^2}{2gR}$$

The value of $z_{\max}$ corresponding to the given typical data is $0{\cdot}069R$, i.e. 440 kilometres. If we had continued to adopt the uniform gravitational field, we would have obtained the value of 412 kilometres for the maximum altitude of the rocket.

The designers of rockets attempt to make the term $c \ln (M_0/M_B)$ as large as possible. The largest value of c obtainable with chemical fuels is of the order of 3500 m s^{-1} and the largest value of M_0/M_B obtainable with present-day designs of the structure of the rocket is of the order of 10 (i.e. $M_F(0)$ is nine-tenths of M_0). Therefore the largest obtainable value of $c \ln (M_0/M_B)$ is of the order of $2{\cdot}30c$, namely 8050 m s^{-1}. This is insufficient for the purposes of lunar missions, for which burnout speeds of the order of 11 200 m s^{-1} (the escape speed associated with the Earth) are essential. The burnout speeds required for lunar and interplanetary missions are obtainable with multi-stage rockets; the payload of the first stage becoming a rocket when the structure of the first stage is abandoned in space at the end of the first-stage burn.

EXERCISES ON CHAPTER 15

1. A body of mass M moves along a smooth horizontal track with constant speed U before experiencing n collisions at $t = T/2n, 3T/2n, 5T/2n, \ldots, T - T/2n$. At each collision a stationary body of mass M/n adheres to the moving body. Determine the speed of the moving body at $t = T$ and the distance travelled by the moving body during the time interval $[0, T]$ in the particular cases $n = 1, 2$ and 4.

Show that, in general, the speed at $t = T$ is $\frac{1}{2}U$ and that the distance travelled during the time interval $[0, T]$ is

$$\frac{UT}{n}\left(\tfrac{1}{2} + \frac{1}{1+1/n} + \frac{1}{1+2/n} + \frac{1}{1+3/n} + \ldots + \frac{1}{1+(n-1)/n} + \tfrac{1}{4}\right)$$

which is an approximation (based on the trapezium rule) to the integral

$$UT\int_0^1 \frac{1}{1+x}\,dx = UT[\ln(1+x)]_0^1 = UT\ln 2$$

2. A body, of mass M and moving with speed U at $t = 0$, moves along a smooth horizontal track and picks up material that is at rest and distributed continuously along the track. The mass of the body is

$$M(t) = M(1 + t/T)$$

Calculate the body's speed at $t = T$ and the distance travelled during the interval $[0, T]$. Show that the body's kinetic energy decreases by an amount $\frac{1}{4}MU^2$ during the interval $[0, T]$.

3. A sledge is propelled by a rocket engine along horizontal rails. At burnout its mass is M and its speed is U. It carries a passenger of mass m and decelerates by picking up water from a trough between the rails. Assume that the contact between the sledge and the rails is smooth, that the rocket engine has burned out before the retardation process begins, and that the maximum deceleration of the sledge is 10 g. Investigate the retardation process when the mass of the sledge is increasing at a constant rate. What is the maximum force needed to keep the passenger in a sitting position (if the passenger is sitting and facing the direction of motion)? What is the force needed to keep the passenger in a sitting position when the speed of the sledge is $\frac{1}{4}U$? What is the average deceleration and the average speed during the time interval in which the speed is reduced from U to $\frac{1}{4}U$?

4. A body moves along a smooth horizontal track and picks up material that is at rest relative to the track and is distributed continuously along the track. Its mass and velocity at time $t = 0$ are M and U. The rate at which its mass increases is $MU(t)/UT$, where $U(t)$ is its velocity at time t and T is a positive parameter independent of time. Show that its mass at time t is $M(1+2t/T)^{1/2}$. Calculate the distance travelled by the body in the time interval $[0, 3T/2]$.

5. A steam locomotive is travelling along a horizontal track and is working at a constant rate P. During the interval $[0, T]$ it picks up at a constant rate water of mass m from a trough between the rails. At $t = 0$ the locomotive's mass is M and its speed is U. If the equation governing the locomotive's motion during the interval $[0, T]$ is

$$\frac{d}{dt}\{M(t)U(t)\} = P/U(t)$$

where $M(t) = M + mt/T$, show that

$$U(T) = \{(M^2U^2 + 2MPT + mPT)/(M+m)^2\}^{1/2}$$

6. A spherical raindrop falls under the influence of gravity through a stationary cloud. Its mass increases with time at a rate proportional to its surface area. If the raindrop starts from rest and its initial radius is zero, show that it falls with constant acceleration $\frac{1}{4}g$.

7. A raindrop falls under the influence of gravity through a stationary cloud, and its mass increases at a constant time rate. The raindrop starts from rest and its initial mass is zero. Evaluate its constant acceleration through the cloud.

8. A raindrop falls under the influence of gravity through a stationary cloud. It starts from rest and its mass increases at a constant time rate m_0/T, where m_0 is the initial mass of the raindrop, and T is a positive parameter independent of time. Show that the raindrop when its mass is m has fallen a distance

$$\tfrac{1}{4}gT^2\{(m^2/m_0^2 - 1) - 2\ln(m/m_0)\}$$

9. A sledge of mass M is carrying n fragments each of mass M/n and is moving along a smooth horizontal track at speed U at $t = 0$. At each of the instants $t = T/2n, 3T/2n, 5T/2n, \ldots, T - T/2n$, a fragment is projected in a horizontal direction so that its speed relative to the sledge is c (i.e. its velocity is $U(t) - c$ when the sledge's velocity is $U(t)$). Determine the speed of the sledge at $t = T$ and the distance travelled by the sledge during the time interval $[0, T]$ in the particular cases $n = 1, 2$ and 4.

Show that, in general, the speed at $t = T$ is

$$U + \frac{c}{n}\left(\frac{1}{1+1/n} + \frac{1}{1+2/n} + \frac{1}{1+3/n} + \ldots + \frac{1}{1+1}\right)$$

which is an approximation (based on the right-hand rectangular rule) to

$$U + c\int_0^1 \frac{1}{1+x}\,dx = U + c\Big|\ln(1+x)\Big|_0^1 = U + c\ln 2$$

10. A rocket-propelled vehicle is moving along a smooth horizontal track. At $t = 0$ its mass is $2M$ and its speed is U. If the gas is ejected at a constant speed c relative to the vehicle, show that the vehicle's speed is $U + c\ln 2$ when the vehicle's mass is M.

The mass of the vehicle decreases with time at a constant rate M/T, where T is a positive parameter. Find the distance travelled by the vehicle during the time interval $[0, T]$. Evaluate the constant thrust of the rocket engine.

11. A sledge of mass M is carrying n fragments each of mass M/n and is moving along a smooth horizontal track at speed U at $t = 0$. At each of the instants $t = T/2n, 3T/2n, 5T/2n, \ldots, T - T/2n$, a fragment is projected in a horizontal direction, and the kinetic energy of the system is increased by an amount e_k. Calculate the speed of each fragment relative to the sledge immediately after the fragment is projected from the sledge, and calculate the speed of the sledge at $t = T$ in the special cases $n = 1, 2$ and 4.

12. A sledge is propelled by a rocket engine along a smooth horizontal track. At $t = 0$ its mass is M_0 and it is at rest. All the products of combustion are ejected from the engine at a constant speed c relative to the sledge. Show that the kinetic energy of the sledge at burnout is

$$\tfrac{1}{2}M_B c^2\{\ln(M_0/M_B)\}^2$$

where M_B is the mass of the sledge at burnout.

What proportion of the initial mass M_0 should the initial mass of the fuel be so that the kinetic energy of the sledge at burnout is maximized?

13. A rocket-propelled vehicle is to be designed which will hover vertically above a fixed point on the surface of the Earth. The rocket engine expels gas at a constant speed c relative to the vehicle. If, at the instant when the vehicle is first in position, three-quarters of its mass consists of fuel, show that it can remain in position during a time interval of length $(2c/g)\ln 2$. In what manner does the mass of the vehicle vary with time during the hovering period?

Evaluate the length of the hovering period when c has the value $3000\,\mathrm{m\,s^{-1}}$.

14. A rocket has a mass M_0 before the engines are started and has a mass $\frac{1}{5}M_0$ at burnout. The mass of the gas ejected per second during the burning of the fuel is a constant parameter β. If the rocket is set to lift vertically, find

(i) the least velocity of the ejected gas if the rocket is to lift immediately after the engines are ignited,

(ii) the least velocity of the ejected gas if the rocket is to lift at all before burnout.

15. A rocket is launched in a vertical direction. Its initial mass is M_0 and its mass at burnout is $\frac{1}{2}M_0$. The engines burn for 42 s and the constant speed at which the gas is expelled relative to the rocket is $2500\,\mathrm{m\,s^{-1}}$. Calculate the rocket's speed at burnout.

16. A rocket is launched in a vertical direction. Its initial mass is M_0 and its mass at burnout is $\frac{1}{4}M_0$. The engines burn for 100 s and the constant speed at which the gas is expelled relative to the rocket is $3000\,\mathrm{m\,s^{-1}}$. Calculate the rocket's speed at burnout.

If the mass of the rocket decreases at a constant rate with respect to time during the burn, determine the altitude of the rocket at burnout and find the constant value of the thrust of the engine during the burn.

17. A lunar module of total mass M_0 is at a height H above the surface of the Moon and is descending vertically with speed u_0, when a rocket is ignited to produce a soft landing. The mass of the fuel decreases at a constant rate with respect to time, and the gas is ejected at a speed of $2400\,\mathrm{m\,s^{-1}}$ relative to the module. If the module touches the lunar surface with zero velocity and the module's mass at the end of the burn lasting 350 s is $\frac{2}{3}M_0$, evaluate u_0 and H. (Assume that the acceleration due to gravity at the surface of the moon is $1{\cdot}62\,\mathrm{m\,s^{-2}}$.)

18. A rocket is fired in a vertical direction from a launching station on Earth. Its initial mass is M_0 and its burnout mass is M_B. The mass of the gas ejected per second during the burning of the fuel is a constant parameter β. The equation governing the rocket's ascent through the atmosphere is

$$M(t)\frac{dU(t)}{dt} = -c\frac{dM(t)}{dt} - M(t)g - k_1 U(t)$$

where $M(t) = M_0 - \beta t$ and k_1 is a positive parameter. Verify that this differential equation transforms to

$$\frac{d}{dt}[U(t)\{M(t)\}^{-k_1/\beta}] = \{c\beta - M(t)g\}\{M(t)\}^{-1-k_1/\beta}$$

Hence show that the rocket's speed at burnout is

$$\frac{c\beta}{k_1}\left\{1-\left(\frac{M_B}{M_0}\right)^{k_1/\beta}\right\}-\frac{M_B g}{(k_1-\beta)}\left\{1-\left(\frac{M_B}{M_0}\right)^{-1+k_1/\beta}\right\}$$

19. Two bags containing sand are attached by an inextensible string which hangs over a smooth peg held in a fixed horizontal position. Initially the mass of each bag of sand is M_0 and the system is at rest. One bag develops a small hole, out of which sand runs; the mass of the bag decreasing with time at a constant rate β. Show that the speed of the system is

$$(M_0 g/\beta)\{2\ln\tfrac{5}{3}-\tfrac{4}{5}\}$$

when sand of mass $\frac{1}{5}M_0$ has run out of the hole.

20. Consider two particles of masses M_E and $M_E/81$ that are fixed and separated by a distance D. A third particle is free to move under the influence of their inverse-square gravitational fields of force. Show that there is a neutral point on the line segment joining the two fixed particles at which the total force experienced by the third particle is zero. What is the distance between this neutral point and the particle of mass M_E?

Use this as a model of a spacecraft moving between the Earth and the Moon. Show that the speed with which the spacecraft must be launched from the Earth so that it travels in a straight line and just reaches the neutral point is

$$\left[\left\{2g_E R_E-2g_M R_M\left(\frac{9R_M}{D-R_E}\right)\right\}\left(1-\frac{10R_E}{9D}\right)\right]^{1/2}$$

and the corresponding speed for a launch from the Moon is

$$\left[\left\{2g_M R_M-2g_E R_E\left(\frac{R_E}{9(D-R_M)}\right)\right\}\left(1-\frac{10R_M}{D}\right)\right]^{1/2}$$

where $D=3{\cdot}84\times10^8$ m, $R_E=6{\cdot}371\times10^6$ m, $R_M=1{\cdot}741\times10^6$ m, $g_E=9{\cdot}81$ m s^{-2} and $g_M=1{\cdot}62$ m s^{-2}. Evaluate these speeds and explain why multi-stage rockets are necessary to launch a spacecraft on a lunar mission from the Earth.

16 Rigid Bodies

16.1 Introduction

To obtain mathematical models in the earlier chapters we have assumed that the motion of a body occupying a finite volume at any instant may be characterized by the motion of a single element set, the mass of the body being associated with this set. In doing this we have introduced the idea of a particle and we have made a study of Particle Dynamics. This process produces acceptable predictions and results in two situations, namely (i) when the motion of the body is translational and (ii) when the size and shape of the body are unimportant. There are situations when the size and shape of a body are important, and the predictions and results of Particle Dynamics are unacceptable. Then we have to allow our mathematical model to accommodate the general motion (having translational and rotational aspects) of a body of finite dimensions.

When a body experiences forces in a physical or engineering situation, the resulting motion of the body is extremely complex. The size and shape of the body may change, and there are forces acting within the structure of the body. Problems of this type give rise to wide areas of study that encompass Physics and Engineering. We shall study a special class of problems, namely some problems concerned with the motion of a rigid body. The distance between any two points of a rigid body is constant for all time and is independent of the forces applied to the body. Clearly bodies that deform are expressly excluded from our discussion, and the size and shape of a rigid body are unaltered in all situations. Do rigid bodies exist in the real world? All bodies are deformable to a greater or lesser degree, but some are almost rigid. A rigid body is a convenient idealization based on a geometrical constraint.

The position of a rigid body is expressible in terms of six coordinates relative to an inertial frame of reference; we say that a rigid body has six degrees of freedom. Three coordinates specify the position of a chosen point of the body, and three angular coordinates specify the orientation of the body. We shall study some problems in which the rigid body is constrained to rotate about a fixed axis. In this special case the rigid body has one degree of freedom.

16.2 Distribution of mass

While considering systems of particles in chapter 13 we became accustomed to a discrete distribution of mass. A system of particles moving subject to the characteristic geometrical constraint is an example of a rigid body. It is often convenient to conceive of a rigid body whose mass is distributed continuously along a curve, over a surface, or throughout a volume.

Consider a rigid body whose mass m is distributed continuously throughout its volume V. The mass per unit volume, namely m/V, is called the *average density* of the body. Suppose P is a typical point of the body and ΔV is an element of volume surrounding P. If the mass of the material occupying the element is Δm, then the average density of the element is $\Delta m/\Delta V$. Taking the limit as the element surrounding P shrinks in size, we define the density at the point P to be

$$\rho(P) = \lim_{\Delta V \to 0} \frac{\Delta m}{\Delta V}$$

When this limit exists and has the same value for all points of the volume V, we say that the body has a uniform density. The unit of measurement of density is the kilogram per cubic metre ($\mathrm{kg\,m^{-3}}$). Similarly we may define the average density and the density at a point in the cases of mass distributed over a surface or along a curve. Here are some illustrative examples.

(i) Suppose mass is distributed along a line segment of length l. Selecting a cartesian coordinate system so that the line segment lies along the x-axis between $x = 0$ and $x = l$, we have

$$\rho(P) = \rho(x) = \lim_{\Delta x \to 0} \frac{\Delta m}{\Delta x} = \frac{dm(x)}{dx}$$

where P is a typical point of the line segment. The total mass is

$$m = \int_0^l \frac{dm(x)}{dx}\,dx = \int_0^l \rho(x)\,dx$$

If the distribution is uniform, the density takes a constant value ρ_0 and $m = \rho_0 l$. When mass is distributed along a curve, the unit of measurement of density is the kilogram per metre ($\mathrm{kg\,m^{-1}}$).

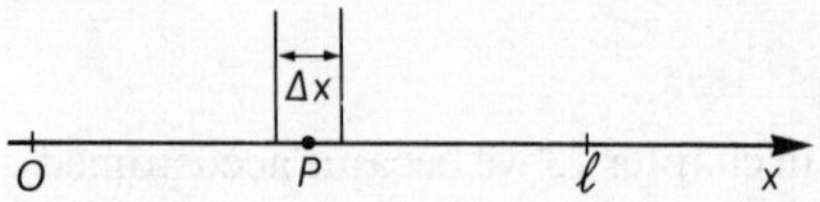

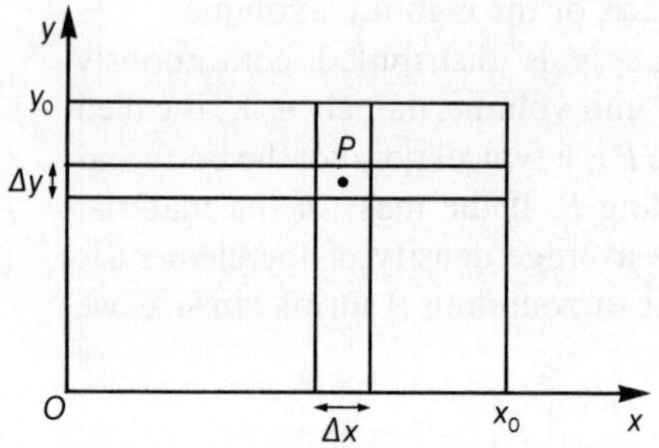

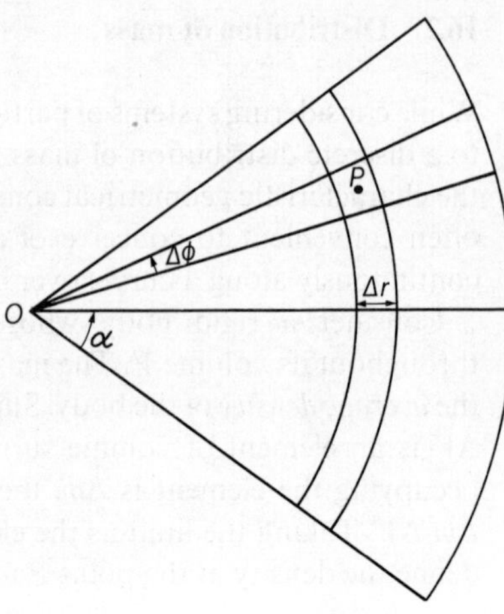

(ii) Suppose mass is distributed over a rectangular surface, the lengths of whose sides are x_0 and y_0. Choosing a suitable cartesian coordinate system, we have

$$\rho(P) = \rho(x, y) = \lim_{\Delta S \to 0} \frac{\Delta m}{\Delta S} = \lim_{\substack{\Delta x \to 0 \\ \Delta y \to 0}} \frac{\Delta m}{\Delta x \, \Delta y}$$

where P is a typical point of the rectangular surface. An extension of the ideas of integration with respect to one variable (based on lower and upper Riemann sums) leads to

$$m = \int_S \rho(P)\, dS = \int_0^{y_0} \int_0^{x_0} \rho(x, y)\, dx\, dy$$

where

$$\int_S \ldots dS$$

is a surface integral over the surface S and

$$\int_0^{y_0} \int_0^{x_0} \ldots dx\, dy = \int_0^{y_0} \left\{ \int_0^{x_0} \ldots dx \right\} dy$$

is a repeated integral. We evaluate the repeated integral by evaluating the inner integral with respect to x and then the remaining integral with respect to y (both by means of standard techniques for one-dimensional integrals). Sometimes it is convenient (and permissible) to interchange the order of integration in the repeated integral and integrate first with respect to y and then with respect to x. An interchange in the order of integration alters the limits of integration unless all the limits are constants. When mass is distributed over a surface, the unit of measurement of density is the kilogram per square metre (kg m^{-2}).

(iii) Suppose mass is distributed over a sector of a circle, the semi-angle being α

and the radius being r_0. It is convenient to introduce plane-polar coordinates. Then we have

$$\rho(P) = \rho(r, \phi) = \lim_{\Delta S \to 0} \frac{\Delta m}{\Delta S} = \lim_{\substack{\Delta r \to 0 \\ \Delta\phi \to 0}} \frac{\Delta m}{\Delta r(r\Delta\phi)}$$

and

$$m = \int_S \rho(P)\, dS = \int_0^{r_0} \int_{-\alpha}^{\alpha} \rho(r, \phi) r\, d\phi\, dr$$

(iv) Suppose mass is distributed throughout a cuboid, the sides having lengths x_0, y_0, z_0. Introducing cartesian coordinates, we find that

$$\rho(P) = \rho(x, y, z) = \lim_{\Delta V \to 0} \frac{\Delta m}{\Delta V} = \lim_{\substack{\Delta x \to 0 \\ \Delta y \to 0 \\ \Delta z \to 0}} \frac{\Delta m}{\Delta x\, \Delta y\, \Delta z}$$

and

$$m = \int_V \rho(P)\, dV = \int_0^{z_0} \int_0^{y_0} \int_0^{x_0} \rho(x, y, z)\, dx\, dy\, dz$$

(v) Suppose mass is distributed throughout a right circular cylinder, the radius being r_0 and the height being z_0. Cylindrical polar coordinates are suitable in this case. Hence we write

$$\rho(P) = \rho(r, \phi, z) = \lim_{\Delta V \to 0} \frac{\Delta m}{\Delta V} = \lim_{\substack{\Delta r \to 0 \\ \Delta\phi \to 0 \\ \Delta z \to 0}} \frac{\Delta m}{\Delta r(r\Delta\phi)\Delta z}$$

and

$$m = \int_V \rho(P)\, dV = \int_0^{z_0} \int_0^{r_0} \int_0^{2\pi} \rho(r, \phi, z)\, r\, d\phi\, dr\, dz$$

(vi) Suppose mass is distributed throughout a sphere of radius r_0. Using spherical polar coordinates, we find that

$$\rho(P) = \rho(r, \theta, \phi) = \lim_{\Delta V \to 0} \frac{\Delta m}{\Delta V} = \lim_{\substack{\Delta r \to 0 \\ \Delta\theta \to 0 \\ \Delta\phi \to 0}} \frac{\Delta m}{\Delta r(r\Delta\theta)(r \sin\theta\, \Delta\phi)}$$

and

$$m = \int_V \rho(P)\, dV = \int_0^{r_0} \int_0^{\pi} \int_0^{2\pi} \rho(r, \theta, \phi) r^2 \sin\theta\, d\phi\, d\theta\, dr$$

16.3 Centre of mass

In our discussion of the motion of a system of particles in chapter 13 we found that the centre of mass had some important properties. We now define the centre of mass associated with a continuous distribution of mass. Suppose a rigid body has mass m, volume V and variable density ρ. The defining relation is

$$m\mathbf{r}_c = \int_V \rho(P)\mathbf{r}_P\, dV$$

which is analogous to

$$m\boldsymbol{r}_c = \sum_{i=1}^{N} m_i \boldsymbol{r}_i$$

where

$$m = \sum_{i=1}^{N} m_i$$

If the bounding surface of the volume V is easily expressible in terms of cartesian coordinates (e.g. in the case of a cuboid), we have

$$m\boldsymbol{r}_c = \iiint_V \rho(x, y, z)(x\boldsymbol{i} + y\boldsymbol{j} + z\boldsymbol{k})\,dx\,dy\,dz$$

and we may be able to evaluate the three constituent integrals of the repeated integral representing the volume integral. In this case we may write

$$mx_c = \iiint_V \rho(x, y, z)x\,dx\,dy\,dz, \quad my_c = \iiint_V \rho(x, y, z)y\,dx\,dy\,dz$$

$$mz_c = \iiint_V \rho(x, y, z)z\,dx\,dy\,dz, \quad \text{where} \quad m = \iiint_V \rho(x, y, z)\,dx\,dy\,dz$$

This is possible because the unit vectors have constant directions. Similarly we may define the centre of mass associated with a continuous distribution of mass over a surface or along a curve. Let us examine some examples.

(i) Consider a rod of length l and mass m, where

$$m = \int_0^l \rho(x)\,dx$$

The x-coordinate of the centre of mass satisfies

$$mx_c = \int_0^l \rho(x)x\,dx$$

If the density is uniform and equal to ρ_0, we have

$$m = \rho_0 l \quad \text{and} \quad mx_c = \tfrac{1}{2}\rho_0 l^2$$

Thus $x_c = \frac{1}{2}l$ and the centre of mass is at the mid-point of the rod. In the case of the non-uniform density $\rho(x) = \rho_0(1 + 2x/l)$, we find that

$$m = \rho_0(l + l) = 2\rho_0 l, \quad mx_c = \rho_0(\tfrac{1}{2}l^2 + \tfrac{2}{3}l^2) = \tfrac{7}{6}\rho_0 l^2$$

and $x_c = 7l/12$.

(ii) Consider a rectangular plate (of negligible thickness), whose sides have lengths x_0, y_0 and whose mass is m, where

$$m = \int_0^{y_0}\int_0^{x_0} \rho(x, y)\,dx\,dy$$

The coordinates of the centre of mass satisfy

$$mx_c = \int_0^{y_0}\int_0^{x_0} \rho(x, y)x\,dx\,dy, \quad my_c = \int_0^{y_0}\int_0^{x_0} \rho(x, y)y\,dx\,dy$$

If the density is uniform and equal to ρ_0, we see that

$$m = \rho_0 \int_0^{y_0}\int_0^{x_0} dx\,dy = \rho_0 x_0 \int_0^{y_0} dy = \rho_0 x_0 y_0$$

$$mx_c = \rho_0 \int_0^{y_0}\int_0^{x_0} x\,dx\,dy = \tfrac{1}{2}\rho_0 x_0^2 \int_0^{y_0} dy = \tfrac{1}{2}\rho_0 x_0^2 y_0$$

$$my_c = \rho_0 \int_0^{y_0}\int_0^{x_0} y\,dx\,dy = \rho_0 x_0 \int_0^{y_0} y\,dy = \tfrac{1}{2}\rho_0 x_0 y_0^2$$

i.e. $x_c = \frac{1}{2}x_0$, $y_c = \frac{1}{2}y_0$ and the centre of mass is at the point of intersection of the diagonals of the rectangle.

In the case of the non-uniform density $\rho(x, y) = \rho_0(1+2x/x_0)$, we find that

$$m = 2\rho_0 x_0 y_0, \quad mx_c = \tfrac{7}{6}\rho_0 x_0^2 y_0, \quad my_c = \rho_0 x_0 y_0^2$$

i.e.

$$x_c = \tfrac{7}{12}x_0 \quad \text{and} \quad y_c = \tfrac{1}{2}y_0$$

(iii) Consider a lamina (of negligible thickness) whose shape is the sector of a circle of semi-angle α and radius r_0. Introducing plane-polar coordinates whose origin is at the apex of the sector, we may write

$$m = \int_0^{r_0}\int_{-\alpha}^{\alpha} \rho(r, \phi)r\,d\phi\,dr$$

and

$$m\boldsymbol{r}_c = \int_0^{r_0}\int_{-\alpha}^{\alpha} \rho(r, \phi)\boldsymbol{r}r\,d\phi\,dr$$

where $\boldsymbol{r} = r\boldsymbol{e}_r = r(\boldsymbol{i}\cos\phi + \boldsymbol{j}\sin\phi)$. Thus

$$mx_c = \int_0^{r_0}\int_{-\alpha}^{\alpha} \rho(r, \phi)r^2\cos\phi\,d\phi\,dr$$

and

$$my_c = \int_0^{r_0}\int_{-\alpha}^{\alpha} \rho(r, \phi)r^2\sin\phi\,d\phi\,dr$$

When the lamina has a uniform density ρ_0, we find that

$$m = \rho_0 \int_0^{r_0}\int_{-\alpha}^{\alpha} r\,d\phi\,dr = 2\rho_0\alpha \int_0^{r_0} r\,dr = \rho_0\alpha r_0^2$$

$$mx_c = \rho_0 \int_0^{r_0}\int_{-\alpha}^{\alpha} r^2\cos\phi\,d\phi\,dr = 2\rho_0\sin\alpha \int_0^{r_0} r^2\,dr = \tfrac{2}{3}\rho_0 r_0^3\sin\alpha$$

$$my_c = \rho_0 \int_0^{r_0}\int_{-\alpha}^{\alpha} r^2\sin\phi\,d\phi\,dr = \rho_0 \int_0^{r_0} r^2[-\cos\phi]_{-\alpha}^{\alpha}\,dr = 0$$

i.e. $x_c = \frac{2}{3}r_0(\sin\alpha)/\alpha$ and $y_c = 0$.

It is worth while to note that it is not permissible to write

$$m\boldsymbol{r}_c = \boldsymbol{e}_r \int_0^{r_0}\int_{-\alpha}^{\alpha} \rho(r, \phi)r^2\,d\phi\,dr$$

because the direction of the unit vector $\boldsymbol{e}_r$ depends on ϕ, a variable of integration. The presentation in terms of the unit vectors $\boldsymbol{i}$ and $\boldsymbol{j}$, having constant magnitudes and directions, is essential.

16.4 Equations of motion

Let us consider some forces that can act on a rigid body and cause a rigid body to move. Gravity is an example of a force that acts at each point of the body. Other forces, e.g. aerodynamics drag and contact friction, act over the surface or a part of the surface of a body. When a force is applied over a small part of the surface, e.g. the force applied by a tug when pulling a ship by means of a rope, we shall adopt the idealization that the force acts at a point. In the case of a volume or surface distribution of force we shall be interested in the total effect of the distribution of force. We shall consider the effect of gravity on a rigid body in the next section.

We shall define the linear momentum of a rigid body and the angular momentum of a rigid body by extending the definitions given for the corresponding quantities for a system of particles in chapter 13. Our definition of the linear momentum of a rigid body is

$$\boldsymbol{p} = m\dot{\boldsymbol{r}}_c$$

where m is the total mass (independent of time) and $\dot{\boldsymbol{r}}_c$ is the velocity vector of the centre of mass relative to an inertial frame of reference. In terms of the volume integral introduced in the previous section, we have

$$\boldsymbol{p} = \frac{d}{dt}\int_V \rho(P)\boldsymbol{r}_P \, dV$$

An alternative definition is

$$\boldsymbol{p} = \int_V \rho(P)\dot{\boldsymbol{r}}_P \, dV$$

which is an adaption of

$$\sum_{i=1}^{N} m_i \dot{\boldsymbol{r}}_i.$$

It is not obvious, but it is true, that the two definitions of $\boldsymbol{p}$ are equivalent. The validity of interchanging the differentiation and the integration processes requires proof. Our definition of the angular momentum (or moment of linear momentum) of a rigid body about a point A is

$$\mathbf{L} = \int_V \rho(P)(\boldsymbol{r}_P - \boldsymbol{r}_A) \times \dot{\boldsymbol{r}}_P \, dV$$

where $\boldsymbol{r}_A$ is the position vector of A relative to the origin of an inertial frame of reference. This is an adaption of

$$\sum_{i=1}^{N} (\boldsymbol{r}_i - \boldsymbol{r}_A) \times m_i \dot{\boldsymbol{r}}_i.$$

Summation with respect to the particles has been replaced by integration over the volume occupied by the rigid body at a given instant. The resulting volume integrals are complicated. We shall restrict our attention to special cases in the subsequent sections.

Newton's Laws of Motion have been our axioms in Particle Dynamics. They do not apply directly to Rigid Body Dynamics. Consequently we have to select alternative axioms. We shall adopt the following axioms, which are analogous to results applying to systems of particles.

(i) The rate of change of linear momentum of a rigid body equals the total external force acting on the rigid body;

$$\dot{\boldsymbol{p}} = m\ddot{\boldsymbol{r}}_c = \mathbf{F}^E$$

where $\mathbf{F}^E$ denotes the total external force.

(ii) The rate of change of angular momentum (or moment of linear momentum) of a rigid body about the centre of mass or a point fixed in the inertial frame of reference equals the total moment of the external forces about the chosen point;

$$\dot{\mathbf{L}} = \mathbf{M}^E$$

where $\mathbf{M}^E$ denotes the total moment of the external forces about the centre of mass (or a point fixed in the inertial frame of reference).

The first equation describes the translational motion of the centre of mass of the rigid body, and the second equation describes the rotational motion about the centre of mass (or a point fixed in the inertial frame of reference). They provide six scalar equations corresponding to the six degrees of freedom possessed by a rigid body in general motion.

16.5 Centre of gravity

Let us consider the effect of gravity on a rigid body. Suppose a uniform gravitational field of force acts on a rigid body of mass m and volume V. Let ρ be the body's density, which may be a function of position within the body. The total force experienced by the body is

$$\mathbf{F} = \int_V \rho(P) g\boldsymbol{k}\, dV = \int_V \rho(P)\, dV g\boldsymbol{k} = mg\boldsymbol{k}$$

where $\boldsymbol{k}$ is a unit vector directed vertically downwards. The total moment about a point A is

$$\mathbf{M} = \int_V (\boldsymbol{r}_P - \boldsymbol{r}_A) \times \{\rho(P) g\boldsymbol{k}\}\, dV$$

$$= g \int_V \rho(P)\{(y_P - y_A)\boldsymbol{i} - (x_P - x_A)\boldsymbol{j}\}\, dV$$
$$= mg\{(y_c - y_A)\boldsymbol{i} - (x_c - x_A)\boldsymbol{j}\}$$
$$= (\boldsymbol{r}_c - \boldsymbol{r}_A) \times (mg\boldsymbol{k})$$
$$= (\boldsymbol{r}_c - \boldsymbol{r}_A) \times \mathbf{F}$$

We see that this volume distribution of force is equivalent to a single force (represented by $mg\boldsymbol{k}$) acting at a point, called the *centre of gravity*. In the case of the uniform gravitational field of force, the centre of gravity coincides with the centre of mass C.

These results are analogous to the corresponding results for a system of particles, namely

$$\mathbf{F} = \sum_{i=1}^{N} (m_i g\boldsymbol{k}) = \left(\sum_{i=1}^{N} m_i\right) g\boldsymbol{k} = mg\boldsymbol{k}$$

and

$$\mathbf{M} = \sum_{i=1}^{N} \{(\boldsymbol{r}_i - \boldsymbol{r}_A) \times (m_i g\boldsymbol{k})\} = \left\{\left(\sum_{i=1}^{N} m_i \boldsymbol{r}_i\right) - \left(\sum_{i=1}^{N} m_i\right)\boldsymbol{r}_A\right\} g\boldsymbol{k}$$
$$= (\boldsymbol{r}_c - \boldsymbol{r}_A) mg\boldsymbol{k}$$

Consider a rigid body consisting of two particles P_1 and P_2 held apart at a constant distance by a rigid connector of negligible mass. Let P_1 have *mass* m_1 and position vector $\boldsymbol{r}_1$ relative to O, and let P_2 have mass m_2 and position vector $\boldsymbol{r}_2$ relative to O, where O is the origin of an inertial frame of reference. This rigid body is an idealization of a dumb-bell. Suppose that the dumb-bell is moving in the inverse-square gravitational field of a particle of mass M, the particle being fixed at O. The total force acting on the dumb-bell is

$$\mathbf{F} = -\frac{GMm_1}{r_1^3}\boldsymbol{r}_1 - \frac{GMm_2}{r_2^3}\boldsymbol{r}_2$$

and the total moment about a point A is

$$\mathbf{M} = (\boldsymbol{r}_1 - \boldsymbol{r}_A) \times \left(\frac{-GMm_1}{r_1^3}\boldsymbol{r}_1\right) + (\boldsymbol{r}_2 - \boldsymbol{r}_A) \times \left(\frac{-GMm_2}{r_2^3}\boldsymbol{r}_2\right) = -\boldsymbol{r}_A \times \mathbf{F}$$

We note that the centre of mass of the dumb-bell has the position vector

$$\boldsymbol{r}_c = (m_1\boldsymbol{r}_1 + m_2\boldsymbol{r}_2)/(m_1 + m_2)$$

and that

$$(\boldsymbol{r}_c - \boldsymbol{r}_A) \times \mathbf{F} = \frac{GMm_1m_2}{m_1 + m_2}\left(\frac{1}{r_1^3} - \frac{1}{r_2^3}\right)\boldsymbol{r}_1 \times \boldsymbol{r}_2 + \mathbf{M}$$

The centre of gravity coincides with the centre of mass if $\boldsymbol{r}_1 = \boldsymbol{r}_2$. Its position vector relative to O, $\boldsymbol{r}_G$, satisfies

$$\mathbf{M} = (\boldsymbol{r}_G - \boldsymbol{r}_A) \times \mathbf{F}$$

It is not obvious that a centre of gravity exists for a general problem. However, for the important problem of a rigid body moving in a uniform gravitational field, a centre of gravity exists and coincides with the centre of mass. The above example concerning the dumb-bell illustrates the difference between the centre of mass (which depends on the rigid body and always exists) and the centre of gravity (which depends on the rigid body and the gravitational fields and does not exist, in general).

EXAMPLE

Investigate the gravitational force between a particle of mass m and a spherical rigid body of mass M, radius R and uniform density ρ_0.

We introduce a system of spherical polar coordinates (r, θ, ϕ), whose origin O is at the centre of the sphere. Without any loss of generality we may suppose that the particle Q is situated on the polar axis, the distance between O and Q being z_Q $(R < z_Q)$. Let P be a typical point of the rigid body, the position vector of P relative to O being

$$\begin{aligned} \boldsymbol{r}_P &= r\,\boldsymbol{e}_r \\ &= r(\boldsymbol{i} \sin\theta\cos\phi + \boldsymbol{j}\sin\theta\sin\phi + \boldsymbol{k}\cos\theta) \end{aligned}$$

where $0 \leqslant r \leqslant R$, $0 \leqslant \theta \leqslant \pi$, $0 \leqslant \phi < 2\pi$. We note that the position vector of Q relative to O is $\boldsymbol{r}_Q = z_Q\boldsymbol{k}$.

The mass of the spherical body is

$$M = \int_0^R \int_0^\pi \int_0^{2\pi} \rho_0 r^2 \sin\theta \, d\phi \, d\theta \, dr = \tfrac{4}{3}\pi\rho_0 R^3$$

The force experienced by the particle Q is

$$\mathbf{F} = \int_V \frac{Gm\rho_0}{|\boldsymbol{r}_P - \boldsymbol{r}_Q|^2} \frac{(\boldsymbol{r}_P - \boldsymbol{r}_Q)}{|\boldsymbol{r}_P - \boldsymbol{r}_Q|} dV$$

where $\boldsymbol{r}_P - \boldsymbol{r}_Q = (r\sin\theta\cos\phi)\boldsymbol{i} + (r\sin\theta\sin\phi)\boldsymbol{j} + (r\cos\theta - z_Q)\boldsymbol{k}$ and $|\boldsymbol{r}_P - \boldsymbol{r}_Q| = (r^2 - 2rz_Q\cos\theta + z_Q^2)^{1/2}$.

Writing the volume integral as a repeated integral we find that

$$\begin{aligned} \mathbf{F} = Gm\rho_0 &\int_0^R \int_0^\pi \int_0^{2\pi} \frac{(r\sin\theta\cos\phi)r^2\sin\theta}{(r^2 - 2rz_Q\cos\theta + z_Q^2)^{3/2}} d\phi\, d\theta\, dr\, \boldsymbol{i} \\ + Gm\rho_0 &\int_0^R \int_0^\pi \int_0^{2\pi} \frac{(r\sin\theta\sin\phi)r^2\sin\theta}{(r^2 - 2rz_Q\cos\theta + z_Q^2)^{3/2}} d\phi\, d\theta\, dr\, \boldsymbol{j} \\ + Gm\rho_0 &\int_0^R \int_0^\pi \int_0^{2\pi} \frac{(r\cos\theta - z_Q)r^2\sin\theta}{(r^2 - 2rz_Q\cos\theta + z_Q^2)^{3/2}} d\phi\, d\theta\, dr\, \boldsymbol{k} \end{aligned}$$

The x and y components of $\mathbf{F}$ are zero because

$$\int_0^{2\pi} \cos\phi \, d\phi = \int_0^{2\pi} \sin\phi \, d\phi = 0$$

Next we make the substitution $D = (r^2 - 2rz_Q\cos\theta + z_Q^2)^{1/2}$ and we note that

$$\frac{dD}{d\theta} = \frac{rz_Q \sin\theta}{D} \quad \text{and} \quad (r\cos\theta - z_Q) = \frac{r^2 - z_Q^2 - D^2}{2z_Q}$$

Thus

$$\mathbf{F} = 2\pi Gm\rho_0 \int_0^R \int_{D_0}^{D_\pi} \frac{(r^2 - z_Q^2 - D^2)}{2z_Q} \frac{rD}{z_Q D^3} \, dD \, dr \, \boldsymbol{k}$$

where $D_0 = (r^2 - 2rz_Q + z_Q^2)^{1/2} = |r - z_Q| = z_Q - r$ and $D_\pi = (r^2 + 2rz_Q + z_Q^2)^{1/2} = z_Q + r$.

It follows that

$$\begin{aligned}
\mathbf{F} &= \frac{\pi Gm\rho_0}{z_Q^2} \int_0^R r\left\{(z_Q^2 - r^2)\left(\frac{1}{D_\pi} - \frac{1}{D_0}\right) - (D_\pi - D_0)\right\} dr \, \boldsymbol{k} \\
&= \frac{-4\pi Gm\rho_0}{z_Q^2} \int_0^R r^2 \, dr \, \boldsymbol{k} = \frac{-4\pi Gm\rho_0}{3z_Q^2} R^3 \, \boldsymbol{k} \\
&= -\frac{GMm}{z_Q^2} \boldsymbol{k}
\end{aligned}$$

We recognize that this result is exactly the same as the result we would have obtained if we had replaced the sphere by a particle of mass M situated at the origin O. We referred to this result in Section 3.4 when we were considering the Earth's gravitational field of force.

16.6 Forces and couples

Consider a system of forces acting on a rigid body. Suppose external forces represented by $\mathbf{F}_1, \mathbf{F}_2, \ldots, \mathbf{F}_N$ act at points $P_1, P_2, \ldots, P_N$ having position vectors $\boldsymbol{r}_1, \mathrm{r}_2, \ldots, \boldsymbol{r}_N$ relative to the origin O of an inertial frame of reference. The total force experienced by the body is

$$\mathbf{F} = \sum_{i=1}^{N} \mathbf{F}_i$$

and the total moment of the forces about a point A, having position vector $\boldsymbol{r}_A$ relative to O, is

$$\mathbf{M} = \sum_{i=1}^{N} (\boldsymbol{r}_i - \boldsymbol{r}_A) \times \mathbf{F}_i$$

The point A is the centre of mass or a fixed point of the inertial frame of reference.

Consider a pair of forces, say the forces represented by $\mathbf{F}_1$ and $\mathbf{F}_2$. The moment of these two forces about the point A is

$$(\boldsymbol{r}_1-\boldsymbol{r}_A)\times \mathbf{F}_1+(\boldsymbol{r}_2-\boldsymbol{r}_A)\times \mathbf{F}_2 = \boldsymbol{r}_1\times \mathbf{F}_1+\boldsymbol{r}_2\times \mathbf{F}_2-\boldsymbol{r}_A\times(\mathbf{F}_1+\mathbf{F}_2)$$

When $\mathbf{F}_1+\mathbf{F}_2 = \boldsymbol{0}$, the above expression for the moment about A becomes

$$(\boldsymbol{r}_1-\boldsymbol{r}_2)\times \mathbf{F}_1 = (\boldsymbol{r}_2-\boldsymbol{r}_1)\times \mathbf{F}_2$$

which is independent of A. If $\mathbf{F}_1+\mathbf{F}_2 = \boldsymbol{0}$ and $\mathbf{T} = (\boldsymbol{r}_1-\boldsymbol{r}_2)\times \mathbf{F}_1$ is nonzero, we say that the pair of forces forms a couple, and we call $\mathbf{T}$ the *moment of the couple* or the *torque of the couple.* We note that a couple does not influence the translation of the centre of mass of the rigid body, but does influence the rotation of the rigid body about the centre of mass.

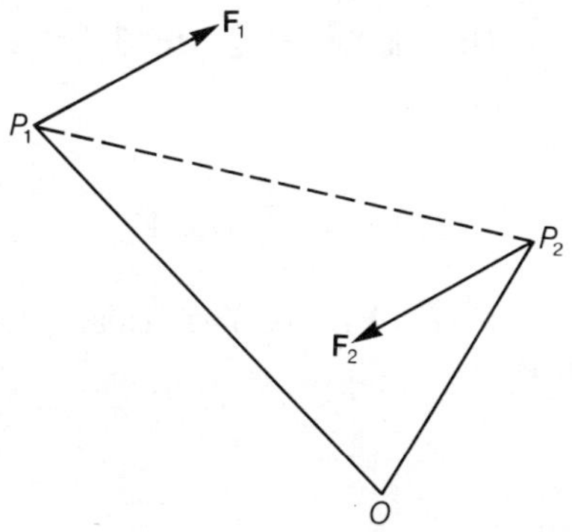

Suppose a single force is acting on the rigid body, say the force represented by $\mathbf{F}_1$. In this case the total force is $\mathbf{F}_1$ and the total moment about A is $(\boldsymbol{r}_1-\boldsymbol{r}_A)\times \mathbf{F}_1$. Consider another situation in which the rigid body experiences a force and a couple, the force having the same magnitude and direction as the single force but a different point of application, say B instead of P_1. Let $\mathbf{T}$ represent the torque of the couple. In this second situation the total force is $\mathbf{F}_1$ and the total moment about A is $(\boldsymbol{r}_B-\boldsymbol{r}_A)\times \mathbf{F}_1+\mathbf{T}$, which equals $(\boldsymbol{r}_1-\boldsymbol{r}_A)\times \mathbf{F}_1$ provided $\mathbf{T} = \boldsymbol{r}_1-\boldsymbol{r}_B)\times \mathbf{F}_1$. Thus the single force at P_1 (represented by $\mathbf{F}_1$) has the same effect on the motion of the rigid body as a force at B (represented by $\mathbf{F}_1$) and a couple (whose torque is represented by $(\boldsymbol{r}_1-\boldsymbol{r}_B)\times \mathbf{F}_1$). We say that the single force at P_1 is equivalent to the force at B and the couple.

Extending this to the original system of N forces, we say that the original system of N forces is equivalent to a single force acting at B and a couple, the single force being represented by

$$\sum_{i=1}^{N} \mathbf{F}_i$$

and the torque of the couple being represented by

$$\sum_{i=1}^{N} (\boldsymbol{r}_i - \boldsymbol{r}_B) \times \mathbf{F}_i.$$

The system of N forces has the same effect on the motion of the rigid body as the single force and the couple. We note that the single force acting at B is represented by

$$\mathbf{F} = \sum_{i=1}^{N} \mathbf{F}_i$$

and the torque of the couple is represented by

$$\mathbf{T} = \sum_{i=1}^{N} (\boldsymbol{r}_i - \boldsymbol{r}_B) \times \mathbf{F}_i = \sum_{i=1}^{N} (\boldsymbol{r}_i \times \mathbf{F}_i) - \boldsymbol{r}_B \times \mathbf{F}$$

It follows that

$$\mathbf{F}.\mathbf{T} = \mathbf{F}.\sum_{i=1}^{N} (\boldsymbol{r}_i \times \mathbf{F}_i)$$

because $\mathbf{F}.(\boldsymbol{r}_B \times \mathbf{F}) = \boldsymbol{r}_B.(\mathbf{F} \times \mathbf{F}) = 0$. The scalar product $\mathbf{F}.\mathbf{T}$ is independent of the point B.

EXAMPLE

Is the system of three forces,

$$\begin{array}{lll} F_0\boldsymbol{k} & \text{acting at} & l(\boldsymbol{i}+\boldsymbol{k}) \\ F_0\boldsymbol{j} & \text{acting at} & l(\boldsymbol{j}+\boldsymbol{k}) \\ F_1(\boldsymbol{i}+\boldsymbol{k}) & \text{acting at} & l(\boldsymbol{i}+\boldsymbol{j}+\boldsymbol{k}) \end{array}$$

reducible to a single force acting at a suitable point?

The total force is represented by

$$\mathbf{F} = \sum_{i=1}^{3} \mathbf{F}_i = F_1\boldsymbol{i} + F_0\boldsymbol{j} + (F_0 + F_1)\boldsymbol{k}$$

Suppose the system is equivalent to a single force F acting at a point B and a couple. The torque of the couple is specified by the condition that the total moment of the system of forces about any point, A say, is equal to the sum of the moment of the single force acting at B and the torque of the couple; i.e.

$$\mathbf{F} = \sum_{i=1}^{3} \mathbf{F}_i = F_1\boldsymbol{i} + F_0\boldsymbol{j} + (F_0 + F_1)\boldsymbol{k}$$

which simplifies to

$$\mathbf{T} = \sum_{i=1}^{3} (\boldsymbol{r}_i \times \mathbf{F}_i) - \boldsymbol{r}_B \times \mathbf{F}.$$

If the system reduces to a single force acting at B, the position vector of B satisfies

$$0 = \sum_{i=1}^{3} (r_i \times \mathbf{F}_i) - r_B \times \mathbf{F}$$

where

$$\begin{aligned}\sum_{i=1}^{3} (r_i \times \mathbf{F}_i) &= F_0 l(i+k)\times k + F_0 l(j+k)\times j + F_1 l(i+j+k)\times(i+k)\\ &= -F_0 lj - F_0 li + F_1 l(-j-k+i+j)\\ &= (F_1 - F_0)li - F_0 lj - F_1 lk\end{aligned}$$

Thus the coordinates of B satisfy the linear equations

$$\begin{aligned} (F_0+F_1)y - F_0 z &= (F_1-F_0)l\\ -(F_0+F_1)x \qquad\qquad + F_1 z &= \quad -F_0 l\\ F_0 x \qquad - F_1 y \qquad\qquad &= \quad -F_1 l\end{aligned}$$

Eliminating z, we find that x and y satisfy

$$\begin{aligned} -(F_0+F_1)F_0 x + (F_0+F_1)F_1 y &= \{F_1(F_1-F_0) - F_0^2\}l\\ F_0 x - \qquad F_1 y &= \qquad -F_1 l\end{aligned}$$

This pair of equations is consistent provided

$$0 = \{F_1(F_1-F_0)-F_0^2\}l - (F_0+F_1)F_1 l = -(F_0+2F_1)F_0 l$$

We deduce that a single resultant force F acts at B (and there is no couple) provided $F_0 + 2F_1 = 0$. We may obtain this condition by noting that

$$\begin{aligned} 0 = \mathbf{F}.\mathbf{T} = \mathbf{F}.\sum_{i=1}^{3}(r_i\times\mathbf{F}_i) - \mathbf{F}.(r_B\times\mathbf{F}) &= \mathbf{F}.\sum_{i=1}^{3}(r_i\times\mathbf{F}_i)\\ &= \{F_1 i + F_0 j + (F_0+F_1)k\}.\{(F_1-F_0)li - F_0 lj - F_1 lk\}\\ &= F_1(F_1-F_0)l - F_0^2 l - (F_0+F_1)F_1 l = -(F_0+2F_1)F_0 l\end{aligned}$$

Thus when $F_1 = -\frac{1}{2}F_0$ the linear equations governing the coordinates of B become

$$\begin{aligned} \tfrac{1}{2}y - z &= -\tfrac{3}{2}l\\ -\tfrac{1}{2}x \qquad -\tfrac{1}{2}z &= -\ l\\ x \qquad +\tfrac{1}{2}y &= \ \tfrac{1}{2}l\end{aligned}$$

and have an infinite number of solutions, namely

$$x = 2l - z, \quad y = -3l + 2z$$

We observe that B is any point on a straight line, called the *line of action of the resultant force.*

EXAMPLE

Calculate the resultant of the system of forces

$F_0(4i+4j+k)$	acting at	$l(i+j+3k)$
$F_0(i-2j)$	acting at	$l(i-j+k)$
$F_0(-3i+j-3k)$	acting at	$l(-3i-j+k)$
$F_0(-2i-3j+2k)$	acting at	$l(-i+2j+k)$

and show that the total moment of the system about any point is zero.

The resultant is

$$\mathbf{F} = F_0(4\boldsymbol{i}+4\boldsymbol{j}+\boldsymbol{k})+F_0(\boldsymbol{i}-2\boldsymbol{j})+F_0(-3\boldsymbol{i}+\boldsymbol{j}-3\boldsymbol{k})+F_0(-2\boldsymbol{i}-3\boldsymbol{j}+2\boldsymbol{k}) = \boldsymbol{0}$$

The moment of the system of forces about any point A, having position vector $\boldsymbol{r}_A$, is

$$\mathbf{M} = \sum_{i=1}^{4} (\boldsymbol{r}_i - \boldsymbol{r}_A)\times \mathbf{F}_i = \sum_{i=1}^{4} (\boldsymbol{r}_i \times \mathbf{F}_i) - \boldsymbol{r}_A \times \mathbf{F} = \sum_{i=1}^{4} (\boldsymbol{r}_i \times \mathbf{F}_i)$$

because $\mathbf{F} = \boldsymbol{0}$. It follows that

$$\begin{aligned}\mathbf{M} &= F_0 l(\boldsymbol{i}+\boldsymbol{j}+3\boldsymbol{k})\times(4\boldsymbol{i}+4\boldsymbol{j}+\boldsymbol{k})+F_0 l(\boldsymbol{i}-\boldsymbol{j}+\boldsymbol{k})\times(\boldsymbol{i}-2\boldsymbol{j})\\ &\quad +F_0 l(-3\boldsymbol{i}-\boldsymbol{j}+\boldsymbol{k})\times(-3\boldsymbol{i}+\boldsymbol{j}-3\boldsymbol{k})+F_0 l(-\boldsymbol{i}+2\boldsymbol{j}+\boldsymbol{k})\times(-2\boldsymbol{i}-3\boldsymbol{j}+2\boldsymbol{k})\\ &= F_0 l[\{(1-12)+(0+2)+(3-1)+(4+3)\}\boldsymbol{i}\\ &\quad +\{(12-1)+(1-0)+(-3-9)+(-2+2)\}\boldsymbol{j}\\ &\quad +\{(4-4)+(-2+1)+(-3-3)+(3+4)\}\boldsymbol{k}]\\ &= \boldsymbol{0}\end{aligned}$$

If a rigid body experiences a system of forces for which $\mathbf{F} = \boldsymbol{0}$ and $\mathbf{M} = \boldsymbol{0}$ for all time, and it is at rest at a given instant, the rigid body remains at rest for all time. We say that the rigid body is in equilibrium or that the system of forces is in equilibrium.

16.7 Rotation about a fixed axis

Consider a rigid body rotating about an axis that is horizontal and fixed relative to an inertial frame of reference. We select a system of cartesian coordinates so that the z-axis coincides with the fixed horizontal axis of rotation, the y-axis is horizontal, and the direction of x increasing is vertically downwards. It is convenient to introduce the system of cartesian coordinates $OXYZ$ that is fixed relative to the rigid body so that the origins of the two systems coincide, the Z-axis and z-axis coincide, and the centre of mass C is on the X-axis (cf. the rotating axes in chapter 12).

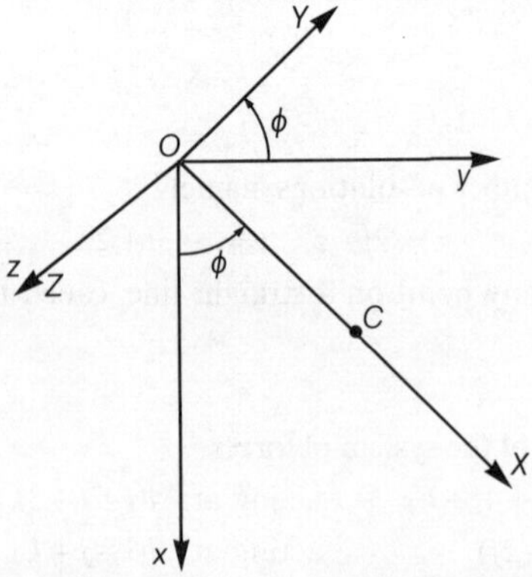

A typical point P of the rigid body has the position vector $\boldsymbol{r}_P$ (relative to the origin O), where

$$\boldsymbol{r}_P = x\boldsymbol{i}+y\boldsymbol{j}+z\boldsymbol{k}$$

The body is rotating about the z-axis so that the z-coordinate of P is independent of time. We may write

$$x = X\cos\phi - Y\sin\phi \quad \text{and} \quad y = X\sin\phi + Y\cos\phi$$

where the angle ϕ depends on time and the X- and Y-coordinates are independent of time. Hence

$$\begin{aligned}\dot{\boldsymbol{r}}_P &= \dot{x}\boldsymbol{i} + \dot{y}\boldsymbol{j} + \dot{z}\boldsymbol{k} \\ &= (-X\sin\phi - Y\cos\phi)\dot{\phi}\boldsymbol{i} + (X\cos\phi - Y\sin\phi)\dot{\phi}\boldsymbol{j} \\ &= -y\dot{\phi}\boldsymbol{i} + x\dot{\phi}\boldsymbol{j} \\ &= \boldsymbol{\omega} \times \boldsymbol{r}_P\end{aligned}$$

where $\boldsymbol{\omega} = \dot{\phi}\boldsymbol{k}$, which is called the *angular velocity of the rigid body*. The centre of mass C has the position vector $\boldsymbol{r}_c$ (relative to the origin O), where

$$\boldsymbol{r}_c = (X_c\cos\phi)\boldsymbol{i} + (X_c\sin\phi)\boldsymbol{j}$$

and

$$\dot{\boldsymbol{r}}_c = -(X_c\sin\phi)\dot{\phi}\boldsymbol{i} + (X_c\cos\phi)\dot{\phi}\boldsymbol{j} = \boldsymbol{\omega} \times \boldsymbol{r}_c$$

Let us consider a particular rigid body, namely a dumb-bell consisting of two particles P_1 and P_2 connected by a rigid connector of constant length $l_1 + l_2$ and of negligible mass. Suppose the dumb-bell is pivoted about O at a distance l_1 from P_1, and its motion is confined to the xy-plane. The particle P_1 of mass m_1 has the position vector $\boldsymbol{r}_1$ (relative to the origin O), and the particle P_2 of mass m_2 has the position vector $\boldsymbol{r}_2$ (relative to the origin O), where

$$\boldsymbol{r}_1 = (l_1\cos\phi)\boldsymbol{i} + (l_1\sin\phi)\boldsymbol{j} \quad \text{and} \quad \boldsymbol{r}_2 = -(l_2\cos\phi)\boldsymbol{i} - (l_2\sin\phi)\boldsymbol{j}$$

The dumb-bell has one degree of freedom (associated with the coordinate ϕ). We shall refer to the connector as a "light rigid rod"; a light rigid rod does not bend, has constant length and has negligible mass.

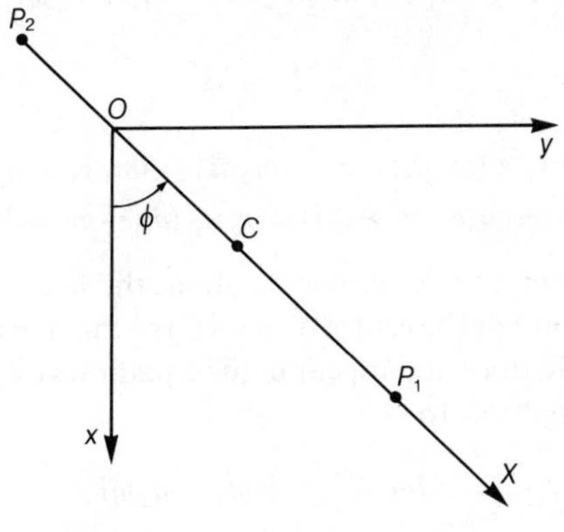

The centre of mass C has the position vector $\boldsymbol{r}_c$ (relative to the origin O), where

$$(m_1+m_2)\boldsymbol{r}_c = m_1\boldsymbol{r}_1+m_2\boldsymbol{r}_2 = (m_1 l_1-m_2 l_2)(\boldsymbol{i}\cos\phi+\boldsymbol{j}\sin\phi)$$

i.e. $X_c = (m_1 l_1-m_2 l_2)/(m_1+m_2)$. The linear momentum of the rigid body is

$$\boldsymbol{p} = m_1\dot{\boldsymbol{r}}+m_2\dot{\boldsymbol{r}}_2 = (m_1+m_2)\dot{\boldsymbol{r}}_c$$

and the angular momentum of the rigid body about the origin O is

$$\begin{aligned}\mathbf{L} &= \boldsymbol{r}_1\times(m_1\dot{\boldsymbol{r}}_1)+\boldsymbol{r}_2\times(m_2\dot{\boldsymbol{r}}_2)\\ &= m_1\boldsymbol{r}_1\times(\boldsymbol{\omega}\times\boldsymbol{r}_1)+m_2\boldsymbol{r}_2\times(\boldsymbol{\omega}\times\boldsymbol{r}_2)\\ &= m_1\{(\boldsymbol{r}_1\cdot\boldsymbol{r}_1)\boldsymbol{\omega}-(\boldsymbol{r}_1\cdot\boldsymbol{\omega})\boldsymbol{r}_1\}+m_2\{(\boldsymbol{r}_2\cdot\boldsymbol{r}_2)\boldsymbol{\omega}-(\boldsymbol{r}_2\cdot\boldsymbol{\omega})\boldsymbol{r}_2\}\\ &= (m_1 l_1^2+m_2 l_2^2)\boldsymbol{\omega}\end{aligned}$$

because $\boldsymbol{r}_1\cdot\boldsymbol{r}_1 = l_1^2$, $\boldsymbol{r}_1\cdot\boldsymbol{\omega} = 0$, $\boldsymbol{r}_2\cdot\boldsymbol{r}_2 = l_2^2$, $\boldsymbol{r}_2\cdot\boldsymbol{\omega} = 0$. We shall use I to denote $(m_1 l_1^2+m_2 l_2^2)$, which is called the moment of inertia of the dumb-bell about the z-axis. The moment of inertia is independent of time. Its dimensions are ML^2 and the unit of measurement is the kilogram metre squared ($\mathrm{kg\,m^2}$).

Next we examine the forces acting on the dumb-bell. There is a uniform gravitational field of force. At the pivot O there will be a reaction on the dumb-bell, a force supporting the dumb-bell. We shall assume that there are no frictional forces acting at the pivot; frictional forces usually combine to produce a frictional couple that opposes the rotational motion of the rigid body about the axis.

The equations governing the motion are

$$\dot{\boldsymbol{p}} = (m_1+m_2)\ddot{\boldsymbol{r}}_c = \mathbf{F}^E$$

where

$$\mathbf{F}^E = m_1 g\boldsymbol{i}+m_2 g\boldsymbol{i}+\mathbf{R} = (m_1+m_2)g\boldsymbol{i}+\mathbf{R},$$

and

$$\dot{\mathbf{L}} = \mathbf{M}^E$$

where

$$\begin{aligned}\mathbf{M}^E &= \boldsymbol{r}_1\times(m_1 g\boldsymbol{i})+\boldsymbol{r}_2\times(m_2 g\boldsymbol{i}) = (m_1\boldsymbol{r}_1+m_2\boldsymbol{r}_2)\times(g\boldsymbol{i})\\ &= (m_1+m_2)\boldsymbol{r}_c\times(g\boldsymbol{i}) = \boldsymbol{r}_c\times\{(m_1+m_2)g\boldsymbol{i}\}.\end{aligned}$$

We have chosen to take moments about the fixed point O (rather than another fixed point or the centre of mass C) so that the reaction of the pivot, represented by $\mathbf{R}$, does not appear in the equation governing the rotational motion, which reduces to

$$I\boldsymbol{\omega} = \boldsymbol{r}_c\times\{(m_1+m_2)g\boldsymbol{i}\}$$

i.e.

$$I\ddot{\phi}\boldsymbol{k} = \{(X_c \cos\phi)\boldsymbol{i} + (X_c \sin\phi)\boldsymbol{j}\} \times \{(m_1+m_2)g\boldsymbol{i}\}$$
$$= -(m_1+m_2)gX_c \sin\phi\,\boldsymbol{k}$$

The differential equation governing the motion of the dumb-bell is

$$I\ddot{\phi} + (m_1+m_2)gX_c \sin\phi = 0$$

This has the same form as the differential equation governing the motion of a simple pendulum, which we considered in chapter 7, namely

$$\ddot{\phi} + \Omega^2 \sin\phi = 0$$

In particular, we note that the period of small-amplitude oscillations about the position of stable equilibrium ($\phi = 0$) is

$$\frac{2\pi}{\Omega} = 2\pi\left\{\frac{I}{(m_1+m_2)gX_c}\right\}^{1/2}$$
$$= 2\pi\left\{\frac{(m_1 l_1^2 + m_2 l_2^2)}{(m_1 l_1 - m_2 l_2)g}\right\}^{1/2}$$

The quantity $(m_1 l_1^2 + m_2 l_2^2)/(m_1 l_1 - m_2 l_2)$ is called the *length of the equivalent simple pendulum.*

It remains for us to calculate the reaction of the pivot on the dumb-bell. Using the equation governing the motion of the centre of mass, we obtain

$$\begin{aligned}\mathbf{R} &= (m_1+m_2)\ddot{\boldsymbol{r}}_c - (m_1+m_2)g\boldsymbol{i}\\ &= (m_1+m_2)\{-X_c(\ddot{\phi}\sin\phi + \dot{\phi}^2\cos\phi) - g\}\boldsymbol{i}\\ &\quad + (m_1+m_2)\{X_c(\ddot{\phi}\cos\phi - \dot{\phi}^2\sin\phi)\}\boldsymbol{j}\\ &= -\{(m_1 l_1 - m_2 l_2)(\ddot{\phi}\sin\phi + \dot{\phi}^2\cos\phi) + (m_1+m_2)g\}\boldsymbol{i}\\ &\quad + \{(m_1 l_1 - m_2 l_2)(\ddot{\phi}\cos\phi - \dot{\phi}^2\sin\phi)\}\boldsymbol{j}\end{aligned}$$

We note that we may obtain $\dot{\phi}^2$ in terms of ϕ by integrating

$$0 = \ddot{\phi} + \Omega^2\sin\phi = \frac{d}{d\phi}\{\tfrac{1}{2}\dot{\phi}^2 - \Omega^2\cos\phi\}$$

with respect to ϕ and using the initial conditions to determine the arbitrary constant.

A special case arises when $m_1 l_1 - m_2 l_2 = 0$. The centre of mass is on the axis of rotation, the rate of change of linear momentum is zero, and the total moment of the external forces about O, which is the centre of mass and the centre of gravity, is zero. Thus

$$\boldsymbol{0} = \mathbf{F}^E = (m_1+m_2)g\boldsymbol{i} + \mathbf{R}$$

and

$$0 = \dot{\mathbf{L}} = I\ddot{\phi}\boldsymbol{k}\,.$$

The reaction of the pivot on the dumb-bell is constant (being equal and opposite to the weight of the dumb-bell) and no oscillatory motion is possible (the angular velocity of the dumb-bell being constant or zero).

One of the purposes of balancing a road wheel of a vehicle is to ensure that the centre of mass of the wheel is on the axis of rotation. If the centre of mass is on the axis of rotation, the wheel can take up an equilibrium position at any fixed value of the angle ϕ.

16.8 Compound pendulum

A dumb-bell is a simple rigid body having a discrete distribution of mass. Let us consider a continuous distribution of mass contained in a plane (e.g. a rod, a hoop, a square lamina, a circular lamina, etc.). We shall proceed as in the previous section, and we shall examine the motion of a lamina about a fixed horizontal axis, the lamina being in a vertical plane perpendicular to the axis of rotation for all time. We shall use the cartesian coordinate systems introduced in the previous section, the $Oxyz$-axes being fixed relative to an inertial frame of reference and the $OXYZ$-axes being fixed relative to the rigid body. In particular the axis of rotation coincides with the Oz, OZ-axes and intersects the lamina at O (the lamina being in the plane $z = 0$). Also the centre of mass C has the position vector $\boldsymbol{r}_c$ (relative to the origin), where

$$\boldsymbol{r}_c = (X_c \cos\phi)\boldsymbol{i} + (X_c \sin\phi)\boldsymbol{j}$$

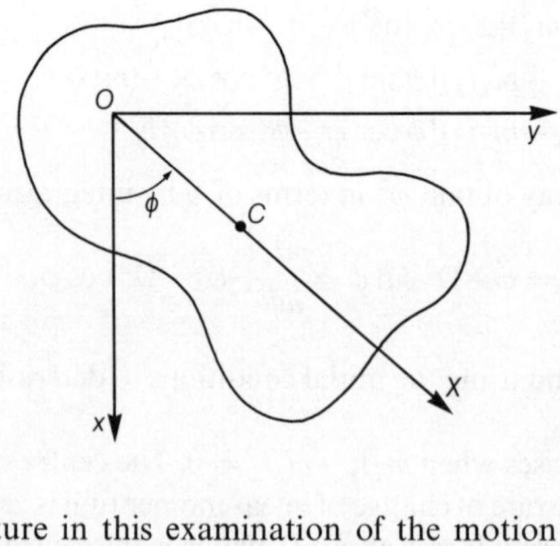

The new feature in this examination of the motion of the compound pendulum is the need to evaluate the angular momentum associated with a continuous distribution of mass. We are assuming that the determination of the position of the centre of mass of the lamina presents no difficulty (cf.

Section 16.3); i.e. X_c is a known length. Let m denote the mass of the lamina, and let S denote the region of the xy-plane occupied by the lamina. Then

$$m = \int_S \rho(P)\,dS$$

where $\rho(P)$ is the density at a typical point P of the lamina. The position vector of P (relative to the origin O) is

$$\boldsymbol{r}_P = x\boldsymbol{i} + y\boldsymbol{j} = (X\cos\phi - Y\sin\phi)\boldsymbol{i} + (X\sin\phi + Y\cos\phi)\boldsymbol{j}$$

The position of the centre of mass is defined by

$$m\boldsymbol{r}_c = \int_S \rho(P)\boldsymbol{r}_P\,dS$$

i.e.

$$mX_c = \iint_S \rho(X, Y)X\,dX\,dY \quad \text{and} \quad mY_c = \iint_S \rho(X, Y)Y\,dX\,dY = 0$$

The linear momentum of the lamina is

$$\boldsymbol{p} = m\dot{\boldsymbol{r}}_c$$

In this example, we have

$$\int_S \rho(P)\dot{\boldsymbol{r}}_P\,dS = \int_S \rho(P)\boldsymbol{\omega}\times\boldsymbol{r}_P\,dS = \boldsymbol{\omega}\times\int_S \rho(P)\boldsymbol{r}_P\,dS$$
$$= \boldsymbol{\omega}\times(m\boldsymbol{r}_c) = m(\boldsymbol{\omega}\times\boldsymbol{r}_c) = m\dot{\boldsymbol{r}}_c$$

i.e. the alternative definitions of the linear momentum are equivalent (cf. Section 16.4).

The angular momentum of the lamina about the fixed point O is

$$\mathbf{L} = \int_S \rho(P)\boldsymbol{r}_P\times\dot{\boldsymbol{r}}_P\,dS$$
$$= \int_S \rho(P)\boldsymbol{r}_P\times(\boldsymbol{\omega}\times\boldsymbol{r}_P)\,dS$$
$$= \int_S \rho(P)\{(\boldsymbol{r}_P\cdot\boldsymbol{r}_P)\boldsymbol{\omega} - (\boldsymbol{r}_P\cdot\boldsymbol{\omega})\boldsymbol{r}_P\}\,dS$$
$$= \int_S \rho(P)(\boldsymbol{r}_P\cdot\boldsymbol{r}_P)\,dS\,\boldsymbol{\omega}$$
$$= I\boldsymbol{\omega}$$

where

$$I = \iint_S \rho(X, Y)(X^2+Y^2)\,dX\,dY$$

To derive this expression for the angular momentum we have used the following results:

$$\dot{r}_P = \omega \times r_P, \quad r_P \cdot \omega = 0, \quad r_P \cdot r_P = x^2+y^2 = X^2+Y^2$$

The moment of inertia of the lamina about the axis of rotation, denoted by I, depends on the distribution of mass and is independent of time.

If the compound pendulum is in a uniform gravitational field of force, the effect of gravity is equivalent to a single force, represented by $mg\boldsymbol{i}$, acting at the centre of gravity, which coincides with the centre of mass C. Letting the reaction of the pivot on the lamina be represented by $\mathbf{R}$, and assuming that there are no forces other than the weight and the reaction, we find that the equations governing the motion are

$$\dot{\boldsymbol{p}} = m\ddot{\boldsymbol{r}}_c = mg\boldsymbol{i}+\mathbf{R}$$

and

$$\dot{\mathbf{L}} = I\ddot{\phi}\boldsymbol{k} = \boldsymbol{r}_c \times (mg\boldsymbol{i}) = -mgX_c \sin\phi\,\boldsymbol{k}$$

Thus we have

$$I\ddot{\phi}+mgX_c \sin\phi = 0$$

and

$$\mathbf{R} = -m\{X_c(\ddot{\phi}\sin\phi+\dot{\phi}^2\cos\phi)+g\}\boldsymbol{i}+m\{X_c(\ddot{\phi}\cos\phi-\dot{\phi}^2\sin\phi)\}\boldsymbol{j}$$

The period of small-amplitude oscillations about the position of stable equilibrium ($\phi = 0$) is

$$2\pi\{I/mgX_c\}^{1/2}$$

and the length of the equivalent simple pendulum is I/mX_c.

It is clear that we have to be able to calculate the moment of inertia of a rigid body about a specified axis, say the z-axis. If the mass of the rigid body is distributed discretely, then

$$I_{Oz} = \sum_{i=1}^{N} m_i(x_i^2+y_i^2)$$

The analogous expression for a continuous distribution of mass occupying the volume V is

$$I_{Oz} = \int_V \rho(P)\{r_P-(r_P \cdot k)k\} \cdot \{r_P-(r_P \cdot k)k\}\,dV$$

$$= \iiint_V \rho(X, Y, Z)(X^2+Y^2)\,dX\,dY\,dZ$$

Let us look at some particular examples.

(i) Calculate the moment of inertia of a uniform rigid rod of mass m and length l about a perpendicular axis (a) through the centre of mass (b) through an end point.

Suppose the rod is on the X-axis between the origin and the point whose X coordinate is l. Let ρ_0 be the uniform density (mass per unit length).

$$m = \int_0^l \rho_0 \, dX = \rho_0 l$$

$$mX_c = \int_0^l \rho_0 X \, dX = \tfrac{1}{2}\rho_0 l^2, \quad X_c = \tfrac{1}{2}l.$$

(a) Let I_{cz} denote the required moment of inertia, where

$$I_{cz} = \int_0^l \rho_0 (X - X_c)^2 \, dX = \tfrac{1}{3}\rho_0 [(X - X_c)^3]_0^l$$
$$= \tfrac{1}{3}\rho_0 l^3 (\tfrac{1}{8} + \tfrac{1}{8}) = \tfrac{1}{12} m l^2$$

(b) Let I_{Oz} denote the required moment of inertia, where

$$I_{Oz} = \int_0^l \rho_0 X^2 \, dX = \tfrac{1}{3}\rho_0 l^3 = \tfrac{1}{3} m l^2$$

We note that

$$I_{cz} = \int_0^l \rho_0 (X^2 - 2XX_c + X_c^2) \, dX$$
$$= I_{Oz} - 2X_c \int_0^l \rho_0 X \, dX + X_c^2 \int_0^l \rho_0 \, dX$$
$$= I_{Oz} - 2X_c m X_c + X_c^2 m = I_{Oz} - m X_c^2$$

The result that $I_{Oz} = I_{cz} + mX_c^2$ is a particular statement of the Parallel Axes Theorem that applies to all rigid bodies.

(ii) Calculate the moment of inertia of a uniform circular hoop of mass m and radius r_0 about (a) a diameter, (b) an axis through a point of the hoop and perpendicular to the plane of the hoop.

Suppose the hoop is in the XY-plane and has its centre at the origin. Let ρ_0 be the uniform density.

$$m = \int_0^{2\pi} \rho_0 r_0 \, d\phi = 2\pi \rho_0 r_0$$

The centre of mass C is at the origin.

(*a*) Let I_{cX} denote the required moment of inertia, where

$$I_{cX} = \int_0^{2\pi} \rho_0 (r_0 \sin\phi)^2 r_0 \, d\phi = \tfrac{1}{2}\rho_0 r_0^3 \int_0^{2\pi} (1-\cos 2\phi)\, d\phi$$

$$= \pi\rho_0 r_0^3 = \tfrac{1}{2} m r_0^2$$

We note that

$$I_{cY} = \int_0^{2\pi} \rho_0 (r_0 \cos\phi)^2 r_0 \, d\phi = \tfrac{1}{2} m r_0^2$$

(*b*) Let A be the point of the hoop on the X-axis and let I_{Az} denote the required moment of inertia, where

$$I_{Az} = \int_0^{2\pi} \rho_0 \{(r_0 - r_0\cos\phi)^2 + (r_0 \sin\phi)^2\} r_0 \, d\phi$$

$$= 2\rho_0 r_0^3 \int_0^{2\pi} (1-\cos\phi)\, d\phi = 4\pi\rho_0 r_0^3 = 2 m r_0^2$$

We note that

$$I_{cz} = \int_0^{2\pi} \rho_0 r_0^2 r_0 \, d\phi = 2\pi\rho_0 r_0^3 = m r_0^2$$

and that $I_{Az} = I_{cz} + m r_0^2$, this being another illustration of the Parallel Axes Theorem. Further we note that

$$I_{cz} = I_{cX} + I_{cY}$$

which is an example of the statement of the Perpendicular Axes Theorem that applies to plane rigid bodies (it being essential that the mass be distributed over a region of a plane).

(iii) Calculate the moment of inertia of a uniform square plate (of negligible thickness) of mass m and side l about (*a*) an edge, (*b*) an axis through a corner of the plate and perpendicular to the plane of the plate.

Suppose the plate is in the XY-plane and is bounded by the X-axis, the line $X = l$, the line $Y = l$ and the Y-axis. Let ρ_0 be the uniform density (mass per unit area).

$$m = \int_0^l \int_0^l \rho_0 \, dX\, dY = \rho_0 l^2$$

(*a*) Let I_{OX} denote the required moment of inertia, where

$$I_{OX} = \int_0^l \int_0^l \rho_0 Y^2 \, dX\, dY = \int_0^l \rho_0 l Y^2 \, dY$$

$$= \tfrac{1}{3}\rho_0 l^4 = \tfrac{1}{3} m l^2$$

(*b*) Let I_{Oz} denote the required moment of inertia, where

$$I_{Oz} = \int_0^l \int_0^l \rho_0(X^2+Y^2)\,dX\,dY = \rho_0 \int_0^l (\tfrac{1}{3}l^3 + Y^2 l)\,dY$$
$$= \tfrac{2}{3}\rho_0 l^4 = \tfrac{2}{3}ml^2$$

We note another illustration of the Perpendicular Axes Theorem, namely

$$I_{Oz} = I_{OX} + I_{OY}$$

where

$$I_{OY} = \int_0^l \int_0^l \rho_0 X^2\,dX\,dY = \rho_0 \int_0^l \tfrac{1}{3}l^3\,dY = \tfrac{1}{3}ml^2$$

(iv) Calculate the moment of inertia of a uniform circular lamina of mass m and radius r_0 about (*a*) a diameter, (*b*) an axis through the centre of the lamina and perpendicular to the plane of the lamina.

Suppose the lamina is in the XY-plane and has its centre at the origin. Let ρ_0 be the uniform density.

$$m = \int_0^{r_0} \int_0^{2\pi} \rho_0 r\,d\phi\,dr = \int_0^{r_0} \rho_0\,2\pi r\,dr = \pi\rho_0 r_0^2$$

The centre of mass C is at the origin.

(*a*) Let I_{cX} denote the required moment of inertia, where

$$I_{cX} = \int_0^{r_0} \int_0^{2\pi} \rho_0(r\sin\phi)^2 r\,d\phi\,dr = \tfrac{1}{2}\rho_0 \int_0^{r_0} \int_0^{2\pi} r^3(1-\cos 2\phi)\,d\phi\,dr$$
$$= \pi\rho_0 \int_0^{r_0} r^3\,dr = \tfrac{1}{4}\pi\rho_0 r_0^4 = \tfrac{1}{4}mr_0^2$$

(*b*) Let I_{cz} denote the required moment of inertia, where

$$I_{cz} = \int_0^{r_0} \int_0^{2\pi} \rho_0 r^2 r\,d\phi\,dr = \int_0^{r_0} \rho_0 r^2 2\pi r\,dr$$
$$= 2\pi\rho_0 \int_0^{r_0} r^3\,dr = \tfrac{1}{2}\pi\rho_0 r_0^4 = \tfrac{1}{2}mr_0^2$$

We note another example of the statement of the Perpendicular Axes Theorem, namely

$$I_{cz} = I_{cX} + I_{cY}$$

where

$$I_{cY} = \int_0^{r_0} \int_0^{2\pi} \rho_0(r\cos\phi)^2 r\,d\phi\,dr = \tfrac{1}{4}mr_0^2$$

We have mentioned in the above examples, the Parallel Axes Theorem and the Perpendicular Axes Theorem. These theorems are important aids. They allow the complicated evaluation of a moment of inertia to be split into a sequence of simple steps. Consider a rigid body having a discrete mass distribution. Suppose there are N particles $P_1, P_2, \ldots, P_N$ having masses $m_1, m_2, \ldots, m_N$ and having position vectors $\boldsymbol{r}_1, \boldsymbol{r}_2, \ldots, \boldsymbol{r}_N$ relative to the origin O. The mass of the rigid body is

$$m = \sum_{i=1}^{N} m_i$$

and the position vector of the centre of mass C is $\boldsymbol{r}_c$, where

$$m\boldsymbol{r}_c = \sum_{i=1}^{N} m_i \boldsymbol{r}_i$$

Let I_{cz} denote the moment of inertia of the rigid body about an axis parallel to the z-axis through the centre of mass C, and let I_{Az} denote the moment of inertia about a parallel axis through a point A, whose position vector is $\boldsymbol{r}_A$. We have

$$I_{cz} = \sum_{i=1}^{N} m_i\{(x_i - x_c)^2 + (y_i - y_c)^2\}$$

and

$$I_{Az} = \sum_{i=1}^{N} m_i\{(x_i - x_A)^2 + (y_i - y_A)^2\}$$

It follows that

$$\begin{aligned} I_{Az} &= \sum_{i=1}^{N} m_i\{(x_i - x_c - x_A + x_c)^2 + (y_i - y_c - y_A + y_c)^2\} \\ &= \sum_{i=1}^{N} m_i\{(x_i - x_c)^2 - 2(x_i - x_c)(x_A - x_c) + (x_A - x_c)^2 \\ &\quad + (y_i - y_c)^2 - 2(y_i - y_c)(y_A - y_c) + (y_A - y_c)^2\} \\ &= I_{cz} + m\{(x_A - x_c)^2 + (y_A - y_c)^2\} = I_{cz} + md^2 \end{aligned}$$

where d is the distance between the parallel axes through the centre of mass C and the point A. This is a statement of the Parallel Axes Theorem. The theorem applies to rigid bodies having a continuous distribution of mass, its proof being analogous with integration replacing summation.

Let I_{Ax} and I_{Ay} denote the moments of inertia of the rigid body about axes parallel to the x-axis and y-axis through the point A. Then

$$I_{Ax} = \sum_{i=1}^{N} m_i\{(y_i - y_A)^2 + (z_i - z_A)^2\}$$

and

$$I_{Ay} = \sum_{i=1}^{N} m_i\{(x_i - x_A)^2 + (z_i - z_A)^2\}$$

If the rigid body is confined to the plane $z = z_A$, we have

$$I_{Ax} + I_{Ay} = \sum_{i=1}^{N} m_i\{(y_i - y_A)^2\} + \sum_{i=1}^{N} m_i\{(x_i - x_A)^2\} = I_{Az}$$

This is a statement of the Perpendicular Axes Theorem, which applies to any plane rigid body. The proof for the case of mass distributed continuously over a region of a plane is obvious.

EXAMPLE

A uniform circular lamina is rigidly attached at a point A of its circumference to a uniform rigid rod AB to form a pendulum. The rod is in the plane of the lamina and is normal to the circumference of the lamina. The circular lamina has mass M and radius r_0 and the rod has mass m and length l. The pendulum is allowed to oscillate in a vertical plane about a fixed horizontal axis through B. Determine an expression for the length of the equivalent simple pendulum.

The pendulum formed out of the rod and circular lamina is a model of a grandfather clock pendulum.

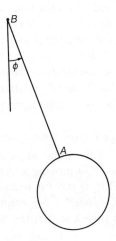

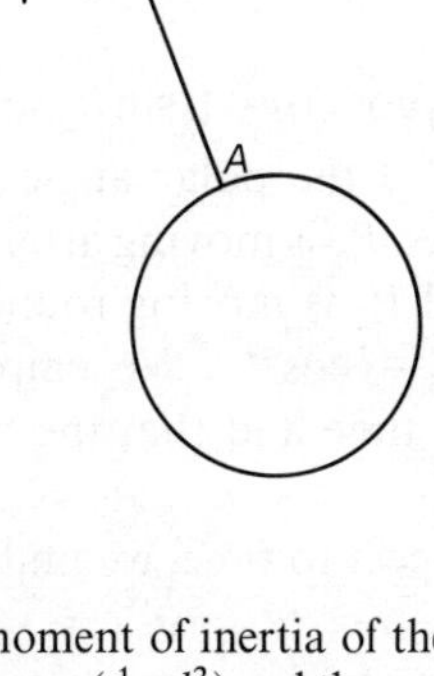

Suppose that we know the moment of inertia of the rod about a perpendicular axis through the rod's centre of mass ($\frac{1}{12}ml^2$) and the moment of inertia of the lamina about a perpendicular axis through the lamina's centre of mass ($\frac{1}{2}Mr_0^2$). Applying the Parallel Axes Theorem we obtain the required moment of inertia of the pendulum about the horizontal axis through B, namely

$$I_{BZ} = \{\tfrac{1}{12}ml^2 + m(\tfrac{1}{2}l)^2\} + \{\tfrac{1}{2}Mr_0^2 + M(l+r_0)^2\}$$
$$= \tfrac{1}{3}ml^2 + M\{\tfrac{1}{2}r_0^2 + (l+r_0)^2\}$$

The equation $\dot{\mathbf{L}} = \mathbf{M}^E$ (involving moments about B) leads to

$$I_{BZ}\ddot{\phi} = -mg(\tfrac{1}{2}l)\sin\phi - Mg(l+r_0)\sin\phi$$

where the angle ϕ has its usual definition (see figure). Thus the length of the equivalent simple pendulum is

$$\frac{\tfrac{1}{3}ml^2 + M\{\tfrac{1}{2}r_0^2 + (l+r_0)^2\}}{\tfrac{1}{2}ml + M(l+r_0)}$$

We note that this result includes many special cases, e.g. a light rod and a heavy lamina ($m = 0$), a heavy rod and a particle ($r_0 = 0$).

16.9 Atwood's machine

In our discussion of Atwood's machine in chapter 13 we ignored the effect of the motion of the pulley by substituting a smooth peg for the pulley. We are now in a position to consider the effect of the motion of the pulley about a fixed horizontal axis. Before we re-examine Atwood's machine, we shall take a brief look at the problem of balancing a road wheel of a vehicle, which we introduced in Section 16.7.

Consider a dumb-bell consisting of two particles P_1 and P_2 connected by a light rigid rod of length $2l$. Suppose that the mass of each particle is m and that the dumb-bell is pivoted about the mid-point of the rod, which is the centre of mass of this simple rigid body. We are interested in the motion of the dumb-bell about a fixed horizontal axis through the pivot O during which the inclination of the dumb-bell to the horizontal axis is a constant angle θ_0. Using the cartesian axes introduced in Section 16.7, we are able to write the position vectors of P_1 and P_2 relative to O in the form

$$\boldsymbol{r}_1 = (l\sin\theta_0\cos\phi)\boldsymbol{i} + (l\sin\theta_0\sin\phi)\boldsymbol{j} + (l\cos\theta_0)\boldsymbol{k}$$

and

$$\boldsymbol{r}_2 = -(l\sin\theta_0\cos\phi)\boldsymbol{i} - (l\sin\theta_0\sin\phi)\boldsymbol{j} - (l\cos\theta_0)\boldsymbol{k}$$

The angles θ_0 and ϕ are the polar angle and the azimuthal angle of spherical polar coordinates. P_1 is moving around a circle of radius $l\sin\theta_0$ in the plane $z = l\cos\theta_0$, and P_2 is moving round a circle of the same radius $l\sin\theta_0$ in the plane $z = -l\cos\theta_0$. We emphasize that ϕ is the single coordinate dependent on time and that the dumb-bell has one degree of freedom.

Differentiating with respect to time, we find that

$$\dot{\boldsymbol{r}}_1 = (-l\sin\theta_0\sin\phi)\dot{\phi}\boldsymbol{i} + (l\sin\theta_0\cos\phi)\dot{\phi}\boldsymbol{j}$$
$$= \boldsymbol{\omega}\times\boldsymbol{r}_1$$

and

$$\begin{aligned}\dot{\boldsymbol{r}}_2 &= -(-l\sin\theta_0\sin\phi)\dot{\phi}\boldsymbol{i}-(l\sin\theta_0\cos\phi)\dot{\phi}\boldsymbol{j}\\ &= \boldsymbol{\omega}\times\boldsymbol{r}_2\end{aligned}$$

where $\boldsymbol{\omega} = \dot{\phi}\boldsymbol{k}$. The centre of mass C is at the origin O because

$$m\boldsymbol{r}_1 + m\boldsymbol{r}_2 = \boldsymbol{0}$$

and the linear momentum of the dumb-bell is

$$\boldsymbol{p} = m\dot{\boldsymbol{r}}_1 + m\dot{\boldsymbol{r}}_2 = \boldsymbol{0}$$

The angular momentum of the dumb-bell about the origin O is

$$\begin{aligned}\mathbf{L} &= \boldsymbol{r}_1\times(m\dot{\boldsymbol{r}}_1)+\boldsymbol{r}_2\times(m\dot{\boldsymbol{r}}_2)\\ &= m\boldsymbol{r}_1\times(\boldsymbol{\omega}\times\boldsymbol{r}_1)+m\boldsymbol{r}_2\times(\boldsymbol{\omega}\times\boldsymbol{r}_2)\\ &= m\{(\boldsymbol{r}_1\cdot\boldsymbol{r}_1)\,\boldsymbol{\omega}-(\boldsymbol{r}_1\cdot\boldsymbol{\omega})\boldsymbol{r}_1\}+m\{(\boldsymbol{r}_2\cdot\boldsymbol{r}_2)\boldsymbol{\omega}-(\boldsymbol{r}_2\cdot\boldsymbol{\omega})\boldsymbol{r}_2\}\\ &= m\{l^2\boldsymbol{\omega}-l\dot{\phi}\cos\theta_0\boldsymbol{r}_1\}+m\{l^2\boldsymbol{\omega}+l\dot{\phi}\cos\theta_0\boldsymbol{r}_2\}\\ &= -2ml^2\sin\theta_0\cos\theta_0\{\boldsymbol{i}\cos\phi+\boldsymbol{j}\sin\phi\}\dot{\phi}+2ml^2\sin^2\theta_0\boldsymbol{\omega}\end{aligned}$$

We note that $\mathbf{L}$ is not parallel to the axis of rotation, namely the z-axis. The terms $2ml^2\sin\theta_0\cos\theta_0\cos\phi$ and $2ml^2\sin\theta_0\cos\theta_0\sin\phi$ are called the *products of inertia*, the first being associated with the z-axis and the x-axis, and the second being associated with the y-axis and the z-axis. Their general forms are

$$\sum_{i=1}^{N} m_i z_i x_i \quad\text{and}\quad \sum_{i=1}^{N} m_i y_i z_i$$

The product of inertia associated with the x-axis and the y-axis has the form

$$\sum_{i=1}^{N} m_i x_i y_i$$

and does not arise in this problem. The term $2ml^2\sin^2\theta_0$ is the moment of inertia about the z-axis, which has the general form

$$\sum_{i=1}^{N} m_i(x_i^2+y_i^2).$$

The above products of inertia associated with pairs of axes of the inertial frame of reference vary with time. However the term $2ml^2\sin\theta_0\cos\theta_0$ is a product of inertia associated with a pair of axes fixed relative to the dumb-bell and is independent of time.

Calculating the rate of change of linear momentum and the rate of change of angular momentum about the origin O, we obtain

$$\dot{\boldsymbol{p}} = \boldsymbol{0}$$

and

$$\begin{aligned}\dot{\mathbf{L}} = & -2ml^2 \sin\theta_0 \cos\theta_0 \{\ddot{\phi}\cos\phi - \dot{\phi}^2 \sin\phi\}\boldsymbol{i} \\ & -2ml^2 \sin\theta_0 \cos\theta_0 \{\ddot{\phi}\sin\phi + \dot{\phi}^2 \cos\phi\}\boldsymbol{j} \\ & +2ml^2 \sin^2\theta_0 \ddot{\phi}\boldsymbol{k}\end{aligned}$$

The equation $\dot{\boldsymbol{p}} = \mathbf{F}^E$ implies that the total external force is zero, and the equation $\dot{\mathbf{L}} = \mathbf{M}^E$ implies that the total moment of the external forces has three non-zero components in general. We deduce that we require a couple to maintain the motion of the dumb-bell about the fixed horizontal axis. The reaction of the pivot and the weight of the dumb-bell act through the origin O and make no contribution to the total moment of the forces about O. The dumb-bell will rotate with constant angular speed ω (i.e. $\dot{\phi} = \omega$ and $\phi = \omega t$) provided (i) we apply a couple whose torque is

$$\mathbf{T} = 2ml^2\omega^2 \sin\theta_0 \cos\theta_0 \{\boldsymbol{i}\sin\omega t - \boldsymbol{j}\cos\omega t\}$$

which depends on time, and (ii) we apply a constant force at the pivot to counterbalance the weight of the dumb-bell. We do not require the application of the couple when the product of inertia (associated with the pair of axes fixed relative to the dumb-bell, namely OZ and OX) is zero. Non-zero products of inertia indicate unsymmetric distributions of mass.

The balancing of a road wheel of a vehicle is done in two stages. The first stage, called the *static balance*, is to adjust the centre of mass to lie on the axis of rotation. The second stage, called the *dynamic balance*, is to ensure that the products of inertia are zero, so that the direction of the angular momentum coincides with the direction of the angular velocity (i.e. $\boldsymbol{\omega} \times \mathbf{L} = \boldsymbol{0}$). Small pieces of metal (of maximum mass 0·17 kg) are fitted to the rim of the wheel at appropriate positions to correct the distribution of mass. Special apparatus is available to indicate the correct mass and position of the pieces to be fitted to make the wheel rotate smoothly.

We shall assume that the pulley of the Atwood's machine is balanced, and that the angular momentum of the pulley is proportional to the angular velocity, the constant of proportionality being the moment of inertia of the pulley about the fixed horizontal axis. The string connecting the two objects passes over the pulley and does not slip, i.e. the contact between the string and the pulley is rough. The constant length of the string and the non-slip condition provide two kinematic conditions.

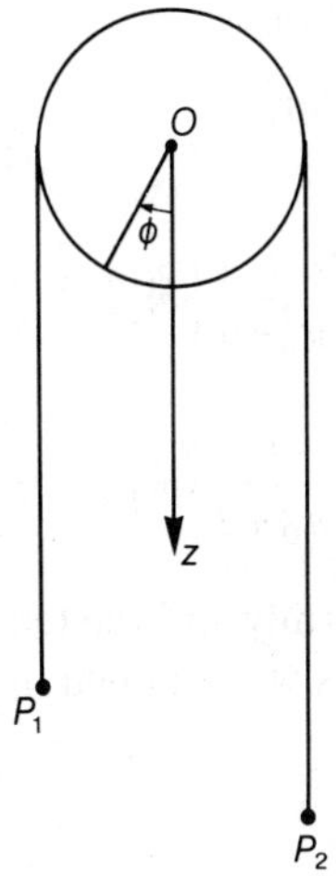

Adopting the notation introduced in Section 13.3, we are able to write the the equations governing the motion in the form

$$m_1 \ddot{z}_1 = m_1 g - T_1$$

$$m_2 \ddot{z}_2 = m_2 g - T_2$$

and

$$I\ddot{\phi} = (T_2 - T_1) r_0$$

where I is the moment of inertia of the pulley about the fixed horizontal axis and r_0 is the radius of the pulley. The constant length of the string implies that

$$z_1 + z_2 + \pi r_0 = \text{constant}$$

and the non-slip condition implies that

$$r_0 \dot{\phi} = \dot{z}_2$$

Thus we have $\ddot{z}_1 + \ddot{z}_2 = 0$ and $r_0 \ddot{\phi} = \ddot{z}_2$. It is important to notice that the rough contact between the string and the pulley causes the tensions T_1 and T_2 to be unequal. Eliminating T_1 and T_2 and using the two kinematic conditions, we find that

$$\begin{aligned} I\ddot{\phi} &= (m_2 g - m_2 \ddot{z}_2) r_0 - (m_1 g - m_1 \ddot{z}_1) r_0 \\ &= (m_2 - m_1) g r_0 - m_2 r_0^2 \ddot{\phi} - m_1 r_0^2 \ddot{\phi} \end{aligned}$$

Thus

$$\ddot{\phi} = \frac{(m_2 - m_1)gr_0}{(m_1 + m_2)r_0^2 + I}$$

$$\ddot{z}_2 = \frac{(m_2 - m_1)gr_0^2}{(m_1 + m_2)r_0^2 + I} = -\ddot{z}_1$$

$$T_1 = \left\{\frac{2m_2 r_0^2 + I}{(m_1 + m_2)r_0^2 + I}\right\} m_1 g$$

and

$$T_2 = \left\{\frac{2m_1 r_0^2 + I}{(m_1 + m_2)r_0^2 + I}\right\} m_2 g$$

The particles accelerate uniformly and the tensions are constant. When we set $I = 0$, we regain the results we obtained in Section 13.3.

EXERCISES ON CHAPTER 16

1. Calculate the position vector of the centre of mass of the system of three particles P_1, P_2 and P_3; P_1 having mass m and position vector $\boldsymbol{i}-2\boldsymbol{j}-\boldsymbol{k}$, P_2 having mass $2m$ and position vector $-2\boldsymbol{i}+\boldsymbol{j}+2\boldsymbol{k}$ and P_3 having mass $3m$ and position vector $3\boldsymbol{i}+2\boldsymbol{j}+\boldsymbol{k}$.

2. C_1 is the centre of mass of a system of particles having total mass m_1, and C_2 is the centre of mass of a second system of particles having total mass m_2. Show that the centre of mass of the combined system of particles is the same as the centre of mass of a particle of mass m_1 at C_1 and a particle of mass m_2 at C_2.

3. A rod of uniform density ρ_1 and length l_1 is joined to a rod of uniform density ρ_2 and length l_2 to form a rod of length l_1+l_2. Determine the distance of the centre of mass of the composite rod from the join.

4. Four uniform rods, each of length l, form a square frame whose vertices have the position vectors $\boldsymbol{0}$, $l\boldsymbol{i}$, $l(\boldsymbol{i}+\boldsymbol{j})$ and $l\boldsymbol{j}$. Each of the two rods meeting at the origin has mass m, and each of the other rods has mass $3m$. Find the position vector of the centre of mass of the frame.

5. Show that the centre of mass of a piece of wire shaped in the form of an arc of a circle of radius r_0 and centre O is a distance $r_0(\sin\alpha)/\alpha$ from O, where 2α is the angle subtended by the arc at O.

6. A uniform flat plate consists of a square plate of side l joined along an edge to an equilateral triangular plate of side l. Find the distance from the centre of mass of the combined plate to the edge common to the square and triangular plates.

7. Determine the distance between the centre of mass of a uniform semicircular lamina, of radius r_0, and the bounding diameter.

8. A square plate of side l is removed from a square uniform plate of side $2l$ in order to make an L-shaped plate. What is the distance between the centre of mass of the L-shaped plate and the centre of the original square plate?

9. A uniform hemispherical shell has radius r_0. Find the distance between the centre of mass and the centre of the circular rim.

A uniform conical shell is made from the same material, the radius of the circular rim being r_0 and the cone's height being r_0. What is the distance between the centre of mass of the conical shell and the centre of the circular rim?

If the two shells are joined to form a convex shell, find the distance of the centre of mass of the convex shell from the centre of the common circular rim of the component parts.

10. Determine the distance between the centre of mass of a uniform hemisphere of radius r_0, and the centre of the plane base.

11. A rigid body experiences a system of forces,

$$
\begin{array}{ll}
3F_0\boldsymbol{i} & \text{acting at } \; l\boldsymbol{i} \\
2F_0(-\boldsymbol{i}+\sqrt{3}\boldsymbol{j}) & \text{acting at } \; \sqrt{3}l\boldsymbol{j} \\
4F_0(-\boldsymbol{i}-\sqrt{3}\boldsymbol{j}) & \text{acting at } \; -l\boldsymbol{i}
\end{array}
$$

Find the resultant (its magnitude, direction and line of action).

12. A rigid body experiences a system of forces,

$$F_1\boldsymbol{i}+8F_0\boldsymbol{j} \quad \text{acting at the origin}$$

$$
\begin{array}{ll}
2F_0 i + F_2 j & \text{acting at } li \\
-4F_0 j & \text{acting at } l(i+j) \\
-6F_0 i + F_3 j & \text{acting at } lj
\end{array}
$$

Evaluate F_1, F_2 and F_3 in terms of F_0 so that the system of forces is in equilibrium.

13. Find the magnitude and direction of the resultant of the system of forces,

$$
\begin{array}{ll}
F_0(i+2j) & \text{acting at } l(i+j) \\
F_0(-3i+4j) & \text{acting at } l(-i+j) \\
F_0(-2i-5j) & \text{acting at } l(-i-j) \\
F_0(2i-2j) & \text{acting at } l(i-j)
\end{array}
$$

Determine the line of action of this resultant. Verify that the point having the position vector $l(i+2j)$ is on the line of action and that the total moment of the system about this point is zero.

14. A rigid body experiences a system of forces,

$$
\begin{array}{ll}
-F_0 i & \text{acting at the origin} \\
F_1(i+2j) & \text{acting at } li \\
F_2(-i+2j) & \text{acting at } l(2i+j) \\
3F_0 i & \text{acting at } l(i+2j) \\
2F_0 j & \text{acting at } 2lj
\end{array}
$$

Determine F_1 and F_2 in terms of F_0 so that the system is equivalent to a couple. Evaluate the torque of the couple.

15. A system of six forces,

$$
\begin{array}{ll}
F_0 i & \text{acting at } li \\
-2F_0 k & \text{acting at } lj \\
3F_0 j & \text{acting at } lk \\
4F_0 k & \text{acting at } l(i+j) \\
-F_0 j & \text{acting at } l(i+k) \\
2F_0 i & \text{acting at } l(j+k)
\end{array}
$$

is applied to a rigid body. Show that it is equivalent to a single force **F** acting at the origin together with a couple of moment **T**. Determine **F** and **T**.

16. Forces represented by

$$F_0(2i-k), \quad F_0(j+4k), \quad F_0(i-3j+k), \quad -F_0(j+k)$$

act on a rigid body, their points of application having the position vectors

$$l(2i+j), \quad lj, \quad 2lj, \quad lk, \quad \text{respectively.}$$

Show that this system of forces is equivalent to a single force **F**. Determine **F** and the point in the xy-plane that is on the line of action.

17. Show that the system of forces

$$-F_0 j \text{ acting at } li,\ F_0 k \text{ acting at } lj,\ F_0 i \text{ acting at } lk,$$
$$-F_0 i \text{ acting at } l(j+k),\ F_0(j-k) \text{ acting at } l(i+j),$$

is equivalent to a couple. Determine the torque of the equivalent couple.

18. Show that the system of four forces

$F_0(\boldsymbol{i}-\boldsymbol{k})$	acting at	$l\boldsymbol{i}$
$F_0\boldsymbol{j}$	acting at	$l\boldsymbol{j}$
$-F_0(\boldsymbol{i}+\boldsymbol{j}-2\boldsymbol{k})$	acting at	$l\boldsymbol{k}$
$-F_0\boldsymbol{k}$	acting at	$l(\boldsymbol{j}+\boldsymbol{k})$

is in equilibrium.

19. The corners of a cube are $A, B, C, D, A', B', C', D'$ (A' above A, etc.). Forces, all of magnitude F_0, act on the cube. Their points of application are

$$A,\ C,\ A',\ C',\ B,\ D$$

and their directions are the directions of the line segments

$$\overrightarrow{AB},\quad \overrightarrow{CD},\quad \overrightarrow{A'D'},\quad \overrightarrow{C'B'},\quad \overrightarrow{BB'},\quad \overrightarrow{DD'},$$

respectively. Show that this system is equivalent to a single force of magnitude $2F_0$ acting at the centre of the face $ABCD$ in the direction of the line segment $\overrightarrow{AA'}$.

20. The total moments of a system of forces about three points having the position vectors

$$l\boldsymbol{i},\quad l(\boldsymbol{j}+\boldsymbol{k}),\quad l(\boldsymbol{i}+\boldsymbol{j}+\boldsymbol{k})$$

are $F_0l(-\boldsymbol{i}+2\boldsymbol{j})$, $F_0l(\boldsymbol{i}+\boldsymbol{j}+3\boldsymbol{k})$, $F_0l(\boldsymbol{i}+2\boldsymbol{k})$ respectively.

Show that the system is equivalent to a single force. Find the components of the resultant force and the coordinates of a point on its line of action.

21. Four particles each of mass $\frac{1}{4}m$ are fixed to a light rigid rod AB of length l, their distances from A being $\frac{1}{4}l, \frac{1}{2}l, \frac{3}{4}l$ and l. The rigid body is free to rotate in a vertical plane about a fixed horizontal axis through the end A. Calculate the length of the equivalent simple pendulum.

What is the corresponding length when N equal particles are similarly distributed along the light rigid rod?

$$\left[\sum_{i=1}^{N} i = \tfrac{1}{2}N(N+1),\quad \sum_{i=1}^{N} i^2 = \tfrac{1}{6}N(N+1)(2N+1).\right]$$

22. A uniform rigid rod of length l is free to rotate in a vertical plane about a fixed horizontal axis through one of its ends. Calculate the length of the equivalent simple pendulum.

23. A uniform rigid rod of length l is free to oscillate in a vertical plane about a point that is a distance d along the rod from the centre of mass. Show that the period of small-amplitude oscillations about the position of stable equilibrium is $2\pi\{(\frac{1}{12}l^2+d^2)/gd\}^{1/2}$. Investigate the manner in which the period varies with the distance d. What is the minimum value of the period?

24. A uniform rigid rod AB of mass m is smoothly pivoted at A. It is horizontal when it is released from rest. Determine the force of the pivot on the rod in the subsequent motion.

25. A rigid rod AB of mass m and length l has a non-uniform density. Its density varies linearly along the length, taking the value ρ_0 at A and the value $2\rho_0$ at B. Show that $m = \frac{3}{2}\rho_0 l$ and that the distance between the centre of mass and A is $5l/9$. Calculate the moment of inertia about a perpendicular axis through A.

Find the length of the equivalent simple pendulum when the rod is free to oscillate in a vertical plane about a fixed horizontal axis through A.

26. A rigid rod AB has periods T_A and T_B when free to perform small-amplitude oscillations in a vertical plane about fixed horizontal axes through A and B, respectively. Show that

$$\frac{g}{4\pi^2}(T_A^2 d_A - T_B^2 d_B) = d_A^2 - d_B^2$$

and

$$\frac{4\pi^2}{g} = \frac{1}{2}\left\{\frac{T_A^2 + T_B^2}{d_A + d_B} + \frac{T_A^2 - T_B^2}{d_A - d_B}\right\}$$

where the distances from the centre of mass (which coincides with the centre of gravity) to A and B are d_A and d_B, respectively.

27. A uniform rectangular lamina has mass m and the lengths of its sides are x_0 and y_0. Calculate the moment of inertia about an axis through a corner and perpendicular to the lamina.

28. Show that the moment of inertia of a uniform triangular lamina ABC of mass m about the side BC is $\frac{1}{6}md^2$, where d is the length of the perpendicular from A to BC. Deduce the moment of inertia of a uniform square lamina of mass m and side l about a diagonal.

29. A uniform square lamina of side l is free to oscillate with its plane vertical about a smooth horizontal axis through a corner. Determine the period of small-amplitude oscillations about the position of stable equilibrium.

30. A uniform square lamina $ABCD$, of mass m and side l, is free to turn with its plane vertical about a smooth horizontal axis through A and has a particle of mass M attached to it at C. If the lamina is released from rest when AC is horizontal, find the lamina's angular speed when AC is vertical.

31. Four uniform rods, each of the same mass and length l, are rigidly joined together to form a square frame. The frame is free to oscillate with its plane vertical about a smooth horizontal axis through a corner. Determine the length of the equivalent simple pendulum.

32. A uniform hoop of mass m and radius r_0 is free to rotate in a vertical plane about a fixed horizontal axis through a point A of the hoop. A particle of mass M is attached to the hoop at the point diametrically opposite to A. Show that the length of the equivalent simple pendulum is $2r_0$.

33. A uniform circular lamina of mass m and radius r_0 is free to rotate in a vertical plane about a fixed horizontal axis through a point A of the circumference of the lamina. A particle of mass M is attached to the circumference of the lamina at the point diametrically opposite to A. Calculate the length of the equivalent simple pendulum.

34. An annular lamina has an outer circular edge and an inner circular edge, which have a common centre and have radii r_0 and r_1 ($r_1 < r_0$). Its mass is m and it has a uniform density ρ_0. Show that

$$m = \pi\rho_0(r_0^2 - r_1^2)$$

and that the moment of inertia about an axis through the centre and perpendicular to the plane of the lamina is

$$\tfrac{1}{2}m(r_0^2+r_1^2)$$

35. A pulley in the form of a uniform circular lamina of mass M and radius r_0 rotates smoothly about its axis, which is fixed and horizontal. An inextensible string passes over the pulley and has two particles of masses m and $2m$ attached to its ends. If there is no slip between the string and the pulley, and the parts of the string not in contact with the pulley are vertical, calculate the acceleration of the particle of mass $2m$.

36. An inextensible string carrying a particle at each of its ends passes over a cylinder, which is free to turn about its axis, the axis being fixed and horizontal. The string does not slip and it is in a plane perpendicular to the axis, the parts not in contact with the cylinder being vertical. Show that the acceleration of either particle is

$$\frac{g}{(1+2/\alpha+\beta/2\alpha)}$$

where m and $(1+\alpha)m$ are the masses of the particles and βm is the mass of the cylinder.

37. An Atwood's machine has a pulley whose radius is r_0 and whose moment of inertia about its axis is I. The bearings exert a constant frictional couple, the torque of which has a magnitude T_F and a direction opposite to that of the angular velocity of the pulley. Determine the difference between the tensions on the two sides of the pulley when the inextensible string passing over the pulley carries objects of mass m_1 and m_2 at its ends.

38. A flywheel has a shaft of radius r_0. The moment of inertia of the flywheel and the shaft about a fixed horizontal axis of rotation is I. An inextensible string coiled round the shaft supports a particle of mass m hanging vertically. The system starts from rest and its motion is retarded by a constant frictional couple, the torque of which has a magnitude T_F. After the flywheel has turned through an angle Φ_1, the string runs off the shaft. The flywheel then turns through a further angle Φ_2 before coming to rest again. Show that

$$T_F=\frac{mgr_0}{\{1+(1+mr_0^2/I)\Phi_2/\Phi_1\}}$$

Determine the flywheel's maximum angular speed.

39. Show that the moment of inertia of a uniform solid circular cylinder of mass m, radius r_0 and length l about an axis through the centre of mass perpendicular to the axis of symmetry is

$$m(\tfrac{1}{4}r_0^2+\tfrac{1}{12}l^2)$$

Show that the moment of inertia of a uniform open-ended circular cylindrical shell of mass m, radius r_0 and length l about an axis through the centre of mass perpendicular to the axis of symmetry is

$$m(\tfrac{1}{2}r_0^2+\tfrac{1}{12}l^2)$$

40. Show that the moment of inertia of a uniform sphere of mass m and radius r_0 about a diameter is $\tfrac{2}{5}mr_0^2$.

Show that the moment of inertia of a uniform spherical shell of mass m and radius r_0 about a diameter is $\tfrac{2}{3}mr_0^2$.

Answers

Chapter 2 (p. 40)

1. 36 km
2. 60 km per hour, $16\frac{2}{3}$ m s^{-1}
4. 20·8 km, 1·067 rad (61°9′) north of east, 0·1805 rad (10°21′)
7. 24 s, 768 m
8. $T = \{2L(A+R)/AR\}^{1/2} \qquad 0 \leqslant L \leqslant U^2(A+R)/2AR$ and
   $T = U(A+R)/2AR + L/U \qquad U^2(A+R)/2AR \leqslant L$
9. $2(D_2T_1 - D_1T_2)/T_1T_2(T_2 - T_1), \quad (D_1T_2^2 - D_2T_1^2)/T_1T_2(T_2 - T_1)$
10. 73·8 km per hour, 82·5 km per hour; an increase of 11·8 per cent
11. $-1/60$, 13/12, 32·5 s, 762·5 m
12. (i) 400 m, 2/3 m s^{-2}; (ii) 382 m, $\pi/6$ m s^{-2}; (iii) 409 m, 3/4 m s^{-2}
13. 91·7 m, 0·66 m s^{-2}, 487 m
15. $|\boldsymbol{r}|^2 = 1, \quad |\dot{\boldsymbol{r}}|^2 = 1 + \sin^2 t, \quad |\ddot{\boldsymbol{r}}|^2 = 4\cos^2 t$
17. $\alpha < 0$, $\beta^2 > 4\alpha\gamma$; $x = X_0 + r_0\cos(\omega t + \varepsilon)$, where $X_0 = -\beta/2\alpha$,
    $r_0 = -(\beta^2 - 4\alpha\gamma)^{1/2}/2\alpha$, $\omega = (-\alpha)^{1/2}$
18. $z = 7 + 3\cos(\omega t - \pi)$, where t is measured from noon in hours and $\omega = 6\pi/37$. The earliest possible time is 4.31 p.m.
19. The trains pass after 25 minutes 45 seconds, at a distance of 49·5 kilometres from A. The second train is delayed by 30 seconds.
20. 4 s, 6 cm
21. 0200 hours. The position vector of the point of collision is $12\boldsymbol{i} + 4\boldsymbol{j}$ (a distance 12 649 m in a direction 18° 26′ north of east) relative to the origin of the frame of reference
22. $\frac{3}{25}$ hours (7 minutes 12 seconds), 4 km
23. $\frac{7}{57}$ hour (approximately 7 minutes 22 seconds)
24. 3·965 nautical miles (at 5 minutes after the first instant)
25. $\{H^2 + u^2D^2/(u^2 + v^2)\}^{1/2}$
26. $a(u+v)\sqrt{2}/(u^2 + uv + v^2)$, $a\{(u^2 - uv + v^2)/(u^2 + uv + v^2)\}^{1/2}$
27. 1815 m
28. $(30 - 6t)\boldsymbol{i} + (35 - 7t)\boldsymbol{j} + (3 - t)\boldsymbol{k}$, 1988 m
29. The direction makes an angle 43° 36′ with the upstream direction; 36·25 s
30. 21° 48′ with the horizontal. 10·77 m s^{-1}
31. 17·09 kilometres per hour, blowing from the direction 35° 50′ south of east
32. $u[\{4 + (\tan\beta + \tan\alpha)^2\}/(\tan\beta - \tan\alpha)^2]^{1/2}$. The direction of the wind is θ east of north, where $\tan\theta = \frac{1}{2}(\tan\beta + \tan\alpha)$
33. (*a*) $2T\{(1 + (1 - k^2)^{1/2}\}/(1 - k^2)$; (*b*) $2T(4 - 2k^2)^{1/2}/(1 - k^2)$

Chapter 3 (p. 58)

1. 0·998, 0·980, 0·826, 0·444, 0·250

Chapter 4 (p. 74)

1. A distance $\frac{1}{2}gt_1t_2$ below P. The speed at P is $\frac{1}{2}g(t_2-t_1)$.
2. 5 s; $12{\cdot}5g = 122{\cdot}625$ (the units being metres)
3. $T = D/U+(2D/g)^{1/2}$ and $D = UT + \dfrac{U^2}{g} - \left\{\left(UT+\dfrac{U^2}{g}\right)^2 - U^2T^2\right\}^{1/2}$; 4·64%
4. $m\{2gD/F(F-mg)\}^{1/2}$; $\{2gD(F-mg)/F\}^{1/2}$
5. $M(A_1+A_2)/(g+A_2)$
6. $\frac{19}{18}H$; $\{(19+\sqrt{19})/3\}\,(H/g)^{1/2}$
8. 16·3 km
9. $2(2H/g)^{1/2}\cos\alpha$
10. The height of the rth ball is $4a_r(1-a_r)H$, where $a_r = \frac{1}{5}(r-1)$ $(r = 1, 2, 3, 4, 5)$
11. The horizontal and vertical coordinates are $\frac{1}{2}X^2\tan\theta/(X\tan\theta - Z)$, $\frac{1}{4}X^2\tan^2\theta/(X\tan\theta-Z)$ respectively
13. $g\{H+(H^2+D^2)^{1/2}\}$; $\tan^{-1}[\{H+(H^2+D^2)^{1/2}\}/D]$
14. (i) $\cos\theta = \frac{5}{7}$; $(245gD-96\sqrt{6u_0^2})/7u_0g$
    (ii) $\cos\theta = \frac{3}{4}$; $(24gD-7\sqrt{7u_0^2})/4u_0g$
    (iii) $\cos\theta = 1$; D/u_0
17. $\cos^{-1}\{U+(U^2+8u_0^2)^{1/2}/4u_0\}$
18. $D\sec^2\theta\left\{\dfrac{\Delta u}{u}\dfrac{gD}{u^2} + \Delta\theta\left(1-\dfrac{gD}{u^2}\tan\theta\right)\right\}$
20. $H\{\sin\theta+(\sin^2\theta+2)^{1/2}\}\cos\theta$; $\pi/6$
21. $2\sqrt{g}$; $\tan^{-1}(\frac{1}{2}) = 0{\cdot}464$
22. 12·3 s; $(34{\cdot}6\boldsymbol{i}-101\boldsymbol{k})\,\mathrm{m\,s^{-1}}$
23. $\dfrac{U^2\sin\alpha\cos\alpha}{g}\left\{\left(1+\dfrac{2gH}{U^2\sin^2\alpha}\right)^{1/2}-1\right\}$
24. $(U-u)(2H/g)^{1/2}$; the aircraft is directly above the ship
26. A distance $4u_0^2/3g$ down the plane from the point of projection
27. $2u_0/g(1+3\sin^2\alpha)^{1/2}$
28. $\frac{1}{2}(\alpha+\frac{1}{2}\pi)$
29. $u_0^2/g(1-\sin\alpha)$; $2u_0\sin(\frac{1}{4}\pi+\frac{1}{2}\alpha)/g\cos\alpha$; yes
30. $\theta = 0$ when $a\Omega^2 \leqslant g$ and $\theta = \cos^{-1}(g/a\Omega^2)$ when $a\Omega^2 > g$
32. No mud on windscreen if
    $D > a\sin\Theta + (U/g)\cos\Theta\{U\sin\Theta+(U^2\sin^2\Theta+2ga-2gh-2ga\cos\Theta)^{1/2}\}$

Chapter 5 (p. 84)

1. Yes; $D = \frac{1}{2}u_0T$ and $D = \frac{1}{2}(F/m)T^2$
2. 0·15
3. $g\sin(\beta-\alpha)\sec\alpha$
4. $mg\{(1-k^2)/(1+k^2)\}\sin\alpha$
5. $7{\cdot}67\ \mathrm{m\,s^{-1}}$
6. 80 m
7. 61 kilometres per hour; 0·50 (e.g. dry road with some loose chippings); 0·26 (e.g. road with a covering of snow)

9. $mg(1+T_1/T_2)$; $\frac{1}{2}gT_1T_2$
10. $\{(F_2-F_1)/(F_2+F_1)\}\tan\alpha$
11. $Mg\sin(\alpha+\lambda)$
12. $F_A/(M+m)g$
13. $4\pi^2av^2/g$
14. $\mu_s > A/g$ and $\mu_s > R/g$

Chapter 6 (p. 98)

1. $\boldsymbol{p}.\boldsymbol{p}/2m$
2. 900 J; $6\,\mathrm{m\,s^{-1}}$
3. $-3mg$; yes, because the field of force is conservative (the work done in this example equals the product of $-mg$ and the difference between the z-coordinate of D and the z-coordinate of A)
4. $\displaystyle\int_{-\pi/2}^{\pi/2} F_0(\boldsymbol{i}\cos\alpha+\boldsymbol{j}\sin\alpha).a(-\sin\theta\boldsymbol{i}+\cos\theta\boldsymbol{j})\,d\theta = 2aF_0\sin\alpha$
5. $\dfrac{3F_0x_0T}{2t_0}$
6. $-F_0x_0-\frac{1}{2}kx_0^2$
7. $M(u^2+U^2)/2UF_0$; $M(2u^3+U^3)/6UF_0$;
$$F=\begin{cases}F_0 & 0\leqslant x\leqslant X_0,\\ UF_0\{U^3+(x-X_0)3UF_0/M\}^{-1/3} & X_0\leqslant x,\end{cases}\quad \text{where}\quad X_0=\tfrac{1}{2}MU^2/F_0$$
8. $\frac{16}{9}T$
9. $\left\{\ln\left(\dfrac{1-\alpha}{1-\beta}\right)-(\beta-\alpha)-\frac{1}{2}(\beta^2-\alpha^2)\right\}\dfrac{mU_{\max}^2}{R_0}$
10. 1250 kW; $0{\cdot}3\,\mathrm{m\,s^{-2}}$
11. $mu_1/(u_2-u_1)$; $mRu_1u_2/(u_2-u_1)$
12. $UP_0/(P_0-MgU\sin\alpha)$

Chapter 7 (p. 124)

1. 0·994 m
2. 6·98 s; 0·164 m
4. Yes (the differential equation is linear)
5. No; $\ddot{\phi}_1+\ddot{\phi}_2+\omega^2\sin(\phi_1+\phi_2) = -\omega^2(1-\cos\phi_2)\sin\phi_1-\omega^2(1-\cos\phi_1)\sin\phi_2$, which is non-zero in general
6. 3·74 N, 18·45 N; $13{\cdot}8\,\mathrm{m\,s^{-1}}$
7. 0 if $a\geqslant 3l/5$, $\{g(3l-5a)\}^{1/2}$ if $a<3l/5$
8. $(7ga)^{1/2}$
9. $(5n^2-1):(5-n^2)$; the contact force has a constant sign throughout the motion provided $n<\sqrt{5}$
10. $\frac{3}{2}a$
11. $\cos^{-1}\{\frac{1}{3}(2+u_0^2/ga)\}$; the particle behaves as a projectile and does not slide on the smooth outer surface of the fixed sphere if $u_0\geqslant(ga)^{1/2}$
12. $(T_M/4\pi^2ml)^{1/2}$; mg
13. $2\pi(l/2g)^{1/2}$; $2mg$
15. 5:3

16.

u_0 \ a	400	800	2000	4000
10	0·025	0·013	0·005	0·003
30	0·226	0·114	0·046	0·023
50	0·567	0·308	0·127	0·064

$(mg|U^2 - u_0^2|)/(g^2a^2 + u_0^4)^{1/2}$

17. $\dfrac{d\dot{\phi}^2}{d\phi} - 2\mu\dot{\phi}^2 = -\dfrac{2g}{a}(\sin\phi - \mu\cos\phi)$

18. No, the angular speed decreases exponentially and is never zero

19. $(aF_0/\mu m)^{1/2}(1 - e^{-2\mu\phi})^{1/2}$

20. 6·59, 43·4, 286; three complete turns

Chapter 8 (p. 144)

2. $9mg/l$; $\frac{2}{3}\pi(l/g)^{1/2}$; $3d(g/l)^{1/2}$

3. π; $2\sqrt{2}$; $3\pi/8$

5. $2\pi(Md/mg)^{1/2}$; $Mg + mg(1 - D/d)$

6. $4\pi^2 mlv^2$; 4% if we ignore second-order terms (4·13% if we ignore third-order terms)

7. Mg; $l + (ml/M)\{1 + (1 + 2M/m)^{1/2}\}$

8. a distance $\frac{3}{2}l$ below the fixed support; a distance $\frac{1}{2}l$ below the fixed support

9. $\displaystyle\int_0^{10} F_A(e)\,de$; 40 600 J; 20 m; 33 m s^{-1}; 54 m s^{-2}

10. $mg < k_1h + (k_1 + k_2)l$; $2\pi\{m/(k_1 + k_2)\}^{1/2}$

11. $2d$

12. $\frac{1}{2}l$

13. $3l$

14. $\{1 + \lambda_2/(2\lambda_1 + \lambda_2)\}l$; yes, provided $\lambda_2 \leqslant 2\lambda_1$

15. $\dfrac{2\pi}{n+1}\left(\dfrac{nml}{\lambda}\right)^{1/2}$; $n = 1$

16. 0·81 s; 48 m s^{-1}

17. $2\pi(ml/\lambda)^{1/2}$; if the amplitude of the oscillations is not small, the governing differential equation has the form

$$m\ddot{x} = \frac{-2\lambda}{l}\left\{x - \frac{xl}{(4l^2 + x^2)^{1/2}}\right\}$$

18. $12mg$

19. $kl/mg >$ the coefficient of static friction

20. mg, $\frac{1}{2}d(5g/l)^{1/2}$

21. $3(\frac{1}{2}gR)^{1/2}$

22. $-\frac{7}{6}$, 0

Chapter 9 (p. 169)

1. $(3gR/2)^{1/2}$; $(8R/g)^{1/2}(\frac{4}{3}\pi + 3^{1/2})$

2. 2370 m s^{-1}

3. $60\,000\,\mathrm{m\,s^{-1}}$
4. about 118 minutes
5. $7770\,\mathrm{m\,s^{-1}}$
6. about 110 minutes
7. H/R, where R is the radius of the Earth
9. $1{\cdot}5 \times 10^6$ kilometres
10. $8{\cdot}8 \times 10^4$ kilometres
11. $(H_2 T_1^{2/3} - H_1 T_2^{2/3})/(T_2^{2/3} - T_1^{2/3})$, 6380 km, $9{\cdot}77\,\mathrm{m\,s^{-2}}$
12. $d(1+\sin\alpha)$, $d(1-\sin\alpha)$
14. 6994 km, about 97 minutes, 0·0532
15. 27 411 km, 0·758, 11 700 km, $10{\cdot}3\,\mathrm{km\,s^{-1}}$, $1{\cdot}41\,\mathrm{km\,s^{-1}}$
16. The period is proportional to $(a^3/GM)^{1/2}$ (and the dimensionless constant of proportionality equals 2π)
17. 89·4 minutes
18. $(gR^2/(R+H))^{1/2}$
19. $28{\cdot}8\,\mathrm{km\,s^{-1}}$, 0·207, $21{\cdot}4\,\mathrm{km\,s^{-1}}$
21. $(128a^3/9GM)^{1/2}$
22. The polar coordinates of the apses are $(a-ae, 0)$ and $(a+ae, \pi)$; $E_0 = -GM/2a$ and $L_0^2 = GMa(1-e^2)$; $\frac{1}{2}a\{(9-8e^2)^{1/2}-1\}$; the new orbit is hyperbolic because there is one apse and the total energy is positive ($E_0 = GM/a$)
23. $(2^{1/2}+1)(\mu/d)^{1/2}$
24. The orbit is hyperbolic, the length of the semi-latus rectum being $(r_0^2 u_0^2/\mu)$ and the eccentricity being $(1+r_0 u_0^2/\mu)$
25. $L_0^2 = \mu$, where $L_0 = r^2\dot{\phi}$
26. $\dot{r} = 0$ at $r = 2r_0$ (but $r \leqslant r_0$ for all time)
29. $r_0^2 \mu^{1/2}$
30. The circular orbit is unstable if $g'(r_0) < 0$

Chapter 10 (p. 200)

2. F/mk; $\dfrac{1}{k}\ln\frac{3}{2}$ and $\dfrac{1}{k}\ln 2$
3. $u = \dfrac{\alpha t}{k} - \dfrac{\alpha}{k^2}(1-e^{-kt})$
4. $\dfrac{1}{2k}\ln 2$
5. F/M; $(F/k)^{1/2}$; $2{\cdot}4 \times 10^7$ kg, $2{\cdot}4 \times 10^6$N and $34\,560\,\mathrm{kg\,m^{-1}}$
6. $U(1-e^{-3kx/m})^{1/3}$, where $U = (P/k)^{1/3}$
7. 0·388 radian
9. $3MU^3/d$; $(\ln 4)MU^3/d$
10. $1/a_1$; $\ddot{x} = -2a_2\dot{x}^3$
11. $n < 2$
12. $(m/2k_1)\ln\{(4k_1+k_3u_0^2)/(k_1+k_3u_0^2)\}$
13. $0{\cdot}025\,\mathrm{m\,s^{-1}}$; 986 m
15. $(U/g)\ln(1+u_0/U)$; $\frac{1}{2}mu_0^2 - mu_0U + mU^2\ln(1+u_0/U)$, where m is the mass of the particle
16. 606 m; $5{\cdot}004\,\mathrm{m\,s^{-1}}$; 126 s
17. $9{\cdot}3\,\mathrm{m\,s^{-1}}$
18. $22{\cdot}7\,\mathrm{m\,s^{-1}}$, 263 m; $5{\cdot}001\,\mathrm{m\,s^{-1}}$, 229 m; 54 s

21. $(u_0/g)\{\frac{1}{4}\pi + \ln(1+2^{1/2})\}$
22. $\frac{1}{2}mu_0^2 - \frac{1}{2}mU^2 \ln(1+u_0^2/U^2)$
23. $u_0(1+bu_0^2/a)^{-1/2}$
24. $(a/2g)\ln(b/a)$; $a = U^2$, $b = u_0^2 + U^2$
25. 133·1 s; 132·9 s
26. 54 s; 26·8 m s^{-1}, 258 m
27. $-5{\cdot}7$, 0·17, 5·8; 9·7 m s^{-1} to 2 sig. fig. (In fact $f(9{\cdot}697) = 0{\cdot}0025$)
28. $\alpha = 1$, $\beta = 2$, $\gamma = 1$
29. $U/N^{1/6}$; $U/M^{1/2}$
30. $\frac{1}{2}u_0$
31. $-U\{1-(1-g\Delta t/U)^n\}$; $-Un\Delta t + (U^2/g)(1-g\Delta t/2U)\{1-(1-g\Delta t/U)^n\}$
32. 53·82 m s^{-1}, 31·4 s; 54·00 m s^{-1}, 29·7 s

Chapter 11 (p. 223)

1. $(c^2 - 4mk)/4m^2$
2. $\{z_0 \cos 4t + \frac{1}{4}(z_0+u_0)\sin 4t\}\, e^{-t}$; $\{z_0 + (z_0+u_0)t\}\, e^{-t}$;
$\frac{1}{3}\{(4z_0+u_0)\, e^{-t} - (z_0+u_0)\, e^{-4t}\}$
3. $(u_0/\omega)\sin \omega t$, where $\omega = (k/m)^{1/2}$; $(mu_0/c)(1-e^{-ct/m})$; $(u_0/\bar{\omega})\sin \bar{\omega} t\, e^{-ct/2m}$, where $\bar{\omega} = (4mk - c^2)^{1/2}/2m$
4. $m\ddot{z} + c\dot{z} + kz = 0$ with $c < 2(mk)^{1/2}$; $d = u_0(m/k)^{1/2}\, e^{-ct_1/2m}$, $\bar{\omega} t_1 = \tan^{-1}(2m\bar{\omega}/c)$ where $\bar{\omega} = (4mk - c^2)^{1/2}/2m$
5. $2d(1-e^{-N\Lambda/2})/(1-e^{-\Lambda/2}) - d$, where $\Lambda = 2\pi a(1-a^2)^{-1/2}$; 0·87, 0·0002
6. $l + g/\delta^2$ below the support; $l + g/\delta^2 + d(1+u_0/\delta d)\, e^{-u_0/(u_0+\delta d)}$;
$l + g/\delta^2$ when $u_0 \leqslant \delta d$ and $l + g/\delta^2 - d(u_0/\delta d - 1)\, e^{-u_0/(u_0-\delta d)}$ when $\delta d < u_0$
7. $m\ddot{x} = -m\omega^2(x-l) + \frac{10}{3}m\omega(U-\dot{x})$; $l + 10U/3\omega$
8. $\{mg + k_1 l_1 + k_2(d-l_2)\}/(k_1+k_2)$; $c^2 < 4m(k_1+k_2)$
9. $\dfrac{5m}{32}\left\{\dfrac{g}{d}\left(\dfrac{125d-9l}{5d-l}\right)\right\}^{1/2} \leqslant c$
10. $u_0 \exp\{-2\pi(4m^2g/k_1^2 l - 1)^{-1/2}\}$
11. $\{F_0/m(\omega^2-\Omega^2)\}\{\sin \Omega t - (\Omega/\omega)\sin \omega t\}$; $\{F_0/2m\omega^2\}\{\sin \omega t - \omega t \cos \omega t\}$
12. $(z_0 - F_0/m\omega^2)\cos \omega t + (u_0/\omega - F_0\Omega/m\omega^3)\sin \omega t + (F_0/m\omega^2)(1+\Omega t)$
13. $(F_0/m\omega)|\sin \omega t_0|$
14. $l - mg/k$; $l - g/\omega^2 + \{F_0/m\omega(\omega^2-\Omega^2)\}(\omega \sin \Omega t - \Omega \sin \omega t)$, where $\omega = (k/m)^{1/2}$
15. Yes, provided $F_0 < 0{\cdot}545mg$
16. $z_0 + \dfrac{F_0}{c\Omega} - \dfrac{m^2\Omega F_0\, e^{-ct/m}}{c(c^2+m^2\Omega^2)} - \left\{\dfrac{m\Omega F_0 \sin \Omega t + cF_0 \cos \Omega t}{\Omega(c^2+m^2\Omega^2)}\right\}$; $F_0/\Omega(c^2+m^2\Omega^2)^{1/2}$
17. $(\frac{4}{3}z_0 + \frac{1}{3}u_0 - 5)\, e^{-t} - (\frac{1}{3}z_0 + \frac{1}{3}u_0 - 8)\, e^{-4t} + 9 \sin 3t - 3 \cos 3t$
18. $2^{1/2}F_0/36m\tilde{\omega}^2$
19. $17^{1/2}F_0/34m\tilde{\omega}^2$
20. $F_0/m\tilde{\omega}^2$ when $\Omega = 0$
21. $\Omega < (2k/m)^{1/2}$
22. $Z_0 + l - g/\omega^2 + d(\omega^2 \cos \Omega t - \Omega^2 \cos \omega t)/(\omega^2 - \Omega^2)$;
$Z_0 + l - g/\omega^2 + d(\cos \omega t + \frac{1}{2}\omega t \sin \omega t)$
24. $\frac{1}{2}d \sin^3 \omega t$
25. $3d/5^{1/2}$
26. u_0
27. 0·286, 0·025, 0·0007

28. (i) $\left[x_0\boldsymbol{i}\cos(3^{1/2}\omega t)+3^{1/2}\left\{\frac{x_0}{6}\boldsymbol{i}+\frac{u_0}{3\omega}\boldsymbol{j}\right\}\sin(3^{1/2}\omega t)\right]e^{-\omega t/2}$;
(ii) $\{x_0\boldsymbol{i}+(\omega x_0\boldsymbol{i}+u_0\boldsymbol{j})t\}\,e^{-\omega t}$;
(iii) $\frac{3^{1/2}}{6}\left[\left\{(2+3^{1/2})x_0\boldsymbol{i}+\frac{u_0}{\omega}\boldsymbol{j}\right\}e^{-(2-3^{1/2})\omega t}-\left\{(2-3^{1/2})x_0\boldsymbol{i}+\frac{u_0}{\omega}\boldsymbol{j}\right\}e^{-(2+3^{1/2})\omega t}\right]$

Chapter 12 (p. 245)

1. $m(g+a)$
2. 12 m; 661 N when $t\in(0,2)$ and 493 N when $t\in(2,4)$
3. $l+\{g-a(1-\cos\omega t)\}/\omega^2$, where $\omega=(k/m)^{1/2}$
4. $-(g+a)(1-\cos\omega t)/\omega^2$, where $\omega=(k/m)^{1/2}$
5. $l+g/\omega^2+(U/\omega^2T)(1-\cos\omega t)$, $t\in[0,T]$ and
$l+g/\omega^2-(U/\omega^2T)\{1+(1-2\cos\omega T)\cos\omega t-2\sin\omega T\sin\omega t\}$, $t\in[T,2T]$, where $\omega=(k/m)^{1/2}$
6. $l-m(g+a)/k+u_0t+\frac{1}{2}at^2$
7. $M/(1+a/g)$
8. 11·02 kg; 8·98 kg
9. 80 kg; 74·5 m
10. $R_\theta^{-1}=\begin{bmatrix}\cos\theta & \sin\theta & 0\\ -\sin\theta & \cos\theta & 0\\ 0 & 0 & 1\end{bmatrix}$, $R_\theta^{-1}\dot{R}_\theta R_\theta^{-1}=\dot\theta\begin{bmatrix}\sin\theta & -\cos\theta & 0\\ \cos\theta & \sin\theta & 0\\ 0 & 0 & 0\end{bmatrix}$
11. $\frac{1}{2}d3^{1/2}$; $(1/\omega)\ln(4+13^{1/2})$
13. $\ddot X+\mu(g^2+4\omega^2\dot X^2)^{1/2}-\omega^2X=0,\quad \dot X>0$, and
$\ddot X-\mu(g^2+4\omega^2\dot X^2)^{1/2}-\omega^2X=0,\quad \dot X<0$;
$\{u_0/\omega(1+\mu^2)^{1/2}\}\sinh\{(1+\mu^2)^{1/2}\omega t\}\,e^{-\mu\omega t}$;
$\ddot X-\omega^2X=-\mu g$, $\dot X>0$, and $\ddot X-\omega^2X=\mu g$, $\dot X<0$
15. Yes; at the rim when $k\leqslant m\omega^2$, at a point whose distance from the centre is minimum $(R_0, kl/(k-m\omega^2))$ when $k>m\omega^2$
16. $\pi/2\omega$; $\frac{5}{8}l$
17. $(1+3^{1/2})/\omega$; $m(g^2+12l\omega^2)^{1/2}$
22. At $t=0$, $X=\dot X=Y=\dot Y=0$
23. $x=\frac{4}{3}d(\cos\omega t-\cos 2\omega t)$, $y=\frac{2}{3}d(2\sin\omega t-\sin 2\omega t)$;
$X=\frac{4}{3}d(1-\cos^3\omega t)$, $Y=-\frac{4}{3}d\sin^3\omega t$
24. $m\ddot X+(k-m\omega^2)X-2m\omega\dot Y=kd+\frac{kl(X-d)}{\{(X-d)^2+Y^2\}^{1/2}}$,
$m\ddot Y+(k-m\omega^2)Y+2m\omega\dot X=\frac{klY}{\{(X-d)^2+Y^2\}^{1/2}}$
25. $m(g^2+\omega^4R^2)^{1/2}$
26. $\dot{\mathbf{I}}=\omega\mathbf{J}\cos\theta$, $\dot{\mathbf{J}}=-\omega\mathbf{I}\cos\theta-\omega\mathbf{K}\sin\theta$, $\dot{\mathbf{K}}=\omega\mathbf{J}\sin\theta$
28. $Z_1(t)=H-\frac{1}{2}gt^2$, $Y_1(t)=2\omega H\sin\theta$, $X_1(t)=0$;
$Z_2(t)=H-\frac{1}{2}gt^2$, $Y_2(t)=\frac{1}{3}\omega gt^3\sin\theta$, $X_2(t)=0$;
$Z_3(t)=H-\frac{1}{2}gt^2$, $Y_3(t)=\frac{1}{3}\omega gt^3\sin\theta$, $X_3(t)=0$
29. $X(t)=u_1t+\omega u_2t^2\cos\theta$,
$Y(t)=u_2t-\omega(u_1\cos\theta+u_3\sin\theta)t^2+\frac{1}{3}\omega gt^3\sin\theta$,
$Z(t)=u_3t-\frac{1}{2}gt^2+\omega u_2t^2\sin\theta$

30. $\dfrac{u_0^2 \sin^2\alpha}{2g} + \dfrac{\omega u_0^3}{g^2}\sin^2\alpha\cos\alpha\cos\theta$;
$\dfrac{u_0^2\sin 2\alpha}{g} + \dfrac{4\omega u_0^3}{3g^2}\sin\alpha(3-4\sin^2\alpha)\cos\theta$

Chapter 13 (p. 266)

1. $7{\cdot}9\ \mathrm{m\,s^{-1}}$, N $18{\cdot}4°$ E
2. constant speed $mu/(m+M)$ around a circular orbit of radius $mR/(m+M)$
3. $t = \pi/|\omega_1 - \omega_2|$, $\boldsymbol{r}_1 = R\boldsymbol{j}$
4. $\boldsymbol{r}_c = \frac{1}{3}(\boldsymbol{r}_1 + \boldsymbol{r}_2 + \boldsymbol{r}_3)$; the equation of a median is $\frac{1}{2}(\boldsymbol{r}_1 + \boldsymbol{r}_2) + \lambda\{\boldsymbol{r}_3 - \frac{1}{2}(\boldsymbol{r}_1 + \boldsymbol{r}_2)\}$ and the point of intersection of the three medians corresponds with $\lambda = \frac{1}{3}$
5. $\{2G(m_1+m_2)(r_0-r)/r_0r\}^{1/2}$
6. Yes
7. $\ddot{\boldsymbol{r}} = -G(m_1+m_2)\boldsymbol{r}/r^3$, where $r = |\boldsymbol{r}|$
9. No
10. $\{G(M+m/3^{1/2})/R\}^{1/2}$; $\{G(M+\frac{1}{4}m+m/2^{1/2})/R\}^{1/2}$
11. $1{\cdot}92$ s
14. $Mmg(\sin\alpha+\sin\beta)/(M+m)$
15. $m_1m_2g(1+\sin\alpha-\mu\cos\alpha)/(m_1+m_2)$
16. $\{(2d/g)(M+m)/(M-\mu m)\}^{1/2}$
19. $(2Mmg\tan\alpha\cos\phi)/(M+m)$
21. $\frac{1}{2}mg(1+l^2u_0^2/r^3g)$
22. $(m_1u_1+m_2u_2)/(m_1+m_2)$
23. l
24. $(k/m)^{1/2}/2\pi$, $(3k/m)^{1/2}/2\pi$; $l(1+\frac{1}{2}\cos(3k/m)^{1/2}t)$

Chapter 14 (p. 284)

1. (i) $F_0\tau\boldsymbol{i}$; (ii) $\frac{1}{2}F_0\tau\boldsymbol{i}$; (iii) $\frac{2}{3}F_0\tau\boldsymbol{i}$
2. 3000 N
3. $\frac{1}{4}u_0$, $\frac{3}{4}u_0$
5. Two collisions; $6u_0/25$, $9u_0/25$, $2u_0/5$
6. At the point diametrically opposite to A; yes
7. $\frac{1}{3}\pi R$; both beads are moving in a clockwise direction, the speeds of B_1 and B_2 being $\frac{1}{2}u_0$ and $\frac{5}{4}u_0$, respectively
8. $u_0(-\boldsymbol{i}+2\boldsymbol{j})$ and $3u_0\boldsymbol{j}$
10. $-u_0(2\boldsymbol{i}-\boldsymbol{j})$, a "head-on" collision
11. $\frac{1}{4}u_0$
12. $\tan^{-1}(0{\cdot}75)$ ($0{\cdot}6435$ rad or $36{\cdot}87°$)
13. $(143/256)u_0$ away from the cushion, $(7/256)u_0$ towards the cushion
14. $eu_0(m+e^2M)/(m+M)$, $e(1-e^2)u_0m/(m+M)$
17. $H(1+e^2)/(1-e^2)$
18. $\frac{1}{2}(1-e^2)mu_0^2\sin^2\theta$
20. $R = H\{(48)^{1/2}-(24)^{1/2}+(30)^{1/2}-6^{1/2}\} = 5{\cdot}06H$
22. (i) $0{\cdot}36$, (ii) $0{\cdot}60$, (iii) $0{\cdot}82$
23. $5mgR/4$
24. $184\ \mathrm{m\,s^{-1}}$

25. $\Omega(d^2-d_0^2)^{1/2}$, where $\Omega=(k/m)^{1/2}$;

$$\left[d^2+\frac{2F}{m\Omega^2}\{(d^2-d_0^2)^{1/2}\sin\Omega\tau-d_0(1-\cos\Omega\tau)\}+\frac{2F^2}{m^2\Omega^4}(1-\cos\Omega\tau)\right]^{1/2}$$

27. $J(2l/m\lambda)^{1/2}$; $\pi(ml/8\lambda)^{1/2}$

28. $2\dot{u}_0$ in the opposite direction; $6mu_0^2$

30. $u_0+(E/10m)^{1/2}$, $u_0-4(E/10m)^{1/2}$; yes, provided $u_0=2(E/10m)^{1/2}$ (i.e. $E=5mu_0^2/2$)

Chapter 15 (p. 304)

1. $n=1, \frac{1}{2}U, \frac{3}{4}UT; n=2, \frac{1}{2}U, \frac{17}{24}UT; n=4, \frac{1}{2}U, \frac{1171}{1680}UT$

2. $\frac{1}{2}U$, $UT\ln 2$

3. $10mg$, $5mg/8$; $5g/2$, $\frac{1}{3}U\ln 4$

4. UT

7. $\frac{1}{2}g$

9. $n=1, U+\frac{1}{2}c, T(U+\frac{1}{4}c); n=2, U+\frac{7}{12}c, T(U+\frac{13}{48}c); n=4, U+\frac{533}{840}c,$ $T(U+\frac{1923}{6720}c)$

10. $T\{U+c(1-\ln 2)\}$; Mc/T

11. $n=1, (4e_k/M)^{1/2}, U+(e_k/M)^{1/2}$;
$n=2, 2(4e_k/3M)^{1/2}, 2(3e_k/2M)^{1/2}, U+(e_k/3M)^{1/2}+(2e_k/3M)^{1/2}$;
$n=4, 4(e_k/7M)^{1/2}, 4(7e_k/12M)^{1/2}, 4(3e_k/5M)^{1/2}, 4(5e_k/8M)^{1/2},$
$U+(e_k/7M)^{1/2}+(4e_k/21M)^{1/2}+(4e_k/15M)^{1/2}+(2e_k/5M)^{1/2}$

12. $1-e^{-2}=0{\cdot}865$

13. $M(t)=M(0)\exp(-gt/c)$; 7 minutes 4 seconds

14. M_0g/β, $M_0g/5\beta$

15. $1320\,\mathrm{m\,s^{-1}}$

16. $3180\,\mathrm{m\,s^{-1}}$; 112 kilometres; $2{\cdot}4M_0g$

17. $306\,\mathrm{m\,s^{-1}}$, 82·6 kilometres

20. $9D/10$; $11{\cdot}1\times10^3\,\mathrm{m\,s^{-1}}$, $2{\cdot}27\times10^3\,\mathrm{m\,s^{-1}}$. The values of $(2g_ER_E)^{1/2}$ and $(2g_MR_M)^{1/2}$ are $11{\cdot}2\times10^3\,\mathrm{m\,s^{-1}}$ and $2{\cdot}37\times10^3\,\mathrm{m\,s^{-1}}$.

Chapter 16 (p. 339)

1. $\boldsymbol{i}+\boldsymbol{j}+\boldsymbol{k}$

3. $\frac{1}{2}|\rho_1 l_1^2-\rho_2 l_2^2|/(\rho_1 l_1+\rho_2 l_2)$

4. $\frac{5}{8}l(\boldsymbol{i}+\boldsymbol{j})$

6. $3l/(8+2\sqrt{3})$

7. $4r_0/3\pi$

8. $l\sqrt{2}/6$

9. $\frac{1}{2}r_0, \frac{1}{3}r_0, \frac{1}{6}r_0(4-\sqrt{2})$

10. $3r_0/8$

11. $\mathbf{F}=-F_0(3\boldsymbol{i}+2\sqrt{3}\boldsymbol{j})$; $-2x+\sqrt{3}y=6l$

12. $F_1=4F_0, F_2=-2F_0, F_3=-2F_0$

13. $F_0(-2\boldsymbol{i}-\boldsymbol{j})$; $x-2y+3=0$

14. $F_1=-\frac{3}{2}F_0, F_2=\frac{1}{2}F_0$; $\mathbf{T}=-(13/2)F_0l\boldsymbol{k}$

15. $F_0(3\boldsymbol{i}+2\boldsymbol{j}+2\boldsymbol{k})$, $F_0l(-2\boldsymbol{j}-3\boldsymbol{k})$

16. $3F_0(\boldsymbol{i}-\boldsymbol{j}+\boldsymbol{k})$, $l(-\frac{2}{3}\boldsymbol{i}+2\boldsymbol{j})$

17. $F_0l(\boldsymbol{j}+\boldsymbol{k})$

20. $F_0(2\boldsymbol{i}+\boldsymbol{j}-\boldsymbol{k})$; $l(3\boldsymbol{i}+\boldsymbol{j})$

21. $\frac{3}{4}l$; $\frac{2}{3}l(1+1/2N)$

22. $\frac{2}{3}l$
23. $2\pi\{3^{1/2}l/3g\}^{1/2}$
24. $-\frac{1}{4}mg\{(10\cos^2\phi-\sin^2\phi)\boldsymbol{i}+(9\sin\phi\cos\phi)\boldsymbol{j}\}$
25. $7ml^2/18$; $0{\cdot}7l$
27. $\frac{1}{3}m(x_0^2+y_0^2)$
28. $\frac{1}{12}ml^2$
29. $2\pi\{8^{1/2}l/3g\}^{1/2}$
30. $\left\{2^{1/2}\dfrac{(M+\frac{1}{2}m)}{(M+\frac{1}{3}m)}\dfrac{g}{l}\right\}^{1/2}$
31. $5(8^{1/2}l/3)$
33. $2r_0(M+\frac{3}{8}m)/(M+\frac{1}{2}m)$
35. $2mg/(M+6m)$
37. $\{(m_2-m_1)gI+(m_1+m_2)T_F r_0\}/\{(m_1+m_2)r_0^2+I\}$
38. $[2mgr_0\Phi_1\Phi_2/\{I\Phi_1+(I+mr_0^2)\Phi_2\}]^{1/2}$

Index